THE PHOENIX PRIEST

CASSIDY CLARKE

Website : cassidyclarkewriting.com
Cover Designed by : COVERDUNGEONRABBIT
ISBN: 9781957993003
First Edition: April 2022

10 9 8 7 6 5 4 3 2 1

~Dedication~

To Caleb, Joshua, Katie, and Alita:

I promise I didn't TOTALLY base the Atlas sibs off of us. But I would go to war for you any day.

Us before all.

CHAPTER 1

ELIAS

"I'm home."

The rasping words cut through the silence that blanketed the rose-scented temple, given life by a broken soldier kneeling at an abandoned altar.

Elias Loch had been searching for a place like this since he and Kallias crossed the border a couple days ago, sneaking past both Atlas and Nyx's forts without much trouble thanks to their combined knowledge of their peoples' habits: a quiet, simple temple down the street from the inn where they'd chosen to stay for the night. The pews were threadbare, the wooden backs were worn from generations of hands that had gripped them for support during hymns, and the floorboards groaned at every step and stiff wind, but the altar was well-cared for.

Every time he'd found himself in turmoil, he'd sought out the inexplicable peace that temples brought him. Maybe it was his upbringing, maybe it was nostalgia, but he always felt at home amongst the candles and incense pots, the pews and stained glass. Even after he'd left Mortem's service, he'd never been absent from temple services for long.

These past months in Atlas were the longest he'd ever been away. And even here, surrounded by frostbitten air and melting snow dripping from his boots…even this altar felt a bit foreign, like some part of it had turned its back on him. Like Mortem was no longer pleased with him.

Well, that was fine. He wasn't feeling too generous with her either. Not after…

Shearing bone. Peaches and smoke. Fire and honey. "I would have said yes."

His dreams had not been kind as of late.

Fire and glass, smoke and sweet, a voice that slowed his heart near to stopping.

"Find me in Artem, Elias Loch…Go to Artem. Find me there."

Elias swallowed past the burning lump in his throat, ignoring the memory of those whispers, forcing prayers out through gritted teeth: "I know you haven't left me. I know you better than that. Even if it feels that way, I know…I know. I trust you're here."

Nothing answered him but the moaning wind and the beating of his own heart. Healthy, strong beating—the poison that had doomed him to an early grave so many weeks ago seemed to have been removed entirely, the thorny, knotted veins of scarring on his arm the only proof that it was ever there in the first place.

Out of habit, he reached up to his chest and fiddled with the token that rested over his heart, pressing it so tightly into his palm that the cool metal bit his skin.

Not his prayer beads.

"It's okay, smartass," he said softly, clinging to that ring with more fervor than he'd ever held those beads. Heat prickled at the backs of his eyes, but he blinked hard, forcing it back.

No weeping. No weakness.

"It's okay," he repeated, the words scraping off the lump in his throat like sparks from a whetstone. "I'm not angry. Not with you."

He was something, though. Something that had tangled his heart in barbed wire and *squeezed*, some terrible and twisted thing he couldn't hope to extricate, a burning coal that wouldn't extinguish. And maybe he didn't want it to. Not until this was over.

Some days it felt like that thing was strangling him. Others, it felt like the cornerstone holding him together.

Soon they'd be in Andromeda, Nyx's crown city, bringing news of necromancers and godwork to Queen Ravenna. Kallias would entreat her for her help, and Elias...

Elias would tell her that her daughter was dead, sacrificed at the altar of an enemy goddess.

His hands clenched against his knees, and he forced himself to breathe through the wave of bone-shattering pain.

No weeping.

Soren had paid for his every breath with all that remained of hers. He wasn't about to waste them on something as useless as tears.

So he swallowed his grief. Steadied his legs as he stood up, turning his back on the altar and the iron-forged icon of a rose-eyed skull hanging on the wall, petals carved in just the right way to make him feel watched.

No weakness.

He walked out without looking back.

CHAPTER 2

KALLIAS

"I really don't think this is a good idea."

Elias didn't even turn around at his nervous hiss. "Neither is starving ourselves for the next few days. Just keep your head down and follow my lead, will you? It's only one night. We'll gather supplies, spend the night in a warm bed, and be gone by morning."

Kallias Atlas scowled at the back of Elias's head, tugging his knit hat further down, running his fingers around the brim to make sure none of his hair had slipped out. Though redheads weren't unheard of in Nyx—he'd seen two or three just entering through this city's heavily-guarded gates—the hair color combined with his decidedly poor Nyxian accent would cause too much suspicion if he was forced to speak at any point. They'd opted on the side of caution.

He hated this city the moment he set foot in it—not for the city itself, but for what it represented. An Atlas defeat.

The city of Delphin had been held by his kingdom for years, up until a few weeks ago, when Nyx had mounted an unexpected assault and stolen it back. Their soldiers had flooded past the walls with a ferocity not often seen after this long at war, shouting out a new battle cry, wearing makeshift mourning braids on their arms. A black cord to represent the Nyxian spy he was currently following through the winding streets…and a red one representing the twice-lost princess. Lost by both his kingdom and theirs.

For Soren!

He could practically hear the echoes of his sister's Nyxian name still bouncing between alley walls, kept alive by the horrifically cold winter wind. The ghostly cries made it near-impossible to walk through this city.

Not that it wasn't beautiful. The streets were paved in black, white, and gray stone, red-brick and ebony-wood houses and shops huddled close together in winding rows, tiny strung lanterns twinkling merrily from windowsills and doorframes. Snow hung heavy on every rooftop and pathway—not as foreign a sight to him as it would have been without his time in the army, but still hard to look at without itching to draw his sword, especially when his eyes caught on burned scraps of Atlas-blue cloth trampled into the snow—remnants of scorched flags discarded after the battle. The scents of pine and frost and smoke braided through every gust of ice-kissed wind, embroidering his breath with a promise that he was far, far, *far* from home.

Though it was night, the city still bustled beneath the light of wrought-iron kerosene streetlamps. Horse-drawn carriages navigated the wide streets easily, bells jingling on the harnesses stretched between horse and carriage, the animals' breath coming out in ghostly huffs as they trotted along. Some houses had wreaths of roses hung on their doors; others had a familiar carving etched into the doorframe instead.

"Mortem is worshiped most prominently here, but Tempest is a close second," Elias broke his near-perpetual, grieving silence to explain as Kallias stopped to run his gloved fingers down the jagged lightning bolt carved into the door of one of the few shops that had already closed.

A light shiver trailed down his neck in time with his fingers, and he pulled away, swallowing down the strange yearning that tightened his throat. "You don't fear him?"

Elias shrugged. "Not in the way you mean. To us, Nature isn't wicked. It just…is."

"My people call him a ship-breaker."

"And if it never rained, you'd call him a harvest-killer."

That was fair, though Kallias had to bite his tongue on a retort. He was tolerating Elias's presence for many reasons—one of which being the fact that he needed him if he was to have any hope of surviving the coming encounter with Nyx's queen—but he still hadn't forgiven the man for all the lies he'd told over these past weeks. When Kallias hadn't known him as Elias, the Nyxian spy, but rather as Eli, a newly recruited Atlas soldier and…and a friend.

What a fool he'd been. In more ways than one.

"Come on." Elias jerked his head, the knit cap tugged over his ears barely budging with the movement. The Nyxian man was bundled up far less extensively than Kallias, his deep scarlet coat with black trim and simple leather gloves the only real defense he had against the cold. Even so, he didn't shiver; he simply looked ahead, eyes dull and resigned, like a man facing down an old enemy he knew he couldn't defeat. "It's getting late. If we don't reach an inn by true nightfall, they won't let us in."

"I thought nightfall was when Nyx thrived."

Elias rolled his eyes, which Kallias didn't think was very fair. "That doesn't mean we're nocturnal. Are all Atlas up at the crack of dawn?"

"*I* am."

Elias sighed. "Just follow me."

Not that he was paying attention—because he wasn't—but Elias had gotten worse since his visit to the abandoned temple they'd passed on their way here. His eyes were stamped with sleepless shadows, and his hands shook every time he used them. He kept tucking his second mourning braid up into his hat to hide it, like he was ashamed of it, like it was a secret he wasn't ready to tell. A ring lined with black and white diamonds hung from a chain around his neck, and though Kallias hadn't asked what its purpose was, he thought he might have an idea.

The echoes of a familiar grief spread through his chest like ripples through a tide pool. The gods may have been proven real, but they'd also been proven cruel. To give his sister back after ten years only to take her away again mere months later…

Worse than cruel. Monstrous.

And that had been before the nightmares started.

Goosebumps rose on his arms that had nothing to do with the deadly Nyxian cold, and he blinked back flashes of screaming lightning and roaring waves. Those dreams were some twisted form of homesickness, nothing more. He wouldn't give them any ground here. When they made it to Andromeda, he would be setting foot on an untested battlefield, one no Atlas had truly breached before. A one-man army with no weapon but his wits.

Gods, he should've let Finn come instead.

As they moved through the city, there was a building energy that buzzed across his skin, uncomfortably familiar: the sense of oncoming battle. Very few common folk wandered the streets, and those who did were all armed; all adults, no children. Soldiers walked in groups or in pairs, never alone, and they too were armed to the teeth. There was little laughter, little gossip—despite the cheery atmosphere, there was a razor edge to the starlight that sparkled off every plate of armor and sheathed weapon.

He remembered the tang of bloodlust from his earliest days in the war. It hung heavy on the air tonight.

But that vicious silence was broken by a strangled gasp—not from him. Not from Elias. From a woman who'd stopped dead in the middle of the street, her features outlined in strips of shadow and kohl, the whites of her eyes shining with utter shock as the various parcels she was carrying thudded in a pile of slush at her feet.

"Elias?" Barely a whisper, a wisp of campsmoke borne on the merciless wind. Then again, louder, a hybrid of sobbing and shouting: "*Elias!*"

For the first time, true emotion broke across Elias's face, disbelief that quickly morphed into something almost like fear. "Evanna—?"

Elias barely got the name out before the stranger crashed into him, fully tackling him into the snow, and Kallias had to jump back to avoid getting taken down with him. Slush splashed.

"*I—am—going—to—kill—you,*" Evanna snapped between kisses peppered across Elias's forehead and cheeks…and punches peppered along his chest. Her sleek brownish-black hair was cut through with what he guessed were dyed streaks of shimmering silver, and the fury in her eyes gleamed behind a shield of tears. Her black leather ensemble clung to her sturdy frame, threaded with silver like her hair, and she didn't seem to care that she was being stared at. "They thought you were *dead*, they told us you *died*, you absolute bastard of an *asshole!*"

"Good to see you too," Elias wheezed from beneath her weight. "Um, Evanna, if you'd let me up—"

"I'll let you up when I'm good and ready. Elias, Mortem save you, we held a *funeral.*" Evanna's voice broke, and she paused in her pummeling to hold Elias's face between her hands. "Mama burned a pyre. Everyone *mourned* you."

"Elias?" Interrupting didn't seem like the best idea—he didn't want to find himself taken down in the snow, too—but he didn't care to be left out of the loop. "Care to introduce me?"

"Right." Elias blinked away the guilt that had started to fester in his gaze, gesturing to the woman helplessly. "This is Evanna—Evanna Loch. My older sister."

"His favorite sister," she corrected, finally swinging herself off of Elias and reaching down to help him up, minding his arm with a gentleness that puzzled Kallias until he remembered the wound that used to be there. She stood to her full height—a whole head below Elias—and held her hand out to Kallias. "And who are you, stranger?"

Kallias opened his mouth by instinct, but froze. Which false name could he use that wouldn't stir suspicion? He could only remember Atlas monikers. "I...ah..."

"Evanna," Elias interrupted, saving him from having to stumble through an answer with his terrible Nyxian accent, "what are you *doing* here?"

"Well," Evanna muttered, brushing snow from her pants, "everybody said you had to be dead, but we knew Soren was still alive because our spies in the city brought the news back to Enna. But that's where it stopped—with Enna. She warned them against spreading it any further because of the ridiculous claims Atlas was making of it, that Soren was actually Princess Soleil and we've been hiding her here all this time. Only it wasn't ridiculous at all, it was *true*, gods save us. Yvonne and Emberlyn confronted her and she told them everything. And once Emberlyn found out Soren was alive, she came to me and said you had to be alive too, because Soren would've killed her way through Port Atlas before she let anyone touch a hair on your head, of course. So we came here with Yvonne and found Captain Jakob and told *him*, and he told your company, and now we're preparing a rescue party. Well, we *were*. But now you're here, and..." She trailed off, her eyes focused on something below Elias's face—when Kallias followed her gaze, he realized Elias's mourning braids had been knocked loose when Evanna tackled him. They now lay in full view.

Horror flooded Evanna's eyes. "No," she said. Then again: "Oh, *no*..."

A tremor ran through Elias's chin, but his jaw flexed, stopping it in its tracks. "It's a long story, Evanna."

"No story is too long for me. Start talking while we walk. The princesses are staying in Lord Bacchus's manor, they'll want to see you. Who's your friend? And your arm—how bad is your—"

Evanna rolled up Elias's sleeve, and Elias choked "Don't—"

But it was too late. Both Loch siblings froze as Elias's sleeve bunched near the crest of his shoulder, revealing the scarred flesh beneath...scars that resembled thorny vines belonging to a goddess not worshipped by Nyx.

Even the falling snow seemed to drift to a halt, the world watching with baited breath.

"Elias," breathed Evanna, "what in the *pits* happened to you?"

Elias snatched his arm back. Tugged down his sleeve. "The manor first," he said roughly. "I don't want to tell this story on the streets."

"Fair enough." But the grief, the terror, didn't abate from Evanna's eyes. As she took a step back, Kallias caught the glint of familiar beads nestled against the collar of her coat. "Follow me."

The journey through the city was a quick one, at least by Kallias's standards; Delphin wasn't half the size of Port Atlas. Not that he would've known it based on the sheer magnitude of the building Evanna led them to—gated and heavily guarded, the manor was an intimidating, stocky thing of black and silver and white, a portrait painted without color that loomed against the night sky, a structure built from shades of shadow.

When they finally reached the gate, Elias didn't wait for Evanna. He stepped forward and signaled to the guards who manned it with a quick wave of his hand, removing his hat and shouting, "Hold! Officer Elias Loch, from the Obsidian company!"

Like they would recognize his name. Like it would be enough to stay their weapons and grant them access to what should have been one of the most closely-guarded structures in Nyx. Did he really hold so much sway in this kingdom?

Though, he had been the battlemate of one of the *princesses*. Maybe that afforded him some higher rank than most officers.

Regret poured into the brew of anxiety already churning in Kallias's stomach. Maybe putting his trust in a Nyxian spy had been a worse idea than he'd first thought.

"Elias!" shouted a male voice, and one of those guards jumped down from his post, rushing toward them as fast as his armor would allow. For one strange moment, Kallias thought he recognized the muscle-bound blond soldier, but when the man threw his arms around Elias with a booming laugh, he shook that sensation off. It had been a long journey, that was all.

Elias thumped the man on the back, a weak laugh cracking from his own chest, and Kallias almost flinched. The sound was like hearing a plate shatter against a stone floor. "*Jakob.* Shouldn't you be home by now?"

Jakob gripped the back of Elias's neck, bumping foreheads with him before pulling back. He was dressed in typical Nyxian armor, black with silver detailing, and his blond hair was cropped close to his head, a tattoo climbing up the left side of his neck and curling around his ear. "Should be," Jakob agreed, not releasing Elias's shoulders as he looked him up and down, awe on his face that Kallias knew all too well from a day he'd spent in this very kingdom. The awe of seeing the dead alive again. "We all should be, really. But it seems two of my *dumbass* soldiers decided to get themselves carted off to Atlas. And even if they hadn't, Varran took an arrow to his shoulder and got himself an infection because he wouldn't go to the physician tent until I went with him—yet another dumbass the universe decided to burden me with—and I couldn't go home without him, and nobody else wanted to go back without us. Then the princesses and your sister showed up planning some half-assed rescue mission, and I had to know for sure. Elias, we thought you were *dead* until they came here. It's been months."

Elias's shoulders tensed, his hand starting to drift toward his neck before it stopped, curling into a fist instead. "It's...it's a long story, Jakob. Longer than you know. I need to speak with Yvonne and Ember."

"Of course." Jakob's eyes flickered to Kallias and narrowed. "Who's this?"

Kallias swallowed, opening his mouth to deliver the story they'd practiced on the walk here to get him through the gates—but Elias caught his gaze. Shook his head. "Tell him. It's all right."

Tell him which part? Did he still claim his title as prince, if only to keep them from killing him right away? Did he tell the whole story of his abdication, of his engagement, of everything that had led him from the battlefield outside Ursa to the site of Atlas's most recent defeat?

"Kallias Atlas," he said finally, carefully removing his hat and giving Jakob the slightest bow he could manage. Enough to convey respect, but not enough to lower himself below them. "Firstborn son of Queen Adriata and King Ramses. I bring news of a danger that threatens both our kingdoms."

He heard the creak of tautening bowstrings before he even finished speaking, and Jakob's face dropped at the same time his hand did, his gloved fingers wrapping around the hilt of his sword. Evanna, too, took a step back and went for her weapon. But before either of them could draw their blades more than an inch, Elias's hand flashed out, catching Jakob's wrist. "No," he said. Then again, louder, to the archers above and his sister beside: "No! It's all right. He's with me."

"He's *with* you?" Jakob repeated incredulously, trying to move forward, pushing Elias a step back as he did so. Still, Elias held firm, his hands braced against Jakob's armor.

"Jakob, if I had any other choice, you know I never would bring an Atlas over the border. He's not lying. Something...something terrible happened. He's trying to help us, as mad as it sounds."

The blond soldier studied Kallias for too long, his lip curling at the corner before he turned his attention back to Elias, reading his face carefully. And Kallias knew exactly when Jakob found the second mourning braid in Elias's hair, because the soldier's face fell into such devastation that it thumped like an arrow in Kallias's own chest.

"No," said Jakob. "Not Soren."

Elias's jaw ticked, but his stony expression didn't falter. "I need to see the princesses," he repeated.

Jakob swallowed, the slightest hint of dampness lining his eyes. He gave Kallias one last look before finally saying, "Fine. But I want eyes and blades on him at all times."

"Wouldn't expect anything less," said Elias.

"I'm used to it," Kallias added dryly.

Jakob snorted softly. "I'm sure you are. Come on, Atlas bastard. You make one wrong move and I'll do my best to find out if that pretty head of yours bounces."

Well, it wasn't the smoothest threat—or compliment—he'd ever heard, but it conveyed his meaning well enough. Kallias followed the Lochs through the gate, keenly aware of Jakob's presence behind him and Evanna's before him, her arm wrapped protectively around her brother's waist. He swallowed the nerves bundling in his throat, pulling his coat tighter around him even though his shivers had long ago stopped. His body had resigned itself to the cold, it seemed.

"Jakob," Elias said over his shoulder as they walked, and Kallias didn't like the sudden caution in his tone, "I don't suppose Raquel is still around?"

Silence held for a beat too long. Then Jakob laughed, a startled bark that grated on Kallias's resolve and stirred that strange sense of familiarity again. "Oh, shit. That's a very good question. I didn't even think of that."

"Who's Raquel?" Kallias had never heard the name from Soleil's mouth or Elias's.

"Pray to whatever gods you love that you never find out," Jakob chuckled. "I don't know if she's still here or not, Pious. I've been sleeping in the infirmary for a week."

"How's Varran recovering?"

"Well, he'll *live*, which is all I can ask for at this point. My better half spends too much time worrying about me and not enough about himself. He keeps trying to kick me out of the infirmary so I can get some sleep."

"Sounds like someone else I know," Elias said pointedly. "Remember when you broke your ankle in Canis? When you ordered Lily to wrestle him into bed at all costs?"

Jakob snorted. "That was different. I can function fine being awake for a couple days. Varran's useless if he doesn't get his eight hours."

Before Kallias could get too irritated about being left out of the loop, they reached the manor's doors. They were more intimidating than any Kallias had seen before, made entirely of iron. Heavy, dense...unbreakable. Looking like they'd been placed there by the hand of a deity, forged with a power not known in this world.

As they stepped into the front parlor, a rush of warm air unfurled itself over him, cinnamon-scented and smokey, surprisingly inviting. This was nothing like the gilded, bejeweled parlor back home; this was a vast room with stone walls and a white brick fireplace on each side, fires crackling in each one despite the late hour. Plush black carpet soaked up the melting snow from his boots as he took another step inside, suddenly unsure if he was being tricked—this couldn't be where the Nyxian princesses was staying. There weren't any guards beyond those he'd seen at the gate, and while it was well-decorated, it was hardly the finery he'd come to expect of royalty.

This...this looked like a home. Albeit a much larger-than-normal home.

There were couches and stuffed chairs scattered throughout the room, arranged around small tables or stools, and dozens of people lounging on them. Not servants, by the look of them—they appeared halfway ready for bed, wearing nightclothes and wool socks, hair unbound and laughter rising above the popping of the logs in the fireplaces. Books, cards, half-empty glasses, and ceramic mugs littered the tables; it seemed nobody was planning on leaving anytime soon.

The sight of the amber liquid in some of those glasses tugged sharply on Kallias's stomach, his tongue drying out. He swallowed hard, biting the inside of his cheek to distract himself.

This was nothing like Atlas's palace, which had been so heavily guarded since the fire that no one made it through the gates unless they were hired onto the staff or a close family member of someone who was. He still didn't know how Elias had managed to get past three guarded checkpoints without getting caught and killed.

"Is it normally open like this?" he hissed to Elias, but when he turned, he found the Nyxian soldier watching the scene with both fondness and indescribable pain etched into his features. Elias swallowed visibly, reaching toward his necklace, tweaking it between his thumb and forefinger, and some of Kallias's irritation faltered. "Hey. Eli—Elias."

Elias jerked as if Kallias had pushed him, his hand falling away from his necklace. "What?"

He gestured to the scene before them. "This is…"

"Homely?" Elias asked dryly. "Quaint? Peasantish?"

"I was going to say *nice*."

Elias shrugged one shoulder, but the sheen of emotion in his eyes betrayed him as he looked back to the groups of friends huddled over games of cards and steaming mugs.

"The manor's lower floor is open to the public at any hour," Evanna explained. "It houses the city's library down the hall. And a lot of the soldiers hole up here to get out from under their captains and generals for a while."

"Come on," Jakob interrupted, jerking his chin toward the staircase. "Ember's staying upstairs. You can leave your coat and boots here."

Kallias blinked at him, not moving even as Elias removed his own coat and boots, revealing a loose-fitting knit sweater that covered his scar and tattoos. "We are meeting with *the princesses*, yes?"

Elias hung his coat on one of the many racks lining the wall inside the doorway, raising one eyebrow at him. "Unless I decide to let Jakob throw you in the dungeon instead."

Jakob laughed. Kallias scowled. "That's not funny."

Elias sighed. "Yes, Kallias, we are meeting with the princesses. Did you forget already?"

"Normally, diplomatic meetings between royals demand a certain amount of propriety. Respect. They're often a matter of life and death, war and peace…and you want me to take off my *shoes*?"

The faintest smirk touched the corner of Elias's mouth. "Welcome to Nyx, Kallias Atlas."

Self-consciousness crept across his shoulders like Elias had slipped a beetle into his shirt, but he kicked off his boots anyway, wishing he hadn't decided to wear the socks Soleil had knit him for this past Saltwater Festival. Not that he didn't love them—he would've loved them no matter what, because she made them for him—but they were the gaudiest amalgamation of yarn he'd ever seen in his life, made entirely of clashing colors and strange patterns, and they drew every single eye his way as they made their way up the wood-and-wrought-iron staircase.

He heard whispers as they climbed, but to his surprise, they weren't focused on him—instead, people watched Elias, their expressions ranging from uneasy to grieved whenever they found that blue-twined braid in his hair. Some even reached out and brushed his shoulder in passing, a gentle, knowing touch that startled Kallias with its familiarity. Most of them had braids of their own—some only one, others multiple. One wore four braids that he could count, an older man who walked alone while many walked in pairs.

A sick feeling stirred in his stomach that had nothing to do with nerves, and he lowered his eyes, lengthening his strides to keep up with Elias.

When they finally reached the right floor, it seemed someone had been warned they were approaching; the guard he'd expected to see downstairs had simply relocated. A handful of soldiers lined the short hallway, all with hands on blades and eyes on him, hatred keen as a razor edge in each and every gaze. There was only one door, a simple wooden thing that stood waiting at the opposite end of the hall. It was open, and standing outside of it, both wearing sleeprobes made from velvet the color of starshine—

Elias bowed. "Princess Yvonne. Princess Emberlyn."

Princess Emberlyn nodded to Elias, but the Crown Princess didn't look at him, not even for a moment. Her eyes found Kallias's and stayed there. And Kallias felt…

Nothing.

He'd expected hatred. He'd expected anger. He'd expected all the grief and rage and sorrow of the past ten years to come surging out of him like a riptide intent on devouring the daughters of the woman who'd held his baby sister captive. He'd expected the concept of allying with them to disgust and terrify him.

But he felt none of that.

Looking into Princess Yvonne's eyes, his body was suddenly taken over by bone-deep, visceral exhaustion. A weariness he only ever felt after the bloodiest of battles, the worst of his losses. And in her, he saw the same—some strange tether stretched between them, some common ground, a thing he couldn't explain but could only feel. He recognized the bearing of another ruler with the weight of a kingdom on her back, though she carried it with an inherent grace that reminded him painfully of Jericho. Her hair was the color of gilded starlight, white with a hint of gold, a color he'd never seen before. Her brows were dark, though, which suggested to him that she might have utilized Nyx's famous cosmetic dyes and tonics to achieve that shade. Her pale face was round and rosy-cheeked, her robe wrapped tightly around her ample form, and the way she rested her hand against her hip suggested that she was hiding a weapon somewhere beneath it. The rumors of her beauty certainly hadn't been exaggerated.

The second eldest, Emberlyn—the weaponsmith, he remembered, once a deadly force in Nyx's army, one of the named targets for their Vipers before she reportedly retired following the death of her battlemate—wasn't hiding her weapons. A belt of varying blades seemed hastily thrown around her narrow hips, and her layers of clothing couldn't hide the perfectly-honed muscle beneath. Her amber eyes studied him in a calm, calculated way that promised she'd already decided exactly how he would die if the situation called for it. Beautiful in a different way than her sister, but lovely all the same.

"First Prince Kallias," said Princess Yvonne. "You're the last person I expected to find darkening my door this evening."

"We have a lot to discuss, Your Highness." His voice came out stronger than he'd expected, and for that he was grateful—that, and the fact that she had named his former title without him having to fumble around the specifics of it. "But I come under a banner of peace."

Yvonne's eyes sharpened. "Atlas baited us with the promise of peace before, and it cost my mother many of her best soldiers. If you wished for a warm welcome, you should have brought our sister back with you. Where is she?"

He caught Elias's flinch out of the corner of his eye.

"I think it's time we do away with pretense." Kallias took a step forward, and every weapon in the hall sang out in a single shared note, steel against sheath, dozens of blades leveled in his direction.

He did not flinch, even as cold sweat began to bead on the back of his neck. There was no room for fear. Fear would lose him this battle before it even began.

"Do your people know her true name?" The words crept off his tongue with a softness that barely reached above the breathing of the guards around him. "Do they know where she came from? Where your mother *took her* from?"

Yvonne didn't flinch, but Emberlyn did, the slightest hint of anger in her eyes—anger he didn't think was directed his way. She stepped to her sister's side, putting a hand on Yvonne's shoulder. "Weapons down," she ordered the guards. "Prince Kallias, please join us inside—just you. It's time this story was heard."

Jakob, who'd been quiet up until now, made a small noise of protest. "Your Highnesses, at least a couple guards—"

"Captain Petrov, please find a place for the Lochs to catch up," interrupted Yvonne. "I'm sure they'd like a moment alone."

Elias raised his head, shoulders still taut beneath his sweater. "Ember, Yvonne, I need to—"

"Later," Yvonne said then, much more gently—and in that one word, Kallias realized the Crown Princess already knew. That her eyes had already read the truth in Elias's haggard face, in the slope of his back, in the second braid twined through his hair. But her voice held strong when she said, "We *will* speak, Elias. But there are some things that have waited too long to be brought into the light."

"All due respect, Your Highnesses," Kallias rasped, "but I am friendless in this kingdom. I will not go anywhere without my ally."

This time every head in the hall turned to Elias, whose mouth twitched downward, an unhappy thing that twinged deep in Kallias's chest.

That was a misstep. He'd just branded Elias as an enemy sympathizer to a handful of his peers, possibly even his friends.

Yvonne cleared her throat, bringing every eye back to her. "Understood. Evanna, Elias, Captain Petrov—you all may join as well."

The part of him that was long-practiced in how to arrange a battlefield in his favor screamed to dig his heels in, to promise her that she would have no audience if she did not even those odds a bit. But the truth of his position was obvious in the shine of torchlight on dozens of pieces of steel: he was outnumbered, outmatched, and he had nothing to bargain with. His youngest sister, their princess, was dead; he could not offer her safe return. He'd forsaken his title weeks ago; he could not barter true peace without his mother's approval. As they likely could not bargain without theirs.

He had nothing to offer but the news of his older sister's foolhardy bargain with powers beyond his understanding, and a warning to prepare for a renewed onslaught from Atlas. These princesses held the key to a mystery that had tortured him for ten years.

So he took a deep breath. Straightened his back. Tried very hard not to wish for a drink in his hand—and almost succeeded, which felt worse than outright failing. "Fine."

The princesses moved to either side, leaving the door to their room open.

The breath stuttered in his chest, his back already aching from a knife that wasn't yet in it, but he walked forward with his head held high. And though his feet shied from that threshold, he crossed it without a beat of hesitation.

He'd promised to lay down his life for his kingdom long ago. This was merely a different sort of battlefield, and he'd take it just the same.

Elias, Evanna, and Jakob filed in after him. The door shut behind them with a finality that sent a soul-deep shiver through his body.

CHAPTER 3

KALLIAS

The Nyxian princesses may not have shared blood, but they certainly shared one thing: a glare that could melt the bones of even the bravest of men, a talent Soren had utilized often during her time in Atlas. Both of them were seated on a couch across from his borrowed chair, staring him down; even in their velvet robes and slippers and rumpled hair, he felt the need to sit straighter, to fold his hands politely in his lap, to look as non-threatening as possible. He knew better than to test the mercy of Nyxians. He'd learned that from his lost sister.

He wondered if any of these girls had families grieving them, too.

"You promised me answers," he croaked when the silence stretched on, long enough that he could hear Elias's breathing behind his chair. The Loch siblings were flanking him on either side, but he only felt safe in regards to his left—Evanna could still sink a dagger into him on the right. "I'd like to have them."

He also wished he could believe that there were any gods left to lend him a hand, because it was going to take divine intervention for him to get through a conversation with *Yvonne, Evanna,* and *Emberlyn* without calling one of them by the wrong name.

Emberlyn looked to her sister, who took in a breath that brought her shoulders near to her ears.

"Ten years ago," Yvonne began, "my mother was ordered to assassinate the Atlas heir. Her father intended to use the fire to wipe all of you out, if possible, but ensuring Soleil's death was his priority. He hoped that by unbalancing the order of succession, he could break Atlas down at its core before ever launching a true assault on your borders. But my mother disobeyed him. She set the fire too late, giving your family the opportunity to escape. But Soleil wasn't fast enough. She got trapped in the ballroom."

The scoff escaped his lips before he could stop it. "You expect me to believe Queen Ravenna was trying to *save* us?"

Yvonne met his gaze steadily. "No. But it's the truth. She and your mother were friends once, you know. And even if they weren't, my mother wasn't willing to see children die for her father's ambitions."

Fire and soot stained the walls of his memory, flashes of screaming and stampeding feet and shouting for his siblings threatening to pull him out of this room. He dragged himself out of that place with a shaky breath, digging his own nails into his leg to ground himself. "But she failed."

"Not in every case," Yvonne reminded him. "You and Finnick and Jericho made it out. But King Byron's men had already locked the ballroom doors by the time Sor...Soleil reached them. She couldn't get out." She was silent for a beat, then: "My mother couldn't bear to leave her there to burn. She ran through the flames, wrapped Soleil in her own cloak, and escaped with the help of her battlemate."

"But she didn't bring her to us." Ah, there was the rage he'd been waiting for. "She *took* her."

"If word had gotten out that she was still alive, Byron would have tried again," Yvonne promised gravely. "And he would have killed my mother for her failure."

"He was her father. He wouldn't have—"

Yvonne glared him down, and he shut his mouth. "He would have," she said softly. "Without blinking."

All the words fled Kallias's mouth, and he could only stare, trying to comprehend that idea. His parents...no matter how badly he failed, no matter how much he disappointed them, they would never have raised a hand against him in anger, let alone a blade.

"My mother and her battlemate separated from the group and fled across the border to Ursa. There's an orphanage there run by a friend of the family—the same place I was raised," she added. So she was legitimately Nyxian, at least. "The plan was to keep her safely hidden there until my mother could make contact with Adriata and smuggle her home without Byron's knowledge, but the border shut down too fast—none of her messengers made it through. And when Soleil woke, she was confused, panicky. She couldn't tell anyone her name or who her family was or what kingdom she was from. All she could get out was *So. Soso, Soso.* She needed to be called something in the meantime, and Soren was the closest Nyxian name my mother could think of."

He heard Elias's intake of breath, sharp but slow, and forced himself to mimic him. His chest ached with held-in air.

"It wasn't safe to take her home," Yvonne continued. "Not until King Byron passed away two years later. Until then, she lived in Ursa with the family who ran the orphanage. They had a daughter about Soren's age and they got along well—they became battlemates later on, in fact. Once Byron was gone, my mother reached out to Adriata and offered to discuss peace. She agreed." Her eyes speared Kallias with muted accusation. "You know what happened then."

He did. Jericho had volunteered to go herself to secure peace, but she'd come home covered in blood and weeping, claiming the Nyxian escort had turned on her and her guards. She was the only one to escape alive.

A lie—all a lie.

"After that, Adriata refused contact," Yvonne concluded, "and the conflict intensified. Princess Jericho had proved herself perfectly happy with the war, and my mother didn't know what else she'd be willing to do. She didn't know how deep her attachment to her crown ran."

Kallias's throat tightened. "She was afraid Jericho would kill Soleil if she came home."

"I won't fully defend her actions, Prince. She was wrong to keep Soren's true heritage from her—and to keep it from us." Yvonne's jaw worked like she was chewing something tough. "We only found out the truth ourselves when we confronted her about why she wouldn't send a rescue party after Soren. And by then it was too late for us to do anything, anyway. But for what it's worth, as the future Queen of this kingdom…I give you my solemn apology. This was handled poorly, and harm was done unnecessarily. I would offer reparations if I had the power to do so. But I know empty words are worth nothing in the hand of one so harmed. I don't ask that you accept my apology, only that you hear it—and take it into account when considering the future of your kingdom's actions toward mine."

He could offer that much to a princess who'd had as little to do with this tragedy as anyone else. "I hear it and accept it, as far as it can go. But I have one more question."

"Ask it."

"What happened to my people? The ones who were living here when you attacked?" He should have seen at least a *hint* of Atlas presence in this city; instead, it looked as if it had never switched hands in the first place.

Yvonne cleared her throat and smoothed her hands over her hair, straightening back up from her apologetic posture. "Many fell in the fight. Most escaped or were allowed to leave after the battle was done. Those who wished to stay—mostly young families who feared to travel with children—were allowed to remain in their homes. Anyone who tries to mistreat them is quickly discouraged—either by guards under my employ, or by me personally…or, if they're quite unlucky, by my sister. We keep no prisoners her—there's no point to it, really." Yvonne took a deep breath, sitting back in her seat, and Emberlyn eased a hand over her shoulder before spearing Kallias's gaze with her own.

"Your turn," said the quieter, more frightening princess. "Tell us what happened in Atlas."

So Kallias did. He told them about bringing Soleil home, about her hostility and her desperation, her demand for something they could not supply. How Finn had jumped in before any of them could tell her there was no such thing as a Viper venom cure, dangling that prospect to make her stay until she could remember who she was. He told them of memory attacks and a spy dressed up as a guard— both princesses rolled their eyes fondly at that part, and he heard the punch of knuckle against arm behind him, followed by a pained grunt from Elias—and of the necromancy scourge that had slowly spread through his city, that had changed from grave robberies to intimidation to assassination attempts. He told her of betrayals and deaths and a goddess made flesh—borrowed flesh. Stolen flesh. And against his better judgment, against the part of him that still wanted to see this kingdom burned to ash, he told them of an alliance with Artem, how that kingdom had offered weapons in exchange for a wedding.

The moment *Artem* left his mouth, Emberlyn's hand fell away from her sister's shoulder, her eyes flaring in horror that seemed personal. "*Artem* agreed to ally with *you*?"

"After they were informed that you were dabbling in necromancy, it seems they were finally persuaded away from their position of neutrality." No easy feat, seeing as Emberlyn was of Artemisian blood—he knew that much about her. Their spies had been increasingly nervous about Nyx possessing any Artem-trained weaponsmith, let alone a daughter of diplomats, let alone one who sat on a Nyxian throne. The day she'd vanished from the battlefields had seen more sighs of relief in the war room than any day Kallias could remember, though the threat of her eventually using her connections with Artem to gain an ally to Nyx's cause still remained.

"They know better than that," Emberlyn argued. "Necromancy is *Anima's* magic. Any Artemisian could tell you that much. Their children are taught every bit of lore on the pantheon from the time they begin schooling—not just Mortem, but all of them."

Kallias's ears burned, and he clenched his fist—the one that glimmered with a band of gold. His claiming ring. He'd wanted to remove it, but Elias had cautioned him against it—he claimed a married man was less likely to be looked at with suspicion, even one who didn't speak. "Let's just say my sister was convincing in her ruse. And my mother made it more than worth their while."

Emberlyn's eyes fell to his hand, and her jaw flexed. "I have to go," she said, turning to Yvonne. "Vonnie, I have to go and speak to the Empress, someone has to tell them they've been misled—"

Yvonne shook her head. "Em, we can't afford to lose any more of us, Soren already—"

"We will lose a *kingdom* if Artem and Atlas come against us as a united front!"

"It may not come to that," Kallias interrupted, working hard not to wince as Emberlyn's simmering gaze landed on him once again. "I've abdicated my throne. I'm no longer First Prince—not by title. My mother's lost me as a bargaining chip, and without that, Atlas may not have enough to secure the alliance."

Emberlyn pinched her lips together. "You're not the only prince Atlas has."

"My brother is new to the position, and he's not yet twenty-one. Even if he was, he's not suited to an arranged marriage to a complete stranger. He would require time before agreeing to an arrangement, and Artem doesn't seem the kind to offer aid in advance. It may fall through."

"*May* is not a risk we can take. And neither can you," said Emberlyn. "Your kingdom, whether it knows it or not, is in the middle of a coup, Kallias. You do see that?"

He held her gaze. "I wouldn't be here if I didn't."

"Someone has to go," Evanna agreed, coming around to sit beside Emberlyn on the couch, wrapping an arm around her waist, "but it can't be you, and you know damn well why. And *I* know damn well why you actually want to go."

To Kallias's surprise, Emberlyn's cheeks darkened a touch. "I want to go to keep my kingdom safe."

"Right. Of course," Evanna said. "And perhaps you're missing the taste of Artemisian fare?"

"This isn't up for debate," Emberlyn snapped. "Someone has to go to Artem, and it should be me. I have blood-claim to them. They won't cast me out no matter what they think Nyx may be involved in."

"You're right, it's not up for debate," said Yvonne. "You're not going. We will send someone else—"

"Who?" demanded Emberlyn, rising to her feet in one swift motion, crossing her scarred arms. "Tell me who could be better suited for this than a daughter of Artemisian diplomats. I know just as much about them as I do us. I lived with them for years. I know them—"

"And they believe that we've broken the most sacred of their—and our—laws," Yvonne reminded her. "They'll likely be furious with any Nyxian face, Ember, Artemisian blood or not."

Their arguing continued, rising in pitch and volume, but before it could reach the point of no return, a voice broke through from behind Kallias:

"I'll go."

CHAPTER 4

ELIAS

*F*ire and glass, smoke and sweet, a voice that slowed his heart near to stopping.

"Find me in Artem, Elias Loch…go to Artem. Find me there."

"I'll go."

He didn't realize he'd spoken the words until every head in the room turned to look at him—and he didn't realize Kallias had said the same in unison until Yvonne addressed the Atlas prince first. "You think they'll allow you in, even without the alliance?"

"The Artemisian delegation isn't supposed to reach Atlas for another couple days," Kallias said slowly, using his thumb to nervously fuss with his beard. "And it's a three-week journey from Atlas. We're closer here. Even if they leave within five minutes of arriving at our palace, it will likely be some time before they make it back with the news of our failed alliance. I can use that to our advantage—buy us time with my engagement to the Empress. We may be able to convince them of our story before the delegation arrives to tell them I've forsaken my title."

"And what will you tell them?" Evanna pressed. "You expect to continue to court the Empress even after you tell her of Atlas's deception?"

"No, but I expect she'll withdraw the engagement on her own at that point. All we need is an audience, and this ring will buy me that."

Yvonne turned her eyes on Elias. "And you?"

Elias swallowed, wishing his tongue didn't taste like soot. "Anima and Tenebrae aren't the only gods beginning to stir. We believe the others may be searching for hosts, as well."

"Not Mortem," Emberlyn said immediately. "She doesn't take hosts."

"No. But be that as it may, I…" He swished the words in his mouth for a moment, tasting them for truth before he let them out. "I believe she's been speaking to me. I had a…a dream, of sorts. She told me to go to Artem. She asked me to find her there."

"And you believe it was a true vision?" Evanna prompted, her fingers clasped tightly around her own string of prayer beads. His shoulder itched. "Not just a dream?"

"I do. It was too real. I woke still smelling smoke, still feeling the heat of the flames, I…" He clenched his fists, his skin pulsing with a brief burst of heat. "I believe it was her."

Yvonne worked her jaw, glancing between him and Kallias. He could see the turmoil churning in her gaze before she said, with surprising hesitancy, "And what of Tempest?"

Elias fought not to look Kallias's way. "We're not sure." Not that he didn't have his suspicions. He'd heard Kallias sleep-talking plenty these past weeks; had seen the ice that crept from beneath his palms when he was nervous or angry, too. Every so often, when he'd pushed the Atlas man a bit too far past the line of cordial bickering, he could've sworn he'd heard a rumble of thunder in the distance, whether the skies were cloudy or not.

Yvonne nodded once, rubbing her own palms together slowly as she gazed into space. He knew the princess's faith—she was not an avid worshipper of Mortem like most Nyxians. She was a worshipper of Tempest, one who bore his blessing, who carried lightning and thunder in her blood. Raquel, the only other Tempest-worshipper he knew, also used to be an aeromancer—a storm-wielder.

She'd sworn off magic long ago, though. He wasn't even sure if she still prayed to her god.

"I will go regardless," said Kallias. "You are not my princess. But I would ask that you let Officer Loch accompany me, if he's willing. He's much more knowledgeable in matters of religion, and I feel that's going to be valuable in a negotiation such as this."

Yvonne exchanged a glance with Evanna, who shook her head so slightly that Elias almost didn't catch it. "You're more than capable of handling these matters alone as First Prince, aren't you?" the princess hedged.

Kallias's jaw flexed beneath his beard. "This matter goes beyond ordinary politics. I was raised as a prince and a soldier, not a priest. Elias has expertise I do not share. He was instrumental in investigating the necromancy attacks on my kingdom, spy or not. I'm confident my appeal would be heard more easily with his assistance…and it would go a long way toward proving your intention to provide reparations to Atlas for the theft of our Heir."

The threat buried in those last words wasn't subtle—Ravenna's intentions might have been good, but that didn't change the fact that she'd harbored a prisoner of war—more or less—for ten long years. Atlas was well within their rights to continue their war effort, no matter what fate Soren ended up suffering. Kallias might not be First Prince any longer, but he still wielded power in Atlas, especially with the common people. He could direct their perception of Nyx any way he liked—in their favor or against it.

"I want to go," Elias insisted. "I need to go." He didn't know how that had become true so quickly, but he felt it in the marrow of his bones: Artem was where he needed to be. There were answers there that he needed to hear, answers to questions he couldn't ask here. And Kallias was right; as much as he hated it, they stood a better chance as a united front. "Evanna, I know she spoke to me. I saw her. If she's calling me to Artem, I have to follow her. I…I owe it to Soren to put an end to this. If I can't save her, I can at least save our kingdom…our kingdoms."

Kallias looked away. So did Yvonne. Evanna merely nodded. "If you must go, you must," she said softly. "But at least stay for tonight. Have dinner with us."

Elias nodded. "We can spare the time for that."

Kallias stood straighter, wiping his palms on his pants, letting out a slow breath. "To Artem, then."

"In the meantime, we should send more soldiers to the border—maybe even to the towns beyond," Yvonne mused. "We could use more ears in Atlas if they're about to escalate."

"I'll go," Jakob said immediately—Elias had forgotten he was still there, hunched against the wall, watching them all with a look of grim determination. "My battlemate is going to be out of the fight for some time anyway. I'll do more good out there than I will sitting on my ass in the infirmary."

Elias glanced to his friend. Since the day Elias entered the barracks—and for years before that, too—Jakob had been trying to get himself sent over the border. Well before Elias joined up, Jakob's brother Jaxon had gone missing after a year stationed as a spy in Atlas, leaving Jakob—barely in training himself, already orphaned—entirely alone. He'd been trying to find an excuse to set foot in that kingdom ever since.

"Jakob, you're still Captain, and the company's already taken heavy losses," said Elias. "They need—"

"I don't take orders from you, Pious, you take them from me."

"We will discuss it, Captain Petrov," said Emberlyn—more diplomatically than before. "Yvonne is right. We need more eyes on this."

"Not in Port Atlas," Kallias warned. He might be a traitor and turncoat already, but Elias guessed that he drew the line at helping them establish spies in the heart of his kingdom. He could hardly fault him for it.

Yvonne's nod was halfhearted at best, and the unhappy frown on Kallias's face suggested he wasn't convinced, but there wasn't much more he could do. He hardly held the power in this room.

Ember stood too, coming to stand before Elias. She took his hands, looking into his eyes, her brows drawn low. "When you get there," she said, "find Havi. He'll be able to help you. I'll send a letter with you asking him to help."

"Havi?" He'd never heard the name.

Shockingly, a touch of blush darkened Ember's skin. "He's a friend. Trust me, you'll need his help for what you're about to go through."

That didn't sound promising. But Elias had chosen this path—now he had only to walk it to its end.

And once he reached that end, he would have to find a new way to survive this hole in his chest.

Luckily, he had an idea of where to start.

* * *

Elias Loch was not a drinker.

He'd told everyone that when he joined the Nyxian army, and it hadn't been a lie. He'd avoided the stuff religiously after his father's death. His mother had always warned him about the danger of drinking to drown something out—whether it be grief, or fear, or anger. When you used it to medicate a condition that could not be fixed, it was too easy to get addicted. To make mistakes. To find yourself in a hole you couldn't drag yourself out of.

But after weeks of rigorous training, he'd been bone-sore and raw-nerved, and at some point the heckling about his holier-than-thou attitude had snipped away the last of his self-control. So when Princess Soren Nyx, young and brash and so gods-forsaken annoying, had taunted him with an invitation she'd known he wouldn't accept, he'd calmly set his book aside and come to join the circle. And that night...

A game of truth or dare Elias should never have agreed to. Lips searching each other out in the darkness of a storage room. The smoky taste of Nyxian whiskey dark and inviting on her tongue, both of them muttering insults into each other's mouths even as she pulled him closer, even as his hands twisted into her hair and tugged—

Tugging. Ripping.

Shearing bone. Peaches and smoke. Fire and honey. "I would have said yes."

Elias swallowed past the burning lump in his throat, lifted Soren's ring—what would have been Soren's ring, if he'd ever stopped being a coward, if she'd been alive to say yes—and pressed his lips to it briefly, squeezing his eyes shut.

Miss you, smartass.

He let the ring fall where prayer beads once hung—in the dip of a throat that had heaved with pleas to the goddess of death who never cared for her devoted anyway—and replaced it with his refilled shot glass, relishing the burn as the liquor washed the lump from his throat. He ran his tongue over his teeth, tasting what traces were left.

Dinner with Evanna and the princesses and what remained of his company had been brief, but welcome; Varran was noticeably absent, thanks to the injury keeping him in bed, as were Lily and Raquel—the former killed in the attack to take Delphin back, the latter simply unable to be found. But the others had all nearly tackled him to the floor in a smothering group hug...then promptly abandoned him to gawk at his awkward Atlas companion.

By the end of the night, Kallias had been laughing, trading joking jabs with Jakob and comparing scars with anyone willing to show one off.

It had been too much, watching Kallias sit in Soren's usual place, hearing traces of her in his laugh, watching his friends take to him like flies to honey. He'd needed to get away.

He'd needed a drink.

So he'd left Kallias to find his way to their guest room in the manor alone, and now here he sat, making mistake after mistake with every lift of his hand for another round, the alcohol doing the opposite of what he'd hoped—pulling his memories into sharp relief rather than muddling them past remembrance. But at least it dulled the sting a bit.

He and Soren never talked about that dare-fulfilling kiss. Not in the year that passed between that game and the deaths of their battlemates, not after they'd claimed each other and taken their new vows, not even in Atlas. Some part of him wondered if it had even happened, or if he'd dreamed it, some cruel fantasy spun to life by the alcohol he'd consumed and the scent of the expensive imported strawberry perfume she'd worn back then.

He ran his fingertip around the rim of his glass, relieved to find the edges of his vision were finally starting to blur, the jagged pain in his chest softening to a dull ache. For the first time in weeks, for the first time since he'd woken up in chains, his lungs expanded enough for him to drag in a deep breath.

His mother was right. It would be far too easy to come back to this tavern on the seedier side of Delphin. To sit on this same rickety stool pulled up to the wooden counter with names and expletives carved into it, to clean his teeth with liquor until he couldn't feel them anymore, to become one of the regulars sprawled in booths or playing gambling games at tables, cigars perched between their lips and their spilled drinks turning the floor sticky.

To drink until he forgot about games and goddesses and the girls whose bodies they stole.

"What're you drinking?"

Apparently, the whiskey was doing too good a job dulling his senses, because he would have sworn on his father's grave that the seat beside him was empty a moment ago. But when he turned his head, there was a girl perched there, watching him with a look he almost would've named disappointment.

She was pretty. Would've been beautiful, probably, if not for the sudden blurriness of the world. Hair the color of grave dirt, smooth brown skin, full lips, a hooked nose, thick dark brows. And her eyes…he'd never seen eyes that dark. Had never felt anything like he did looking into them, like his soul was slowly being unspooled from his body, like something was draining from him, his limbs going weak and cold.

No. He had felt something like it…once. But he couldn't remember when.

She broke away from his gaze, sipping her own drink—water with ice—and he snapped back to himself, his strength returning all at once. Unease punched hard into his chest, and he rubbed at the sudden gooseflesh prickling at his arms. Nausea fluttered in his belly, and he didn't think it was because of the liquor.

"Who wants to know?" he rasped.

She gave him a long once-over, but didn't look him in the eyes again. "A friend."

"Go to the pits." He didn't have the decency left to feel guilty for swearing at a strange woman. Especially not one that came to a tavern to order a water and judge its patrons, though he could practically hear Soren laughing and ribbing him for being hypocritical. He'd probably done the same a million times in her company. "I've never seen you before in my life."

"It's not possible to remember every face you've ever seen."

Elias squinted at her. Maybe that made sense…did it? Gods, that last shot had been one too many. "A name might help."

She only smiled, a bitter thing that smelled of secrets. "Elias Loch, you're the last person I would've expected to find drunk in a Delphin tavern."

His left hand tensed on the counter. His right drifted toward one of the pitch-dark daggers at his belt. "You have five seconds to answer me. How do you know my name?"

This girl, whoever she was, didn't seem fond of words. She merely dug her hand into the pocket of her plain black dress and pulled out a string of beads—black, with a matching skull at the bottom. A skull with bloodred roses instead of eyes.

The tension bled from Elias's muscles, and he rested both palms on the counter, his own beads burning a hole in his pocket. "You serve in the temple."

A wry chuckle. "You could say that."

He eyed her slowly—not because he wanted to look like a shameless ogler, but because his eyes refused to take her in quickly. Every movement felt sluggish, like tar was jamming his joints.

Right. This was why he didn't drink. He was, as Soren affectionately used to put it, "such a lightweight, it's an utter embarrassment."

"You don't talk like a priestess," he mumbled, motioning to one of the bartenders for another refill. The woman started to open her mouth—probably to tell Elias he was cut off—but the other bartender, a woman with a mourning braid pinned above her ear, gripped her partner's shoulder and shook her head.

"He's got a fresh braid," he heard the woman murmur. "Leave it until you can't."

"If he passes out, you're the one dragging him upstairs," the other mumbled back, but she poured Elias's drink.

No weeping. No weakness.

Shame—that was what he should have been feeling. Shame and disgust at the lack of strength he was displaying, the lack of honor to his battlemate. The lack of courage.

But Soren wasn't here to kick his ass for it. And she never would be again.

So instead, he downed that next shot with the rigor of a seasoned reveler.

The priestess, if she was even that, watched the movement with a scowl. "Is this how far you've fallen? Drinking yourself into oblivion in a den of vice?"

An accusation like that should've brought him to his senses. As it was, all that mattered then was that whiskey tasted better than grief. Elias snorted, a chuckle wrenching painfully out of his chest. "This is hardly a den of vice."

The priestess jerked her chin to the gambling tables. "Greed." She nodded to a pair of lovers in the corner who appeared to be trying to consume each other's faces. "Lust." She gave him a look sharper than his knife, gesturing at him with her glass, water spilling over the edge. "Gluttony."

Everything in him grew very, very cold. Cold as a temple floor, cold as a makeshift deathbed.

"You," said Elias, slamming his shot glass down, "do not know a damn thing about me. You don't know where I've fallen from, or what pushed me off that edge. Besides, judgment is for Mortem alone to deal out, isn't that right?"

The priestess only sighed, long and loud, her shoulders slumping forward as if he'd burdened her with his reply. "Doesn't seem fair that she has to bear that task alone."

To Elias's surprise, a laugh rose up—a real one this time. He swallowed it back, twisting on his stool, propping his elbow against the bar. "Well, if you hate it so much, why are you here?"

"Looking for you." A blunt answer, not that it made any sense. "Priestess Kenna has been praying for you, you know. Every night since you and the princess disappeared."

Even liquor wasn't enough to shield him from that blow. He squeezed his eyes shut, rubbing his head. "I'll pay her a visit soon."

"See that you do." The priestess was quiet for a moment. Then: "The loss of a loved one is never easy. I didn't mean to make light of it. Soren was a bright girl. She'll be missed."

Elias merely grunted. He started to turn away, to raise his arm to ask for another round, but before he could even lift his hand halfway, her words hit him:

Looking for you.

The death of a loved one is never easy.

No one from his home temple should've known he was home yet, let alone be able to find him here in Delphin. No one else should've known Soren was dead. He'd only just told the princesses.

Adrenaline catapulted through his veins, burning out the musty haze the alcohol had brought. Slowly, he turned to look at the girl beside him.

Her drink was gone. The simple dress was gone.

And in its place, fire.

Flames licked up the girl's body, from her ankles to the tops of her shoulders. Flames that danced like feverish worshippers, climbing toward her neck, traces catching in her hair. Her face belonged to a mourner, upturned, streaked in soot, mouth poised as if to wail sorrows to the uncaring skies.

A girl born of a funeral pyre. Or maybe she was the pyre itself.

Her gaze was locked on him, lips pressed thin in displeasure, and where there had once been nothing but a void in her eyes…now there were twin gold flames, flickering with life of their own, glowing in the dimness of the dingy chandeliers that lit the tavern.

He tasted ash on his tongue. He smelled incense on her breath.

Elias's knees cracked against the floor before he even realized he was kneeling, his palms shoving against the roughshod floor so hard splinters dug in under his callouses, his liquor-flushed forehead barely kissing the wood.

Because she'd been right. He did know this stranger, this girl, this creature of fire and ruin.

He once spoke to her every morning, every evening. He'd been sworn to her service as a child. He carried her beads in his pocket.

Not a girl after all, but a goddess.

"Off your knees, Elias Loch," said Mortem, Goddess of Death. "Find me again in Artem. And pray that I never find you wasting your potential so appallingly again."

Even at his lowest, his angriest, he did not dare look a goddess in the eye and ask her to explain herself. And it wouldn't have mattered anyway, because by the time he dragged his eyes up from the sullied floor, by the time he found the words to beg forgiveness or ignorance, she was gone—the seat empty and covered in a thin layer of dust, as if it had never been sat in at all.

And he wished that the whole tavern wasn't staring at him, because he was definitely, definitely going to be sick.

CHAPTER 5

KALLIAS

"Hang on. I'm sorry, I don't think I heard you right. Go through it one more time."

Kallias paced across the washroom floor, trying to ignore the sound of Elias vomiting into the toilet—for the fourth time in the past two hours. He'd guessed when the Nyxian zealot had abandoned him in this pleasantly cozy guest room that he'd come back in some sort of state, but he hadn't thought Elias would be foolish enough to drink himself *this* sick.

Then again, Kallias was hardly one to talk.

"I had a vision," Elias groaned, hauling himself up from the floor and dragging himself to the sink. He leaned over it, his sweat-soaked hair falling limply against his forehead as he rinsed his mouth out. He pulled back after several seconds to spit and add, "Mortem spoke to me."

"Spoke to you?"

"Yes."

"Out *loud*?"

Elias glowered blearily at him, snatching up a ragged washcloth and rubbing his face vigorously. "I thought I was the one who was lacking his faculties. Try to keep up."

"You're a mean drunk."

"You're a sad drunk." Elias threw the washcloth at him. "Believe me, after that experience, I'd rather be mean."

Kallias blinked. "Excuse me?"

"Never mind," Elias sighed. He dragged a stepstool over to the sink—the sort of thing that smaller children used to reach the faucet—and sat down on it, rubbing the back of his neck wearily. The liquor may have been purged from his system, but he still smelled like stale beer and cigar smoke. The taint of vice must've clung more tightly to holy men.

"If Mortem is visiting me," Elias said at length, "and Anima is…around…it's safe to assume the other gods are stirring as well."

"And you're sure you didn't…I don't know, fall asleep at the bar? Drunken dreams?"

Elias shook his head. "I know what I saw."

Unfortunately, Kallias believed him. He crossed his arms over his chest. "Fantastic. Who does that leave?"

Elias leaned his head back against the sink, closing his eyes. "Tenebrae, but we know something about his whereabouts from Jericho. So that leaves Occassio and Tempest. Time and Nature."

"Allies or enemies?" When had his life become a godsforsaken fireside story? *Allies or enemies?* They were gods-damned…*gods*! They were legends, barely more than stories. Not something to discuss in terms of strategy.

Elias shook his head, rubbing the heels of his hands against his eyes. "Hard to say. Occassio isn't known for her loyalty. She'll likely choose whichever side is winning. Tempest…I know how Atlas feels about him, but our stories paint him mostly as a benevolent god, generally in favor of keeping balance. So…ally, maybe. He's closely associated with Anima in the stories, though."

Kallias blew out a long breath, sinking against the wall, the toes of his boots touching Elias's. "So. No idea, then."

Elias's chin dipped against his chest, a low, bitter chuckle rumbling from him. "None whatsoever. Some priest, hm? The one thing I'm supposed to be useful for and I can't even..."

"Hey," Kallias said. "This isn't anything you've encountered before. We're all treading new waters here."

Elias closed his eyes. "But I'm the one who's supposed to know how deep they go."

Any further protest died on the back of Kallias's tongue, turning any words he could've said bitter. So instead he asked, "What did she say to you?"

"She told me to go Artem again. That she'd find me again there."

"Nothing we weren't already planning on, then. And we're sure she's not on Tenebrae's side?"

Elias's head came back up, an incredulous look buried beneath the woozy drunkenness still glazing his eyes. "Mortem would *never*."

He should have known better than to suggest Elias's goddess was anything less than benign. He rubbed one hand down the side of his face, scowling at the scratch of his unkempt beard. "If you say so."

They sat together in silence after that, Elias bent nearly in half with the weight of alcohol and exhaustion, Kallias watching him carefully in case he bent too far and passed out. He'd been on that side of grief—had taken a disastrous detour into it a couple weeks ago, in fact. Which was unfortunate for many reasons, not the least of which the fact that he couldn't begrudge Elias this particular vice. Not when he was barely clinging to the edge of the wagon himself. They'd taken days longer to get out of Atlas than they should have, thanks to the withdrawal that had consumed him with raging shivers and constant nausea, making him unfit to travel. They were gods-damned lucky his mother's search parties hadn't caught up with them.

"Drink some water," he said finally. "Sleep it off. Everything will look better in the morning."

Elias shook his head. Another dark chuckle ground out of his chest. "Somehow I doubt that."

Kallias hated that he couldn't offer something more than empty proverbs and halfhearted hope. But there was nothing else he could dredge up...not even a more substantial bit of hope. So when Elias stumbled off to bed, all he could do was make sure he didn't collapse on his way there.

* * *

Smothered in pure darkness, Kallias couldn't breathe.

Petrichor and burning metal seared his nose. Someone had tied anchors to his eyelashes, and the bed had vanished from beneath him; instead his bare back pressed against damp sand, so cold his skin ached, goosebumps shuddering up and down his limbs. Torrents of rain and hail pounded divots into his body, droplets like daggers pelting every inch of exposed skin. When he opened his mouth to scream, water welled up from *inside* him, a spring bubbling to life in his throat, choking out his very breath.

Kallias heaved upward with all his strength, nails clawing deep furrows into the sand. A ragged, burbling cry forced its way through his throat, washing his teeth in water so cold and pure he knew he'd crave its taste even as it drowned him.

But his body didn't budge. His back only arched, his limbs pinned down by something breathtakingly hot.

No—not hot. So cold that it burned.

Somewhere in the back of his mind, he knew this wasn't real. Knew he was still safe and sleeping in the manor. But that was in the back of his mind, and when one was in danger, one tended to focus on things in the very front—things, for instance, like the fact that one *couldn't breathe.*

His thoughts looped in frantic, teetering circles. It wasn't real. It wasn't real, it wasn't real, it wasn't—

Prince, boomed a voice that was not a voice. Then, softer: *Kallias.*

His eyes flew open.

Above him, black clouds roiled, writhing as if in pain. Below him, snow-white sand cradled his body, soaked and ever-shifting. Beyond, the dark sea heaved and crashed, attacking the shore with the ferocity of a starving lion.

And Kallias was trapped in its path.

He jerked his neck side to side, trying to take in his surroundings, trying to find a way out—

His eyes caught on a glassy, gleaming surface.

Oh gods, his arms…

His arms and legs were frozen, nearly numb, encased all the way around in ice so thick he couldn't lift his limbs.

He tugged. Nothing—no movement at all. Dead weight.

Panic flooded his chest like a burst dam. He tried to twist, to gag up the water in his lungs, but it just kept *coming*, a river flowing from his mouth, tasting of rock and ice and *fear*—

Worse, he recognized that tang, that strangeness slithering through the shell of his body, wearing him like an oversized coat.

It was that gods-damned *magic*. That feral thing he'd sensed stirring the moment he'd crossed Nyx's border. A wordless promise that tantalized and terrified him.

This was what lay at the end of that path. Utter consumption. Losing himself to sea and storm. *Becoming* sea and storm.

Spent, his nose and eyes burning, Kallias crumbled back against the sand, blinking dully up at the sky. He couldn't feel his lips, his fingers, his toes. They'd melted away, now part of the ocean clawing its way toward his body.

Thunder snarled. Lightning screamed across the sky, once, again, again, again—

Then it struck downward.

White-blue fire slammed into Kallias's chest, igniting his bones, fire and ice colliding as *agony* blazed through him—

Darkness.

And in that darkness, a voice.

This doesn't have to be your fate, it whispered, purring with power. A voice like the roar of the waves and the rumble of thunder. *I can help you, Prince. But only if you let me.*

"Kallias!"

Elias's shout smothered the fire, shattering the dream, dragging him kicking and screaming from that predatory storm—

To find that even in wakefulness, even dry and warm in his bed, he still could not breathe.

His vision was consumed by dark eyes glazed with revulsion.

Dizzy terror drove adrenaline through him from head to toe, and he clawed at the hands trying to crush his windpipe, bucking his body to throw his attacker off. But they held on, tightening their legs around his hips to keep their balance, their fingers curling in—

Another shout from Elias, and the weight disappeared from atop his body, leaving him gagging and gasping for breath as he scrabbled up on the bed. Elias and the shadow tussled on the floor, but he'd barely managed to reach over and light the lamp on his nightstand before the two pulled apart, the attacker vaulting back over the bed before Elias could catch them, and—

Steel nipped the back of his neck.

Not wielded by Elias, who now stood in front of him, his eyes wider than Kallias had seen them in a while. His hands were up and out, reaching toward Kallias, fingers splayed to show he was unarmed.

"Wait," Elias began. "Don't—"

"Elias," said an unfamiliar voice, "either help me hold him down or leave."

Gods above. He'd never heard a voice like that—coarse and lovely and filled with such rage he barely registered the words past the emotion in them. Something about it called to that *thing* making a home out of his unwilling body. Frost crystallized in his palms, static lifting the hairs on his neck. That voice lit him up from the inside, an unbearable twist of agony and brilliance...a lightning strike stabbing him through the heart.

"Kallias," said Elias, a resignation on his face that Kallias didn't much care for when there was a *blade* at his gods-damned neck, "this is Raquel Angelov. Raquel, please do me a favor and don't kill him yet."

Yet?

"Hello," he said carefully when that blade did not retreat, and in fact pressed in harder. "I'm—"

"I know *exactly* who you are, Atlas bastard," hissed the woman behind him...*Raquel*. "You're Prince Kallias Alexandros Atlas, firstborn son to Queen Adriata. You are twenty-five years old. That is eight years older than my sister was when you murdered her with a sword through her back. She was a *child*, and you *killed her*."

He didn't know why Elias was *smirking*, as if anything about this was even remotely funny.

"Alexandros?" asked the Nyxian peasant that he should have run through weeks ago.

"You're one to talk, Elias *Tiberius* Loch."

That wiped the smirk off his face. "Who told."

"Finn."

"Excuse me!" Raquel snapped, and skin gave beneath the tip of her knife. Blood ran down Kallias's back...blood as cold as snowmelt. Any urge to laugh about ridiculous names dribbled away with it. "Listen, Loch, I don't know what they did to you there, but you'd better have a damned good reason for suggesting I spare his life, and you'd better give it fast. You have thirty seconds. Tell me why all of Delphin is talking about the First Prince of Atlas walking the streets of this city *unscathed*."

"Give him a minute," said Kallias over his shoulder. "He can't form a coherent thought that fast."

The knife twisted, wrenching a groan out of him. "Twenty seconds."

Ah. Right. That was why he couldn't be a smartass like Finn—he wasn't any good at it.

"He's Soren's brother," Elias said.

Raquel's grip didn't relax. "Soren doesn't have a brother."

"Yeah, it was news to her too. Raquel, *please* let him go."

Knifetip scraped bone at the base of Kallias's neck. Every muscle in his body jerked, adrenaline flooding him at that *noise*, vomit burning the back of his throat. He still remembered the way it sounded when bone collided with steel—would never forget it. The battle against puppeted dead outside his home had ensured that.

Elias shifted almost infinitesimally—Kallias only noticed it himself because he'd been on the receiving end of his attacks before, thanks to their sparring sessions. His shoulders tensed. His jaw twitched. His dark eyes searched the stranger for weaknesses, and Kallias didn't like the way his mouth twisted at the corner—like he hadn't found anything helpful.   Elias's hand drifted toward one of the daggers ever-strapped at his hip, and his voice pitched upward, angrier, almost fearful: "Angelov. He's not an enemy."

"I know exactly what he is." The blade pressed in further. "What is he to *you*?"

Elias hesitated, and in that silence, Kallias heard a hundred answers he could have given. A hundred things he might've said to save Kallias's life. A hundred things he might've said to end it.

"He's an ally," Elias said finally, "and as of right now, he's under the protection of our princesses. Raquel, I swear I'll explain everything, I will, but I need you to *let him go*."

Silence fell, with only Kallias's roaring heartbeat in his ears to break it. He held his breath, waiting to see which would fall first—the knife, or his head.

"Killing him now would be considered *treason*," Elias added pointedly.

There was a hot puff of breath against his neck, a Nyxian curse he didn't understand and didn't particularly want to. Then the pressure lifted away and a hand shoved his shoulder, pushing him into Elias's reach. Elias caught Kallias and pushed him behind in one smooth motion, putting his own back at Kallias's chest, his empty hands raised to the woman before them.

And gods, what a woman.

He'd never considered that comeuppance might have a face, let alone that it would be so starkly beautiful. But this woman, Raquel, she was a thing of sharp edges and hatred, her eyes—no, *eye*, the right one was glass—absolutely blazing with it, her teeth gritted and her fists clenched like she had too much of it to carry in one place. Her hair was split into two thick braids, and while it looked black in the shadows of their guest room, every flirt of lamplight against it brought out an almost blue cast—Nyx was known for its dyes, both clothing and cosmetic, so it wouldn't surprise him if even its warriors indulged now and again.

He took a brief moment to thank whatever gods that *weren't* trying to kill them that Finn had never had access to such things. He would've woken up with green hair one day, no question.

A soft pang of homesickness rattled his ribs. He hadn't expected to miss his brother, not so much that he actually regretted telling him to stay behind.

Raquel took one step forward, keeping her knife ready, if lowered. There were sleepless circles stamped around her bloodshot eyes, and after a moment he realized why: there was a third braid that swept from her right temple to the back of her head, hair twined with a pinkish strip of cloth. A fresh mourning braid, something he recognized now thanks to Elias.

She cocked her head to the side, studying first Kallias, then Elias, who was still shielding him with his own body. Her left ear was half-mangled, and there were stripes along that side of her scalp where no hair grew, like she'd been swiped by the claws of some great beast. She wore simple training clothes, mostly black cloth with leather reinforcement in vulnerable areas, but no shoes—likely how she'd snuck in without alerting either of them.

"Where's Soren?" she asked.

Gods, he wished people would stop asking. The way Elias *slumped* every time, like the question dragged what fight he had left out of his bones…it was getting harder and harder to remind himself that Elias was wrong, that Soleil wasn't dead, that they simply had to find a way to get that goddess out of her.

She'd already survived death once…twice. After what he'd seen when he found her on that battlefield, he was never going to bet against her again.

In that lifeless voice Kallias was really beginning to hate, Elias quietly explained the whole story to this Raquel—in a little too much detail, *alarmingly specific* details about Atlas he would rather have seen left out—but the woman

41

merely listened, and watched Kallias like a jungle cat on the hunt. Her knife was practically salivating for his lifeblood. But when Elias got to the end of the story— when he spoke about his own death in a voice softer than a spy's footfall— Raquel's eyes snapped to him. Horror tightened her lips and widened her eyes.

"Your spine," she breathed. "Gods. But you're obviously not dead, so..."

"Soren made a deal with Jericho. Her life for mine." Elias spat the words out like they tasted foul. "And Jericho invited Anima to make herself at home in Soren's body."

Raquel took a step back, cursing viciously. "*Elias.*"

"I know." Seeing Kallias's confusion, Elias explained, "Raquel's another...acolyte, of sorts. She's Tempest-blessed."

That explained his reaction to her presence—maybe. "You have magic?"

Raquel glared at Elias like he'd revealed an embarrassing secret of hers, shifting on her feet, her toes stirring up dust. "I don't use it. So...that's why you're going to Artem?"

Elias scowled back, equally displeased. "Is Evanna getting in the habit of telling everyone my business?"

Raquel crossed her arms, tapping that knife lightly, her body still turned toward Kallias. "Just answer the question."

"Yes, we're going to Artem. And I need Kallias to get me past the border, which is why you *can't kill him.*"

Raquel tilted her head, her eyes drifting over Kallias with slow, predatory focus. The glass one was painted with such precision, he wouldn't have known it was false if not for the slight lag in its movement. His throat tightened, his hand itching to lunge for his sword, but Elias was still standing too close. Shield and barrier. Keeping Kallias safe and keeping him in check.

"All right," she said, indifference snapping into place over rage. "When do we leave?"

"Excuse me?" The words burst out before Kallias could stop them.

Raquel gave him a look with more venom than any Viper's blade. A tendril of cold air coiled around the base of his neck. "If you're under orders from my princesses, it would be treason to kill you now," she said softly, twirling her knife before tucking it back in its sheath, "but the moment it's not, Kallias Atlas, you will meet Mortem at the end of my blade. Until then, I'm not letting you out of my sight. And besides that..." Her gaze drifted to Elias and softened slightly— snow instead of ice, gravel instead of stone. "If Soren has really found her way back to my sister's side, I owe it to her to make sure you make it home safely, Loch. Whether you care to or not."

Elias jerked back a bit, like Raquel had punched him in the chest. Kallias shot out a hand to brace him—

Searing heat bit into his palm through Elias's skin. A pulse of power not entirely unlike the skyfire he'd endured in his dream.

Cursing, he jerked his hand back, pain throbbing in the heel of his hand. He looked down to find a red welt already rising.

Before he'd even fully registered the pain, it cooled. That same breeze that had wound itself around his neck slithered downward, twining around his hand, sapping the heat from the burn. Another curse slid through his teeth and he batted the breeze away, clutching his hand against his chest. This was quickly climbing from ridiculous to absurd. "Elias?"

Elias shook himself like a man emerging from a dream. "Fine," he said, walking toward his pile of blankets on the floor without a backwards glance— leaving Kallias utterly exposed, standing with arms outstretched and jaw halfway to the ground.

"She's not coming with us!" he snapped. He was willing to be in the company of exactly *one* Nyxian for this mission, and that Nyxian was not this blue-haired, beast-slaying woman with a bigger chip on her shoulder than the one his mother had carved into him.

"Does she look like she's giving us a choice?" Elias threw over his shoulder as he burrowed himself back in his blankets. He'd refused to use the other bed offered to them, opting for the floor instead, claiming it was somehow more comfortable. He'd done the same in every inn they'd visited throughout their journey.

Kallias slid his gaze over to Raquel, who was indeed already claiming the empty bed, baring her teeth at him in a grin that was all threat and no smile. Dread chilled the blood in his veins worse than his nightmares ever had, the back of his tongue drying out, remembering the taste of that ever-flowing spring inside him.

Maybe it was time to make his peace with the fact that he was never going to see his kingdom again. One way or another, it seemed Nyx was determined to put an end to him, either by blade or by the hand of their second-best god.

The blood on his neck had finally warmed and dried, at least. Maybe he'd imagined the bite of frost creeping through it before.

A quiet snort blew out of his nose, warming his upper lip a bit. As if he'd get that lucky. The things he wanted to be false never were, and so many things he depended on to be truth had let him down. Jericho's loyalty to Atlas. His mother's reliance on him preventing any arrangement for his hand. The silence of the gods, which he'd never considered something to be grateful for until it was taken away.

No, he'd been born thoroughly without luck. Had likely been born under a ladder, first shown his reflection in a broken mirror, had taken his first steps toward a black cat he saw in the street. With the way luck shied from his touch like an untamed stallion, he must have been coated in misfortune from the moment he entered the world.

He ran his hand over the column of his throat one last time, his insides still longing for the cold, gloriously fresh wellspring from his dream. His stomach pinched nervously, recognizing that ache from a different craving, a different vice, but he shook it off.

He didn't sleep a wink that night, Raquel's shadow ever-present on the other bed, her eyes fixed on him exactly as she'd promised.

CHAPTER 6

FINN

First Prince Finnick Aurelius Atlas, Trickster and Deceiver and wearer of hundreds of names, was pissed off.

Not because he'd just woken from his fifth nightmare in as many hours, though he had. Not because the knocking at his door had become constant in the past few weeks he'd borne this ridiculous title. Not because there was a goddess puppeteering his little sister's body like nobody would ever be the wiser. Not even because his older sister had betrayed them all and his older brother had abandoned him to play hero in the kingdom of their enemies, leaving Finn a new role to learn without so much as even letting him get a peek at the script.

No. No, right at this moment, Finnick Atlas was pissed off because he couldn't get his damned *shirt on.*

The tremors in his hands had started after the battle to drive an undead army out of his city, and despite enduring multiple healing sessions with the Anima-blessed in the infirmary, they hadn't yet stopped. Every time he emerged from a nightmare—waking or sleeping—the shakes seized his hands in an unrelenting grip, rendering him unable to button a shirt or safely wield a dagger.

He clasped his fingers once more around the top button of his shirt, picking at a chip in its glazed exterior.

Mirrors and magic and a maze of false walls. Impish giggles and star-kissed curls and a face he could never remember. "Not long now, Trickster."

He ripped himself free of those flashes, stopping his fumbling with his buttons to lean against the wall, fingers splayed, letting out a slow breath through rounded lips.

He couldn't let this happen. He needed his steady hands almost as much as he needed his steady mind. They couldn't both be failing him at once.

"Get out of my head," he rasped into the wall. "I'm not my sister. You don't have anything I want. Anything that could have broken me is already gone."

Right on cue, that rasping murmur crawled through the back of his mind, lovely and taunting: *"Everyone can be broken, Trickster. Just because you don't know your weakness doesn't mean I won't find it."*

He pressed his forehead harder against the wall until his skull began to ache, until the pain forced the voice out. Until he felt less like a man sleepwalking through a dream and more like a prince with a very real migraine.

He opened his eyes to let a slit of the world back in, wishing that winter had clung on a bit longer to Atlas, that the sun wasn't so gods-damned *bright.* But unfortunately—suspiciously—winter had released the world much earlier than usual, spring tiptoeing in with warm breezes trailing in its wake and flower buds cradled in its hands.

He guessed it had less to do with luck and far more to do with the goddess dressed up as his dead little sister.

Pushing off the wall, he ducked to snatch up his purple sweater off the floor, pausing for a moment to rub his thumb over the thick, hand-knit yarn. The sleeve had a poorly-done patch in it, a hasty thing grafted over the days he'd been wracked with fever and delirium, nightmares-turned-visions crowding the space between his ears until rambling prophecies leaked from his dangerously loosened lips.

You made me a sweater?…I love it. Honest.

Good. I expect you to wear it everywhere.

Another round of knocking shattered his silent connection with the *thing* that had invaded his most sacred space. He growled under his breath, shrugging out of the shirt with all its buttons. He'd been doing his best to form a new mask, one that looked like a dutiful son performing his duties as First Prince, but that mask might have to include wearing his usual sweater if his hands wouldn't cooperate. "I'm coming! Give me a moment, for Anima's sake!"

"Sorry, love. Take your time."

He froze with his sweater halfway over his head at the sound of his mother's voice. She *never* came to fetch him herself, not even on her best days. He couldn't remember the last time she'd stepped foot in this hallway.

He tugged the sweater on the rest of the way, relieved that his arm, at least, had healed. The scar from the undead's bite remained, a gnarled knot of flesh in the center of his forearm, but it didn't burn like pit-fire anymore. Another thing he owed to his traitorous sister.

Rage simmered low in his gut, but he tamped it down with half a thought. It wasn't time for that—not yet. Not yet.

"Come in, Mama," he called, striding across the room and sliding into the chair at his desk, hiding his bare feet in the gap between desk and floor. He scooped his glasses up with one finger and quickly perched them on his nose, letting them slide to the tip as he flipped open a random journal and started writing down a list of every tavern in the lower city from memory. So long as she didn't look too closely at his notes, he'd look the part he'd been playing for these past weeks: the perfect, proper First Prince, not a soldier or a diplomat like his brother—not a traitor, either—but a scholar, a deep thinker, a good son eager to please his mother and queen.

Traitor. No matter how much he tried to quell those rumors, they slipped out in drunken slurs and angry whispers from the mouths of lower city gossips: *The Traitor Prince of Atlas. Helped that Nyxian death-worshipper escape after he almost assassinated the Heir a second time.*

In the upper city, those whispers were few and far between. People knew his brother there; knew him well, called him friend. Many of them believed Kallias had been kidnapped, or coerced into helping Elias through some dark Nyxian magic. At the very least, they weren't calling for his neck in a noose. He could manage a kingdom halfway turned in the wrong direction, but once the tide took them all, there would be no fixing his brother's reputation.

47

Though, who knew if he should even bother fixing it. Kallias hadn't thought much of it when he'd abdicated his crown and fled the kingdom.

Queen Adriata Atlas slipped into his room with unusual caution, her body half turned back like she thought he might order her out. Her hair was down for once, hanging in supple scarlet waves down her back, her pale chiffon pants and sapphire-blue satin blouse more casual than she usually dressed. Her own reading glasses were perched on her nose, and she had a book tucked beneath her arm. "Are you busy?"

"Never too busy for you." He set aside his journal and tossed his quill away, removing his glasses to rub his eyes like he was fatigued from working. Every tiny gesture helped. "Do you need something from me?"

Adriata's mouth twisted unhappily, but she nodded. "Come walk with me?"

Finn's ribs tightened around his heart, the muscles in his abdomen tensing like he was about to take a blow—something he'd been getting more and more used to lately. He stood up to join her, sliding on his sandals before Adriata led the way into the hall. She was silent until they rounded a corner into a quiet corridor, empty of palacefolk and guards alike. Then, with a resigned sigh, she said, "Artem's delegation just left."

He had to bite back a curse. "They came early."

She nodded, pushing her glasses back up her nose with one finger. "I had to tell them Kallias is...absent." Her tone was abrupt, businesslike, but she fussed uneasily with the hem of her blouse, frown lines carving deeper into her cheeks. She could play angry all she liked, but she couldn't hide the mother's frantic worry buried beneath. He was the only one who knew the absolute truth of Kallias's departure, and until it was proven that he'd left the kingdom of his own free will, Adriata had chosen to believe he'd been tricked or enspelled to do so.

"And they weren't willing to renegotiate?"

"They may yet be, but due to the circumstances, they must obtain permission from Empress Idris before engaging in further arrangements."

Understandable. The Empress of Artem couldn't risk giving away all for nothing, especially not when choosing a side in such a long and bloody war. "So what now?"

He felt the change in her silence like a shift in the tides—subtle but strong, a nudge that changed the entire composition of the sea.

That wasn't good. "Just tell me, Mama."

"I know you're not yet twenty-one," she said, "not for a few more months."

He knew exactly what thought was in her head—had guessed it would come from the moment Kal's crown passed on to him. So instead of dragging it out, instead of playing dumb like he tended to do, he simply said, "Which kingdom, Mama?"

The tension loosened in her shoulders. "Lapis."

That surprised him. "The Mirror Queen wants to be *married?*"

"Not particularly, but she grows increasingly paranoid. She claims a consort would ease her mind."

No, a consort would simply put another body between her and a blade. But Finn didn't say that, because that was a Second Prince thing to say, not a First. "Queen Esha is how old?"

"Younger than all the rest. She's eighteen. She was orphaned at ten, crowned queen two years ago when she came of age. She nearly fell prey to a coup performed by the minister who ruled in her stead during her childhood, and she's received death threats ever since she quelled the uprising. They've never been willing to ally with another kingdom at war because they've been too busy preventing civil unrest in their own."

He stayed quiet, letting that turn over in his head. He'd already known all that, but it helped to hear it out loud. Lapis was a kingdom steeped in mystery, with closed borders and closed negotiations. The Mirror Queen would not be an easy woman to share a throne room with.

He'd spent nearly a decade learning every nerve and artery and bone of his city. To be torn away and forced into a place with entirely different patterns to learn… "You know I can't guarantee it would be a good match. It would take time for me to decide. I would have to get to know her. She would need to be willing to—"

"Which is why I'd like to accept her request now," Adriata interrupted. "She agreed to come here in order to complete the negotiations, and I think we could persuade her to give us until your birthday to finalize them. That would give you time."

"And if I refuse?"

Adriata was quiet for several seconds. "I would not force you, love. You have a choice, just like Kallias had a choice. When he turned twenty-one, he agreed to go wherever I asked him to go. You…I'm asking much of you. I know that. But if Nyx is employing necromancers, they have an advantage we can't hope to counter. We need help from *somewhere*, and unless Artem comes back with another offer, Lapis is our better bet."

"Will Artem come back?" He knew the answer.

"I don't believe so. Idris specifically asked for Kallias. She's looking for a warrior to sit on the throne beside her." Adriata's lip quirked up, a cluster of freckles disappearing into her dimple. "And we both know your strengths don't lie in bladework. You're better suited to Lapis."

No argument from him. "And if I can't agree at the end of those months…"

"Then we'll find another way. We have time. I may be able to secure her alliance without offering your hand."

"I would greatly prefer that."

"As would I, love."

Well. He'd expected it, but he hadn't expected it so soon. This was a game he'd never played before, the one sort he wasn't entirely sure he could pull off. Unlike Kallias, he didn't have a line of admirers of all sorts lined up outside his door. He didn't find courtship easy or particularly desirable. But he had a role to play, and if he wanted to pull it off, he had to be what Kallias had been for so long—obedient, dutiful, compliant. Willing to do whatever he must to earn his mother's favor.

So Finn hid his shaking hands inside his pockets. Tipped his head back to stare at the ceiling, blinking away a hint of pink that danced on the edge of his periphery. "Tell her to come. We have nothing to lose."

Adriata's eyes drifted away from him, and he followed her gaze toward Kallias's bedroom door. It was closed and locked—as it had been since Kallias had left. Like Soleil's had been for the ten years following her death. Like there was no expectation of its occupant returning.

"No," she whispered. "There's always something more to lose."

CHAPTER 7

ANIMA

S and—that was another thing Anima had forgotten to put on her list of things she'd missed while being without a body.

Sand, and grooves of tree bark against her fingertips, and dirt embroidering the spaces beneath her nails. The velvet kiss of flower petals and the stickiness of honey gluing her lips together. The way an ocean breeze felt different than a forest one, how the air at the ocean had weight and heft, how she could run her fingers through it just the same as running her hands through her hair. The gentle tickling of flicker-fish pecking at her feet and ankles as she waded in the shallow part of the ocean, her laughter carried back to shore by a friendly breeze that lifted the layer of sunbaked heat from her skin.

But most of all, more than anything else in the entire world, she'd missed being able to see *color*.

She knelt in the foam-lipped crystal-green waves, burying her fingers beneath the stodgy ridges of sand beneath, strands of her gold-kissed red hair flying in her eyes despite the ribbon she'd used to tie it back. The water was surprisingly warm, thanks to her—the wind had been cold this morning, winter hanging onto Atlas by the edge of its fingertips, not quite ready to be replaced by warm spring breezes. But she'd gently coaxed the weather a different way. She was hardly her older brother Tempest, who possessed a much more complete command of nature, but she and the sun had a bit of an understanding; wherever she walked, spring tended to follow like a trained dog at her heels. The palace was buzzing with excitement over the early thaw.

You can't call it a thaw if there was never any ice.

The joy burbling in her chest dampened in an instant, and she curled her fingers into fists, puddles of sand squelching in her palms. "I can call it whatever I like."

It had been weeks since she'd first realized her body's old owner was still around, clinging like a cobweb to the back of her mind. Weeks since their first fight, since the awful creature had drawn blood. Weeks she'd spent hiding the intruder from her oldest brother Tenebrae. She knew what he'd tell her to do if he found out. And she didn't want anything to do with it.

Soren's voice was bored, tired, and Anima could almost picture her lounging in a hammock somewhere at the back of her skull, swinging gently while she tried Anima's patience. That dark wall between her consciousness and Soren's may have kept them from hearing each other's deeper thoughts, but it didn't stop the cobweb from offering her own nosy, often vulgar opinions. *You should go back inside before Jericho chases us down.*

"I'm a goddess. She can't do a thing to me."

Then why did you sneak out of our room this morning?

"*My* room. And I didn't sneak." She'd simply moved with the natural grace afforded to a goddess.

Sure, Goddess Great.

As if her cobweb's words had summoned her, the voice that had so often reached out to Anima in despairing prayers called out to her again, this time with considerably less respect than she was used to: "You know you're not supposed to be out here, *Soleil.*"

Anima groaned as another wave pushed against her knees, threatening to throw her off-balance. She pulled her hands from the muck and let the saltwater wash them clean, glancing over her shoulder at the scarlet-haired princess who'd beseeched her to heal her beloved's wasting body. First Princess Jericho Atlas stood several feet back on the shore, her mouth twisted into a tight knot, her arms folded over the bodice of her lavender cotton gown. The fabrics Atlas made use of were strange; Anima was used to royalty wearing much finer things than simple cotton. But she supposed the balmy weather of this particular kingdom would require some adaptations.

"I just wanted to see the water. Sorry." Then she groaned once more, silently this time, already feeling Soren preening in satisfaction at her apology. So much for *Goddess Great.* What was she doing, apologizing to one of her worshippers? Jericho would have nothing at all if not for her.

It had been like this ever since she'd taken her first breath with these new lungs: Jericho insisting she had to remain in Soren's room, that she had to practice being harsher, louder, angrier. That she was too soft to play the part of the lost-and-found Heir of Atlas. She'd spent hours in front of the new mirror in her room, practicing her scowl, trying to bare her teeth like a wolf, and all she'd managed to do was make Soren laugh until Anima's side clenched with a psychosomatic cramp.

"You need to come inside," said Jericho, avoiding her gaze. "We're having a family meeting over breakfast."

"I thought you said—"

"I know what I said. But it's been weeks now—the Heir can't stay out of official matters forever, no matter what kind of betrayal she's suffered. We've run out of time. We just have to hope you're ready."

Soren's mirth vanished as quickly as Anima's confidence, and Anima's fists clenched closed of their own accord. She still remembered the crushing, frantic feeling of the Mortem-worshipping boy trying to choke the life from her new body. He couldn't have succeeded even if the older Atlas prince *hadn't* hauled him off to the dungeons, not with her magic reaching beyond all natural laws to keep her heart beating, but even goddesses were prone to human fears every now and again. Especially when she was so out of practice with mortality. If not for the magic thrumming through her veins, she would still be wearing the bruises around her throat.

You underestimate him. He'll find a way, magic or not.

Anima bit her tongue on a retort. He was nothing but a boy, regardless of who he worshipped or how strong his hands were. She was eternal. She was dangerous. She was—

Another wave shoved against her back, tipping her forward past the point of being able to save herself, and she crashed face-first into the water.

Oh, yes, I'm quaking in my boots, Soren deadpanned as Anima flailed and sputtered, coughing out salt and sand until she managed to push back up to her feet, waving her splayed hands to correct her stance.

"It's your clumsy body," she hissed under her breath, ducking her head to squeeze out the thin cotton shift she'd donned this morning to cover the scandalous set of swimclothes Soren seemed to prefer over the more modest wetsuits most of the Atlas population wore. Blood rushed into her cheeks at the muffled laughter other beachgoers hid behind their hands—some princess she was turning out to be. Princess of falling on her face.

So much for natural grace, huh?

Anima shook her head to clear the cobweb away and staggered back to shore, her legs struggling to find purchase in the sludge, those nippy flicker-fish fleeing from her lumbering strides. Rot and ruin take her, she'd never felt less graceful, not in any of her other bodies.

"Why—are—you—so—ridiculously—tall?" she hissed between steps.

When my mother was teaching me how to ride a horse, I fell off, but my ankles got caught in the stirrups. The horse started bucking and it tossed me around so much that my body got stretched out.

Horror nearly rooted her into the sand. "Holy gods, that's awful! How did you even—oh," she said suddenly, understanding darkening the blush in her cheeks as amusement leaked from Soren's consciousness into her chest. "You're joking."

Very clever, Goddess Great. Soren's voice was still mocking, but tiredness gnawed at the edges, dulling her usual sharp wit. That was the one mercy Anima had been given: Soren may be clinging to life well past her welcome, but she couldn't talk for very long without wearing herself out.

This had to stop. She couldn't get caught losing a battle of wits to a wisp of soul who hadn't had the decency to die all the way.

That was how Mora—Mortem—would have put it. *"How exceptionally lazy she must be, to not even give proper effort to her death."*

Her jaw clenched up at the thought of her sister, but she forced herself to loosen those muscles. The teeth-grinding was something she brought with her into every body—it was purely her own bad habit. Maybe that was what made it so hard to break.

When she finally reached the shore, Jericho tossed a towel over her shoulders and started rubbing them dry as they walked back up the beach. To anyone else, it would look like two sisters sharing a tender moment, but...

"Has he said anything else?" Jericho breathed into her ear, the stink of desperation buried under the coconut-and-sugar perfume she'd dabbed in the hollow of her throat.

Tension curled Anima's shoulders inward, away from her worshipper's arm, but Jericho held fast in spite of being shorter and weaker. "You know what I know."

Jericho's nails anchored painfully in her skin. "I don't understand. You said when you had a host, you would heal him. You *promised* me that—"

"*We* said that if you found someone fit and willing to be my host, I would assist you in keeping your husband alive. I have—I've kept your little war going. But he doesn't get healed until Tenebrae has a host, too." Those were the terms her brother laid out for her; her tone even took on the nasty edge that Brae's often did when he dealt out threats. She didn't like it—it made her stomach queasy—but this body's voice seemed better-suited to hostility than the deity that currently governed it. Soren had been a soldier, after all. And from what Anima had learned about her in these past weeks, she had no trouble believing the body's old owner was more than capable of such things.

Jericho flinched and her arm finally fell away from Anima's shoulders. "That won't be enough forever. His cravings get worse every day."

"Then you should think long and hard about how long you plan to keep my brother waiting." Even that sideways threat took effort, her tongue stumbling uncertainly over the more sinister suggestion buried beneath. It was what Brae had told her to say, but threatening someone into taking on this burden wasn't the way it was normally done.

Soren's quiet huff echoed off the back of her skull, but the cobweb didn't say anything. She'd likely used all the energy she had poking fun at Anima's gullibility.

You were born to bring beauty into the world, whispered a voice that wasn't Soren's, wasn't Anima's. *Now look what you've become. Body-stealer. Heart-breaker. Blackmailer.*

The echo of someone else's screams dredged up from deep inside this new mind, a memory of bloody soil and dark, beautiful, empty eyes. But when Anima tried to grasp it, tried to see it through to its end, it vanished like a swirl of mist.

Sweat broke out on the back of her neck. She hurriedly dashed it away with her fingers, wishing it wasn't so warm, wishing it didn't feel like blood.

These hands remembered something her mind could not. They shook even as she balled them into fists at her sides.

I am nothing that I have not been forced to become, she said silently to the voice with no life behind it. *And when this is all over, I can become something better again.*

Only silence answered her. Not even Soren had anything left to say, it seemed.

She and Jericho walked in silence the rest of the way up the beach, Anima silently reveling in the burning of hot sand against her bare feet until they reached the palace's private boardwalk, where she'd left her sandals behind. She slipped them onto her feet, marveling at the way the heat immediately fled from her skin, leaving behind tender spots but no real burns.

Every little sensation was worth basking in. Who knew how long she'd have the privilege of feeling everything, even pain?

The gentle hum of insects droned on in the background, and when she tilted her head back to snatch one last look at the sky, it blazed with vivid blue, patched up with cotton-clump clouds.

"Do we have to go?" she found herself saying, longing aching in her throat.

She didn't hear an answer, and when she looked down, Jericho had already vanished inside. "I'll take that as a yes," she murmured under her breath.

She hurried into the palace's grand mudroom—which didn't seem like the sort of thing a palace would ordinarily have, not that she'd been in all that many—and tugged her clothes from where she'd stashed them in one of the cubbies lining the long wall. Anyone wanting to use the palace's private stretch of beach went through here first, a large room with tile floors, plentiful storage for belongings, and washrooms off to the side for changing clothes and washing the beach from their bodies before returning to their duties. A handful of palacefolk were gathered there as well, preparing for a quick swim between their shifts; they each gave her a polite smile and nod, which she returned with what she guessed was a tad more enthusiasm than Soren normally would, because they all looked surprised by her eager hand-waving.

"Tone it down, Ani," she muttered firmly after sequestering herself in one of the washrooms, scrubbing off the sand on her feet and tugging on her emerald-green woven gown, pausing briefly to admire the flowering vines embroidered on the bodice, hem, and sleeves. One advantage of play-acting as the former owner of this body: she hadn't had to procure herself an all-new wardrobe while guessing at her new measurements.

Not that she would've done the procuring back then. Anything that involved sleight of hand or fluttering eyelashes or an innocent smile was always offered up for Cassi's clever mind to conquer.

She wished—not for the first time—that her older sister was here with her now. Cassi had the advantage of a mirror-like mind; she was all reflections and facets, every edge sharp enough to cut cleanly, every smile and laugh as much a weapon as any knife or razor wire or poison she kept in her pockets. Cassi didn't need magic; it was just another in her long list of assets. She could conquer a kingdom with a smile and a hand slipped into the right pocket.

But Cassi wasn't here. Brae had trusted *Ani* with this task—silly, sweet, sunny Ani. He was counting on her to be more than that now. She had to be better than the littlest sister in a brood of five, had to be ruthless, had to be *brave*. All the others were scattered. She was filling the shoes of four now, and she couldn't leave room for error.

Cunning like Occassio. Cold like Tempest. Fierce like Mortem. Invincible like herself.

Terror nibbled at her like those flicker-fish in the water, but she shook herself free of it, inhaling a long breath that smelled of warm water and rosemary soap.

Something about that scent...

She pressed her palm to her nose, inhaling deeply, letting her eyes drift shut. *"You still trust me?"*

"With my life," a low voice murmured, warm breath stirring her hair. Her head rested against someone else's, a flicker of russet skin and pitch-black hair in the corner of her eye, his scarred, strong hand twined with hers. *"Just not with your own."*

A soft, strangled gasp tore out of her chest when her eyes flew back open. Her left hand was still clamped over her nose and mouth, the sharp sweetness of rosemary lingering on her skin...but her right hand was extended, fingers splayed, searching for a hand that wasn't there and had never been in the first place.

A memory. She'd finally *remembered* something from Soren's life.

She waited with baited breath and flushed cheeks, straining to hear any sign of distress from her cobweb, but Soren seemed to be sleeping. Nothing but silence crept past that steel-and-shadow barrier between them.

By the bones of the old gods, her heart was pounding, pumping heat through her veins from the memory of that hand...that smell...that *voice*.

His touch was much more pleasant when he wasn't trying to kill her.

Ani scrambled to the sink, snatching up the bar of soap, catching it with a whispered *oops* when it slipped out of her grasp the first time. She sat down against the wall, curling her too-tall form into a smaller knot of long limbs, trying to shrink herself to a size she was more comfortable with. All it really managed to accomplish was cutting off the blood supply to her extremities, but that was all right. She could still think with numb fingers and toes.

She held the bar of soap to her nose, pleading silently with her borrowed mind to cooperate.

You belong to me now, she coaxed. *It's all right. Show me who you were before.*

But even with that, even when she breathed in the scent until dizziness spun her thoughts into cotton drifting on spring breezes, even when she silently begged for another glimpse of the boy with sweet-smelling hair and a voice like crackling embers…her mind did not give anything else up to her.

That was fine. She had time. She'd waited centuries to taste life again. She wasn't going anywhere.

Jericho wasn't waiting when Ani finally walked barefoot into the palace proper, but someone else was—someone who sent phantom beetles scurrying down her back and made the cobweb in the back of her mind stir from her silent rest.

Prince Finnick Atlas offered her an easy smile, the corners of his eyes crinkling up, cocoa-brown gaze gleaming behind gold-framed glasses he'd perched dangerously low on the bridge of his nose. He was less sun-kissed than his sisters, but one could still find clusters of freckles here and there. He was more tanned than Soren was, even with Ani's constant escape attempts lately. His handsome face and lean form were clearly more suited to scholarly pursuits; she could practically smell old parchment and knowledge seeping from his pores, and she couldn't recall ever seeing him without a book in his hand.

Still, though…he had never regarded her with anything but affection, or at the very least patience, but there was something about his eyes that gave her goosebumps. The angle of his smile never tilted right. He didn't seem entirely settled in his own skin. He reminded her of someone she used to know.

Soren's deeper mind was still hidden, locked behind that dark wall she had formed to protect herself; for a wisp of soul, for something barely there, Soren defended the last vestiges of her mind with the ferocity of a tiger standing guard over its cubs. But this body had memory, too, and her fingers never failed to clench into a fist at her hip whenever this particular Atlas brother came near. Around him, her hands felt less like gardening tools and flower-pickers and more like sword-swingers. More like eye-scratchers. Adrenaline could make a weapon out of anything, even an unwilling vessel.

"You're late," he said, propping his shoulder against the wall, giving her a quick once-over. He was wearing that same purple sweater he always wore, but today it was rumpled, the hem tucked and gathered haphazardly in the waistband of his golden-brown corduroy trousers. And he did, in fact, have a book hanging from his slender fingers. She tilted her head to try and catch the title, but he tucked it under his arm with a deft twist of his wrist. "Mama was getting worried."

"I lost track of time in the water." An excuse she'd heard more than once in this ocean-obsessed kingdom. "Where's Jericho?"

"She went on ahead. I told her I'd escort you."

"Oh."

"You sound disappointed."

"No!" The word burst out far too loudly, and Finn raised one eyebrow. She cleared her throat, hurriedly adjusting her walk to a swagger instead of a skip, hoping she didn't look like a complete fool as she reached his side. What did Jericho say to do? *Scowl, slouch, arms crossed, walk like you'd rather be going anywhere else but where you're going.* "No, not at all. I just don't think I still need to be babysat after all these months."

Finn ran his eyes down her stance once more, and she hoped to the gods…well, maybe not the gods…that she didn't look like one of those twisted bread things she'd found in the kitchens the other day. She certainly felt like one.

Pretzel, Soren contributed helpfully. She must have woken up when Finn arrived.

"Please be quiet," she pleaded.

Now Finn's other eyebrow jumped up to join its twin. "I didn't say anything."

Rot and ruin *take* her, may the old gods have *mercy.* "I wasn't talking to— never mind. Sorry. Can we just walk?"

Finn rounded his lips in a low whistle, pocketing the hand that wasn't carrying his book, leaning sideways to peer past her down the hall. "Well, we'll see. It's a big palace. You think you can carry me if I get too tired?"

A giggle tried to force its way out, but she didn't think this feral skin would find it agreeable, so she contained herself to a smile that showed her teeth. It didn't feel quite like the wolfish thing Jericho had tried to teach her, but it was close as she could get. "I'll do my best. You'll have to put the book, down, though. Looks like it weighs half as much as you all by itself."

Finn's good-natured smile faded at the corners, and he pulled his free hand back out of his pocket to scratch behind his ear. "It seems I have some studying to get done."

Curiosity twined around her ribs like a creeping vine, and she fell into step beside him as he began to walk. "Aren't you too old for schooling?"

"It's not the formal sort of studying." He tossed her the book, and she fumbled to catch it, a quiet *oof* knocked from her chest as the heavy tome thumped against her. Thankfully this body—*her* body, she had to start calling it hers—had the musculature to take the hit.

She took in the foiled text on the cover, frowning a bit. "Lapis?"

Finn kept his eyes fixed on something at the end of the hall, his gait steady and sure. "Mama's wasted no time in searching out a replacement for Kallias's failed arrangement."

That jerked Soren awake, her voice drowning out Anima's thoughts, a sharp ache circling her head like a crown: *She did* not. *He's got to be lying.*

"She—she *betrothed* you to someone?"

"That's a very fancy word for you." Before she could scramble to recover from yet another misstep, Finn sighed, plucking his glasses from his nose so he could rub his eyes. "Not yet, but that's the intention."

Gullshit! yelled Soren, and another aching pain radiated through Ani's skull, pressure squeezing at the edges of her brain.

Stop it, she snarled silently, and Soren shockingly obeyed, though the fury leaking beneath the edges of her wall was enough to set Ani's heart pounding uncomfortably.

This was a surprise, but it didn't change her plans. She and Tenebrae didn't need Finnick for what came next.

Though she kept her eyes fixed straight ahead, intent on ensuring she didn't trip on her own ankles yet again, she still felt it when Finn's gaze slid to her. Every hair on the back of her neck stiffened at the weight of his scrutiny.

"How are you doing?" he asked. "With Elias gone."

Elias. The boy with death in his eyes and smoke trailing on his heels. The boy who'd held Soren's hand and washed his hair with rosemary soap.

The presence in her head shrank back a bit—like Soren was holding her breath.

"I'm fine," she said. "I chose Atlas. He chose Nyx. He tried to kill me. End of story."

Finn's hesitation didn't feel like a disbelieving one. It felt like the stomach plunge before a long drop. It felt like the dip before a symphony's crescendo.

It felt like the breath someone took before they delivered terrible news.

"Has anyone told you yet?" Finn asked.

Soren was wide awake now. Anima could feel her more strongly than ever, her presence crowded up against the wall between them, like she had one ear pressed to the door that led to Anima's side of the mind. It made her temple throb.

Dread pulsed through her veins, cold and thick, and she didn't know which of them it belonged to. "Told me what?"

Finn turned away from her, but she still caught the scrunch of his brow, the anger in the clench of his knuckles. "Elias has branded you a traitor in Nyx. He told them to kill you on sight."

Fear struck her stomach at the same time Soren's heart crunched painfully, an autumn leaf flattened beneath the toe of a boot.

He really thinks I'm gone, Soren whispered.

I think he proved that when he tried to strangle *us, yes,* Anima thought back.

Smugness overtook sorrow. *Did you just say* us, *Goddess Great?*

"Me," she corrected hastily.

"Yes, you," Finn said, looking confused.

Anima had to swallow a groan. "No, I didn't—I wasn't—" She let out a harsh breath through her nose. "Sorry. I…it's fine, Finn. Let him talk all he wants, it won't do any good. They can't reach me here, can they?"

Soren's consciousness flinched behind the unbreakable wall in their—*her*— mind. *They already did it once. With an Atlas prince's help, it probably wouldn't be hard for them to do it again.*

Finn reached out and put a hand on her shoulder. "They won't get anywhere near you," he promised. But the squeeze of his fingers around her scarred skin was a little too tight to be soothing. More of a warning than a comfort as he met her gaze, eyes gleaming with promise. "We're not taking our eyes off you."

CHAPTER 8

SOREN

After her first day of training for Nyx's army, Soren had limped back to her bed in the barracks convinced that she would never feel that tired ever again.

And until now, that had held true—even when she was dying on that Ursa battlefield, even with lifeblood coating the gaps between her fingers and her guts touching fresh air for the first time, she hadn't felt as bone-deep tired as that night. She'd collapsed into her bed with pain throbbing in muscles she hadn't even known she *had*, every bone splintered at the edges, every pore utterly empty of sweat.

This was worse. This went deeper than a body-tired, a muscle-tired. She was soul-tired, and that was a kind that sleep and salves couldn't cure.

She was supposed to be dead.

Which, to be fair, was sort of becoming the theme of her entire life. But this time should have stuck. She couldn't think of anything that should have shielded her against the presence of a goddess.

Jericho had said it herself, a hushed whisper amidst a crackling fireplace and a pile of pastries and Vaughn's gentle snores: *"Even a body built for godhood cannot hold two souls. The stronger soul will always win, and there's no fighting a soul drenched in divinity."*

But here Soren was. Not that she'd asked to be. Not that it mattered.

There were days she didn't remember any of her names. When she didn't remember why she was even there, why she was living in the dusty corner of someone else's head.

Anima—her host's name was Anima.

Or was *she* the host? Was this Anima's body or hers? Was she Anima, or a prisoner, or a daydream that had overstayed its welcome?

The forgetful days were bad. Those were the days she nearly gave up, and only the faintest trace of dark eyes and a rough-hewn voice kept her awake. Only the quiet, ever-lingering certainty that there was some reason, some memory, some *person* she was still here for.

The days when she *could* remember were almost worse.

The days when steel and blood were pinned between her shaking hands, when the sound of a spine snapping sent a pang through every nerve, a wave of agony that she didn't need a body to feel. The days when fire licked at her back, flames twining around her body like a purring cat, charming her toward a hazy sleep that promised an end to the pain.

Soleil Marina Atlas. Soren Andromeda Nyx. Two different girls with two different griefs. Two different lives. Two different deaths.

She didn't know how to reconcile them. Didn't know where one ended and the other began. Didn't have the strength to figure it out.

So she had no choice but to stay here, huddled in some empty crevice deep in her head, bodiless and barely alive. No choice but to watch Anima smile and laugh and joke with the Atlas family in this sunny breakfast room painted a pastel orange, the curtains cream-colored and embroidered with flowers, golden lacquer shimmering in the table grain. No choice but to watch her fail spectacularly at playing the part of Soren, and watching it work anyway, because none of these people really knew her to begin with.

The Atlas family. *Her* family.

Stop that. Anima's voice was grating—Soren's voice, but too soft, bordering on a whine. *You're being depressing.*

Soren wanted to growl, but that was hard without access to her throat. *Yeah, well, I'm depressed. Sorry to bring you down, O Venerated One.*

The goddess sighed. *My name is Anima.*

Of course. My apologies, O Honored Parasite.

Anima didn't growl, but she did groan. *I'm not a parasite. You consented to this, in case you've forgotten.* A pause. *Oh. Sorry. I—have you forgotten? I don't know—*

No need to play nice, Goddess Great. I remember what I did.

The goddess wasn't wrong…Soren had given her consent, had allowed the goddess to make her home inside her body. Not that there was much of a choice, not with Elias's broken neck cradled in her hands, his lifeless eyes promising a much worse pain if she didn't agree.

Anima chewed on her lip—something she'd picked up from Soren's old habits. *I don't. You won't let me see.*

You don't want to see. And there was no gods-damned way she was going to let her see that love—that weakness.

Not hers. Elias's. If Anima knew how deep that bond ran between them, what Elias was willing to do for her…who knew what she'd do with it. Who knew what she'd try.

Affection, exasperated and grief-trimmed as it was, swelled what bit of her heart remained her own. Her Elias, loyal to the last. It was going to get him killed.

It *had* gotten him killed.

I wouldn't have been able to get in if you hadn't, though, Anima continued, as if Soren cared, as if she was even listening. *Consent is imperative. We can't settle into an unwilling host.*

How benevolent of you. Please shut up.

Anima gritted their teeth, a grinding that buzzed up through their skull. *Hey, it's not my fault you're stuck in there. If you'd just faded away like you were supposed to…but you didn't. So now you get to listen to me.*

Whoopee.

They were only a few minutes into breakfast, an affair that had almost been the end of Jericho already, because an offhanded remark from Finn—*Damn, Soleil, seven pancakes? That's one godly appetite you've got there*—had caused Jericho to choke on her juice. Soren had never appreciated her brother more.

So, Anima said, interrupting her thought as she sawed at that stack of pancakes, *your boy is still trying to kill you.*

He thinks I'm already dead. It's not the same.

Still. Anima hesitated for a moment. *I'm, um…I'm sorry. I know that—*

You don't know a thing about me, Goddess Great. Leave me alone.

Anima was right. Elias had told them to kill her. But could she blame him, really? She knew his beliefs, knew that he had no idea she was hidden away in the back of Anima's stolen skull. He was trying to put her to rest in the only way he knew how.

There was no saving her. He knew it. She knew it.

And yet she was here. And she had no gods-damned idea *why*.

If we're a target for Nyx, we're done for anyway, she said to Anima, curling back as far as she could get away from the wall between her and the goddess. She couldn't feel it so much as she could sense it, a nascent void that roiled gently like a thundercloud laden with toxic rain, a barrier that had shut her out of her own body.

But at least it was a fair tyrant. At least it kept Anima out of her thoughts unless she allowed her to hear them.

How so? Anima's voice pitched all wrong in her ears, reminding her of the nasally tone she used to take on when she wanted to mock someone's words back to them.

You haven't exercised properly in weeks, let alone hefted a blade or done any combat training. Do you even know how to hold a weapon?

Anima swallowed down a mouthful of syrup with a hint of pancake, tapping her empty fork lightly against the edge of her ceramic plate. *Why would I need one? I have my magic.*

Right, sure, but you're also pretending to be me, dumbass. Do you think your brother's going to be happy if you reveal yourself that soon?

A pause, a pulse of uncertainty from the other side of that wall. But Anima didn't get the chance to answer, because Adriata set her silverware down just then, picking up a butter-yellow napkin to dab at her lips before saying, "Soleil, I'm sure Finn's already discussed it with you, but you should know that there will be a delegation from Lapis arriving here fairly soon to discuss an alliance…a marriage alliance. You'll need to be part of those talks."

She wasn't surprised that Adriata had fallen so thoroughly for Anima's ruse. Wasn't really surprised by Ramses, either, mostly because Anima had been going out of her way to avoid him; the one smart choice she'd made in all these weeks.

But then there was Finn.

He knew *something*, she could tell that much. Besides his pointed comments and masked smiles, he was kinder to Anima than he'd ever been to her, and the way his face twitched sometimes when Anima said something particularly out of character…yes, he knew the person speaking wasn't truly her. Whether Elias had told him or he'd figured it out on his own was anyone's guess. And gods only knew what he was doing agreeing to an *engagement*.

If she knew one thing about Finnick Atlas, she knew this: anyone who agreed to marry him would have to be pits-damned *insane*.

"He mentioned it," Anima said—then cleared her throat, forcing her voice down a notch. "I'm afraid I don't know much about them. Nyx didn't have many dealings with Queen…um…"

"Esha," Finn supplied, his tone coated a façade of helpfulness, though his eyes narrowed with snakelike precision on her face.

"Esha," Anima echoed, and Soren wished she could laugh as flush-petals unfurled over their cheeks, heat that had nothing to do with the morning sun. "Sorry. I didn't sleep well last night."

All urge to laugh vanished with that fleck of truth.

It was true; in sleep, the barrier between them thinned, and nightmares were one of the unfortunate things they shared. Not all of her memories were kind, and in spite of her shield, sometimes they slipped through to Anima unbidden.

Anima couldn't know why Soren dreamed of broken necks and dead dark eyes so often, and Soren had no idea why Anima was so terrified of the sound of splintering wood. But either way, she knew they were both tired of waking up sobbing and gripping the empty sheets beside them, tired of vomiting their guts up at the image of crooked spines or hands so bent and twisted they were near-unrecognizable, tired of spending their nights shivering in a cold sweat on the bathing room floor.

Both grieving losses the other hadn't suffered.

I hate this, Anima muttered, her thoughts clearly following along the same path.

If you hate having me around so much, maybe you should let me have my body back.

You'd like that, wouldn't you?

Gods, she'd never wished so badly that she could punch herself in the face.

Shockingly, yeah!

Anima snorted, quickly masking it with a cough. But it was too late—Soren had heard her.

Did you just laugh at me? She wasn't sure if she was more miffed or surprised.

Sorry. You sound like Occassio, I…nothing. Never mind.

She tried to cast her thoughts back to Elias's lectures, but she hadn't really been able to recall them even at the height of her mental acuity. He hadn't been a fan of this goddess, she was mostly sure about that. She could *almost* recall a look of disdain when he said that name, but…well. Disdain wasn't an uncommon sight on her judgmental best friend's face. *Occassio. Which one is Occassio?*

Anima's breath caught in their throat, and a flood of images vaulted over the wall between them.

Sleight of hand and twist of tongue. Crystal balls and weighted dice. Dark curls and darker eyes. Incense smoke and candlelight playing on too-white teeth. Eyes like a fox and a grin to match. Lullabies and tickle fights.

None of your business, Anima whispered faintly.

What you use my *brain to remember is certainly my business.*

"Soleil?" prompted Jericho, and Anima turned their head to find the princess staring them down, her polite smile clashing with her twitching eyelid. A sprig of rosemary had sprouted in the gaps between her fingers; she fiddled with it while she stared them down, her mauve-painted nails contrasting sharply with the fresh greenery. "Where do you keep wandering off to?"

Where, indeed.

Soren settled back in the crevice that now served as her prison. Anima would get no help from her. This was—

Anima slouched a bit, pulling in a butter-scented breath before flashing a sticky smirk toward Jericho, licking a drop of syrup off one of her fingers. A near-perfect mimic. "What, so Finn can pretend to be useless, but I can't?"

Soren froze.

Jericho blinked. Her eyes jumped to Finn, something worse than uncertainty dimming her eyes: suspicion. There and gone, nothing more than a glint, but it was there, and—

And if she saw it, Finn did, too.

Anima had meant it as a joke. Jericho had read it as a warning.

Finn laughed, the corners of his eyelids crinkling as he popped another bite of his breakfast in his mouth, garbling, "Hey, that's rude! I'm not pretending anything. My uselessness has been honed for years. I've put *work* into it."

Joking. Perfectly at ease. But Soren knew—Soren could see the panic, the rapidfire glances in Jericho's direction as he tried to read whether his bravado had done the trick.

Why did you say that? she snarled to Anima, reeling, rageful. Her brother's games had nothing to do with Anima, and for her to throw him to the wolves that way—

What's the problem? Anima demanded in return, though her snips always came with an undercurrent of doubt. *You said it yourself, he's a liar.*

You can't say that to them, *you'll put him in danger! He's got nothing to do with you, why would you—*

I didn't know that! Anima's voice rose in pitch, so warbling and confused she didn't really sound like Soren anymore at all. *Besides, he's not my family. What do I care if they know he's a walking trunk of trouble?*

She'd been doing so well protecting Elias. Had been so focused on him that she'd forgotten there were others her memories could put in danger—others she couldn't let Anima reach.

Kallias was safe, but Finn...Finn was not. And that look Jericho had given him...

She couldn't let that happen again.

You will not have him, she choked. *Not any of them. Not from me.*

Anima tensed, their whole body strumming with sudden fear. *What do you mean?*

She didn't answer. Didn't give herself time to think, to dread, to wonder if this was a mistake.

She closed her eyes, released her grip on herself, and retreated until darkness took over.

CHAPTER 9

SOREN

*Y*ou *will not have them. Not from me.*
"Hey."

She retreated as far back from the wall as she could. Instead of pushing against it like she'd done for weeks, trying to whittle her way back into her body, she did her best to shrink herself, to hide all thought and memory from the intruder across that impenetrable wall neither of them had made.

Something hard jabbed into Soren's side—it felt like the toe of a boot. But she didn't move...wasn't sure she even could. Wasn't sure if there was enough of her left.

"All right, Little Miss Drama, you've thrown your fit. Up and at 'em. We've got things to do."

A frown tried to wrap itself around her numb lips. That voice…

A long, impatient groan from above her head. "Soren Andromeda Nyx, I swear to the gods I will sit my pretty ass directly on your back and pull on your hair until it pops off your head if you don't wake up."

She found her lips. Found her voice. "I don't know…that sounds like it could be—"

"There she is!" A hand ran over her back, patting between her shoulder blades. "Come on, look at me. I don't want to stand in this stuff any longer than I have to."

It was only then that Soren realized she was no longer floating in some indeterminate space, numb everywhere but her heart. No, she was sprawled out in a heap of limbs that she could feel, something shifting beneath her as she tried to move, something that managed to soothe and scratch at the same time.

Sand?

Her eyes fluttered open to what did indeed look like the steel-plated toe of a boot.

A hand reached down, cutting off her vision—a hand the color of teakwood, with permanently bruised knuckles and chipped nails chewed down nearly to the quick.

Oh, gods. She knew that hand.

She looked up to meet black-coffee eyes and a smile that shone with more energy than four cups of that particular drink. A pretty face with stern features that had always let her fake an air of authority she'd never really possessed. Dark brown curls that haloed her head and fell over her forehead, nearly obscuring her thick brows.

"You," said Jira Angelov, crossing her arms, "have some explaining to do, Princess Soleil-Soren-whoever-you-are."

Soren's throat sealed up so fast it cut off the joyful laugh that tried to make it out of her mouth. "Jira."

The disbelief and desperation that tumbled through her body woke up every part of her that was still numb, and she sailed to her feet, rocking on unsteady ankles before flinging herself into her sturdy battlemate's arms.

Her long-dead battlemate's arms.

Oh.

Some strange lump formed in the base of her throat—she couldn't tell if it was sorrow or relief. She clung on tighter to Jira, resting her chin on her friend's shoulder. "So. I'm dead, then?"

"Not quite."

"That's a terrible answer."

Jira laughed, and heat welled behind Soren's eyes at the sound. She hadn't realized how much she'd already lost in the two years since Jira's death; how could she ever have forgotten what that wicked, cackling laugh sounded like? How often had they been shushed in their classes because of it, Jira's boldness coaxing a quiet, fire-scarred orphan into mischief right beside her? "There's not really an answer to give you yet. I mean, you're definitely less alive than you were."

"Yeah, well, a goddess decided to shuck me out of my body, so..."

"From what I saw, the goddess tried. You're the one who decided to retreat."

Soren's stomach cinched tighter, and she let go of Jira, wrapping her arms around herself. "It would've happened eventually. And there are things I know that I can't let her see."

"Hmm." Jira crossed her arms again, jerking her chin somewhere behind Soren. "Where'd you bring us?"

"I didn't..." The words died on her lips as she turned, bare feet sinking deeper into the sand, toes finding their way from sun-warmed grains to cold, water-seeped sludge. The ocean unfurled itself before her, glimmering green waves lapping past her ankles.

Atlas. She was still in Atlas.

"I thought Infera was supposed to be a firepit," she said without turning.

"You think I got tossed into Infera?" Jira snorted. "Please. Mortem wouldn't dare. I'd steal that throne right out from under her prudish—"

"Jira! Please tell me what in the pits is going on."

Jira's hand settled on her shoulder, carefully turning her back around. "You know how they always talk about your life flashing before your eyes before you die?"

"I guess." Though, if this was to be a trip through what memories she had, they'd started in the wrong place. "Are we starting with the end?"

"No." Jira's murmur was almost lost beneath childish laughter carried past them by the sea breeze. "Seems whoever hid your memories is busy elsewhere now."

Cold adrenaline stabbed Soren as well as any knife. "What do you mean, whoever—"

"Shh, will you? This is important." Jira gripped her by the shoulders, pushing her sideways a bit. "We're starting with what you've forgotten."

"Wait up!" shouted a boyish voice, and Soren turned all the way around just as a gaggle of redheaded children bundled past—three of them. A girl with freckles and ribbon-tied braids was in the lead, untying her frilly dress and tossing it aside to reveal a wetsuit beneath. Behind her were two boys, one eager and gangly, one small and struggling to keep his footing in the sand. The older boy was holding the younger one's hand, keeping him upright when his chubby legs threatened to fail. The older boy looked about eight. The younger couldn't have been more than three.

"Slow down, Kallias!" called a laughing voice from further up the beach. "Let your brother keep up!"

"Slow down!" the smaller boy agreed, clutching his brother's wrist as tightly as his hands could manage.

Soren's heart plunged into the sand below.

Kallias. Which made the little boy...and the older girl...

"Finn?" The name barely made it out of her mouth. "Jericho?"

None of them reacted to her shaky, rasping voice. Instead they kept going, laughing and squealing as they plunged into the sea, Kallias scooping Finn up to keep him out of reach of taller waves that might have knocked him over, Jericho promptly diving under and disappearing from sight.

"I swear to the gods, Ramses, those three are going to be the death of us," sighed that voice again, the one who'd called to Kallias from far away. When Soren whipped back around, Jira had disappeared, and in her place, picking their way across the sand...

Ramses and Adriata.

Mama, her heart corrected—or at least, those words echoed where her heart should've been. There was no rhythm, no beat, just an empty cavern between her lungs and her ribs. Papa.

They both looked young—so much younger than the king and queen Soren knew now. Adriata wore a wrap dress made of pale blue cotton, the straps thin, baring freckled shoulders to the morning sun. Her scarlet hair tumbled in loose waves down her back, her green eyes shining, not a line or wrinkle to be found on her face. And in her arms, clinging to her dress with one fist and her hair with the other, craning her neck to watch the other three children...

Soren's breath caught as she met that little girl's gaze. No older than two, pink-cheeked and wide-eyed, her hair a shock of gold-red atop her head. She strained against Adriata's hold, making an impatient noise when her squirming didn't earn her a swift release.

"Mama, down," protested the girl, pushing against Adriata's shoulders. "Let me down, Mama!"

"Soon, Soleil," Adriata said distractedly before raising her voice again, cupping one hand around her mouth. "Kallias Alexandros! Don't go any deeper until Papa takes Finn, understand?"

"Yes, Mama!" Kallias called sheepishly, quickly making his way back into the shallower waves, though his body bent back longingly toward the deeper waters. Seemed that much hadn't changed.

Ramses chuckled, slinging his arm around his wife's waist and pulling her close, capturing her lips in a hungry kiss that sent heat flushing through Soren's ears. Memories or no memories, watching her parents kiss wasn't exactly something she cared to do. "We made some good kids, you know."

"We made wild kids," Adriata corrected him, finally letting Soleil down. The tiny girl wandered a bit closer to the water before happily plopping herself into the wave-soaked sand and digging around in it, plucking shells out from the muck. "Gods, wasn't it just yesterday that Jericho was born?"

"Feels like it." Ramses ran a hand through his own reddish-gold hair, sighing through pursed lips. It was tousled and messy on top and shaved on the sides, much shorter than Soren remembered ever seeing it. Honed muscle flexed in his arm as he lowered it—a swordsman's arm.

No, her mind corrected this time. A fisherman's arm.

"Can you believe Jer's nearly twelve?" Ramses continued, a hint of sadness in his voice. "She'll be off to the Academy before we know it."

"We're getting old, my love." Adriata leaned into his embrace, weaving her arm around his waist.

Ramses snorted. "Thirty is hardly old."

"The Nyxian princess is only eighteen, did you know that? It'll be her first summit this year."

"Mm. What's her name, again?"

"Ravenna. Here's hoping she's not as bloodthirsty as her father."

"King Byron hasn't shown signs of hostility in some time. Maybe he's aged out of violence."

Adriata snorted softly, her eyes fixed on her children. "You don't age out of whatever's wrong with that man."

"Mm." Ramses pressed his lips against her temple, smiling into her hair. "Come back to me, love."

"I'm right here."

"Mm-mm. My queen is right here. I'm looking for my wife."

Adriata's posture loosened a bit. She pushed her hand against Ramses's chest, jerking her head toward the water. "Go save Finn before Kallias accidentally drowns him, will you?"

Ramses chuckled, giving her a playful swat on the backside before jogging forward to avoid her retaliating slap, calling over his shoulder, "Stop Soleil from eating the sand!"

"Easier said than done!"

Only when she took a step back did Soren realize that she was shaking. Panicky quivers trickled up and down her arms and legs, rendering her absolutely useless, unable to move.

She wanted to run to them. She wanted to run away.

"What is this?" she tried again, much weaker. Gods, why wouldn't Mortem just let her die?

Jira's voice drifted back into her ear, softer, sadder: "It's a mercy—and a choice."

Before she could ask again what in the pits that meant, the scene faded away, plunging her into blackness once more.

CHAPTER 10

FINN

I t had been weeks since Finn had looked in a mirror, and gods, was he paying for it.

Days after his talk with Anima, gazing into the eyes of his own reflection, he found little that he recognized: his hair was unkempt, tangled and dull, like a fishing net piled in the corner of some long-abandoned ship's hold. His face was pale, a permanent divot driven between his brows, and there were dark circles stamped beneath his eyes like wax seals on the last of his sanity. His lip was near-bruised from being chewed on, and his eyes…

He rubbed them, cursing quietly, trying to blink the cleverness back into them. Trying to polish them from dull to gleaming again.

Gods, this was useless. He wasn't Kallias. He wasn't used to having a hand in running his kingdom; at least, not the proper way. Losing his easy access to the city's underbelly hadn't just robbed him of his favorite pastime; it had rendered him nearly useless, clumsy, fumbling his way through every meeting as he tried to paint on a new mask—trying to make this new role fit over the shoddy frame of his old one.

It wasn't working, not even a little bit. And it was damned near driving him mad.

Cursing again, he plucked his glasses from where he'd tossed them on his dresser that morning. The glass would at least partially shield him, and might imitate that gleam he'd been missing for gods-knew how long now.

The Lapisian queen was arriving today. A clever, conniving woman who supposedly traveled surrounded by an outer circle and an inner circle of bodyguards—Daggers on the outside, Mirrors on the inside. The Daggers, he'd been told, were highly-trained soldiers not unlike their Vipers, though what was so special about their training, he couldn't be sure. Poison wasn't Lapis's style, so that was anyone's guess. The Mirrors, on the other hand, were not soldiers, but handmaidens—a tight circle of women who were ever by their queen's side, each one rumored to be Occassio-blessed. After all, who was safer than someone surrounded by a pack of seers? No enemy would ever have the element of surprise so long as their queen remained in Occassio's favor.

He needed to be in top form today. Needed every card he could shove up his sleeves, every cheat he could dredge up from his tavern-going nights, every mask polished and fit to perfection. He was inventing a new act today, and that would require every bit of his concentration. Esha would be no ordinary adversary. All rumor and gossip suggested she was at least his equal in cleverness, and he'd never gone up against an equal before, not truly. Soleil was the only one who'd ever come close, and even she was too brash to really play his games. She had a gift for seeing straight through any shield he threw up, which made her dangerous to him, but he'd never worried that she would be capable of beating him. Not unless he let her.

"Don't put that mask back on…it doesn't work on me. I still see you."

Something spasmed in his chest, and he rolled the sleeves of his sweater up over his elbows, rubbing at the cramp over his heart. His fingers trembled against the yarn and he cursed quietly, gripping a fistful of it and squeezing until his bones felt steady again.

He couldn't meet the Lapisian queen like this. He needed a win first. He needed to get out of this palace. And luckily, based on the note that had been passed under his door a few minutes earlier, there was finally something worth risking a solo trip into the city for.

He tugged on a pair of boots and threw on a plain dark cloak, forcing all emotion-tainted thoughts from his mind. There was no room for grief today. No room for anger or fear or confusion. This meeting was more important than any he'd had in some time, and no one could catch wind of it. Not Jericho. Not his parents. No one.

The city was bustling when he made his way onto the streets, clusters of people all moving in the same direction: the beach. The unseasonal warmth of the day was chasing everyone from their homes and into the water.

Perfect. That meant, with any luck, the taverns would be empty.

Sweat quickly gathered in the small of his back beneath his sweater, heat trapped inside the dark cloak he wore, but he didn't remove it. Better to be sweaty than seen.

Just as he'd hoped, the Broken Conch tavern, nestled between a sugar-spinner's shop and a small library, was practically deserted; the mahogany tables were polished to perfection, the carved-shell napkin rings gleaming where they encircled pristine cloth napkins beside every seat, sunlight leaking in through every window. The Broken Conch was considerably nicer than most of the taverns he frequented; upper city folks preferred a bit more finery with their debauchery. The only people inside were the bartender—Felix, a slight man barely into his twenties with hair like dark silk and bright white teeth he bared often in genuinely pleased grins—and two figures seated at the same table, matching in build and wariness, each monitoring either side of the tavern as they sipped glasses of what appeared to be brandy. Early in the day for it, but out of everyone in the city, he supposed these two had earned it.

He pulled out the third chair at their table, letting the legs screech against the wooden floor to announce his presence. "Felix," he called, and the bartender looked up from where he was wiping down the counter. "A water for me, please, and two more of whatever my friends are having."

"Right away."

"And pour one for yourself," he added, tossing a coin bag filled with at least twice the money the drinks were worth. "The usual arrangement."

Felix offered him one of those too-bright smiles, scooping up the bag with a reassuring wink. The usual arrangement—silence on all that happened from here on out.

Finn settled back in his chair, propping his feet on one of the curling table legs, knocking back his hood as Felix hurried to lock the tavern doors. Good man. "Welcome home, Vidia. Vash."

The pair lowered their hoods, as well, revealing nearly identical faces, dark eyes gazing at him with something he'd almost call warmth, brown hair pulled back in precise plaits. One had a beard crawling up his light sienna skin, his features squarer than his sister's—Vash Maren, four years Finn's senior and a good foot taller. Vidia Maren was just as tall and twice as funny as her brother; she leaned across the table with a ready grin, eyes gleaming without fear. "Finnick Atlas. You've gotten taller since we last saw you. Still need help reaching the high shelves in the shops?"

"Vidia," sighed Vash, "please stop trying to piss off the Second Prince."

Finn tried not to smile, but the Maren twins had a way of pulling out his good humor. "First Prince, now, actually."

Vash's slight smile flickered out like a blown-out candle. "What? Where's Kallias?"

"He's not—" Vidia started, but Finn held up his hand.

"Not dead," he said. "And I'd like it to stay that way. Which is why I summoned you home."

Vidia and Vash exchanged looks. "Explain," said Vash.

The Maren twins were Finn's favorite resources—not only captains in the army, but the captains of *his* army. The part of it that had been his idea, his invention, the one ounce of revenge he'd allowed himself after Soleil's first untimely death.

Vidia and Vash, Fangs of the Vipers.

He'd created the Vipers after losing his sister the first time. It seemed only right he summon them now that he'd lost her again.

He shook off the dark cloud that tried to creep over him once more. He'd already grieved his sister once; he refused to do it again. He refused to redo work he'd already done.

He was not sad. He was not broken. He was not angry. He was not the boy he'd been back then, the boy whose idea of revenge had stopped with a blade in a Nyxian back his arm could never reach. He was older now, patient, cunning, cruel. And they'd done worse than killed his sister—they'd tortured her. Ruined her.

Dangled Elias's life as bribe and blackmail and forced her to choose: her life or his.

It hadn't even been a choice for her. He knew that as well as anyone, had documented that weakness early on and held it ready for his own designs...before memory fits and hand-knit sweaters and hot chocolate on rooftops had changed everything.

Fury, his irrational and unfamiliar new companion, tightened a noose around his throat. He barely managed to swallow past it, curling his fist around the edge of the table to anchor himself. Not yet—not yet. This was a long game. He had to play it right, step by step, knight over rook.

There was nowhere they could run. No place they could hide. When one had Finnick Atlas as an enemy, all time was borrowed.

"Has any word from home reached your outpost in the past couple months?" Finn asked first. No use telling a story they'd already heard.

"Only your warning to keep all our Vipers away from Port Atlas," said Vidia, settling back with her head tilted at a cocky angle that pinched him in a place he couldn't reach. "We ceased accepting communications after that. Felt too risky."

Smart woman. "Then you haven't heard about Soleil."

Vidia stilled, her smile freezing in place. "What about her?"

For a woman who made her living in reconnaissance, Vidia's emotions were painfully obvious, spelled out for all to see. He'd tried to train it out of her, but it was useless—her face wasn't built for masks. They didn't stick to her skin; she repelled anything that wasn't genuine. But he'd still chosen her as Fang for a reason; what she lacked in tact, she made up for with her silent feet and masterful poisonwork. Vash was much better built for Finn's side of things, made up of shadows and scales and blades that struck in the dark—the reason the Vipers were called by that name, capable of shedding any skin and replacing it with one that better suited his needs.

Two sides of the same coin. Honesty and Deceit. He would've been lying if he said he hadn't chosen them out of something more than calculation, if he said they didn't remind him of another pair of inseparable siblings.

"We found her," Finn said quietly.

Vash leaned in, eyes gleaming dangerously. "What do you mean, you *found* her?"

Vidia looked like she might be sick. "Her bones?"

He almost wished they had. It would have been better than getting her back and losing her again. Better than sitting on a cliff at sunrise and thinking that maybe, just maybe, the gods still possessed some modicum of mercy…only to find out they were crueler than anyone could have guessed. Only to find out he was more of a fool than he should've been capable of managing. "No. Kallias found her fighting on a Nyxian battlefield under their flag. We found her *alive*."

"A decoy," Vash said immediately, while Vidia picked up her cup and drank deeply, squeezing her eyes shut against the tavern lights. "Has to be."

"I thought the same. But I was…wrong." The confession burned on his tongue, scraping painfully past his gritted teeth. He'd never said those words before; had never needed to. "It was her. Truly her. Nyx didn't kill her, they stole her. And when we brought her home, she had no memory of us, or of her life before. She was going by a different name—Soren."

Vidia choked on her drink, and Vash thumped her back until she managed to sputter, "The Nyxian *princess*? The one they've turned into a battle cry?"

"We assumed she died," Vash said, his fingers twitching toward his own glass, which was about as close to a true reaction as Finn ever seen from him. "We never thought that…Occassio bless her, she's alive?"

An itch tweaked the back of Finn's ear, and he scratched it away, resisting the urge to snap at Vash for invoking the name of that particular goddess. "What do you know about the gods and their hosts?" he asked instead of answering.

Vidia snorted, finally lowering her empty glass, tapping her chipped nails against it. "That's nothing but a legend. The gods don't walk among us anymore. They haven't in hundreds of years, if they ever did at all."

Vash shot her a cautious look. "That we know of. Just because they weren't documented doesn't mean there weren't more." He looked back to Finn. "Why do you ask?"

Finn didn't have the time to waste giving him everything, so he did his best to cut it down to basics: Vaughn's necromantic magic, Jericho's treachery, Elias's death, Soleil's sacrifice, Kallias's abdication. And when that was over, he said, "You two are the only ones I've told—the only ones in my confidence." He carefully molded his tone into a point, a promise, a threat. "So if it gets out, I'll know exactly where to look."

Vash simply nodded. Vidia, who normally took offense to his withholding of trust, looked too horrified to think much else. "Gods, Finn. Are you…I mean, are you all right?"

A wild, ridiculous laugh bubbled in the hollow of his throat, but he swallowed it down. That wouldn't make him seem any saner. "I'll be better when that goddess is out of my palace. If possible, I'd like for you two to come under my command for the time being. If Jericho and Vaughn are traitors, I have very little confidence in most of my palace informants, and I've had to avoid most of my lower city contacts since taking on the title and scrutiny of First Prince. I need eyes and ears I can trust."

"Eyes," said Vidia.

"Ears," Vash agreed. "We're owed a leave, anyway." He leaned across the table, gazing at Finn with uncomfortably knowing eyes. "There's something lurking behind your gaze, Prince Finnick. Is there more we need to know?"

Finn held his gaze without flinching. "I don't owe you all my secrets, Maren. Unless you'd like to hand over yours."

The corner of Vash's mouth twitched upward, only briefly. He leaned back with a nod of acquiescence, his silky hair shifting as he settled in his chair. "Understood."

Finn shifted his gaze to Vidia. "Vash, I need in the palace with me. But Vidia, I have another task for you, if you're willing."

She perked up immediately, her eyes gleaming with anticipation. She was never one to say no to a challenge. "Name it."

This was a risk. More than a risk—an outright gamble, a bluff on a horrendously bad hand. But he'd been losing this game long enough. It was time to reclaim his crown.

So he fixed his favorite mask in place, with a confidence so absolute even he believed it. Of all the names he'd created for himself, *spymaster* was the one he felt best suited to. This was just like every other scheme and heist and con he'd pulled in the past decade. He just happened to be going up against players who were a tad more immortal than he liked.

He sat forward, holding Vidia's gaze. "How hard would it be for you to get over the Nyxian border?"

CHAPTER 11

ANIMA

"Why aren't you *doing* anything?"

It took effort not to shrink at Jericho's vicious voice, pretty silk sewn with thorns in the hem. Anima forced her fingers to stay on Vaughn's sweaty forehead, his fever pulsing madly beneath her hand, his magic writhing beneath his skin. The necromancer was gasping for breath, every inhale rattling terribly in his chest, his eyes bloodshot and focused on some faraway thing none of them could see. Flickers of green glowed within the gray of his eyes.

Guilt nibbled deep in her stomach.

Her magic had done this. The parts of her power that lived within the world had given this man a gift that could only ever end in tragedy, one way or another. In the ages when war was commonplace across all kingdoms, necromancy hadn't been the scourge it was now—there was always enough death to feed necromancers back then. They were employed among the people who cleaned battlefields and restored them; it was much easier to enspell the dead to follow a necromancer to a mass grave than dragging the bodies one by one, and they never lacked for work. But in this era of widespread peace, it was no wonder he was killing himself with his resistance. A good man who needed death to survive…she guessed it was only thanks to Jericho's intervention—and hers and Tenebrae's—that he was still alive at all.

"There's not much I *can* do yet," Anima said as calmly as possible, but a hint of threat crept into her voice. This body wore menace much better than sympathy. "My powers are more limited when I'm mortal. You know that."

"But you're still ten times more powerful than any medimancer here. More powerful than *me*. Can't you—?"

"Jericho," breathed Vaughn, his eyes drifting shut. "Let her be. She's trying."

"My magic is still settling," Anima whispered, shame blotting out her attempts at sounding powerful. It was getting harder and harder to connect with her host's sharper side with Soren huddled as far behind the wall as she could get. Not that she was complaining—the quiet was nice—but it was beyond frustrating that her cobweb was so determined not to give her another memory. She was never going to get the hang of playing this part without full access to her host's mind. "It's going to take time. Besides, you know the deal. We don't heal him until—"

Jericho slapped the wall with her open palm, her face contorting in fury. "I know the deal! I know. I could recite the gods-damned deal in my *sleep*."

A hand cracked across Ani's cheek, so fast and hard she didn't even feel the pain at first.

"Calm down, Ani. Just do what I tell you," murmured a gentle voice, that hand cast soothingly over her hair, "and we'll fix this. All right? We'll fix all of it."

"Mora and Peter won't help us." Her voice shook, and she winced, waiting for another slap, another well-meaning but painful attempt to end her hysteria.

Instead, that hand settled on the back of her neck, forcing her to meet her brother's dark, determined eyes. "They will. They won't have a choice. We just have to make them see."

Vaughn's moan of agony tugged her back to reality. She swallowed hard, gently soothing his hair back, trying to ignore the phantom stings prickling across her cheek. It was like her freckles had become hundreds of tiny bruises. Memory was powerful—so powerful it could sometimes transcend lifetimes. Transcend bodies. "I can ease his pain, but that's all. He needs to use his magic."

"No," Vaughn ground out through gritted teeth. "Not again. Not ever again."

Jericho's face shifted from rage to pain. She pushed off the wall and stood over her husband, framing his face with her hands, wiping away a drop of sweat from his temple. "Vaughn, we're so close now. Don't—"

Vaughn jerked his head away from her hands as best he could, squeezing his eyes shut, refusing to look at her. His voice came out soft, the softest anger Anima had ever heard: "Please leave."

Jericho's eyes filled with tears, and she reached out again, hands shaking. "Vaughn, please—"

"I asked you to *leave*."

Jericho's face shuttered, from devastated to emotionless in moments. She wiped her palms off on her glittering blue gown, brushing past Anima as she fled into the hallway, slamming the door behind her.

Anima swallowed hard, letting her magic seep through her fingertips into Vaughn's skin, seeking out the more vicious power tearing him apart from the inside. "Do you want me to go, too?"

Vaughn was quiet for so long that she'd just moved to check his pulse at his neck when he finally spoke. "I love my wife."

She awkwardly patted his shoulder. "I know."

He opened his eyes again, seeking hers out, pain of a different sort darkening his gaze. "I loved my little sister, too."

Her fingers stilled, her heart stuttering at the shame in his eyes. The guilt.

"I love my wife," he said again, "and I won't let her sacrifice any more pieces of herself for me. Not to Tenebrae. Not even to you."

Pity clenched her chest. He had no idea how little chance he had in that fight. To challenge the gods was to lose, and lose greatly—especially when that god was her eldest brother. "Do you want me to go?" she said again, softer. She didn't need to kick him when he was down. He'd lost enough. Had more yet to lose.

As her magic settled beneath his skin, his muscles loosened, and a slow breath of relief escaped his lips. He let his eyes drift shut, nodding in a single exhausted bob. "Yes."

After she washed his sweat from her hands and slipped into the hall, she found Jericho waiting, hollow-eyed and angry—like she'd been every day lately.

"I don't understand," she said.

Anima blew out a breath, turning away from the princess, letting her feet lead her toward the door at the end of the infirmary hall. "I already told you, my magic hasn't—"

Long nails dug into the back of her shoulder, forcing her to turn around and meet blazing green eyes. "I don't *understand*," Jericho repeated, clutching Anima's shoulder too tightly. Pain pierced her skin, and she knew without looking that Jericho had drawn blood. She tried to pull away, but Jericho held fast, pressing in so close Anima could smell the desperation on her breath. "I've worshipped you my whole life. I've knelt at your altar and planted offerings in the garden boxes. I prayed to you every single night, even when I was so tired I couldn't keep my eyes open, even when I could barely speak for weeping. I betrayed my family for this. My sister *died* for this. I trusted you. I believed in you. You're supposed to be this all-powerful, gentle, loving *goddess* with ancient magic beyond our imagination, but you...you're just a *child*."

Child. Child. Child. That word echoed in her head, finding its mark in old wounds she'd forgotten were even there.

Magic purred dangerously beneath her skin, power curling in her veins like a vine wrapping itself around a gate, anger digging in like unpruned thorns. This woman was toeing a line no mortal should ever *dare* to cross. "I," Anima said softly, stepping into Jericho's space until they were nose-to-nose, "am not a child. *Everything* you have, I gave to you. Your magic. Your husband's life. Your *war*. And with one word, I could take it all away. Do you want that? Do you really want to *push* me that far?"

It was only when Jericho tried to speak and her words came out as a strangled gasp that Ani realized vines had manifested from thin air and twisted up Jericho's body, winding around her throat and squeezing.

All that anger vanished in an instant, and Ani stumbled back, quickly clenching her fist and jerking it back like she was casting something behind her. The vines released Jericho, and the princess dragged in a breath, the redness fading slowly from her face.

Horror prickled in Ani's palms, but she buried them in her skirts, taking another step back. "I'm so sorry. I didn't—I—"

"Don't apologize, Ani," said Jericho—but it wasn't Jericho's voice that rumbled from her chest, a feminine tone underlaid with a deep, dark timbre. Wasn't Jericho's eyes that rose to meet Ani's, narrowed in amusement, gold flickering through the green.

Something relaxed and tensed in Ani at the same time. "Brae?"

"She disrespected you. She had to be put in her place." Brae straightened Jericho's posture, looking Ani up and down with a distinctly unimpressed look. "This host doesn't suit you, you know."

Ani flushed, slouching a bit further, again cursing Soren's height. "I know."

Jericho's—Brae's—eyes gleamed, and he leaned against the wall, folding Jericho's arms. "Don't worry. We're going to fix that."

It took her a moment to read his relaxed stance, his slight smile, his patient air while he waited for her to catch up. A gasp escaped her in a delighted whoosh, and she jumped forward, gripping his arms tightly. "You know where to find them?"

"I do." He pushed up off the wall. "Sort of."

"Sort of?"

He jerked his head, moving down the hall. "Follow me. I'll show you."

CHAPTER 12

ELIAS

E lias would give this to Artem: they certainly picked a good place to build
their kingdom.

While Tallis was considered the Stone Kingdom—their cities tucked
between crags of rock, scattered amongst various valleys with manmade roads
paved between each one, its people hardy and resourceful and withdrawn from
the bloodshed in the other kingdoms—the largest of its mountains crept past the
Artem border. It was within the looming giant of Mount Igniquit that Artem had
carved out their tunnel-city, a capital protected by its own outer shell. The
Artemisian people were world-famous weaponsmiths, glassblowers, ironworkers,
and all other kinds of craft that relied on fire and elements of the earth. Between
the mines in the roots of the mountain and the desert sands beyond, they never
lacked for materials.

Igniquit. Fire-Breather.

"Are we there yet?" called Kallias from further down the winding mountain path, every word punctuated by a wheezing gasp. When Elias looked over his shoulder, he found Kallias leaning against a boulder, clinging to it like an anchor, his lips tinted blue. He was so pale his freckles were like dots of ink splashed across his face.

Prissy.

"What's the matter, Prince? Bit out of shape?" Raquel called from ahead. Letting her take the lead had seemed like the best plan; Elias trusted her with his life, but Soren had trusted her with Kallias's death, and he wasn't willing to risk everything on Raquel's restraint.

"The air's thinner here than he's used to," Elias mumbled.

"Forgive me if I'm not weeping for him." Her boots crunched gravel, her leather gloves creaking as she braced herself against the mountainside and turned to face him. "When did you start defending Atlas bastards instead of killing them?"

"Since Soren found out she shares blood with them."

Raquel averted her gaze, tugging her thick cloak tighter around her shoulders. "Blood isn't everything."

She of all people would know, but Elias didn't say anything; he couldn't waste precious oxygen arguing with her. The air *was* thinning up here, rapidly, and his lungs were beginning to burn.

Don't burn me, Elias. You can bury me wherever you like, with as many locks on my coffin as you need, but don't burn me.

His boot caught and slid on loose gravel, sending him skidding back down the path. One hand slammed down, palm stinging as it scraped against rock and dirt, and he dug his nails in, cursing until he finally managed to find a new foothold. His boot stopped barely an inch from the lip of the path.

Kallias's hand touched his back, guiding him away from the edge. "Are you all right?"

Bone separating from bone. Agony incomparable. The worst and quickest pain he ever felt in his life.

He shoved Kallias's hand away with such ferocity that he startled himself; but even with the prince's steadying hand gone, heat remained, pulsing in the marrow of his once-rent spine.

Not pain, not anymore. Just a memory. Just a scar. A death blow undone.

"I'm fine." The words scraped out of him like he'd swallowed gravel instead of tripping on it. He wiped at the sweat gathering beneath the edge of his knit hat, wishing these desert mountains were a bit colder. "Keep up. We should be about there."

And they were. It was barely minutes later that Raquel crested the ridge, paused at the top, and called down, "Come up slowly. Seems they're expecting us."

The tension hidden beneath her casual tone told him all he needed to know: weapons were drawn and aimed. Any sudden movement would be the last they ever made. Artemisian steel bit deeper and harder than any other; legend claimed their blades drank the blood from their victims, and every kill reinforced the steel past all natural laws.

But he had already seen what waited beyond the tunneling of blade through body. Had already breathed in the chill of the grave. Still carried a piece of it deep in his chest, next to a heart that wasn't entirely sure whether it was allowed to continue beating.

He carried Artemisian blades on his belt. And he knew they did not drink blood; at least, they hadn't seen fit to drink his.

So when he joined Raquel and found a semicircle of guards in burnished red armor waiting, spears and swords at the ready, he did not flinch. He did not fear.

No weakness.

"State your names, your kingdom, and your business here," said a woman, stepping out from behind the semicircle of what he assumed were guards. Her hair was the color of coal, tied in a bundle of thick, silky braids, bits of gold strewn throughout the strands. Her skin was rich russet brown, and he could just make out the tattoos winding up her arms—similar to Ember's, coils of winding fire climbing from her wrists to her shoulders. She wore golden cuff bracelets on each of her wrists with rubies studding the metal and similar cuffs on the tops of her arms. There was a small gold hoop piercing her septum, and rubies glinted at her earlobes—Artem imported quite a bounty of jewels from Lapis. Her features were soft, her face round and gentle, but her eyes were smoldering flames, dark as his own, lined sharply with kohl and some other shimmering gold cosmetics. Her uniform was crisp and pressed perfectly, finer than any other kingdom's he'd seen, scarlet and orange silk threads held together with brass buttons and detailing that appeared to be diamond-studded.

She wore more weapons than he'd ever seen any one person carry: a spear in her hands, twin swords sheathed on her back, an array of daggers belted at her hips. If he had to guess, she likely had many more stowed where they couldn't see them. If it wouldn't have gotten him killed, he would've drawn his own daggers, though they suddenly felt a paltry defense in comparison.

"My name is Elias Loch," he said, offering her a bow. "And my friend here is Raquel Angelov. We're escorting Prince Kallias Atlas to an audience with his betrothed, Empress Idris Artem. I believe we're expected."

The woman's sharp brow rose. "We sent an escort ahead to bring him here. There are much easier ways up the mountain." Her smooth accent pitched her voice low, danger coiling around every word, every flicker of muscle in her jaw or arms telling him he was one false word away from losing the tongue he spoke with.

"Time is of the essence. There are things Empress Idris must hear. We couldn't wait for your escort."

"And where is Prince Kallias?"

"Down here," came the wheezing words from below. Elias closed his eyes and took in a breath through his teeth.

I can't disrespect him in front of Artem. I can't disrespect him in front of Artem.

Kallias's hand appeared at the edge of the ridge, and Elias turned to help him up, realizing a moment too late that he'd turned his back on people who had yet to decide if he was an enemy. But he couldn't very well leave Kallias down there, and Raquel wasn't going to be the one to help him.

The woman's eyes followed Kallias as he joined them, her mouth thinning in displeasure at whatever she saw. "You travel with an Atlas prince," her eyes trailed back to Elias, "but your accent is Nyxian. We've heard terrible rumors about you as of late. Have you anything to say about those, boy?"

"Like he said," Kallias interrupted before Elias could speak, "we have much to share with Empress Idris. I can vouch for them, on my honor as First Prince."

The woman gave Kallias a long, lingering once-over, the disapproval in her gaze never once flickering. She glanced at Elias and paused, moving closer, her hand hovering between them. The air wavered around her fingertips like the haze of heat over a lit stovetop. "You are searching for more than you say. Death has touched you. Mortem's fingerprints don't fade easily."

A chill ran down Elias's spine, snuffing out that burning heat. His chest tightened. For a single heartbeat, he thought he smelled roses. "I don't know what you're talking about."

"Hmm." But the woman pulled back. "I'm General Star Aquila. You are right that we've been expecting you. However, no one reaches the Empress without first speaking to the High Priestess. I will take you to her."

His heart lurched at the sound of that name—*Aquila*. "Would you happen to be related to a Sera Aquila?"

For the first time, surprise broke through the emotionless shield in the general's eyes. "You know my sister?"

"Is everyone in these kingdoms related somehow?" Kallias mumbled behind his back. The heavy silence didn't hold an answer, but Elias knew Raquel was drilling holes into the prince's head. Angelov glares were weighty as a mace and twice as deadly.

"Sera is my mother," Elias said quietly. He'd known she had family here, but she hadn't mentioned that family was *quite* so high in the pecking order of Artem. "She opened her own ironwork shop in Nyx. She married my father there."

"I know. I should have recognized your name." A slight smile bent across Star's face. "I visited for your parent's wedding. Evan Loch was a good man. Too quiet for my sister, I thought, but gods did he adore her."

A duller pain thudded gently in his chest—a healed-over wound, a grief nearly five years old. "He did."

"You have his face. But your eyes are your mother's." The general gestured at her guards, and they all lowered their weapons. "Come with me. Weapons stay on your belts."

Surprise rooted his feet to the ground. "We can keep our weapons?"

"It's disrespectful to ask a warrior to part with their weapons. If you draw them out of turn, you'll be dead before your blade makes it out of its sheath." No boasting—cold, simple confidence. He believed her wholeheartedly. "Now walk, or I'll leave you all out here to die from exposure, family or not."

He wished she would stop talking about *death* so much. His heart lurched with every utterance, like it remembered when death was more than a word to him, like it could outrun anything that tried to halt its rhythm again.

It couldn't beat past a broken neck. Vaughn had proven that much for him.

In any case, they didn't have much choice but to obey. He pushed past Kallias to take the lead, flashing a warning look when the prince tried to protest— if there was any trouble, Elias preferred to be the one closest to it. Threats or no threats, Star might be less willing to gut her sister's child. From the stories his mother had told him in their shop between each clang of shaping hammer against iron, they'd been close as children; he was willing to risk this much on his mother's word.

"General," he heard one of the other guards hiss, a man with a captain's regalia and rings of tattoos around his neck and wrists. "We can't just let them in.

Nyxians showing up with the Empress's betrothed mere weeks after news arrives of them dabbling in necromancy? He could be their prisoner."

"I have this under control, Captain Janus," said Star smoothly. "The prince does not appear to be under duress. Besides," she added, casting a warning glance over her shoulder, "even if they are, we have no bodies for them to puppet here."

Another advantage Artem held over anyone dabbling in dark magics: they didn't bury their dead, or even entomb them. Every dead body in Artem was burned beyond any potential for resurrection, necromantic or otherwise.

"Appearance means nothing. They could have been whispering threats in his ear all the way up the mountain. They—"

"*They* can hear you," called Raquel from the back of the line. Elias bit his lip to hide a smile. Ever since losing her eye, Raquel's hearing had sharpened enough that nobody in their barracks dared gossip about her. "And believe me, sir, if we intended to harm the prince, we wouldn't have gone through the trouble of marching him up the mountain. You think two of us would be enough to take you all down? You have that little faith in your own skill?"

The captain scowled. Star's eyes glimmered in amusement. "Nyxian wit still knows no bounds, I see. Come."

Gravel gritted in the soles of Elias boots as they followed the Artemisian warriors a bit further up the peak until they reached a gaping maw of darkness in the side of the mountain. To Elias, it seemed the darkness breathed—warm air rolled out from within, dry and spiced with smoke and incense and iron. It smelled like the forge. Smelled like...home.

They stepped into the mouth of the great stone beast, and as Elias's eyes adjusted to the darkness, more details swam into focus: at the far end of the cave stood towering black marble columns, feathered wings carved into the base and head of each one. Two mighty doors stood beyond them, at least thirty feet tall, also black marble. The left one was decorated with the visage of Mortem—a graceful woman with fire cradled in her hands, a skull charm worn around her neck and a rose crown on her brow. It was...an uncomfortably accurate rendering. The eyes seemed to stare at him in disapproval all over again.

The right door, however, was etched with the image of a great bird, its wings spread and talons out, flames trailing in its wake and lining each painstakingly detailed feather.

Not a bird at all. A phoenix.

A creature long-extinct, if they'd ever existed at all, but still Artem claimed it as their patron. Priestess Kenna had always taught that phoenixes were Mortem's favored mounts, that she was the one who'd gifted them with an ability no other creature possessed: the power to resist death. Legend said that death was as sleep to a phoenix, and when they woke, they woke in a storm of flame and light, a flash so brilliant it lit the night up like day.

Deathless.

Elias's fingers drifted back toward his stomach, but Kallias bumped him from behind, and he shook off those thoughts. Nothing was deathless; the fact that those birds were now extinct was proof enough, supposedly hunted out by people who'd become convinced that their feathers or blood or whatever else could gift them immortality.

Star whistled loudly, a shrill sound that bounced off the cave walls, and the handful of guards that stood by the doors immediately pulled them open. Another blast of hot air flared out over them, drying out Elias's eyes, and Kallias drew in a hitched breath behind him.

"You all right?" Elias asked over his shoulder.

"Fine," said Kallias, but his voice was tight. "Just regretting all these layers."

"An Atlas complaining about heat?" Raquel snorted, but sweat was already glittering on her brow as well. She swung off her cloak to reveal black leather traveling armor beneath, glaring down an Artem soldier who started to protest the sudden movement. "Believe me, sweetheart, if I'm drawing a blade, you'll know."

"Leave your coats and cloaks here," Star ordered. "You won't need them in the city."

"Gladly," Kallias mumbled. Elias tensed a bit, giving him a quick once-over. He seemed fine enough, but his face *was* flushed, the creases in his coat soaked through with sweat already. They hadn't even stepped foot inside yet. Raquel wasn't wrong—this was a far cry from teeth-chattering and complaints stuttered through shivers when they first crossed the border into Nyx. Kallias should have been reveling in the heat. Instead, he tore off his thick coat with such haste that a couple buttons ripped off, clattering to the floor in a series of thin echoes.

He should have done more when the man had woken him up screaming and hacking like he was choking on his own breath, clawing at his throat so viciously Elias had feared he would rip his own skin apart to escape whatever threat he faced in his mind. But Elias had been so preoccupied with his own nightmares...

Another fierce shake of his head dispelled those memories. *No weakness.* Kallias's problems would keep until they were settled in here. They would talk once he was sure they weren't going to be killed for trespassing or imprisoned on suspicion of necromancy and kidnapping the First Prince of Atlas.

He shed his own coat. Forge air and mountain wind collided, wrapping around his body in a rapid dance, heat and cold gliding over his skin like they were fighting over which got to settle inside him.

He shook them both off. He belonged to nothing and no one. He had followed Mortem's summons here because it was the only gods-damned bit of direction he'd been offered, and he'd always been a follower, never a leader. First his parents, then the priests and priestesses, then Kaia, then Soren…he'd never had to question which direction to march. He'd always taken up the role of shadow, following dutifully behind whoever shone the brightest in his life like a moth drawn to flame.

This light was half as vibrant as the one he'd been shadowing before. Still, he followed it—straight through those thick, heavy doors. When they shut behind him, the impact rattled every untethered thing in him, and it took effort not to reach for the ring dangling from his neck.

"Kallias Atlas, Elias Loch, Raquel Angelov," said Star, "welcome to Artem."

CHAPTER 13

KALLIAS

A rtem was utterly terrifying.

Beautiful, too, certainly. But first and foremost? *Terrifying.*

The heat was *suffocating*, even though it was dry, nothing like Atlas's water-laden winds that trapped heat inside humidity, the air practically seared his skin. The layer of sweat that had coated him outside dried almost instantly, though more was seeping out from every pore. Everyone they passed was dressed in at least *partial* armor—gauntlets here, a chestplate there, a belt of daggers or quiver of arrows on nearly every hip and back. Not one person unarmed. Every single one likely capable of killing him before he even knew it was happening.

It truly was a city—the entrance tunnel led into a vast cavern, so huge he couldn't make out the end of it. The common space at the bottom milled with people, as did the long, smooth paths that wound from level to level, steady inclines that never grew too steep or treacherous, with handrails on the far side of each. On each level, there appeared to be dwellings or shops; some entrances were sheathed with only tapestries or beaded curtains, others had doors, others appeared to have no cover at all. He wondered if those were true caves with nothing in them, or if the owners of those particular establishments had an admirable amount of trust in their people.

In the common space, he spotted dozens if not hundreds of firepits—that was where the heat was coming from, he guessed. Some seemed to be for social gathering, but others were surrounded by people wearing gear he recognized as forging equipment.

Star led them down the path until they reached the common space. It reminded him a bit of the parlor in Delphin's manor; the atmosphere was similar, relaxed and companionable, people calling across the room to each other or tossing tools back and forth between workstations.

"Safi!" Star called, and a young woman raised her head from where she bent over one of the fires, her crown of braids tied back with a leather headband, the firelight glistening gold across her dark brown skin. The woman lifted a hand to wave, then moved back from the fire—not on her feet, but in a wheelchair, an invention that had been a joint effort between Arborian medimancers and Artem inventors. Though Artem wasn't neutral in the same way Arborius was, they'd made certain that every kingdom had the designs and trained craftsmen to make them.

The woman wheeled herself over to them and tugged her protective spectacles up, tipping her head and narrowing her eyes at Kallias. "I didn't think we were expecting you so soon, First Prince Kallias."

He offered his hand to shake, not bothering to ask how she knew who he was, and she took it. It took all his control not to flinch away from the heat in her skin from working by the fire—gods, what was wrong with him? He could barely think straight for sweating. "Circumstances changed, I'm afraid. And you are?"

"Safi Aquila. I'm the general's daughter." She let go of his hand and rolled up the sleeves of her smoke-stained work shirt as she looked to her mother, one brow raised. "You're looking for the High Priestess, then? She's in the chapel. I'll come along, if you don't mind." Safi flashed him a grin and a good-humored wink. "Not too often we get princes tromping around here."

A blush heated Kallias's face even worse than before, and he hoped desperately that he wasn't visibly sweating. "It's not too often that I get to do any tromping."

"Save the flirting for later, Kallias," said Elias tiredly, and if Kallias wasn't exhausted himself, he would've punched the Nyxian for that. "We've come a long way, and we're in a bit of a hurry."

"This is Elias Loch," Star told Safi, her bangles rattling as she crossed her arms. "He's your Aunt Sera's son."

"Elias and Kallias?" Safi's grin widened. "Your names rhyme a bit. Was that done on purpose? Do they match guards to princes by name?"

"I'm not his guard," Elias muttered at the same time Kallias said, "Oh, depths. I didn't even realize—"

"Later," Elias pleaded, and Safi laughed.

"Come on, cousin, we'll show you the way." She gave Elias a quick pat on the arm before pushing herself past him, leading them down the wide paths between fires. "Those are some fine blades on your belt," she added, eyes flicking to Elias's daggers. "Do they have a crest on them?"

Elias drew one of his daggers and studied it. "Yes. A circle with an arrow inside it and three flames above it."

Safi barked out a delighted laugh. "I knew it! Those are one of my sets."

"You're a weaponsmith?"

"Well, I wasn't sitting by that fire to keep my ass warm."

Kallias chuckled, and even Raquel cracked the slightest smirk. "Weapon of choice?" she asked.

Safi shrugged. "Bow and arrow, though I'm not half-bad with a set of throwing knives, either."

"My sister favored knives," said Raquel, and Kallias's neck ached with the urge to look her way, but he kept his eyes glued straight ahead. He could feel her stare burning into his temple, anyway. "She could hit a fly on a board thirty feet away."

"Talented girl." Safi took in a deep breath. "So, are either of you Nyxians the necromancer that's had my whole kingdom buzzing with ridiculous gossip for over a month?"

"Safi," snapped Star, but the woman waved her mother off impatiently as she stopped in front of a black marble door similar to the ones that guarded the entrance to the Kingdom of Fire. This one only had an etching of Mortem; no phoenix to be seen.

"Mother, it's *fine*. They'd be no threat to me until someone died, anyway." She smirked at Elias, but he avoided her gaze, his knuckles paling as he tightened his grip on his dagger. "The High Priestess is inside. If she's praying, wait to approach until she summons you to the altar. She gets cranky if she's interrupted."

That didn't strike him as promising. They needed this priestess no less than welcoming if they were going to make it before the Empress, and optimism had decided to crawl down his bones and hide in the soles of his feet rather than settle in his stomach. More and more often lately, fear had decided to make itself the foremost among his emotions. Fear, then anger, then doubt.

But Atlas needed better than that; it needed bravery, needed calm, needed confidence. He was their best Heir here, crown or no. He was their only advocate.

And yet, he was here to deliver news that would paint them in treachery to the one kingdom that had bothered to offer a hand of alliance in ten long years.

His head felt heavy, threatening to bow with shame, the weight of his new title bearing down on his spine.

Traitor.

He didn't need to be in the Atlas streets to hear the whispers. His heart still lurked in the sea-kissed breezes, and it felt the change in the wind as surely as a sail. But he had sworn an oath to protect his kingdom—and its Heir—at all costs. If he let Artem ally themselves with Atlas against Nyx, this war would never end, and Soleil would be lost to them forever.

He'd failed her once, twice, three times now. He *would not* fail her again.

His boots brushed gently against scarlet-carpeted floors as he slipped into the chapel, Elias at his back, Raquel presumably and unfortunately following along.

He halted almost immediately, the flicker of flame rooting his feet to the floor, the sight alone enough to turn his stomach.

Fire. Everywhere he looked, fire.

In the brass braziers bookending the black stone altar. In the colorful blown-glass lamps lining every wall. In the stained-glass fireplace in the center of that altar that cast chips of ruby and amber and sapphire light across the walls. This place was built to glorify the thing that had stripped away his family, his home, everything he'd ever known and loved.

New sweat poured down his back. His shirt clung uncomfortably to his skin, and for a second he had to fight the absurd urge to peel it off.

Elias whispered into his ear, his breath another brush of smoke-scented warmth: "You're here for your people. Head high. You can do this."

The Nyxian's words shouldn't have meant something, but for some reason they brought his chin up a bit higher.

"And remember," Elias added, "if you don't, both our kingdoms are forfeit."

"Oh, thanks," he mumbled back. "No pressure."

Elias pinched the back of his shirt and gave a sharp tug, pulling it away from his sticky back. "Best manners on hand, Your Highness. We get one chance."

Kallias's cheeks flushed hotter, and he shrugged Elias off, suddenly feeling a bit dizzy. "You're not helping."

There was a figure kneeling at the wide steps of the altar. As they halted just shy of the edge of the altar space, she stood in one swift motion. As she slowly lifted her head, Kallias's mouth dried out.

A diadem of living flame wavered atop her head.

The High Priestess turned to face them, and his breath caught in his chest. The firelight glinted across her rich onyx skin and hair, luminous as a raven's feathers. Her locks fell past her waist, decorated with bits of gold and silver and a couple other precious metals he couldn't identify. She wore a thick necklace of hammered gold shaped like a ring of flames, gold and silver rings on most of her fingers, and several golden hoops in the lobes and cartilage of her ears. Her gown was some hybrid design, cloth and metal working in tandem to create a type of garment he'd never seen before: scarlet and gold, armored at the bodice and other vulnerable places, thin chiffon-like fabric sheathing everything else. It was a dress designed to be fought in, breathable and unbreakable. Geometric tattoos a shade darker than her skin bordered every edge of her: her forehead, her fingers, her collarbone. He guessed there were more hidden beneath the layers of her armored gown.

If this was the woman they had to pass to get to the Empress, then Idris must be imposing, indeed.

"Prince Kallias," she greeted him, her voice low and level. It reminded him of the honey Jericho added to her tea every morning. "We weren't expecting you so soon."

"High Priestess." He offered a respectful nod. "You know my name already, so allow me to introduce my companions. Officer Elias Loch and Officer Raquel Angelov from Nyx."

Her brow peaked. "An Atlas prince traveling with Nyxian guards?"

"I'm afraid I bring troubling news for Empress Idris." Careful to put the emphasis on *Empress Idris*. "I—*we* must speak to her immediately."

"I'm afraid the Empress is taking no audiences at this time."

He held to his composure, even though he sensed Elias tense to his left. "When will she be taking audiences?"

"It's impossible to say. The Empress is in mourning. I'm sure you heard of the late Emperor's death."

Kallias was careful to keep his face neutral, though his stomach dropped to the soles of his feet at her words. The oppressive heat spun his head in circles as he tried to regain his bearings. "Her father, yes. We were saddened to hear of his passing. But respectfully, Priestess, it's been months since his death. Surely the period for mourning is over."

The High Priestess raised both thick brows this time. "Yes. And it's been ten years since your younger sister's death. When will Adriata's mourning period be over, I wonder?"

Elias twitched—the slightest flinch Kallias had ever seen. He sucked in his dry bottom lip, chewing on it for a moment. "I assumed she intended to meet me before she agreed to my mother's terms of alliance."

"And she will. But it will be on her time, *Prince*, not yours." Cold. Cutting. A reminder of his place.

But he'd spent his whole life lashed by that exact tone. It no longer bent his back; instead, it straightened it. Strengthened it. "I understand perfectly, Priestess. But our news won't keep for long. It has bearing on the alliance your kingdom is entering into with mine."

"Be that as it may, you must...you. Boy. What was your name?"

Kallias blinked to find the Priestess's attention was no longer on him. Her gaze had focused on Elias, her head cocked slightly in curiosity.

Elias took a hesitant step forward, keeping his chin tilted down in respect. "Elias Loch, Priestess."

The Priestess's brow twitched. "Are you a worshipper of Mortem, Elias Loch?"

The answer should have been quick and easy. But Elias hesitated a moment too long before saying, "I am. I—I was. I grew up in the Andromeda temple, under the tutelage of Priestess Kenna."

The High Priestess tipped back her head, regarding Elias down the bridge of her nose. "Come forward."

To his credit, Elias only looked mildly uneasy as he stepped forward, coming to a halt before the Priestess. He was only taller than her by an inch or so.

"Take off your shirt."

"What?" The word came from both Elias and Kallias at once, Elias confused, Kallias incredulous.

The Priestess regarded them both without expression, gesturing at Elias expectantly. "Take off your shirt. Let me see your tattoos."

"How do you know I—?"

"Let me see them, please."

Elias's throat bobbed visibly, but he slowly did as the Priestess asked, rotating to show her his back. Kallias had to swallow at the sight of his tattoos: runes mingled in geometric designs like the Priestess's, like Star's, like Safi's. Not Nyxian after all—Mortem's designs, belonging to no particular kingdom or crown. The tattoos were considerably sparser than the Priestess's, though; they only spanned Elias's upper back and shoulders.

But the longer Kallias looked, he realized that wasn't quite true. There was another mark there, one that hadn't been present when Elias was strung up in the Atlas dungeons after his identity was uncovered—a dark etching of a bird with flaming wings outstretched, stamped at the base of his neck. It looked less like a tattoo and more like...a branding. Like it had been burned into Elias's skin rather than inked.

The Priestess's eyes widened, and she breathed a soft, reverent prayer—or a curse. Kallias wasn't sure which. "Cleric."

"What?" Again, that word bursting from his mouth and Elias's in tandem. Kallias bit down on his tongue, awkwardly folding his hands behind his back. How had this gone downhill so quickly? When had his formal request to meet with his betrothed devolved into ogling Elias?

"This," she said, touching her fingers to the mark on Elias's neck, "is the mark of a cleric. Mortem has marked you as hers."

"As a host?" Kallias made the only guess he could, dread burrowing deep in his belly.

Both the Priestess and Elias shot him looks of warning, and Elias said, "Mortem doesn't take hosts, remember?"

"She doesn't," agreed the Priestess cautiously, her gaze drifting between the two of them with new suspicion. But she continued anyway: "Mortem took a host once and only once. Instead, historically, she's chosen a priest or priestess to carry out her will by proxy. And you, boy...she's marked you as her next."

Elias's expression shuttered. He pulled away from the Priestess, scrunching up his shirt before unfurling it and tugging it back over his head in one smooth motion, the hem settling over his waistband. "I don't want it. She'll have to pick another."

"It is the honor of a lifetime."

"I don't *want it*."

The Priestess glanced toward Kallias with a look that unsettled him. That, or the spinning of his head was starting to turn his stomach, as well. The flames above her head fluttered higher, then calmed again. "I will offer you a compromise, Prince. You'll have your audience with Idris…if your guard agrees to undertake a task from me."

"I'm *not* his guard," Elias said again, at the same time Kallias said, "What task?" They exchanged a look from the corners of their eyes, Elias annoyed, Kallias apologetic.

"He has been claimed as Mortem's cleric. That branding won't fade, whether he wants it or not. It's the mark of the phoenix—the mark of someone who has set foot in Mortem's realm and was allowed to walk back out." The Priestess's eyes settled on Elias, silent challenge burning in their depths. "The last of Mortem's clerics underwent three trials here, as has every cleric who has ever served her—a Trial of Blood, a Trial of Fire, and a Trial of Death. At the end of these three trials, Mortem lays final claim to her chosen. They determine your worthiness as her weapon and will. If you succeed and accept her calling, you join the ranks of the Mortem-blessed. If you fail…you are subject to her mercy. Either way, until you're granted that audience, that discomfort you feel in your own body, that strange burning in your chest…it won't ever stop, Elias Loch. You will never feel fully alive again."

Elias's hand clenched over his chest. "How did you—?"

The Priestess interrupted him by raising one hand. With a quick flick of her wrist, fire burst to life and climbed from her wrist to her palm, tendrils crawling up each finger and flickering in talon-like protrusions from her nails. She studied it with halfhearted interest. "I have my ways. If you complete the trials, you'll have your audience. I promise you that."

Kallias caught his breath against a surge of fear. It was ridiculous; he knew Mortem-blessed wielders carried fire in their hands…but he also hadn't seen one since the night Soleil died. Only a glimpse, but he could still see them in his mind's eye: a flash of dark leather sleeves and fingers lit at the tips like matchsticks, trailing along the walls of his palace like a student dragging their nails down a chalkboard to annoy a schoolteacher.

"So?" asked the Priestess. "Do we have an agreement?"

The voice that peeled out of his throat was thinner than a sheaf of paper, whittled to nothing by the sight of that flaming hand. "He's my ally, not my guard. It's not my choice to make."

Elias was quiet for several moments, black eyes drifting from the Priestess to the altar, stopping on the hearth in its center. The reflection of those flames danced deep in his eyes, and Kallias didn't think he liked what burned behind them.

"If I complete the trials, we'll have our audience," Elias said. "Whether I take on Mortem's blessing or not. If I *complete* them, success or failure, Prince Kallias meets with Empress Idris immediately after. Are we agreed?"

The Priestess dipped her head, the slightest hint of some odd satisfaction in her gaze. "We are."

"Then let's get this over with. Tell me what I have to do."

"All in good time." The Priestess jerked her chin toward the door. "General Aquila will show you where you'll be sleeping for the duration of your stay. For tonight, rest. Tomorrow, we'll discuss your first Trial."

Kallias wanted to speak again, to protest that they didn't have the time for this, that his kingdom could be falling apart at the seams while they forced Elias to take part in some godly game. But his voice had faded from thin to useless, trapped inside his aching chest, sweat pooling beneath his arms and pouring down the small of his back. Even the backs of his knees and neck were slick with it, his hair and pants and shirt all *sticking* unpleasantly to his skin, heat and frustration and fear pushing him toward an edge he didn't want to set foot over.

He needed food. He needed sleep. He needed an ice-cold shower.

So he obeyed when the Priestess gestured for them to leave. And when she twisted her arm in a grasping motion, snuffing out every fire but the hearth in the heart of the altar, he was grateful for the shiver it sent down his spine.

CHAPTER 14

FINN

T he violins were not helping his headache.

Nor was the stiff, strangling collar of his uniform—his brother's old military jacket, tailored to fit him instead. Tailored a bit *snug*, if he said so himself, but beggars couldn't be choosers. His brother's medals had been removed, the jacket thoroughly cleaned and pressed until the Atlas-blue cloth practically sparkled, the gold thread and buttons shimmering in the light of the ballroom's many chandeliers.

All part of the costume. All part of the show. Lapis was expecting a First Prince, and by the depths, he was going to give them one.

"You need to fire the tailor that did this," Finn muttered to his mother, tugging at his collar *again*, silently and soundly cursing his brother for being so gods-damned noble.

"It was a rush job," Adriata murmured back, reaching over and pulling his hand away from his collar. "Stop fidgeting."

"It's a *shoddy* job, is what it is—"

"Hush."

"It's not their fault you're skinny as a reed," Jericho mumbled from his other side. She was scowling worse than he was, her arms crossed tightly over her chest like she was shielding herself from view. Vaughn was still resting in the infirmary, fighting off his latest bout of pain from his *wasting sickness*.

Gods, it was an *ache*, the urge to tear his sister's ruse apart. To tell her he hadn't fallen for it. To prove his mind was still the sharpest in this palace. But this was a long game. His pride would just have to pinch a bit longer.

So he feigned hurt instead, pressing his hand over the stiff coat, pleased to find that his hands were holding steady—at least for now. He needed to come up with an excuse in case they started trembling while he was speaking with the Lapisian delegation. That would hardly present him as *king* material, a boy whose hands quivered before a queen. Perhaps he should have worn gloves. "I've been bulking up!"

Anima leaned around Jericho, flashing a smirk that was so clearly practiced he nearly laughed out loud. This goddess was the worst actress he'd ever seen. "Bulking up what, your ego?"

"Hush," hissed Adriata once more as two attendants began to pull the heavy ballroom doors open. "What's gotten into the three of you?"

His stomach clenched, and the urge to laugh vanished as quickly as it had come, his eyes catching Anima and Jericho's winces in his peripherals. What *had* gotten into them, indeed.

Normally Kallias was the one who kept them all in check. Kallias was the one who caught twiddling hands and hissed warnings into ears and pleaded quietly to the gods for patience, because their mother hadn't bothered to do so in gods-knew how long. And Kallias had ensured she'd never needed to—had done his best to make sure Finn never felt the lack.

At least, he had after the incident.

Before Finn's flawless memory could pull him into a loop of shattering glass and the reek of old wine and *screaming*, his mother put her hand on his shoulder and squeezed. "Remember," she said into his ear, "be yourself. Everything will be fine."

Himself. Please. After so many years shuffling through masks and personas like a card player stacking a deck, he wasn't even sure if he *could* remove them all. Wasn't even sure there was a *himself* left at the bottom of the pile.

He opened his mouth to give her the answer she wanted to hear, but the words died in his throat as he caught the first flash of light beyond the door.

Lapis was here.

The Daggers entered first. Six of them, all men, dressed in sleek silver uniforms inlaid with shimmering thread. Not one weapon in sight, but he noted the way each of them walked, the places they favored and the way they positioned their arms. Not one of them walked without added weight. They each wore their blades in different places from what he could see, but they were all armed to the teeth—their uniforms were likely designed with hidden compartments rigged to open if the Dagger prompted them. Pockets that would likely allow them to pass any gate inspection without giving up anything important.

Assassins. Bodyguards. Deadly with or without a weapon in hand. But they weren't his to worry about—they would be Vash's mission.

Then came the Mirrors.

Aptly named. Each of the women wore gowns with tight bodices that flowed into floor-length silk skirts—at least, he thought it might be silk. But each dress was so bedecked in reflective jewels of all sizes and cuts that he could hardly see cloth for color. Six of them filed in one after the other, each one wearing a different gemstone—ruby, emerald, sapphire, opal, topaz, aquamarine. They flared out in a fan-like arrangement in the spaces between the Daggers, backs straight, eyes cold, staring straight ahead at the Atlas royals on the dais before them. Each of them wore mirrors on their wrists like Luisa did, but these women went steps further; they wore mirrors hooked in their ears, belted around their waists, strung around their necks. The sunlight refracted off of them like their very essence resisted it, dappling the floor and ceiling with white-gold droplets of light. Every eye in the ballroom was on them—figuratively and literally. The suspicious eyes of the crowd of palacefolk reflected back at him from each of the seers' dresses and jewelry.

Dozens, hundreds, thousands of eyes surrounding him.

"No more masks, trickster," Occassio's voice purred in his ear. *Fingertips trailed down the back of his neck.* *"This oughta be fun."*

He gave his head a quick jerk, gritting his teeth until they stopped buzzing with the urge to speak all his long-buried truths, resisting the urge to scratch the itch behind his ears.

Not here. Not here. Not *now*.

A flicker of purple caught his eye at the end of the row of Mirrors—not six women after all, he realized as a head poked around the others, eyes wide with curiosity. Not six—seven. He'd missed one; not because he wasn't paying attention, not because his vision had stolen valuable seconds from him, he assured himself, but because she was so...*short*.

She was just slightly out of line, smaller than all the rest by at least a foot, not quite as perfect, not quite as polished. She wore just as many mirrors as the others, her dress coated in amethysts, but her gaze wasn't half as cold. Her feet shuffled in place, her fingers tweaking nervously at the mirror hanging on a chain around her neck. Her multifaceted pink glass slippers shimmered distractingly in the sunlit ballroom as she fidgeted, keen eyes sweeping the crowd with nervous energy. Her shoulders were tilted a bit too far back—an overcorrection for a natural tendency to slouch, perhaps—and her thick, dark ringlets were strewn with tiny jewels in all colors, tossing glimmering chips of light against the wall when she moved her head. A spray of freckles decorated her warm brown skin, and when she caught his eye and offered him a shy, almost reflexive smile, the tip of her tongue poked through a gap between her front teeth.

Younger than the rest, by the look of her. Newer. An apprentice, maybe. She hadn't learned how to spot a snake yet. So Finn smiled back, carefully tucking his own tongue behind his teeth where she couldn't see him hiss. *There you are.*

A chink in the Queen's armor. She'd be his way in.

"I want those dresses," Jericho mumbled.

"Those dresses cost as much to make as this ballroom cost to build," Ramses said from Adriata's right, but there was no mistaking the longing gleam in his father's eye; it was hard to kill a thieving instinct, even when it was buried inside a king. Finn tried not to smile. One of those dresses might end up going *missing* in the wash during Lapis's stay here. His bet was on the ruby one.

Before he could lean over and suggest that very thing to his father, a new rush of sundrops spattered across the ballroom floor, followed shortly by the very woman they'd been waiting for: the Mirror Queen herself.

Esha Levine.

Young, like his mother said. Her sleek ebony hair framed a pale face made up of all angles: sharp cheekbones, sharp eyes, sharp nose, sharp brows. Even her thin-lipped scowl seemed honed to a bladed edge, a threat with no words, a promise with no warmth. Her crown was a cluster of all sorts of gems and precious stones pressed into clear-cut crystal, and her dress…

Diamonds. Hundreds and hundreds of them, some so large he actually had to swallow down some pickpocket's drool of his own, his sleight-ready fingers quickly dipping into his own pockets instead. But his heart dropped a moment later as realization dawned:

Diamonds on white silk. A wedding gem backed by a bridal color.

Esha had come dressed all in white from head to toe. And knowing what he did of her, knowing this queen did absolutely nothing by accident, he could guess exactly what that was meant to imply.

She'd come here searching for a consort. And she wouldn't be leaving until she found one.

"Welcome, Queen Esha." Adriata stepped out of their own line, spreading her arms in greeting. "Welcome, all of you. We're happy to have you here."

Esha dipped her head just barely enough to be polite. "Queen Adriata," the Mirror Queen said, her voice like a pealing bell, clear and melodic. "I heard many stories about you from my mother."

"Lyria was a good friend."

"I hear you were all friends, once. My mother. You. Queen Genevieve." The queen's eyes gleamed. "Queen Ravenna, even."

Adriata's smile was fixed perfectly in place, but her eyes hollowed out with anger. "We were young then. Please, make yourselves at home. Dinner will be served shortly. Until then, allow me to introduce you to my family."

The crowd relaxed a bit as Adriata descended the dais, followed closely by Jericho and his father, and more reluctantly by Anima, who seemed determined not to meet any of the Lapisians' eyes. Slowly, cautiously, folk began to find their seats at the various tables set up around the dance floor. But most gazes still lingered on their visitors.

His mother would expect him to follow her and his family. He was the reason Esha was here. The First Prince needed to be present, ever at his Queen and Heir's side. But as Esha leaned to the Mirror and Dagger closest to her—the ruby-dressed woman and, surprisingly, the youngest of the men—and offered a soft word that seemed to be a dismissal of all but them, he watched the amethyst-clad Mirror awkwardly start to follow the other Mirrors away as they split off to mingle; and they all turned their backs on her and went their own ways, leaving her alone in the midst of a foreign kingdom's people, a look of near-panic on her face.

Perfect. This was going to be easier than he thought.

He bided his time carefully—drifted from table to table, picking at hors d'oeuvres and keeping himself out of sight of his mother and Esha, letting the discomfort settle on his target's narrow shoulders. Her hesitant steps brought her to the edge of more than one table, but her timid greetings either went unheard or ignored. By the time he saw her heading for one of the balconies adjoined to the ballroom with a champagne glass in one hand and a pile of frosted cookies in the other, there was a sparkle in her eyes that suggested tears were on the way.

Poor girl. It was almost enough to make him feel guilty for what he was about to do.

Almost.

Glancing over his shoulder, he caught sight of his mother trading terse words with his father, who was craning his neck over the crowd, eyes probing for his missing son. When his father did catch his eye, Finn raised one finger to his lips, doing his best to convey a plea with only his eyes.

Ramses's expression softened. He offered the slightest dip of his head—*I'll buy you time.*

Finn blew out a quiet breath of relief and nodded back. *Thanks, Papa.*

He waited until Ramses drew Adriata's attention away, pointing in the opposite direction of the frosted-glass balcony doors, catching just enough of the movement of his lips to understand that his father was suggesting he might have ducked into the hall to get some air. He really didn't give his father enough credit for his ability to fool Adriata—he was a terrible liar, but never once did Adriata doubt him.

Finn pressed his palm to the balcony door, pushing it open so softly that the hinges didn't even creak. The Mirror was seated at the edge of the balcony, her skirt pulled up past her knees and her short, freckled legs dangling through the bars on the railing. Cookie crumbs were piled in the spaces between the gems on her skirt and stuck in the gloss on her lips; she was munching glumly, three more cookies still cradled in one hand, the other braced on the floor beside her champagne glass. She gazed out at the sea, clearly lost in thought, clearly unaware of his presence.

With quiet precision that a hunting cat would have envied, Finn lowered himself down beside her, sitting cross-legged, carefully angling himself to stay just outside her periphery. He arranged his leg so it was beside her champagne glass, took a deep breath, and loudly said, "Now *this* looks more like my kind of party."

The girl started with a shrill squeak, her hand knocking into the champagne glass. It bumped into his leg, some of the liquid splashing across his pants, and she quickly snatched the glass back up. "I'm so sorry! Oh, gods, I'm so—" The girl scrambled up, but her skirt caught on one of the bars, causing her to stumble and spill more champagne into Finn's lap. "Oh, that's worse. Oh no."

Well. That could not have gone any better.

"No, it's all right!" Finn gestured for her to stop, trying not to wince as cold, sticky liquid soaked through his pants. "It's all right. I snuck up on you, that's—I asked for that."

The girl stared at him, brown eyes wider than dinner plates, her cookie-filled hands covering her mouth. "I am *so sorry*, Prince Finnick."

He cracked a sheepish grin, scratching the back of his neck. "Damn. That obvious?"

"If you want to fool anyone, you might want to get rid of the crown. And besides, I just saw you inside. Five minutes ago." The girl forced a nervous, warbling laugh that made him think of morning birds. She lowered her hands before seemingly remembering that she'd stolen a considerable amount of sweets; she quickly hid her hands behind her back, offering him a quick but suitable bow. "You're to be betrothed to my queen."

He let his smile falter. No need to hide this. He stood and plucked the crown from his head, rotating it slowly in his hands. "That seems to be the intention, yes." He glanced down, tugging the soaked cloth away from his skin. "However, I'm not sure she'll be so keen on a consort that wets himself in front of pretty girls."

The girl's laugh was genuine that time, an ungraceful snorting sound followed by a bubbling giggle. "I'll be sure to let her know it was entirely my doing, Your Highness."

"Finn," he corrected her, offering his hand. "I don't care much for titles."

She snorted again, more delicately this time, shifting her cookies to one hand and shaking his with her other. "Good luck being king-consort then, huh?" Her eyes widened, her cheeks darkening with a blush, her free fingers fidgeting with her skirt. "Pardon me. That was out of turn."

"Not at all." Hm—surprising. The girl had a sharp tongue hidden behind that shy smile. He shoved his hands into his pockets to hide their impatient twitching, nodding back toward the ballroom. "You don't seem to be enjoying yourself in there."

She lowered her gaze, her glass shoes tapping at the floor. "I didn't mean to give that impression—"

"Don't bother, really. I hate parties too." He cleared his throat, pulling her attention back up to him. "You got a name, Fidget?"

She wrinkled her freckled nose. "Fidget?"

He nodded to her piano-key fingers, and she quickly stilled them. "Nicknames are sort of an Atlas tradition. And since I don't know your real name..."

"My name is not *Fidget*." But her lips tweaked with mirth.

"Then what?"

She tipped her head, her eyes narrowing a bit on his face. "From what we hear in Lapis, you're supposed to be the smartest member of the Atlas family. Why don't you try to guess?"

He snorted quietly. "I'm not familiar with Lapisian names, Fidget."

"Stop that!" she laughed, pinning her twitching fingers under her arms. "Mirrors and Daggers aren't supposed to tell people our names. It's a rule. But if you can guess it...well, that wouldn't be my fault, would it?"

He'd known that, but he'd wanted to see how long this girl had been in training with the Mirrors. Long enough to stick to their code, anyway: faceless, nameless. Mere reflections of the queen herself, shadows and shields, nothing more.

He cocked one eyebrow at her. She met his look with a crooked grin.

"It could be fun," she added. "If you're to court my queen, we'll be seeing a lot of each other. Might be a good way to pass the time."

In spite of himself, his own mouth quirked upward. That undercurrent of loneliness in her voice was *exactly* what he needed. "Fine. I'm game. But I need *something* to call you in the meantime."

"*Not* Fidget."

"I got that, thanks." He studied her briefly, careful to linger a bit too long on her face, careful to worry his bottom lip with his teeth. Her eyes, as expected, dropped to his mouth—good. He'd learned something from watching Jericho and Kallias make fools of themselves, then.

Seduction wasn't a chess piece he utilized often; he'd never been like Kallias, who saw beauty in just about anyone and lost his head entirely in the face of it. Finn acknowledged beauty, understood it, could appreciate it from a distance, but the fluster, the heart-pounding heat, the head-spinning...that had only happened once, with a diplomat's daughter from Arborius, a wild-haired fiend of a girl he'd befriended during the three-year stretch her parents had lived in the palace. And even then, it had taken time. He'd only started to feel those flutters of attraction after a year or so, when they'd spent a night stealing pastries from the kitchen and sneaking out into Port Atlas, their bare feet warmed by the summer heat still gathered in the cobblestones. And after he'd shown her all his secret places, after he'd introduced her to the kingdom he ruled over all on his own, she'd looked at him with shining eyes and said, "Finnick Atlas, you may just be the most dangerous person I know."

Before Soleil had come crashing back into his life, Astrid Thorne was the only one who'd ever gotten a true peek beneath his mask. And even though they'd both agreed it was useless to pursue an official courtship when their kingdoms were already allies, they enjoyed the year and a half they had. And even when she left, they stayed close—now a diplomat herself, having taken on her father's position when he retired, she often wrote Finn asking for advice or sharing particularly entertaining stories.

Finn would never last as a diplomat. He didn't have half the patience of his coy, careful friend.

"Prince?" The Mirror's voice cut through his memories like a carved-crystal knife, one of her bejeweled eyebrows raised. "You're staring."

Damn, he had to stop. These bouts of absentmindedness were going to ruin him. "Freckles?" he suggested, and her nose wrinkled again.

"I guess that's better," she allowed. "But...mm..."

"Not a fan of nicknames?"

"Not a fan of yours."

He chuckled. "Well, if you're not going to like any of them, I'm sticking with Fidget."

The girl considered him for a few moments. Finally, she nodded. "If you insist."

Just as he was about to say something more, the balcony door opened, and his mother's furious face poked out. "Finnick Aurelias Atlas. Inside. *Now.*"

Oh, depths. Even the Trickster Prince of Atlas didn't go up against his mother when the middle name came out. He quickly offered one last bow to his new friend. "Fidget."

She offered him a smile still dotted with cookie bits, bowing in turn, crumbs scattering across the balcony as her skirt shifted. "Prince Finnick. Good to make your acquaintance."

He offered her his best roguish grin before his mother dragged him back inside, anger fuming off her like smoke from a fire. "What happened to you?" she scolded, reaching up to rub the furrow from between her brows when she caught sight of the state of his uniform. "Gods, you're all going to make me wrinkle before my time."

"You're nearly fifty," he reminded her. "There's not much more *before* your—"

She gave his cheek a quick, sharp pat. "Do not finish that sentence. Go to your room and change. *Now.*"

He buried his laugh with a quick cough. "Yes, Mama. Sorry, Mama."

The moment he stepped into the hall, he sensed the presence of a shadow behind him. But he walked anyway, not looking back. "Well?"

"The Daggers are well-trained and impeccably scheduled," said Vash, his voice quiet. Finn couldn't even hear his footsteps on the lacquered floor. "I was hoping to replace one of them, but I'm not sure it'll be possible. I haven't caught an entry point yet."

"Careful. These are Occassio-blessed people. They're trained to see through illusions."

The slightest rasp of breath before Vash responded—Finn couldn't tell if it was a laugh or a scoff. "I worship Occassio, too. They won't see through mine."

"Good. Give it time; they've only been here a couple hours. You'll find an opening." A reassurance and an order. "And Vidia?"

"Gone this morning. Seamus and Alia?"

"Waiting on my word. I'll meet with them once things have settled."

"And you?" Vash prompted. "What did you find?"

He nearly smiled, flicking a stray cookie crumb from his fingers. "Exactly what I was hoping for."

CHAPTER 15

ANIMA

"A phoenix feather. A mirror that shows no reflection. A bloom from the heart of the forest. A shard of ice that never melts. And a music box that plays a song of chaos." Ani cast herself onto the fainting couch at the foot of Jericho's bed, moaning into the frilly pillow propped at the end, twitching her nose at the tickly brush of fabric. "This is going to take *ages*."

"You're sure that's all he said?" Jericho asked from where she was bundled under the covers, the shadows beneath her eyes nearly matching her dying husband's. Vaughn was asleep, as he seemed to be more and more lately; Nyx and Atlas had yet to engage in another battle, and the guard on the city cemetery was constant and excessive. There would be no grave-robbing anytime soon.

Ani lifted her head, the itch in her nose building until it erupted into a sneeze. She jumped, startled by the force of it. "Oh!"

Jericho frowned. "What?"

Ani swallowed down her embarrassment, quickly looking away, fussing with the hem of her skirt. "Sorry. I, um…that's the first time I've…sneezed. In a while. Just forget it."

To her surprise, Jericho's mouth actually quirked upward—very nearly a smile. "It's all right. You were saying?"

"Each relic is in a different kingdom, of course, because nothing can be easy about this." Blowing out a breath, Ani clambered onto her knees, leaning her elbows against the foot of Jericho and Vaughn's bed. "Only Tallis doesn't have one." That made sense, at least—Tallis worshipped no gods at all. It was the only kingdom that hadn't been founded or guided in some way by her or her siblings.

"So at least one of them is here." Jericho's eyes gleamed. "Yours?"

"No. Mine would be in Arborius, I think…the bloom at the heart of the forest. Tempest's might be here."

Jericho's eyes dimmed as fast as they'd lit. "Tempest is hardly worshipped here at all anymore. Many of his worshippers moved to Nyx well before the war."

Ani's heart sank. "You think his relic might have been taken too?"

"We can check the old temple, but it was stripped of anything valuable long ago." Jericho thought for a long moment. "But…"

Ani's ears perked, and she leaned closer, Jericho's footboard digging into her ribs as she stretched over it. "What?"

"Lapis is here."

"Yes. So?"

"So…" Jericho's eyes slowly started to gleam again, that hint of a smile returning. "The Mirror Queen. Who else is more likely to have a priceless relic of Occassio?"

"But she wouldn't have brought it here," Ani protested. "She'd leave it in her palace to protect it."

"Most would, but not her. She's paranoid. Her kingdom is split in two. Most of the people she trusts are likely here with her—you think she'd leave such a prized possession in the hands of her would-be enemies?"

Hope, fragile as a butterfly's wings, began to flutter in her belly. "A mirror with no reflection."

Jericho nodded, jaw set in determination. "It's somewhere in this palace."

Ani gathered fistfuls of the duvet to quell her excited shaking. "Then we need to find it."

Jericho swung her legs around, hopping lightly out of bed. "And I know just the person to help search."

CHAPTER 16

ELIAS

Trials.

He should never have agreed to come.

Star and Safi took them up two floors, then down a long tunnel lit by more stained glass lamps. Safi chattered with Raquel the whole way, keeping her occupied with talk of weapons, and Elias was grateful—it kept Raquel from snipping at Kallias, who was still flushed and sweaty, his gait slow and faltering, his breathing labored and heavy. Star asked more than once if he needed a physician, but he simply shook his head and tromped on.

It wasn't Elias's place to challenge him on it; not with these particular listening ears. But the moment they were alone, he needed to have an honest talk with the Atlas prince. Spontaneously exhibiting magic well into adulthood was already strange, but paired with these symptoms, with these nightmares…

There hadn't been any signs with Soren, which suggested to him that she hadn't been a target until the temple. Jericho's plan had changed somewhere in the empty moments after Vaughn snapped Elias's neck—the only attempt at mercy the Prince-Consort had been able to offer. Somewhere in the small eternity Elias spent walking to the edge of Mortem's realm, Jericho had realized what Soren's body could bear, what she could offer as a sacrifice to her goddess, and bent his battlemate's will using his life as a weapon at her heart.

All because he'd walked through those gods-damned doors.

He shook himself as Star and Safi brought them all to a halt by a door at the far end of the tunnel. He didn't have time for regret today. Trials or no trials, he was responsible for unraveling the godly side of this horrific tangle of bloodshed. They were already juggling enough deities as it was. If Tempest was laying claim to Kallias, they had to stop it, and *fast*. Even if Tempest could be counted as an ally—or at the very least, not an active threat—he wasn't willing to give up one more life, especially not to one of the more vicious gods.

Kallias fumbled into their room with a quick mutter of gratitude, his eyes already halfway to closing, and Raquel went to follow him. Elias caught her left arm quickly, giving it a brief squeeze. He knew better than to come at her from her blind side. "Raquel." She didn't look up, but he pressed on anyway, lowering his voice. "Raquel, I know what you're feeling. But you really can't kill him."

"He killed my sister," she said softly.

"I know. But he's the only thing standing between Nyx and all five of the other kingdoms. You know how seriously they take necromantic threats."

Raquel's jaw worked. She wouldn't look at him. "Why do you think he's still breathing?"

A slow breath slipped from between Elias's teeth, and he gave her arm another squeeze—gratitude instead of warning. "I need to take care of one last thing before I turn in. Can I trust you to keep your blade in its sheath while I'm gone?"

"I don't need a blade to kill him."

"*Raquel.*"

"*Yes*, Elias, he will still be breathing when you get back. I'm not a fool." She finally looked up, dark eye gleaming, the lamps bringing out the blue buried in the black of her hair. A cold flame burning in the dark. "Hurry back."

It was the best he would get from her, but he still wasn't settled when he finally turned back to his cousin and aunt. When he asked them about the *Havi* Ember had mentioned, surprise overtook him at the confused—and slightly alarmed—looks on their faces. But when he mentioned that Princess Emberlyn had sent along a letter for him, both of them relaxed, Safi going so far as to roll her eyes. "Why didn't you say so to start with? Gods, you're going to make his whole month." When he shot her an inquisitive look, she smirked and added, "My big brother has a soft spot the size of this mountain for that particular princess."

Elias blinked. "He and Ember are...?"

"It's a bit hush-hush, so don't take it back to Nyx with you, but yes. Why they didn't wed before she went home is anyone's guess."

"She seemed to think he'd be helpful with..." he gestured helplessly back down the tunnel, "...all this."

Safi narrowed her eyes, exchanging a look with her mother, who shrugged. "I see," Safi said. "Well, his shop should still be open for a bit longer. I'll introduce you."

Again, her skeptical reaction twinged a cord of disquiet in his stomach. Who exactly had Ember sent him to see? A powerful Mortem-blessed wielder? Maybe a priest? A weaponsmaster? Gods, he should have read her letter before he came.

Safi wheeled herself back down the hall, taking him down one floor using one of the long, gently sloping ramps built into the stone walls. Once they reached level ground once more, she said, "So. Artem-forged daggers, Nyxian accent, Atlas prince. Sounds like quite the story."

A noise escaped him—he wasn't sure if it was a laugh or a scoff. "Not one I'm at liberty to tell."

"Understood. So are you his prisoner, or is he yours?"

Gods, this woman didn't mince words. "Neither. Though I was his for a time."

"Well, that is just...unbearably vague."

"Like I said, I'm not at liberty to say much to anyone but your Empress."

"Not even for your favorite cousin?"

"I met you an hour ago."

Safi pouted. "Still. I've got to be close."

To his own surprise, something that might've been a smile touched on his lips. "Not for *any* cousin, favorite or not."

Safi narrowed her eyes at him, but didn't push…though he could see in her eyes that she wasn't the type to give in easily. Instead she said, "Here. The shop on the left with the iron sign."

Elias had expected the sight before him to some extent: a metal door set into the wall, a sign above it reading *The Sugar Spinner*, the glow of fire reflecting in the single frosted-glass-paned window built into the wall.

He hadn't expected it to smell of yeast and sugar. Or to hear the sound of singing through the cracked-open window, deep bass flowing beneath the hum of people milling about, a molasses-smooth harmony to the melody of this kingdom's people.

Safi knocked on the door with a gloved fist, and the singing cut off abruptly. "Havi! Quit showing off and let me in!"

"Can't I show off *while* letting you in?" countered that same bass voice, no longer musical in tone but somehow still soothing to the ear.

"Don't be smart. I have a *guest*."

The door opened to reveal a man who appeared to be a few years past twenty, maybe a little older than Kallias. He stood taller than the actual door; he had to duck down a bit to look out at them, his thick black locks swinging with the movement, a blinding grin digging twin dimples into his mahogany skin, a little bit of powdered sugar caught in his well-groomed beard. Dark eyes sparkled behind spectacles perched on the bridge of his nose, laughing eyes that spoke of a joy that didn't often fade. Flour stained the simple black apron tied loosely around his hips, and his sleeves were pushed up to his elbows, baring arms tattooed from the wrists upward with blooming roses. He leaned one broad shoulder against the doorframe, offering Elias his hand after surreptitiously wiping it clean—or at least, clean*er*—on his apron. "My apologies. I'm Havi Aquila. And you are?"

Elias took his hand slowly, mind racing through a hundred reasons why Ember might have sent him to a *baker*. "Elias Loch of Nyx."

"He's Aunt Sera's kid," Safi offered. "And he comes bearing gifts."

Elias nodded quickly, letting go of Havi's hand to dig around in his pack. "I have a letter meant for you, sent from Princess Emberlyn."

The man's swift intake of breath was almost comical. The moment Elias managed to maneuver the letter out of his pack, it was gone from his hand. Havi quickly slid a finger beneath the lip of the envelope, breaking the wax seal and holding it up to better light, adjusting his glasses to read. He scanned it with the exact level of eagerness and adoration Elias would've expected on the face of a man seeing the sun after years of darkness.

The small oblivion in his chest pulsed with memory, and he bore down on it, pressing his fist over his heart until the pain faded from sharp to soft. From breaking to bearable.

After a handful of minutes, Havi's eyes darted up to him, then back to the letter, then back to him. He slowly folded it and tucked it into his back pocket before moving aside from the door, gesturing inside his shop. "Why don't you come inside for dinner? It's getting late, and I'm sure you've had a long journey."

Elias hesitated, taking a step back. Family or not, he didn't truly know these people, and he was still suspected of being a necromantic sympathizer. Even if Ember trusted them… "Oh, I, ah…I wouldn't want to impose…"

"Oh, you're not," Safi reassured him, wheeling past him into the shop. The door was built wider than most—he guessed it was meant to allow easy access for her. "We're imposing on you, cousin. Get in here. You're skinnier than a polearm."

She wasn't wrong; he'd wasted some while in Atlas. Illness had carved away muscle and mass until his skin clung uncomfortably close to his bones…and his lack of fondness for fish hadn't helped any. One sniff of the sea or one loose scale on his plate was enough to kill his appetite beyond salvaging, and since Soren…since everything happened, not even Nyxian fare had managed to revive it to its original health. Everything tasted like dust in his mouth.

"All right," he relented. "But only for a few minutes. My…my allies are waiting for me in our quarters, and—"

Before he could finish, Havi wrapped a thick, strong arm around his shoulders, giving him a surprisingly friendly squeeze. "Do you like flatbreads?"

Elias frowned, hoping that the man couldn't feel the raised, ugly scar beneath his sleeve. "What's a *flatbread*?"

Havi broke into a beaming grin, his eyes shining with anticipation. "Mortem bless you, I was hoping you'd say that."

CHAPTER 17

KALLIAS

The baths in Artem were very different than what he was used to.

He sank deeper into the water, wiggling his toes against the oddly smooth stone floor, wishing this bath wasn't quite so warm. He hadn't thought to specify temperature when requesting water, and had only just managed to swallow his groan of despair when they'd brought it in steaming hot. A kindness to anyone else, but he would have sold his soul to be back in Nyx, the wind kissing his face with frost and forcing all unnecessary heat to take its leave.

But to complain would have been impolite at best, offensive at worst, and he was still a prince at heart if not in name. So instead he'd stripped down to his undershorts and sat at the edge of the rock basin that appeared to have been carved right out of the wall, watching the steam curl off the surface of the water until it finally vanished entirely. Lukewarm was better than near-boiling, at least.

A clatter outside the washroom door brought his chin up, his hand twitching instinctively toward his sword leaning against the craggy sides of the basin, steam-fed condensation dripping down the blade. He'd brought it just in case; Raquel may have promised not to kill him—yet—but he wasn't foolish enough to believe her. Promises were easier to break than bones these days, and even if they weren't, the way she kept eyeing him gave him the shivers. Not the good kind.

The sword blurred as his eyes unfocused, led down paths of thought that darkened and twisted with every passing moment.

This was supposed to be *his* mission. Artem was supposed to be his battleground to claim, a political dance with him leading the steps. Instead, the Priestess had clapped eyes on Elias and promptly lost interest in Kallias altogether. He hadn't even managed to meet the woman his mother had seen fit to sell him off to.

A frigid tendril of air teased the back of his neck, and a cold, coarse voice rolled like thunder in his ear: *Kallias Atlas. Always doomed to be less than you were born to be. Aren't you tired of waiting your turn?*

And now he was hearing gods-damned voices.

Eyes closed, body submerged in slowly cooling water, he curled his fists against the stone floor of the basin. Instead of shoving that voice out, instead of telling himself he was only mad or lonely or delirious with hunger, he whispered back: "Patience is a virtue."

A rumbling chuckle called every hair on his nape to stand at attention, goosebumps erupting down his arms. *Diplomatic as ever. But you can't fool me, Prince. There's a storm brewing in your blood. Can't you feel it?*

His dreams came back to him all at once: ice encasing his hands and feet. His body dissolving into sand and sea. Lightning tearing into the center of his ribcage, mauling him like a starving animal, lighting every bloodpath and bone with brilliance, with agony...

With *power*.

You could be so much more, the voice murmured. *I could give you everything you want.*

"And what do you think I want?"

I could make you a king.

All at once, his throat and mouth parched, dry with a craving that had taunted him since his nightmare of drowning. "Tell me your name," he said, too loudly.

The shuffling from the outer room dropped into sudden silence, and he held his breath once more, silently cursing himself. It was hardly going to work in his favor if Raquel thought he was the sort of person that talked to himself in the bath. That definitely wouldn't make him look too imposing.

It was there in the silence that Kallias heard, softer than the shifting of sand: *You know my name. You're only afraid to admit it.*

He squeezed his eyes more tightly shut. Loosened his fists. Whispered into the still air of the bathing room: "I don't."

You do.

Kallias shook his head with a low groan, thumping his hand into his head like he was trying to knock water loose from his ears. The voice didn't speak again, but its words echoed, a promise that chilled his spine with dread.

And then his headache came back with a vengeance, a throbbing that felt like it was trying to crack right through his skull. Scooping up a container full of some rose-scented concoction—shampoo, he hoped—he lathered a handful into his dirty hair, sighing in relief as the serum seeped between the oily strands and lifted the grime from his scalp. Dirty hair was the bane of his existence.

He was exhausted, that was all. Exhausted and hungry and dizzy with heat. Probably dehydrated, too. Any one of those things could cause hallucinations. Depths, he'd already seen what sleep deprivation could do to him just a handful of weeks ago.

He drew in another long breath through his nose and ducked under the surface of the water, letting his head settle at the bottom so the water could coax the shampoo from his hair. This basin was less of a bath and more of a small pool, big enough for him to stretch all the way out—a significant feat, considering he was over six feet tall—and deep enough that he could fully submerge.

If he kept his eyes shut tightly, he could almost imagine he was back home, settled on the floor of the sea; that the headache was from a day spent too long in the sun, that his toes were brushing against the bristling shells of live sand dollars or passing crabs rather than simple stone.

But this wasn't home. No matter what his mother might have intended, this mountain could never be his, throne or no throne. Not this far from his precious sea.

Sighing internally, he gathered his wits back about him, then sat up, ready to break the surface of the water—

His forehead collided with a solid wall, knocking his head back *hard* into the stone, pain exploding from both sides of his head. A startled cry escaped his lips before he clamped them closed again, holding what little remained of his breath, his lungs straining in protest. Fighting against a wave of dizziness and the pressure of the water, he forced his eyelids open.

His heart stopped.

Above his head, stretching from one end of the basin to the other, a thick sheet of ice had formed, cutting off all access to the surface.

He was trapped.

He dashed his fist against the ice. Nothing. He kicked, thrashed, knocked elbows and knees and knuckles into that barrier, panic building with every fruitless hit. Not one crack appeared—the ice might as well have been steel.

No. No. No. This couldn't be happening.

Another bubble of air escaped as he got knocked back by his own blows once more, ghostly ribbons of transparent red wavering in the water where blood leaked from the scrapes on his limbs. Frantic, he clawed at the ice with hands that felt bruised, his skin thrumming from multiple hits on the rock-hard surface of the water, but still it held.

He couldn't die like this. The firstborn prince of Atlas, lover of the ocean, master of the waves, a skilled swimmer since he was barely a toddler—drowned to death in a gods-damned *bathtub?*

His lungs burned. His vision began to darken at the edges. His thoughts dimmed, half-formed shadows that didn't quite make sense, robbed of coherence by the lack of air…

In one last desperate grasp for life, he opened his mouth, letting out his final breath in a roar for help. All that came out were soundless bubbles.

His eyes drifted shut. He sank to the bottom. And because his body couldn't bear it any longer, because he was too close to unconsciousness to care, he breathed water into his dying lungs.

And he exhaled.

And he inhaled.

And he exhaled.

What in the depths?

Relief flooded his lungs as he took in a deeper breath, a harsh gasp that hurt in a different way, a curious twinge that eased the more he gulped in. His arms braced against the craggy sides of the basin, his fingers digging in like anchors. Shakes slowly began to seize him as he took in another breath…two…three…

He was breathing.

He was breathing *underwater.*

Time came to a grinding halt as he lay trapped beneath the ice, the water slowly growing colder and colder, the tremors ebbing and flowing through his body with every impossible breath he dragged into his chest.

He was dead already. He had to be. There was no way this could be real. It had to be some cruel joke by Mortem, some mockery for having dared set foot into her realm—

Something impacted the ice from above. Cracks shot out from that central point, and Kallias flinched away from it, hands coming up to shield his face.

Another impact—when Kallias opened his eyes again, peering through his fingers, he saw a blade-shaped shadow plunge downward.

This time, the ice shattered entirely, bucking beneath the pommel of his own sword. Moments later, a hand plunged through the hole, snagging Kallias around the back of his neck and tugging him up and out.

A horrible round of thick, congested coughs bent his body in half the moment true air touched his lungs again, and he vomited up mouthfuls of water, his throat burning, his tongue curling against the sickly sweet taste of shampoo and soap. The instant he broke the surface, the hand that had saved him jerked away, leaving him huddled in the basin, wheezing through absolutely uncontrollable shakes.

Raquel's gravelly voice reached past his waterlogged ears, pinning him in place with the disbelieving fury in her tone: "What in the pits was *that*?"

Blinking water from his stinging eyes, he raised his head to glare back at her through the curtain of hair hanging over his face. "What did it look like?"

She met his glare without flinching, but there was a pinch to her mouth that didn't match that bit of composure. "*You're* Tempest-blessed?"

"Did you do that?" he demanded, rage of his own rising up to meet hers. Elias had said she was an aquamancer, hadn't he? "Did you really try to drown me? After you promised Elias—"

"I did nothing but *save* your cowardly, undeserving ass, you Atlas *bastard*. You're the idiot who froze the damned bath." She shoved away from the edge of the basin, and it was then that he realized the front of her outfit was sopping wet, the right sleeve of her sapphire-blue velvet tunic soaked and sticking to her skin.

His mouth, still tasting of soap and panic, went a bit dry. "Oh."

Raquel averted her gaze, snatching the towel he'd been given off a nearby stalagmite and tossing it at him. "It was too easy of a death for you. And too early for what Elias needs."

Of course she hadn't saved him out of the goodness of her heart. If she even had one.

"Get yourself decent," she added in a mutter. "I have questions, and you're going to answer them."

"And what if I don't?" He caught the towel, doing his best not to blush as he realized exactly how *much* of him this murder-hungry woman had likely seen. He stood quickly, wrapping the towel around his hips.

"You will. I may not be allowed to kill you, but that doesn't mean I can't make you suffer." Raquel stalked to the door, the sound of a smirk in her voice as she added, "And I've just gotten a pretty good look at where to start."

* * *

As he emerged from the bathing room, dressed in simple dark pants but forgoing a shirt thanks to the smothering heat that hadn't abated any with the fall of night, he found Raquel seated at the foot of one of the two beds in the room. She watched him steadily, sitting cross-legged, sharpening one of her many blades with a whetstone. The scraping stirred a flutter of nausea in his stomach; he didn't know if it was the memory of cutting through bone again, or if he hadn't fully purged the soap-tainted water from his body.

He slowly lowered himself onto the bed opposite hers, toweling off his hair. "All right," he said carefully, praying to anyone that *wasn't* trying to steal his or anyone else's body that he could handle this with poise. And that he'd come out of it without a knife in any part of him, lethal or otherwise. "Ask your questions."

She didn't blink as she slid the whetstone down the blade once more. "You were breathing beneath that water."

"I don't know how that happened."

"What are you blessed with?"

"What?"

"When your magic first manifested as a child," Raquel clarified, and Kallias's tongue curled at the word *manifested*, his throat drying out further at the wine-soaked memory of his argument with Jericho only a few short weeks ago, "what sort of magic were you told you had?"

"I wasn't told." At the lazy drift of her blade through the air, the tip aimed toward him, he hurriedly added, "My magic didn't…manifest…as a child. I've only had it for a few weeks."

A harsher stroke of her whetstone, sparks falling to the floor. "Lying is not a good way to—"

"It's not a lie," he snapped. Her grip tightened on her blade, and he blew out an irritated breath, bracing his palms against his legs. "It started small at first. Every time I got upset, wherever I put my hands...ice started appearing."

"Just ice?" she asked. He nodded. "No wind, no lightning...?"

Fragments of a dream barely survived clattered through his mind again, and he cringed, his hands flexing on his knees. "No."

"Hm. Aquamancer, then. But the breathing..."

"Is that not normal?"

"Not in the slightest. In fact, I've only ever heard of people breathing underwater in texts on Tempest taking a host." Now she broke from his gaze, just in time to miss the way he flinched at the word, at the confirmation of the dread that had been fermenting in him ever since he'd bled cold back in Delphin.

He swallowed hard, trying to tame his riling panic. This was nothing he hadn't already guessed. If Elias's knowledge was true, the gods required permission before they took possession of a body, and he would *never* give permission. Not to Tempest, not to any of them. He'd spent enough time being used by others. His body was his and his alone, no matter how much magic Tempest tried to tempt him with.

No matter how dreadfully he still thirsted for that unnatural wellspring of water.

Just then, the door ground open, and Elias stepped in with a paper-wrapped parcel trapped under his arm. The smell of food wafted to Kallias's still-sore nose, and if he wasn't utterly drained from both the climb up the mountain and his fight against the ice just now, he would have run to Elias and wrestled it right out of his hands.

"What happened to you?" Elias demanded, his eyes immediately falling to Kallias's scraped arms and hands that were already beginning to purple with bruising.

"How long were you going to wait to tell me he's Tempest-blessed?" Raquel shot back before Kallias could answer, her voice seething with fresh anger.

Elias, to his credit, didn't flinch. "When it became relevant."

"It's relevant," Kallias mumbled, scratching his beard.

"Why?"

"Because about ten minutes ago," Raquel said tersely, setting aside her whetstone but keeping her hold on the blade, "your new friend here almost drowned himself."

Elias's gaze shot back to Kallias, incredulous. "You *what?*"

"Not on purpose," he said quickly. "The water froze above me. I couldn't break the ice."

Elias's shoulders slumped. He ran one hand through his hair, looking to Raquel with tired eyes that screamed out his desperate need for a nap. "You got him out?"

Raquel flipped around to lie on her stomach, feet propped by her pillows. Bitterness leaked into her voice, bleeding over the anger until the two were inseparable. "He's gods-damned lucky I was here. And that Tempest seems to have taken a liking to him."

Tension stretched between Kallias's shoulder blades at the same time Elias stiffened. "What do you mean?" asked the Nyxian spy, dangerously deliberate, setting each word down with a caution that toed the line of fear.

Kallias swallowed past his raw throat. "This might go down better after food."

Elias gave him a disparaging look, but tossed the paper parcel to him. "Courtesy of Safi's older brother Havi. He was kind enough to make us dinner."

Raquel sat a little straighter, some of that burning resentment cooling a bit. "Ember's Havi?"

"How do you know about him and I don't? Soren never—"

Soleil's Nyxian's name cut through the air like a thrown punch, and Elias's mouth fumbled it, running out of air toward the end like he'd changed his mind about saying it just a second too late. He swallowed, emotion trying and failing to drag itself across his features. "Yes," he said instead, softer, more distant. "Ember's Havi."

Sorrow threatened to wrap its thorned fingers around Kallias's stomach too, digging uncomfortably into his appetite, but he forced it away. They were going to find a way to get her back. Just because Elias had given up didn't mean he had to.

It surprised him, the fury that crested as he took in Elias's empty eyes, his bent shoulders. The posture of a man who had nothing left to fight for. It pissed Kallias off—because if the circumstances had been different, if it were Elias whose body had been hollowed out and made a home for a selfish and malevolent deity, they would've needed to break every bone in Soleil's body before she gave up on bringing him back. Maybe not even then.

His sister, who had tried to capture him on a blood-soaked battlefield, who had nearly died for the attempt, who had spent months in the home of her enemies trying to steal the Viper antidote from them...if there was one thing she had proven beyond doubt, it was that as long as Elias breathed—and even when he didn't—she would do whatever it took to save him.

He'd never thought Elias would be incapable of returning the favor.

He swallowed down the anger. He was too tired to spend it properly, and Elias looked too tired to put up a fight, anyway. Better they eat and sleep on it before anything else.

His fingers peeled back the paper to reveal four oval-shaped disks of bread, well-baked from what he could tell, each one smothered in a reddish sauce, some kind of cheese, and assorted meats and vegetables. Water flooded his mouth—not the drowning sort this time—at the smell of garlic and other spices wafting from inside. "What are these?"

"Havi called them flatbreads," said Elias with a shrug. "Two of them are for you. I told him you've made it clear you're on the edge of starvation."

Kallias looked up swiftly, just in time to catch the absolute *faintest* hint of a smirk on Elias's face before it flickered out.

"Thanks," he said, too surprised by the kindness to poke fun back. Damn it. Now he felt a bit guilty for thinking such barbed thoughts at him. "Does it matter which ones I take?"

"Not unless Raquel decides to be picky." Raquel *hmph*ed, but didn't move to stop him or inspect the flatbreads, so he took that as permission to pull out two before handing them back off to Elias, who handed them to Raquel before coming to sit beside Kallias. He sniffed loudly, then asked, "Why do you smell like a perfumery?"

He scowled at Elias, who was smirking again, sitting all smug with his clothes smelling of woodfire and pastry. "I used what they gave me. Besides, I like it. It's fancy."

"You smell like a florist's shop vomited all over you."

Kallias elbowed him, and Elias clapped him upside the head before ducking out of the way, anticipating Kallias's attempt at a grapple. It was easy to tell that Elias had a sibling or five of his own.

"Hey!" Raquel barked, tossing one of her pillows in just the right way to hit them both. "Enough. I'm not putting up with roughhousing. This isn't the barracks, Loch, and he's not Soren."

Kallias bit his tongue on a sharp remark, his heart sinking as the brief mirth on Elias's face drained back into a blank slate. Raquel could wish him dead all she liked—that was fair—but there was no call to smother what little remained of Elias's light.

Raquel seemed to realize what she'd done. The irritation in her eyes dulled, her fingers tapping lightly at the bottom of her flatbread. "Sorry, Elias," she said after a long pause. "I just meant—"

"I know what you meant." Elias got up without taking his own flatbread, kicking off his boots before heading for the bathing room and closing himself inside.

Kallias glared daggers at Raquel. "Don't do that again."

She blinked at him, as if she couldn't believe he was speaking to her. "Do what?"

"Bring her up like that. He's grieving enough. He doesn't need you riling him."

Raquel scoffed quietly. "You have no idea how he grieves."

"And you do?"

"I do. I was there when he lost his first battlemate."

Kallias paused, his anger guttering. He'd known Elias lost a battlemate before Soren—he'd seen the two mourning braids as they were traveling to Nyx—but he hadn't considered that Raquel might have been privy to that process. "What was he like?"

"Angry," she said. "Just as he is now. Angry at anything and everything, but...quiet. He would've let it eat him alive if Soren hadn't dragged it out of him."

"What did she do?"

To his surprise, Raquel's mouth curled into a nostalgic smile. "Her mother forced her to a pick a new battlemate, and she chose him. Normally pairs aren't forced, but Soren needed back out there, and she couldn't go without a battlemate. She wanted Elias or no one."

That sounded like the Soleil he now knew. "So what happened?"

"He refused to train with her for weeks after. Would just sit on the sidelines and ignore her when it was their turn to spar. So one day she went out there and started taunting him. She said all sorts of things: about his faith, about his dead father, about his mother. Nothing budged him." Raquel sucked in a breath. "Then she told him Kaia—that was his first—was better off in Infera than she was when she had him as a battlemate. I've never seen Elias move that fast, before or since. Shot out of his seat like a gods-damned arrow and punched her right in the nose. It never sat quite right after that, but she deserved it. She *wanted* it. They fought for *hours*."

That *definitely* sounded like Soleil. "Then what?"

Raquel shrugged. "No clue. We all got tired of watching after a while and left. All I know is that the next day, and every day after, they were absolutely inseparable. Never saw one without the other, especially after Elias's Viper bite."

He opened his mouth to ask more, but it seemed that Raquel had realized who exactly she was opening up to. She clamped her mouth shut, scowling as she rolled over, sitting up against her pillows and tucking a dagger beneath them.

"You owe me a life debt, Kallias Atlas," she said. "Twice over. And I *will* collect it."

She would try. Of that, he had no doubt. "I guess we'll see whose blade is fastest, Raquel Angelov."

She only snorted, turning over and tucking herself under the covers, her storm of dark hair hiding her face from view.

It could have been minutes or hours before Elias emerged from the bathing room. His hair was still dry, as were his clothes, but there was a look in his eye and a tautness to his jaw. When he raised a hand in silent acknowledgement, there was a trace of dark mottling along his knuckles.

"How'd the wall take it?" Kallias asked.

Elias's jaw flexed. Instead of answering, he snatched up a pillow and extra blanket from the bed.

"You are not about to sleep on this floor," he protested. Though he'd done so at every inn they'd stopped at on their journey, even when the cots were perfectly decent, this floor would be considerably less forgiving.

"I've slept on worse. You made sure of that."

"I don't mind sharing."

Elias rolled his eyes. "Well, I do."

"Can't stand sharing space with an Atlas bastard?"

Elias's throat bobbed, and his hand wandered toward that ring he always wore. "It's not that," he said quietly. And nothing else after.

Well, there wasn't much he could say to that. Elias had a way of ending arguments by simply being too gods-damned cryptic for him to come up with a retort he was confident in. He heaved a sigh, pulling himself to his feet and grabbing a blanket of his own, wrapping it around one arm. "Fine. Then let me take the floor."

Elias outright *laughed.* "No."

"Why not?"

"Because I'm not going to listen to you complain about your backache all day tomorrow, that's why not. Take the bed. I prefer the floor."

"Elias—"

"I can't sleep in a bed without her in it, Kal."

The hushed, almost blurting admission stopped Kallias in his tracks. He paused with his hand still wrapped up in one of the pillowcases, his eyes tracing the hollowness in Elias's eyes, the shuffling of his feet, the bruising on his knuckles.

"All right," he said finally, setting the bedding back down. "I hear you. But at least take another pillow, will you?"

Elias relaxed a bit, nodding once, offering one last almost-smile as he took the pillow Kallias offered him. "Missing Finn?"

His brother's name hit a painful chord in his chest, but he forced a laugh. "How could you tell?"

"You're fussing. I'm a big brother too, you know. I know what it looks like."

"If you're going to call me prissy again—"

"Will you two quit flirting and go to *sleep?*" Raquel hissed from beneath her pile of pillows.

"But I'm so good at it," Elias deadpanned, and Kallias snorted out a laugh.

Eventually his companions found sleep, soft snores rumbling from Raquel's side of the room, quiet murmurs from Elias's makeshift bed on the floor. But Kallias found himself unable to sleep; every time he shut his eyes, every time he began to drift off, the memory of ice crept over his thoughts. His lungs ached no matter how deep a breath he pulled in, and fear whispered that it was because they might be hungering for something other than air.

I could make you a king.

He had a very bad feeling about this.

CHAPTER 18

FINN

After Kallias had fled the palace and before Anima had been released from the infirmary, Finn had moved Soleil's treasure box.

Anima already had his sister's body, her mind, her room, her gods-damned *sweaters*. She wasn't about to have this, too. She could force it out of his cold, dead hands—or, preferably, leave it in his warm, alive ones. Even if she *did* know it existed, even if she'd pried it from the depths of Soleil's memory, it didn't seem like the sort of thing a goddess would be interested in.

Before, he'd protected it because it was proof of his one great weakness. But what use was that now? Soleil was dead. Kallias was gone. Jericho and Vaughn were traitors. His parents didn't seem to be targets of whatever scheme they were pulling. He had no weaknesses left to find. So now it served another purpose: keeping him company through every hour of his sleepless nights. Steadying his hands, busying his fingers with something other than the shakes that plagued him.

He rolled the pen between his fingertips, ink seeping into the ridges of his fingerprints as he stared down at the freshly scrawled letter in the journal.

Soleil,

You would have hated every second of this day. Well, not every second. You would've enjoyed the food. I ate a cinnamon pastry in your honor.

That's a lie. I ate it because it was gods-damned delicious. We hired on a new pastry chef recently, and she's criminally underpaid for her skill. I'm going to talk to Mama about a promotion as soon as I can get her alone, which is…easier, weirdly, since Kallias left and you…well.

I haven't told her or Papa yet. That you're gone. That the thing walking around wearing your body is our kingdom's most popular goddess. Speaking of her, by the way, her impression of you is pitiful. All bark with no bite, and it's more whine than bark. Either Jericho's a terrible teacher or Anima's a terrible actress.

I told her Elias turned on you. Or…I tried to tell you he did. It was all I could think of to see if you were still kicking around in there. Foolish, I know. But it wasn't just for you. I told everyone I could reach by the border to act in kind. They were under orders to smuggle Kal and Elias out if they saw them, and to report the Nyxian wanted your head if anyone asked. Safer that way. My mother won't make him a target of our spies then.

Anyway, the ball.

I met this girl.

Fidget's cookie-crumb-coated smile flashed in his mind, her trusting eyes already promising he'd picked the perfect mark. He rubbed his eyes, forcing his eyelids to rise in spite of the exhaustion dragging them down.

She reminds me of you a bit. Hates parties. Sweet tooth. Not half as clever, but that's all right. It's better that way for what I've got planned.

I will beat them, Soleil. Whatever it takes.

The *s* at the end skidded a bit, the pen's point digging so hard into the paper that it nearly tore a hole through the page. He cursed, throwing the pen away and pinching the bridge of his nose between his thumb and forefinger.

He didn't mean to close his eyes.

Darkness deeper than any sea surrounded him, suffocated him, pressing in on all sides until he couldn't see his own hand in front of his face.

"I shouldn't be here!" shouted a voice from far away, a ragged scream that jolted him from his breathless panic. "You have to let me out! Just let me die, for gods' sakes!"

"*Soleil?*" *he shouted back to the darkness.*

"*What is it? Huh? You want me to fix it? To kiss it better, is that it? Do you want me to save you, Finn?*" *The sound of a fist breaking through wood sent him staggering back, hands desperately seeking purchase behind him and finding none, fingers searching his pockets for a weapon and coming up empty. "I can't save you! No one can save you! Stop looking at me like that! Stop looking at me, Soleil!*"

"*Kal,*" *he choked out, but before he could find the breath to shout for help, for his parents or Jericho or even Vaughn, his older brother's broken screams morphed into a different voice. Softer. Somehow more menacing.*

"*So much pain, Trickster Prince. Where do you keep it all? Isn't it hard, carrying all this agony inside you?*"

Fingers pressed into his temples on either side, buzzing with energy, pink light flaring in his peripherals as the voices quieted. The pain dulled. Even his hands steadied.

"*I can take it all away.*" *Occassio drew so near he could feel her breath in his ear, could smell the spicy-sweetness of it. "If only you'd let me in.*"

He strained to block out her voice, muttering his answer through gritted teeth: "You will not have me."

Her giggle tumbled through his head like gems poured from a jeweler's hand. "Won't I?"

A knock—gods, another knock, another of the unending gods-damned Anima-cursed knocks—shattered the darkness that held him captive. He burst upward into bright late-morning light, sweaty palms digging into sweaty sheets, his legs knotted up in cotton and silk. Soleil's journal rested on his stomach, still open to his latest letter, the pen nowhere to be seen.

Something warm trickled from his nose to his lip, salt and iron seeping between his lips to touch his tongue. Instinct had him wipe it away, and when he peered at it, thoughts still heavy with grogginess, scarlet flashed bright against his skin even in the darkness.

His nose was bleeding.

Lovely.

He yanked the pillowcase off one of his pillows and jammed it against his nose, a low, pounding pain traveling from one temple to the other, stretching a strumming cord of discomfort between the sides of his skull. He squeezed his eyes shut against the pain, warm stickiness slowly soaking through the pillowcase, his heart beating in time with the flow of blood and the pulse of pain in his head.

At least he'd finally gotten some sleep, restful or not.

"Finn?" His mother's voice sounded tinny and muffled through the door, but he couldn't tell if it was due to the wooden barrier or the ringing in his head. "Anima's budding pits, love, are you still asleep?"

Despite the blood making his lips sticky, they still managed to tweak upward at his mother's profanity. He'd learned his ridiculous blasphemies from her while sitting cross-legged beneath the desk in her office as an ever-curious boy who hadn't yet learned viciousness and trickery, who'd been better-versed in mischief and imagination. She'd laughed endlessly at his childish voice mimicking her groans and curses, though she'd faked stern disapproval when he uttered them within earshot of anyone else. "Not asleep, Mama. Just a bit indisposed."

"Are you decent?"

"Sometimes."

"Ill?"

"Only in the head."

"Finnick, if you don't give me a good reason not to, I'm coming in."

He held his silence, not sure if he was all right with her seeing him hunched over and bleeding, but this was the second time in a week his mother had come to see him. He didn't know if it was guilt or something else that drove her, and he wasn't going to rest easy until he knew.

Adriata entered after precisely three seconds of silence, the door opening slowly and closing much faster. "Tell me that's not blood."

"Seems the dry spell's gotten to me," he garbled through the cloth, trying to raise his head to meet her gaze. But the blood only gushed faster, and he quickly jammed a fistful of cotton back against his face.

"Let me see." Before he could protest, his mother sat down beside him, gently but firmly peeling the bloody pillowcase away. "Gods, did you break your nose in your sleep?"

"No, but that would've been pretty impressive."

"Mm." She forced him to tip his head back and pinched the bridge of his nose with her own fingers. "Keep stanching it."

Her tender touch took him off guard, and words blurted out without his consent: "How do you know how to treat a bloody nose?"

"Back when we were courting, your father got himself into more than one skirmish in the streets before he moved into the palace." Her voice lilted in amusement. "And I may have gotten myself into one or two with him."

Oh, *this* he had to hear. "*Queen Adriata Atlas*, getting into alley brawls?"

"Well, no one else was going to save your father's sorry skin, were they?"

"How did Appa and Amma feel about that?"

Adriata snorted softly. "Well, they didn't catch us the first two times. But the third time we both came home bleeding, Genevieve told on us. I thought your Appa would toss your father out with the fishermen's chum. Instead, he invited him to move into the palace with us. Got him away from his bastard of a father, treated him like his own son…" She shook her head fondly. "They were thicker than thieves, those two. They went out fishing on your Appa's boat every single morning before he fell ill."

His perfect memory petered off just at the cusp of that time, the edges ragged and hazy; his grandfather had died when he was only four years old, too young to really have grieved him, and his grandmother had passed only a year later. But he remembered Appa bouncing him and Soleil on his lap in the middle of meetings, remembered seeing him play-sparring with Kallias and wearing the flower crowns Jericho made for him. He'd never heard a single untoward rumor about his grandparents' rule in all the years he'd spent with his ear to the walls of musty taverns and upper-city parties alike. Queen Cordelia and King-Consort Samuel Atlas had been well-loved.

"Mama," he said, and he sensed more than saw his mother go very still at the caution in his tone, "why did you come here?"

"A mother can't come sit with her son without an ulterior motive?" Finn raised one eyebrow at her, and she softened a bit. "You're too clever for your own good, you know. You inherited a double portion. My perception and your father's common sense."

"I just got lucky Kallias and Jericho didn't take any of it."

His mother laughed, a cackling thing punctuated by snorts that reminded him too much of the one sibling he hadn't named. He curled his fingers more tightly around the bloodied pillowcase.

"So," he said, "guilt or boredom?"

"Neither," she said, then hesitated. Sighed. "Fine. Guilt, a bit. But mostly…" She took her fingers away from his nose, and he lowered his head, surprised to find the blood no longer gushed. Even more surprised to see that she was staring at him with what he would've called tears in her eyes if he hadn't known better. "I know you agreed to this Lapis business, but…"

The sorrow hidden in her eyes, the tired lines digging between her brows… "But Kallias agreed too," he guessed—a risky move, a wild leap towards the other end of a board he hadn't finished considering the angles of yet.

She flinched. *Checkmate.* "Every morning I wake up afraid," she confessed, running the tips of her fingers through his bed-rumpled hair. The tender gesture made everything in him tense, waiting for the reveal, waiting for the trick. His mother hadn't been soft with any of them since Soleil died.

Well, that wasn't entirely true. She'd barely left his side after he was bitten by that gods-damned undead body. "Afraid of what?"

"Afraid that I'll wake up to find you've run away, too. That I'll wake up to another two-sentence note and another empty bed in this hall."

His heart pinched, a pain sharper but smaller than his headache. "Mama, you didn't force me into this. I chose it."

"So did your brother."

Maybe it was the headache pounding out the sense from his mind like a hammer beating the flaws from steel. Maybe it was her fingers untangling his hair. Maybe it was just one too many masks for him to wear at once. But instead of letting that comment lie, he said, "That's not necessarily true. You knew he didn't want to leave."

Adriata's eyes dimmed. She leaned back, her scarlet curls falling away from her face as she braced herself against his bed, her gaze fixed on the ceiling like a child searching for a wishing star. It didn't fit with her frown lines and furrowed brows. "Your brother thinks I blame him for Soleil's death."

His stomach twisted like a coiling snake rearing to strike, and he bit back the words that wanted to come out. He'd already gone well past his quota for truths revealed in this conversation; he didn't need to show her any more cards in his hand. "Do you?"

Her answer didn't surprise him, but the honesty in it did. "No."

It had to be a lie. His mother may have distanced herself from all of them in the years following Soleil's death, but she'd only turned cold toward Kallias. She'd coddled Finn, spoiled Jericho, but Kallias? Kallias had tried again and again to reach out to her, to make up for his failure that ash-ridden day, and every time she'd managed to find a new way to make him feel less-than. He'd spent enough years watching his bold, confident, outspoken brother fade into a quiet, subservient son to know that Adriata hadn't exactly been nurturing toward him. "Mama, you have to be—"

"Do you remember the day of Kal's incident?" she interrupted, eyes still fixed on the ceiling.

Empty wine bottles shattered on the floor. Bloodshot blue-green eyes staring wildly into his, glazed and glassy and teeming with hate. "Stop looking at me, Soleil!"

The heat of adrenaline dried out his throat, making his next word a rasping whisper. "Yes."

They didn't talk about that day—the day Kallias had nearly broken whatever semblance of *family* they still had after Soleil's death. Kallias had asked for forgiveness already, and they'd all given it...or at least, they said they had.

"Kal?"

Finn knocked again on his brother's door, shivering, the winter chill from the floor traveling through the soles of his bare feet all the way up to his knees, sneaking beneath the hem of his flannel pajama pants. He tugged his sleeves down to cover his knuckles, bouncing back and forth between each foot to try and stop his shaking while he waited for Kallias to come to the door. He'd tried Soleil's first before he'd woken up all the way and remembered that there was no one behind it who could answer.

It'd been over a year already. Her birthday had come and gone without a party, without cakes or presents or even flowers for her grave. His father had gathered them all into the dining room of their country home instead, where they quietly ate a meal together while Ramses tried to coax them into sharing their favorite memories of Soleil. Not one of them had managed to dredge up their voices to tell a story.

He knew she was gone. But this was his first night back in the palace since the repairs had been completed, and his mind might have known she was dead, but his feet hadn't quite figured it out. Her room was still the first place they thought to go.

"Kal!" he hissed again, knocking harder. "Kal, it's me, are you awake?"

"Go 'way," came his brother's muffled voice through the door. It sounded funny, lazy, his words melting together into a sludge.

"Can I sleep in there with you? I-I brought my own blanket. I won't kick or anything."

Silence.

Finn finally turned the knob himself, tired of waiting for his brother to wake up enough to understand what he was asking. He shuffled his bare toes past the threshold, shutting the door behind him, hauling his thick, heavy blanket over one shoulder. Ever since Soleil had died, he hadn't been able to sleep without it, a specially-crafted quilt with weighted beads sewn into it. Aunt Genevieve said it was good for children who were anxious or restless, or who had been through terrible things...like the fire that had stolen his home and his sister.

Soon it would steal his brother, too, if Kallias had his way. He was adamant on convincing their mother to let him fight with her and their army, even though he'd only just turned seventeen a few days back.

Kallias wasn't in his bed like Finn had expected. Well, he was, but not asleep; he was sitting on the edge of it, feet on the floor, hands wrapped around a big glass bottle wedged between his knees. He stared at Finn—through Finn, really, as if he couldn't really see him. His eyes were glassy and red-rimmed, his lips parted slightly.

Finn looked at the bottle, frowning a bit as he read the label. "We're not supposed to drink that. Mama said not until we're eighteen—"

"I don't give a shit what Mama said."

The dark, venomous bite in Kallias's voice dragged his feet back a step toward the door. "We're not supposed to say that word—"

"What're you going to do about it? Run to Mama and tell on me? Do your worst." Kallias swayed a bit as he shifted and picked up the bottle, putting it to his lips, swallowing several times before lowering it again.

Finn swallowed hard himself, hugging his blanket tighter, the comforting weight pressing against his chest like a shield. "No. I just—I—"

"Why are you here, Finn?" Kallias had never spoken his name like that before, like he was sick of Finn being there, like he was tired of him after only one minute.

Finn shuffled his feet, a pinching feeling in his stomach making him want to run. Embarrassment softened his words to a mumble: "I had a nightmare."

Kallias's shoulders slumped, and for just a second, that angry gaze softened. But just as Finn started to relax, just as he started toward his brother, Kallias lurched up from the bed and stumbled away from him, moving toward the window on his far wall. "What do you want me to do about it?"

Uncertainty wrapped its hands around his ankles, tugging him to a stop. "I just…you said, after the fire, you said if I needed you, that I could—"

"What is it? Huh? You want me to fix it? To kiss it better? Do you want me to save you?" A horrible laugh clawed out of Kallias's chest, and Finn scuttled backward as quietly as possible, reaching for the doorknob as his brother ranted, every word coming out more frenzied than the last. "I can't save you. No one can save you! Stop looking at me like that! Stop looking at me, Soleil!"

Kallias spun in a teetering arc, flinging the bottle directly at the door—directly at Finn's head.

Finn let out a terrified scream, lacing his fingers behind his head, ducking his face into the floor as glass shattered against wood. Pain bit into his back as shards ricocheted off the door and rained down on him, clinking out a deceivingly pretty melody as they scattered across the floor. Finn kept his head down, shaking, his tears dampening the space between his skin and the floor. Even when silence fell, even when Kallias's pacing footsteps halted, he didn't move. Couldn't move. Terror had glued every joint in place, like one of his tin toy soldiers whose hinges had rusted beyond salvaging.

Just beyond the racing heartbeat in his head, he heard Kallias speak, his voice wavering and small: "Finn?" And when he didn't answer, Kallias's voice pitched higher, louder, horror pulling it up to a shout: "Oh gods, no, no—Finn?!"

Before he could draw in the breath to answer—or to call for his mother—Kallias's hands were on him, flipping him over, probing desperately at the crook of his jaw. When they locked eyes, Kallias's voice cracked on a curse as he wiped away Finn's tears with his sleeve. "Oh, thank Anima. Thank Anima. Oh gods. Finn, I'm so—I'm so sorry, I didn't know you were—I didn't see you move, I didn't—"

Finn's voice finally caught against the flint of his throat, sparking a shout to life: "Mama! Mama, Mama—"

He scrambled away from Kallias just as the door flew open, glass flinging to the side as Mama burst in, the broken wine bottle crunching beneath her slippers as she took in the scene: Kallias swaying on his knees, panic and confusion both holding ground in his bleary gaze; Finn scooting backward, his shoulders shaking with sobs, droplets of something warm sliding down his back and shoulders, cold air slipping in through the slits in his pajamas.

"What did you do?" Mama scooped him up into her arms so fast it dizzied him, her fingers probing the stinging places on his back. She hadn't picked him up in years, not since he'd turned seven and declared himself too big to be carried around, but he was still small for his age. She didn't even falter at his weight. "Kallias! What did you do?!"

The memory of her panic, her *rage*, brought him back to the room. Brought him back to her hand on his back, just like it had been then.

It was shortly after that night that he'd first wandered into the city. That night had taught him a lesson well beyond doubt: he could only trust himself now. The only sibling he could rely on was nothing more than ash beneath the newly repaired floorboards of the palace, and Kallias was right in the end: he couldn't save him. *No one* could save him.

"I have *never* blamed him for Soleil's death," Adriata said softly, refusing to look at him. "But I have never forgiven him for breaking you."

That confession thumped into his chest, piercing like an arrow tipped with Artemisian steel, lodging itself deep in the center of his heart. "He didn't break me."

Adriata was already shaking her head. "Soleil's death hurt you. Out of all of us, it hit you the hardest. We all knew that. But you were still *you*. You were still the little boy that memorized all our rules so you could learn exactly how to break them best. You were still my mischief-maker. It was the one solace your father and I found in our grief, that piece of Soleil that lived on in you." Adriata's jaw flexed, a tear hovering just at the edge of her eye. "After that night, it was like a stranger wore your face. There was no light left behind your eyes. It took months for you to talk to Kallias without looking like you wanted to run. It took years for you to start *smiling* again."

Finn pulled away from her touch. He couldn't quite breathe right. "Mama, that's…"

"I know. It's not what a mother should do, is it? Holding grudges against her children. I know it's not fair." There was no humor in her laugh. "Don't misunderstand me. I love Kallias more than he will ever know. But I'd already lost Soleil. Losing you…"

"You didn't lose me." He hadn't meant for the words to snap off his tongue like the strike of a whip, but that cold bit of steel hadn't come free from his chest yet, the strangest ache he'd ever felt throbbing alongside it. He didn't understand that feeling, couldn't name it, and that frightened him more than anything. "Mama, it was an accident. He didn't mean it. He's more than made up for it. I mean, gods, he was just a kid, and he was grieving. Guilty, too. He—"

"It sounds to me," his mother interrupted softly, "like you've said all this before. Maybe to yourself. Maybe more than once. Finn, whatever he was, it doesn't make what he did all right."

She was seeing too much, piercing him too deeply. He had to stop her before she landed a blow he couldn't shake off. "I think you should leave."

She stood, hand drifting to brace against her ribs like she had an ache somewhere inside too. "Finn—"

"I need to get ready for the day," he said curtly. "I'm already late for breakfast with the Lapisian delegation. Esha doesn't strike me as the type to graciously forgive a second failure to present myself, now does she?"

Adriata's eyes shuttered, all softness and sorrow vanishing. She gave a clipped dip of her chin before striding out and shutting the door behind her, bloody fingerprints left behind from her ministrations to his nose.

She did not look back, and he did not care.

CHAPTER 19

FINN

B reakfast, as it turned out, was even more awkward and unbearable than the welcome feast had been.

He sat at the foot of the table, Esha at the head. The Mirror and Dagger he'd marked as the leaders sat on her right and left respectively; he had Seamus to his right, Alia to his left. His mother had raised an eyebrow at his request for Alia—she didn't hold a particularly high rank in the guard—but hadn't protested beyond that. It was a bit foolish to let these people see those he kept close at hand, but as captain over the entire palace guard, it would have been more suspicious to exclude Seamus from this event…and he always did better work with Alia at his side.

Alia, to her credit, looked considerably more comfortable than Finn had expected. She held herself with impeccable poise, graceful as a swan and silent as a stone. Seamus looked less at ease, but that was just Seamus. He was used to guarding the door, not sitting at the table.

Next to Alia sat his target.

Fidget wasn't wearing her bejeweled gown today, nor was she quite so made-up. Still, tiny bits of sparkle winked off her long, dark lashes as she fixed her gaze on her plate, her heather-colored tulle sleeves sheer and cuffed just above the mirrors lashed around her wrists. She had two cinnamon rolls on her plate, which wouldn't have been something worth noticing if the cinnamon rolls weren't the size of his face. He could've used one as a passable shield if the need truly arose. The rhinestones on her lacquered nails were dulled with a coating of icing, and he almost laughed when she thoughtlessly licked it off. Maybe it helped soothe her shyness.

Finn couldn't argue with that. His own sweet tooth often ached a bit harsher when he was feeling less than himself.

"So," he said, "Queen Esha. I trust you slept well?"

"I did." Brief. Clipped. Cold.

"Were your quarters to your satisfaction?"

No words this time, just a stiff dip of her sharp chin.He just barely kept himself from sighing out loud before carefully cutting off a piece of his waffle and popping it into his mouth, the buttery sweetness seeping across his tongue.

This wasn't going to work if he couldn't get her to talk…or at least look him in the eye. She was the one who wanted this wedding, wasn't she? Why was he doing all the work?

Time for a new tactic.

"What's your favorite color?" he asked through that mouthful of syrupy waffle.

All soft chatter at the table came to an abrupt halt. Slowly, the queen raised her eyes from her plate, locking her black gaze on his. Out of the corner of his eye, he saw Fidget freeze, her mouth still open, her hand partway to her lips with another hunk of cinnamon roll perched in her fingers.

"What was that, Prince?" asked the queen, every word deliberately placed.

Finally, he'd caught her off guard. "What's your favorite color?" He leaned back casually in his seat, stopping just short of propping an ankle on the fine silk tablecloth. This was their formal dining room, after all, not the secret sibling one. He had some boundaries he needed to hold to.

For the first time, there was a hint of curiosity in her hunting-hawk eyes. "Yellow. Yours?"

He risked cutting a glance toward Fidget, propping one corner of his mouth up in a suggestive smile. "Purple."

Her cheeks darkened as she hurriedly broke his gaze, studying her remaining cinnamon roll like it had just promised the world's most tantalizing secret if she only paid it her whole attention.

"Hm." Esha's own mouth coiled a bit, but he wouldn't have called it a smile. She leaned forward and clasped her hands together, resting her elbows on the table, her iridescent silk sleeves dragging across the tablecloth. They were shaped like calla lilies, cupping her forearms in just the right way to reveal the opal bracelets cuffed around each wrist. She tipped her head to one side, her long hair fanning across her shoulder; it was the smoothest hair he'd ever seen, thin and fine and black as kohl, the chandelier light gleaming off it like polished metal. She wore no crown today.

"Favorite food?" he chanced.

"Rosemary chicken. Yours?"

"Fried fish sandwiches."

Her small nose barely twitched, the slightest crinkle of distaste. "I don't care for seafood."

"Well, that's because you've never had Atlas cuisine. Our seafood is fresh-caught every morning, you know. You'll never eat a fish older than a day here."

Esha's eyes narrowed. "You sound like a street hawker."

"Well, that's what this is all about, isn't it?" He swiped up his cup of orange juice and took a slow sip, holding eye contact with her all the while. Then he lowered it a bit, licking his lips, noting Fidget watching him from beneath her lashes. "Selling you on Atlas as an ally. Selling you on me as a consort."

"Indeed." Esha leaned her chin on her folded hands, her gaze never breaking from his. "I'm pleased to see the rumors of your cleverness haven't oversold you, Prince."

"I'm pleased to meet expectations, Queen." He raised his glass without blinking. "Perhaps in time, I'll exceed them."

Now Esha smiled. "We shall see."

Finn offered her his best smile over the top of his glass, lifting it back to his lips.

One crack in the Queen's icy demeanor, one in Fidget's shyness. Now he only had to find a gap large enough to slide his fingers into, and a lockpick that fit the entrance to their respective secrets. One from each, and he'd once again hold the power in this palace.

So after the meal, once Fidget had excused herself and left the dining hall, he made his own excuses and followed shortly after.

He made it into the hallway just as she disappeared around a corner, the tip of her trailing skirt teasing across the floor like the flicker of a snake's tail as it slithered beneath a bush. Quick little thing.

Just as he was about to follow, a hand landed on his shoulder, and Seamus's voice hissed in his ear: "We have a problem."

"Don't we always?" Finn muttered, but he followed the blond soldier into an empty side room, Alia slipping in shortly after them. She shut the door and locked it with an artful twist of her wrist, biting her lip as she turned to face them. Her ink-smudge eyes were troubled.

"I heard Anima and Jericho talking yesterday," she said, running her hand down her long, dark braid—a nervous habit. "But it wasn't *Jericho* talking."

Dread punched low in his stomach. "Do not tell me—"

"Her eyes aren't gold," Alia added quickly, scratching absently at her sternum where she'd gotten the illusion-breaking tattoo Elias had taught him. He still wasn't sure how that worked, whether the power was in the symbol or the ink, what sort of magic might have imbued it—or if Elias had just been messing with him—but it seemed to have worked. Alia was one of his best palace spies, the only one he trusted enough to assign to Jericho and Anima, and he couldn't have her fooled by a divine breed of the masks he loved to wear.

Well. *Trusted* was a stretch. She was his best among the guard, and she was the one he held the most collateral for. He was decently sure she wouldn't betray his confidence with the cards he wielded over her head. Seamus was the same.

"If they aren't gold, then why—?" Finn began.

"They *aren't* gold now. But they *were* gold then," Alia explained, making an erratic gesture he took to mean *move* before she sidled around him, tucking herself beneath Seamus's arm, her head at just the right height to rest against his chest. Seamus wrapped that arm more tightly around her, his cautious blue eyes never leaving Finn, a quiet warning buried in them.

Finn eased back a bit, giving Seamus the slightest dip of his head. Alia's anxious days were hard enough without him tugging on her loose threads. "What were they saying?"

Alia's face was a bit wan, her brown skin sallow with dread, her eyes circled in sleeplessness. That didn't bode well; he hadn't seen her this unnerved since her first night working for him. "Anima called her Tenebrae," she said in a hushed, distracted voice, anchoring her fingers in Seamus's shirt. He pressed a kiss to the crown of her head, and Finn tried very hard not to let his impatience show. He didn't blame the guard for his worry, but the sooner Alia got this out, the sooner they could all get back to their business. "And they were talking about relics."

"Relics?" Seamus echoed.

"I only heard bits and pieces, but I think they're some kind of objects associated with the gods. One for each. I couldn't hear them all, but I know they mentioned a mirror, and a music box, and a shard of ice. They think the mirror is here somewhere. They think the ice is in Nyx."

"Did they say why they want them?"

Alia shook her head, and he swallowed down a curse. "Only that they need to find them before *the others* can stop them."

"Others? The other gods?"

Alia shrugged helplessly. "From what I saw, it looks like Tenebrae can only keep control of Jericho for a few minutes at a time. She fainted before they finished talking, and when she came to, her eyes were normal again."

Finn rubbed his temples, a dull pain beginning to build between them.

"A phoenix feather. A mirror that shows no reflection. A bloom from the heart of the forest. A shard of ice that never melts. And a music box that plays a song of chaos."

"Prince Finnick!"

He opened his eyes to find Alia and Seamus's faces hovering *over* him instead of in front of him, both of them staring wide-eyed, their faces screaming *the First Prince just died in front of us and we're alone in a closet with his corpse.* He would have laughed at their misplaced panic if his head didn't *hurt* so damned much.

"I'm fine," he said.

"You dropped like a sack of potatoes," said Seamus.

"That doesn't change what I said."

"Your ears are bleeding," Alia said softly.

He reached up to find warm, sticky rivulets trickling from his ears. *Fan-damned-tastic.* "They do that. I really do need to see about getting a new pair."

"Prince," Seamus began, "if you're falling ill—"

"Trust me, Seamus, you will know when I'm ill. There will be great moaning and sorrow and gnashing of teeth. You will hear my demands for blankets and soup across the land."

The two of them exchanged looks as he sat up. If they hadn't been the only palace informants left that he still trusted enough to use, he would have fired them both.

"If they need these *relics*," Seamus said finally, "and one of them is in Nyx…"

"No," Finn said immediately.

Seamus's eye twitched. "If they think one is here, they'll go after that one first. We could get ahead of them if we just—"

"You know very well why that won't be allowed, *Seamus*," he said, letting his voice wrap pointedly around the bends and dips in that name, stretching it out to the point of discomfort. He was the only one in Atlas who knew exactly how poor of an idea it was to let Seamus cross the border into that kingdom—the only one in Atlas who knew *Seamus* wasn't the name he'd been born with.

Well, him and one other.

Alia gave Seamus a look of her own—Finn couldn't tell if it was sadness or hurt feelings—but her voice was steadier when she said, "What should we do, then?"

Finn wiped the blood from his jaw and neck with the handkerchief Alia offered him, rifling through his mind for an answer. This was why he'd stayed behind: to foil any designs Anima, Jericho, and Vaughn might have for his kingdom. The Lapis game was an afterthought, an unfortunate byproduct of his need to play Kallias's part. He was wearing two crowns on one head, and balancing them would require all his focus. He had to prioritize.

"Nothing yet," he said. "We don't know enough. Keep on them, Alia. They'll tip their hand eventually. But take today off, will you? You look like you haven't slept in days."

Her brows scrunched up, and she pulled away from Seamus's supporting grip. "I'm fine."

"You're not, and that wasn't a request. It's not pity, either. I need you at your best, and you've been on overnights all week. Seamus, you too."

Seamus still wore bitterness on his breath from Finn's reminder of his place when he said, "If we're off resting, who's going to be keeping an eye on things?"

"I have eyes and ears elsewhere."

Seamus looked unhappy—what else was new—but he nodded. "Before we go…any word from Kallias or Eli?"

"Not yet." And that worried him more than it should. It wasn't easy to get word through the Nyxian border, let alone people, so it wasn't surprising he hadn't heard from his brother yet. But he would have liked to know if Kallias had succeeded in convincing the Nyxians of what had happened here or if he was currently convalescing in their dungeons while Finn sat on his ass and ate waffles with crystal-worshipping queens. "You'll know when I do."

Seamus nodded once more, tugging gently at Alia's braid. "Let's go, then. He's right, you look dead on your feet."

Alia snorted softly, catching his hand and pressing his knuckles to her lips. "We all know what the dead look like on their feet, Shay. I hope I don't look half that terrible."

"'Course you don't. Maybe a quarter that terrible."

The two continued to banter in soft, teasing tones as they left the room, leaving Finn with blood crusting his collar and a new idea beginning to churn in his head.

Priorities. It was time he figured out exactly where his stood.

CHAPTER 20

ELIAS

"Hey, jackass." Toes dug into his side and wriggled, an impatient voice huffing morning breath directly into his ear. "Wake up. I want breakfast."

He smiled into his pillow, reaching up without looking and shoving Soren's face away, chuckling at her choked noise of protest as she flailed to regain her balance. "Then go find it, smartass."

She bounced on the bed, shaking the whole mattress beneath him. "But you make the pancakes so much better."

Oh, there she went with the pout. That just wasn't fair.

He kept his eyes tightly shut. If he didn't look, she couldn't work her puppy-dog-eyed magic on him. "But you cook the best bacon."

"I'll cook *your* bacon, if you know what I mean."

"I honestly, *genuinely* don't."

An exasperated huff warmed his ear again just before her entire weight collapsed on top of him, limbs akimbo, her hair falling across his face like a tickly curtain.

"Soren," he said. No answer. She'd moved on to the silent treatment, it seemed. "*Soren,* for the love of Mortem, get your ass off me."

Still no answer. Once she'd committed to the bit, there was no budging her.

He sighed, letting out all his breath in one long whoosh before twisting himself around, careful not to throw her off. "Are you done being a—"

Lifeless, bloodshot green eyes stared back at him, lips parted in silent scream, blood streaming from her eyes and nose and mouth.

"Elias," pleaded her voice with no mouth, a breathless thing that floated from her throat with no movement of lips or tongue. "Don't burn me, Elias. Don't burn me."

But it was too late. Because this bed was no longer a bed, it was a woodpile—no, it was a *pyre,* and he stood in the center of it, cradling her emaciated body in arms that could not save her, that *had not* saved her, that could *never* save her—

He woke up already screaming, already retching, horror wringing his stomach out like a damp towel, putting all of Havi's generosity to waste. He barely managed to roll out of his tangle of blankets before vomiting up his entire dinner from the night before, his elbows scraping painfully against the stone floor as he dragged himself away from his belongings.

Within moments, cold hands settled on his bare shoulders, Kallias's urgent voice coming from somewhere above his head: "Elias? Elias, what's wrong?"

"Nothing," he tried to say, but all that came out was another gag, the image of Soren's lifeless face hitting him deeper than any blow ever could.

"What did that baker give you? Angelov! Are you feeling sick at all?"

"I'm fine, Atlas, move over." Raquel's hand settled on his back, her voice much calmer than Kallias's, but still tense. "Elias, are you feverish? In pain?"

Kallias's voice came again, frightened, angry: "Did they poison him? If they poisoned him, I swear to the gods—"

"They didn't poison—" Elias broke off into a retch. All at once, their voices, their hands, all of it was too much. He flung one arm behind him, desperately shoving at their arms until they let go, leaving him kneeling and trembling on the floor, the burning taste of vomit clinging to the backs of his teeth.

Dead. Dead. Dead.

"I'm fine," he finally managed to say, gritting his teeth against another wave of nausea. "I-I have to walk."

"Eli, that's not a good—"

He shoved himself to his feet, wiping his mouth with the back of his hand, refusing to meet either of their gazes. If he saw anything of Soren in Kallias right now... "I have to *walk*."

He blindly made his way out into the cave corridor, shutting the door on Kallias's continued protests. He leaned back against the cold metal door, letting it sap the heat from his sweaty back, shuddering breaths building in speed until he caught himself hyperventilating, his hands splayed against the door as his lungs clawed for any scrap of air to clean the scent of blood and decay from his nose.

Something pulled tight in his throat, something that thinned his breaths and hitched deep in his chest, something that ached so sharp and savage that he almost buckled to his knees right there in the hall.

No weeping.

He cleared his throat until that hitch released.

No weakness.

He breathed until his chest no longer heaved, until the dizziness abated, until his stomach no longer churned with acid and his skin no longer crawled with spidery revulsion.

I'm sorry, smartass. Another deep breath. It tasted like bile and smoke. *I'm sorry. I won't burn you. I swear to the gods, I won't burn you.*

He still remembered the day she'd asked that of him, an ice-coated day mostly spent on a battlefield. Their first battle. Their first testing ground as battlemates.

Dark clouds had burgeoned above, slinging hail at the opposing armies with remarkable aim, Tempest meting out judgement on both sides as fist-sized globes of ice pelted them without mercy. Soldiers had fallen left and right, dead from no weapon held by man. Soren had taken one to the head and crumpled into a heap beside him, blood pouring down her temple—gods, he still remembered the feeling that had coursed through him, he might as well have taken the blow himself for how he'd shouted—and he'd dragged her back to the physician's tents while propping a stolen shield over the both of them like a steel parasol. And when she woke up with physicians hovering over her and him praying in her ear, she'd started to cry.

"Don't burn me, Elias," she begged, half-conscious and terrified, confusion muddling her gaze from vivid emerald to winter-dulled pine as it met his. She fumbled for his hand, and he

gave it, his heart cracking as she clung to him, hysterical sobs jerking at her shoulders. "You can bury me wherever you like, with as many locks on my coffin as you need, but don't burn me, please don't burn me, not like them, not like them——"

"I won't," he swore, bringing her fist to his lips and kissing her knuckles, never breaking her gaze. "I swear on my life, Soren, no one's going to burn you. You're fine. You're fine, smartass. It's just a head wound, all right? Looks worse than it is."

Her tears spilled over, soaking in the streak of blood across her face, dripping red from the edge of her chin. "Not like them," she repeated, his fingers beginning to tingle as she squeezed them with all her strength. "I don't want to die like them."

He came back to the stone halls of Artem with a blink and a shudder, his hand flexing at his side, his bones still remembering the imprint of Soren's grasping, distraught fingers.

She was so afraid to die.

His stomach lurched up into his throat, but nothing rose up with it; he'd already lost everything he had to give. He braced himself against the wall, dry-heaving until his body finally seemed satisfied, until it acknowledged that he was indeed empty.

Empty.

He ran shaking fingers over his forehead, dashing away the beads of sweat that gathered there.

He was right. He needed to walk.

So walk he did, bare feet padding silently on the stone floor; he must have kicked his socks off in the midst of his fitful sleep. Every muscle in his legs protested as they stretched and loosened and stretched again, scraping uncomfortably against each other, tender from the long climb up the mountain yesterday.

Somewhere along the way, his feet chose a path for him—the only path they knew here, really—and he found himself walking past Havi's shop. He expected the windows to be dark, but to his surprise, warm light glowed beyond the frosted glass window, Havi's gentle bass humming above the pop of burning wood.

His traitorous stomach rumbled at the smell of blueberries and cinnamon, and he swallowed back the saliva that tried to pool beneath his tongue. Even if he'd been decent for company right then, he wasn't about to give his body more fuel to purge from itself. But just as he turned to go back to the chamber, the door creaked open behind him. "Morning, cousin."

Too late to run now. He cleared his throat, turning around on his heel to meet Havi's concerned gaze. The baker slung a dishtowel over his shoulder, studying Elias carefully from head to toe. Gods knew what sort of state he was in.

"Rough night?" The baker's voice was unbearably gentle. It prickled uncomfortably at Elias's neck.

"I just needed some air," he hedged. "I didn't mean to disturb you. I didn't think anyone would be awake."

Havi jerked a thumb over his shoulder with a sheepish smile. "Well, these muffins aren't going to make themselves, you know." Elias's stomach growled again, audibly that time. Havi chuckled and moved aside, gesturing Elias in. "Come on in. I could use a taste tester, anyway. This is a new recipe."

Elias's feet hesitated, self-consciousness sticking them to the stone. "I, ah…I'm not really decent for…"

"I've got a shirt you can borrow."

No route left for escape. He followed Havi's pointed finger inside.

The shopfront itself was sparkling clean: there was a long glass case that separated customer space from curator space, and the stone floor had been sanded down and covered in brick pavers instead. Dark wooden display shelves were built into the walls, affixed to natural ledges in the rock, showing off glass-domed cake stands and branched bits of metal that seemed to be designed to display batches of muffins or cupcakes. Glass globes hung at various heights from the ceiling, each containing a flame with no fuel—spheres of sourceless fire that kept the shop well-lit.

That glass case, to his surprise, was already full; pastries and breads of all sorts gleamed and glistened behind the transparent barrier, organized by type with handwritten tags announcing the name of each. Sourdough, rye, garlic, rosemary and sea salt, honey wheat…the list went on and on. And that was just the breads.

Havi pushed past the swinging wooden gate that allowed him access behind the glass counter, motioning for Elias to follow. "Come on into the back."

Elias obeyed, rubbing the ridged scar on his right arm, hoping Havi hadn't spotted it. Scars were nothing to be ashamed of, and he'd never tried to hide one before, but…this one was a mark of something other. This one bore Anima's essence, a vine of thorns that didn't fit with his Mortem-honoring tattoos.

It spoke of a stolen miracle, and he wanted nothing to do with it.

Something rumbled dangerously deep in his chest, and he slipped the tip of his finger through Soren's ring, pressing it tightly between his fingers until it left a throbbing imprint in his thumb.

How many months had he begged Mortem for mercy? How many nights had he lain awake, whispering to the goddess he'd served his entire life, pleading with her to halt the poison's path?

Too many for her to have ignored his prayers that way. Too many for *Anima*, a goddess he'd never trusted in or prayed to, to have been the one to save him instead.

A flash of heat seared down his neck, a burning that leaked from his nape like molten ore pooling in that branding on his skin. He swallowed hard, bracing himself against it as he followed Havi into the kitchen. His cousin had started singing again, an old hymn he recognized from his time in the temple…something about melting down a flawed blade, purging all dross and forging what remained into something stronger than before.

He'd never liked that hymn. He'd never cared for the implication that things always had to get worse before they got better. He liked it even less now that he was trapped in the *worse*, with no real hope of ever achieving *better*.

The kitchen was just a bit too far past cozy to be comfortable, the giant wood-fired oven against the back wall belching heat in relentless waves. The butcher-block counters were clearly well-used, scored with scratches and stained in places, but still beautiful somehow. None of the storage was on the floor—all the walls in the kitchen had been smoothed out and paneled in wood, with cupboards and shelves covering nearly every inch of them. The only spot that wasn't dedicated to storage was a framed square of glass hung above what he guessed was Havi's more formal workspace, a corner desk that jutted out from the lower right corner of the kitchen. Within the frame was…

"Is that Ember?" Elias moved closer, forgetting his discomfort in favor of awe. The painted portrait was utterly lifelike, an incredible rendering of the Nyxian princess from the shoulders up. She was smiling.

Havi's singing cut off with a cracked note, and he cleared his throat, rubbing the back of his neck as he circled the counter to approach the desk. "It is. Safi painted that before she left."

"Safi paints?"

"A woman of many talents, my little sister." Havi gazed at the portrait, his mouth tilted at a fond angle. "She's also quite skilled at being annoying."

"Aren't all little sisters?"

"Ah, so you have one yourself?"

"Three, actually."

Havi whistled low, shaking his head, the metal bits twined in his locks clinking together. "Gods help you."

"They haven't so far," he muttered without thinking, then cursed himself for being an idiot when Havi's eyes narrowed in thought.

"Come on. These muffins should be ready any minute. Oh, here—you should meet Cherry. Cherry! Out of the oven, girl."

It took him a moment to make sense of those words—and another moment to process the sight of a red-scaled creature suddenly stirring in the depths of the oven, ruby chips of light undulating beautifully as it bent itself in a catlike stretch, batlike wings unfurling with a snap that sent embers and ash flying.

Havi groaned, waving his hand toward the oven until the creature padded out, its ears flicking as it turned curious scarlet eyes on Elias. Between those ears were two tiny horns, and as it hopped down to the floor and shook itself clean of soot, it butted Havi's shin with a growling chirrup.

"Ah, stop it. Don't be grouchy for our guest." To Elias, whose eyes felt nearly as wide as the plates on the shelves, Havi added, "This is my dragon, Cherry. Forgive her sour manners, she's a terrible grump when I wake her from her nap."

"A dragon," Elias echoed. "You have a pet dragon?"

"I do indeed. Not common in Nyx, I know."

Not common anywhere, but he refrained from saying so. "Is she friendly?"

"Well, she won't bite unless you try to take food from her."

Elias leaned down to tentatively scratch behind Cherry's ears as Havi grabbed a log from the pile beside the oven, earning himself what seemed to be a purr while Havi worked. Havi placed his palm on top of the log for a moment, closing his eyes; adrenaline bolted through Elias as a flame leapt up between Havi's fingers, lapping hungrily at his skin and the wood beneath.

Havi didn't flinch. And as he ducked down and stuck his *entire arm* inside the oven, a cry of protest leapt unbidden to Elias's lips—but Havi simply set the log inside with his bare hand, a stunt that would have left most men with ruined skin, potentially even a lost limb. He calmly nudged the wood that was already burning into a better position, cradling embers in his fingers and placing them near the new log. And when he pulled back to meet Elias's wide eyes, he offered a serene smile as he brushed ash and soot off on his apron. "Don't you have Mortem-blessed wielders in your kingdom?"

"Yes, but…" Controlling fire was one thing. Being *impervious* to it was another. "Can all pyromancers here do that?"

"Of course." At Elias's choked noise, Havi let out a booming laugh, putting his hands on his hips and bending back to make more room for the sound. "I'm joking, cousin. No, not everyone. Some, but not everyone. It's a rare gift among pyromancers."

Unbelievable. "How does it work?"

Havi stuck his arm back into the oven, expression never shifting, and pulled out a living ember, rotating the pulsing gold-and-black chunk of wood in his hand. Not one flinch, not one cry. "Some say when Mortem loves one of her worshippers, they're more likely to find themselves sent to an early grave. Others claim that she grants her favorite worshippers protection from her own touch." A wry smile as he lifted the flame up and pressed a kiss to it before tossing it back into the oven. "I've never been too keen to find out the true answer. I'd hate to find out my goddess isn't very fond of me."

A trailing itch stirred beneath the venom-scarred flesh on Elias's arm. He cleared his throat, crossing his arms tightly. "About that shirt you mentioned…"

Havi smacked his forehead with a groan, leaving behind a streak of soot. "Of course! Sorry, let me get that for you."

As Havi shuffled away, ducking into a closet off the side of the kitchen, Elias's eyes fell to the ring encircling his fingertip. He swallowed hard, squeezing it till his knuckles paled, his mind darting back to what had driven him here in the first place.

The nightmares were always the same, yet always different. Soren was always dying, but sometimes they were back on the battlefield outside Ursa. Other times he found her head, but it happened to be missing a body. Other times she took her last breath in wheezing pain, dark veins pulsing beneath her skin, poison wracking her with agony until her heart finally gave up, her pulse puttering out beneath his fingers.

Whether it was his grief fueling those dreams or his mind trying to *somehow* explain Soren's absence by telling itself they'd seen her die in a way that made sense to it, he didn't know; but he never dreamed of Anima speaking with his battlemate's mouth. He never dreamed of a stranger's smile on his Soren's face. The memories were worse than any nightmare his mind could throw at him.

He'd endure. And when this was over, when he succeeded in these trials and turned down whatever purpose Mortem was trying to saddle him with, he'd find some way to come to terms with a death that he hadn't truly witnessed.

Kallias would never stop fighting to save Atlas, not until his final breath was driven from his body. Between him and his conniving brother, they'd find a way to put an end to whatever godly scheme was brewing out there…if Kallias just held his ground against whatever Tempest tried to lure him in with. People braver and better than Elias would end this before it could go any further, and once they did…

Maybe Kallias would be kind enough to allow him to witness her true burial.

"Elias?"

He jerked his head up to find Havi gazing at him cautiously, that discomfiting gentleness in his eyes once again. He held out a shirt. "This should fit you."

"Right." The word could've been drowned out by the footfall of an ant. "Thanks."

Havi continued to watch him as he pulled the shirt on, and he was grateful, not for the first time, that he didn't wear embarrassment easily on his face. "You look like your mind wandered off to a bad place. Do you want to talk about it?"

Elias hesitated. "It's…personal."

"Of course. No pressure, but the offer stands." Havi grabbed a sturdy wooden stool in one hand and set it down for Elias, motioning him to sit as he moved back to the oven. "I find it's easier to face unpleasant things if you don't give them the power of your silence."

"What do you mean?" Elias slid onto the stool, incredulity gluing his eyes to the oven as Havi pulled out a pan of blueberry muffins bare-handed. Cherry immediately jumped up to reclaim her napping nook, curling up in the flames and closing her crimson eyes.

"Our minds are the most easily plied parts of us. It's why *instinct* is such a powerful thing—our bodies aren't half as easy to trick." Havi set the pan down on two potholders arranged on the butcher-block counter. "If you talk about the thing that's hurting you, it becomes easier to battle. You make it tangible. You bring your body into the fight. And," he plucked a muffin from the pan, set it on a small plate, and passed it to Elias, "by telling others, you gain allies."

Reluctance slowed his fingers as he took the piping hot muffin, even as hunger moaned in his gut. He tore it open and let the heat pour from it in wafts of blueberry-scented steam. "You don't even know me."

"Don't have to. I know what it looks like when someone's fighting for their life." Havi leaned against the counter, dark eyes suddenly gouging Elias with merciless kindness. "And anyone who chooses to wander a foreign kingdom in the dead of night, alone and unarmed, is fighting one abysmal battle."

Grief thinned his blood, his heart slowing as Havi's words reached into his chest and clenched down, a fist squeezing out whatever remained of the denial he'd been clinging to since he woke up. "I...lost someone. Recently."

"A battlemate?" When Elias looked up in surprise, Havi fingered one of his own locks in demonstration. "Ember wears a braid like yours too. I saw it last time she visited."

That fist released his heart to grip his throat instead. "Yes."

"What was their name?"

"Soren."

Havi blinked, a flicker of horror crossing his face. "Ember's sister Soren?"

Elias nodded, popping a piece of muffin into his mouth to buy himself more time to speak. His throat was too tight to get a word out just then, and—oh, Mortem *save* him, that was a fantastic muffin. Blueberry and sugar exploded on his tongue, washing away all memory of the tongue-curling fish he'd had to endure for all those weeks in Atlas.

He was so distracted by the magic happening in his mouth that he almost missed Havi leaning against the counter, hands gripping the edges so tightly his knuckles flexed, frustration and sorrow bleeding into his eyes. "She didn't mention that in her letter."

"What did she mention?"

Havi shrugged one shoulder, distraught eyes drifting to his desk and the portrait that sat on it. "Just that you were friends of hers, and she wanted me to make sure you didn't get killed out here. She suggested I feed you whenever possible. Gods, Em...she must be devastated."

At least she hadn't seen it happen. At least it wasn't her fault.

Elias bit into his cheek, the muffin in his mouth suddenly turning, sweetness twisting into something a bit sickly. He swallowed. "I saw it happen, and it just...it's been difficult to...sleep. Since."

Havi nodded, tearing his gaze away from the portrait to find Elias's eyes again. "Nightmares?"

"Yes."

"I might have something to help, if you like."

Elias frowned. A baked good that could help with nightmares? "Like what?"

"It's a tea my mother used to make us when we were children. I had gods-awful night terrors as a boy, and with my magic..." Havi's mouth bent at a sheepish angle. "I burned up a lot of beds."

Elias tried not to shiver. Even though Mortem had never seen fit to bless him with magic of his own, he'd never felt lesser or left out because of it; there'd always been something about magic that frightened him, an element of wildness that he'd never been sure he would be capable of controlling. He'd heard tales of pyromancer children burning down their houses by accident, aeromancers throwing fits that summoned storms that could wipe out entire towns, aquamancers accidentally freezing entire harvests to death. Magic was as dangerous as it was miraculous, and he'd never cared to have a share in it. "And tea really helped with that?"

Havi chuckled. "It's a good tea."

"It doesn't have anything…you know…illicit?"

Havi blinked. "Illicit?"

"Well, you know…herbs that…have an effect on…"

Havi snorted then, sudden understanding in his eyes. "Cousin, if I wanted to drug you, I would've slipped it into those flatbreads last night."

That comment gave him pause, his stomach twinging a bit at the memory of his vomiting session and Kallias's urgent voice promising retribution if he'd been poisoned. "But you didn't, right?"

Havi chuckled and put a hand over his broad chest, the warm light teasing against his sleeve of rose tattoos. "I did not. Mortem strike me down where I stand if I'm lying." They both waited for a beat, then Havi shrugged with a good-humored grin. "Seems I'm still honest. That's a relief."

A quiet laugh snuck out of Elias before he could stop it. He looked back down to his half-eaten muffin, absently flicking loose crumbs from his fingers.

"I'll get you some of that tea to keep in your room. And feel free to take as many of those muffins back as you like—or send your friends down to get some themselves. Safi will be here to help me later."

Elias had to bite back another laugh at the idea of Kallias trying to have a conversation with both Aquila siblings without blushing or stammering his way through it. "I'll see if they're up to a trip later today."

Solemnity suddenly claimed Havi's face, his arms crossing, baring those tattoos once more. "You start training today for the trials, don't you?"

"I assume so." Not that anyone had bothered to tell him where to go, or who he'd be training with, or what he'd be training *for*.

Two more muffins landed on his plate. "Eat. This isn't something you're going to want to tackle on an empty stomach. Especially when you're used to fighting in a pair."

Dread curled his ribs inward, the edges poking into his stomach. "So it is a fight?"

"I couldn't tell you. I wasn't yet born when the last champion attempted them. But I know they're not easy. I know there's potential for failure. And I know it's not the kind of failure you can come back from."

There it was again, the cascade of molten heat down his spine, filling every notch and bend with a burning that nothing could soothe. He bent back a bit, pain forcing him to sit straight, all that fire gathering in the brand he'd spent some time studying in the mirror the night before.

A phoenix with its wings spread, wearing fire like a royal mantle. *Deathless.*

He ate both muffins. And when Havi piled more food on his plate, he ate that too, relishing familiar tastes he'd never take for granted again.

If he was going to enter this blind, he'd at least do so with a full stomach for once.

CHAPTER 21

ANIMA

The beach was still Ani's favorite piece of Atlas, but she hadn't seen the city yet. And by the old gods, it was *beautiful*.

Cheerful fiddle music floated on a sun-kissed breeze, gently brushing Ani's cheek as it tumbled past, tugging a couple strands free from her neatly-twisted bun. She'd managed to pull back her heap of hair early that morning, securing it with a leather band before tying a colorful headband closer to the crown of her head. She'd chosen one with a floral design, jade-green silk patterned with pink and yellow hibiscus flowers, something that made her smile every time she caught a glimpse of herself in a shop window. In her pale yellow shirt with sleeves cuffed at her biceps and pale blue trousers cuffed above her ankles, the headband in her hair and jingling gold earrings flashing at her earlobes, she finally looked...herself.

The city was alive with chatter and laughter, the early-spring sun coaxing vendors out into the streets to sell their wares. Kites and toys and clothing of all colors hung from portable carts, a tapestry of smells unfurling on every blow of that beautiful breeze. Sugar and spice, pastry and meat, perfume and cologne. She could have spent the entire day just sitting and *breathing*.

"Keep up," Jericho hissed to her. The princess was dressed much less happily than Anima, her deep mauve dress cut in strange, sharp ways. Sheer black material stretched over slits on either side of her waist, just above her chest, and at her elbows, sweat gathering on her forehead and the base of her throat. She'd put on cosmetics today, smoothing every crease and dark spot and sleepless shadow, but there was a glaze to her eyes that only people on the verge of sickness or sleep wore. Even her lips were wound up poorly, the corners barely managing to lift with every attempt she made at a smile. "We're nearly there."

"Can't we get some breakfast first? Those doughnuts smelled so wonderful, and there was a strawberry tart—"

"Later, Soleil." A warning more than a promise. Ani scowled, scraping her sandals across the cobblestones for a moment, the tantalizing smell of all that food calling her back, but Jericho was right; the Lapisian delegation was set to go on a sunset boat trip tonight, out into the ocean. If the mirror with no reflection was in the palace, tonight was their best chance to pilfer it.

Jericho didn't stop at any of the stands, though many people called out to her and raised their hands in greeting; she simply lifted her hand in return and moved on, a crimson-tinted shadow flickering through sun-drenched streets. Ani rubbed a hand over her flyaway curls, wishing that Soren—or Soleil, or smartass, or whoever—had been a friendlier person. It was driving her mad to follow Jericho's dismissive example.

Soleil was what everyone here called her. But her body's old owner had never used it. In her own head, she was Soren and no one else.

A body with too many names even now.

Jericho turned onto a quieter street, leaving the colorful vendors and shouts of street hawkers behind. This street was lined with houses instead, and the voices and laughter came from a handful of towheaded children sprawled on their knees or stomachs on the street, pastel lumps of chalk gripped in their chubby hands. They were covered in chalk dust and play-scrapes and grass stains, reedy voices raised in excitement as they built worlds with their combined imaginations.

Ani remembered playing like that once, a long time ago. Remembered chalky hands and green-tinted knees and giggles that made her stomach hurt in a good way. Remembered imaginary friends and pet rocks and potted plants to fill the lonely gap that yawned whenever her siblings were away.

The problems had only begun when Anima's imaginary friends stopped being quite so imaginary.

As they approached, one of the older children—a girl in a daisy-patterned sundress and two neat braids on either side of her head—saw them coming. She scrambled to her bare feet and whispered quickly to the rest of the children, who followed her example. They jumped up with haste, shoving chalk into pockets or casting it off down the street in a fit of panic.

"Princesses," the girl greeted them, offering a surprisingly fine curtsy. Her siblings quickly followed suit, the two younger boys bowing, the two younger girls attempting to mimic their sister's curtsy. The youngest, a girl of barely three years, wobbled on uncertain ankles as she dipped and bobbed, her skirt slipping through her fingers more than once as she tried to spread it out.

Jericho, to Anima's relief, softened at the sight of the children. "Hello, Hanna. Is your mother home?"

Hanna nodded eagerly, pointing to a house near the end of the row with a sky-blue door and potted plants strewn about the porch. "Yes, Princess."

"She's baking us cookies," offered one of the boys, who quickly received an elbow to the ribs from Hanna.

"Oh, that's lovely," Ani said, and the children's eyes all moved to her, widening even further.

The littlest girl wobbled over, arm firmly wrapped around a matted stuffed toy of indeterminate species—Ani thought it might have been a cat at one point, or a bear—and her other thumb in her mouth, chalk dust rimming her lips as she mumbled around her finger.

"What was that, little one?" Ani prompted.

The little girl released her thumb for a moment. "You'we petty," she said softly, her childish voice skimming right past the *r* in favor of the rest of the word.

Ani giggled, pushing a strand of her hair back into the nest of her bun. "That's very kind. So are you."

The girl beamed, showing off her teeth. "I'm a pincess, too! Mama says so."

"Oh, are you?" Anima peeked after Jericho; the First Princess had already moved down the line of houses, beelining for the one they'd come to visit. "Well, do you know what every princess needs?"

The girl shook her head, thumb slowly returning to her mouth.

Ani checked once more; Jericho still wasn't watching, and no one else was out in the streets. So she knelt in front of the children and bent over a bit to shield her hands. She squeezed her eyes shut as she pinched her fingers together, the warmth of the sun and the leftover dirt from her time in the garden this morning mingling in the cradle of her fingertips. With speed and subtlety, she wove that warmth and light and earth together, smiling a bit as the gentle thrill of magic stirred just beneath her skin.

When she opened her eyes, a neat stack of five flower crowns was nestled in her palms, and the children were all staring at her with open mouths and shining eyes.

"Magic," breathed Hanna, the oldest.

"Again!" squealed the youngest girl, clapping her hands eagerly. "Do it again!"

"Oh, I'm afraid that's a one-time trick, little one. But here." Ani carefully set one of the wildflower crowns atop her head, then passed the rest to the other children. "Now you're all honorary royalty! But shh. This is a *secret*, understand? Do you all know how to keep secrets?"

Each child nodded with great solemnity, even the youngest, donning their crowns with a reverence that warmed her deep in her stomach.

"Good." She hopped to her feet, offering them one more smile and a finger to her lips.

"Soleil!"

Rot and ruin take her, couldn't Jericho give her five minutes? "Coming!"

The house wasn't anything particularly fine, but Ani loved it the moment she saw it. Ivy crept up every wall, and wildflowers dotted what patches of grass there were. Jericho hurried up the steps to the door and knocked, a hurried *one-two-three* beat of knuckles against old wood.

Within moments, the door swung open, the smell of baking cookies drawing water from Ani's mouth. The woman who peeked out at them was small, even shorter than Ani used to be; her head barely reached past Jericho's shoulder. Her brunette hair fell in a long, straight ponytail down her back, a wildflower tucked behind her ear and another in the pocket of her apron. Her suntanned skin was lined at the eyes and mouth, and her cocoa-brown eyes tired, but she lit up when she saw Jericho. "Princess! It's been too long!"

"Oh, none of that. It's Jericho to you forever." Jericho gave her a quick hug before gesturing for Ani to approach. "Soleil, this is Briar. Briar, you've met my sister, but I'm not sure…"

"Not since she was recovered, no." Briar reached out and took Ani's hands with the gentlest touch. "I'm so happy to see you home, Soleil."

Strangely, even though the sentiment wasn't meant for her, tears pricked at the back of Ani's eyes at that sweet smile, the soft touch. She clung on to Briar's hands for a moment, offering a feeble smile back, wishing it felt stronger. "You're very kind. It's good to meet you again, Briar."

"Briar studied at Ivycreek Academy with me," Jericho explained. "She was in contention for top of the class."

"Well, as much as I could be with two dual-wielders ahead of me," Briar accused good-naturedly, bumping Jericho with her hip. "How is Daphne these days? I don't see her in town."

Jericho's eyes dimmed a bit. "Last I heard, she was serving in the battlefield tents, traveling with the army. But she seemed well last I saw her."

Briar's throat bobbed, and her hand went to her chest. "Anima keep her."

Anima keep her, Anima keep her, Anima keep her.

Prayers. Even though she couldn't grant them half as well in a physical body—there were limits to what magics humanity could bear, even those hardy enough to hold a deity—the prayers of her worshippers still lodged themselves deep in her heart. She swallowed hard, folding her hands in front of her.

Daphne Ivera was still alive, she could sense that much. A wielder of medimancy and biomancy, just like Jericho. Ambitious, fierce, and certainly talented. But she couldn't tell this woman that, no matter how much her tongue ached with the weight of the answer to her prayer.

"Briar," Jericho said, interrupting Ani's thoughts, "I have a job for you."

Briar frowned. "A job your palace healers can't manage?"

Jericho crossed her arms. "A job that has more to do with your other talents."

Briar's gaze darted past Jericho to her children, still playing on the street. "No."

"Briar—"

"I don't do that anymore." Finality rang like a struck gong through Briar's voice, and Ani turned to go, disappointment hanging her hands at her sides. At least they'd tried, but the woman had every right to turn them down.

Jericho shot out a hand, catching Ani's shoulder to stop her, but her eyes never left Briar's face, pleading, taking on a bit of that desperate edge. "Briar, please. It's not for me. It's for Vaughn."

Briar's eyes flickered, but her jaw stayed taut. "I don't *do that* anymore. I don't even think I *could.*"

"Don't sell yourself short. We both know...please, Bri. I have gold. It's not a favor, it's a *job.*"

Briar held Jericho's gaze for a long moment. Then: "Paid?"

-"Dearly."

"Anonymous?"

"Thoroughly."

"When?"

"Tonight."

Briar glanced toward her children once more, fingers flexing, fussing with the wildflower tucked inside her pocket. Then, in a voice with far less softness than before, she said, "Come in. Close the door behind you. And for Anima's sake, keep your voices down."

CHAPTER 22

FINN

I f he spent one more night trapped within the four walls of his room, drinking black coffee like water and writing in a dead girl's journal, he was going to go madder than Occassio's influence could ever make him.

Useless energy coursed through his limbs, his leg bouncing, his fingers tapping on the windowsill as he sat in his windowseat and gazed out at the city. His fifth cup of coffee was somehow both too much and not enough, and the hollow rumbling in his stomach reminded him that he'd missed dinner in favor of research.

Divine relics. Tempest take him to the depths, this was only getting worse.

Chatting with the priests and priestesses of the palace's private temple had gotten him nowhere. They'd told him nothing more helpful than what Alia had already gathered, and the way they'd looked at him had suggested further questioning would land him in hot water. They were closer with Jericho than with him by quite the margin, and he found templefolk were harder to bribe into silence; he couldn't risk word of his questions getting back to her.

His next sip of coffee was slower, letting the brew seep into his tongue, relishing the curl of bitterness it carried with it. He'd lost a bit of his taste for sweet in these past few weeks. Every waft of chocolate and sugar brought with it the memory of abrasive laughter and keen eyes that saw too much for their own good.

So he downed the last of his coffee, ignoring his taste buds pleading for cream, picturing the chess board he'd gotten himself trapped on. There was only one other person he still trusted who might actually have an answer for him, and she couldn't be reached from this palace. He was out of clever, foolproof moves; it was time to take another risk. It was just a matter of deciding which one he could afford to gamble on.

At least he knew Luisa wouldn't tell on him to his traitorous sister. But getting caught outside the palace in the dead of night in company of a seer…that would bring about all sorts of questions he wasn't prepared to lie his way through.

He glanced up from his tapping fingers, meeting his own gaze in the windowpane, his exasperated exhale stirring the hair that fell across his forehead. "What's our plan, huh, genius?"

Nothing answered him but the orchestral song of crickets and the faraway lapping of waves, his breath bouncing off the window and fogging up his glasses. He took them off, sheathing his thumb and forefinger with his sweater and pinching the lenses between them, rubbing in circles until the glass was clear again. He heaved another sigh before he slid them back on, looking back up to the window—

His own dead, rotting face stared vacantly back at him, skin curled back from his mouth to reveal bared teeth and bone.

The shout tore from his throat before he could even think of swallowing it. He kicked at the wall, tumbling off the windowseat with a *thump* that knocked the breath clean from his lungs, scooting several feet back before he caught himself against the foot of his bed, staring wide-eyed at the window.

Empty. No festering face, no undead grin, no milky eyes staring straight to his soul.

Breath punched through his chest with a painful gasp, and he squeezed his eyes shut, rubbing them fiercely with the heels of his hands.

Poor Trickster Prince, tsked that voice dripping in moonlit madness, a playful hiss that dipped in and out of Finn's mind like a sewing needle in the practiced hand of an embroiderer. *Having nightmares again, are we? That's only going to get worse, you know. Minds don't take kindly to magic like mine.*

"Get out," he hissed, clamping his hands over his ears.

You can't out-trick the Trickster Goddess, handsome. But I do enjoy watching you try.

"Get *out!*" he roared, digging his nails into his skin until Occassio's giggles were drowned out by a low droning sound, pain leaking from his ears down his neck as his nails dragged down, down—

He only realized what he was doing when his collar began to stick strangely to his skin.

Like a lever clicked into place, the ringing in his ears stopped. Occassio's voice vanished, leaving him huddled against the foot of his bed with a quiet mind, shaking hands, and blood trickling from scratches that burned behind his ears.

Fear tried to tighten its noose around his neck. He swallowed past it, quickly getting up and stumbling to his private washroom, taking in the state of himself with bloodshot, sleepless eyes.

At least they still had life in them. At least they weren't rotting out of his head.

Blood ran from his head in thin rivulets, soaking into his sweater and drying in the yarn, stiffening the collar in strange ways. Its rusty remains were buried beneath his nails.

He'd pierced his own flesh in his frenzied attempt to claw her out of his head.

Luisa. He had to talk to Luisa *now*, risk be damned.

He cleaned himself up in a hurry—at least the scratches were superficial, the bleeding had already stopped—and wrapped his scarf around the lower half of his face before fastening on his cloak and tossing the hood over his head.

He barely paid attention as he snuck through the palace halls toward the kitchen exit; he'd followed this exact route so often that he didn't have to spare half a thought to avoid the guard patrols and the night shift of palacefolk.

Unfortunately, he was barely out the door before a voice called out to him, too loud, too certain: "Prince Finnick!"

He kept walking. Maybe if he ignored them...

"Prince Finnick, *wait*!" Louder that time, more insistent. He swallowed a curse, palming the dagger at his belt as he turned around to face the unlucky soul who'd had the misfortune of seeing him. That wasn't something he could allow, especially not now.

But the person running after him, her hair tied in a bundle of curls atop her head and her skin sparkling in the moonlight, cursing as her crystal-cut slippers snagged on every cobblestone between him and her...

He knew her. And unfortunately, she wasn't someone he could dispose of with a dagger and a handful of gold in the hand of the nearest guard.

His grip loosened on the dagger. Just a bit. "Fidget?"

The Lapisian girl plucked off her shoes and tossed them unceremoniously into the plain knapsack knocking against her hip, her breath escaping in gasping huffs like she'd been running. And run she did—or rather, she skipped, hurrying toward him with a hasty smile that didn't match her desperate eyes. "I don't mean to bother you at this hour, Prince—"

"Finn."

"—Finn, sorry, I knew that, I just—ugh! I can't think straight. Give me a moment." The girl dropped her knapsack to the ground, wincing a bit at the sound of shattering crystal. Besides her now-hidden footwear, though, she was dressed far less ostentatiously than before; she wore an outfit of muted grays and purples, simple pants that cuffed above her bare ankles, a loose heather tunic with sleeves that flowed past her wrists, and a linen scarf tied around her neck. He guessed her mirrors were hidden beneath for the sake of remaining anonymous to onlookers— it was what he would've done.

"Fidget," he coaxed, "I really need to know why you're following me."

"My name isn't Fidget."

"We've established that."

"Then stop using it! It's silly."

"You're changing the subject." Danger dropped his voice low, and he took a step toward her, placing himself in the best offensive position he could. This girl held no weapon he could see, and he was reasonably confident his blade was still faster than any magic she might be able to wield. "Tell me why you're following me. I am not asking."

Finally, her face dropped with a comprehension he always cherished seeing: the realization that Prince Finnick Atlas wasn't nearly the fool he pretended to be. Flirtatious ruse or none, he needed his anonymity far more than he needed her help getting to the Mirror Queen's secrets, and he wasn't above threatening her to keep it, whether he could actually carry out those threats or not.

The girl cleared her throat, taking a single step back. "I need your help."

Help? What could a Lapisian Mirror, even an inexperienced one, need from him?

Against his better judgement, curiosity creeped in. He eased his hand off his dagger, raising one eyebrow. "At this hour? Can't it wait until morning?"

Fidget flushed, brushing a few stray curls out of her eyes. They bounced right back into place. "I wouldn't have bothered you if it could. Someone stole something from my queen's quarters tonight, and I need your help getting it back."

Interesting. He crossed his arms, stretching a bit to his full height, staring down at her with a gesture of invitation. "You have my attention."

Fidget's shoulders dropped in relief. "You'll help me?"

"I didn't say that. I said you have my attention." He jerked his chin at her. "You have one minute of my time. Convince me your problem is worth more than that."

For the first time, he caught a hint of more assertive emotion on the girl's face: offense. "I thought Atlas princes were—"

"Whatever you think you know, it's my brother you've learned it from, not me. He's the dashing hero." He took a step inward, leaning forward, letting his snakelike smile be the backbone of his threat. Fear was always a better tool than flirting, anyway. "Take a guess what I am."

Surprise ruffled his stomach as she stepped forward to meet him, mirroring his movement with precision, her eyes narrowing. Softly, she said, "I am not a fool."

"I never said you were."

"And neither is my queen," she added, as if he hadn't spoken. "We know what you are, Prince Finnick. More than anyone in your own kingdom knows, if I had to guess."

"Hmm." So there *was* a sharp edge to this Mirror. "Something tells me you don't."

"Don't what?"

"Have to guess." He loosened his posture, shoving his hands into his pockets, picking absently at a fuzz buried within. "Your goddess tattled on me, I presume?"

Fidget pressed her lips together, and that was all the answer he needed. But she said, "Occassio *reveals* things to us as needed, yes. Especially my queen."

"So she tattled."

A smile tugged on Fidget's mouth, and she relaxed a bit, her busy hands burying themselves in her scarf, picking at loose threads in the weave. "Yeah, she tattled, Trickster Prince."

A terrible chill rolled down his spine, but he held himself still, clenching his fists against the tremors that tried to seize them. "Unfortunate." Understatement of his gods-damned year. "Because I guard my secrets very carefully, Fidget. And I'm not too keen on people giving them out without my permission."

Fidget's throat bobbed, but she kept her chin high—well, as high as she could. Finn wasn't an especially tall man, and still the top of her head barely reached his shoulder. "And my queen doesn't take kindly to people threatening her Mirrors. So it seems we're at an impasse."

Regrettably, she wasn't wrong. The murder of a foreign dignitary a mere handful of feet from his palace…as fast as he was, she was on her guard. Someone would hear her scream. Someone would remember seeing him leave his room in the middle of the night. Someone he'd paid off in the past would have a crisis of conscience. It was only a matter of which loose end would come undone first.

He didn't have an iron grip on his palace like he used to. He'd dropped too many threads in the wake of Jericho's treachery, of Kallias's escape. He was running this con with a skeleton crew, and it wasn't enough to pull off a politically-charged assassination without embroiling Atlas in a second war.

Another tactic, then.

"Your minute is up," he said. "I'll give you one more, but only one."

The salt-soaked air between them hummed with tension and cricket-song, the only witness to their standoff the faraway moon. Unfortunately for him, though, the moon was a dirty snitch, and she was currently fighting on any side that wasn't his.

His middle finger itched to do something about that, but he didn't think that would get him any further with his new friend.

Fidget angled her feet to the side like she was preparing to run, and his legs tensed, adrenaline readying him to dart after her before she could give news of his threats to her queen. But instead, she took in a bracing breath before saying, "Is there a place we can talk while we eat?"

He blinked at her. She blinked back at him.

"You're not great with instructions, are you?" he asked.

Her eyes crinkled playfully at the corners. "You said I get a minute to convince you. You didn't say I had to use it *now*."

Oh, clever little vixen. She had him there.

Maybe it was curiosity about her plight. Maybe it was the unexpected pleasure of being surprised by someone for once. Maybe he just happened to be hungry himself. But before he could really think it out, he heard himself saying, "As a matter of fact, I just might know a place."

CHAPTER 23

FINN

It was official: Finn had finally met his match. A title he'd borne for nearly his entire life was being torn from his grasp, passed triumphantly to the curly-haired chatterbox seated across from him, her legs crossed and her bare feet bouncing to the beat of the tavern music, her lacquered toenails shining in the chandelier light.

He could no longer out-eat anyone who dared challenge him.

"How," he groaned, leaning back in his chair as he watched Fidget devour her tenth cookie in as many minutes, "are you *doing that?*"

"I have a second stomach that holds desserts." She licked her fingers around a victorious smile, tugging off her scarf and shaking the crumbs out of it before tossing it to him. "If you're going to vomit, Prince, feel free to catch it in that. I'd rather the poor barkeep not have to mop it up."

He scoffed. "I'm not throwing up in your scarf."

"Suit yourself." She propped her ankles up on the table, grinning at him over bare toes. Her current state was a stark contrast to his: he was cloaked and hooded, his own scarf only pulled down enough so he could eat. She was barefoot and bare-shouldered, the removal of her scarf revealing a sleeveless corset top hidden beneath. The mirrors on her wrists and around her neck reflected the tavern and his own face back at him, making it easy to fake another round of flirtatious ogling. All he had to do was drop his gaze to his own reflection in her mirror necklace for her to blush, mistaking the object of his attention.

He'd seen Kallias do this exact thing a time or two, though his brother was subtler about it, more polite in his admiration. Finn didn't have time for manners. Still, he didn't linger long. He wanted to come off as interested, not sordid. And beyond that…as he'd learned earlier this evening, even staring at his own reflection for too long was a risk these days. Gods knew what he was going to see staring back.

"So," he said, taking her scarf and wrapping it around his own neck, the scent of lilac and sugar floating from the linen, "what did they take from my lovely wife-to-be, hm? Jewels? That diamond dress?" If so, he could only begrudge them for beating him to it. That gown could fund his schemes for the rest of his life and then some.

Fidget's face grew grim, her teeth worrying her lip, her eleventh—gods, *eleventh*—cookie dangling from her fingertips. She propped her wrist on her cocked knee, glancing over his shoulder before she murmured, "A mirror."

The groan escaped before he could stop it. "Please tell me you didn't drag me away from my business for a *mirror*. We'll happily replace—"

"Not just any mirror." She flipped that cookie between her fingers like he would've done with a card, her brows coming together in a deep divot. "It's blessed by Occassio. It once belonged to her."

His stomach dropped into ice-cold recognition. *A mirror with no reflection.* Jericho and Anima.

"What does it do?" he asked, leaning forward a bit.

"I couldn't tell you. Only Queen Esha knows, but I do know that it is…beyond precious." Fidget swallowed hard, that keen edge of desperation sharpening her voice once more, ending in a bit of a wobble. "And I…*we* need it back as soon as possible."

Finn regarded her for several seconds, careful to keep the truths he knew from showing up in his eyes. Then: "It's your fault it was taken?"

Her shoulders slumped, and he held in a breath of relief. He hadn't lost his touch entirely. "Everyone else was taken on a sunset ship tour this evening with King Ramses. One of the Daggers and I were left to protect it in Queen Esha's absence. I went to get dinner for the two of us, and when I came back…" She shrugged helplessly. "He was unconscious, and the mirror was gone."

"And where's the Dagger?"

"Nursing his concussion in his room."

"And why didn't your queen take this to my parents? If someone in the palace is responsible, a royally sanctioned investigation is the best way to—"

"My queen would prefer that this knowledge did not reach the ears of other royals. This relic is extremely powerful. She keeps it at her side always."

"No other royals, and yet you came to me." None of this was adding up.

Fidget…well, fidgeted…uncomfortably, finally breaking eye contact with him. "You're to be her consort. It's different. It's…"

Comprehension dawned, and he had to swallow a curse. "It's a test."

"Not a planned one, but yes. Of sorts. She wants to see just how much truth there is to the rumors we've heard…and the claims Occassio has made." She took a bite of her cookie, watching him carefully while she chewed, the barest hint of an apology shining in her eyes.

His fist clenched the edge of his seat, but he kept his voice light, careless. "And what claims has the great and powerful Cassi made of me, hm?"

Fidget choked on the bite of cookie, crumbs spewing across the table. "*Cassi?*"

"She knows what she did."

"Finn, you can't give a goddess a *nickname*. You're asking to be smitten—smote? Smited?"

"Smote, I think."

"*Finn.*"

He smirked in spite of himself. "So we're past the *Prince* thing now?"

Fidget blinked at him. "You have a death wish. Nobody told us you were *mad.*"

"It's a new development." And it was that exact goddess's fault, so he wasn't about to offer up any apologies.

All at once, exhaustion swept over him, the combined fatigue of too many sleepless nights digging in behind his eyes. Even the gentle flicker of the tavern lights burned, a dry scalding that dragged his eyelashes downward, blurring everything into a muddle of purple silk and cookie crumbs and his own jumbled features in Fidget's mirror pendant.

Too much. All of it was too much. A couple months ago he'd been swindling people in taverns for fun, had gotten himself caught cheating at cards because he was *bored*, had foolishly declared out loud that he didn't have enough to think about. It wasn't supposed to be a *challenge*, gods damn it.

"So?" Fidget's voice jolted him back to this moment, this tavern, with his chin resting on her stolen scarf and his hands trembling violently against his legs.

"So?" he repeated, trying to clench his fingers closed. Not one muscle obeyed his silent command; his hands remained splayed, stiff and shaking.

Toss me in the depths and drown me twice, not now.

"Will you help me find it?" Her limpid brown eyes watched him, wide and eager and pleading, her own hands tapping the table, plucking at the grooves like a pianist at their keys.

Finn had never truly envied anyone before. But just then, watching her fingers pick and prod without a single twitch or tremor, jealousy possessed him so utterly he actually had to sink his teeth into his tongue to keep from saying something he would absolutely regret.

Gods, this wasn't like him. He never *felt* things like this, never got overwhelmed by irrational anger, was never so gods-damned tired that he couldn't *think*. But all he could focus on was the rigidity stringing his muscles to his bones, tarring his knuckles so he couldn't hope to bend them. And she was just sitting there, smiling at him, moving her gods-damned fingers, *looking* at him—

"Stop looking at me, Soleil!"

"Fine," he snapped, then cursed silently as her face fell, one glossy lip pouting out a bit in what appeared to be genuine hurt. *Pull it together, you ass.* He couldn't be losing his grip on this game already. It was a long con, but not much longer than any he'd pulled before. He shored up the gates of his restraint, forcing an apology out of his mouth. "Sorry. It's been a long day. Gods. Yes, fine, I'll help. But only because I'm sincerely afraid that you'll eat me if I don't."

Fidget's posture relaxed into her more natural slouch as she laughed, her hands easing off the table. "Oh, no, I could never. I've only got the one extra stomach."

"Princes don't count as dessert?"

"*You* certainly don't."

He offered his very best imitation of Jericho's pout, complete with a flutter of his lashes. "I can be sweet when I want to be."

Her eyebrow cocked. "Maybe one day you'll prove it."

Oh, he definitely needed more sleep. Because when she smiled again, hopeful, almost teasing…he found himself smiling back. A curve of his lips that didn't feel as false as it should have. "I guess we'll see, won't we?"

She held out a hand. "Can we start with you returning my scarf?"

"Oh, no, I'm keeping this." He patted the scarf—at least that was something he could do with an uncooperative hand. "If I'm going to be putting myself on the line to help fix your mistake, I'm going to need some collateral."

"Hm. Fine. But if I'm going to risk my reputation by teaming up with you, I'm going to need a bit of my own." Swifter than a flicker-fish, her fingers darted out and snatched his scarf right off his neck, a deft bit of thievery that left him blinking at her, one hand coming up *just* too late to block her.

She grinned again, looping his scarf around her neck. The rich brown yarn somehow managed to compliment her ensemble of purples and grays, adding a splash of warmth to her outfit.

"Seems fair," he finally said. Gods, she was quick. "You sure you didn't steal that mirror?"

A snort. "Don't I wish. Then all my problems would be solved."

Yet again, a smile tried to pull at his mouth. He forced it back down. "You know your own way back to the palace?"

"Absolutely not."

He'd figured as much, but he'd hoped all the same. A sigh heaved from his chest as he stood, quickly tucking his hands into his pockets. "I'll take you back. But we enter separately, through different doors, and if anyone asks…"

"I haven't spoken to you since this morning," Fidget assured him.

"That's the spirit."

It wasn't until he was safely back in the palace, running his cramped hands under warm water and attempting to kick his boots off, that a thought occurred to him:

He'd forgotten to seek out Luisa.

He hadn't decided against it. He hadn't changed his mind. He'd *forgotten*.

As he slowly raised his eyes to meet his gaze in the washroom mirror, cold dread pumping into his blood with every beat of his heart, a quiet chuckle rumbled in the back of his mind.

Within the hour, he removed every last mirror from his room. He drew every curtain and dirtied anything reflective with wax or dirt or whatever he could find. And once that task was done, once he couldn't find his own reflection anywhere at all, he barely managed to clamber into bed before his eyelids finally gave up the fight.

And he slept.

And slept.

And slept.

CHAPTER 24

KALLIAS

He might have questioned Elias's tastes on most things, but he had to give him this: these were the best gods-damned muffins he'd ever tasted in his entire *life*.

"You," he said to Havi, already reaching for another muffin, "are an artist. I don't suppose you're looking to relocate?"

Havi snorted before laughing, sliding onto the stool across from Kallias, leaning his elbows on the table between them. "Afraid not. Not to Atlas, at any rate. Too humid for me."

"You've been?"

"Once, before the war. The Emperor had business with your mother, and my mother had to tag along. I was...gods, sixteen? Seventeen? I don't remember. Anyway, Safi loved it. She talks about moving and starting a shop of her own out there all the time, but until the war's over…" Havi shrugged. "Too dangerous to be crossing borders right now without dire cause."

"Pity. Atlas would be better for either of you."

"Don't start," Safi called from the door. She was greeting customers as they came in, holding a tray of samples nestled in paper wrappers, looking rather impatient. From what Kallias had gathered, she worked a shift here at the Sugar Spinner in the mornings, and Havi went to assist her with her forgework in the evenings after the bakery closed. "Elias warned us about your flirting, Prince."

"He's just jealous because I don't flirt with him," Kallias called back dryly.

"Can't blame him, either, handsome." Safi offered a wink, and heat flooded Kallias's face.

"Safi," Havi sighed, "he's engaged."

Safi rolled her eyes, waving her free hand dismissively, the samples in her other hand sliding to one side as the tray wobbled. "I know."

"To the *Empress*."

"I *know*."

A chuckle got caught behind his next bite of pastry. He swallowed hard to clear the way. "Any advice on that front?"

"Oh, absolutely not." Havi pulled at his collar a bit with a gulp, his smile taking on a sympathetic but nervous edge. Kallias held in a groan; that wasn't at all the reaction he'd been hoping for. "Idris is…well. Let's just say that's far above my head."

"A rare occurrence for you, I assume," Kallias joked. The baker was even taller than him—it was anyone's guess how he managed to avoid feeling claustrophobic in this kingdom of caves. But even as he forced the humor, his stomach pinched. He'd hoped Havi would say something closer to *oh, yes, Idris? What a sweetheart. Incredibly reasonable. Wonderful listener. Doesn't mind a bit of dishonesty to gain an audience with her. Super good at god-killing, if that's what you need.*

Well…to be fair, maybe he'd let his daydreaming go a little too far.

Another booming laugh, and Havi slapped his knee, eyes shining with merriment. How long had it been since he'd seen someone laugh so easily? "You're funnier than I expected, Prince."

Discomfort latched tighter to his ears the more that title reached them, and he cleared his throat again, shaking his head. "Kallias, please."

Havi's mouth tilted in a concerned frown, but Safi said, "First name basis with a prince? Is that something we can put on a sign? I feel like that's worth putting on a sign."

"Safi," Havi groaned.

Safi ignored him, setting the tray up on the counter and wheeling over, stopping to wave her now-empty hand in demonstration as she recited, "*Come get your pastries from Havi at The Sugar Spinner, the only bakery officially endorsed by the future Emperor of Artem!* Come on, that'll definitely drum up some business."

"We are not going to use our *new friend* as a business gimmick."

Kallias wanted to laugh—would have, if all his senses hadn't been veiled with dread the moment those words left Safi's sharp tongue.

Future Emperor.

He wasn't the future Emperor. He wasn't the future *anything* anymore. Just a man with no crown, no throne, no use for the royal blood lying dormant in his veins, settled at the bottom like sediment in a riverbed.

But crown or not, that blood didn't fade. He was still his father's son in the ways that mattered: Ramses Atlas, a master of holding diplomacy in one hand and a blade in the other, prepared to battle or bargain depending on which hand his adversary chose to take. He was his mother's son in every other way—hers in the loyalty to Atlas that had stitched his heart irrevocably to the shore, hers in the way his brow ached for a crown, hers in the way he'd cut down anyone who dared lay a threatening hand on what was his, kin or kingdom.

But for this, for the aid of this kingdom that had no obligation to offer it, he would dig up the parts of him that belonged to his father. He would exchange hubris for humility if it bought Atlas a chance.

So he forced out the laugh trapped in his chest, getting it out barely a second later than he should have. He gestured with the half-eaten muffin in his hand. "If it will get this magic into the hands of more people, I'm happy to be used however you see fit."

Safi grinned triumphantly, but her gaze slid past Kallias to the door. "Don't look now, but you've got company. And she doesn't look half-pleased."

A groan caught in Kallias's chest as he turned to spot Raquel standing stiffly at the back of the line, arms crossed and scowl held at the ready. She wore lighter clothes today—leather pants still, but her shirt was crafted from thin gray silk, the straps about two inches thick, baring her collarbones and the deep scars down the side of her neck and her left shoulder. Thicker than Atlas garments still, but more suited to the dry heat of Artem's mountain. Her belt of weapons shifted as she did, ever-fastened around her hips, and—

Kallias blinked, cursing silently as he came back to himself and realized he was staring.

Raquel was dangerously beautiful, there was no arguing that, and Kallias always had a weakness for both those things—especially when they were working in tandem. But there was a difference between danger and death, and he knew which waited at the end of a path where he indulged in any further thoughts about this Nyxian warrior woman. The fire-kissed Empress was a *far* safer place to fix his attention.

If he ever got to meet her, anyway.

Elias was back in their chambers, bathing and preparing for his meeting with the High Priestess to be debriefed on his first Trial. Kallias still didn't like the idea, but his words in the chapel had been true; it was Elias's task to take on or turn down, and if it got them their audience with the Empress, he had little choice but to let it happen.

Even if his mind had kept him awake all night with horrible, lurid, half-conscious nightmares of Atlas in shambles, his family dead or possessed, his people slaughtered and forced to become lifeless puppets with Vaughn's magic animating the bones beneath their rotting flesh.

"Angelov!" he called, and he watched Raquel close her eyes and heave out a long sigh before she turned to meet his gaze, annoyance twitching in her jaw. He met the glare with one of his own, crooking a finger to summon her out of line.

She stayed instead, defiant gaze lingering on Kallias the entire time, until she reached the counter and purchased her own food. And even when she had it, she dawdled, leisurely taking bite after bite of her chocolate-drizzled croissant as she crossed the bakery. Kallias's knuckles tightened as he gripped the edge of the table, forcing patience to soothe the riling irritation tying knots in his temper. If he let her see that she was goading him, she'd only do her best to waste more of his time.

"Is Elias on his way to the Priestess yes?" he asked carefully as she picked up a chair one-handed, dragging it around to sit beside Safi and straddling it with her elbows propped on the back. She took another bite of her croissant before letting it dangle from her hand, dark eyes spearing him in place.

Gods, the oven in the kitchen must have been burning ridiculously hot. These waves of heat washing over his face were almost alarming.

"He was still preparing when I left," she answered finally. "He seems nervous."

"Better than nothing." The apathy he'd grown so used to seeing on Elias's face was beginning to worry him. "Did he say if he had a—?"

"I'm not a messenger hawk, Atlas," Raquel interrupted, snideness souring her voice. "If you have questions for him, go ask them."

"You know, I think I should go check on the oven," Havi announced at a volume that was just a bit too high to be casual. He stood, offered a graceful bow to Kallias and a kind smile to Raquel, then ambled off to the safety of the kitchen. Kallias had never envied someone so much.

"Coward!" Safi called after her brother, but her eyes were apologetic as she shot Kallias a smile. "Actually, I should go too. Don't want the flies to get the samples. Don't kill each other in the bakery, all right? It's not sanitary."

"I'll do my best," said Raquel, though the way she was tapping her fingers against the hilt of one of her knives suggested her *best* might not be something to count on.

Safi shook Raquel's hand and bumped Kallias's fist with hers before wheeling back to the counter, abandoning him to the mercy of Raquel Angelov.

Somehow, he didn't think this woman held that particular virtue in abundance.

Raquel swung out of her chair and moved into the one that Havi had abandoned in his hasty getaway, pulling one of her ankles up and resting it on her opposite thigh, her eyes flickering down to the tabletop. The corner of her mouth curled up—not in a friendly way. "Your magic betrays your manners, Atlas."

He looked down to find frost outlining his fingers and quickly dashed it away, hiding his fists beneath the table. "And I suppose you never have any problems with this?"

"Never." She shrugged, and he hated the self-righteous smugness that lined her shoulders. "I mastered my magic years ago."

"How lovely for you. As I mentioned, mine just decided to start causing trouble a few weeks ago, so can we chalk this up to a learning curve?"

Her head tipped to one side, black shimmering blue in the light. "You speak so prettily for a murderer."

And there it was again. "I'm *not* a murderer."

"Then I'd love to know what exactly you think you are." The table creaked as Raquel leaned a bit closer, her elbows digging into the smooth wood. "You killed my little sister."

And didn't that story sound familiar.

Pain ached in his cheek as he bit down on it, reading the simmering hate in her gaze, watching the clenched fingers that no doubt wanted to be wrapped around his neck. He knew that look, that posture, the need buried in those grasping hands. He'd felt it every day of the ten years he'd grieved his own little sister. He'd felt it even worse in the eight he'd spent fighting for his life on battlefields and fighting for his soldiers in war rooms.

"Do you even remember her face?" rasped Raquel.

"You're asking me to remember a soldier I saw once, years ago, in the midst of battlefield chaos." Kallias stood with one swift movement, shoving the chair back as he did. This was a useless conversation, and it could only end badly for him. "I am sorry for your loss. I am sorry for what part I played in it. But it was war—it *is* war. Your sister, whoever she was, knew what she was signing up for. And if given the chance, I know she would have just as soon seen her blade in my heart as I would have seen mine in hers."

Simmering hate came to a raging boil. She stood in a flash, slamming her fist against the table, rattling the silverware and plates sitting empty. "The only reason you still draw breath is because Elias is a very good friend. The moment you turn on him, the moment you remember my kingdom is your enemy, I will be resolving that."

Kallias closed his eyes, dove past his father, his mother, himself…and found a lesson he'd learned from Finn buried somewhere near the bottom of his mind. "You need to get better threats," he said, wearing that lazy confidence his brother was lucky enough to possess. "You're starting to repeat yourself."

He turned away and walked out, wishing he was wearing armor, wishing he could feel braver about exposing his back to her.

Before he could make it back to their chamber, an unfamiliar voice called out behind him: "Prince Kallias!"

Kallias turned, a ready smile halfway sprung to his face, an old princely instinct kicking in before he even saw who was coming for him: a man who appeared to be a handful of years his senior, brown hair short and styled to spike a bit at the front, wearing a fine military uniform decked in shades of flame. The reds and golds played well with his pleasant hazel eyes, distracting from the burn-scarred skin on his neck and jaw that turned Kallias's stomach—not because he minded scars, but because his family and many palacefolk still bore marks of the very same.

"Captain Janus, yes?" he asked, remembering the man from the day of their arrival. He'd protested against letting Raquel and Elias in.

The man brightened. "Good memory. Captain Zaccheus Janus." He offered his hand, and Kallias gave it a firm shake. "I was hoping to reintroduce myself after my rudeness when you arrived."

"Not rude at all. It's…an odd circumstance. I don't blame you for being vigilant."

"That's putting it mildly." Zaccheus paused, casting a look over his shoulder before meeting Kallias's gaze, the sparkle in his eyes dimming to something more contemplative. "Would you walk with me for a moment, Prince?"

Alarm blazed in Kallias's mind. "For what purpose?"

"I have questions for you…not the sort I feel you'd be comfortable answering honestly with so many idle ears about."

Honestly, he didn't feel comfortable answering most questions with honesty these days. But the look on Zaccheus's face intrigued him. "Of course. Lead the way."

They made their way down to the common area, following a wide path toward a quieter district of the mountain-city; mostly residential, from what Kallias could tell. Some abodes were carved out of the rock like the shops above; others were made of more typical constructs, mainly brick and stone. Fire-resistant materials.

"I'm sorry to drag you all this way for my own curiosity," Zaccheus said; his hands were folded behind his back, but every slight movement had Kallias's fingers inching toward his sword. "But I couldn't help overhearing your conversation with Safi in the Sugar Spinner."

Kallias blinked. "What about it piqued your interest?"

Zaccheus turned to meet his gaze directly, his eyes utterly serious. "The fact that you so clearly don't wish to be Emperor."

Panic hooked into Kallias's heart, tugging him to a stop, his hands coming up like a shield of denial. "Oh, no, I didn't mean to give that impression. I'm honored to have been—"

"Lies," sang out a new voice from somewhere behind them.

Kallias turned as a woman twirled out from the shadows at the side of one of the houses, wearing a teasing grin on scarlet lips. Her skin was pale as snow, but she was covered in midnight-dark freckles a shade lighter than her hair. Her eyes were greener than his mother's, rich emerald that glimmered with intrigue. "It's all right, Prince. We're not going to tell anyone."

He took several steps back as she hurried to Zaccheus, planting a kiss on his cheek that left a red print behind. Zaccheus mock-groaned, his stern features softening some as he rubbed at the lipstick on his cheek, pulling the woman close to his side. "Apologies. Prince Kallias, this is my wife, Esmeralda Janus. Mal, I think you scared him."

"Not at all," Kallias interjected, subtly removing his hand from his pommel. "It's a pleasure to meet you, Lady Esmeralda."

"Just Mal, please." Esmeralda held out her hand, and he took it, brushing a polite kiss over her knuckles, surprised by how warm they were. She beamed, pulling her hand back with a look at her husband. "Did you see that? Such nice manners. Remember when you had those?"

"No."

"Me neither." Esmeralda grinned at Kallias, patting her husband's chest sharply before pulling away from him. Her top was dark red chiffon, one-shouldered, revealing similar scars to her husband's on her bare shoulder, trickling down to her elbow. "Take a deep breath, Prince Kallias. I'm concerned for the health of your heart."

"And what do you know of my heart?"

"Mal is a sanguimancer," Zaccheus explained with a warning look at his wife.

The warmth drained from Kallias's face, but before he could say anything, Esmeralda chuckled. "I haven't felt a heart skip like that since Zac saw me on our wedding day!"

Sanguimancers. People with power over the blood. Another class of magic Kallias had thought extinct. "I don't want any trouble," he croaked, taking another step back, "but I need you to tell me why you've brought me here."

"Exactly what I said. You don't want to be Emperor." Zaccheus glanced to his wife, whose grin faded at the corners until she looked just as grim. "As it happens, our interests seem to align."

"And how is that?"

"We—and many of our people—would see this alliance forsaken. I'm sure you know we're a mere twelve years past a war of our own with Tallis." Zaccheus's eyes darkened with memory, and Esmeralda somehow paled even further, her scarred shoulder shrugging as if by habit. "We fought one war under the flag of zealotry already. Our Empress seems prepared to enter another, but our people have yet to fully recover from the first. I have voiced my concerns to General Star and the High Priestess to pass on to Idris, but based on your arrival, they seem to have gone unheard." He clenched his fists. "She refuses to put aside her grief to hear the needs of her people, preferring to leave it in the hands of others."

"I see," Kallias said slowly. "And why do you think I would give up aid for my people for my own selfishness?"

"I've been following you and your friends a bit," Esmeralda said without shame. "There's more to this than meets the eye, clearly. The three of you are tenser than a troupe of cats clinging to the edge of a bath."

Zaccheus sighed. "What my wife means to say—"

"Your wife said exactly what she meant, thank you."

"—Is that we think with our combined efforts, Prince, we may be able to come to an arrangement that will serve us both. You've grown up in a war-riddled kingdom. Can you blame me for wishing to spare my own people from that?"

He couldn't. "And what is your suggestion?"

"Not here." Zaccheus glanced around as if just remembering to search out eavesdroppers. "Idris has loyal ears on every corner. I'll meet you tonight outside your chamber; if you're amicable to hearing our offer, be ready just after midnight."

"And if I'm not amicable?" Kallias dared ask.

"Then I'll swear on my life to my superiors that this conversation never happened." Zaccheus's eyes took on a dangerous gleam, burning away all pleasantry. "And you'll lose your chance to have a voice in our plans. I hold no ill will toward your kingdom, Prince, but neither do I care much for its fate. I think you'll find this arrangement will benefit your people far more than any Idris will offer."

"You would betray your Empress?"

"Never. But her judgement has been clouded by grief—something I'm sure you understand. I won't let her narrow vision harm my people."

His own words to his mother came back to him in rushing-tide whispers: *If you won't set your pride down to protect Atlas…if you won't save our people…then I will.*

He may as well have been looking in a mirror for how well Zaccheus's conflict and determination reflected his own. He could practically see the weight of this decision buried behind the stranger's eyes, *Traitor* and *Savior* twining hands until they were inseparable from each other. And in all truth, their interests *did* align…he was here to request that Idris withhold aid from Atlas anyway. But from what Zaccheus was saying, it didn't entirely sound as though she would be willing to hear him out.

It couldn't do any harm just to listen.

"All right," he said. "After midnight. I'll be ready."

Relief gleamed in Zaccheus's eyes. "I knew you struck me as reasonable."

Kallias nearly snorted. "If my brother heard you say that, he'd choke on his own laughter."

"Well, in any case, I'm grateful." Zaccheus offered his hand once again, and Kallias shook it with more decisive force this time. "I have a feeling this is the start of something good, Prince."

Kallias shared no such feeling. But Idris was out of his reach; if he would find no help in the throne room, maybe he would find it in her halls.

Or he would simply dig himself a deeper hole. But it was a risk he was willing to take for the sake of his kingdom.

Just one talk. That was all he'd promised. That was all he'd give.

CHAPTER 25

ELIAS

"Your first trial will be the Trial of Fire."

The Priestess's voice cut through the sleepless haze in his mind, nudging his thoughts back to wakefulness. He stood before the altar in the stained-glass chapel, his toes flexing uneasily in the sheath of his boots, his hands folded against the place where the branding pulsed gently above his skin. It had lit with strange, unappeasable heat during his bath today, and no matter what creams or salves the physicians offered him, nothing had cooled it.

The Priestess stood on the altar, the fire behind her rendering her in silhouette shadows. She gazed down at him without feeling, her hands held out in front of her as if in supplication or offering. A globe of fire danced between her palms, growing and shrinking with every breath she took.

"Fire," she began, gently stroking a fingertip over the flame like a child petting a newborn kitten, "is a fickle friend. Difficult to control, dangerous to wield. One stray ember can burn down a kingdom." Her eyes caught and held his, that flame lighting her eyes up with lambent gold. "One carefully placed flame can start a war."

A bitter taste washed over his tongue as he bit down on barbed words, their spikes digging into him instead.

"This first trial will bleed directly into your next." The High Priestess cupped her hands together and twisted her wrists deftly. When she pulled them apart, the flame had vanished, leaving behind no mark or wound. "Your success in the second will depend entirely on how well you do in the first. If you fail here, you will almost certainly fail there as well. And failing any two trials results in—"

"Failure?" It came out much more sarcastically than he meant. He bit down harder on his tongue as the Priestess raised one eyebrow at him.

"More or less," she said.

Just perfect. "Tell me what I have to do."

The Priestess descended the altar, her feet oddly silent against the stone steps before settling on the carpeted floors. As her skirts swished back in place, he caught a glimpse of bare toes circled with gold and silver rings. Even barefoot, she nearly overtook him in height, her eyes level with his. "You will be given access to your own forging equipment, your own workspace, and a limited amount of materials. You will have three days to forge a weapon—or weapons, if you prefer to dual-wield—to take with you into your second trial, the Trial of Blood. Whatever weapon you have at the end of those days is the one you will have to use, no matter how flawed it may be. And if you ruin all of your materials and end with no weapon, you will fight with only your hands. The rules will not change to your favor or to your detriment either way."

He nodded. Crossed his arms. Tried to ignore the dull-toothed beast in his chest that felt like it had clamped its jaws over his heart.

It didn't hurt, not the way it should have. The raw agony had dimmed into something almost worse, a sort of dragging down, a numbing pressure that felt like it was trying to slow his heart back to a stop.

He *should* have cared about whether he succeeded or failed in this. He should have cared if he was about to be shoved into a fight with only his fists to defend against blades.

He didn't.

"When do I start?" he asked.

The Priestess frowned a bit at whatever she heard in his voice—or perhaps what she *didn't* hear, no fear, no feeling—but she simply said, "Now."

CHAPTER 26

ANIMA

The morning dawned warm and sunny, birdsong pulling her gently to wakefulness, her eyelids fluttering open to a rumpled pillowcase, drool gluing her cheek to the silk. She smacked her lips sleepily, frowning a bit as the sleep-blurred room shuddered into focus.

Brown eyes blinked five inches away from her face, one auburn eyebrow raised. "Wakey wakey."

Ani shrieked, snatching up the first thing her hand touched—one of her feather pillows—and flinging it as hard as she could at the intruder. Magic fizzed to life in her fingertips, but she forced it back, silently cursing old habits. Instead, she forced her voice awake long before it was ready. "Guards! Guards—"

A hand deftly slithered over her mouth, clamping down over her scream. That head popped back up, looking considerably more annoyed this time. "Will you stop? It's just me, Soleil."

Ani's breath stuttered on a frustrated sigh as she finally recognized him. Shoving his hand off, she choked, "Finn, why are you in my room?"

"Well, I *was* coming to tell you that breakfast is ready, but—"

"I thought you were having breakfast with Esha."

"If I have to endure one more meal where I'm the only one bothering to make conversation, I'm going to go madder than you."

Ani pouted a bit; at least she and Soren had that reaction in common. "I'm not mad."

"Debatable. Please throw an utterly ridiculous hissy fit and demand that I eat breakfast with you."

"I don't know the first thing about throwing a *hissy fit*. I'm a *princess*."

"I hear that kicking and screaming is usually involved, and hey! You're already halfway there this morning."

Now her pout was genuine. "You startled me."

"I gathered." Finn pulled away and stood, crossing her room to fling her closet door open, burying his top half inside. "What outfits do you own that scream *spoiled*?"

"Why don't I just trade with you?"

Finn looked over his shoulder at her, then down at his outfit, loosing a pout of his own. "I look classy. It's different."

He did look different today. Instead of his usual sweater, he wore a finely tailored military jacket with gilded buttons, the material a soft shade of gray that set off his brown eyes. The collar was unbuttoned and folded neatly, but the rest was properly buttoned up, snugly hugging his frame. He'd shaved and trimmed his hair a bit, slicking it back with a bit of pomade, and his glasses were perched neatly on his nose, not sliding off like they were often prone to do. A heather-purple scarf was tucked neatly into his collar like a cravat.

"You look like you slept well," she offered, and he did—there was a gleam of energy in his gaze, and the shadows she so often saw playing beneath the skin below his eyes had faded some.

Finn cleared his throat, smoothing a hand over his hair. "I did." No further comment was offered, and Anima bit her lip. *Why do you have to be so bones-cursed awkward, Ani?*

"I think," she said slowly, "that if you eat breakfast without me today, I shall wither away and die from lack of attention."

Finn smiled, but it wasn't an entirely pleased thing, his eyes probing her room one last time before settling on her. "Fantastic. I'll wait outside."

Finnick Atlas had yet to cease being a mystery to her. Jericho had promised that not one person in this palace was onto them, that they were perfectly safe to continue their ruse, but the way Finn looked at her sometimes…

She shook her head. It was paranoia, that was all. Finn had been perfectly pleasant to her. There was no reason for him to suspect she was anything other than what she claimed to be.

"Is everyone else going to be at breakfast too?" she called through the door as she dressed in a hurry, pulling on a dress with a halter neckline and tiny gold crystals frosting the entire bodice. The skirt was bare but beautiful, layers of chiffon tumbling in sheets of sunset colors, deepening in color and vibrancy the closer to the ground the fabric fell.

"As far as I know, yes." Finn sounded distracted, and she frowned a bit.

From what Tenebrae had told her, Soren and Jericho weren't the only Atlas siblings capable of hosting a god. And she knew the signs to watch for: she still remembered the dark, terror-blurred days after their magic had first awakened. Still remembered being trapped inside a tiny hovel with her four older siblings fighting for their lives.

Brae, his body wracked with pain as his chaos magic tried to rearrange every organ and muscle and bone, blood pouring unceasingly from his nose and mouth; Mora, burning with a fever so hot her skin caught fire to every blanket that touched her, her throat too dry to even ask for water; Peter, his body slowly freezing, so cold that he risked huddling close to their blazing sister just to stay alive; and Cassi, hunched in the corner of the room with her hands clamped over her ears and bloody furrows scratched across her eyes from her attempts to claw them out of her head, alternating between mad giggles and horrified screams as visions danced a garish rhythm through her head.

Ani could hear a hint of that same madness at the brink of Finn's voice: a chip in the edge of his lazy confidence, a crack that threatened to collapse into a scream.

It seemed their siblings were already stalking the Atlas brothers, and that could either spell doom for their plans…or bring them another step closer to their goal. It all depended on where Peter and Cassi—Tempest and Occassio—decided to make their stand.

Mortem wouldn't help them; she knew that much already. Her sister refused to take hosts, even willing ones, even for a greater purpose, and Tempest and Tenebrae hadn't spoken in centuries. He'd likely settle himself on whatever side their stricter sister landed on. But Cassi…they might be able to get Cassi to stand with them, if she ever decided to show herself. It would take a god far older and wiser than Ani to even begin to sus out the Trickster Goddess's loyalties.

But it didn't matter anyway. Once they gathered all the relics, she would be one step closer to getting them *all* back, whether they agreed with Tenebrae's methods or not.

Not Tenebrae, Tempest, Mortem, Occassio, and Anima…but Braeden, Peter, Mora, Cassandra, and Annelisa.

They *would* be a family again. Brae had promised her, and he never broke his promises.

A lump dropped into her throat like a tulip bulb, and she braced her hands against her torso, fussing with the crystals, the texture soothing the restlessness in her hands.

This body didn't like to be still; that was another thing to get used to. Her fingers were always seeking out something to fiddle with. It reminded her of the way Cassi used to crinkle her nose and bite her lip and play cat's cradle to keep her hands busy.

"Soleil!" Finn's annoyed voice cut through those thoughts with a three-beat knock on the door.

"Coming!" Gods, this family had no *patience.*

But as she and Finn walked together toward the private dining hall, a sharp whistle pulled both of their attention back to the hallway behind them. Ramses was standing in the door, his hair pulled back in a neat ponytail at the nape of his neck, an easygoing grin crinkling the corners of his eyes. He was wearing a wetsuit.

"Don't bother," he called. "Go get changed. We're eating breakfast by the water."

Finn groaned, but Ani was already running back toward her room, joy carrying her feet like she walked on the wind. Finally, *finally,* a chance to get back outside.

She brushed past Ramses with a murmured *sorry, excuse me,* but before she made it all the way through, he caught her and planted a kiss against her hair.

"You look happy, Sunbeam," he said, that eye-crinkling grin growing. She guessed there were dimples hidden somewhere beneath his beard.

Cheeks heating, she offered a quick smile, pushing the rest of the way past without hugging him back. "Just excited to get in the water."

Something about Ramses made her feel…guilty. Like she'd been caught in a lie and was waiting on her punishment. She tried to skirt around him whenever she could, often claiming headaches or business with Jericho when he tried to catch Soleil for a meal or a walk. But he doted on his children; his presence wasn't going to be avoidable for long, and if she kept ducking him, someone was going to notice. Soleil's mind had yet to give up more than surface memory, but she knew the princess had been close with her father, even in the wake of everything that had happened.

He wasn't Anima's father, and he had no idea that she wasn't his daughter. Even so, the hidden hurt in his eyes pinched at her heart. But he smiled past it, if smaller than before. "Of course. Hurry up. Maybe I can give you a quick refresher on surfing."

Soleil knew the sea. Soren knew the sky. Neither belonged to one more than the other, and for the first time, with the sea below and the sky above, her blood settled in her veins. When she spotted an unbroken wave, she swam to it and positioned herself in front of it. When she felt the back of the board lift, she jumped to her feet, knees cocked for balance—

And just like that, like she'd always known how, like she'd never stopped, she caught a wave.

"That would be great," she said with a hurried smile before ducking back into her room, pressing her back to the door to close it, her breath escaping in a whoosh.

She could do this. It was just breakfast, and Soleil's body did most of the acting work for her anyhow. It was fine. She was *fine*.

CHAPTER 27

SOREN

B reakfast by the water would have been pleasant, if she wasn't trying so hard to ignore it.

She'd spent much of the past few days sleeping—as much as she could sleep with Anima's thoughts making a racket just past the nebulous wall. But since her dream of Jira—and of the Atlas family, young and happy and so tantalizingly familiar it hurt—she'd been floating in darkness, waiting for something that didn't seem to be coming.

No matter how hard she tried, she couldn't seem to die.

So instead she hid, her consciousness curled up in the very back of her own skull, trying not to think too hard about her own formlessness. If she focused too much on her lack of body, that nauseous panic became all she could focus on, and the urge to slam herself against that wall until it broke or she did became almost unbearable.

Minds weren't meant to be without bodies. If she lost herself to this *wrongness*, this feeling that she shouldn't exist, she might just drive herself mad.

If she wasn't mad already.

"Soleil?"

Soren's head turned toward Finn without her command, and her lips stretched into a smile against her bidding. "Yes?"

Finn was stretched out on the picnic blanket beside her, keeping her—them—company while Adriata and Ramses walked hand-in-hand through the waves, Ramses kicking water at his wife's ankles, her laughing and threatening to do far worse if he continued to act up. Jericho and Vaughn had declined to join them. What a shock.

"If you're not going to eat your pancakes," Finn said, his eyes locked on her untouched plate, "I'll happily take them off your hands."

Anima tugged the plate closer. "Keep your grubby hands off my breakfast."

Gods, that almost sounded like her.

"Papa used to make these for us, you know," Finn said nonchalantly. "Do you remember that? At the country house?"

Anima rattled off something—some excuse or lie, Soren didn't know. Didn't care. Because exhaustion finally came to visit once more, a wave of darkness that promised a reprieve from being crammed into this gods-damned cage of existence.

She let the darkness take her where it would.

* * *

Soleil

"I call the top bunk!"

Soleil burst into the country house with unquenchable purpose fueling her limbs, bolting up the stairs before Finn even crossed the threshold behind her, his footsteps pounding in pursuit as she careened into the bedroom the two of them always shared when they took their trips west for the summer. She could hardly breathe for giggling as she launched herself at the ladder, her teeth rattling with the impact as Finn flung himself after her, his own laughter wheezing in his lungs as he tried to grab her ankles.

"You got top bunk last year!" he protested. "Mama said it's my turn!"

Soleil kicked his hand away, propping herself on the edge of the bunk and clinging tightly to the wooden barrier around the mattress. "But I called dibs. That's more important!"

"It is *not!*"

"Hey!" Kallias popped his head inside the room, his bag slung over his shoulder, giving them a stern look. "We literally just walked in the door. Can you guys keep from fighting for, I don't know, ten minutes?"

Soleil and Finn exchanged looks, then looked back at Kallias. "No," they chorused.

Kallias sighed, rolling his head around on his neck before walking off to find his own room. Jericho trailed after him, somehow lugging three bags despite her skinny arms, her hair mussed and eyes bleary from napping on the carriage ride over. "Mama said it's Finn's turn, Soleil."

Soleil pouted as Finn cackled triumphantly, somersaulting onto the bed behind her and planting his foot into her back, nearly shoving her straight off the bunk. "I'm king of the top bunk! I hereby banish you to the Bottom Realm!"

"Kids!" Adriata's voice echoed down the dusty hall, freezing them all in their tracks, Finn's foot still dug into Soleil's spine, her body hanging halfway over the edge of the ladder. "Behave, will you? You can all drive each other mad once your father and I have slept off the trip."

"Yes, Mama!" they chorused, Soleil's tongue heavy with the weight of the blood rushing to her head in a dizzying flush. She managed to right herself, scrambling down the ladder with a final scowl thrown at Finn, who simply flashed her a gap-toothed grin. He'd bragged endlessly about his top two teeth falling out before hers, but at least she could still say *seashell* without whistling.

After unpacking their things, Soleil left Finn to lord over his new domain while she padded down the hallway, the creak of floorboards beneath her bare feet nearly drowning out Jericho and Kallias tossing good-natured insults back and forth between their rooms. The summer house still smelled like dust and disuse, but that wouldn't last long; once her father gathered his energy enough to go see what few palacefolk they'd brought along had stocked the kitchen with, it would soon smell of breakfast for supper, one of her favorite holiday traditions. Her father so rarely cooked—the palace staff took care of that back home—but Soleil loved it when he did. He made pancakes shaped like daisies for Jericho, smiling faces for her and Finn, and swords for Kallias, who always pretended he was too old for it before he picked one up and slid it down his throat, miming like he was a sword-eater at a carnival, drawing giggles from the whole family. Adriata most of all, though she still groaned and warned him against choking through her laughter.

But the kitchen was silent and lifeless when Soleil peeked inside, void even of palacefolk. She frowned, quietly closing the door and doubling back to the bedrooms, struggling to remember from previous trips which room her parents preferred to stay in.

Finally, she heard their voices coming through the first door to the left at the entrance to the hall. But when she laid her hand on the knob, she paused, the tone of their voices warning her against opening the door.

"I'm telling you, we shouldn't be away from Port Atlas right now," Adriata said, her tone all tension and no teasing. The flutter of clothes and the click of trunks unbuckled with a bit more force than necessary filled in the spaces between her words. "Not with Nyx circling the border like a flock of vultures, trying to bait us into a fight."

"A wake," said Ramses.

"What?"

"A group of vultures, it's called a—"

"*Ramses.* I'm serious."

"I know." What little laughter had pushed its way into her father's voice tumbled away with those two words, and suddenly he sounded tired. "But it's safer for the children here. And remember, Genevieve is keeping an eye on things. She has this well in hand. She'll send word if we're needed."

"We should tell Jericho and Kallias, at least."

"And what good would that do? They'll only worry, and it would only be a matter of time before one of them slipped up and told the other two. Nyx hasn't proven themselves a threat yet. Increased presence at the border could mean any number of things."

Adriata was silent for so long that Soleil pressed her ear to the door to make sure she wasn't missing anything. Then: "I don't want them to think we lied to them."

"We aren't lying. Addie, look at me." Ramses's voice softened, the sort of tender that usually warned Soleil and her siblings to cover their eyes before the kissing started. "It's going to be *fine*. Nyx has no reason to start causing trouble."

"King Byron has proven time and time again he doesn't need a *reason*. Ramses, something is wrong here. I *know* it."

"And I trust your instincts. But what I said stands: if any trouble is coming, it's better that we're here. And you know that."

"I don't like putting ourselves over our people," Adriata mumbled.

"Neither do I. But we have the kids to think about."

"You like to talk in circles, Ramses Atlas."

"Mm." Soleil wrinkled her nose at the smacking sounds that followed her father's murmur of agreement. "Only when I'm right."

"You think you're always right."

"I *know* I'm always right." He paused. "Just like I know we have a little eavesdropper at the door."

Soleil started to flee down the hall, but her father's hands caught her shoulders, anchoring her in place. "Where do you think you're running to, Sunbeam?"

Soleil's face went hot, and she covered her face, her throat already aching with unshed tears. "I'm sorry, Papa, I wasn't trying to spy, I just—"

"Oh, no, no tears," Ramses groaned as he lifted Soleil into his arms, rubbing her back while she dissolved into a puddle of guilty sobs. "It's all right! Soleil, it's all right. Why are you crying?"

"I-I don't kno-ow," she blubbered, burying her face in his sleeve, the smell of his cologne soothing the knot in her stomach—but only a little. "I don't feel good. I-I wanna go home."

"Oh, love…" Adriata's words reached Soleil before her hand did, joining Ramses in patting her back, something pinched tight in her voice. "How much did you hear?"

"N-nothing," she tried, but she was a terrible liar. Her father's arms tightened around her, and she felt his breath hitch, a pause that made her stomach twist up all over again.

"Addie…"

"Ramses. Let me have her."

Her father passed her off into her mother's strong arms, and she hid her face in her mother's neck, listening to the gentle tap of her shoes on the floor as she carried her into the bedroom.

Adriata sat down, straightening her skirts with a harried swish of her hand before settling Soleil in her lap, tucking Soleil's hair behind her ears with her fingertips. She held Soleil's face gently, giving her a firm look, probing her face for any trace of childish untruths. "Tell me what you heard, little one."

Soleil couldn't hold her mother's piercing gaze. "Y-You said that Nyx wants us to fight them. And Aunt Genni is watching the castle for us."

Adriata's features pinched, but whether it was sadness or determination stitched in the creases of her forehead, it was impossible to tell.

And then Adriata told her of a kingdom called Nyx. A kingdom ruled by a terrible king who wanted very much to make their kingdom his.

* * *

Soren

"I don't understand."

Soren stood on the threshold of that bedroom door, watching Adriata—so different from the Adriata she'd met in Atlas, so young, so tender, but equally fierce—attempt to explain the intricacies of a war threat to the child queen seated at the foot of the bed, her big green eyes filled with tears she didn't understand, her arms wrapped around a stomach that ached for no reason she could discern.

"What is there to not understand?" Jira propped herself against the opposite side of the doorframe, side-eyeing Soren with a judgmental brow-raise. "I told you before—these are your memories."

"Not mine. Soleil's."

"Semantics." Jira turned to face her fully. "By the way, I've been keeping an eye on all this Soleil-Soren drama from a distance, and I gotta say: so unfair that you had the hot brother card hidden up your sleeve all this time."

Soren scowled. "Kallias *killed* you."

"I was talking about Finn."

"That's—no. Ew."

"And don't even get me *started* on your gorgeous father."

"*Jira!*"

"Look, Soren…" Jira rubbed her temples as if she had a headache—as if Soren *was* the headache. "Your mind is trying to heal itself, okay? This, all this…this is what you've been missing for ten years. This is your childhood. Don't miss it by analyzing it to death, will you? You're always so busy looking for a threat that you miss the bigger picture."

"And you don't know when to stop keeping a secret."

Jira grinned so widely that her eyes crinkled at the corners. "Who says I know the truth of this one? I'm just a guide, dearest."

She blinked. "A guide."

"Well, more of a contingency. If you decide to let the goddess keep your body, I'm here to escort you out to the next world. Battlemate privileges."

Soren blinked. "If I *decide?*"

"I told you, this is a choice. A gift, too, but a choice all the same."

"A choice between what?"

Jira's eyes glimmered. "Between living or dying. Between fighting or losing."

"This isn't a *fight*, Jira! She's a goddess! I can't fight her, I can't..." All the strength went out of Soren's voice all at once, and she looked back to Soleil, some flimsy thread of memory tying their pain together, her stomach pulsing with the ache that had accosted her years ago. "There's nothing to fight for."

Elias was far away, safe beyond the borders of Atlas. And everyone else...they were better off if she vanished entirely, taking her memories and their secrets with her.

"Mmm." Disappointment weighed Jira's voice down from cheerful to disapproving. "Fine. Let's move on. You can't make a choice until you believe there's a choice to be made, can you?"

"Jira—"

But it was too late. The memory dissolved into darkness, and Soren could do nothing but follow its leading.

CHAPTER 28

ELIAS

Artemisian steel was notoriously finicky. Elias had forged with it only once, and had ruined the project so thoroughly he'd been too embarrassed to even let his mother see it. He'd never bothered to try again, because why risk wasting money and time on metal he couldn't work with? It was too expensive to allow for trial and error.

So of course, when he walked into the private forge he was borrowing for the trial, he found only Artemisian steel waiting. And not nearly enough of it for his comfort.

"I still don't get why she won't allow you any help," Kallias said as he walked in behind Elias, carrying an impressive amount of equipment in his arms. The Atlas man looked put out, but at least he wasn't sweating incessantly or about to pass out anymore. One more reek of rose-tinted sweat in Elias's nose would bring about another vomiting session faster than any nightmare.

"He's vying for a goddess's blessing," Raquel said as she came in after them, her arms crossed—it seemed she was letting Kallias do the heavy lifting this time around. "If he succeeds based off of another's help, he hasn't earned it."

"But if someone could at least—"

"Kallias," Elias interrupted, already tired of other people's voices, "it's fine. What're you going to do in a forge, anyway? Do you know how to heat steel? How to avoid cracks and warps? Can you pick up a knife and show me where the *tang* is?"

Kallias lowered the materials to the floor before folding his arms, hurt and determination battling for dominance in his eyes. The lack of power still dogged him, Elias could tell; a man used to authority didn't let go of it easily, and though Kallias had only been First Prince and not Heir, it was still a loss. "Fine. So you have to do it alone. That doesn't mean you have to *be* alone while you do it."

A piece of the mire coating his heart flaked off, something softening along the edge. But he steeled himself against it. "I *want* to be alone."

Kallias's arms dropped to his sides. "Fine." As he turned and skirted around Raquel, he tossed over his shoulder, "The tang is the part that connects to the handle."

Guilt settled in the bottom of his stomach, weighing it down. But he didn't call Kallias back—couldn't. His name snagged against the teeth of the beast curled in Elias's chest.

Raquel gave him a long, long look.

"Don't start," he warned. "You should be happy. You didn't want me keeping Atlas company anyway."

A soft snort. "I wasn't going to say anything."

"Mm."

"Elias." When he didn't say anything, focusing on sorting through the tools in front of him, she came forward and put a hand over his, halting his work. "There's nothing wrong with needing time to learn how to stand alone."

Her words scraped another piece of that miasma away from his heart, and a bit of pain leaked through, tainting the numbness that had become his shield. He clenched his fist beneath her hand, his sore knuckles protesting against the rasp of her palm. "How have you been since Lily?"

Her hand tensed over his before pulling away. "So you did hear."

"I had my ear to the ground in Atlas as much as possible. It buzzed with her name for a week or two after you all took back Delphin." Along with accusations of their newfound princess feeding Atlas knowledge back to the kingdom that raised her. "I'm so sorry."

Raquel's breath escaped in a trembling sigh, but her voice came out strong, held up with beams built of dark satisfaction: "Good. Maybe he'll remember *her* name, at least."

"Raquel, he's not—" Elias caught himself before he could slide too far down that slope, biting down hard on his tongue.

What was he doing? Kallias didn't need him to defend his honor, and he didn't really deserve it, anyway. Raquel was right; Kallias had put a blade in Jira's back, breaking Raquel's heart and nearly ruining Soren. He was the one who'd dragged Soren back to Atlas. If he'd just left her on that battlefield…

And whose fault is it that she went after him alone? whispered a voice that sounded like all his harshest thoughts, all his darkest moments. A flood of memories poured in after it—a snowy battlefield, prayer beads wrapped around his knuckles, bloodied red hair, and dying green eyes gazing at him with a softness that scared him. Desperate pleas and a sprint for help and torn armor found empty. *Who was too busy praying to his goddess to realize that she'd left?*

He swallowed hard, squeezing his eyes shut against those images, a nightmare he'd had the misfortune of living through.

No. He couldn't blame Kallias for Soren's fate. If it had been one of *his* siblings lost in the ranks of Atlas…gods, he would've torn the world apart to bring them home. Besides, Kallias had believed Elias when he'd made his claims about Vaughn and Jericho. He'd saved him from a certain execution in the belly of Atlas's dungeon. And he'd put aside the crimes Ravenna had committed to give Nyx a fighting chance to survive this war. He'd turned traitor against his own people for Elias's. For Soren's.

"Raquel," he croaked, "I'm not asking you to forgive him. But try to remember that he's betrayed his people to help ours."

Raquel's jaw ticked dangerously. "Are you suggesting that makes up for—?"

"No. Of course not. I know what he did then. I'm just asking you to give consideration to what he's doing *now*."

Raquel dragged a hand through her hair, fingers snagging in her tight plait. She was quiet for a beat, then: "You keep asking me for favors, Loch. I can only give you so many."

A sigh escaped before he could catch it. "I know."

He turned away, back to his equipment, tracing his fingers over well-loved tools and sleek new steel. The feel of them filled him to the brim with homesickness. What he wouldn't give to have his mother and siblings here. What he wouldn't give for...

"Did you tell her?" Raquel's voice was so hushed he almost didn't catch it over the crackle of flame in the forge. "Before she died, did you tell her?"

That shield split away from his heart with an audible tear, and Elias had no time to brace himself before white-hot agony ripped away all rhyme and reason.

Worse than a blade tracing deadly patterns in his gut. Worse than unholy magic rending his spine in two. Worse than...

I was going to ask you to marry me.

I would've said yes.

He couldn't breathe. He couldn't *breathe.*

The ring was in his hand before he knew it, the jewels digging so sharply into his palm that warm blood bubbled in the creases of his skin, the only outward sign of his suffering the awful catch of breath in his throat.

No weeping. No weeping.

"Yes." The voice that came out didn't belong to him. It belonged to the beast, the creature of ruin and rage that made its home between his ribs. "I did."

"What did she say?"

I would have said yes.

You kept your vows. Now let me keep mine.

"It doesn't matter." It *couldn't* matter. "I have to get to work."

Raquel's boots tapped lightly against the floor, but she lingered—he felt her eyes burning between his shoulder blades, threatening to brand him a second time with her stare. Then, without so much as a goodbye, the door clicked gently into place.

He forced his hand open, flexing his fingers, watching blood leak from the jagged divot left behind by the gem of the ring. He swallowed past a sandpaper tongue, the last vestiges of anguish draining away as he braced himself against the wall, dragging in a deep breath.

"Soren," he whispered into the stone, his hot breath warming his own face. "I don't know if you can hear me, but—"

"She can't."

Adrenaline rammed through his veins, chilling whatever remained of that fiery pain. His breath caught like he'd been caught in a sin, his heart hesitating before tentatively stepping into its next beat. He didn't turn. "I did what you asked."

"Almost." Cold fingers tapped his branding, and the heat that had been dogging him all day suddenly dissipated. In its place spread a tingling cold, a numbness not unlike the one wrapped around his chest. "You came to Artem, yes. You agreed to take on my trials. Yet I seem to recall warning you not to continue wasting your potential."

He blinked. "I've barely begun to—"

"And yet you've already lost." Those fingers dropped away from his back, but the cold continued to climb, sinking beneath his skin to trail up his spine. Goosebumps rose on his arms, and he tried not to shiver as she continued, "This trial requires more than knowledge. It requires commitment. It requires passion. It requires *faith*. None of which I see in you now."

"I've lived my whole life by faith," he rasped. "And in the end, it earned me nothing."

"It earned you time when you were ill." The softest brush of slipper against stone. "It earned you a second chance to live your life."

"I didn't ask for that."

"You did. More than once."

Now he twisted around, jaw clenching against an onslaught of words he still couldn't bring himself to throw at her. Mortem stood before him with her plain black dress and death-dark eyes, her head held high, her lips pinched in displeasure. Sparks scuttled along her shoulders and tumbled down her arms, gathering in bracelet-like rings around her wrists.

A month ago, he would have been on his knees. Pits, a couple *days* ago he would have thrown himself at her feet and hidden his face until she gave him permission to stand, just like he did in that tavern.

Not today. Today, he was tired. Today, he was griefsick.

Today, he was *angry*.

"I never wanted it at the cost of her," he snarled. "You *know* that."

She cocked her head like a curious bird. "She paid the price to bring you back. Would you have had me deny her?"

"*Yes*." Anger tasted like ash. Like soot staining his teeth. Like the flames of the forge had caught and spread in his gut, a bonfire smoking out every part of him that remembered reverence. Every part of him that would have cowered beneath the glare of a goddess.

She could do no worse to him than he had already endured. There was no suffering that could compare to this.

He used to be battlemate, believer, brave. Now he was nothing but dust carried along by Soren's last breath, trying to fulfill a promise he hadn't managed to make to her while she was living.

Mortem watched him for a long, long time. So long that the sparks ringing her wrists began to flare into proper flame. "Elias," she said, and the gentleness in her tone caused his ire to falter, "I did not take her from you."

His fists clenched so hard that his nails broke through the skin. "Do you remember what I promised you when we were on that battlefield in Ursa? Were you listening?"

"I always listen to the prayers of my people."

"*You will have whatever you ask of me, but not her.* If you'd just saved her, I would have given you *everything.* Now she's gone, and you still expect me to fulfill my end of a deal you didn't see through?"

"You forget that your prayer was answered that day. She lived through that injury."

"Because Kallias brought her to medimancers."

"Because *I* held her death at bay long enough for him to make it." Mortem came closer, hands folded demurely in front of her, but there was a bite to her voice that burned. Her hair floated back, strands lifting as if stirred by a sourceless breeze, ink bleeding into air. "Her insides were spilling out of her. She was an inch from my realm when you left her behind. You know as well as I that she shouldn't have survived the journey back to her birth kingdom."

When you left her behind.

When he didn't answer, unable to untangle apology from accusation, she sighed softly. "Consider carefully who truly led your beloved to her fate. Until you acknowledge the truth of that, you will have no peace."

"*Soren* was my peace."

Mortem gave him a long, knowing look, a sadness to her smile that made his branding itch. "Faithlessness doesn't suit you."

A bitter laugh caught on his collarbones. "I am not faithless. I'm here, aren't I?"

"Believing in me and having *faith* in me are two different things." Before he could argue, she held up a hand, her smile hardening. The shadows at the edges of the room seeped down the walls, blunting the edges of the forge-light, a dimness reminiscent of death. "My patience has limits, Elias Loch."

Righteous anger and stupidity were two different things, too, and Elias was only in possession of one. He shut his mouth.

"Remember," she said, "fire is not kind. It purifies, yes, but the purging is never painless. It will scorch away all that is false. Make sure that the truth of you can stand the test of flame."

The shadows thickened all at once, smothering the room in darkness, drowning out even the glow of the forge. And when Elias blinked away that darkness, lungs gasping in a reassuring breath against the *thud-thud-thud* of his heart, he opened his eyes to find himself alone.

CHAPTER 29

FINN

"Come on. We don't have much time."

He tossed a cloak at Fidget as he walked past her in the opposite direction—her heading for the guest dining room, him heading for the kitchens. She caught it with an audible splutter, and he kept walking, smirking to himself as mild cursing and hurried footsteps followed. "Where are we going?"

"Out."

"We're supposed to be at dinner!"

"I just ate with my parents, who think Esha preferred to dine alone this evening, and your queen thinks I'm in bed with a truly abominable stomach bug— not appropriate to speak of in pleasant company, if you catch my meaning."

"Ew." Her short strides finally brought her to his side, one of his steps covering the same ground as two of hers. "I could've done without knowing that."

"Rule number one while working with me, Fidget: always have an alibi, and always keep your story straight with your partner."

She grinned. "Partner?"

"Colleague," he amended.

She didn't stop grinning. "So what am I doing in this alibi, then, partner?"

Great. He'd started something. "Playing nursemaid for me, naturally."

"Ha-ha. No, seriously, what am I going to tell Queen Esha?"

"That's up to you. I don't know your life." And he was doing her a favor, not the other way around. He wasn't going to do *all* the work here. "We have a problem. The mirror's not in the palace."

He sensed more than saw Fidget's grin twist downward. The corner of the cloak he'd handed her flickered in his periphery as she swept it around her shoulders, covering her sparkling ensemble—pink today—in a quick swoop. To his surprise, she pulled out his scarf from gods-knew-where, looping it around her head and tying it beneath her chin like a kerchief, the yarn hiding the bits of sparkle in her hair. After that, she plucked a kohl pencil from her pocket and quickly but precisely ran it across her lower eyelid, then licked a finger and smudged it until it looked like she'd been wearing it for hours.

"We knew that," she said impatiently, completing her transformation with a few curls tugged haphazardly from beneath the scarf. She no longer looked like a Queen's handmaiden; instead, she looked like an ordinary city girl, potentially walking home from a long shift at a shop or tavern. "That's why I need your help."

Impressive. What exactly did these Mirrors have to do for their queen in Lapis? Were some of them spies as well as bodyguards?

"No," he corrected her, quickly flipping up his own hood and adjusting his walk to be slower, more tired, matching her look rather than asking her to imitate his; he knew better than to expect that much of someone. "We knew it was missing from your queen's quarters, but the thief is inside the palace. I thought the mirror would be too."

"How do you know they're in the palace?"

"You had to go through our checkpoints when you arrived, yes?" After her nod of confirmation, Finn continued, "Atlas's palace is the most secure in all the kingdoms. No thief could get in and out without losing their head."

Just a particularly determined Nyxian spy. But he knew exactly how Elias had managed to get into the palace without getting caught, and he knew it had nothing to do with his skill—something the man himself likely wasn't aware of.

Fidget slipped in front of him as they entered the kitchens, apparently remembering which door to take from their encounter the other night. Finn nodded to the head chef and flipped him a coin—then, after consideration and a glance at the Mirror in his company, flipped him a second one. He couldn't be too careful.

"Well then," Fidget said, crossing the threshold with a cheerful skip and a spin to face Finn, that cheeky grin already back in place, "we'll just have to figure out how to track down a ghost."

He narrowed his eyes at her as he shut the door behind him with a swift tug, forcing patience to hold condescension back. "A ghost?"

"Sure. Who else could slip past your guard so easily?"

A goddess, maybe, he thought, but instead he said, "You make a good point."

Too many thoughts going unspoken these days. His tongue was starting to scar from all the biting it had endured lately.

Just a bit longer. It'd been long enough that Kallias must have reached and subsequently left Nyx; the news of Anima's infiltration and Jericho's treachery must have made it to someone who could help by now. His brother may have given up his crown, but he knew Kallias better than that. Atlas was his only true love in this world. He'd come back—he *would* come back, and hopefully he'd have an army behind him when he did. Or at least someone who knew how to wrest a goddess back into whatever ether she'd crawled out of. He couldn't do another ten years of kneeling by a grave with no body.

This would all be over soon. Finn just had to keep the game going until Kallias gave them the tools to end it.

Casing the streets with a shimmering, sugar-addicted girl whose idea of espionage seemed to include *skipping* likely wasn't what Kallias had in mind when he'd asked Finn to hold Atlas together while he was gone. But then, Kallias had given that order without having any idea that Finn had been doing that very thing for most of his life. He'd been claiming these streets as his nearly as long as Kallias had been conquering battlefields, both of them generals in their own right. Finn's army just happened to be more...scattered. And as of tonight, a bit more sparkly.

"So what's our next move?" Fidget asked, trading skipping for tiptoeing, delicately picking her way through the streets without touching a toe on the gaps between the cobblestones. Completely contrary to her shy, bubbly demeanor, her body moved with sinuous grace, a dancer's form hidden beneath her ducked head and bashful mumbling. The lights of the ballroom her first night here had shrunk her to nearly nothing, but she seemed to come alive in alley shadows.

Unexpected. But not unwelcome, especially not with the business they had to carry out tonight.

"We're going to meet a friend of mine," he said. "If anyone's going to have an idea of where to find something of Occassio's, she will."

"A friend?"

He sighed. "Colleague."

"Of course." She suddenly careened to the side, bumping him with her hip, and his foot caught on a cobblestone as he stumbled sideways.

He blinked at her incredulously, brushing off his cloak. "What was *that* for?"

She bounced on her heels, looking for all the world like she was seconds away from launching into a cartwheel. Where did she keep all this *energy*? "Trying to get you to *lighten up*. There's nothing wrong with having friends, you know."

"Oh, yes, because you have so many."

That earned him another one of her now-familiar pouts. "I have lots of friends!"

"Name three."

Fidget hesitated, worrying her lip, the night-blooming flower drooping a bit beneath his scrutiny. "Um…well…there's, ah…we're not supposed to say our names, remember?"

"You don't know anyone other than the other Mirrors and Daggers?"

That pout had dipped into something much sadder. She cleared her throat, looking away. "It's…not really a job that's conducive to friends."

A feeling touched his heart that almost felt like pity. Almost.

"Neither is being First Prince." He wielded his smile like a lockpick, flashing it at her as they turned down the next alley. "This way, partner."

He could practically hear the click of tumblers moving into place as the sadness lifted from her face, her dimpled grin shaken loose by his manipulations. She followed him, her steps taking on the occasional skip once again. "What's your favorite thing about Atlas?"

So much for being shy. "The scenery. Walking along the beach and nearly stepping on a dead jellyfish? Nothing like it."

She scowled. "Be *serious*."

A dramatic gag. "Oh, gods forbid. If you ever spot me being serious, I want you to wield that diplomatic immunity of yours and kill me where I stand."

She blinked. "I have that?"

He stabbed a warning finger her way. "Whoa, now. You just got way too excited about that. I expect you to use that information responsibly."

She nodded solemnly. "Mercy killings only. Cross my heart."

He almost—*almost*—chuckled again. Who would've guessed a Mirror had a sense of humor? "Deal."

Fidget's hand smacked into his chest, fingers splayed. She twirled to face him, eyebrows raised expectantly.

He raised his eyebrows back, not sure what she was waiting for. "What?"

"In my kingdom, we seal deals with handshakes."

"They do that in every kingdom, you know." But he reached for her hand, fingers outstretched—

She tugged her hand away, sighing, her frustrated breath stirring the curls cloistered along her forehead. "No, no, not like *that*. It's got to be different for every deal. Don't you know anything?"

"I didn't exactly get a lot of time to study your customs, Fidget." Plus, he was almost entirely sure she was making this up as she went.

"Here. Make a fist." Once he obeyed, she did the same, then bumped the top of his fist with the bottom of her own. "Okay, now trade places."

Intrigued, he did as she asked, his hand switching places with hers as he tapped the top of her fist. She then gripped his knuckles and turned his fist sideways, gesturing for him to hold his hand in place, a look of utter concentration on her face before she lightly bumped knuckles with him. Slowly, still not entirely certain she wasn't messing with him, he bumped her knuckles back.

And gods, he might as well have handed her the moon set in a golden ring. Her entire face lit with nose-crinkling joy, her lip curling back to show off the gap between her teeth. "Perfect! Now it's a promise."

He gave her a long, long look, slowly pulling his hand back. "You're a very strange girl, you know that?"

"Better strange than boring, don't you think?"

And oddly enough, he did.

It took an hour to reach Luisa's—between Fidget's weird avoidance of the cracks in the street and his intentional wrong turns to throw her off the correct path, they made terrible time—but eventually they came upon the tucked-away shop. Fidget's laughing questions halted in their tracks, as did her bare feet, her toes digging into the alley floor as she cocked her head at the wall—staring directly at the place where Luisa's true sign was hidden.

"Your seers have to hide here?" she asked, her voice much quieter than before. Unnerved, maybe. Her ankle rotated a bit as she stared at the wall.

"They don't have to. Most don't. But Luisa likes her privacy. She doesn't normally take clients here. You have to know someone in her confidence to be invited to a private session."

"And you know someone?"

He smirked. "Better. I'm the someone you have to know."

A breathy laugh, and she fell back on her heels, shaking her head. "So Occassio told the truth about that, at least."

"About what?"

"You hold more power than you pretend to. It's strange."

"No stranger than a girl who uses handshakes to seal her secrets."

Fidget smiled a bit, but it dug into her dimples strangely, like a frown wearing a cheap festival costume. "Most people pretend to have more power than they have. Not many men care to be looked down upon."

"I'm not many men. I'm just one." He walked to the door, fist already up to knock. "And in my experience, one man does better work without an audience."

Fidget's impressed *hmm* was drowned out by another voice, louder, annoyed: "Finnick Atlas, what are you doing bringing strangers to my shop?"

He turned a heartbeat before Fidget did; she took a step back as he took a step forward, placing them side by side as he casually crossed his arms. "What are *you* doing using my full name out in the open?"

Luisa stood a few feet back, cloak thrown back to reveal her cloud of sleek ebony curls, her deep blue gown nearly black in what little moonlight managed to spill into the alley. She opened her mouth—to scold him further, presumably— but then she took in the full measure of Fidget, and her scowl dropped away in an instant. All composure drained from her face as she pressed her arms to her chest, shielding the mirrors on her wrists from view. "You're a—"

"An ally," Finn interrupted quickly. "Can we talk in the shop?"

Luisa's eyes were absolutely glued to Fidget, her throat bobbing like a fishing lure. "Finn," she said breathlessly, but Fidget stepped forward with her hands up, an anxious tilt to her head.

"It's okay! I'm a seer too. I'm a Mirror, see?" She batted aside her cloak and flashed the mirrors on her wrists and neck. "I'm from Lapis."

"That's why she's spooked," Finn mumbled out of the corner of his mouth.

Fidget's reassuring smile faltered. "What?"

Luisa watched her carefully, her hands slowly lowering back to her sides, though her fingers stayed clenched in fists. She dipped her head, never taking her eyes off of Fidget. "You're…new."

"Yes."

"Is Ruby still your facet leader?"

Fidget gasped with far more excitement than the situation required—or even allowed for, really. "You know her?"

A bitter laugh from Luisa. "I did, once."

"Why does she have a name?" Finn demanded, and Luisa shot him a disparaging look.

"That's not her real name. It's just what we called her."

He looked to Fidget. "And you don't have one because…?"

"I have one," she said defensively. "But it's only for use among other—"

"Forget it." He turned his attention to Luisa, trying not to frown as he took in her shaken demeanor, one of her hands now wrapped around the strap of her leather satchel like she thought Fidget might snatch it away. Or like she was preparing to run. "Lu. She's only here for your help, you hear me?"

"If she tells her queen—"

"She won't." Finn caught Fidget's gaze. It was difficult to deliver a threat with only the eyes, but he'd been doing it long enough now. The furrow he dug into his brow promised a ruin of some kind if she gave up Luisa to Queen Esha. Good allies were few and far between these days, especially for him, and he couldn't lose his seer friend to her former kingdom's dungeons if they chose to punish her for deserting.

He'd known about Luisa's past for some time now—had caught her once on a bad night, huddled in her shop with a pipe full of sweet-smelling herbs and a shimmering, near-invisible wall thrown up between her desk and the rest of the shop. It was the first and only time he'd seen her use her other talent, her auramancy—a magic of manifestations very few Occassio-worshippers were blessed with. Illusions, mainly, but more powerful wielders could project physical things into the world…often protective things like shields, from what Luisa had told him.

She'd once been a Mirror herself, she'd told him that night as she took in several long draws of her pipe. She'd fled when the late queen and king had been killed and Esha's traitorous minister had seized control, and she'd never looked back. That night, she'd seen a vision of Esha's crowning and the impending coup attempt in her birth kingdom. It had taken hours for him to convince her that going back was no good, not to her or the young queen, no matter how loyal Luisa had been to the late Queen Lyria.

"I won't tell anyone you're here," Fidget agreed, tracing a finger over her chest. "Cross my heart."

Luisa stood silent for a moment, looking like there was nothing she wanted more in the world than to melt into the alley shadows and never be seen again. Finally, the hard line of her shoulders eased a bit. "All right. Get inside, quickly."

Luisa slipped inside with a swoop of her cloak. Before Finn could follow, a quick tug yanked on the back of his cloak, halting him with one foot over the threshold. He looked over his shoulder at Fidget, whose hands were both clutching his cloak with pale knuckles, nerves shaking her body slightly. "What's the plan?" she whispered.

Patience, he reminded himself as annoyance sparked in his fingertips. He gently extricated his cloak from her grip, letting his hands linger on hers just long enough for her to glance down, for her eyes to unfocus a bit, shyness softening her fear.

Gods, he was brilliant at this. He needed to give himself more credit.

"Listen carefully," he said with impeccable seriousness, and she leaned in, eyes widening a bit. She was so close that he could see tiny flecks of brownish-gold buried in the dark pools of her gaze. He spread his fingers, enunciating carefully as he counted off each one. "We go inside. We sit down. You say nothing. I say a lot, and you act like I'm the cleverest person you've ever met. Laugh at every joke, even if it's not funny, as if that's possible—don't look at me like that, will you? I'm hilarious. Now, are you listening? This is important. If I say the word *blobfish*—"

Her lips formed that pretty pout she so liked to wear. "You're making fun of me."

"Oh, absolutely, yeah."

A squeaky noise of frustration came out of her before she ducked past him, bumping his elbow with her shoulder. She probably meant for it to hurt; instead, she may as well have tickled him with a feather for all the impact it offered. He chuckled under his breath before following her in, shutting the door behind them.

Luisa's shop was one of his favorite places. The air hung heavy with magic and herbs, an effervescent bundle of smells latching onto the insides of his nose as he took in his first deep breath of the night.

Magic. He'd never known the name for what wove itself through the air of Luisa's abode, the thing that gave the shop a sense of selfhood, a certain presence that always lurked over his shoulder. But now, with Occassio's claws dug into his mind and her lurid daydreams thrusting his mind into a future he didn't want to see, he knew exactly what it was that gripped him by the back of the neck with an invisible hand and coaxed the hairs on his nape to stand tall.

At least the crystal ball on Luisa's desk—a very *expensive* piece he'd replaced after his newfound magic had shattered the old one—was covered with a violet suede cloth, and no other reflective surfaces were visible in his eyeline.

Fidget slipped off her cloak, revealing her sparkling pink tunic once more. The skirt slashed across her body asymmetrically, cut high on her hip on one side and reaching past her knee on the other. Her leggings were pearlescent white, and she wore clear crystal shoes once more; seemed she hadn't shattered her only pair, then.

Luisa eyed her outfit with no lack of envy. "Gods, I miss Lapisian fashion."

Fidget's smile came and went faster than Finn could blink. She cleared her throat, standing before Luisa's desk with her hands clasped behind her back. "Finn seems to think you can help us."

Luisa arched one eyebrow at him, mouthing, *Finn?*

He shrugged one shoulder, mouthing back, *Familiarity breeds trust.*

Luisa narrowed her eyes, but a quick one-two blink told him she understood. "Help you with what?"

He fell into the chair across from Luisa's, shooting Fidget a warning look, his best reminder that he'd told her to let him do the talking. Luisa held more of his trust than most, but that was still only a paltry bit. This needed to be handled delicately. "Something's gone missing from Queen Esha's quarters. Stolen. I don't suppose you've heard any whispers about people who can pull off jobs within the palace?"

Luisa snorted. "That is a *very* short list, Finn."

"Fabulous. Then it shouldn't be difficult for you to remember." She extended her hand. He groaned. "Come on, Lu—"

"I think better with gold in my hand, sir, and you know that. You brought plenty with you—ah! Don't start," she added when he opened his mouth again, empty hands splayed in innocence. "You can't lie to a seer, Prince. Gods, it's like you don't even know me anymore."

Scowling, he dug around in his pocket with a string of muttered curses before plopping a depressingly heavy coin bag into her palm. "There, you greedy goose. Will that do?"

"Call me a *goose* again, and the price goes up next time." But Luisa tucked the coins away with a mollified look. She folded her hands on her desk, her gaze occasionally wandering to Fidget, who looked thoroughly uncomfortable with standing still. Her shoes were scraping unpleasantly against the wooden floor, her hands fussing with her skirt, her eyes darting anywhere but to Luisa's. After a moment, Luisa leaned back, finally meeting Finn's gaze. "It really is a short list. Only two names come to mind: Colin Rath and Briar Holbrook."

"Holbrook's been out of the game since before I started running," Finn protested. "She's got a family. Five kids and a husband."

"You didn't ask if they were still operating, you asked who could pull it off. I told you. Colin's got the skills, but Briar's got the connections. She worked at the palace her first few years out of the Academy."

He knew that already. Briar had been in Jericho's class at Ivycreek Academy, the institute where medimancers were trained in the craft of healing the human body. If Jericho and Anima were behind this theft, Briar was likely the one Jericho would have gone to first. From what he knew of Colin, he was hard to find and even harder to hire. He was barely older than Finn, but his particular skill set earned him quite a high starting pay for any job he was brought on for. Finn had only hired him once, and the cost he'd demanded…exorbitant wasn't the word. It made Luisa's continuously rising prices look like pocket change.

He blew out a breath. "I really don't want to interrogate a mother of five."

"Nobody said you had to."

"If she's the one who lifted it, she's the one who knows where to find it."

"It's not likely she's going to hold on to it," Fidget interjected; her fingers were now thoroughly tangled in her skirt, but she looked more focused than before. "We might be better off staking out places where people are selling goods. Every city has a black market buried in it somewhere. We just have to find Atlas's."

Luisa chuckled. "If it's black market you're looking for—"

"I know where to go," Finn interrupted. "In the meantime, Lu, can you do me a favor? A *paid* one," he cut her off with a groan as she opened her hand again. "Occassio's diamond toenails, you're lucky I can afford you." Both women made noises of protest at his disrespectful curse, but he made a louder noise of protest to drown them out, waving his hands to silence them. "Fine, fine! I get it. No more Occassio-themed curses. I *get it*. Gods above and *below*, you two. Fidget, give us a moment, will you?"

240

Once Fidget had left and Luisa's hand was heavy with yet another pile of gold, she listened carefully to his request. And when he was done, she let out a long, slow sigh. "Too many games, Prince. I keep telling you."

"I'll stop playing when I stop winning." He stood, leaning across the desk to give her a quick kiss on the forehead before he scooped his cloak off the back of his seat, slipping it back around his shoulders. "Stay safe."

"I'd tell you the same, but there's no point," sighed Luisa.

He cracked his best trickster smile, relieved that his mouth sank into the familiar notches with ease again. Being out of the palace was good for him, it seemed. "Safe doesn't get the job done."

"Finn," Luisa called just as his hand touched her doorknob. She had her eyes on her covered crystal ball, but he could sense her attention was fully trained on him. "Be cautious of Esha…and her Mirrors. They're not like your usual marks. They're trained to withstand your kind of work."

"This one's new."

"Still. Don't get cocky."

"Far too late for that, I'm afraid." He blew her another kiss before opening the door, stepping out with one last promise thrown over his shoulder: "I'll see you soon."

He thought she muttered something else as he shut the door. But the thud of the door drowned out whatever it might have been, and something told him he didn't really care to hear it, anyway.

CHAPTER 30

KALLIAS

Midnight came just in time.

Raquel had just returned to the room with a plate of leftover food and a slightly more pleasant attitude—pleasant in that she merely grunted in greeting rather than throwing an insult at him—when the clock struck the hour he'd been waiting for. He muttered something about going to check on Elias as he passed her, his sleeve brushing hers. She smelled like the inside of a tavern, smokey and laced with the bite of liquor, but her gaze was stone-cold sober as it followed him out. Even when he closed the door, he couldn't quite shake the sensation of watching eyes.

Barely a minute passed before a casual whistle echoed down the corridor. He looked up to find Zaccheus waiting at the bend, leaning against the stone wall, watching him with a surprised grin.

"That's a good chunk of coin I just lost to my wife," Zaccheus sighed as Kallias approached, glancing over his shoulder to make sure Raquel hadn't peeked out after him. "I didn't think you'd come."

"I didn't either," Kallias admitted with a forced laugh. It ground uncomfortably against his throat, and he swallowed to smooth it out. He'd debated the benefits and detriments to accepting Zaccheus's invitation all day…he'd even considered telling Elias about it and requesting his counsel. But the Nyxian man had made it very clear in the forge that he didn't much care what Kallias did.

Still, he guessed Elias wouldn't have a favorable opinion toward taking this risk. But if Idris wasn't taking audiences, perhaps he could seek them elsewhere.

"I hope you're hungry," Zaccheus said as he led Kallias back down the corridor. He'd changed out of his uniform, the sleeves of his forest-green linen shirt rolled up to reveal even more burn scars, tendrils of ruined flesh wrapping around his forearms and disappearing beneath the sleeves. "Mal goes a bit nuts when we entertain."

"Starving," Kallias admitted. Every kind of craving seemed to have sharpened since his nightmare in Nyx—thirst and hunger alike.

"Good. We'll get that fixed."

Zaccheus led him back to the bottom level of the mountain-city and into the same residential district they'd visited earlier in the day. Somehow, it was more beautiful at night—glass lamps dancing with sourceless flame hung by every doorway, streetlamps lit the same way lining the path between the rows of houses, casting a golden glow over the darkened streets. There were chips of something reflective buried in the path's paving, making it look as if they walked over living embers.

Beautiful as it was, it still stirred nausea in the pit of his stomach. He wasn't sure he'd ever stop wanting to run from the sight of fire.

Zaccheus picked up his pace as they neared the end of the row, jumping up to the porch of one of the stone houses. It wrapped around the entire construct, crafted from beautifully engraved metal, and a dark shape was huddled on the rug in front of the door. At Zaccheus's approach, the bundle of black scales sprang up from its sleep, pouncing toward him with a strange warbling sound.

"Watch out!" Kallias cried, but Zaccheus only laughed, catching the creature's collar in one hand and stretching to open the door with the other. Light flooded the porch, revealing an impossible sight: a creature that Kallias had only seen in storybooks, its body covered in obsidian scales, leathery wings folded tight against its back. Its pointed ears were strangely mobile, swiveling behind horn-like crests, its bright eyes filled with surprising intelligence as it greeted Zaccheus with a soft series of chirps.

"Sorry about Iggy. He's a bit excitable, but harmless to friends. Ignis! *Sit*, boy." Zaccheus raised his voice, though he still seemed perfectly at ease—a feat Kallias couldn't fathom considering what sat at his feet. "Mal! Come get your dragon!"

"*My* dragon? I'm sorry, but I seem to remember *you* being the one who brought home an—oh!" Esmeralda stopped at the door, her hands wrapped in a dishrag, face now void of cosmetics, hair braided neatly down her back. Her lips stretched into a smug grin. "So he did come!"

"Yeah, yeah," Zaccheus grumbled, finally pushing Ignis into the house, though the dragon—the *dragon*, somehow only grown to the size of a hound, his head barely reaching past Zaccheus's waist—still craned his head around his master, eyeing Kallias with an expression he could only describe as *eager*. "Come on in, Prince. Make yourself at home."

Kallias blinked, his feet still rooted to the porch. "That's a dragon."

Zaccheus blinked placidly back at him. "Yes."

"In your *house*."

Zaccheus frowned. "Do you not have dragons in Atlas?"

Kallias swallowed, his throat even drier than before, his voice barely squeaking out. "Decidedly not, no."

"Well, Iggy's a good first, trust me. Iggy! Say hello to our guest."

Before Kallias could protest, the dragon bounded back to him, rearing up and planting taloned paws on Kallias's chest. He flinched away as the dragon's maw opened, baring razor-sharp teeth—

A sandpaper tongue rasped over his bearded cheek.

Kallias forced himself to peek, finding marble-like eyes gazing back at him, the dragon's head cocked to one side in a way Vaughn would have likely found adorable. Vaughn had many pets growing up, cats and dogs and all sorts of other creatures, but Kallias had never really understood the appeal of sharing one's living space with an animal.

"Hello," he croaked.

The dragon chirruped as if in reply, licking him once more before dropping back to all fours and trotting to Esmeralda's side, brushing up against her legs and arching its back. Esmeralda scratched behind its ears, smirking at Kallias. "He likes you."

And he was incredibly glad to hear that.

"Come on in," Esmeralda added, stepping aside so he could come over the threshold. "Everyone else is already here."

"Thanks, love." Zaccheus caught her around the waist and pressed a casual kiss to her cheek as he moved past her, gesturing for Kallias to follow. Eyeing Ignis carefully, not quite trusting his gleaming teeth and innocent eyes, Kallias obeyed.

The house was spacious, but somehow still cozy; the foyer was warm, not uncomfortably so, and the hall led straight into an open living area. The floor was polished ebony wood, the walls painted a soothing shade of blue, and a white-and-black marble fireplace was built into the wall. Kallias braced himself to feel the punch of adrenaline that often came with the sight of flame, but to his surprise, this fire burned differently—the flames glimmered blue and green and white rather than red and gold. Like the driftwood bonfires they built on the beach in Atlas.

"Mal noticed you were set off a bit earlier and took a guess," Zaccheus said quietly, noticing where his attention went. "She struggles with fire too sometimes, so we keep some things on hand to change the color. I hope that's all right."

No one had taken such care on his behalf before. "Tell her thank you for me. Please."

"Of course."

A burst of laughter called Kallias's attention to the fact that they weren't alone. The furniture in the living area was packed full—an armchair that housed two men on either arm and a woman sitting cross-legged on the cushion, a couch that had at least four people piled on top of each other, limbs tangled as they wrestled for possession of a pillow, and several more sitting or sprawled on the gray and white patterned rug on the floor, chatting and joking and sipping from glasses of wine or mugs of what appeared to be coffee or tea.

"Can I get you anything?" Esmeralda's voice in his ear startled him, her hand catching his shoulder before he could spin around. "Sorry! Sorry. Didn't mean to startle you."

"You're fine…sorry. I'm out of sorts today." Today and every day since his city had been attacked by creatures formed from living bone.

"It's no problem. Anything to drink? Coffee? Wine or tea to settle your nerves?" Her eyes twinkled with teasing that had an edge of knowledge to it, eyes that saw more than he'd like. Or maybe it was her magic that recognized what he needed.

His tongue twisted to form the word *wine*, but he forced it to say, "Tea would be lovely."

"Coming right up." She patted his shoulder, squeezing it for a moment, and some of the tension there eased. His chest loosened a bit, and he pulled in a deep breath, unsure whether to be grateful for her help or wary of it. "Find a seat anywhere. Don't be afraid to push these animals around, either."

Noises of protest came from the assembly, and he almost smiled. Rather than taking Esmeralda up on her offer, he found an empty sliver of rug near the wall and folded himself into it, pressing his back against the wall and drawing his knees to his chest to make room. It wasn't the most comfortable position, but it kept him out of everyone's way—and allowed him to take in the whole room at once. He couldn't be sure yet that he was among friends. Exposing his back felt dangerous.

Barely a second passed before a surprisingly warm snout bumped against his leg, and he peered over his knees to see Ignis staring at him with those dark, expectant eyes.

"Hello," he rasped.

Ignis bumped him again, squeaking in a manner that almost sounded impatient.

Slowly, Kallias lowered his legs, crossing them instead. Ignis promptly wriggled into the gap between him and the fireplace, stretching out beside him and settling his head in Kallias's lap, his maw opening in a yawn that revealed his rows of truly terrifying serrated teeth.

Fear rooted him in place; any sudden move could draw those teeth to his flesh.

"Aw, does the little lizard want scritches?" cooed a new voice. A girl no older than sixteen scooted over to Kallias, her blonde hair reflecting the blue-tinted firelight as she scratched at the corner of Ignis's jaw.

The scaled creature started *purring*.

"It's okay, he won't hurt you. He can tell you're nervous, that's all." The girl smiled up at him. "I'm Ivory, but you can call me Rory. That's Vicor, and that's Farrah, and that's Erevis, and that's—"

Kallias really did try to keep up as Rory introduced each person by name, but even with them raising their hands when their names were called, he lost track after four or five of them. Luckily, before Rory could quiz him, Zaccheus came to stand at the front of the room, backlit by the fire. He clapped his hands with a sharp whistle, pulling all attention to him and hushing all conversation.

A man respected, and not just for his rank. They all looked to him with eyes that gleamed with fervent loyalty, every breath baited, waiting to hear what he had to say.

He knew that look. He used to be on the receiving end of it.

The next time his people's eyes sought him out, he guessed they wouldn't be so warm.

"Thank you all for coming," Zaccheus began. "You all might have noticed we have a guest tonight. Prince Kallias, thank you for agreeing to hear us out."

As Zaccheus spoke his name, he watched the color drain from Rory's face first, her shock reflected in each of her friends' faces. Kallias's heart skipped a beat, dodging a blow from fear as it tried to stop it entirely, and Ignis buried his face against Kallias's shirt, his scales growing warm with a gentle heat that rumbled out with his constant purr. Soothing, if odd.

Kallias cleared his throat, offering a nod of acknowledgment and nothing more. This was not his committee, and neither Zaccheus nor his people would take kindly to Kallias speaking out of turn.

While Zaccheus spoke with his people about some things Kallias didn't fully understand, something about storehouses and activity near their border with Tallis, Esmeralda crossed the room with silent grace, tiptoeing between crossed legs and propped elbows until she reached Kallias, handing him a mug of tea with a reassuring smile and a kind wink. Kallias closed his eyes and inhaled deeply, letting the fragrant steam soak his senses. He sipped at the tea, blinking in surprise at the explosion of herbal flavors that seeped into his tongue. Maybe everything in Artem tasted better than ordinary fare.

"Kallias." Zaccheus's raised voice brought Kallias's attention back to him. "As it stands, you're arranged to be married to Empress Idris within a month or so. From what we've discussed, I believe that arrangement isn't exactly to your liking?"

Kallias worked a muscle in his jaw, chewing on his words a bit while he thought them over. "I don't believe it to be in the best interest of my kingdom," he answered diplomatically.

"We agree on that front." Zaccheus looked down at his group, crossing his arms, tapping one of the scars stretching across his forearm. "Idris would see us returned to war for the sake of outdated religious zealotry. The involvement of necromancy—this perceived affront to Mortem's authority—is all that she required to change her stance on our neutrality. I have raised our concerns to General Star. I have reminded her—and through her, our Empress—that our land

and our people still bear the scars of our last holy war. I have asked them, begged them, to reconsider their stance. And here we are still." Zaccheus's gaze settled on Kallias. "I cannot pretend to understand why you would wish to strike down a hand of alliance offered to your people, but I understand the look in your eye, Prince. Whatever your reasons, you do this for your kingdom. So do we. I feel if we put our heads together, we can find the solution to our mutual problem."

That scornful tone scratched a nerve. "Have you something against faith, Zaccheus?"

"Nothing against faith. Only something against it being used to justify subjecting innocents to the horror of war." Zaccheus's eyes grew cold. "I didn't see Mortem fighting beside us on battlefields we stormed in her name. Only good people who didn't deserve an early death."

Kallias only vaguely remembered the conflict between Tallis and Artem; he'd barely passed a decade of life when it started, not yet interested in the events of kingdoms beyond their borders. But he knew from what little he had gleaned and from what lessons had been taught during his schooling afterward that the conflict had come about because of Tallis's desire to possess Mount Igniquit. The hulking mountain was the only one that didn't fall under their rule, but Artem had refused to negotiate a potential land trade or shifting of the border on the grounds that the mountain was considered a holy space belonging to Mortem. The godless Tallisians hadn't cared for that answer, and war followed after yet another border skirmish resulted in the death of King Denali's lover.

When his silence stretched on, Zaccheus turned back to his friends. "I know it's a risk to trust him," he said, as if Kallias wasn't there. "But this could be the chance we've waited for. We need to find a way to *delicately* dismantle this alliance. Now that he's here, Idris would need to officially deny the arrangement on her end." Zaccheus looked to him once more. "I assume your mother already completed her side of the treaty."

"It should be arriving in a couple weeks with the delegation your Empress sent to fetch me," Kallias agreed, careful to word it properly, conscious of Esmeralda's riveted attention. If she could sense a lie, then he needed to tiptoe around the truth.

It should be arriving—but it wouldn't. Not unless the delegation had suggested reworking the treaty to exclude marriage, and he honestly wasn't sure what else his mother could offer them.

"If it helps," Kallias ventured, "I believe I have something that will persuade her to end the arrangement. But for my kingdom's sake, I'm only able to share it with Idris herself."

Zaccheus narrowed his eyes thoughtfully. "Secrets don't make friends, Prince."

Kallias held his gaze. "And are you entirely without secrets, friend?"

Zaccheus's mouth twitched, and Kallias caught a chuckle from Esmeralda's direction. "Fair enough. So. You have an ace up your sleeve, but you can only win the game if Idris bothers to show up to play?"

"Yes."

"Isn't your friend going through these trials to earn you an audience?" Esmeralda asked with a frown.

"He is, but we have no idea how long these trials will go on," Kallias explained. "If they aren't over before my mother's treaty arrives, it may be too late to stop Idris from agreeing to it. I can't be sure she intends to meet with me before she does so."

Esmeralda found her husband's gaze, raising one eyebrow. "Then we need to find another way for you to get her attention."

Zaccheus smiled for the first time all evening, and in it, Kallias saw a scheme that could save or doom him. "Give us a day or two, Prince. I'll think of something. But first..." He turned back to his people. "All in favor of working with Prince Kallias?"

Hands went up around the room, though not all of them. Kallias took care to note which ones didn't raise a hand and which ones hesitated a beat too long before doing so, reading the reluctance in their eyes, the doubt on their faces.

This wasn't his brightest idea. It was a risk he didn't fully need to take. But he understood Zaccheus's fear—understood the anger that came with watching a ruler subject their people to unnecessary bloodshed.

He had yet to save his people. He would feel better if he could at least prove himself capable of saving someone else's.

"The yeas have it." Zaccheus turned back to him, that rare smile broadening. "Welcome to the Hearth-Keepers, Prince Kallias. We're happy to have you."

CHAPTER 31

FINN

D aytime was no friend of Finnick Atlas, but it was certainly a friend of Jaskier Lionett, and that was who strutted through the Port Atlas streets on this fine and fabulous morning with dark-dyed hair slicked to the skies and scarlet cape fluttering behind him. He stalked through the crowded upper city shopping district with a scowl fixed sharp and pretty on his face, heeled boots clicking on cobblestone, warning people out of his way with a haughty wave and a warpath walk.

Hidden deep beneath the guise of Jaskier, Finnick Atlas plotted in the shadows.

He'd spent another awkward breakfast with Esha this morning, trying and failing to get something—*anything*—useful out of the Mirror Queen. But even his ridiculous questions hadn't coaxed a sliver of truth out of her mouth, and he was running out of locks to try and pick. He'd known that she didn't trust easily—how could she, as a young queen ruling a kingdom torn in two?—but he normally could break even the most complicated of codes if given enough time.

His birthday was still a long way off. He still had time. But he'd hoped to put an end to this game far earlier than that, and she was testing even his well-practiced patience.

At least Fidget was a safe easily opened. One properly placed *partner* and a sultry smile was all it took to pop that lock. She'd proven herself clever and capable, but luckily for him, naivete could still exist among traits that ordinarily warned it off.

He'd get what he needed from her soon. Today, he had a different game to play.

The shop he needed wasn't too far down from the Broken Conch, and when he reached the entrance beneath a bright red awning, he swung through the door with all proper gusto, flinging his arm out with a showman's flourish. "Where is my favorite tailoress?" he snapped impatiently, soaking his tone in familiarity he didn't dare hold with most shopkeepers and careful to paint the undercurrent of his words with the arrogance this character required.

A graying head poked around the side of a half-dressed cloth mannequin, her neatly-wrinkled face lighting up at the sight of him. She pinned the garish garment to the side of the mannequin with the artful stab of a pin, clapping her talented hands before flinging her arms open as she approached. "Jaskier Lionett, light of my life! Where have you *been*, gorgeous?"

"Francesca Serna!" He greeted her with a kiss to each cheek, and she reciprocated before ushering him further into the shop. The smell of fresh linen and overpowering blackberry perfume wafted from her, a scent that reminded him of his late Amma Cordelia. "Where have *I* been? Where have *you* been? I feared you dead in those dreadful attacks, your shop's been closed so long!"

Francesca shuddered, but even that loss of composure betrayed a certain poise to her. The best tailoress in Port Atlas had come by that title honestly; every inch of her was in stern possession of style, from her coiffed silver hair to her matching silk suit. Even the wrinkles of her face seemed to be pressed just so, accentuating her features rather than drawing away from them. She plucked her tiny glasses off of her nose and polished them with a soft cloth for a moment before placing them back on her face, her beady blue eyes focusing on him with grave purpose. "Let's not dirty this day with talk of such things, shall we? I'm alive, you're alive, we're both still beautiful, what more is there to talk about? Come, come, tell me something new! *Fiona, Selena!* We have a guest, my loves!"

Francesca's assistants bustled out from the back room, letting out squeals of delight when their gazes found him. Selena was a pale-skinned, dark-haired woman, which often set her on the receiving end of Finn's best vampyre jests, all of which she bore with good-natured humor. In contrast, Fiona was a sculpture cast in gold, her hair, skin, and eyes all glimmering like treasure hoarded in a chest.

"What gossip do you bring today, Lord Lionett?" Selena asked, her amused voice revealing only a hint of true interest. If he needed a rumor spread, he could always count on the ladies of the Silken Siren to do the job.

"Well." Finn paused, counting a few beats until the girls leaned in a bit closer, feeding on their gazes burning with desperate curiosity. "You won't believe this, but it's true, every word. I swear it on my nan's grave, Anima bless her soul." Privately, he sent a silent apology to his Amma for sullying her so.

"Go on," Fiona urged, taking his cape when he offered it to her, Selena and Francesca already busy wrapping measuring tapes around his body. They had this routine down pat.

"Now, you didn't hear this from me," he warned, and all three women nodded in unison, "but you know that Prince Finnick is currently courting the Mirror Queen?"

"How could we not?" Selena snorted, letting the measuring tape recoil with a sharp *snap*. "The whole kingdom's abuzz."

He held his silence for a beat, enjoying the catch in their breathing as they hung on his next words. It was rare he had anyone quite so invested in what he had to say. "Well...I heard from a friend that his attention is straying. Rumor has it one of the Mirrors has caught his eye."

A chorus of gasps. "Which one?" Fiona demanded at the same time Francesca uttered a fervent prayer to Occassio for mercy, fanning herself with a free hand. Finn was just relieved she'd set down the pincushion beforehand.

"The little one in purple. Can't sit still, doesn't talk much, jewels in her curls?"

Fiona visibly deflated in disappointment. "I haven't seen her." She snatched up a sample of blue cloth and held it up to his skin before making a dismissive noise and tossing it aside, digging in her basket for a different shade. "I saw that emerald girl when I delivered some garments to my cousin, though. He's one of the palacefolk working in their wing. He says they're a terrifying lot. Polite, but terrifying."

"I've heard the same." He winced as a pin poked into his side, and Selena murmured an apology. "I've never heard of anyone turning his head before, have you?"

"No, never," Fiona said with breathless glee. "Oh, that's unbearably romantic. A forbidden love affair amidst an arranged marriage? He's living in a novel!"

"Hardly," Francesca chided. "This isn't a fairytale, dear. These things have consequences in the real world."

And that was exactly what he was counting on.

"The poor man," Selena murmured. "Can you even imagine?"

It took effort to keep from smirking. "Not at all. Poor sap. But enough of that...have you ladies heard anything about a sale going on?"

* * *

"We need to talk!"

He barely processed Fidget's panicky hiss before she tugged him into a supply closet, shoving the door shut behind her, effectively smothering them in darkness.

"I talk better in the light," he lied.

A frustrated growl from her, and an orb of pinkish light sputtered into existence between her palms, tracing her features in rose and quartz. She glowered at him, fury contorting her ordinarily sweet face. "What have you been telling people?"

He leaned back, tracing his fingers over his jaw, watching her while biting his lip on a grin. "You know, it's really hard to take you seriously with those little sparklies in your eyebrows."

"This isn't funny! Finn, Queen Esha asked me today what's *going on* between us!"

"What did you tell her?"

"What did *you* tell her?"

He put his hands up in mock surrender. "You've heard every word I've ever spoken to her, Fidg."

"If you start shortening *Fidget*, I'm going to murder you."

253

"With what? A pretty pink bubble? I'm shaking in my shoes." He poked at the illusion her auramancy had wrought, his finger sliding right through it.

She snatched her hands out of reach, her pout looking a bit more scowly than usual. "This isn't funny."

"You mentioned."

"Finn, she thinks you *like* me."

"I do like you! You're quite pleasant company when you aren't *yelling* at me." He made as if to snatch the orb, and this time it dissipated, dropping them back into darkness.

Fidget growled again, and he couldn't help thinking of that time he'd witnessed two stray kittens play-fighting in the street, their high-pitched mewls feeble attempts to practice threats. "She thinks you *like-like* me."

He had to pinch his lips together to hold back a laugh. "*Like-like* you? Gods, I thought I left that kind of talk behind in school."

Fidget groaned, and her foot stamped down on his; he thought about acting like it hurt to make her feel better, but he wasn't sure he wanted to encourage her. "You're being mean."

"I *am* mean. I thought we covered this."

"You have to tell her it's not like that."

"Oh, yeah, that'll make great breakfast conversation! *Good morning, Your Royal Stuffiness—*"

"Please don't call her that—"

"*—By the way, just wanted to let you know that I do not like your newest and purpliest Mirror, and I most certainly do not, as the young people say these days, like-like her—*"

"Okay!" Fidget groaned, clapping her hands to summon her orb back, that fancy bit of auramancy leaving him blinking against the brightness. He reached out to try and swat it out again, just to drive her a bit more crazy, but to his surprise, his palm smacked against something solid.

"Impressive," he said, while silently cursing his own stupidity. New or not, she'd been chosen as one of the most elite bodyguards in the kingdoms. Of course her magic went beyond simple illusions.

She averted her gaze. "It's not really."

"Sure it is. Illusions are one thing, but from what I've heard, you've got to be a powerful auramancer to make them real."

"And what do you know of auramancy?" Fidget pulled her orb away from his hand, hugging it tight against her chest.

Not nearly enough, that was for certain. "A fair bit."

"Hm." Fidget crossed her arms, and when she removed her hands from beneath the orb, it stayed put, hovering in the air with a gentle hum. "Prove it."

He blinked. "Prove it?"

She jerked her chin at him. "Go on. Show me what you know."

"I said I know about it, not that I can perform it!"

"You didn't have to." Fidget tapped the side of her right eye, and a shimmer of purple-pink light winked in that eye before blinking out again. "Occassio says you can."

He gritted his teeth, the urge to laugh vanishing in an instant. "Occassio likes to tell you a surprising amount of lies about me."

"It's not a lie. I've already *seen* you do it." Fidget smirked, a thing so baiting and haughty that he blinked a bit, wondering if she'd seen him playing his part as Jaskier today. "So do it."

"Auramancy *and* divinimancy?" Just his luck. "You should be higher up on the ladder, you know."

"You're trying to distract me, and it's not going to work, sir."

"Neither is me trying to wield auramancy. Look, I'll have a word with your queen, okay? I'll make sure she knows nothing untoward is going on." He paused, quirking one eyebrow. "Although, if you keep shoving me into closets, people are bound to start questioning—"

One alarmed yelp later, and he found himself shoved out of the closet, the door shutting hard on a squeaked-out apology. He caught his footing quickly, straightening his shirt and glancing around the empty hallway.

"There's no one out here," he said. "You can come out."

"Nope," came her muffled voice through the door. "Not until you leave. I'm not being seen with you."

"Well, that's just hurtful."

No answer.

He sighed dryly, leaning against the wall beside the closet, kicking his foot back to brace himself as he studied his nails. "So I suppose you don't want to hear about the auction happening tonight?"

The door cracked open, and a single brown eye peeked out. "What kind of auction?"

"The black-market kind. The getting-a-godly-artifact-off-your-hands kind."

Another inch. He could just catch a sliver of her nose now. "Tonight?"

255

"Mmhm. The palace is putting on a fireworks show to entertain Queen Esha, so the entire city's going dark to watch. We—what? What're you looking at?"

The door opened fully now, Fidget starting at him with a look of utter longing. "*Fireworks?*"

He scratched the back of his ear. "Well, yes, but that's not really—"

"Oh. Right." He'd never seen a person deflate so fast; he could've sworn tears peeked out the edges of her eyes before she blinked them away. "We'll be busy."

"You like fireworks?"

"I love them. When I was a girl, me and my family, we used to climb up on rooftops to get a better view when there were shows in our city." Pained fondness danced in her eyes just like her magic had moments ago. "We never could get the view we wanted, but it was enough. It was something."

He paused. The undercurrent of loneliness in her voice wasn't unfamiliar; he'd caught it plenty of times before, had plied it just so to serve his own ends throughout this entire ordeal. But something about it sounded different now. Something about it sounded...

Like him.

"Where's your family now?" he asked.

Her silence stretched on for miles. "Gone," she said finally. "Long gone."

"I'm sorry. Brothers? Sisters?"

"Both."

It shouldn't have mattered. It shouldn't have changed anything. But he knew that pain in her eyes, the grief that tweaked just a bit differently, the agony she couldn't fully bury beneath a smile and a teasing laugh. And the thought of not only losing Soleil, but losing Jericho, losing Kal...

But then again, he had lost Jericho. Had lost her long before he'd ever realized it. She'd dug her own grave the day she chose to sacrifice Soleil for her own selfish needs, and he didn't have the time to waste standing vigil at the wake of a traitor.

He had stolen, manipulated, lied, killed by proxy. Until this, until now, he'd been the worst of the Atlas brood by a wide margin. But he'd never sullied himself by wearing the title of *betrayer*.

"I am sorry," he croaked. "Truly. I can't imagine that."

"You don't want to." Anger had never graced this girl's voice in his presence before, but he heard it now: the barest whisper of rage buried beneath the sadness and grief and sweetness, a blistering fury that tapped on his shoulder and demanded to be recognized.

He watched her for a long moment, leaning further into the wall until his shoulder ached. "Who betrayed you?"

Her eyes flickered with surprise, her lips rounding briefly before she pressed them back together. "How did you know?"

Bloody temple floors, smiles full of foreign shyness, eyes that glimmered gold like coins in a fountain. "Let's just say I'm familiar with the feeling."

Fidget gnawed absently on her bottom lip, her hands kneading each other, her silence wearing pain like a perfume. She avoided his eyes. "We were trying to build a better life. We grew up on the streets after our mother died, and we came up with a plan to…"

Again, hesitation, a beat of fear.

"I won't tell Esha," he said quietly. "It's okay. You can speak freely here." The promise rolled off his tongue easily, each word infused with earnest reassurance, a lie he'd told hundreds of times before.

This time, though, it was different. This time…this time he meant it.

Fidget's throat bobbed, her mirror pendant rising and falling with her bracing intake of breath. "We planned to rob the palace treasury. We just wanted enough to get us somewhere we could be better off. But one of my siblings…fear got the best of her, I guess. Or she couldn't handle the guilt on her conscience. She reported us to the Daggers. They were waiting when we showed up. They separated us and threw us in the dungeons, even the sister who reported us. I…I made a mistake. I tried to pick the lock with my auramancy. It didn't work, the guards caught me, and when they realized I was doubly blessed by Occassio…they took me to Esha. She offered me a place training to join the Mirrors."

His heart may as well have been made of rock as it dropped into his stomach. "*You* were going to try and steal from a queen?"

"Not alone, but—"

"*You?*"

Fear traded places with something closer to offense. "Yes, *me.*"

"You said you weren't a thief."

"I said I wasn't *the* thief, not *a* thief. Just because I didn't steal the mirror doesn't mean I've never stolen anything." She paused before digging in her pocket, holding out one hand, fingers splayed to reveal a gilded pen in her palm. A pen engraved with a curving *F* at the end—a pen that had *absolutely* been tucked into his pocket this morning.

Shock tugged his hand into his pocket, feeling out the empty space, disbelief numbing his tongue into a stutter. "How did you—when—*how*."

Nobody pickpocketed Finnick Atlas. Nobody was halfway good enough to pull that off. Nobody had ever dared *try*.

Fidget smiled sheepishly, rubbing the back of her neck with her other hand. "Sorry."

"Give me that." He snatched the pen away and shoved it back into his pocket, trying to quell the uneasiness in his stomach. He didn't have the excuse of visions or fevers or delirium this time. There was no pink haze over his vision or tremor in his hand. How had she managed to get her hand into his pocket? Was she just that good? Was he truly losing his touch?

"So your siblings are in prison?" *Distract, distract.* He couldn't let her see how much that rattled him.

"No." There it was again, the anger that sounded so wrong in her sugar-sweet voice. "I got word shortly after I accepted her offer that they were all put to death. Hung."

"*Hung*? Just for conspiracy?"

Fidget shrugged, her gaze bleak, distant with unpleasant memory. "Conspiracy is the birthplace of rebellion. Esha shows no mercy to those who even whisper of plans against the crown."

Interesting. Horrific, obviously, but interesting too. He filed that knowledge away for later, hand still flexing against his pocket, mind racing over the last day for any hint of when she'd plucked out that pen.

"I'm sorry," he said again, pushing off the wall and curling his hand around her shoulder, giving it a gentle squeeze. Another move he'd learned from watching his brother. "That's…I'm sorry."

Fidget shrugged the shoulder he wasn't holding, her gaze suddenly snapping to his with surprising intensity. "Who betrayed *you*, Finn?"

"Jericho tricked her. Promised her my life if she gave up hers to Anima. Now they both have what they want—Jericho gets to have her war, and Anima gets to have a body."

Bile burbled in the hollow of his throat, and he released her shoulder. "Meet me outside the kitchens once everyone else has left for the fireworks. Dress as wealthy as you can. Go over-the-top. We're not hiding tonight."

She took a step toward him as he took a step back, one hand extended—the same hand that had slipped past his defenses somehow. "Finn, wait—"

"Don't be late," was all he said in return, shoving his hands into his pockets as he walked away, ears trained behind him for any sound of pursuit.

She didn't follow him. But someone *did* fall into step behind him somewhere along the way, a phantom drifting across the palace floor without a sound, judgment poisoning the air between them.

Annoyance ticked a muscle in his jaw. "I don't have the patience for passive-aggressiveness today, Vash. Say what you want to say."

"Something is off about all of this. I have a bad feeling. I don't think you should go to the auction."

Finn held back a sigh. Vash had always been cautious, but this was toeing the line of paranoia. And he should know—he was the gods-damned prince of paranoia. "You know that's not an option. Whoever took that mirror needs to find a way to pass it off to Jericho somehow, and this auction is the best place to do that."

"So let her take it. Get it back once she has it in her quarters."

"We don't know what the mirror *does*. You want to risk Tenebrae and Anima having it in their hands for even a short time? Because I don't. Intercepting it at the auction poses the least risk."

"Not to you."

"Risk is my middle name."

Vash sighed. "Your middle name is Aurelias."

Finn mimed a gag. "You didn't have to remind me."

"It seems I did."

"You're fired."

"I work for the queen, technically. You can't fire me."

"*Technically*, I'm going to send you and Vidia to the Bogs for your next tour if you keep giving me attitude, Maren."

Vash actually cracked a smile—or at least, he cracked a halfway-decent imitation of one. "We'll just flee elsewhere. I hear Arborius is beautiful in the summer."

"You'll be tried as deserters."

A scoff. "You'll never find us."

That much was true. If Vash and Vidia decided to disappear, it would be a waste of resources to even try tracking them down. He was half-sure Vash could turn invisible at will, and Vidia could traverse through trees and across rooftops better than any bird. "You're a pain in my ass, you know."

"But a useful one."

Finn made a noise of dismissal, waving his hand in exasperation. "You sound like your sister. Can I count on you to be there tonight or not?"

Vash's mouth moved, but no sound came out.

Finn frowned, blinking hard and rubbing at his ear. "Come again?"

Vash's mouth continued to move, but instead of his voice, there came a buzzing—a loud, horrible whine that built and built, a rush of sound that reminded him of cicada screams, a commotion that vibrated deep within his ears until pain drowned out all sound. He clamped his hands over his ears, a roiling nausea bearing down on his stomach, and when he tried to take a step—

"Kal, stop!"

Kallias stood straight and tall before him, his bare shoulders facing Finn. He wore no shoes, no shirt, only a ragged pair of trousers that stopped halfway down his calves. A gale from the sea whipped his hair around his head, tears streaming freely from his eyes—stirred by the wind or by the unnamable emotion that painted his face in equal measures of desperation and thrill, Finn couldn't tell. He was poised at the edge of a cliff as if about to dive, surrounded by nothing but the elements themselves: wind circling him, storm above, untamed sea below.

"I have to try," Kallias said, and Finn didn't know why, but terror bloomed in his chest at the words, at the way Kallias said them—like it was some kind of farewell.

"Don't," Finn blurted, trying to go to his brother, trying to tug him back from the edge, but his feet were rooted to the stone. Even as the storm roared and battered them both, even as rain lashed Finn's face and flattened Kallias's hair to his head, Finn tried. "Stop it, just—come back, come away from the edge, we don't need this! You don't need this!"

Kallias looked over his shoulder. Met Finn's gaze briefly, barely a blink, the barest imitation of a smile on his face.

Then Kallias, still smiling, turned and walked off the cliff.

"No!" Finn shouted, lunging forward, and now that it was too late, now his feet moved. He shot to the edge of the cliff, dropping to his knees, clinging to the edge as he leaned over—

And watched Kallias plunge toward the sea below, waves rearing up like gaping jaws ready to devour him.

Finn jerked in place, his heart punching against the wall of his ribs as he came back to his senses. But he wasn't in the hall anymore; he wasn't with Vash. Instead, he blinked to find himself in his shelf-lined room, dust mites bobbing lazily through the reddish rays of the sunset. His knees were digging into the floor beneath him, his hands pressed into the floorboards like they were trying to reach through them, and no matter how hard he thought, no matter how hard he tried…

He couldn't dredge up one memory of the hours that had clearly passed between his conversation with Vash and now.

Panic tried to pull his chest taut, but he shook it off, deliberately dragging in a breath until the strings of terror loosened. He untied them one by one, taking in breath after breath until it came easily again, until his thoughts cleared, until he could ease himself up from the floor without losing his balance.

It was almost over. They were going to keep that mirror out of Jericho's hands, Kallias would be home soon, and everything would be set right. Whatever that took, whatever it cost, he was going to get his gods-damned life back.

One godly scheme foiled at a time.

CHAPTER 32

ELIAS

"Tell me what you're thinking."

Warm skin pressed against his as Soren nestled in closer, silken curls bundled against his chest, his fingertips gliding lightly between her bare shoulders. A tired smile spread across his face as he traced patterns down her back, his hand finding the dips of scars and the dimples at the base of her spine.

"I'm thinking," he said with a contented sigh, "that you're beautiful."

Soren raised her head, green eyes glimmering like emeralds in the candlelight, that fiendish grin he loved and despised in equal measure flashing across her face. She pushed herself up by shoving her fists into the bed on either side of him, hovering over his body, her nose an inch from his. "Well, I knew that, jackass. What else?"

"As you've so astutely pointed out many times, my mind can only handle one thought at a time." He nipped the tip of her nose, grinning as she wrinkled it, groaning in protest. "And unfortunately, you're just too damned distracting."

"Mm." She dipped downward and pressed her smiling lips into his skin, a thrill of heat searing straight through him as she left a trail of kisses along his collarbone. "Would it help if I put some clothes on?"

"Probably not," he admitted, and her cackle soothed what little tension still remained in his aching, tired body. He couldn't remember what had left him in so much pain—a training session, maybe, or a day in the forge with his mother—but Soren never failed to offer a peaceful end to a grueling day. She was a balm, a blessing. He didn't know what he'd do without her.

"Well, then, here." She settled herself back on top of him, reaching up with one hand and covering his eyes, her callouses rasping against his eyelashes. "Maybe that'll clear your mind."

He heaved a sigh, her body lifting and falling with his. "Well, now I'm thinking about how annoying you are."

Her laugh was more of a bark that time. "Yeah, knew that too, jackass."

"Fine. Then what are you thinking about, smartass? Enlighten me."

"I'm thinking," she mused, leaning in close, her cinnamon-and-whiskey breath tickling his nose as she kissed him, finishing her sentence against his mouth, "that you're wasting time talking when you could be kissing me."

Her teeth sank lightly into his lower lip, drawing a groan from his throat as he tugged her closer, capturing her mouth with his. He slid his hands up into her hair, tangling his fingers in her curls, her body melting into his as if they'd been made to fit together.

It hadn't been like this the first time they kissed. The first time had been awkward and aggressive, his head bumping into the shelves in the barracks closet, her elbows sticking out at awkward angles while she tried to help him fix his form. But practice made perfect, and now he knew her like the back of his hand, knew exactly how she liked to be kissed, knew exactly how she liked to be—

Wait.

Icy adrenaline put out the slow-burning fire in his veins, and he pulled away from her kiss, even as his body begged to linger. He opened his eyes to find her frowning at him. "What's wrong?"

He didn't know. He didn't know, but something was, something was shaking the bars that kept his instincts in check, screaming at him to remember why this couldn't be happening. Why this couldn't be real.

"We haven't done this," he began, but she shushed him, trailing a finger down his lips.

"We *are* doing this," she said. "We're doing it now. So what's the problem?"

"No, we…" His mind raced. "Soren, I haven't…this isn't right."

Her frown deepened as she shifted, propping herself up once more to look into his eyes, her brow furrowed in concern. "What's wrong, Elias?" she asked in a voice too soft to be her, all sweetness and sugar, her breath smelling of fresh blooms and rotting corpses.

When she smiled at him again, her eyes flickered gold.

This time when he woke up gagging, Kallias was already there, shoving something beneath his face just as his stomach somersaulted into his throat, pouring all of its contents right back out of him.

"Well," said Kallias with a sigh and a gentle pat to Elias's back, "better this end than the other, right?"

"That's disgusting," Elias rasped before his body bent in half again, emitting an ugly retch that almost worsened the nausea.

Kallias slid an arm around him—a fearless gesture, really, since Elias wasn't entirely sure how good his aim would be if he vomited in earnest again. "Let it all out. Have you been drinking that tea Havi gave you?"

"Not yet." Gods knew he hadn't had a chance, what with the High Priestess throwing him straight into an impossible challenge. This was the first bit of sleep he'd been able to snatch in two days, propped against the forge wall. He wiped his mouth with the back of his hand, slowly sitting up and pushing the receptacle— one of the now-empty crates the steel had been brought in—away from him. "What're you doing in here?"

Kallias shrugged one shoulder, his hand still lingering cautiously on Elias's back, rubbing absent circles between his shoulder blades—a gesture Elias recognized from his own time nursing his siblings through a stomach sickness. "Thought you might have changed your mind about having company. Didn't want you to feel alone."

A bit of warmth threatened to poke through the numbness Elias was beginning to rely on, so he said, "You just didn't want to spend the night alone with Raquel, did you?"

Kallias hesitated, his hand pausing its rotation on Elias's back. "I can be here for two reasons."

Elias grunted, unable to argue. He stood slowly, shaking off Kallias's hand, rubbing the sleep from his eye as he gazed down at the Atlas prince. "Seriously, why are you here, Kal?"

The nickname tumbled off his sluggish tongue without thought, and he silently cursed himself. He didn't know when he'd picked it up; probably when nightmares had rendered him so sleepless that forcing his way through the entirety of *Kallias* was just a bit too much to endure.

To his credit, Kallias didn't say a word about it, didn't tease him for being so informal or scold him for dipping that far into familiarity. He simply stood alongside Elias, leaning back until his spine cracked with an audible *crick* that turned Elias's stomach in another somersault. Kallias rolled up the sleeves of his black sleep tunic before crossing his arms, shrugging a bit. "I meant what I said. I really didn't think you should be alone. And I genuinely think that Raquel might just bludgeon me with a rock and blame a cave-in if I try to sleep in there."

Elias shook himself, striding to his workstation and snatching up his water canteen, pouring a bit and swishing it around his mouth, hoping to catch the last of the stomach acid in its wash. He hated the way water tasted after vomiting, a cloying sweetness that almost burned a bit going down, but he hated the feeling of grime lingering on his teeth even more. "Fine. You can stay. But there are rules."

Kallias brightened. "Name them."

"No asking about the nightmares."

"Done."

"No talking while I'm working."

Kallias wrinkled his nose at that one, but he nodded. "Fair enough."

"You get in my way, you're out. No second chances."

Kallias raised one eyebrow. "Anything else, Your Highness?"

A sigh wound its way out of his bile-scalded throat, and he turned back to his work with a final remark thrown behind him: "You're buying breakfast."

"I don't know about that. Sure your stomach's not going to waste my money?"

Without looking, Elias chucked the now-empty canteen over his shoulder. And when the hollow *thunk* of metal hitting skull echoed back to him, when Kallias snarled in protest and pain, he almost started to laugh.

* * *

This was his last chance.

Elias bent over the forge, his chapped lips burning at the unceasing onslaught of heat, his sleepless eyes stinging with every heavy blink. Everything around him had tunneled, blurring at the edges until it was only this: just him, the forge, and this hunk of metal that was proving to be prissier than Kallias could *ever* manage.

He'd turned out two other blades in the past two days, and neither had come out to his satisfaction. One had warped after he'd plunged it into the quenching barrel and had resisted correction no matter how much he worked with it; the other had formed cracks, and though he'd ground them out, the grain of the metal was too large, too fragile. It would've broken after any strong impact.

Which left him with this: his final blade, the final chunk of Artemisian steel he hadn't ruined.

He glanced away from the superheated metal to find Kallias slumped in the corner, his head knocked back against the stone wall, hair removed from its bun and splayed limply down his shoulders, snores grinding from his open mouth. His own sword was propped across his lap, his wrists dangling limply over the edge of the sheath. He never went anywhere without it.

He had to give it to Kallias: the man had shown more endurance than he'd expected. Assisting with the process of forging, especially without experience or proper rest, could be almost as grueling a task as the actual forging, and Kallias had made it nearly as long as Elias without closing his eyes.

All because he didn't want Elias to feel alone.

A slow sigh escaped him, and he blinked hard to clear his eyes, looking back to his final bit of steel.

It wasn't fair, the way he'd been treating Kallias since they'd left Atlas. He knew that. The former prince had shown him nothing but kindness, and he'd gone out of his way more than once to support Elias through his grief even as he clung staunchly to his own belief that Soren was savable.

Kallias Atlas shouldn't be a friend to him. He'd killed Jira, Soren's battlemate, Elias's sister-in-arms, Raquel's blood sister. Had definitely killed many other precious people on gods-knew how many other battlefields. Had stolen Soren to Atlas, unintentionally setting her on the path to her own destruction. If anything, he should have hated Kallias even more than Raquel did.

But there was no hate in him when he looked at Kallias, snoring quietly in the corner, poised to wake at a moment's notice if Elias needed him. All his animosity was now aimed in more divine directions. He didn't have enough left over for anyone still trapped in the cage of mortality.

And if he was being honest with himself…he knew full well the blame for Soren's death rested on someone else's shoulders. Kallias was hauling enough guilt without Elias throwing extra burdens on him that weren't his to carry.

The next few hours went by in a blur, the seconds flying away with every strike of his hammer against red-hot metal, coaxing it into the most basic blade shape he knew. He didn't have any faith in his abilities past that, not with a material like this, and there was no one left for him to offer prayer to. Mortem had made it very clear she would offer no support. Anima and Tenebrae were holding his battlemate's corpse captive. Tempest was potentially toeing the line of Kallias's soul, trying to coax the man into the same pyre Soren had burned on. And Occassio…it didn't matter what side the Trickster Goddess was on. He knew better than to trust her with something as vulnerable as his prayers. She might answer them, but her favors never came without cost, and he couldn't afford to have even one more thing ripped from his grasp.

Remember, Elias, murmured a voice he hadn't heard in nearly four years, bringing with it the memory of swordfighting lessons in the yard and tickle wars in the house, an echo of the delighted cries of his siblings as all seven Loch children piled on top of their father, newly returned from the battlefield. *Your prayers are your best weapon. To invite Mortem into your battles is to gain an ally no one can wrest away from you. Humility and faith, Elias—these will win the battle every time.*

His father was wrong. Faith had lost him every battle he'd fought in the past four years. Placing his fate in the hands of another had only seen him lost…had only seen him *dead.* Faith had proven itself a useless weapon, warped and cracked, riddled with flaws. No more. He fought for himself now.

Heat, hammer, heat, hammer. Quench, flare, cool. The world melted away to a distant hum, memory and thought and worry replaced by a singular focus that sang between his mind and his hands, a harp string perfectly tuned stretched between them, and before he knew it—

Before he knew it, he was holding a sword.

Nothing fancy, not by any means, but Artemisian steel had an inherent beauty in any form. He swung it through the air, listening to the melodic swipe with near-hysterical giddiness bubbling like spilled champagne in his veins.

He'd done it. He'd *done* it. And without a single fingerprint of the divine touching the blade.

"You see that, smartass?" he breathed, the words floating off a tongue blackened with smoke and heretical prayers. "I did it."

The blade twirling in idle circles as he crossed the forge, he picked the target he'd chosen as his tester: a training dummy built by Safi herself, a well-armored hunk of vaguely human-shaped material she'd fondly named *Zed the Stationary*.

An apt title, to be sure. And despite her warnings against damaging it beyond salvaging, Elias had spent weeks wishing desperately that he could put a sword through the goddess that had stolen his Soren from him. And while she was so far out of his reach, too great a distance for this blade to cross, Zed would make a damned good surrogate.

He stood before the dummy with steady hands despite his utter exhaustion, carefully sliding his boots into the proper stance, his muscles rearing back without hitch or hesitation, memory guiding them through motions he hadn't properly followed through in too long. There was a stiffness, the pop of something releasing, and then—

His first strike drew a snuffle from Kallias's corner, the ring of steel against steel bringing a tear to Elias's eye as surely as any fine symphony or tragic play performed at the Andromeda Grand Theatre.

He'd done it.

The second strike pulled a full-fledged complaint through Kallias's teeth, though it was thoroughly slurred with sleep.

A strange jerking sensation pulled at Elias's chest. Once. Twice. Again. Feet scrabbled against floor as Kallias tugged himself up, his groggy voice barely intelligible. "What in the depths—?"

Elias paid him no mind. Because for the first time in gods-knew how many weeks...

He was laughing.

It wasn't pleasant to the ear, but it was laughter: thin, manic, stomach-sore laughter that shook the cage containing the sleeping beast in his chest. Laughter that made him realize just how long he'd gone without it; laughter that didn't feel forced or false.

It still wasn't quite right; it sounded hollow somehow, incomplete, a harmony missing its melody, the gaps normally filled in by Soren's wild, snorting cackle more obvious than ever. But it was a laugh. And it was his.

He swirled the blade in a complicated twist just for fun before bringing the blade down once more, bitter satisfaction thickening in his blood like a sludge—

On the third strike, the blade *shattered*.

All sound vanished from the cave as the pieces rained down around his feet. He didn't hear the grinding, awful sound of that laughter coming to an abrupt halt. He didn't hear the clinking of metal chunks scattering across the floor. He didn't even hear Kallias, though he could see the man's mouth moving, his freckled brow furrowed in concern as he crossed the cave, tiptoeing carefully around the ruined blade with one hand outstretched.

The entire world was shaking.

Elias's knees hit the ground, his skin barely registering the bite of steel shards. He scooped up a handful in his unsteady grip, staring down at them like they might find their voices and explain themselves to him.

But no such explanation came. And in the depths of that unnatural silence, the muffling of the world that only utter desolation could bring, he could almost hear the faintest strain of that missing melody, a lure that would drive him mad if he let himself chase it.

CHAPTER 33

KALLIAS

After hours spent watching Elias kneel in the midst of his shattered sword—which had come directly after hearing the worst sort of laughter clawing itself free from whatever depths-dark pit Elias had shoved it into—Kallias had finally managed to convince him to go and sleep on the problem of the second trial, which was due to commence tonight. A battle, Elias had said, he was meant to forge his own weapon for.

And failing that, he would be expected to fight with his bare hands.

But that didn't matter, because Kallias wasn't going to let it go that far. What good was this damned ring on his finger if it only granted him permission to sit on his ass in this kingdom he was supposed to be preparing to rule? No, he was going to work with Zaccheus to get himself into that throne room, wherever it was, and he was going to stop this before it went any further.

But first, breakfast.

It really was unfortunate that Havi's establishment was the only real bakery in Artem's crown city. Unfortunate for his purse, because he'd developed an addiction to those blessed blueberry muffins, his stomach growling like a mountain cat on the hunt every morning until he devoured at least two. And unfortunate for his safety, because Raquel seemed to have developed a similar taste for Havi's chocolate croissants, which saw them eating breakfast in the same place every morning, watching each other from opposite ends of the bakery while pretending they had no clue the other was there.

This was ridiculous. He was a *prince*, for gods' sake. She could be hostile and rude all she liked, but he was raised better. He may have set down his crown, but he was still in possession of *manners*, gods damn it. One of them had to take the high road.

One visit to the counter later, he crossed the bakery, slipping between patrons and muttering *excuse me* until he reached her table in the corner. She was leaning against the back of the chair, her boots propped up on the seat opposite her to prevent anyone trying to sit in it, taking small and slow bites of her croissant as she read through a book that looked new.

She didn't glance up as he set a mug down on her table, rotating it so the handle faced her. "For you."

"I don't want anything from you, Atlas."

He bit down on his cheek, breathing patience in. *Manners. Manners.* "It's coffee. Black. Fresh, from what Havi said."

"What's in it?"

"I'm assuming coffee. Likely black. Hopefully fresh."

Now she looked at him, glaring from beneath thick brows, eyes darker than the drink he'd brought her. "Why?"

He steepled his fingers awkwardly, hot blood flooding his face. Still, he did his best to cling to the confidence that had driven him in this direction. "When you got coffee the other day, you didn't add anything to it, so I just assumed—"

"Not *that*." Her boots fell to the floor with a sharp *clap*, her spine straightening as she speared him with those bitter-brew eyes. "Why are you being kind?"

That was a very good question, one he should've asked himself a bit sooner. There was a difference between manners and foolishness. *High road, Kallias.* "You saved my life the other day. I wanted to thank you."

"I told you, it's only so I can kill you better later on." But her fingers crept toward the mug, nails clinking lightly on the ceramic. "And a coffee hardly equals a life debt."

"Well, you also saw me naked, and I normally try to *precede* that with a drink, so…consider it a reinstatement of propriety?"

Shock bolted his heart to the back wall of his chest when Raquel snorted—something so close to a laugh it almost toppled from annoyance to amusement. "If you're concerned about me telling your future wife that she doesn't have all that *much* to look forward to, I really don't care enough to bother."

Heat flamed through his cheeks. "Could you please just say *thank you* like a normal person so I can go back to my breakfast?"

She hesitated. Lifted the mug. Peered into it briefly before her gaze snapped back up to him. "I'm immune to twenty-seven types of poison."

He blinked. "Congratulations?"

"I'm just saying that whatever you put in here probably isn't going to do the job."

"Fine," he sighed, waving her off as he turned to go back to his own table. He'd done his due diligence. If she didn't care to accept it, it wasn't his problem. "Enjoy your breakfast. Waste the coffee if you want."

It wouldn't do him any good to keep pushing. If Raquel Angelov was determined to be his enemy—if she was determined to wear his death on her hands like a signet ring, his blood the ink that would seal her sister's loss with retribution—he could hardly talk her out of it. He was beginning to discover a common trait among Nyxians: a certain resistance to diplomacy, a tendency to dismantle a locked door rather than knocking and politely asking to be allowed in. They were not a patient people, and manners only wasted their time.

When he came back to his table, he found Safi already there, his half-empty plate in one hand as she wiped down the table with the other. But when she saw him, she paused mid-polish. "Oh, sorry. Were you not finished?"

"I *should* be. I already had two before that one." He cut his hand through the air to stop her when she tried to lower the plate back onto the table. "Don't worry about it. I don't want to make another mess for you."

"You're sweet." But she set down the plate anyway. "Just eat over your plate like a big kid, all right?"

He tried for a smirk, but pain rippled through his stomach, loneliness piercing his insides like bait on a hook. "You remind me of my little brother, you know."

Safi's nose wrinkled, and she blew a strand of hair from her eyes, pouting a bit. "That's hardly what a girl likes to hear from a pretty boy, you know."

That time he laughed. "Sorry, no, that's not what I—I just mean that he's funny like you. He makes these ridiculous jokes, I don't know where he gets them from...none of the rest of us are funny."

Safi nodded thoughtfully, flipping her towel over her shoulder. "Hm. Is he single?"

"As far as I know."

"Pretty like you?"

A grin cracked across his face, and he offered a sultry wink, one he'd practiced an embarrassing number of times in the mirror as a youth, play-acting with his reflection as he imagined meeting his future partner someday. "No one's pretty like me."

Safi mock-groaned, dramatically pretending to swoon back against her chair, swiping a hand across her brow before plucking the towel off her shoulder and flicking his arm with it. "It's just gods-damned unfair that you're marrying my Empress, you know. You shouldn't flirt so freely. You're going to break too many hearts."

He chuckled. "Sorry. Listen, if you ever do relocate to Atlas, I'll find you someone nice to make up for it."

"Oh, no. Nice is boring, Prince. Get me someone *interesting*, then we'll talk."

He opened his mouth to keep bantering, but his eyes slid past Safi's shoulder, catching on a group slowly beginning to mingle just past the bakery's door. He frowned a bit, leaning forward, catching the glint of torchlight on strange weapons hanging from their belts and the grim expressions on their faces.

"What's going on there?" he asked.

Safi turned her chair, following his gaze with a frown of her own. "Hm. Looks like Zaccheus is taking a group out to the fields."

"The fields?"

"We don't stay in the mountain all the time, you know." Safi's gaze stayed glued to Zaccheus, who was standing at the head of the group, calling out over the chattering voices, seemingly organizing them into smaller bands. "We get most of our crops from farms scattered along the plains beyond the mountain. But lately they've been...disappearing."

"Disappearing?"

"Destroyed, actually. Our storehouses are being burned." Safi turned her chair back toward him, concern shrouding her normally excitable face in darkness. "We can't figure out who's responsible. Zaccheus thinks mercenaries hired by Tallis…my mother says there's no evidence of their direct involvement, but Tallis hasn't exactly made it a secret that they'd like to have all the mountains to themselves. It irks King Denali to this day that we're in possession of Mount Igniquit. But he hasn't had the courage to make his displeasure formally known once again, seeing as we thrashed them so thoroughly before, so it's anyone's guess if this is his halfhearted attempt at putting himself out there."

"Mm." He'd met the Tallisian king once—him and his twin children, Everin and Raini. Everin was kind enough, a known peacemaker; he'd have to be, considering King Denali and his daughter were notoriously bad-tempered. He absently twisted the end of his braid around his fingers, remembering Raini's threats to scalp him where he stood if he called her *grumpy* even one more time. "What's Zaccheus going out there to do, then?"

"Mortem only knows. My mother won't tell me." Safi scowled. "Says it's *crown business.*"

"Huh." He was quiet for a moment, thinking that over. As he did, he caught Zaccheus's eyes flicking to him, then away; then to him, then away. A subtle gesture. "Crown business. Well, I happen to be in possession of a crown."

"I wouldn't—" Safi started, but Kallias was already moving.

A dozen pairs of eyes bored into him as he approached, quiet mutters whispered between friends as they huddled in close, forcing him to a halt on the outskirts, circling the knot they'd formed before their leader. He only recognized two of them from the meeting two days before—Esmeralda, who was helping one of the younger members of the group adjust the straps on their pack, and Rory, who offered him a beaming smile.

"Can I help you, Prince?" called Zaccheus over all the mumbling. Not for the first time, Kallias silently tossed up a quick prayer of thanks to whichever god had granted him his height; it allowed him to make eye contact with Zaccheus above the crowd's heads without having to push around anyone.

"I was about to ask you the same question," he called back.

"We're all set here, thank you." Zaccheus's smile was a tight thing that suggested Kallias was already pushing too far past a boundary, but his eyes were calm, prompting Kallias to go on.

Was he testing Kallias? Maybe afraid to show favor to another kingdom's prince in front of his people?

"My friend Safi mentioned you've had some trouble with burning storehouses," Kallias ventured, unsure of his place in this dance.

Zaccheus narrowed his eyes, displeasure tweaking his mouth beneath his beard. "Safi knows better than to be gossiping with foreign princes."

"I'm sure she does." Kallias offered him a polite smile, reaching up to scratch at his beard, careful to show off the claiming ring on his finger. "But this was a discussion between the general's daughter and the Empress's betrothed."

Zaccheus's smile vanished like a barely-formed daydream. "I see."

"Really, you'd be doing me a favor," Kallias admitted, loosening his posture a bit further, softening the pointed edge of his half-threat with a friendlier laugh. "It's been days since I've seen the sun. I'm going a bit out of my mind."

Finally, the tattooed guard's arms eased out of their cross, his eyes taking in Kallias's full form with something like approval. Then: "Homesick?"

Pain rolled through Kallias's body like a riptide, trawling a net through him, dredging up every lonely pang and desperate worry that had buried itself in him over the past few weeks. "You have no idea."

"All right, fine. Tag along if you like. But don't stray from the group, and don't mistake that ring on your finger for a crown. Out there, if I give an order, you follow it."

More and more like home with every passing minute. "No argument from me."

"I'd like to come as well," said a now-familiar voice, the harbinger of the thundercloud ever-lurking at Kallias's back. He closed his eyes, breathing in through his nose before he turned to face Raquel. The Nyxian soldier had her thumbs tucked into her blade belt, her eyes regarding him with near-boredom as always, but the steel behind them was unmistakable.

"I don't think that's wise," he said placatingly.

"See, that's funny, because I didn't ask for your permission, Atlas. You think I'm letting you out of my sight so you can run back to your mother?" Raquel gave him another rendition of that tight-lipped smile that somehow managed to gain more grimace at the edges every time she wore it. She leaned to the side a bit to catch Zaccheus's gaze. "Care to add another?"

"I don't see why not." Kallias tried to snag Zaccheus's attention again, to gesture and mouth *no*, but Zaccheus's eyes were fixed curiously on Raquel. "But we're leaving now. Whatever you have on you is all you get."

"Fine," he and Raquel chorused, and before she could throw a nasty look at him again, he pushed further into the group, ignoring their uncomfortable shifting. He'd rather have any one of these Artemisians at his back than her.

Rory and Esmeralda made space for him, Esmeralda giving him a look that said *I'll handle it* before engaging in friendly conversation with Raquel.

The first step outside the mountain city nearly drove him to his knees, a heavenly gasp of cold air barreling into his lungs with his first breath. The mountain chill coiled around him like a python, lifting the oppressive heat from his limbs like it had been waiting for him to emerge.

One breeze strayed away from the whole, a curious wisp of wind tickling his ear with a crackling breath: *Welcome back, Prince.*

Goosebumps cascaded down every limb, but he just shook his head, dismissing that whisper with a huff of breath. Despite the cold, he was nearly tempted to strip off his outer tunic, half-desperate to let the wind buffet as much of him as was decent to reveal here. But somehow, he didn't think Zaccheus or his people would take too kindly to him suddenly undressing. Besides, he wasn't sure his dignity could take one more pointed insult from Raquel.

"Afraid of heights, Atlas?"

Speak of the depths-dweller. He took in the deepest breath he could, letting the fresh air dust the floor of his lungs before he answered, "Not in the least, Angelov."

"Hm. Not many mountain peaks in Atlas, are there?"

To his surprise, when he turned around to answer, he found her with her face tipped back, eyes closed, one hand dragging through her hair to loosen it from its plait. She breathed out a gentle sigh, shaking out her blue-tinted waves, letting the breeze slip its fingers through the strands. The early-morning light lit her skin with a gilded sheen, and he watched as the slightest of smiles coaxed her lips into a curve, her head tipping into the wind like she was leaning into a lover's caress.

His heart stuttered in his chest, and his retort tripped and fell right off the tip of his tongue.

She peeked one eye open, scowling. "What are you gaping at?"

He snapped his mouth shut. "Lost my path of thought. Sorry."

Another one of those almost-laughs. "How? Must be one lonely path."

That was an insult. He knew that, but the knowledge didn't make it deep enough into his head before he blurted, "Have you ever seen the ocean?"

Raquel blinked, and for the first time, fumbled for an answer. "I...no. I've never been."

"But you're an aquamancer."

She rolled her sleeves up before starting after the rest of the group, her hair flowing down her back, an impossibly vivid waterfall tumbling from crown to waist. "Your ocean isn't the only water in the world, Atlas."

"But don't you…" He hesitated. There was no reason for him to push her, no reason for him to risk reaching the end of her patience, but she just…*baffled* him. Mere weeks with this magic had left him dry, desperate, willing to do almost anything if he could just touch a toe back in the waves. If she shared the same power, the same longing, how could she bear the cravings without an ocean nearby to quell them? How could she bear the hunger for salt when the sea was so far out of her reach?

He was withering beneath the burden of a month apart from the sea. She was still standing strong after a lifetime.

"You worship Tempest, don't you? God of nature. God of the ocean. Doesn't it…I mean, doesn't it call to you? Doesn't it *ache*?"

"No." No hesitation. The answer bolted from her mouth almost before he was done asking the question. "I've never cared to see it. Besides, I haven't prayed to Tempest in years."

"What stopped you?" Kallias skidded down the slope after her, gravel showering around her ankles in a cloud of dust as he put himself back at her side.

Raquel was silent for so long that he'd just accepted she was back to ignoring him when she said, with surprising softness: "Most people use faith to help. Others use it to harm. To manipulate. To take advantage."

His breath pinched in his throat. "Someone hurt you."

A wry, mirthless laugh. Raquel absently reached up, running her fingertips along the scars torn across her temple. But before he could ask after the rest of the story, a gate crashed down in her eyes, stiffness returning to her shoulders. "Come on, Atlas. We're falling behind."

So close to answers, yet further than he'd ever been. He frowned, but followed after her, queasiness twisting in his stomach as he trailed his gaze along her torn ear, her scarred scalp, the glass eye in her socket.

He shouldn't have cared to hear her story, but something about her…it was like the moment her knife dug its point into him, she crawled in after it. She was under his skin like a thorn, irking him, irritating him…fascinating him. He couldn't shake her off. The mystery of her called to him the same way the sea called to his magic, a strange tether of sameness hooked behind his ribs that kept tugging him closer no matter how wide a berth he tried to give her.

Whatever it was in her that wanted his attention, he couldn't seem to get a grip on it, and that bothered him. She wanted his heart mounted on the end of her blade. No part of him should want *anything* to do with her.

And yet.

"I thought that was exactly your taste when it comes to women?"

Vaughn's amused voice echoed in his mind, and he tried not to flinch, a harsher kind of betrayal brushing up against his heart. He put a hand over his aching abdomen, his stomach swaying back and forth like a ship on unsteady waters.

He still couldn't reconcile his gentle, loving brother-in-law with the horrific events that had nearly torn his city apart. Couldn't even *begin* to put Vaughn and those undead creatures in the same space in his head. Vaughn was always the kindest of them, the most careful, the most compassionate. He'd never borne a harsh word from Vaughn's mouth. Had never once doubted his loyalty, his love.

And Jericho…

His sister had never been the same after Soleil's death, he'd known that. Not one of them had escaped that night unscathed. But beyond simple grief, that attack had also halted any ambition Jericho had of escaping Atlas, shackling her to the throne by the crown on her head.

He alone had been privy to her plans. She'd told him everything back then, or so he'd thought—that Vaughn was ill, that their Arborian relatives hadn't managed to find anything that could help, that they planned to flee even further west on a ship headed for continents well beyond the Six Kingdoms to look for answers.

He'd helped her plan, helped her pack. He'd organized the guard patrols to clear her a path. He'd ensured there would be a ship waiting. He'd even come up with a plan to keep their family from noticing her departure by having them leave the night of the Saltwater Ball.

The night Soleil burned.

He'd been saying goodbye to them in Jericho's room when the screams started. And by the time the sun rose, hazy and red from the smoke that hadn't yet blown out to sea, everything had changed. Jericho became the Heir…and though that at least meant her tryst with Vaughn no longer had to be kept secret, though it meant they could marry whenever they chose, it also meant there would be no seeking help from people beyond their continent's borders. It meant Vaughn's illness would only continue to worsen over the years. It meant Jericho was trapped.

No wonder she'd gotten desperate. No wonder she'd sought help from places she shouldn't have.

He hadn't seen it. Hadn't noticed that while he was busy soaking in the muck of his own misery, Jericho was drowning in waters too deep and dark to tread alone.

A lump swelled in his throat, tightening to the point of pain, and he stopped in his tracks, his boots crunching against the stone path.

How had he missed it? How had he managed to fail not one, not two, but *all three* of his siblings in the time between that cursed night and now?

"Keep up, Prince!" called Zaccheus from further down the mountain, dragging Kallias back to Artem, back to the cold air and the rocky peaks and a blood-hungry woman who'd never seen the ocean. He steeled his stomach against memory and betrayal, swallowing the swill of anger and guilt burning the back of his throat; he couldn't change the past, and Jericho had made her own choices. He could only take steps to ensure she didn't drag the rest of his kingdom down with her.

He caught up with Zaccheus. "I assume you actually wanted me to come along, yes?"

"Yes, sorry about that." Zaccheus's face remained neutral, but his one-shouldered shrug was sheepish. "I have to be cautious about how many of my dealings are noted by others. Idris is not the most merciful when it comes to criticism, and if people caught wind of my allying with a foreign royal…it could be misconstrued."

"Understood. But how will this help me earn an audience with her?"

"Safi was right, we're investigating a burning. You have some…unique experience with such things. If you could offer some insight and assist with naming the culprits, I think the Empress would care to thank you personally." Zaccheus glanced over his shoulder. "What's the deal with you and the Nyxian woman?"

Kallias scowled. "There's…old animosity there."

"Ah. My wife sensed some…" There was an amused sort of tension in the pause Zaccheus took, and Kallias didn't care for it one bit. "Energy."

"Energy of the violent sort, I'm afraid."

"Of course." But Zaccheus was still smiling, and Kallias's face heated—not just because of the sun. He cleared his throat and fell back, planting himself between a couple strangers, suddenly glad for the uneasy silence.

By the time they made it off the mountain, that sun was much higher in the sky, and any relief he'd found in the fresh air had been washed away by a fresh coating of sweat. He could feel the heat of a newly bloomed sunburn sinking into his skin, and both his knees and lungs were on the verge of collapsing beneath the strain. Mortem had raised a threatening hand against him more times on this mountain than she *ever* had on any battlefield.

"Shouldn't it be easier to go downhill?" he gasped out, pausing to brace himself on his trembling knees.

"It is. Your lungs are just weaker than ours," said Rory, with an untimely amount of cheer. Somewhere ahead, he thought he picked out Raquel's snort.

Rude. But probably true.

Sighing, he forced his feet back into motion, striking up casual conversation with the Artemisians he'd joined near the back of the group. But after about an hour of walking—on flatter ground, blessedly—a scent suddenly stopped Kallias in his tracks, an acrid tang in the air he could almost taste. That nausea from before came back with a vengeance, and he had to force down a gag as the smell of scorch forced itself into his nose and mouth. His eyes took in too much, too fast—the blackened remains of a field, the soot-stained bones of what might have once been a farmhouse scattered across the ground, thin tendrils of smoke still curling off bits and pieces of debris.

Zaccheus cursed, picking up his pace, and his group followed. But Kallias couldn't move. The scar on his skull pulsed with memory, his ears remembering the hungry snarling of flame, his back remembering agony as his skin curdled beneath the touch of fire.

This was a mistake. He'd signed himself up to investigate a *burning*? And for what, a breath of cool air and a little relief from boredom? A small *chance* to meet Idris face-to-face?

"Atlas?" Raquel's voice caught his path of thought, dragging it back up from the muddle of memories clamoring for his attention. He blinked at her, slowly, trying to comprehend the look she was giving him, like she'd said something and was waiting for an answer.

"What?" he asked blankly.

"You're white as a sheet."

"I…me and fire, we don't really, ah…get along." A gurgle in his stomach told him his muffins were threatening anarchy. "I shouldn't have come."

He'd just started to turn when her hand clamped down hard on his shoulder. Even through his tunic, even with his newfound affinity for the cold, her fingers were so chilled that he nearly shivered beneath her touch. She turned him back to face her, meeting his gaze, her jaw set against her usual scowl. Her expression was serious, but not angry, not mocking.

"We need them to respect you if we want our message heard," she said, hushed, for his ears alone. "Fire is their ocean. You can't let them know that it repulses you."

"It doesn't repulse me." His voice was so hoarse he almost couldn't hear himself.

Raquel tipped her head to one side, studying him up and down, her fingers still anchored in his shoulder. Her eyes landed on his hands—trembling, tightly clenched—and her brow smoothed a bit. "You're afraid."

"Yes." No use lying. He was shaking like a leaf caught up in a hurricane.

He should have ripped away, should have made some excuse and started the trek back up the mountain. Even more than the Artemisians, Raquel was the absolute last gods-damned person he needed to show weakness to. But her hand was still on his shoulder, and she was still staring at him, pinning him in place, watching his every breath and blink.

"There's no fire here," she said quietly. "Only the aftermath of it."

"That's almost as bad." Gods, his chest hurt, his heart straining with all its might to outrun the memory of a different blaze.

"I know." She glanced over her shoulder, sparing him from her scrutiny for a moment. "Keep your eyes up and breathe through your mouth."

"What?"

"Watch the sky, not the fields, not the wreckage. If you breathe through your mouth, the smell won't be so bad. Keep your eyes on the clouds. I'll walk behind you and watch your path."

Fresh apprehension washed over him, prickling uncomfortably in his shoulders. "You want me to trust *you* at my back?"

"I don't think these people would take too kindly to me assassinating their future Emperor, Atlas." Raquel released his shoulder, her arm brushing his as she moved to stand behind him. He could feel her breath against his neck as she leaned in, her voice brushing cold and confident against his skin: "I'm not a coward like you. You'll be looking me in the eye when you take your last breath."

That shouldn't have been comforting. The fact that it was suggested there was something very wrong with him. But he did as she said: he focused on the sky, pulled in a breath through his mouth, and started to walk.

They circled the burned buildings, the farmhouse and the storehouse several paces away. But Kallias barely saw a thing. He watched the clouds like Raquel said, and was more than a little irked—and, if he was being honest, relieved—to find that it helped.

But averting his gaze couldn't block out his ears, and the mutters of the group still reached him.

"Don't know why Zaccheus brought him along," a young man muttered.

"I don't know why the Empress thinks we need an Atlas king," an older woman said, and it took effort to keep his eyes glued to the sky. Hopefully no one was watching him mouth-breathe. "What use do we have of Atlas alliance? All this will do is drag us into a war we have no business being in."

"Nyx is hiring necromancers to do their war-work now," protested a different man. "That's not only Atlas's problem to bear. Eventually that death toll won't even be enough, and they'll start turning their eyes elsewhere, whether Nyx wants them to or not. Necromancy is banned from every kingdom for a reason. Nyx made this our fight when they broke that rule."

"Necromancy is an Anima-blessed magic," the older woman disagreed. "If you ask me, Atlas is framing Nyx to gain allies to their own cause. Queen Adriata has proven herself ruthless in pursuit of her vengeance. I wouldn't put it past her. And Prince Kallias has been the spearhead of her war room since he was old enough to step foot on a battlefield."

That woman was more discerning than Kallias's entire kingdom. He had to stop himself from congratulating her on a job well done. She was very nearly right on all counts.

"Yet he showed up here with a Nyxian escort," countered the older man.

"The whole thing smells rotten to me," the younger man sighed. "The Empress hasn't even granted him an audience yet. And then there's the business with the Trials for the Nyxian man, General Star's nephew. We're expecting to go to war with Nyx, yet we're allowing one of them to pursue Mortem's blessing?"

"You know why that's being allowed," the older man said, a hint of reproach and awe touching his tone now. "His father was Evan Loch. The blessing is his to pursue by birthright. Besides, we can hardly argue when Mortem marks someone for her Trials. What else could the Empress do but allow him to try?"

Kallias's ears burned with curiosity, and he inched closer, intent on hearing more. What could this have to do with Elias's father?

But that exact moment saw Zaccheus returned from his investigation, and Kallias took a step back, grimacing as he bumped Raquel. "No survivors," Zaccheus said curtly. "But I'm seeing evidence of *vellanguis* activity around the bodies. Back up the mountain. We'll have to come back once they've been picked clean."

That was it? They'd trekked all this way for *that*?

He didn't know whether to be more miffed or relieved as the group turned back to the mountain. The idea of taking that climb a second time was nearly too much to bear.

"What's a *vellanguis*?" called Raquel as they started to walk.

"A terror that migrated here from the Tallisian crag-forests," answered Esmeralda with a shudder. "A furred snake with venom in its fangs. Even a graze can kill a grown man within a few hours without treatment."

Kallias's stomach plunged. He knew those creatures by a different name— viper-cats. Their venom was a key ingredient in the poison their Vipers doused their blades in.

"You all go on ahead," he croaked as they reached the base of the path, his chest clenching as he saw the steep incline ahead. "I need a minute longer."

The naysayers he'd overheard earlier exchanged looks that practically screamed *See? Some Emperor he'll be. Pathetic,* before they followed Zaccheus up the path; he dismissed Kallias with a nod as they left.

Well, depths take them, too. They could think whatever they liked. He wasn't long for this kingdom, anyway, no matter what the ring on his finger claimed.

Esmeralda, however, paused and touched his shoulder. "Don't listen to them. You did well out there." A quiver rattled her hand. "I know...I know it isn't easy, facing the thing that hurt you so deeply. Thank you for doing it anyway."

Kallias offered her a nod, watching her go before settling himself on his haunches, back pressed to the uneven mountainside, closing his eyes while the breeze wound itself around his neck once more, cooling the sweat beneath his thick hair. At least this one was quiet.

A pair of boots appeared in his periphery as he stared down at the path. "I thought the First Prince of Atlas would be made of sterner stuff."

He held in a sigh, a fragile wall of self-control like a sailor's desperate prayer cast up against a coming stormfront. "And she's back. That was fast."

"I never left."

"You were almost helpful for a second there."

"You were about to lose the respect of these people. And now you've lost it anyway, so thanks for being a waste of time."

An old wound twinged beneath those words, and he stood with a lurch, meeting her burning eyes with fists clenched. "You know, I've tried to be kind to you, but you're making it really damned difficult."

She barked out a laugh, that ever-present anger barreling back to the forefront. "*What?*"

"I'm trying to make peace with you here. I've been as decent as I—"

"You think I care if you're *nice* to me?" Raquel shoved him back a step, her fury a whetstone struck against her voice, grinding a deadly edge onto anything that had softened during their journey up and down the mountain. "My sister is two years dead, and do you know what that's costing me? I'm starting to forget her laugh. Her smile. The jokes she used to tell. And you? You can't even be bothered to remember—"

"Her name was Jira. Is that what you want to hear?" A whetstone could sharpen more than one kind of blade, and he snatched that fury out of her hands, wielding it as his own as he took a step forward, meeting her where she stood, towering above her. He clenched his fists tightly shut, glacial anger freezing his joints in place. "Her name was Jira Angelov. You want me to remember her face? I'm guessing she looked a whole damned lot like you. There. Done. Does that make it better? Are you *happy* with that, Raquel?"

Her chest shuddered and heaved, an erratic motion that reminded him of death throes. She pushed in so close that her fist was pressed against his heart, snarling up at him with her nose an inch from his, tears of rage glimmering like diamonds in her eyes. "I will be happy when this—" she beat her fist on his chest, breathing heavy and hoarse through her tears, "stops beating. I will be happy when this—" her hand shot up and gripped his neck, a snake-strike blow that caught him off guard, "is slit straight through. I will be happy when you are *dead*, Kallias Atlas, and not a second before."

Ice crept over his heart, cooling the skin beneath her hand. But instead of locking his anger into place, it soothed it. Calmed it. Chilled it into something different…something dangerous. "Do you know who I remember, Raquel?" he asked softly, sliding his hand beneath hers, pulling it away from his throat. "I remember Soleil Marina Atlas."

The furious blaze in her eyes sputtered. "This isn't—"

"*Soleil Marina Atlas.* Her hair made up half her height. Her feet couldn't reach the floor when she sat at the dinner table. Her laugh sounded like someone set a malicious pixie loose on the world and ran for cover. She used to tell the most ridiculous jokes—and really, I do mean the *most* ridiculous, they were awful jokes, you wouldn't believe it. But we laughed anyway, because gods, one look from those big green eyes? It didn't matter how terrible it was. You couldn't let her down by not laughing, you know?"

He couldn't breathe, but these words didn't need breath, didn't need any effort. They'd been holed up in him for ten long years, hanging from hooks in his heart, trapped in the neat spaces between his ribs where they could never fully break him. And now...now they were free.

"Do you remember *her* name?" he whispered, clutching her hand so tightly that he heard her knuckles crack. She didn't flinch. "Do you remember *her* face? Your sister was sixteen. She signed up for this war. If she was Soleil's battlemate, I'm betting she *begged* to be out there fighting. But my sister? *My* sister was barely nine years old when your people stole into my castle and tried to murder my *entire gods-damned family.*"

Raquel said nothing. Did nothing. He didn't even think she breathed. She simply stared at him, diamond tears drying on her lashes, her hand frigid cold in his. It was the first time in months someone else's skin had felt cold to him.

"How many of my people did you put to the sword, hm?" he breathed, nose to nose, eye to eye. "Do you know their names? Do you remember their faces? You think you have the high ground here, Angelov? *I lost my sister too!*"

He didn't choose to shift his voice from whisper to roar. Didn't choose to finally let that anger have its head. It broke free all on its own, and he had no reins with which to tame it now.

"So if you want your revenge, Raquel," he finished, no longer shouting but still guttural, "I'll give you the chance to earn it. I'm sure we can arrange that once I'm done saving *your* gods-damned kingdom. But you need to know that when that day comes, I'll be fighting just as hard for *my* cut of flesh. *My* share of revenge. And if you don't care to risk meeting your sister in the afterlife a bit early, then I suggest you start thinking about bartering a peace between us. Because this will be the last time—the *last time*—that I offer you the chance at a parley. Think carefully. I'll be waiting for your answer."

When he finally released her, there was a coating of crystalline frost circling her hand. But she hadn't flinched, not once in the entire time he'd been speaking—she'd simply stared. And was still staring now, her other hand hanging limply at her side, watching him as he turned and stormed away.

He'd barely made it two steps before a scream echoed further up the path.

CHAPTER 34

KALLIAS

Wﻪhen Esmeralda had described the *vellanguis,* Kallias had pictured a snake no bigger than the usual sort.

He hadn't expected to come upon a viper the size of a gods-damned *house.*

The monstrous creature was half on the path and half stretched up the mountain face, the end of its tail still hidden in a gaping hole Kallias guessed was its cave. The rest of its body was covered in bristling, mottled fur, shades of gray that offered it camouflage against the stone. As Kallias skidded to a halt, swearing so colorfully his father would've cuffed him over the head for it, the viper-cat reared its head, baring fangs nearly the length of Kallias's sword. Its body undulated in slow, smooth movements, its tongue and teeth stained with blood.

The group had backed down the path, sword-wielders forming a wall while archers had fallen a bit further back. Three black arrows already stuck out from the snake's shuddering form; as Kallias reached the back of the group, they released another volley, two missing and one landing true. The snake reared again, and its echoing screech jittered his bones beneath his skin.

Esmeralda was kneeling beside Rory, who gasped through pain, Esmeralda's hands clamped down around a deep pair of puncture wounds in her shoulder and chest. Esmeralda's brows were furrowed with concentration, her green eyes veined in red, and when Kallias peered over her shoulder at Rory's wound, he saw branches of bruise-tinted red extending from the wound.

"What are you doing?" he croaked, unable to look away even as Raquel shoved past him, her own sword drawn.

"Filtering out the venom." Cold sweat beaded on Esmeralda's forehead as she let out a slow breath, scarlet slowly drowning out the green in her eyes. "Go help Zac. We need that thing out of our way."

And how exactly they were going to accomplish that, Kallias had no idea. The massive snake took up the entirety of the path, blocking the only avenue for escape. No way around. Possibly no way through, either. Those arrows didn't seem to be doing much more than angering it.

A fifth arrow buried itself in the snake's furred hide, and this time it snapped back, catching one of the Artemisians in its jaws. The man's horrible scream cut into a sickening gurgle as the snake's fangs dug down. Before any of them could even begin to fathom a means of saving him, the snake's jaw unhinged, its head snapping back—

And swallowed the man in a single gulp.

Kallias heard Raquel's string of truly abominable curses even from the rear of the group. Horror lent a nauseating sway to the world, his stomach sloshing with a seasick unsteadiness.

They had to get off this mountain.

"Retreat!" he and Zaccheus shouted with one voice.

The group didn't need to be told twice. They sprinted one by one back down the path, ushered by Zaccheus and Kallias both, Raquel passing by without so much as a glance his way. Death by this monster's fanged jaws probably struck her as a justifiable enough fate for him. The river of people parted around Esmeralda and Rory, still huddled in the middle of the path, Esmeralda trembling with the effort of using her magic.

"Mal," Zaccheus panted as he stared up at the snake, only he and Kallias left. The beast seemed content to ignore the fleeing people so long as it still had stationary prey in front of it, and Kallias's veins thrummed with terror as he stared into its flat, dark eyes, knowing any movement would bring those glistening fangs down on him. "Mal, you have to go."

"The poison's not clear yet," Esmeralda said through gritted teeth.

"That wasn't a suggestion!"

"Neither is this. I'm not leaving Rory!"

"Mal—" Zaccheus whipped around to face his wife, and finally the snake darted forward, jaws parted.

"Move!" Kallias barreled his shoulder into Zaccheus, knocking him back just far enough to avoid the snake's blow, the fangs flashing an inch from Zaccheus's body. It writhed with shocking speed, its solid form slamming into Kallias with a force that drove the breath from him, sending him skidding across the path—

Until suddenly, there was no path left beneath him.

Panic escaped in a breathless shout as Kallias's palms slammed down on the edge of the path, his entire body dangling off the side of the mountain. They hadn't climbed terribly high, but it was high enough; he didn't need to look to know he'd be nothing but a sack of broken bones if he fell from this height.

Zaccheus and Esmeralda's voices calling his name were overtaken by the viper's hissing as it slithered around to face him, its head peering over the edge, venom-laced saliva dripping from its fangs. A droplet landed on Kallias's arm, burning his skin as it seeped through his sleeve.

As the snake prepared to strike, Kallias thought he heard thunder.

Skyfire seared through his mind, and as he squeezed his eyes shut, his veins lit with the memory of lightning's brutal stab through his heart. Desperate, near-feral with primal fear, he flung one arm toward the sky. "*Tempest!*"

Blinding light. A clap of thunder that nearly deafened him. A shriek that withered into a dying rattle.

Nothing.

Nothing.

Then hands.

Hands wrapping around his one arm, his fingers digging into the stone so hard they hurt, pulling him over the edge and back onto solid stone. His other hand brushed something stiff but yielding, like the bristles of a brush. The smell of burned hair cut into his nostrils.

He opened his eyes to lolling serpentine jaws.

"Depths!" He jerked back so hard that he nearly plunged off the side of the mountain once more, but Zaccheus caught him.

"Whoa! Whoa, there, Prince. You're all right." But it didn't sound all right—Zaccheus's voice was flat with shock, edged with something that sounded unnervingly like suspicion.

Kallias blinked hard, forcing himself to take in the scene: Esmeralda was still bent over Rory, but her wide crimson eyes were focused on Kallias, her lips parted slightly in awe—or fear. Zaccheus looked about the same, and when Kallias slowly turned his head…

The viper-cat lay limp across the mountain path, a circle of burned hair and flesh scorched straight through the center of its head.

"That was lucky," he whispered.

Zaccheus shook his head, watching Kallias too closely. But before Kallias could scramble for a better argument, an unfamiliar voice called up from further down the mountain: "Zaccheus! What was that?"

Zaccheus raised one eyebrow at him. Kallias swallowed and shook his head, hoping his plea came across clearly in his eyes. *Don't say anything.*

"Not sure," Zaccheus called back, eyes still fixed on Kallias. "Let's call it a boon from the gods. Come up here and help me move this damned thing."

The group straggled back up to them, helping Zaccheus fling the viper-cat's body from the side of the mountain, but Kallias couldn't raise a hand to help. Every muscle was quivering like *he* was the one who'd been struck, every hair on end, every sense heightened. Like he was either going to crow with exhilaration or hyperventilate until he blacked out.

He wasn't entirely sure how they made it back up the mountain; he only knew it happened without any further incident. His mind was too caught up in the *luck* of that lightning strike, his entire body still buzzing uncomfortably with energy that didn't feel like it belonged to him.

But he had no time to think further on it. Upon their entrance into the mountain, Safi came careening toward them, running into a couple people's feet, cursing at them to move out of her way until everyone cleared a path. She wheeled over to him faster than he'd yet seen, chest heaving, eyes wide.

"What's wrong?" he asked, sensing Raquel as she came up behind him. She hadn't said a word the entire way back up the mountain, but he'd felt her eyes on him.

"It's Elias." Safi took in a sharp breath, hand shaking as she settled it over her chest.

Kallias's heart plunged sickeningly. "What did he do?"

"He didn't *do* anything." Safi looked between them both, apology and dread braiding together into a wrinkle between her brows. "The High Priestess just fetched him from the forge. His second trial starts now."

CHAPTER 35

ELIAS

D eep in the heart of the mountain, knees aching, sleeplessness burning like acid splashed in his eyes, Elias Loch knelt at an altar of his own making.

This was the first time he'd been divested of his weapons in Artem, and Star had seemed apologetic while explaining the rules of the trial were the only exception to their customs. He'd failed the Trial of Fire, and there were consequences to any failure.

Like they had to tell him that. Consequences were all he knew these days. His *life* was a consequence of his own failure, for gods' sakes.

So now he was here, cloistered in this quiet cave laid out like an armory, various weapons hanging from the walls. He couldn't tell if they were tokens left behind by previous victors who *had* succeeded in the Trial of Fire, or if they were the surrendered weapons of people who had never come back from whatever battle lay in wait for him beyond this cave.

The thought pulled his throat tightly shut, a twinge of pain pinching the back of his neck.

In any case, the daggers Soren gave him were propped on top of a shelf of rock he'd chosen to kneel before, her ring's chain wrapped around his fingers, a sensation that was slowly becoming more and more familiar. At first his skin had balked at that strange contact, the creases of his palms and the dips of his knuckles used to the caress of prayer beads rather than diamond rings. But after all these weeks of his prayer beads gathering dust in the bottom of his pack, his hands were beginning to catch up to what the rest of him had already decided: no god or goddess had saved his life. Soren had done that. If anyone deserved a prayer, if anyone deserved his faith, it was her.

So he knelt. And he prayed.

"Hey, smartass," he croaked. Not a conventional start to something meant to be reverential, but he didn't know any other way to talk to her. "So, I'm sure you've noticed, but I've…I've gotten myself into something here. Something dangerous. Not that that's a surprise to you. You've always said I'd be lost without you."

Nothing answered him but the gentle drip of condensation from cave rock.

"I always thought you were the reckless one. Turns out you were just quicker to make the reckless choice than me. Without you around, there's no one to beat me to it." A laugh tried to fly through the air, but it fell flat, not even bothering to echo off the rock. "This will be the first battle I've ever fought alone."

Those words *did* echo—in this cave, in his head, in the pit of his chest where the jagged-toothed beast with no name had made its home.

It was true: he'd never gone into any fight alone. There'd always been a sister, a brother, a battlemate there to watch his back and guard his flank. Now there was no one left.

He had no one left.

No one to pick up the slack if he made a mistake in this fight. No one to grieve him if he met his true death out there. No one to carry his ashes back to his family.

A chill ran provocative fingers down his neck, that ache in his spine building with every moment he spent on the ground, his bent posture sending a bolt of irrational panic through his body. If it kept bending, if it didn't stop, if that bone rent itself in half again—

He stood with a lurch, straightening his back and rolling his shoulders, goosebumps erupting over his suddenly clammy skin as he set his spine right again, his fingers fumbling up his shirt to feel for any wounds or cracks. Nothing; the skin was intact, the indentations of his spine still arranged in their proper place.

His next breath wobbled, and he ran shaking hands over his face, wincing at the prickle of his beard beneath fingers still sore from forging. He hadn't shaved in some time now; honestly, he couldn't remember the last time he'd looked in a mirror. Maybe if—

Heat licked up the back of his neck, a flash like he stood before a bonfire, and Mortem's now-familiar voice drowned out his thoughts: "For someone so loved, you seem determined to stay lonely."

He bit into his cheek to stop himself from cursing. "For a goddess of death, you seem determined to hold dominion over my life."

Mortem circled around him, and in spite of everything, his knees trembled a bit when he took her in: today she looked more goddess than girl, her hair braided back and laced with the same fire that consumed her entire form from the neck down, a gown of flame dripping in riling layers along her body. Her fingers, wrists, and neck were all encircled with rings of strung-together sparks. A circlet of roses crowned her in scarlet, and the reddish cast of flame somehow darkened her eyes from ebony to oblivion.

His legs shook, his knees begging to hit the floor, his head threatening to bow. But he braced his spine. Held his ground.

How very much he'd changed in just a few short weeks.

"Why are you so angry with me, Elias?" Mortem asked, her voice soft as smoke as she folded her hands behind her back, watching him with those eyes that made his soul shudder with the memory of being tugged out of his body, gathered into the next world like thread pulled from a spinning wheel.

"I gave you my entire self for my entire life," he whispered. "I have made my path wherever you asked me to walk, even when it hurt, even when it *killed* me. And all you have done in return is take, and take, and take. All you have done is demanded proof after proof of my faith, with nothing given in return. Did you think I would keep blindly giving?"

"I think you're observing your life through a very narrow looking glass."

"I think you're *wrong*."

Saying that was a mistake; he knew it even before the words sprang from his tongue. But it was too late to take back, too late to save himself from the consequences of challenging a goddess.

Mortem raised one eyebrow, curved like a scythe and just as much a harbinger of coming death. But instead of smiting him where he stood, she took a step forward, the flames that outfitted her dimming and sloughing away until they revealed a dress dripping in feathers: black as a raven but four times as long, flame peeking between each one. Her hands reached out, hovering over his face as if in question; when he did not retreat, she framed his face with them, holding his jaw in a gentle but firm grip.

"I do not blame you for your grief," she said quietly. "It is...the least bearable of the gifts love grants us. And it touches each person differently. Some pretend it isn't there. Some would rather feel nothing. Others become angry, others try to put it right by their own actions, and some...some lucky few find their way to acceptance."

As she spoke, images tumbled through Elias's mind: Kallias's grim, determined expression when he promised Elias they would find a way to save Soren; his own face in the mirror, devoid of feeling, blood leaking between split knuckles that didn't even sting; Raquel's fury as she held that knife to Kallias's neck, still burning just as hot after two long years; Finn's eyes as he agreed to Elias's request that he make Anima pay for what she'd stolen, a scheme to balance the scales already taking shape in the deceivingly soft brown of his gaze.

And lastly, he saw his mother's face.

He saw her caring for her children in the wake of her husband's death, bearing each wave of grief openly, allowing them to witness her navigating that endless wilderness of pain. Most parents would have done so privately, put on a brave face for their children; but his mother had allowed them to take part in every step of her journey to healing, and it had given them permission in turn to feel whatever they needed to feel, to scream when they needed to scream, to weep when they needed to weep. He couldn't count the number of nights they'd cried together, ranted together, broke plates and bowls and walls together, laughed at old stories and smiled in spite of their sadness together. His mother had ensured not one of them journeyed that loss alone, and by the time she found her peace with her husband's death, all of them were trailing just behind her.

And then he thought of his first lost battlemate. He thought of Kaia: her starshine-bright smile, her hair dark and straight as a slick of oil, her blue eyes always lit with at least a sprinkle or two of joy. Kaia, whose nose he often joked turned up at the end because she always had it buried in a book, whose glasses never seemed to stay propped on her nose, whose arms were the first he'd run to when he'd heard the news of his father's death. Kaia had been his best friend since childhood, every spare moment between their schooling sessions spent playing games of pretend in the shared plot of grass between his mother's forge and her father's art gallery. They'd gone into Mortem's service together, and when Elias chose to abandon his calling in favor of the army, Kaia had wasted no time packing her own bags. And her death had altered him in ways even his father's hadn't managed.

"You have walked this path before," Mortem said, as if she could see where his thoughts had wandered, "but you did not lose yourself then. Why is this different? What are you running from? What are you *hiding* from?"

Why was this different? Because the last time he'd walked this path, Soren had done everything in her power to make sure he didn't walk it alone.

Kallias's concerned eyes and Raquel's steadying hand flashed through his mind, there and gone, the faintest hint of reason quickly tempered by a fresh wave of anger. He ripped himself away from Mortem, rubbing off the cold traces of her touch like splinters left behind from pyre-building. "I'm not running from anything. I'm here. I'm taking your trials."

"So you've said. But you failed the first. And here you are now, sequestered in the depths of this mountain, about to face a battle with no weapon on your belt and no ally at your back." Baring her knuckles, she struck the place where his blades usually hung, then the small of his back, the branding there flaring beneath her touch. "Yet instead of strategizing with your friends or putting yourself through your training paces, you're praying like a man about to taste his last breath. Like you've already given up."

Elias looked away. "There is no version of a fight against Artemisian weapons where I win with only my hands."

"But there could be a version where you *try*." The heat in Mortem's voice caught him off guard, an ember at the heart of the forge rather than a stone on the floor of a crypt. She stepped forward, smoke seething through her clenched hands. "It seems to me that ever since you escaped the grave, you've been doing your damnedest to dig yourself a new one."

The beast reared to wakefulness all at once, barbed edges and serrated teeth tearing up the tender flesh that lined his chest and throat, gnawing his voice down to a gravelly rasp. "So what if I am?"

"Your battlemate gave everything to keep you alive. To be careless with that gift is to spit on her sacrifice."

Endless, blistering fury cut whatever tether remained on the beast, and it roared with Elias's voice: "You know *nothing* about my damned battlemate!"

His fist dashed into the rock wall, something snapping within his hand, but he felt no pain. No fear. Even the anger cooled faster than a doused campfire, the molten core of him hardening once more to stone. He leaned against the wall, chest heaving through every breath Soren's blood had purchased, lungs aching with the weight of her loss.

"Leave me," he whispered. "I want nothing more to do with you. I rescind myself from your service. I will complete this trial only because it might save my kingdom. *Leave me.*"

Mortem's eyes darkened—not anger. If he didn't know better, he would have called it sorrow. "As you wish."

Between one blink and the next, she vanished into the air. And even though he'd asked for it, demanded it…

Some inner warmth blinked out along with her, some quiet companion he'd never noticed until it was gone, a simmering certainty that he was never truly alone slipping away like a happy dream. A presence he had carried all his life…banished with a thoughtless, desperate word.

Dread struck deeper than any blade, an overwhelming sense that he'd just made his last and worst mistake. But there was no time to think on it, either to beg for forgiveness or to convince himself he'd done the right thing, because a horn sounded outside the cave; a distant, resonant bellow that called to a base instinct buried deep in his blood. It lifted the hairs on the back of his neck, a burst of adrenaline barreling through every strained muscle.

Every soldier knew that klaxon wail, whether it came from a horn or a war drum or the mouth of a commanding officer.

A call to battle.

It was time.

CHAPTER 36

ELIAS

A *battle is no different than a song.*

Vibrations scuttled through the stonework beneath his boots as he marched down the hall, escorted by two Artemisian warriors wearing dress armor and grim expressions.

A battle is a partnership—yes, even between you and an enemy. You make a covenant when you step into their space, when your blade or fist meets theirs, when you shed each other's blood. With that mutual sacrifice, you render a battleground holy.

Every step worsened the aching hollow in his middle, cold and dormant, a wasteland with no marked path home.

A battle is a duet.

Boot against stone. Sheath against armor. Empty hands brushing through air that refused to find its way to his lungs. They all melded into music, a funeral procession that bore him ceaselessly toward the end of the corridor.

Toward failure. Toward peace. Toward escape from this thing eating him alive from the inside out, one way or another.

Even before they reached the iron doors, Kallias's voice boomed out past the metal barrier, arguing with someone just past it: "I understand that you've already issued the summons, Priestess. I'm telling you to de-issue it. My friend hasn't slept in days, he's barely eaten…"

"Be that as it may, Prince—"

"He's not well!" The crack in Kallias's voice brought Elias's feet to a halt, faint surprise trying to raise its head beneath the weight of his resigned heart. He hadn't heard Kallias defend anyone so fervently before, not even himself. "Can't you see that? He's grieving. He's traumatized. He needs rest, not trial by combat!"

"It is not for you to decide what he needs, Prince Kallias."

"But you can?" That was Raquel's voice, hushed but hoarse with anger, a tone he'd only heard her throw at Kallias, not share with him. "Who died and made you queen?"

If Raquel and Kallias were taking up arms together against the Priestess, they must have precious little faith in him, indeed.

Before the argument could worsen to the point of losing Kallias his claiming ring and them all being thrown from the mountain, Elias pushed through the door, finding Kallias, Raquel, and the High Priestess waiting just beyond it. They were gathered in another corridor that cut off abruptly at its end, opening up into a much wider space, the clamor of footsteps and voices echoing within a vastness that pinched Elias's nerves into something trying to be genuine fear.

He'd seen this sort of architecture before—a massive cavern eroded into a rounded space, reminiscent of an amphitheater. But rather than a stage, there was a stretch of smooth rock cut out in a rough rectangle from one side of the cavern to the other, spectator stands climbing from ground to sky on every side, reaching toward an enormous hole in the mountain that revealed a stretch of sky and sunlight beyond, blue and gold that threatened to blind him after so many days of fire and shadow.

This was where he would fight for his life: in the very peak of Mount Igniquit.

Scattered along that space were various obstacles, jagged fangs of rock plunging up from the sediment like he stood in the jaws of a creature born deep beneath the crust of the earth. They vaulted well above his head, darker than what made up the floor beneath him, obsidian rather than slate.

"Elias." Kallias's voice, urgent but soft, brushed against his ear at the same time the man's hand touched his shoulder. "You don't have to do this. We'll find another way to get the Empress's ear. She can't grieve forever."

Elias had it on very good authority that she could. "I gave my word." And his honor was one thing, at least, he hadn't yet lost.

"I am not going back to Nyx to tell your family that I let you get killed."

"Then don't go back."

"I'm not doing it either, Loch." Raquel wore every single one of her weapons within easy reach, her face dark as a summer storm as she came to stand just behind Kallias, their shoulders nearly touching—forming a wall of stubborn muscle and two pairs of eyes that blazed with the promise of oncoming lightning. They both looked a little worse for wear, scuffed and dusty and scratched in places; but even so, when Elias saw clouds like that, he usually did his best to find quick cover. "If you're determined to do this, fine. But you'd better walk away from it when it's over. Sera can't take another loss in this lifetime."

Somehow, the sight of them standing together, united against him, was even more worrisome than watching them threaten to kill each other. On opposite sides, they were merely claps of thunder trying to out-scream each other; together, they fashioned a formidable stormfront. "Raquel…"

"I know," she interrupted, turning her head a bit like she was favoring the side that bore her mourning braid. "Believe me, Elias…I know. But we're still needed here, you hear me? We're not done yet. You're not done yet."

You're not done yet.

Those words should have bolstered him. They didn't.

He wanted to be done. He was tired, tired down to his bones—deeper. Tired all the way to his soul.

The grave had never really let him go—it had only let him wander for a little while. And his feet were weary of it. He was ready…no, he was desperate…for rest.

No more nightmares. No more nausea, no more aching lungs, no more burning heart.

He wanted sleep.

He wanted Soren.

But because he wouldn't get past Raquel and Kallias if he said those things, if he gave voice to the terrible truths that had been devouring him from the inside out for weeks now…he gave her a nod. Clasped Kallias on the shoulder, and tried to smile when the man gripped his arm back. "I'll win you your audience," he vowed, not quite meeting Kallias's gaze. No matter how oblivious the Atlas prince could be sometimes, he was no fool, and Elias didn't lie well with his eyes. "And then you save our kingdoms."

Kallias's fingers squeezed his bicep. "We save our kingdoms."

He offered no answer, only a smile that barely even managed to be a grimace. He released Kallias, bumped foreheads with Raquel, then moved past them to the High Priestess, folding his unarmed hands in front of him. "I'm ready."

The Priestess nodded. Rather than a diadem of flame, today she wore a more tangible circlet, a twisted but artful piece of gleaming gold that settled atop her locks like it had been fit specifically to her head. "Stand in the center of the Forging Grounds, please, Priest Loch."

His throat itched with the urge to correct her, but he swallowed past it, bowing his head and striding into the center of the arena. The moment he stepped past the line that separated shadow and sun, light spilling over him for the first time in days, the crowd came to a sudden and discomfiting hush, silence settling over them like a sheet over a cadaver's prone form.

The light dragged every ugly piece of him into sharp, awful relief: the bruises on his swollen knuckles from repeated thrown punches against a wall that wouldn't give beneath his blows. The blistered burns from his days of failed forging. The grime buried deep beneath his overgrown fingernails. The heat even prickled beneath his unshaven cheeks, reminding him how long it had been since he truly stopped to look at himself…since he'd even cared to worry over what he might look like.

He could taste the pity in the silence of the crowd. Its sickly-sweet film coated his tongue, forcing a shameful lump down his throat.

He did not deserve their pity. Everything that had seen him here was his own doing.

A gong rang out over the cavern, its ear-shattering clang ricocheting from one wall to the next. When Elias looked up, he found the High Priestess standing on an outcropping far above his head, looking down on him with eyes utterly void of feeling.

That was a relief, somehow. If she'd offered him a hand of sympathy as well, he might have lost all semblance of pride.

"Elias Loch has accepted the Trials of Mortem," she called, her voice magnified enough to ring impossibly far, touching every edge of this place carved within the mountain's skull. "The first to set foot in the Forging Grounds since his father, Evan Loch. Mortem keep him."

"Mortem keep him," the crowd echoed solemnly, a chorus of voices lifted above the sudden silence in his head.

Elias stopped breathing.

The shaking began in his toes, working its way up and through, like an earthquake shattering through the heart of the world. It built and built and built, a vicious tremoring he hadn't experienced since that first night without Soren, when he'd lain awake in agony, staring at the wall from the time the sun sank to the moment it raised its head the next morning to check and see if he'd closed his eyes.

His father. His father had been...

"The Trial of Fire was a test of faith." Was he imagining the knowing lilt in her voice, a subtle acknowledgment of his failure? "The Trial of Blood is a test of fortitude. Death is no easy burden to bear, and Mortem's will is no easy thing to carry out."

There was no time to shout up to the Priestess, no time to wrestle with this new revelation of his father, no time to even catch his breath against the disbelief that had dug its fingers into his bones, jostling them as if trying to split them away from the tendons holding them in place.

No time for anything as a grate lifted across the space, shedding dust and pebbles as it went, a horrific metallic whine splitting through the hollow hum between his ears. But even when the grate came to a halt, that awful sound didn't abate; if anything, it grew louder, and louder, until his eardrums pulsed with pain, until—

No.

Oh, pits take him, no.

He saw the steel first. Plating that took on the shape of something he'd only seen in storybooks, a body that moved with strange, joint-jerking steps.

All metal. All wrong. All reptilian in design, an elongated neck and tail capping either end of it, wicked-sharp blades curling out of the feet like talons.

Stepping back in horror, Elias clenched his fists at his empty sides as a gleaming metal myth paced free from its cage, the sunlight deceivingly pretty against its shiny steel hide. A least thirty feet in length and ten feet in height. Ruby eyes sparkled menacingly in the sockets cut into its face, its snout inching back layer by layer to bare serrated teeth in Elias's direction. Something gold flickered deep in its gullet.

And when the dragon-shaped automaton opened its mouth, emitting a flame with a grinding screech that rose above the raucous cheers of the crowd, exhaustion was the last gods-damned thing taking up residence in Elias's body.

"Oh, shit," he whispered.

Then the gong rang, the dragon lunged like a spring uncoiled, and the Trial of Blood began.

His body moved without any command from him, adrenaline striking him like a battering ram, and he tumbled out of the way just as the creature of steel and flame barreled past, knife-teeth bared, tiny infernos sputtering behind the rubies that made up its eyes. Its claws screeched abominably against the rock floor as it stopped and twisted with shocking agility, its movements lightning-quick despite their jerky, click-gear rhythm. His knees and palms burned as he skidded across the floor, pulsing with friction burns as he shoved himself to his feet and launched into a sprint just as the dragon pounced again.

A battle is a duet. Well, Elias was out of practice and out of tune, and his hands were entirely the wrong instrument for this particular melody.

A gods-damned automaton.

They were supposed to be mere theories, nothing close to steel-clad reality. His mother had always said such things wouldn't exist until well after her lifetime; likely his, too.

It seemed Artem had seen themselves ahead of the curve.

Another earsplitting roar accompanied a gout of flame he barely dodged, and even then, the smell of burning hair let him know that the heat had seared off the hair on his right arm, maybe even a bit of his eyebrow. Even with mindless battle instinct pumping through his body, his hand shot up to his mourning braid, puffing out a breath of relief when he found it intact.

What do I do what do I do what do I do—

Think, jackass! Use the room!

His eyes caught on the protrusions of stone scattered about the cavern. Memory crashed into his mind with a speed he wasn't used to, rapid flashes, barely pictures: a training session with Kaia, a dodge he hadn't expected, a collision, a concussion it had taken weeks to recover from.

There was no time for better ideas. The dragon was hot on his heels, a cacophony armed with fire and blade.

He bolted for one of the boulders, heart trying to punch free from his chest, sweat flooding from every pore, his clothes sticking like someone had coated him in oil.

Who taught you how to run? I could go faster than this, and I'm dead!

"Shut up, smartass," he wheezed, his senses lost to the roar of blood in his ears, the empty space at his back, the plumes of heat he only barely managed to dodge every time.

Thirty feet from the rock. Twenty. Ten.

He heard the telltale rattle as the automaton's jaw unhinged, heard the bubble of flame catching to life deep in its hollow throat.

Eight feet. Five. Two.

He threw himself into the air, fingers barely seizing a gap between lips of stone, and he hauled ass up the boulder in one swift thrust just before the dragon caught up.

Crunch. Whir. A roar of approval from the crowd. He crouched at the top of the rock and peered over, mouth open, heaving in frantic gasps of air.

The dragon had collided headfirst with the chunk of stone.

For one wild moment, just one when he briefly remembered hope, he thought the contraption might simply crumple in a heap of sparks and steel. But of course he wasn't that lucky; it lurched back from the wall, wagging its head as if truly dazed, one ruby eye missing. Now that socket blazed with fire alone. It slowly leaned its dented head up to look at him, its warped jaws chittering like it was suffering a muscle spasm, sparks spitting from between its teeth.

Somehow, even among hundreds of other voices, he could still pick out Kallias's shout from somewhere in the stands, booming like thunder: "Eli! Move!"

Elias rarely defied orders, and now wasn't the time to make an exception. He hurtled across the uneven surface of the boulder just as a spurt of flame crashed around it, the heat setting the branding on his back ablaze as he jumped back to the ground, rolling to absorb the impact. Still, an ache cracked through his ankles, and his bark of pain was drowned out by the automaton's twisted, distorted scream as it wheeled around to find him, smoke huffing from its smashed-in snout, its jaws not quite able to close completely.

Slowly but surely, he found his rhythm, guiding the music of the battle until he was the melody and his adversary the harmony, his note ringing through the air just before the dragon's; he repeated his strategy twice more, taunting the dragon into smashing itself into the boulders scattered around, and he was just beginning to allow himself the madness of thinking he might succeed after all when the unthinkable happened.

The fourth time he tried to scale the boulder, the dragon was faster.

Five curved blades sank deep into his calf, agony tunneling through skin and muscle, and he couldn't tear himself free before the dragon dragged him back down the rock, the stone slicing open the skin beneath his fingernails as he tried and failed to cling to the edge. The dragon slammed him down to the ground, starfire exploding in his head, coating the entire world in blazing, beautiful white light.

This could be enough.

The thought tumbled through his dizzy head as the automaton clutched his leg in its claws, pulling him along the ground like a wildcat who'd finally snagged its prey.

It wasn't as gentle as his first death. There were no arms wrapped around him, no emerald eyes gleaming with fury and tears and terror, no love pulsing so fiercely through his chest that he thought it might stop his heart anyway. No confessions left to make. No mercy left to beg for.

But it was quick enough. Honorable enough. It was enough.

But there it was again, Kallias's roar from somewhere he couldn't see, a prince's authority shoring up his voice with furious, fearsome power.

No.

Not a prince.

Something more. A different kind of crown.

"Elias, get up!"

He tried. He did. Even as his body relaxed into the newly familiar sense of death approaching…for some reason, when Kallias asked, he tried.

But it hurt so gods-damned much.

Not his leg. A different agony he was desperate to escape. A different pain that promised to take up residence in his chest for as long as he had the nerve to draw breath past his time. For as long as he lived with the broken shards of his battlemate vows embedded in his heart.

"Eli!" Kallias's voice broke this time, a desperate howl he'd never heard from him before. "Get up!"

Not the command of a royal.

The plea of a friend.

That burning beast in his chest snarled, and the simmering heat in his branding traveled upward, magma creeping slow but steady through his mended spine.

"On your feet, Loch!" Raquel this time, and when he forced his eyes open, he finally saw them: both leaning forward like they were ready to jump into the arena to save him, both held back by more guards than should have been necessary for two people. And even that number seemed to be struggling to contain them: sea and storm, lightning and thunder, their gazes afire with such similar fury that he blinked.

"Don't stop!" Havi, further away and out of sight, but he still recognized that bass call bouncing off the rock.

"Kick its ass, cousin!" Safi, screaming from the same direction as Havi, her voice alone infused with the thing he'd forsaken in that corridor:

Faith.

But not faith in any god or goddess. Faith in him.

Their voices rose above the cheers and groans and shouted suggestions from the crowd, twining together to reach him, four hands held out in supplication and demand.

A battle was a duet, but they'd turned it into a symphony.

For him.

Hey, jackass.

A fifth voice. A fifth note. A fifth hand that settled above his heart, her fingers coiling over the ring that dangled there.

He squeezed his eyes shut as the dragon snarled above him, gears clicking within as it prepared to finish him. Its talons released his leg to pin down his shoulders instead, but he felt no pain this time. *Hey, smartass.*

The memory of her laugh tumbled through his mind, a sound he missed so badly even the thought of it carved another piece out of his chest. *What in the pits do you think you're doing?*

I'm tired, Soren.

You can rest when this is over.

I can't. His eyes ached, and he squeezed them more tightly shut. No weeping. No weeping. *You know I can't.*

Not without dreaming of her death. Not without losing her over and over and over again, a different kind of death blow he was doomed to forever relive.

I know you're tired. Softer, this time. Soren was so rarely soft with him, but she always knew when he was too close to shattering to take her blows. Even when she was nothing but a figment of memory and grief. *I know. But Raquel was right, jackass. You're not done. You can't be done.*

Soren...

For me, jackass. I didn't die for you so you could lie down and let a hunk of metal be your end. You're. Not. Done.

The heat from his branding traveled up through his spine, catching hotter and brighter along his tattoos, a fervor that spread through every limb, every vein, lifting his chest in a deeper breath than he'd taken in weeks.

Air only fed flames. And when it flooded into his lungs, when it touched the raw, ever-blazing hole in his chest...

The very marrow of his bones caught fire.

For me, jackass.

His eyes flew open to blazing ruby, whatever flammable substance coated the dragon's throat dripping down on him like superheated rain, its serrated teeth an inch from his nose.

When the liquid touched his skin, it sizzled. Flared. A dozen tiny fires sprang to life across his body, pinpricks of pain that shook him from his daze.

For me.

The beast in his chest spread its wings and roared.

Elias roared with it, a guttural scream that echoed out from him as he shoved his hands up against the dragon's metal body.

The final tatters of a broken vow. A mourning song. A war cry.

His battlemate's name.

Something gave beneath his palms. And then the world burned red.

CHAPTER 37

ELIAS

All Elias knew was fire.

Crimson and sapphire and persimmon and gold. Smoke and heat and pain and *fury*, endless and endless, a tarlike anger that just kept pouring and pouring and pouring.

The fire was flooding out of him, and it would not stop.

Wave after wave of heady rage melted his bones down to molten ore and set his blood to boiling. Breath after breath of thick smoke dragged into his chest, but his lungs welcomed it—almost craved it, as if it was pure as the air that trailed behind a Nyxian blizzard.

He burned and he burned and he burned.

No weeping. No weakness. The fire scorched away all chaff, all dross. *Make sure that the truth of you can stand the test of flame.*

Well, here was the truth of him: nothing left but this. Rage and ruin. Wretched and wrong.

He burned and he burned and he burned.

Somewhere past the inferno, he thought he heard the faintest notes of that symphony beyond, the cries and shouts of his friends telling him to *stop. You can stop, you can stop, Elias it's over you can stop—*

It was only then that he realized he was wrong: he wasn't being consumed by the fire.

No. He *was* the fire.

Flame surged endlessly from his hands—not just his hands. His mouth was still open, loosing an unending shout, and fire flowed out after it like a howling wind.

Firebreather, whispered a voice he only barely recognized, satisfaction coating the word in saccharine syrup.

Pyromancy.

A shocked hiccup brought the fire in his throat to a sputtering halt, spurring a fit of horrid coughing. And just as quickly as the fire ignited, it extinguished, leaving him standing but shaking, hands splayed in front of him, ragged gasps sending splintering pain through his chest.

He blinked his dry, aching eyes to find nothing left of the automaton but a half-melted lump of superheated steel.

Soot coated his outstretched hands, the taste of ash gritty and unpleasant on his tongue. And as he stepped back from the mangled automaton, the world swaying like he'd climbed atop a rocking chair, he suddenly felt horribly, horribly cold.

The last thing he saw before blessed blackness took over was Kallias finally breaking free from the Artemisian guards and running for him, his lips forming Elias's name as Elias's knees slammed into the stone with a sharp, startling crack.

For the first time since he looked into a goddess's golden eyes, he did not dream.

CHAPTER 38

KALLIAS

S o.

That had gone poorly.

Kallias sat at Elias's bedside while Artem's physicians worked on him, staring dull-eyed at his unconscious friend. Elias had taken a beating in there: his leg had to be stitched, bruises mottled the entire left side of his face, his shoulder had to be wrenched back into place, and two of his fingers were fractured. There were blistered burns sprayed across his torso like water droplets cast against glass, but they were so small they couldn't have been caused by the fire itself. Half his hair had to be cut off, that metal beast's fire having scorched it beyond salvaging, and half his eyebrow on the right side was missing.

But worse than all that was the shivering.

Kallias had never seen a man shiver so hard for so long, nearly convulsing in his infirmary bed, cold sweat trailing from his forehead to soak his pillow, his teeth chattering audibly behind the seemingly-permanent grimace that cut across his face. They'd bundled him in countless blankets and warmed him with their magic, but the shivers refused to stop.

It was normal, or so they told Kallias. When a person expended their magic to its very limit, it often drove them to the point of exhaustion or illness. All things considered, they said, seeing as Elias was newly blessed, he'd come out of it relatively unscathed.

Kallias didn't know if he believed them.

"How is he?"

He didn't even jump at the sound of Raquel's voice; he was getting unnervingly used to her sneaking up behind him, which didn't bode well for any future attempts at avoiding a knife in his back. He shrugged, absently poking his fork into the blueberry muffin Havi had brought him a couple hours ago. He had yet to take a bite. "They say he's going to be fine."

"He *will be* fine," one of the physicians corrected, giving him a pert scowl as she finished bandaging Elias's injured leg. He offered an apologetic smile, but she simply turned her nose up and left.

Raquel raised one eyebrow. "Still not making any friends here, I see."

If he hadn't known better, he would've thought she was actually trying to joke with him. "No, that's actually normal. Physicians and I don't get along."

"Only a man with a death wish argues against his physician."

"I don't argue with *mine*. Just…the ones caring for others."

"Mm." Raquel came around the bed to sit in the chair the physician had vacated, directly across from Kallias. She leaned forward, elbows on her knees, twin braids hanging down to brush Elias's bedsheets. "So. Seems we now have a pyromancer on our hands."

He shuddered, the memory still threatening to stop his heart: Elias screaming like he was being burned at the stake, fire erupting from his hands and mouth and consuming the steel dragon, his once-dark eyes ablaze with golden light.

Godly light.

"What in the depths am I doing?" he moaned, dragging one hand down his face. "This is all beyond me."

"I think it's a bit beyond all of us."

Kallias shook his head, helplessness flooding his stomach like a storm swell. "I don't know what to say to him when he wakes up."

"At least he will wake up. At least he succeeded." Raquel's eyes wandered up Elias's form from his toes to his head, then paused. "Where are his mourning braids?"

Wordlessly, Kallias held out the pieces of cloth he'd taken from the physicians—the reason he was on their bad sides now. He'd threatened them with worse than death if they undid the braids...and after they told him in no uncertain terms that the hair had to go, he'd threatened the same if they tried to throw away the strips of cloth Elias had tied into it. "They had to cut away a lot of damaged hair. I saved these, but that was all I could do."

Raquel stared at them for too long, a crease slowly deepening between her brows. But before he could demand to know what he'd done wrong, she nodded once. "Thank you. That will mean everything to him."

He blinked. "Did you just *thank*—"

"Don't make me regret it, Atlas."

"I'm sure it's too late for that."

Raquel allowed one of her rare smiles to take form, and he offered one back—if only in thanks for what she'd done in that cavern. If only because she'd fought for Elias just as fiercely as he had.

Suddenly, with awkward force, she held out the mug she'd carried in. He peeked into it to see steaming coffee inside, though this cup had been lightened with cream. He raised his eyes to find Raquel staring at him impassively.

"It's a peace offering," she said bluntly. "I'm accepting your invitation to parley."

"I'm only immune to three types of poison, so I'm going to pass, thanks."

Raquel sighed. "I deserve that. Look, you..." He watched in fascination as she fidgeted a bit, looking as if she was in absolute torturous agony for a moment before she controlled herself, running a smoothing hand over her hair. "You were right," she ground out.

"Pardon me? I don't think I caught that."

"Please don't make this more painful than it already is."

"Why? That's all you've been doing for the past week."

"Again, I deserve that." She splayed her hands flat on the bed. "You're right. We've both lost. We've both killed. And we're both owed our shot at revenge. But right now, Elias needs us *both*. As much as I hate to admit it, I can see him leaning on you."

She saw more than Kallias could, then; because to him, it seemed Elias was doing everything in his power to push everyone around him away. "So what's your offer?"

"We act as allies until the war is over. The moment our common purpose is eliminated, you and I will settle this elsewhere. Blood for blood. Winner gets to walk away."

"This sounds a lot like what I've been suggesting all along."

He had to bite back a smirk as her eye twitched. "Where *do* you keep all that pride of yours?"

"My legs. My brother says they're only so long because I needed more storage space for my ego."

To his surprise, she laughed. A harsh, single chuckle, but a laugh nonetheless. "I almost think I would like your brother."

"He's a better man than me."

"That's not saying much." She held up a hand before he could say a word. "Sorry. I'll catch up. This is going to take some time to get used to, that's all." Silence reigned for several minutes, then Raquel added, "My sister was better than me, too."

Without the scaffolding of anger holding up the walls of her words, he almost didn't recognize her voice at all. "From what I've heard, my sister loved yours very much. So I don't doubt it."

Raquel smirked a bit. "Your sister was an absolute imp. Her love should not be the metric by which other people's morality is measured."

His lips twitched in response, and he raised his coffee in a toast. "You'll hear no argument from me." Mostly because he had none to offer. How could he? He'd only known her as a girl, bucktoothed and bubbly instead of brutish and brazen.

"It's not fair, all right? How am I supposed to accept that you remember everyone else more than me if you keep acting like you're trying to get better? Enough's enough, Soren. Give up the act. You don't know us, and you'll never know us . . . in fact, I'm not even sure that you don't still want us all dead!"

Shame dried out the core of his stomach, a scalding thirst crawling up to settle in his throat. A thirst that begged for the sour, soothing taste of wine, the musty aftertaste cloying his tongue and softening the talons of guilt.

As ashamed as he was of his outburst the night he'd told her the truth about the Viper venom—the same night he'd caught Elias with Nyxian prayer beads wrapped around his hand—he'd told the truth. She didn't remember him as well as the others; she always sought out Finn and Jericho's company rather than his. She'd warmed to him some, certainly, but there was never time for him to start getting to know the sister he'd dragged back home on the brink of a second death. The sister he'd sat awake beside the entire journey home from Ursa to Atlas, giving her water whenever her pain-delirious eyes found his, too afraid to close them for fear of her vanishing. He'd been half-convinced that if he blinked too often, her features would rearrange themselves into a stranger, an unfortunate woman with the right hair color whose face had warped in his war-torn vision until she appeared to resemble his lost sister.

But that hadn't happened. And out of respect for her dignity, he hadn't told her of the nights he'd spent sitting by the fire with her bundled in furs beside him, ensuring the battle-trained medimancers kept her from slipping into Mortem's hands in the night. Because he guessed she didn't remember—and likely didn't *want* to remember—how often she'd reached the cusp of consciousness on that journey, her mind fighting and failing to reach true wakefulness; how often he'd soothed her during fits of pain and feverish panic, bathing her bloodied face with a soaked rag and telling her old seamen's stories until her whimpers quieted, until she stopped mumbling unfamiliar names under her breath, until she settled with her head cradled against his knee and her glassy green eyes fixed distantly on his face.

"Can you do something for me?" he rasped to Raquel, wrapping his hands around his mug, letting the warmth leech away the cold that had crept in.

"Depends on what it is."

Kallias swallowed, keeping his eyes glued to the dark liquid in his cup, swirling it around a bit, biting back the wish that it had something stronger mixed into it. "Could you...could you tell me about her? My sister."

Silence. Then: "What do you want to know?"

"Anything." Desperation sharpened that word to a plea, and he cursed silently, doing his best to rein himself back in. "Anything you're willing to tell me."

When he looked up, he found Raquel gazing into space, a light crease wobbling between her brows as she chewed on her top lip in thought. The sight was almost enough to distract him from the craving tightening his throat, a different kind of wanting tugging at his gut when his eyes rested too long on her lips.

"Well," Raquel said after a long pause, "has anyone told you the story about her sneaking into an Atlas war camp and painting obscenities on the general's tent?"

Kallias's jaw dropped so far it should've rattled the bed. "That was *her*?"

He *had* heard that story—straight from the mouth of the general herself. He, Finn, Jericho, and Vaughn had spent the entire meeting exchanging rapid glances and hiding laughter behind coughs or well-timed sniffles. Vaughn's face had been red with contained mirth by the end of it, to the point that Adriata had pointedly asked him if he was feeling all right. They'd all had to flee to the hall before they burst into hysterical giggles. Finn *still* talked about it sometimes, with such admiration and thoughtfulness that Kallias had often considered begging all artists in the city to put a ban on any purchases from the Second Prince.

A flutter of loneliness tried to take flight in his stomach, remembering breakfasts spent scolding Finn to get his shoes off the table and laughing at Vaughn's dry quips while Jericho made sure they were all eating enough. Before Soleil's return had turned everything upside down and inside out, *us before all* had truly been the mantra of their lives—the four of them did everything together. It had taken years for them to manage it, to be able to stomach the starkly empty fifth seat, for it to stop feeling like a betrayal to laugh in the presence of Soleil's ghost. But eventually, even if only for a short time, they'd almost found a way to be a family again.

And then he found Soleil on that battlefield. Then Eli. Then necromancy and assassination attempts and terror struck into the heart of his city. Then goddesses made flesh and betrayal beyond words.

"It was her and Jira." Raquel grinned fondly, the crease in her brow smoothing out as she lost herself to memory, fiddling with the end of her braid. "Gods, Jakob was *livid* when they came back. They could've been killed, but they giggled through his whole lecture. I used to think they were born without fear, those two. But Soren wasn't always like that."

"No?"

"No. She lived with my family for a time, you know. When she was first found." Raquel paused for a long moment. "Looking back on it, I think my mother knew…who she really was, I mean. She was so jumpy those days. Asked Soren every day if she'd remembered her real name yet."

"You didn't know?"

"No. Not a clue. Even if she might've told me, I…I wasn't home much then."

His ears pricked at the shift in her voice. "Where were you, if you don't mind me asking?"

"I mind," she said stiffly. "Besides, do you want to hear about Soren or not?"

"Sorry. Go on." But his curiosity remained piqued.

"She was a quiet kid for the first few months. Barely spoke. Barely ate. My mother tried everything to coax her out of her shell, but nothing worked. She looked so…lost."

Pain wracked down his ribs with ice-tipped claws, a new, worse sort of guilt that threatened to dredge up what he'd already swallowed of his coffee. He could see it so clearly in his mind's eye: Soleil, tiny and terrified, sitting at a stranger's table with bandages wrapped around her healing burns, presented with unfamiliar food in an unfamiliar kingdom, her memories muddled beyond her reach. And all the while, he and the rest of their family had grieved over an empty grave, packed what belongings hadn't been destroyed in the fire, and moved to the country house to wait out the rebuilding of the palace.

And she'd been *right there*. Hidden just past their gods-damned border.

"When did that change?" he whispered.

"When Jira got sick of Soren moping around the house instead of playing with her. Poor kid got dragged into all kinds of schemes that were entirely Jira's doing. I think eventually she just decided that if she was going to be getting into trouble, she might as well deserve it." Raquel started pulling apart split strands at the end of her braid, and he watched as the angry lines that normally crinkled the corners of her eyes softened into something he hadn't seen her wear yet, not truly: grief. "They did everything together. Jira even insisted on moving to Andromeda when the queen officially adopted Soren a couple years later. My mother sent her to some fancy boarding school there just to let them stay together."

"You sound…jealous."

Raquel peered up at him from beneath her lashes, narrowing her eyes a bit. Her glass eye was painted with such precision that he often forgot it was false. "I was," she said without shame. "But it didn't matter. I escaped and moved to Andromeda a few years later."

His fist tightened around his mug. "*Escaped?*"

Raquel blinked. Swallowed. For the first time, he saw a hint of nerves in the blink of her eyes, in the twitch of her fingers. But before he could push further, a new voice joined the conversation.

"I must be dead," rasped Elias; when Kallias turned, he found the man peering at them from beneath half-closed eyelids with a frown. "No way in Infera are you two *getting along* now."

"Not quite dead," said Raquel dryly.

"Despite your best efforts, you bastard." Kallias thumped his fist into the shoulder he knew would be sore, scowling as Elias hissed in pain. "Don't ever scare us like that again."

"Don't scare *him*," Raquel corrected. "I knew you'd be fine."

"Oh, is that why you've been pacing the hall for the past hour?"

Raquel scowled at him, and the familiar sight was almost a relief. At least one thing hadn't changed irrevocably today. "I was keeping watch."

"Don't," Elias interrupted before Kallias could get even half a retort out, giving a tired wave of his hand. "You'll never get the last word there."

Frowning, Kallias set aside his coffee and untouched muffin, crossing his arms. "How are you feeling?"

A harsh breath slid through Elias's chattering teeth, and he pushed himself up against the headboard, tugging the blankets more tightly around his bare shoulders. The physicians had already discarded his tarnished clothes. "Cold. What happened?"

"You don't remember?"

"Bits and pieces." Elias squinted, his half-burnt eyebrow bending in a way that would've made Kallias laugh if he wasn't so tense. "The automaton. I fell…there was fire…"

He trailed off, and in the widening of his eyes Kallias practically saw the scene repeat itself: the dragon preparing to finish Elias off. Kallias and Raquel fighting to reach him, Kallias threatening war if they didn't let him through, Raquel promising something worse right beside him. Elias's feral, ferocious scream halting them in their tracks, and then…

"I burned it," Elias said faintly. "That…I was…I used…"

"Pyromancy," Raquel said softly. "But I've never seen anything like that before."

"What do you mean?" Kallias looked at her sidelong, gripping the side of Elias's cot to brace himself against whatever she had to say. How could every single thing they encountered somehow be without precedent? Gods, he just needed *one thing* that had happened before, one thing that already had a proven and easily accessible solution. Just one problem that was easy enough for him to solve.

"Most pyromancers can't create a blaze that size, not while maintaining the heat required to melt steel that way." Raquel looked to Elias, her mouth digging downward. "And I've never seen one *breathe* fire."

Elias's hand wandered to his neck, his throat bobbing beneath his fingers. "I thought I imagined that."

"No." Kallias swallowed hard himself, remembering hours of vomiting up soapy water after he'd spent mere seconds breathing it in. "That definitely happened."

Silence left them all to their own thoughts for a moment.

"They had to cut your hair," Raquel said finally.

Elias's eyes blew wide with a panic like none Kallias had ever seen before, his hand flying up to the shorn edges of his hair. His chest started to heave. "They—"

"I tried to stop them," Kallias said quickly, "but they said it wasn't negotiable. But I saved these. They—"

Elias snatched up the strips of cloth the second he offered them, staring down at them with a strange look in his eyes that set every one of Kallias's instincts tingling with warning.

"Should I not have done that?" he asked hesitantly. "If it was an overstep—"

"Thank you." Elias's voice was flat, not one chink of emotion pitching it up or down. "I'd like to be alone for a bit, please."

Kallias and Raquel exchanged looks, and he saw his same thought reflected on her face. "Elias, we want to be here," said Raquel.

"And I want to be alone." There, right at the end, was a tremor of feeling that twisted Kallias's stomach. It brought back the memory of his own grief-blurred and wine-soaked days after Soleil's death, days he only remembered in blurry snatches, days he'd tried his best to forget completely.

He knew what that kind of grief did to a person. Knew isolation only cleared the way for it to spread and fester, an infection no medimancer or physician could touch. But Elias wouldn't look at him; he merely clenched those strips of cloth in his palm, holding them against his chest, right over the ring Kallias had also insisted could not be removed from his person. The physicians had allowed that much, at least.

"Please," Elias rasped. "I need time."

Kallias glanced at Raquel again, a silent question of whether they should push further. She gave the slightest shake of her head.

"All right," Kallias said, squeezing Elias's arm and standing. "But send for us if you need anything. We'll bring food later."

Elias only shrugged his unhurt shoulder, eyes dull and distant, and Kallias wasn't even sure if he'd been heard.

CHAPTER 39

SOREN

"Kal, wait up!"

Soleil struggled after her brother, her feet pattering unsteadily on the sand, the weight of her board dragging her side to side every time it wobbled in her grip. The day was cool, summer bending into fall, but her long-sleeved wetsuit kept her warm enough.

A chuckle came from somewhere above her head, and the weight suddenly lifted from her hands. Kallias shouldered her board alongside his, grinning down at her with one brow raised. His short, wavy hair was wind-tousled and vibrant, sticking out against the backdrop of sky and sea, red blazing against blue. "You know, we could still get your baby board if—"

"I'm not a baby." She stomped on his bare toes. "I'm just *small*."

"Hey!" Kallias jumped away from her, still laughing. "Watch it, or I'll carry you too, and then it'll really be like when you were a baby."

Soleil pouted. "You were too little to carry me."

"I was six when you were born, silly. That's almost as old as you now."

"I'm *eight*. That's so much bigger than six!"

"Sure, Minnow."

Only Kallias ever called her *Minnow*. Finn said it was because she was small and annoying. Kallias said it was because she was too quick to catch.

The stretch of beach before the palace was empty; Finn was stuck making up a lesson he'd missed thanks to a sneaky trip into the kitchens to steal afternoon snacks, and Jericho was assisting her old teachers with a class at Ivycreek, so Soleil and Kallias were the only ones out today. Soleil didn't really mind it—Jericho and Finn never liked to go out very far, but Kallias wasn't afraid of the water. He always took her out where the good waves were.

The water was still warm when it washed over her bare feet, taking the edge off the slight chill from the damp sand. She plunged into it headfirst, scaring off a cluster of actual minnows, crawling across the sand until the water deepened enough for her to swim without hitting her knees on the ground. Kallias followed, slower thanks to the burden he carried, but eventually they both made it beyond the safety of the sandbar, wandering over the dropoff where Soleil's toes dangled into a layer of colder water that shot a thrill of adrenaline up her back. Kallias passed her one of the boards, and they cut forward together, Soleil trailing behind now; Kallias was the faster swimmer by a considerable margin, but he never got too far ahead, always pausing to wait while she paddled furiously with her much-shorter limbs.

They spent most of the afternoon catching waves beneath their feet, Kallias coaching her on form and balance, each of them competing for who could ride the largest wave. Kallias always won; the ocean picked favorites, it seemed, and where Soleil's status of Heir bought her favor in most things, the ocean didn't care for crowns.

Soleil's competitive nature tired of losing quickly. She feigned being tired, and Kallias paddled back to her, both of them moving into calmer waters to stretch on their boards and float.

"So," Kallias said after a long period of listening to gull cries and their own breathing, "your birthday's coming up. Have you thought about what you're asking for yet?"

Soleil frowned, folding her hands over her stomach, gazing up at the clear sky. "Finn's birthday is first."

"We already know what he's asking for. Books and candy."

Soleil giggled. "If he makes his bookshelves any heavier, they're gonna fall and squish him."

"Like the bug he is."

Soleil splashed him. "Don't call him a bug!"

Kallias grinned easily, taking her blows without protest. "Sorry, sorry. If I promise to be nice, will you tell me what you want?"

"You just wanna beat Finn."

"He gets you your favorite present every year! I've gotta beat him somehow."

Soleil crossed her arms. "Finn's good enough to guess."

"Well, we all know he's smarter than me. Not my fault you're an enigma."

Soleil wrinkled her nose, sitting up on her board, wobbling a bit before reclaiming her balance. "What's an *igma*?"

"It means you're mysterious."

Soleil preened a bit. "I like being mysterious."

"Then I guess you're not getting a present from me this year."

"*Nooo—*"

They bickered a bit longer, splashing each other and laughing between jabs, until they finally quieted, staring up at the sky again.

"Mama and Papa are getting me a new crown," Soleil whispered. "It's supposed to be special for the Heir or something."

Kallias glanced at her, frowning. "You don't sound excited."

She shrugged one shoulder, trailing her fingers through the water. "I like the one I have."

"Well, you don't have to throw it away or anything."

Soleil just shrugged again, focusing on the droplets resting on her bare toes. Jericho had painted her nails blue a couple weeks ago, and they were just beginning to chip.

Kallias made a quiet noise, and she looked over to find him already watching her. "Are you worried about what it means?"

Soleil hesitated. "I don't know."

Kallias paddled a bit closer, watching her with an uncharacteristically serious expression. "You can tell me, Minnow. I won't say a word to Mama and Papa."

Soleil gave him a look. "You tell Mama *everything*."

"Not this. Cross my heart. May Tempest take me to the depths if I break this promise." He dashed an X across his chest with his pointer finger, and she giggled a bit as he mimed drowning in thin air, grasping at the sky as if trying to catch a rope.

"Mama says I have to start extra lessons soon," Soleil confessed. "Stuff the Heir has to know."

Kallias nodded. "And that scares you?"

"It's not *scary*. But I don't wanna have longer lessons. Finn already gets out earlier than me."

"I know it's no fun. But being queen someday—"

"I'm not gonna be any good at it anyway! I hate sitting still, and I hate meetings, and Mama almost never gets to go swimming with us."

"Queens get to wear the best dresses, though."

Soleil considered. "That's true."

"They get the best desserts."

"Well—"

"And they get to marry anyone they like."

"Doesn't everybody get to do that?"

Kallias laughed, scratching the back of his neck. "Not everybody."

Soleil hesitated. "Do you?"

Kallias shook his head. "Probably not. Someday Mama's going to pick another kingdom for me to go to, and I'll marry someone there."

Panic bolted through her, and she sat straight up. "You're going to *leave*?"

"Not for a long time, Minnow. And not forever! I can visit all the time, and—"

"But I don't want you to leave. I—I won't make you leave. I'll be queen, and then—"

"You probably won't be queen yet."

"Then—then what if I—can we change it? We can change it. You can be the Heir, and I'll just be a princess, and then you don't have to leave!"

Kallias snorted softly. "That's not really how it works."

"I'll *make it* how it works. Hang on."

"Soleil—" Kallias tried, but she'd already rolled off her board, diving beneath the water in search of her quarry.

When she resurfaced, clumsily crawling back onto her board one-handed, she leaned over and solemnly crowned him with a sprig of seaweed. "I, Soleil

Marina Atlas, crown you Heir Kallias Alexandros Atlas. You will be king forever and ever."

Kallias sighed, but his smile widened as he submitted to her crowning. "And what price do you demand for this incredible gift, milady?"

"I only ask that you trade desserts with me every day."

"A fair trade, surely."

Soleil sighed, her shoulders slumping as she took in his obliging smile. "I have to be queen, don't I?"

"I'm afraid so, Minnow."

Soleil groaned. "Well, I'm still not letting you leave. That's what I want for my birthday, okay? I want you to promise you'll stay."

Kallias reached out and took her hand, squeezing it tight. "I promise I'll stay as long as I possibly can. If it's within my power, I'll never leave you behind."

Soleil smiled a little. "Good."

Kallias smiled back—just as she tugged hard on his hand, toppling him from his board and plunging him into the water before he could even shout.

* * *

Soren

"Shh. Shh. You're all right. Just breathe."

Breathing wasn't something that felt possible just then. Every inhale only brought more pain, a blade that drove deeper into her stomach every time she moved.

"Shh." A hand soothed over her hair, and she jumped, a cry of pain cracking free from her dry throat. "You're safe now, Soleil. Hey, look at me. Look at me."

She opened her eyes to a blur of firelight and wrinkled brows and anxious eyes beneath them. A bearded face hovered above her, and she couldn't blink it into focus, couldn't find a name for it—couldn't even find a name for *her*. Everything was a muddle of pain and terror and confusion, her memories of before clouded with agony and the trickle of blood down her middle.

"They're just changing your bandages," said the unfamiliar voice, and she clung to it, following the sound of it back to the face gazing down at her. He didn't look angry; she didn't think he was the one hurting her. "It'll be over in a second, I promise. Just breathe."

She tried. "Ow." The word was shaped more like a whimper, and the face above her flinched.

"I know. I'm so sorry."

Burning pain lanced from one side of her to the other, and the strangled cry that curdled at the back of her throat nearly choked her. She writhed against it, but that only sharpened the pain, building until she could do nothing but sob helplessly, not even able to remember how to beg them to stop.

Hands pulled her from the ground, and when she blinked away the film of tears, she found her head cradled in the crook of a knee, someone stroking gloved fingers through her matted hair. "Hey…do you remember the story of the sailor and the siren?"

Her brow furrowed. There was no strength left in her body after that struggle against whoever was trying to torture her, but she managed the barest shake of her head.

"It used to be your favorite. I'll tell it to you, but you have to stay awake for me. Deal?"

She nodded once. A flush of fever heat spread beneath her skin, but a cold cloth brushed across her forehead a moment later, taming it from a flame to an ember. Her sigh of relief blended with his, and he adjusted beneath her, easing her into a more comfortable position.

As he wove a tale of alluring creatures beneath the sea and the one sailor who was immune to their song, she drifted in a daze, her half-delirious mind filling her head with dreams of the story as it unfolded. And when his tale came to its end, darkness putting the beauty to death just as her pain eased, the part of her that knew him whispered, "Stay."

He shuddered beneath her, and his hand smoothed over her hair again, his beard prickling her skin as he leaned down and brushed a kiss against her forehead. "I promise," he whispered. "I'm not leaving you behind."

* * *

Soren

"Are you getting it yet, pretty girl?"

They sat on the other side of the fire, watching Kallias bathe sweat from her brow and tell her stories to take her mind off her pain. Seeing herself from the outside—a version of herself she recognized, not Soleil—tickled sickeningly at the pit of her stomach, but she forced herself to keep watching. To take in this memory stolen not by fire and ash, but by pain and bloodloss, much more familiar adversaries. "I didn't like that nickname when I was alive, and I like it less now, Jeejee."

Jira scowled. "Mean."

Soren rolled her shoulders. "Ehh."

"You'd like it if Pious was calling you that."

"*Ha.* Elias would choke before he ever got it out of his mouth."

"Poor little prude. I do miss him sometimes."

She missed him every second. "Honestly, it's nice to have a break."

"You're funny." Jira hugged her knees to her chest, watching Kallias with her head cocked to the side, the firelight setting an orange cast against her brown skin. "So that's the prince who killed me."

Soren's stomach pinched tighter. She nodded once, her neck stiffening against the action. Some part of her suddenly felt reluctant to admit that; what, did she want to *defend* Kallias now? Protect him from the hatred Jira was certainly owed? All because he'd taken her surfing and told her a story while she was fighting for her life?

It's not just that, chided her own voice in her mind. *You know that.*

She did.

"Soren, look at me." Reluctantly, Soren obeyed. Jira was gazing back at her with a knowing look, her thumb rubbing absent circles over her own wrist while she thought. "I don't blame you for loving him. He's your family. It was war. It just as easily could've been my blade in his back."

"But it wasn't."

"But it could have been. And what if you'd found out who he was to you after that? Would you have hated me?"

Soren snorted softly. "I could never hate you. You wouldn't have known."

"And he didn't know, either. It's okay for you to forgive him." Jira shrugged one shoulder. "I already have."

She didn't know if it was really that easy. Forgiveness had never been something easily wielded for her; stubbornness was much more fun to cling to. Anger kept her warm on winter nights when she needed something to keep her going. Forgiveness usually felt like a surrender of some kind.

"Besides, look at that face," Jira added. "Could you stay mad at that magnificent face?"

Soren groaned. "*Jira.*"

"Sorry. Thought it might lighten the mood."

They were both quiet for a beat, Kallias's murmuring barely reaching past the crackle of fire.

"I remember him," Soren croaked. "I couldn't before."

But with that one memory of a glittering ocean on a fall day came more, gushing out in a tumbling flood: nine years of surfing lessons and piggyback rides and bedtime stories told to her and Finn, Kallias and Jericho working in tandem to weave tales of adventure and whimsy, both of them pitching their voices up and down to create a cast of characters, Jericho using her hands to create shadow puppets on the wall while Kallias narrated. Nine years of extra desserts snuck onto her plate and sneaking into his room after a nightmare and pushing him into the deep end of the pool whenever he got too close to the edge. Nine years with her big brother, a precious treasure she hadn't known she'd lost until it was found.

She could suddenly see that day in Ursa so much more clearly: could see what it *should have* been. When Kallias let his sword fall, when he called her by her Atlas name, she should have run into his arms right there on the battlefield. She should have clung to him and wept into his shoulder, a lost girl finally found, a sister reunited with the brother she'd thought dead.

Instead, she'd tried to kill him, his face as foreign to her as any other in the enemy's army. And the pain in his eyes had only been half to do with the wound she'd left in him.

"You're not done yet," Jira said softly, reaching over to squeeze her shoulder. "Let's keep going."

CHAPTER 40

FINN

Fidget was late.

As darkness fell the night of the auction, so did rain, which effectively put a halt to the planned fireworks display. But the snarling of thunder as it stalked from cloud to cloud promised that the auction would go on regardless, so Finn now stood outside the kitchens, waiting impatiently for her arrival, counting lightning strikes and precious seconds they were losing. At least the darkness lent a mind-sharpening chill to the otherwise humid night.

There was a shuffle just beyond the door—thank the gods. He was starting to think she'd gotten caught.

"Where were you?" he demanded as the door swung open, turning to face her. "We're going to be la—what in the depths are you wearing?"

He took a step back as Fidget flounced through the kitchen door, splashing in a rain puddle as she landed. Her lip stuck out as she leaned back on her heels, wobbling a bit while she took herself in, plucking at her skirt with deft fingertips. "You said dress rich."

"I said rich, not royal."

Fidget lit up with a smug grin, shifting smoothly from heel to toe and performing a flawless pirouette before settling back on her slippers, throwing her arms wide in a ta-da gesture. "You think I look royal?"

Finn groaned, burying his face against his hand, peeking between his fingers at her beacon-esque form: she shone from head to toe, moonlight catching in the fabric of her lavender-tinted opalescent dress, the skirt falling in tiers of varying height from waist to ankle, the shortest layer stopping just above her knees. A circlet of amethyst and silver and dangly diamond earrings crowned her in finery, along with her usual sequined hair and eyebrows. She might as well have wrung the shine out of the moon and painted herself with it.

"You know," he sighed, "for just a second the other night, I thought you might actually be capable of espionage."

That excitable smile shriveled at the corner, and her throat bobbed self-consciously, the toe of her slipper digging into the cobblestone as she turned slightly toward the door. "I...I mean, I can go change, if—"

A smile formed behind the shield of his hand, and he sighed into his palm, running his fingers down his face as he gave her another once-over. "No, don't. I'm just being an ass. You look perfect."

The blurted compliment surprised him almost as much as it surprised her; he'd meant to craft something more poetic, something sure to make her swoon.

Pull it together, Finn. You can do better than that.

As Fidget giggled shyly and stammered out thanks, he tore his attention away from her and back to himself, eyes searching his own outfit for any flaw, any hint to his true identity. Francesca and her girls had done beautiful work, as always; Jaskier was decked out perfectly for a black market auction. Ebony cloth with elegant silver detailing covered him from head to toe, a finely-tailored dress jacket fit snugly to his form, a more sophisticated version of his brother's borrowed military coat from the welcome ball. A black silk cape floated behind him with every step, and even his boots were perfectly polished, the laces capped in silver.

He'd dyed his hair dark for the occasion, finishing off the look with a rim of kohl precisely applied around his eyes.

Between the outfit, the makeup, and the darkness, there was no possibility of anyone recognizing him.

No more slip-ups. No more losses. The Trickster Prince was going in with a full sleeve of cheats and a foolhardy plot, and that was exactly how he worked best.

And no scoundrel or thief in the world could beat Finnick Atlas at his best.

"Tell me the plan," he said to Fidget as he nudged her forward with a light brush of his knuckle against her back. Her skin heated infinitesimally beneath his touch, her breath catching just a bit, and he caught his smile just before it could take full form.

Good. So his gossips were working their magic after all.

He needed her flustered, distracted, convinced she was the focus of an attention she was forbidden to hold. Rumors from the mouths of others—and that questioning by her queen—would do better to convince her than any false confessions from him. Women knew better than to believe sweet nothings straight from the source.

"The auction is being held in the cellar of one of the lower-city taverns," Fidget recited, visibly holding herself back from dancing ahead of him. A measured gait was not exactly her favored mode of transport. She had her shoulders pulled back too straight to be natural, stiff as a drawn bow. "You're Lord Jaskier Lionett, visiting from the city of Rivermouth."

"And you're Lady Jade Lionett, my blushing bride." He stopped her with a hand on her shoulder, pushing it down a bit. "You look like a kid trying to be taller than they are. You can slouch."

"But you said nobles—"

"I said they walk with pride. You look like you're about to snap your own neck, just—here. Watch me."

She huffed, but stopped where she was, crossing her arms and settling her eyes on him. He flashed her a smirk and a wink before turning on his heel, snapping out his cloak so it would flutter like a sentient shadow as he walked. He sank effortlessly into the familiar skin of Jaskier, stalking down the street with languid ease, taking each step with the confidence of a man who owned every stone his toes touched—which, he supposed he did, technically.

"See?" he called over his shoulder. "Nothing to it. Half the trick to a good lie is convincing yourself that it's true. If you believe it, so will your mark."

He twisted on heel and bowed to her with a flourish, sweeping his cape around one final time for good measure. When he straightened, he found her watching him differently than before—one eyebrow quirked, a curious smirk tilting her lips sideways.

"You're enjoying this," she said.

"Oh, every second, my dear." He flashed Jaskier's cocky grin, offering her his hand with a wiggle of his fingers. "Come along, Lady Lionett. We have business to attend to."

She took his hand with a firm confidence that made him blink, that smirk fixed in place, her eyes glimmering with a hint of wicked humor he'd seen in her only once or twice before. "Of course, my love. But do hurry it up, will you? Your wife needs her beauty sleep."

Delight and surprise thrilled through his veins—she'd picked up on her part quickly, almost flawlessly. Even her accent had slipped from Lapis's crystal-clear musical tones to Atlas's salt-soaked drawl. He brushed a kiss against her knuckles, winking up at her. "Any more beauty sleep, my dear, and you'll start getting mistaken for a siren. You'll be luring men to their deaths out here."

"As if any man could turn my head with you at my side, my love." Even her giggle was different—still shy, trimmed with the lovesick nerves of a newlywed, but the tone was deeper, bolder, more seductive.

Huh. Maybe she'd be able to play this game beside him, after all.

They walked the streets arm in arm, bantering back and forth and exchanging mooning looks and flirtatious laughter by every cluster of people they passed. And the more he watched Fidget find her footing, the further she dipped into the role of Jade, a more troublesome thought tickled at the fringe of his mind.

He'd thought before, after watching her transform herself the night they'd gone to see Luisa, that Fidget might have something more to her. And the longer he lingered near her, the more he watched and listened and learned, he was beginning to realize he might not be the only one wearing masks. She was smarter, quicker, more cunning than she pretended to be. She'd proved that much by pickpocketing him, by the ease with which she was wearing this made-up skin he'd offered her for the evening. But she was also smiley, and naïve, and easily embarrassed. She twirled circles through dangerous streets and wore sparkles in her hair.

She was a person of softness and sharpness pasted together, a meld of danger and daydreams. And that, he guessed, was what the Mirrors were training out of her—the side of her that reveled in the taste of sugar on her tongue and sang along with every bar song that drifted their way on the evening breeze. The side of her that nearly wept at the memory of fireworks and taught him a special handshake to seal their secrets.

And somehow…somehow, that didn't sit right with him.

"Jade?" He hadn't meant to speak. But she looked at him expectantly, lips already poised to make a sultry joke, her eyes lit up brown from the light emanating from nearby shop windows.

"Yes, my love?"

"There's not nearly enough joy in the world." Why was he talking? Why did it matter? "It would be a shame to lose any more of it."

She blinked. Frowned. "What do you mean?"

Gods, he had no idea. He shook himself internally, forcing himself to smile. "Nothing. Never mind. Let's keep walking."

And walk they did, their heels clicking on the rain-soaked road, light from the surrounding shops dancing merrily in the puddles beginning to form beneath their toes. He felt the ripple of tension go through Fidget's body every time they skirted around them, her knees bending a bit, some childish instinct pulling her away from the task at hand.

Finn let go of her arm to grip her shoulders instead, firmly steering her onward. "No puddle-jumping, dear. You'll ruin your dress."

"I'll ruin your dress," she mumbled, but it was a glum threat, already resigned to his eventual victory.

"Ah, you'll never find my dress. That's for a different role."

"Well, now you've got me intrigued."

He chuckled. "Pull this off, and maybe I'll tell you the story over a drink."

A bit of the playful light in her eyes snuffed out. But before he could figure out why, before he could scramble to understand which of his remarks had landed poorly, they came upon the tavern they were looking for.

The Drunken Sun was hardly known for its hospitality, nor its drinks, nor its food. But it was known for several other things that made it useful: for being located in a quiet corner in the lower city where the guard shift was thin at night, for being owned by a greedy pair of women whose silence and morality were easily bought, and for having magically soundproofed walls in its rather sizeable cellar. All things Finn knew intimately from repeated visits for various exploits of his own; often interrogations that needed to be performed outside the palace dungeons.

Seamus still wouldn't wander into the lower city, even after all these years. He hadn't quite forgiven Finn for that first week, but it was hardly his fault—what was he supposed to do when a Nyxian spy tried to waltz into his palace, just let him linger?

Well…perhaps he could have. He'd done it with Elias. But that was different. He'd needed Elias alive for the game against Soleil to even be playable.

"Have you ever had a best friend, Finn?"

"Once."

"What would you have done if you lost them?"

His teeth sank into his tongue, pain blurring the memory of Soleil's all-seeing glare and his own silent promises made to a piece of paper in his bedroom.

Whatever it takes. That was the promise he'd offered to the memory of a girl twice dead. And after tonight, he'd finally have the tools to keep it.

He escorted Fidget into the tavern, ignoring its darkened windows and painted, rotting-wood sign that had been turned to read Closed. The tables were empty, all the chairs flipped upside-down and set on top of them, the only light a single lamp lit by the door behind the bar itself. The smell of damp wood and old drink wafted into Finn's nose, cutting through the constant cloud of Fidget's lilac perfume.

He half-expected her to turn around and declare herself unwilling to go any further. But to his surprise, the moment he let her go, she practically vaulted the bar, bracing her hand against it and swinging herself over. She landed with all possible grace on the other side without so much as rattling the glasses arranged atop it, her head just barely reaching above the high-top counter. She smiled at him, her face distorted comically through the stack of glasses, sort of like the warping mirrors he and Soleil used to love when traveling carnivals visited Port Atlas. "This way, right?"

Dumbfounded, he could only shake his head as he circled the counter himself, following her when she ducked into the open door. Trouble, this girl. Trouble in a triple helping.

Within the stairwell were more lamps, three of them mounted on sconces set at intervals down the wall bordering the staircase, another mounted on the closed door at the bottom. Fidget started to make her way down without hesitation, but Finn flashed his arm out and caught her, shaking his head with a finger pressed to his lips.

"Let me lead," he mouthed.

She frowned, and he couldn't tell if it was suspicion or curiosity that darkened her gaze this time. "Why?"

"These people know me—know Jaskier," he corrected himself, still barely breathing any volume into his words. Just enough for her to hear. "If they see a stranger catapulting into their secret event, they may stab first, bury you later, and never bother to ask questions."

Some of the confidence melted out of her posture. "Fair enough," she whispered back, shimmying around him on the narrow landing, taking up position behind him. Her breath was warm and fragrant over his shoulder; something about the scent jiggled at his memory, but he couldn't place it, and now wasn't the time, anyway.

They made their way down the stairs, and just before they entered, Fidget's tiny hand slipped into his. Magic buzzed between their palms, pink sparks drifting like confetti on the edges of his vision for a moment—magic brought on by her nerves, if he had to guess. Her skin was cold and clammy, her long nails digging into his palm a bit, but he couldn't bring himself to pull away. It was the smart thing, really—besides the fact that they were posing as spouses, he needed her calm, whatever that took. If she spooked at any point tonight, all could be lost.

So he gave it a quick squeeze, a comforting touch he'd caught Elias offering Soleil on occasion when he thought he wasn't being watched. "Remember," he whispered, "Lady Jade Lionett."

She nodded, the briefest dip of her chin. "Lord Jaskier Lionett," she breathed back.

Finn smiled reassuringly, leading her across the threshold, hand in hand— And immediately came to a halt at the click of a crossbow bolt sliding into place, the shiny metal tip inches away from his nose.

CHAPTER 41

FINN

"Jaskier Lionett," drawled a voice that sent spiders crawling on furry legs through Finn's stomach, annoyance and caution fighting for dominance. A hulking man stood just behind the crossbow, a wall of mindless muscle that took him back to a couple months ago: an unseasonably warm winter day, a card game gone sour, a favor done for Luisa just before the world fell apart at the seams.

Drag him to the depths and drown him twice, not *again*.

He put on his most nervous smile, releasing Fidget's hand to put both of his in the air. Still, the flutters of her magic twinkled in his periphery, making him a bit dizzy. "Tomas! My, it's been some time. How are you? How's the family?"

"You shut your cheating mouth," snarled Tomas, inching forward until that crossbow bolt just started to nibble at the tip of Finn's nose. "I want my money back."

"Good sir, I think you're mistaken," Finn rambled, wincing a bit as a drop of blood pearled down his nose to catch against his top lip. "You see, as I recall, I won that money fair and sq—"

"*Fair,* my ass. We both know you cheated at every hand that game." Tomas threw a sneer over Finn's shoulder, and Finn tensed a bit, feeling Fidget duck a little closer to him. Gods, he shouldn't have brought her here; he could've managed this himself. What was he thinking, dragging a girl made of light into his shadow kingdom? He could find his way out of this somehow, but if Tomas threatened *her*…

"Give me my money, or I'll take something else. Maybe your head…" Tomas's gaze dropped to a region Finn really didn't care to have ogled. "Maybe something lower."

"Oh, I'm afraid I'll have to insist against that," said another voice over Finn's shoulder—a voice so unfamiliar that for half a second, he was absolutely convinced a third person had come down the stairs behind them. But no, that was Fidget who curled around from behind him, Fidget who'd spoken such bored, commanding words, her smile void of feeling and her eyes glimmering in a way that reminded him of the flirt of moonlight on steel. He nearly shivered at the expression on her face—no longer smiles and sugar. Crystal and ice. Cunning and cruelty.

"Move aside, Lady." Tomas tracked her out of the corners of his eyes while he kept his weapon trained on Finn. "My quarrel ain't with you."

"Oh, but it is with me. You see, that's my husband's manhood you've threatened, and that's the part of him I'm really most fond of." She tsked, wedging herself between Finn and Tomas, forcing the other man to step back. "Come now, Jaskier. More cheating?"

"Ma'am, you really need to—"

"Now, darling, let's think this through, shall we?" Fidget interrupted Tomas, tipping her head to one side as she pressed her fingertip into the point of the crossbow and coaxed it to aim at the floor instead. "You see, you're not just in the presence of a Lord, here. You're in the presence of his Lady. And it would be terribly uncouth to kill a man in front of his wife, don't you think?"

Tomas stuttered, his mouth opening and closing like a fish gasping for air. "I—"

"Now, if it's money you're worried about, of course I'll see to it that this is made right. My husband—" she tossed a glare at Finn, "—has a bit of a problem. Two problems, really. He has a bad habit of gambling, and testing his wife's *very thin* patience."

Finn lowered his head, hoping to whatever gods didn't hate them that he looked appropriately contrite. His heart pounded like a hammer trying to nail his ribs into his stomach.

No way she was pulling this off. No way small, shy, sweet-toothed Fidget was about to save his ass.

"Now," Fidget continued, utterly indifferent as she plied her diamond-studded earrings out of her ears and tossed them to Tomas, "I have no clue how much he took from you, but these should certainly fetch a pretty penny wherever you fence them. I hope that will suffice?"

Tomas blinked at her once. Twice. Still dull as a brick, it seemed.

"May we get on with our business?" Fidget coaxed with the sweetest damn smile he'd ever seen on a person wearing such cold, careless eyes. His heart stuttered, an odd rhythm that struck his chest differently than before. Not fear. Something else. Something worse.

Something *so much worse.*

Later. We deal with that later.

Finn glanced between them with baited breath as Tomas weighed the earrings in his hand, considering. Slowly, his fingers curled closed. "Fine." The crossbow lowered entirely, and it was only because he was still in character that Finn allowed himself a gushing breath of relief. But no sooner had he started to step forward than Tomas stopped him with a hand on his chest, leaning in so close that Finn could make out every dirt-filled pore in the man's bent nose. "Say thank you to your Lady, friend." He grinned, his breath curling the hairs in Finn's nose. It took work not to gag. "She just saved you, one way or another."

"Of course," he managed, swallowing down the bile threatening to climb his throat like a ladder. "I will...absolutely do that. Of course. From the bottom of my heart, my dear, thank you."

Fidget only sniffed, turning her nose up and away from him. "Let's just find our seats, please. Try not to embarrass me any further tonight, will you?"

Only when Tomas had melted into the crowd—and everyone else's eyes had drifted off of them, losing interest now that violence was off the table—did Finn grab Fidget's wrists and whirl her around, pushing her quickly into an empty corner before releasing her. "How did you do that?"

"I don't know!" Every cold thing he'd seen on her face melted away in an instant, her eyes wide with gleeful terror, her chest heaving visibly, sweat gleaming on her skin. She clutched at her clavicle with a shaky hand, laughing breathlessly as she sank against the wall, covering her mouth with her other hand. The halo of her magic finally faded, settling the dizziness in his head. "I just—I did what you said! I thought about it really hard, and I just…I believed I was her. I was Jade Lionett, and Jade Lionett's a *badass*!"

A full-fledged grin cut across his face, and for the first time in gods-knew how long, he did absolutely nothing to hide it. She'd earned it. More than earned it. "She most certainly is. Thank you. You saved my ass."

Fidget blushed through a mischievous grin. "Well, to be fair, I think his target was a bit more front-facing."

Finn shuddered. "Thank you, thank you, *thank you thank you thank you*."

Fidget giggled, but her eyes slid past him to the front of the cellar. Her hand lifted from her chest to fan her face. "We really should sit down. I think the auction's starting, and I…"

"Are your knees about to give out on you?"

"Definitely, yeah."

"Totally normal. The first time I pulled off a con, I couldn't stand for an hour." Finn took her by the elbow and guided her to a table, careful to wear the guise of an utterly humiliated man begging for forgiveness, careful to shield Fidget's shaken visage from the rest of the crowd. He found them a table near the back, pressed against a wall; they wouldn't have to worry about watching their backs there, and any eavesdroppers would be safely within his line of sight. "Really, though, I mean it. You were brilliant. That was…unbelievable."

"I know!" she burst out gleefully—then, at his warning look, lowered her voice with an apologetic smile. "Sorry. Thank you. I hope I never have to do it again. His breath smelled like…"

"Like a compost bin threw up in a morgue?"

"Oh, gods, that's it *exactly*."

He chuckled under his breath, reaching out and tweaking her empty earlobe. "Sorry about your earrings. I'll replace them."

"Oh, don't bother." Her eyes gleamed with delighted satisfaction. "They're just cheap crystal. Fake diamonds."

Finn folded his hands in a praying position and pressed them to his lips, gazing at her in awe. "You're kidding."

She giggled, shaking her head. "He might get a pinch of copper for them, at best."

"You're my new favorite person in the entire world. Don't tell Luisa."

"Your secret's safe with me, *Lord Jaskier.*"

Their combined laughter, hushed as it was, was drowned out easily by the call of the auctioneer at the front of the room. He clapped his hands in a quick three-beat, pulling everyone's attention forward. "The usual rules are in place," he called in a voice only worn by those utterly bored by life and everything to do with it. "No threats, no murder, and absolutely no bidding outside your means. Break these rules, and you're banned from all future auctions. Failure to pay will result in…additional consequences."

It was rather telling that murder wasn't at the top of the *forbidden* list. Finn exchanged a look with Fidget, but she seemed distracted now, twirling her mirror pendant while she gazed blankly into space. Before he could ask her if something was wrong, the auctioneer began his rounds, and reading the room absorbed every drop of Finn's attention.

It was more than seeking out trouble—it was watching to see who wanted what, who was bidding and who was biding their time, who had seemingly infinite coin and who clutched the clasps of their purses closed with iron-clad fingertips. It was seeking out the rule-breakers, those who slipped between tables to deliver a whispered threat to stop someone's bidding on a particular item. It was keeping track of who wasn't there to bid at all…the people who lingered in the shadows cast by the shelves of wine and casks of ale, the ones who wore triumph or disappointment in their eyes depending on what price each item sold for. These were the suppliers of this auction, the thieves who relied on these bids to keep themselves fed and housed.

Briar Holbrook and Colin Rath were both among them.

There was a clear difference between them: Colin lit up at the sale of more than one item, an eager young man watching his various conquests buy him a better life. Finn knew full well the man had his sights set on moving into the upper city district, and judging by the pleasure glazing his eyes, Finn guessed he might have just earned enough to buy himself out of this life.

Briar didn't so much as blink. Not once. Not at any sales. She simply loitered in the darkest shadows, drawing no attention and paying no mind to the others, looking for all the world like she was waiting for someone to put her out of her misery. She had her eyes on only one person—a figure hooded and cloaked, seated close to the front of the stage who'd arrived shortly after their run-in with Tomas.

He'd seen no more than a couple bids from that patron, each of them halfhearted, neither on the same item. A ploy to disguise the fact that they'd come here for one piece in particular.

Found you, Jer.

At least, he guessed it was her; the build was right, the way she sat, the clear discomfort lining her shoulders. And he doubted Jericho would have trusted anyone but herself to fetch this object. Briar must have told her where to go.

It was almost sad, watching her try to play his game without knowing any of the rules. He would have pitied her if he had any room in his heart to feel sorry for depths-damned traitors.

He hooked a finger into the hood of his cape, tossing it quickly over his head. If it *was* Jericho, she wasn't going to be fooled by a shoddy dye job and some kohl around his eyes.

Finally, the auctioneer gestured toward the side of the room, and Briar pushed herself off the wall, picking up a cloth-covered object she'd been shielding behind her legs until now. Tension tugged at Finn's muscles as he shifted forward just an inch, trying to snatch a glimpse beneath that cloth, but one didn't gain a reputation like Briar's without having deft hands. She kept it covered even as she traded it off to the auctioneer, her mouth moving in what he guessed was a whisper of warning.

"Finn," Fidget breathed from behind him, leaning forward herself, desperate eyes clinging to that covered object. "That's it."

He reached out and pushed her carefully back into her seat. "I've got it," he muttered, glancing over to take stock of the figure he'd noted earlier. She too had shifted forward, all her body language pointing to the sheet-covered oval now mounted on a stand at the front of the room. "Easy," he whispered to Fidget, keeping his hand on her shoulder, pinning her to her chair with a feather-light touch. "Be patient. We'll get it."

The auctioneer tugged off the cloth to reveal exactly what Finn had expected to see: an oval mirror, its frame pure silver, crusted with jewels and precious stones of all kinds and colors. But it was bigger than he thought it would be—at least two feet across the middle and three feet in height—and just as Fidget had said, when the auctioneer dipped it so they could get a better look, there was no reflection pressed between the panes of glass. The lamplight bounced off the surface the way it should, but instead of a reversed rendition of the room, the glass seemed to contain a pool of quicksilver in its middle. With every movement, the pool shimmered and shifted, an illusion trapped in a pretty casing.

He and Fidget let out their caught breaths at the same time, and he exchanged a look with her, mouthing, *Let me handle this.*

Her brow pinched nervously, but she nodded once, handing him control of the game once more. He eased himself back in his seat, cocking his head at a lazy angle, letting his shoulder drop a bit so she could see past him without leaning too far forward and betraying her own interest.

"This," said the auctioneer, "is a once-in-a-lifetime find, plucked from the chambers of the Mirror Queen herself. Rumor claims the glass is infused with Occassio-blessed magic."

Finn's fist tightened against the table, his steady breathing tripping a bit. "Which magic?" he breathed to Fidget out of the corner of his mouth.

"I don't know. Esha's never said. I don't know if she's ever used it."

He didn't have time to press her further. Because by the time he recentered himself and turned back to the task at hand, the bidding had already started—and not just started. *Soared.*

Everyone wanted a chance at that mirror, and it irked him that Briar had been quite so open with the auctioneer about its nature, but it couldn't be helped. If it had been his to pass off to a client, he would've done his best to strike a balance between intriguing and ordinary to keep interest low enough for his client to dominate the bid. But then again, Jericho was First Princess of the kingdom. She hardly lacked for funds. Maybe Briar was simply trying to get a higher cut than what she'd originally been offered.

"Why aren't you bidding?" Fidget hissed into his ear.

"I'm biding my time." He didn't take his eyes off that figure at the front, silently weighing the heft of everyone else's hidden coinpurses against the potential of hers.

"But you said—"

"Tell me what mistakes she's making."

"What?"

Finn dipped his head in the direction of the figure. "What's she doing wrong? Tell me. Anything you notice at all."

Fidget made a quiet noise of frustration under her breath, but she leaned forward, following his gaze. "Um…she sat at the front. That put her in full view of everyone who wants the item she's bidding on."

"And what did that make her?"

"A target." Fidget's voice rounded out with understanding as she spoke, her hand settling on Finn's shoulder, fingers digging into his sleeve. "Everyone knows who to look for afterward if they want to—"

"Steal it," he finished in tandem, smirking as her gasp of delight told him she'd followed his path of thought to the end.

"You're not bidding because we're not going to buy it."

"Why spend my coin when they can do it for me? That's not an easy object to transport safely through the lower city. They probably brought a carriage or a wagon. We can slip inside and slip back out before they even start driving off. Well, you can, I mean."

Her eyes widened in faint alarm. "*Me?*"

He chuckled. "Anyone who can pick my pocket can pull off a carriage lift in their sleep, Fidg. You'll be fine."

The bidding went on for an hour, and the amounts being named off by the auctioneer were high enough to make even Finn's deep pockets cringe. To his surprise, though, the figure he'd marked stopped bidding just short of a victory, their clenched fist on their table the only sign of their fury. The mirror went to a black-cloaked man parallel to Finn and Fidget's table instead, and after he claimed his prize and paid his price at the end of the auction, he rose and swept back up the stairs without hesitation. Clearly he knew there would be a target on his back.

The figure Finn had marked as likely to be Jericho stormed toward Briar, who looked dismayed even with the remarkable schooling of her features throughout the night. Before the two could reach each other, Finn nudged Fidget up from her chair, wrapping a casual arm around her shoulders and guiding her toward the stairs, his heartbeat calming now that the path ahead of them was clear.

"New plan. I'll follow him out and around," Finn breathed into her ear. "You count to thirty, then follow me. Be ready to catch and run. Or cause a distraction, if needed."

"What kind of distraction?"

"How loud can you scream?"

She groaned. "I don't like this plan."

"I hear that a lot. Just follow my lead. It'll be fine."

As Finn stepped back into the eerily dim-lit tavern, the puttering lamp on the wall allowing a grayish cast to seep over his skin, he caught sight of his target walking swiftly away, the flash of moonlight on his cloak the only giveaway that he wasn't just another shadow.

Got you.

Finn bided his time, placing his steps in time with his target's, measuring his paces so he wouldn't get too close or fall too far behind. The man who'd purchased the mirror was certainly familiar with the lower city; he took turns down secret alleys and hidden pass-throughs that even Finn barely knew existed.

It was down one such alley that Finn finally made his move; he teased his dagger free from its sheath with a flex of his fingers, the blade emerging without so much as a whisper to echo off the brick and cobblestone. Even the alley rats didn't balk at his presence, his steps lighter than theirs. But even so, when he bolted forward and shoved his quarry's much taller body into the wall, driving the man's breath free from his chest, his blade met skin at the same time cold steel settled atop his own throat.

"Well," he said against the nip of metal, "this is a bit awkward. Seems we're at an impasse—"

A dirty curse from beneath the hood, and the man threw it back, revealing black-silk hair and moon-kissed sienna skin as he lowered his knife from Finn's neck. "*Prince?*"

A curse of his own slid through his teeth. "*Vash?* What in the depths are you doing here?"

"You asked me to be there, remember?" Vash held up the covered mirror, his brows deeply creased, expressing more emotion than the Viper usually wore. "You told me to get the funds needed from the treasury before Jericho could gather them. I assumed you meant for me to purchase—"

"What kind of herbs have you been chewing? I told you nothing of the—" Finn's voice jammed to a halt in his throat, caught by a hook of sudden terror.

He hadn't told Vash anything like that—not to his memory. But maybe he had, the command buried somewhere in those missing hours between his morning talk with Vash and his awakening at sunset. He'd assumed he'd simply passed out, and that Vash had dragged him to his room to save him from scrutiny.

Had he been conscious all that time? What else had he done, said, revealed? Just how *much* had he forgotten?

"Ah," he said, so weakly that even he wanted to roll his eyes at himself. "Yes. Right. I remember now."

Vash narrowed his eyes. "Prince, something isn't right."

Understatement of his gods-damned *life*.

"I know," he rasped. He meant to lie, to come up with a quip or an excuse, something that would save him face. But terror had stolen any confidence from his words, his mind still wandering back into the fog of those lost hours, desperately probing the haze for something, *anything*—

A scream echoed through the lower city streets, stirring the rats to scurry into their holes and shaking Finn violently from his daze, turning on his heel so fast he nearly twisted his ankle.

He knew that voice. And in spite of his humor, he knew that scream was no joke, no distraction. The fear in it rang true against the Port Atlas walls, honing his panicky mind back into calm, cruel focus even as his stomach dropped straight through to his toes.

"Follow me!" he barked to Vash, sprinting out of the alley and toward the source of that shriek, not caring that his dagger was still drawn, flashing telltale in the light of the nearly full moon. Not caring that his hood had fallen back, leaving his face open to anyone wandering the streets, not caring that he was going about this the most gods-damned foolish way possible.

Because he knew that voice. And if she was hurt, or worse than hurt, it was all his fault for dressing her up to play pretend in a game that should've been his alone to gamble on.

The next few moments stretched out like hours, like *days*, Finn's chest pinching more tightly closed with every breath he took, mounting fury pumping through his veins like a poison whose cure was just beyond reach. Every alley he barreled into, every shopfront he peeked inside—every place he *didn't* see a dress wrought from moonlight and a smile that could turn sweet or scathing at the gentlest tilt of her lips—that venom flowed thicker and sharper.

Where are you where are you where are you

"Fidget!" He shouldn't be risking a shout, but gods damn it, how far could she have possibly gone? How far could they have possibly dragged her without being noticed?

You know how far, his sensible side reminded him, annoyance the only poison it kept on hand. *She's a hundred pounds soaking wet and her hair takes up half of that. They could've tossed her in a cart and driven her a mile away by now.*

And if they had, he would never catch them, not on foot. It would take days to track her down, days he didn't have to spare, days *she* wouldn't have to spare—

Pink light seared across his vision, sharper and brighter than it had ever been, and in the glare left behind on his eyelids, he saw it: an alley back in the direction of the Drunken Sun, a quiet little thing he'd likely missed with his sole-minded focus on Vash earlier.

Go get her, snarled a voice he hadn't heard since covering all reflections in his room, since this hunt for the mirror had started. He'd almost begun to think Occassio had given him a bit of a break. But of course she wasn't that kind.

He didn't waste time questioning her direction. He ran.

And when he finally came to the mouth of the alley, the sight within caught his feet at the ankles, snagging them to the street like he'd stepped in tar.

Fidget was pressed flat to the alley wall, her entire body cringing inward, her fingers feeling desperately along the wall as if one of the bricks would magically loosen and drop into her hand. Her eyes were blown wide, her chest fluttering like a hummingbird's bobbing flight around a flower, and looming above her, thick hands braced against the wall on either side of her, his leering face pushed right up to hers—

Tomas.

Finn did not think.

He did not feel.

He simply moved.

Like a crossbow bolt shot by a marksman unmatched, he arrowed toward Tomas, flipping his knife in a single smooth motion—

Before Tomas could even see him coming, before Fidget could get the breath to scream again, Finn dragged that dagger in a silent arc across Tomas's throat. No hesitation. No thought in his head but *not her. Not her.*

There was a splash. A gasp. A drowning, dreadful gurgle. Finn's hands grew very, very warm.

And then there was nothing at all.

Tomas's body crumpled almost before Finn's knife finished its precise path along his thick neck, but Finn barely spared him a glance. Barely took in the bugging eyes, the slack jaw, and the second mouth—much fleshier, much newer— that gaped just a few inches below Tomas's chin.

He took it in with a blink, there and gone, and that was it. Because Fidget was there, and since the scream that had drawn him here in the first place, she hadn't yet made a sound.

And that terrified him.

"Are you hurt?" he demanded, reaching out to grip her shoulders, realizing too late the warmth that had coated his hands was actually Tomas's vile blood. His handprints soaked into Fidget's dress, but she didn't even flinch, her wide eyes fixed on his face.

"What?" she asked blankly.

"Answer me!" Finn shook her, urgency pitching his voice higher, his heart stumbling to a halt the longer she stared at him in silence. If Tomas had hurt her, truly hurt her—

Death was too good. Death was too fast.

"Fidget!" he snapped again when she only blinked. "*Are you hurt?*"

"N-no—"

"Did he touch you?"

Her shivering sob was the only answer she managed, her face shocky and sick. Her trembling fingers clung on to his bloodied shirt, and he moved to brace her elbows even as he continued probing her with his eyes for any sign of injury. Blood, so much blood, but he couldn't tell if any of it was hers.

"I'm sorry," she rambled, finally finding her voice as she leaned into him, her chest hitching with tiny hiccups trying to be sobs. Fury drove its blade into his heart again at the sight of her tears, but there was no throat left to rend, no blood left to spill. He could do nothing but hold her steady now. "I'm so sorry. He came out of nowhere, I-I didn't see—"

"*You're* sorry?" He tried to laugh, but the noise stuck in his throat, coming out as a choke rather than a chuckle.

It was then that he realized he couldn't breathe.

His chest was drawn tighter than corset strings, his stomach turning slow somersaults, bile and illness brewing in the vat of his throat, waiting their turn behind the laugh he still couldn't quite shake free. He looked down at his scarlet hands, his mouth drying out.

He'd caused plenty of deaths before—had threatened them, arranged them, paid for them in coin on the most desperate of occasions—but his own hand had never borne the blade. His own clothes had never been stained with someone else's scarlet remains. And that warm slickness sliding down his fingers, staining the fingernails he'd chewed down to the quick in fits of absentmindedness, the hot smell of iron and salt and a hint of sour death flooding his nose, his mouth—

He hadn't even hesitated.

"Finn?"

Fidget.

Her hands were touching him, one pressed to his chest, the other to his cheek, her eyes wide with worry. The arterial spray across her dress looked a bit like a firework.

"Guess you didn't miss them after all," he muttered. Everything was so slow. So quiet. Had she always had that little cluster of freckles right between her eyebrows? No, wait, that was another blood spatter. Gods, she was covered in it. He'd covered her in it. He'd killed someone. He'd *killed* someone.

"What?" Fidget's brow pinched, congealing that spatter into a droplet, its path carving down her face like a gruesome tear. Slowly, as if in a dream, he reached out and caught that tear, adding it to the slick of lifeblood that felt like it was seeping through his skin, staining his very bones with the mark of a murderer.

He didn't have the chance to explain himself. As her other hand dropped from his face, darkness swallowed him whole, and for once, he fell into it gladly.

CHAPTER 42

ELIAS

T he days following the Trial of Blood passed in a colorless blur.

His wounds ached and burned and itched as they started to heal, and the soul-deep shivering didn't stop for two entire days, no matter what broths or medicinal brews the physicians forced down his throat. He just kept shaking. And shaking. And shaking.

It was because his magic had only just woken, or so they told him; because he'd plunged into it headfirst instead of testing the waters with a toe, and his body hadn't been prepared. He hadn't built up any sort of stamina.

Shock, they said. His body had gone into shock.

That was certainly what it felt like. The gaping hole in his chest that had been trying to rip him apart before now lay dormant; now that he'd released the many-fanged beast, its den had become a vacant oblivion, a part of him that knew neither pain nor anger nor grief.

It was a relief. Whether it should have been or not. Whether it should have worried him or not.

He felt...nothing.

And he was glad for it.

After they released him from the infirmary early one afternoon, there was no excuse left to keep him from returning to the chamber he and Kallias and Raquel shared. But everything in him cringed away from that idea. Kallias, with his anxious eyes and gentle touches and reassurances that Elias was not alone, was the biggest threat to this impassive new creature that had stretched itself out luxuriously in the den abandoned by the other monster, a much quieter beast that simply snuffed out any feeling or fire before it could form to completion. Kallias wanted to slay that beast, to force Elias to feel and feel and feel until something finally broke. Until something finally changed.

But Elias liked the quiet. So instead of going back to that chamber, he went to Havi's bakery. At least he knew Havi wouldn't force him into anything.

The hours between lunch and dinner were slower in the bakery, and when he limped in, favoring his still-healing leg, he was relieved to find it empty. Havi was seated on a stool behind the counter, a pair of spectacles propped on his nose. He had a book in one hand and a coffee in the other, his hair tied in a bundle of locks atop his head. He wore a beige sweater draped over his tall form, peace emanating from him like ripples in a puddle, sweetening the very air with a sense of contentment.

Suddenly, the nothingness in his chest felt less like peace and more like the lack of it.

This was a mistake.

He turned to go, but as usual, Havi's senses were oddly well-tuned for a man who'd chosen baking over bloodshed in a kingdom of weaponsmiths.

"Elias!" His cousin's excitement changed to offense on his behalf when he turned around. Havi's gaze ran over him in disbelief, and he stood up, kicking the stool back and setting aside his book. "You look terrible. When was the last time you ate?"

"Um—"

"No, stop. If you have to think about it, it's been too long. Mortem help you, we were just starting to get some meat back on your bones." Havi muttered

347

as he placed his coffee on the counter before gesturing for Elias to join him. "Kitchen. Now. I'll make something for you."

He could have argued, but from previous experience, he knew that the one thing Havi didn't allow was for anyone to leave his bakery hungry. He sighed inwardly, reluctantly obeying his cousin's summons.

Once he was seated in the back, the heat of the oven a welcome balm to his still-cold bones, Havi faced him down as he set a bowl on the counter. "Are you here to talk, or do you need to listen to someone else for a bit?"

Relief loosened a band of tension he hadn't even known was there. Being given a choice, when he'd had so many robbed from him lately, was a comfort he hadn't known he needed. "Listen."

"As you wish. Pass me that whisk there?"

Before long, he'd left the seat entirely, assisting Havi in the process of whatever it was he'd decided to craft today. This gentler kind of busyness was good for him—good for his hands, too, which still ached from forging and fleeing that automaton, but had started to grow restless after days of doing nothing.

While they worked, Havi talked. And Elias listened.

"I haven't seen Ember in a while," he said, dumping what Elias could only describe as an unholy amount of chocolate chips into the bowl. "She's only visited twice since she left, so it's been…"

"Difficult?"

"Beyond imagining." Havi shook his head as he stirred in the chocolate, his hand clenched around the spoon with a determined sort of strength. "But it won't be like this forever. I promised her that. As soon as I can afford a ring for her…"

"That's the reason you didn't marry her?" That couldn't be it. That couldn't be the only obstacle. "Ember doesn't care about that. She'd probably prefer a blade, anyway. Why would you…?"

Why would you waste what little time you may have for such a ridiculous reason?

"It's not that." Havi hesitated, setting the spoon in front of Elias with a soft clack. "Here. You can eat that clean if you want."

Elias's mother would've smacked him into the dust if he even thought about touching a tongue to one of her cooking spoons. He picked it up, the slightest bit of childish satisfaction preening through him as he licked off a chunk of dough. "Then what is it?"

"She's a princess. You might have noticed, but she's considerably high above my station." Havi gestured around his bakery with a sheepish smile. "But

I'm proud of what I have. I love this life. And she offered to do it all: to relocate here, to leave Nyx behind, to marry me and become Nyx's ambassador to Artem."

"So why did you refuse her?"

"I didn't. But she'd be giving up everything, Elias—everything she knows, everything she loves, for my sake alone. What kind of man would I be—what kind of husband—if I didn't do everything in my power to prove to her that I'm willing to sacrifice on her behalf, too?"

"But she didn't ask that of you."

"She didn't have to." Havi gave him a small smile, his gaze soft, distant with memory. "When you love someone, sacrifice isn't a question. It's a foregone conclusion. Everything I have would be hers if she only asked."

Darkness writhed in the pit of Elias's stomach, that chunk of cookie dough in his throat suddenly feeling like a lump he couldn't swallow past. "And you don't think she'll resent you for that?"

"For what?"

"For sacrificing yourself when she's already chosen to do it for you. For refusing to let her save you."

Havi blinked at him, and Elias realized too late that he'd revealed something with those words. "Is that how you feel?" Havi probed gently. "That Soren didn't let you save her?"

Elias's face burned, all notions of cold melting away under Havi's piercing gaze. "We're talking about you and Ember."

"I don't know if we are."

"I-I said I don't want to talk." He hated how his voice shook with a stammer at the beginning.

Havi studied him for a long moment, then turned back to his bowl. "All right. You don't have to. But if you still want to listen...I'd like to say something instead, if that's all right."

There was no telling what was about to come out of Havi's mouth, and that scared him more than anything. But he braced himself against it, clinging with both hands to that blessed nothing dulling every sensation in his chest. He'd waited weeks for any semblance of rest to come. He could not lose it so soon. "Of course."

Havi was quiet for a time, eyes glazed over as if lost in thought, his hands going through the motions of dumping the cookie dough onto the counter and beginning to roll it into rounds without any thought behind the action. Elias silently took up the task beside him, butter and sugar prodding his empty stomach until it gave a warning growl.

"There's a saying here in Artem," Havi said finally. "When you ask one thing of Mortem, there are ten thousand things she must do in order to make it happen. We so often forget that miracles do not come about easily."

Elias looked away, back to the row of cookies. "What are you saying?"

"I'm saying," said Havi, reaching out and covering Elias's hand with his, giving it an encouraging squeeze, "that if you have asked something of Mortem, and she has not yet granted it...have patience. Ten thousand tasks take time, even for a goddess."

Elias squeezed his eyes shut, emotions trying and failing to shred through the guard he'd placed around his heart. "I told her to leave me."

Havi hesitated, and in that silence, Elias heard a hundred sentences that would condemn him, that would tell him he had gone too far, that would name him traitor and heretic and faithless. But instead, Havi simply said, "I think you'll find Mortem is not so easily dismissed."

"I felt her go."

"Out of all the pantheon, Mortem is the most protective of a person's free will. You know that. It's why she doesn't take hosts. She will offer you a choice just the same as I did when you came in here. If you choose to remove yourself from her service, she won't force you to stay. But she will spend the rest of your life hoping that you choose to come home."

Elias's eyes burned. No weeping. No weakness. "I don't know if home exists for me anymore."

"Home is not something given to us. Home is something we build. If your old one is gone, then start trying to imagine what you'd like your new one to look like. Just because you're not ready to rebuild yet doesn't mean you'll never be." Havi's smile tinged with grief, but it wasn't the ruination that Elias had seen in himself these past weeks—no, this grief was softer. This grief looked like the sad side of hope. "Someday you'll grow tired of playing dead. And when that day comes, you're going to want something to run toward."

Elias hesitated. His voice wobbled, but for once, he didn't have the strength to be angry about it. "I don't know if I'm playing at anything, Havi."

It was the same thought he'd had just before the trial—that he hadn't really been allowed to walk back out of Mortem's realm. Not all of him. His lungs drew breath, his heart still beat, but ever since they'd stopped for a short while, he hadn't truly felt alive. No, he was some halfway thing, caught in a purgatory he couldn't escape, one foot in the world and one in the pyre. And worst of all was the thought that he was no better than those shambling, decayed shells Vaughn's magic had puppeted through the Port Atlas streets. Just another sick imitation of life, held aloft by a magic that should never have been in the first place.

Just another dead thing walking.

Havi looked at him, and Elias looked back, unblinking. Letting him see just how empty these past weeks had left him. Letting him see every claiming fingerprint left behind by Death's fickle hand.

"You don't have to talk if you don't want to," Havi said again. "But I think you have a story to tell, Elias. And I'm willing to listen, if you'll let me."

He didn't know what would happen if he finally gave voice to the fears that had been dogging him since he'd found out exactly what happened in that temple. But his throat ached with the weight of the words, and suddenly, the idea of clinging to that burden any longer was just as unbearable as the idea of facing down whatever third trial the Priestess had in store for him. "How much time do you have?" he rasped.

Havi smiled. "As much as you need."

CHAPTER 43

KALLIAS

The knock on the door of their chamber roused him from a too-short nap—he could feel it in the almost-pain fogging up his mind, in the iron-lined weight to his bones as he dragged himself off his mattress. Raquel was sleeping on her own bed across the chamber, her bedhead the only visible part of her, her unscarred ear peering through the half-dismantled braid on that side of her head. She didn't stir when he stumbled to the door, rubbing one eye as he cracked it open. "Yes?"

Zaccheus stood there, face impassive. "You busy?"

Kallias straightened, grogginess dissipating. "No."

"Good. Come with me."

After throwing on a shirt, Kallias obeyed, rubbing the back of his neck as he followed Zaccheus down to the main level of the city. People no longer stared as he walked by, though they occasionally cast curious looks his way; he guessed they were surprised by the company he kept. Zaccheus had been careful thus far to paint them as reluctant acquaintances; that he'd summoned him so openly didn't bode well.

Zaccheus took him to a quiet apothecary void of customers, heavy with the smell of herbs and spices. After a quick word to the clerk and a handful of coins dropped into the tip jar, the clerk locked the door and slipped to the back room, hurriedly nodding to them as he went. Kallias swallowed, the taste of the air mixing with his fear, turning his tongue sour. "What happened?"

Zaccheus turned to him, genuine sorrow in his eyes. "Word just arrived of a battle between your people and Nyx."

Kallias's breath caught. His hand dropped instinctively to his sword's sheath. "Where?"

"Vulpecula."

Another border city, this one not nearly as well-defended as Ursa. Kallias relaxed a bit. "How many dead?"

"Not sure. More Atlas than Nyxian, that's for certain."

The statement made no sense. "Come again?"

Zaccheus hesitated, then gently added, "Atlas lost the battle. Soundly. Nearly half their force was wiped out. Seems the Queen anticipated the attack and sent a hearty force to defend her borders."

Kallias's heart plunged, falling endlessly through empty space, horrid realization numbing his insides against the pain of the crash.

His fault. He'd warned them to watch their borders, to prepare for a renewed Atlas assault.

Atlas deaths. His fault.

Kallias pressed a hand over his mouth and nose, the smell of the shop suddenly turning his stomach. It took several minutes of breathing through his hand for his mind to clear again, for his heart to slow its descent, for the horror to stop crashing over and over like a hungry riptide.

He was here for the sake of his people. More would have died if he'd stayed home those three extra weeks, if he'd been content to let Jericho wage her war in order to keep his name clean on the tongues of his people, if he'd come here and sealed the alliance with a ring and a cap on the secrets bottled up within him.

But even so…

Atlas deaths. His fault.

His title of traitor was now cast in steel. There would be no breaking free of it.

"Thank you for telling me." He hardly recognized his own voice.

Zaccheus shrugged. "I would want to know if it was my people." Anger darkened the man's hazel gaze. "War is the most wicked of evils. The cost is never worth the reward."

Kallias wasn't sure he agreed with that. There were things worth fighting for, worth fighting against; he would wage a hundred years of war to pry Tenebrae and Anima's hands away from his kingdom, would sully himself with a hundred sins if it bought his people freedom from their machinations. But he merely nodded. "Did you tell Idris about the mountain?"

"I shared the story with Star. But if you haven't been summoned yet, I assume it wasn't enough to catch her attention." Zaccheus shook his head, raking a hand through his hair. "We don't have much time left."

"Elias has only one trial left. He may be our best bet."

"He's still recovering from his second. Gods know when he'll be well enough." Zaccheus bit his lip. "I'll need to think on it...I'll come up with something. Just be ready, will you? My people can't suffer another conflict of this scale...I fear it will break our kingdom beyond repair."

"If I could ask a question?" At Zaccheus's nod, Kallias continued: "You are a people of weapons experts. Your military is unmatched. Yet you speak of them as if they're fragile."

Zaccheus hesitated. His hand floated to his opposite arm, fingertips grazing his scars. "There's more than one kind of breaking. Would we win? I'm confident. But would the cost be worth winning a war for a kingdom not our own? I don't think it would be. In the war with Tallis, I watched friends struck down with arrows through their throats, their laughter at some joke still hanging in the air when they fell dead. I came home and watched orphanages fill past their brims. You can see shadows lurking in nearly every gaze. And Mal and I..."

Kallias frowned when the normally stoic man shuddered. "What happened to you two?"

"Our company was captured by Tallis. Tortured for days. We all suffered, but Mal bore the brunt of it. She was the daughter of the general who served before Star; she knew more than we did. We were the only two that survived." A soft, humorless laugh. "We were practically strangers before that; I was a no-name kid trying to make some coin, she was practically royalty. After Tallis, we never left each other's sides." Zaccheus shook his head, helpless anger flickering in his gaze. "They used fire on us...our kingdom's element, our favored tool. There are days she can't leave the house because she can't take the sight of all the fires. I can't use my magic at home without warning her first. It's why she has Ignis; she has to take him nearly everywhere in case she has an episode while she's out. He's trained to get her to a safe place and stay with her until she's able to calm down."

Esmeralda's words on the mountainside—and how shaken she'd been by the burning—suddenly made sense. No wonder this man was so terrified of war. No wonder he was willing to toe the line of treason to keep his people out of it.

"We'll figure something out," Kallias croaked. "Idris can't keep me at bay forever."

Zaccheus's throat bobbed, and his voice darkened when he finally said, "We won't let her."

Something about that look unsettled him. But before he could probe further, Zaccheus put his hands on his hips. "While we're on the subject of gods...do you care to tell me what happened out there with the *vellanguis*?"

Kallias winced. "I...I don't know."

"I've been painfully honest with you, Prince. I only ask you return the favor."

It was barely even a lie to say he didn't know. This business with Tempest was only just within the grasp of his understanding.

"I...I have had the misfortune of being blessed by a god my kingdom fears," Kallias said slowly. "It's not something commonly known." No lies. Just the barest shavings cut from the whole truth.

"I see." Zaccheus didn't look convinced. "Would you consider yourself to be...favored, in any way? More than others?"

"I'm not sure what you're implying." Gods, he hoped he wasn't sweating visibly. Zaccheus couldn't suspect the truth of his connection to Tempest—not when he barely knew of it himself.

Zaccheus didn't look convinced. But he simply said, "I understand. I'll keep it quiet, if that's what you want."

"I would appreciate it. My people wouldn't take kindly to it."

"Of course." And before the conversation could go further, Zaccheus called the clerk back to his business and took his leave, parting with barely a goodbye.

Kallias rubbed his chest, letting out a slow, bracing breath.He wasn't sure he should be handling this business with Zaccheus on his own any longer. He needed to tell Elias.

CHAPTER 44

KALLIAS

After searching for his Nyxian companion all day, irritation turning to worry as the day wore on toward evening, Havi finally directed Kallias to a tucked-away establishment a few shops down from the *Sugar Spinner* when he stopped in to get himself some coffee. The moment he heard the name—*On the Rocks Tavern*—he knew exactly what he was going to find, and he wasn't looking forward to it. But he thanked Havi anyway, resigning himself to what he was about to face.

Before he could turn to walk away from the counter, Havi caught him, his brows knit with concern. "Kallias…is it true?"

"Is what true?"

"Is Atlas in the middle of a coup?"

His stomach dropped into a winter sea, plunging through frigid waters with no bottom in sight. "Elias told you?"

Havi nodded once. "I see now why your news must go to Idris first. Honestly, Safi and I thought you were just being…"

"Prissy?"

"That wasn't the word she used, but—"

"I said you were being *entitled*," Safi supplied helpfully, suddenly appearing at Kallias's side, bumping his ankle with her chair.

Kallias swore under his breath. "How do you *do that*?"

"I am the shadow that stalks you at night, the monster who hides beneath your bed. You'll never know I'm there until I've already—"

"Safi," Havi sighed.

She smirked. "You're just tall enough that I can sneak right beneath your periphery, I think. How's Elias doing? Has he forgiven me for my dragon almost incinerating him yet?"

Kallias blinked at her. "*You* made that monstrosity?"

Safi paused, her lips pressing together in an awkward knot. "Uh…no?"

"You *made that*?"

Safi flung her arms up in a gesture of surrender. "Listen, when the Priestess asked if she could borrow it, I didn't know she planned on feeding *Elias* to it!"

Tempest save him. This woman was a mad genius. "What even was it?"

"It's called an automaton. It's a mix of magic and gearwork all forged together with metal. First and only of its kind." Safi's lip pouted out. "At least, it *was*, before Elias melted him down to scrap. My poor sweet Alden."

"Alden?"

"Alden the Automaton. That was his name. Pride of my heart. My best work, utterly irreplaceable—"

"Don't listen to her," said Havi. "She has another one stashed in the back of her workshop."

Safi shot him a look of utter betrayal. "Will you *hush*? I'm trying to get compensated for my losses!"

"You should probably take that up with the Priestess." Kallias hardly had the coin to spare, not when he was cut off from his kingdom's coffers and would continue to be for the foreseeable future. "I should go find Elias before he ends up facedown in his cup."

"Kallias," Havi said, stopping him again as he started to leave. "Don't give up on him, all right? He's close."

"Close to what?"

"I don't know exactly. But something's about to give." Havi's eyes gleamed with worry. "Just make sure someone's there to catch him when it does."

* * *

Just like he thought, he found Elias seated on a barstool, his eyes focused on the shelves of liquor behind the bar, backlit by bits of pyromancy-born fire that burned heatlessly within glass globes.

Kallias's throat spasmed, saliva drying up at the sight of those gleaming bottles. Temptation tied a knot around his middle and tugged, pulling him into the seat beside Elias. The Nyxian man didn't so much as offer him a glance; his bruised hand was wrapped tightly around a glass of whiskey, and judging by the bleary glaze to his eyes, it wasn't his first. His other hand kept wandering up to feel the now-vacant patch of his scalp where his braids used to be. Kallias's eyes caught on a new addition to the chain around Elias's neck—two braided circles of cloth hanging on either side of the ring.

"What can I get you?" asked the barkeep, a fair-haired, fair-skinned man with so many piercings Kallias couldn't count them all, sporting a truly impressive number of diamonds within his jewelry. He leaned on the counter with one brow raised, propping his chin on his hand while he waited for Kallias's answer. No doubt he'd spotted Kallias eyeing the top-shelf bottles with wistfulness bordering on need.

Kallias dredged up every ounce of self-control he'd ever had. "Water for me, please."

The barkeep grunted at the cheap order, but Kallias offered him a winsome smile, and that seemed to earn him some goodwill back. The barkeep passed him the water with a wink before going back to his more lucrative patrons, and Kallias blew out a low breath, taking a long drink, the ice bumping gently against his lips.

"Why are you here?" Each word plunked from Elias's mouth like a lodestone, his breath utterly soaked in whiskey.

"Because you are."

"I don't need a damned babysitter."

"No, you need a friend," Kallias retorted. "And I'm trying my hardest to—"

"You are not my friend."

The prince who'd bitten his tongue for ten years in Atlas would have left. He would have packed up his smarting pride and hurt feelings and walked out, scolding himself for even daring to think he might have actually mattered to someone. But he'd cast that prince aside along with his title, with his crown, with his throne. That prince was locked away in a vault with no key, and Kallias would never—*never*—be him again. Least of all with Elias.

So instead, Kallias leaned forward, forcing Elias to meet his eyes. "Maybe I'm not your friend, but you are mine. And I don't leave my friends to suffer beneath their burdens alone."

Elias glared balefully at him, his hand flexing against his glass.

"Elias," Kallias said firmly, "this has to stop."

"I don't know what you mean."

"Yes, you gods-damned *do*."

Another spasm of his knuckles, like he was fighting the urge to hit something. Probably Kallias's face. "You are the *last* person who gets to judge me for how I choose to cope."

"I'm not judging you. I'm trying to help you." Kallias grabbed the glass, but Elias tightened his grip, both of them pulling in opposite directions and going nowhere.

"Let go," Elias rasped.

"Do you remember what you told me back in Atlas?"

"Was it something along the lines of *piss off*?"

"You asked me if I saw so little worth in myself that I was willing to be sold off for a pile of steel. And you told me that if I truly loved my people, I would fight for what they needed."

"Isn't that what I've been doing?" Elias tried to tug the cup away again, but Kallias tightened his hold. Elias's skin flashed hot beneath his palm, but Kallias didn't flinch.

Elias might have had fire in his blood, but Kallias had ice in his heart. He wasn't afraid of him. "I'm not talking about your people. I'm talking about Soren."

The pain that shattered across Elias's drink-dulled face at the mention of Soleil's Nyxian name was indescribable. His skin warmed once more beneath Kallias's grip, so hot it nearly hurt. "I'm not doing this with you—"

"You love her," Kallias said, a reminder and an accusation. "I can see that. The entire gods-damned world can see that."

Elias finally jerked hard enough that Kallias lost his hold on the cup. Where their hands had touched, there was a patch of steam on the glass. "I *loved* her."

"You *love* her," Kallias corrected, trying to control the bite trying to creep into his tone. So easy these days to let his words grow teeth. "So why aren't you fighting for what she needs, hm? Why are you so damned determined to act like she's gone? We should be—"

It all happened so fast that Kallias had no chance at stopping it. No chance to even try.

Something hard cracked against his cheek, throwing him off the stool, his hand just missing the counter as he scrambled to try and catch himself. His back slammed into the floor, the impact snatching the breath straight from his lungs in a pained wheeze that cut off when Elias flung himself on top of him, pinning him down in a shockingly tight hold for how intoxicated he was. His liquor-sharp breath soured in Kallias's nose as he leaned close.

"Soren is dead," Elias hissed, but the anger in his voice was completely separate from the anguish in his eyes. His hands shook as they held Kallias's in place. "She is *dead*. There is *nothing* I can do for her now but try and save our people."

Kallias tried to shove him off, footsteps reverberating through the floor as the other patrons of the bar hurried out, making room for whatever fight they thought was about to ensue. Even the barkeep ran past, likely to fetch a guard. And based on the way Elias was snarling at him, that might just be the right move.

Anger of his own bore up words he might've swallowed at any other time in his life. "If it was you who was taken by a goddess, do you know what she would have done?"

"You don't *know her*. You have no idea what she would've—"

"She would *never* have stopped looking for a way to get you back," he spat, rearing against his hold, but Elias held fast. Cold anger trickled down his limbs, the winter storm of his rage butting against the wildfire of Elias's. "Don't even try to pretend otherwise. You know what she would've spent all these weeks doing? Hunting down scholars. Finding answers. Searching for something, *anything*, to get that goddess out of you. She would've pulled off some mad scheme *weeks* ago, and it probably would've worked! And what have you done? Nothing. You've already given up on her. You'd *rather* believe she's dead, because if she's not, then you *abandoned her*. And you can't bear to think that, can you? You can't handle the idea that I might just be *right!*"

Elias's eyes flared, and when he exhaled in a sharp growl, his breath no longer smelled of liquor.

That was the only warning Kallias received, the only sign that he'd gone too far.

"You," Elias seethed, "are *wrong*."

Something seared into Kallias's wrists, and his heart dropped, terror stealing all his self-righteous words right off his tongue. "Elias—"

"Not one person, not one in the entirety of our histories, has *ever survived* a god or goddess taking them as a host. Do you understand that?"

He tugged against Elias's grip, gritting his teeth as the skin beneath screamed for release. "You're hurting me—"

"How dare you. How *dare you* suggest I am *wishing* her dead? Do you know what I'd do to bring her back? Show me the door to Infera, Kallias, and I'll crawl through every firepit on my hands and knees if it means she gets to come home! You think I wouldn't? I'd tear down the gods-damned world *myself* if I thought it would do any good! But it won't, do you get that? It won't, because she's dead, she's dead, she is *dead!*"

Elias's roar of that last word erupted out with a tide of fire.

Heat and light and ruin lunged for Kallias, a mountain cat with claws outstretched, an old enemy that had been waiting for its second chance to put an end to him.

Ice and wind and water rose within Kallias to meet it. He jerked his hands free just in time to thrust them upward, and everything *exploded.*

CHAPTER 45

KALLIAS

When Kallias blinked, he found himself face to face with Raquel.

His cheek stung, and it took him several seconds too long to process that she'd slapped him awake. Several seconds longer to realize that she was shouting.

"Atlas!" She shook his shoulders with a curse. "Get up, you useless lump of muscle. Where's Elias?"

Memory flooded back in with an urgency that stole the breath from his chest: the fight, the fire, the power that had barreled through his body like a tidal wave carrying a city away. He lurched up unsteadily, his feet seeking purchase as he searched the immediate area.

The tavern was burning.

He lurched away from the burning wood and smoke-stained windows, the screams drowning out the pop and crackle of flame, the—

Wait.

"What do you mean, where's Elias?" he choked. "He was in there with me, he—"

Raquel's face dropped. "He's still *in there*?"

"We were fighting." Gods, his head hurt, and his hands were shaking like he'd plunged them into a snowbank. "He was…I think his magic…how did I get out—?"

Raquel didn't wait for him to pull together the scattered threads of his thoughts. She vanished like a stroke of lightning, there and gone, only the thunderous screams and shouts of onlookers left in her wake.

The world tilted dizzily as he twisted after her, his stomach tossing in a swirl of terror. "Angelov, don't!"

But she was already snatching one of the water pots someone had brought and bolting through the door into the tavern, her form swallowed by the flames before he could finish saying her name.

All at once, the clamor and chaos hit him at just the right angle, a sail tugged in such a way to catch the wind, that stormy gale waking a part of him he hadn't used in far too long: the sailor's knots that tied his fortitude in place when seas grew rough. The steady hand and keen eye of a captain ready to command his crew through an unfriendly host of clouds.

Prince Kallias Atlas whipped around on his heel, shouting, "*Someone get me Havi Aquila!*"

Someone whose name he didn't know did as he asked without so much as questioning, and Kallias only took a moment to feel grateful for the commanding bark he'd learned from generals and queens alike. Then he stormed forward, guiding people wielding water buckets to the best places to pour, ensuring they kept the entrance as open as possible. All the while, his gaze roved over those flames, searching for the returning shadow of Raquel.

"Kallias!"

Before he could fully register that voice—coming from completely the wrong direction, reaching his ear from behind—Elias's hand clutched at his shoulder, forcing him to turn, his eyes locked in horror on the burning tavern. No haze of alcohol or anger remained. "What happened?"

"Where in the depths did you come from?" Kallias snapped, catching Elias by his shoulder, both of them holding each other up. "Did Angelov find a way out?"

Elias blinked at him, brow creasing. "Raquel?"

"She went in after you! I didn't see you come out, which way did she——?"

"Kallias, I woke up outside!" Elias's eyes widened, fresh panic pouring in. "One of the windows was broken, I think I——what do you mean she went in after me?"

Kallias's throat closed up. He shoved Elias to the ground with one hand, gesturing for him to stay put. "Do *not* move from this spot, do you understand me?"

Elias's eyes drifted back to the tavern, and he gripped the knees of his smoldering trousers, a bone-deep shiver nearly tipping him sideways. He might not have been drunk anymore, but shock could unbalance a person just as well. "Kallias, did I do this?"

Kallias's lips parted, ready to reassure him, but lies were too thick to slip past the block in his throat. Instead he said, "Stay here. I'll be back."

Elias merely stared, and Kallias moved back to the front of the tavern, watching the entrance with baited breath, his memories still fighting to decide where he was. If he stood on stone or sand. If he waited for his sister or a stranger.

His heartbeat thudded in deep, hollow beats against his ears. And he waited. And he waited. And he waited.

Raquel didn't come back out.

"Angelov!" A beat. Nothing. His heart lurched oddly in his chest, and he jumped up on an empty water pot, searching the entrance for any movement as he cupped his hand around his mouth. "Angelov?...*Raquel?*"

Nothing but the crackle of flame and the cries of onlookers organizing themselves. Surely Artem was a kingdom that dealt with fires all the time——they had to have some kind of procedure in place, but...

He'd sent for Havi because of the man's immunity to fire, but he wouldn't get here in time for Raquel. And even though Zaccheus had arrived and was shouting his own orders, his voice much calmer than Kallias's, more official help wouldn't be ready in time, either.

Swearing, he jumped down from the rock and tugged off his loose tunic, leaving just his undershirt beneath. He plunged the tunic into one of the full water pots, pulling it out and wrapping one end around his fist, cool liquid seeping between his fingers. He could've sworn it chilled beneath his touch, the cloth stiffening a bit where it brushed against his skin.

"What are you doing?" shouted Zaccheus as Kallias approached the burning tavern, beating down the flames that blocked the entrance Raquel had plunged through too many minutes earlier.

"One of my people is still in there!" he shouted back.

"Then it's already too late for them!"

Maybe. Maybe.

But it hadn't been too late for Soleil. And he couldn't have one more death on his conscience. Not even Raquel's.

Groaning deep in his chest, he plunged forward into the tavern, ignoring Zaccheus's and Elias's shouts behind him as smoke swallowed him up.

Scarlet heat consumed the entire world, the hair on his bare arms curling away from its bite, sweat pouring down his back, warm and slippery like a gush of blood. Smoke tore into his throat, replacing breath with grit, and he coughed against it as he struggled to find a path to place his feet on. Above flame and fear, above the tremors wracking his bones and the haze of heat blurring his vision, he shouted, "*Raquel!* Tell me where you are!"

For what felt like an eternity, his entire world was the slap of soaked cloth and the vicious teeth of fire gnawing at whatever part of him it could reach, his feet barely finding purchase on the ashen floor. But for every blaze he smothered, another sprang up in its place, a many-headed monster entirely unwilling to die.

Breath scraped into a strangled cough that nearly dropped him to his knees. Head spinning with memory, he collapsed against the first empty space he found, barking in pain when his elbow plunged right through the wooden façade of the wall, colliding with stone beneath. He craned his neck, desperately searching for a gap, for a bit of light, for a flicker of blue hair...and found nothing but smoke and inferno and death.

He'd trapped himself inside.

Cloth creaked in his fist as he tightened his fingers around it, what had once been soaked through now dry and stiff from beating a path.

You know what to do, Kallias.

A tremulous breath wobbled from his throat, and he curled further against the wall, skin begging for relief from the unbearable heat. "I can't."

You can. Focus. Breathe.

"*I can't.*"

Then let me. I can get you out of this. Trust me.

Kallias squeezed his aching eyes shut, sinking his teeth into dry, chapped lips.

Trust. He didn't know who he trusted anymore, didn't know who deserved it, wasn't really sure if anyone had earned it. But one thing he knew for certain: he couldn't trust the gods to keep their word. Even at the cost of his life, he could not—

Something reached his ears. A grating cough, nearly buried beneath the crackle of the fire.

Angelov.

"Raquel!" he shouted again, as loudly as his raw throat would allow, shoving up from the wall and searching through the blinding tornado of scarlet and gold and amber. Searching the shattered glass, the scorched bar—

There. A flicker of movement beneath scattered debris on the other side of the room.

"Here." Her rasping voice was rougher than usual, quieter than he'd ever heard it.

The strength of the relief that flooded him nearly took him off his feet, but he held himself in place. "Can you move? Can you get to me?"

"No." Even quieter now, thin and vaporous, threatening to tumble off the edge of consciousness. "I'm pinned."

Thoughts whirled through his head like a shell caught in the curl of a wave, adrenaline waking up every nerve in his body. He pulled the tunic through his hands, fingers searching its surface until he came across one last damp spot.

Water bends easier than earth and air, said the voice of a storm-summoner, a king-maker. *Stone is too set in its ways. Wind is too wild. But water is moldable, guidable. Water likes to play.*

He clutched that section of tunic, said a pointless prayer, and tried to coax the water out.

Inch by inch, the moisture peeled itself away from the fabric, condensing into a quivering droplet that hovered just above it. He dropped the tunic, and the water stayed, bobbing gently toward his outstretched hand.

There was no time to marvel. All he had left in this Mortem-pit of a place was instinct, and he followed that thread, pinching his fingers together and pulling like he was stretching out a strand of taffy. The water followed, extending from droplet to tendril, rippling with every tug of his will like it only bowed to him begrudgingly. But bow it did—obey it did. And not only the water he'd brought with him; when he looked down, he found a puddle seeping across the floor, rearing up and reaching to join hands with the bit he'd managed to pull from the tunic. The water the rescuers had thrown several feet away, back at the entrance…it heard his call, too.

Ecstasy flooded him with such heady triumph he nearly staggered, his body remembering how it felt to be six shots deep and spinning over the edge from tipsy to drunk. But this was different—not hazy or dull, but vivid and visceral. Not falling asleep, but waking up. Not drifting into dreams, but pulling free from a nightmare.

It was relief, rebirth, a changing that rattled his bones. Something he had always been, but never known. Something he'd always had, but never used.

When Kallias threw out his hands, the water obeying his command as if it shared his very mind, he found its name crouching at the tip of his tongue, ready to be claimed at long last:

Power.

Within the span of a blink, ownership of the tavern changed hands from roaring fire to silent ice. The slick, glassy surface poured over the flames like wax into a mold, dimming the tavern from lurid red to dull browns and grays, smoke and steam pluming from floor to ceiling until a wind with no source slithered through like a snake, dissipating the haze so the air was clear enough to breathe.

And finally, *finally,* he could see her.

Raquel was trapped beneath one of the beams that had held up the chandeliers in this cave masquerading as a tavern, her eyes fixed on the ceiling, her chest heaving as she gasped for air against its weight. One hand was pinned at her side, holding something so tightly in her fist that her knuckles looked ready to tear straight through her skin; the other was pressed to her mourning braid. She was mouthing something, but he didn't realize what it was until he skidded gracelessly on ice of his own making, landing on his knees beside her. The water had left a perfect circle around her, a place where no ice had crossed—like she'd repelled it somehow. Or maybe even the elements feared to put themselves on Raquel Angelov's bad side.

She was praying. For calm winds, for gentle seas, for a smooth path back to her sister.

"Tempest, please take me home," she breathed, the break in her voice as good as a sob.

His stomach pinched, and he caught up the beam in his hands, muscles bunching as he dragged it aside, groaning when something twinged deep in his back.

Raquel's eyelids fluttered, her glass eye stopping just short of him, her other eye finding him with the same spearing intensity it always did, even as she fought for breath past her pain. "Go away."

He tossed the beam aside with a gush of breath, kneeling over her, his palms pressed into the wooden floorboards on either side of her head while he searched her for wounds. "As usual, your expression of gratitude is impeccable."

"I don't want your face to be the last thing I see before I die."

"Well, I have good news for you, then: you're not dying. So the whole argument is moot."

Her mouth twitched, even as her eyelids sank another notch lower. "I hate you."

"Empty words by now, I'm afraid." After searching for mortal wounds and finding none, Kallias pressed his fingers into the crook of her neck; her pulse was strong, but slowing. She might not be dying, but she still needed help. And luckily, he could hear that very thing coming, people tentatively stepping foot through the entrance to investigate the sudden death of the fire. "You're going to have to live long enough to prove it."

"Kallias." His name on her lips was an ice-tipped spear to the chest. "Thank you."

Before he could say anything back—or scrape his jaw off the floor—her eyes closed. And judging by the sudden exhaustion that crawled over his bones, carving notches to collapse every joint, he wasn't too far behind.

"Help her," he croaked, easing back as help rushed in, faces and hands blurring when they came close. "I'm fine, I'm...help her. Help her."

He didn't pass out; he felt it when they pulled him to his feet, when they eased him onto a stretcher and carried him somewhere else. And he heard the whispers, the quiet awe—and suspicion—as they breathed the words *Tempest-blessed*.

He didn't pass out. But he couldn't force his eyes open, either.

Even so, he wasn't sure he ever stopped whispering, asking, *ordering*: "Help her. Help her. Help her."

CHAPTER 46

FINN

When the world returned to him, it arrived singing.

That was the first thing that struck him as his senses filtered back in, sound and touch and smell finding their way back to his body: a quiet melody, a surprisingly low-pitched hum while tender touches brushed over his rigid hands. The music stroked his ears like a lullaby, interrupted only by the occasional splash of water and the faintest snag in the breathing of whoever tended him now. He smelled harsh soaps and softer tonics and sweetness tinted with smoke—the scent of candles recently lit. His mouth still tasted of blood.

Sight came back to him last. And when he blinked, he found Fidget seated across from him, her eyes focused on his hands while hers wielded a washcloth carefully between his fingers, her teeth worrying her bottom lip as she concentrated on cleaning him up. The humming was coming from her.

There were still traces of Tomas's blood drying in the creases of his knuckles.

His hushed intake of breath brought her head up, and her shoulders drooped, her brow smoothing in relief. "Finn? Are you there?"

"Where else would I be?" Gods, his voice sounded like he'd ground it down with a mortar and pestle and dropped it into a bag of rocks. "What are you doing?"

"Your friend had to help me sneak you into the castle. You lost your senses for a bit—he said you were in shock—and you kept trying to wander off, you kept mumbling about having to get cleaned up but we didn't want anyone to see you covered in blood like that so we—"

He held up a hand to stop her babbling, studying her as best he could in the dim candlelight. They were in a bathing room—*his private bathing room*—him seated on the lip of the bath, her seated on a short stool she'd likely dragged in from beside his bookshelves. She'd already cleaned herself up: her hair was wet, and she wore a pair of simple muslin pajamas that were several sizes too big for her, clearly not made to fit her form, and—

"Are you wearing my pajamas?" he asked blankly.

She flushed. "I couldn't get back to my room without being seen. I panicked."

"You're wearing my pajamas."

"Yes."

"You're wearing…"

"Mmhm?"

"My pajamas."

"Are you still in shock?" Fidget demanded, her warm hand wrapping around his wrist, her fingertips seeking out his pulse. "Your heartbeat's still wonky."

A smile tugged at his mouth. "Wonky?"

"Are you my echo now?" But she smiled too. "I'll return the pajamas, I promise. But I really can't put my other clothes back on. They're…" That smile faded. "Let's just say those stains aren't coming out."

His fingers flexed, remembering the glaze of blood against skin, sticky like the coating of a candied apple. *Gods, that's the absolute worst comparison.* "Are you all right?"

"I'm fine, thanks to you." With a shaky breath, she set aside the cloth, and he tried not to look at the rusty stains soaked into it. He'd never been squeamish about blood before. "I'm sorry I—"

"Stop." He held up the hand she wasn't still holding, relieved to find it was clean. "I don't want to hear it."

Her shoulders drooped. "But I—"

"Fidget, I'm the one who's sorry." A word that had hardly ever passed his mouth. It fit all kinds of wrong on his tongue, but he forced it out anyway, because he was mildly certain *sorry* was the proper name for the feeling stuck between his ribs, a pinching that couldn't decide whether it wanted to be guilt or nausea. "I shouldn't have taken you with me."

Her mouth curled into a stubborn frown. "I wanted to go."

"I should have told you no."

"I would've followed you."

A quiet laugh. "I would've caught you."

"Finn." Her fingers released his hand only to reach up and brush the line of his jaw, a touch so soft and unexpected that he blinked. She held them there, gaze uncharacteristically serious as she looked at him. "I *wanted* to go."

Without meaning to, he leaned into her hand a bit, exhaustion swaying him toward anything offering rest. "You really are a bit mad, you know."

Her laugh, musical and magical, lifted the corner of his mouth against the weight of the blood he'd spilled tonight. Something about her laugh made everything feel a bit easier to bear. "Better mad than boring," she said, planting a kiss on his forehead before releasing his face to take his hands once more.

He couldn't argue with her there.

Silence fell, a thick curtain draping around Mirror and man, sheltering them within the cover of candlelight and cautious touches while Fidget finished cleaning his hands. And he...he only watched her.

This should have terrified him. Letting someone see the affliction that had plagued him these past few weeks...letting someone see him *weak*...

He should have ordered her out. He should have put on his meanest mask and scared her so thoroughly she would never think to utter a word about what she saw tonight. He should have been burning these bloody clothes and paying off anyone who might have seen him stumble into the castle with a Mirror and a Viper in his company.

But somehow, he couldn't tear himself away from her velvet-soft fingers. Her lilting voice humming some foreign lullaby. That little wrinkle between her brows that puckered around a stray sequin.

Finnick Atlas was not a man who knew peace. But he thought it might feel something like this.

"I knew you were blessed by Occassio," said Fidget suddenly, dipping her washcloth back into the basin of soapy water beside her and squeezing it out before pressing it to his neck, her tongue poking between the gap in her teeth as she concentrated on her task.

Get out, was what he should have said. *I can do that myself,* was what he should have said.

But that would require looking in a mirror.

"So I've been told," he rasped, reluctantly surrendering to her ministrations. It was a necessity and a convenience, that was all; better for her to do it than for him to attempt it himself with his hands like this.

"I knew you were blessed by her." Fidget's troubled brown eyes flickered up to his. Even after the night they'd had, she still smelled like lilac and sugar; maybe her perfume was Occassio-blessed, too. "I didn't know you were resisting her."

"Of course I'm resisting her. I'm quite fond of my mind, thanks."

"Resisting the visions only makes them worse. Hasn't anyone taught you how to receive them? You're a prince. I would've thought proper instruction would be made available to you."

He swallowed down a sigh, shifting his hips to put some distance between them. She was leaning so close her nose nearly brushed his neck. "Until a short time ago, nobody knew I was having them. Including me."

"You're a late bloomer, then." She tapped the side of his neck. "Turn a bit. I can't get this spot here."

He obeyed, craning his neck to the side, his hair falling across his forehead while he watched her out of the corner of his eye. The washcloth rubbed against his skin, leaving behind a trail of warm water that rapidly cooled as she dabbed and uttered soft curses under her breath that threatened to make him smile again. Maybe he *was* still delirious. "Is that something that can happen?"

"Not usually." Her washcloth-sheathed hand circled the back of his neck, and she paused there, seemingly noticing for the first time how close they still were. Her nose nearly brushed his as she sat up a bit straighter, the stool propping her up enough to put her at eye level with him. "You should probably get these clothes off."

In spite of the unsteadiness plaguing his body and the memory of Tomas's spilled throat engraved on the backs of his eyelids, he managed to curl his mouth into some imitation of a smirk. "Trying to get me naked isn't going to do a thing to save you from all those rumors about us, you know. Though I can't blame you, it is quite the impressive view—"

She snorted, then burst into laughter that was just a pitch too loud for his comfort. He shushed her, and she quickly lowered her voice to a whisper, shaking her head in disbelief. "How do you always have some gods-awful joke prepared, hm? Do you lie awake at night piecing them together?"

"I bought a book, actually. *Jokes to Make Mirrors Blush.*"

"Sounds like a riveting read."

His smirk widened into something uncomfortably close to a genuine grin— were his lips always this pliable when he was tired? "It hasn't led me astray so far."

"Hmm." Her fingers tickled absently at the back of his neck, and the air in the room suddenly felt a bit thick. He cleared his throat while she finally dropped her hand away, tossing the sullied washcloth into the bath's basin and standing. "Seriously, though, you need a real bath. Can you manage it alone?"

"I can manage most things alone." Even if he couldn't, that was a kind of vulnerability he wasn't willing to allow her to see, not even for the sake of his game. This was one hand he wouldn't fold on, no matter how terrible the cards.

"So I've learned." Fidget smiled as if to herself, a half-formed thing that didn't quite touch her eyes. "I'll wait outside. Let me know when you're decent."

"Oh, but then you'll be trapped out there forever," he said, the joke falling much flatter than his last as he rose, silently cursing his quivering knees.

What in the depths was wrong with him? This wasn't nearly the first kill on his conscience. The first one on his hands, true, and the first to leave his clothes sopping red and his own knife discarded in a crimson puddle on the pale tile floor—but far from the first that could be traced back to his order, his coin, his well-placed whisper in the ear of a tavern gossip.

So how come he still couldn't breathe without a hitch in his lungs and a catch in his ribs?

He braced himself against the wall, listening behind him for the click to let him know Fidget had closed the door. Once he heard it, he shed his bloody clothes, relieved when his fingers finally bent to his command, peeling the sticky, smelly material away from his skin and tossing them in a pile over his knife. He'd have to scour the floor later, but that could wait. For now, he needed a bath more desperately than he'd ever needed one in his life. And he was including the time Kallias and Jericho had convinced him and Soren that they'd come down with a case of *pixie pox* and only bathing themselves in maple syrup would keep them from becoming weightless and floating away from Atlas on a stray wind.

Hot water coursed down his body as he twisted the faucet on, a shiver of relief stirring goosebumps along his arms as his cold, clammy body reveled in the soothing rain-beat of showerfall against skin. His joints slowly loosened as the steam cajoled them out of their stubborn stand at attention, his fingers shaking off the last of their rigor just as he reached for his half-eroded bar of sandalwood and citrus soap. He had to order it specially from a vendor in a town far outside Port Atlas—nobody else made soap quite so fine, and nobody else made it with the little beads of texture he found so mollifying on his skin. And he was doubly grateful for it tonight; it turned out dried blood required a tad more scrubbing than other things might have.

Once he was clean and the heat of the shower had calmed his outward shaking, he climbed out and toweled off. The realization that he hadn't thought to grab fresh clothes had only just crossed his mind when he spotted a pair of pajamas folded on the counter.

While he tugged on his fresh clothes, he took a brief moment to be thankful that in spite of Fidget's teasing earlier, she'd made sure he wouldn't have to strut out in a towel with her still waiting in the chamber beyond—and that she'd had the foresight to choose a pair of pajamas with no buttons to fumble with. It was odd, for someone to have put such consideration into something for him. For someone to have picked up on *his* needs for once.

Even as the cloth floated over his head, the scent of clean laundry and his favorite soap drowning out all else, his fingers kept flexing, picking at themselves, seeking any fragment of gore he or Fidget might have missed. He couldn't seem to shake the traces of death from his flesh, and the discomfort of that made his bones cringe.

Something had changed tonight. He'd never, *ever* flung himself into a fight like that, had never been taken over so utterly by mindless rage…had never been taken over by a *mindless* instinct of any kind.

Well, maybe one other time, he allowed, recalling the lumpy scar left behind on his arm in the shape of a dead thing's mouth…but that was different. That was for Soleil. Beyond that, he always thought before he acted; that was what kept him alive.

But not tonight. Tonight he'd seen Tomas towering over little Fidget, his meaty hand planted so close to her face, her eyes filled with terror and tears, and he'd just…snapped.

This girl was worse than trouble, worse than danger. She was inching treacherously close to becoming his ruin, and that was something he could not, would not, allow.

It was time to bring this game to its end. But first...first he needed to sleep.

He stumbled out of the bathing room silhouetted by steam, rubbing his eye and hoping the goop he flicked out of it wasn't another fleck of blood. But he paused just outside the door, catching himself on the doorframe before his foot could fall too heavily against the floor.

Fidget was curled up on the floor in front of his hearth, her body coiled a bit like a cat's to fit her form to the plush oval rug spread out before the fire. Her curls were wrapped up in the brown scarf she'd stolen from him days ago—gods, had it only been days?—and the girl herself was enveloped in a blanket stolen from his window seat, a forest-toned knit quilt his Aunt Genevieve had sent him one or two years ago, a gift for the cold days that always followed shortly after his end-of-autumn birthday.

And she was fast asleep. Not just dozing, but a deep, uninhibited sleep that saw her snoring, her shoulders rising and falling, outlined in golds and reds by the light of the fire.

Warmth leaked into his chest, and he let it out in a whoosh of breath, leaning fully against the wall as he took in the strange sight.

He'd never really found fire beautiful; not after all it had taken from him. But just then he found it in his heart to offer just the slightest hint of appreciation, his eyes skimming the line of Fidget's sleeping form with a reckless affection that he was absolutely, utterly *certain* was a mere product of the absolutely senseless night he'd just suffered through.

Not one thing had gone to his plan. Not a single damned detail. But watching her as she slept peacefully on his floor, his pajamas and blanket and scarf sheathing her in a protective cocoon, her lips parted in a truly abominable, guttering snore...suddenly, he couldn't find it in him to regret what he'd done to Tomas at all. Suddenly, the blood staining his hands felt less like a condemnation and more like a warning to anyone who might yet underestimate him, who might have still thought him less dangerous than his big brother who'd stopped uncountable hearts and rived several stranger's throats.

Finnick Atlas had drawn first blood in a war of his own waging. And that had only been a rehearsal.

The gods should be shuddering in their depths-damned shoes.

CHAPTER 47

ANIMA

"What do you mean, it was *taken?*"

A flinch threw Ani back against the wall to avoid Tenebrae storming past, fury cresting from him with every turn like a wave of flies stirred by the swish of a horse's tail. She pressed her back flush to the wall, her sweat turning the paint clammy.

"Jericho was outbid," she said weakly. "We tried to track down the buyer, us and Briar, but we couldn't find him, and by the time—"

Brae slammed his fist—Jericho's fist, technically—into the wall, careening around to face her, his face contorted so terribly she feared he might split skin. "This is why I didn't want you involved. You're too soft, Ani. And now you're telling me—"

"It wasn't our fault! Jericho didn't have enough—"

"*Damn* the money! This princess is twice-blessed, and you're a *goddess*. You could have slaughtered everyone in that tavern before they even had time to *blink*. And instead you let someone walk away with a *twice-damned relic?*"

Shame coated her tongue in a bitter film, and she hugged herself tighter, trying to push her ribs into a shield around her heart. "I know. I-I know. But you told me to keep my head down, and there were so many people, and I didn't want them to see me, and I just—I'm sorry."

"Sorry." Brae scoffed, waving erratically as he twisted on his heel again, scarlet curls tumbling loose from his braid with every stalking step. "Sorry is not a word we use, *Anima*. Gods have no need for *sorry*, because we are supposed to be *infallible*. Have you forgotten so much already? Did I make a mistake allowing you the privilege of a body?"

Anger nipped at her heels, forcing her to grind them into the floor to halt a fit of temper before it started. Even as distant as she'd become, Soren's emotions still rose to the surface sometimes, dredged up most often by Brae's presence. If it was up to Soren's fighting instincts, they'd have done something completely foolish by now. "No. W-we'll find it. We'll get it back."

Brae's eyes narrowed, and she braced herself for another shout, another put-down. Instead he sighed, the exhale shifting him from imposing to tired. He walked up to her and put his hands on her shoulders, leaning down to press his forehead to hers. "No, you won't. I didn't mean to lose my temper. Just...it's on me. This is why I wanted you to stay here. I never should have let you go. I should have waited until I could handle it myself."

Those words were scalding oil poured over her skin. She curled away from his hold, but he held fast.

"No more excursions," he said, his firm tone brooking no argument. "You stay in the palace from now on."

"But Brae—"

"Don't argue with me, Anima." There wasn't an ounce of willing compromise in his golden gaze. "You don't leave the palace walls. Am I clear?"

But what is the point of being human if I can't be human?

She lowered her head to hide the tears. "Yes, Brae."

"Good girl."

CHAPTER 48

FINN

The first thing Finn did when he woke the next morning was burn his and Fidget's sullied clothes.

Fidget herself was still asleep, nestled in his bed now instead of on the floor; he'd moved her there in a rare fit of chivalry, making a cot out of his windowseat and settling himself there, bunching a pillow up between the sill and the bookshelf beside it. But at the sound of his bare feet shuffling across the floor and the logs crackling beneath the weight of the fabric he fed to the fire, she stirred with a yawn and a full-body stretch, her toes reaching for the footboard and her hands reaching for the ceiling. The muddled groan that escaped her lips brought a smirk to his. "Ow."

"Sore?" he guessed.

"I feel like I got flattened by a carriage." Then she seemed to realize exactly where she was: she scrabbled to her feet, clumsily wriggling out of the blanket cocoon, a flustered look tugging her eyes away from his. "Did I fall asleep?"

"You did. It's all right. I have an excuse ready for you."

"Oh? Pray tell." She shook the last clutching edge of the blanket free from her ankle, stepping out of the lump of yarn, the sleeve of his pajama shirt slumping down her arm to bare one freckled shoulder. Even in the misty haze of morning and his absent spectacles—he rarely wore his glasses out on jobs and hadn't yet put them on this morning—that sight was clear as a shard of crystal, sticking just as sharp in his stomach.

Heat flushed up his neck, and he stepped back a bit from the smoldering clothes, averting his gaze. Damned fire. His skin couldn't handle being this close to the hearth. *Pull it together, Finn. Gods above.*

"You went exploring in the city last night and got caught out by the storm." It wasn't a complicated story, but sometimes simple was best. "You found an inn and sheltered there for the night."

"And you?"

"If you and Vash did a good enough job sneaking me in last night, as far as anyone else knows, I never left this room. Where did you stash the mirror?"

"I didn't." Fidget's lips twisted into a displeased knot. "Vash insisted on taking it with him until you came back to your senses and could tell him otherwise."

Gods, Finn could've kissed that trustless bastard. "I'll go fetch it today. For now, just...lay low. Reconnect with your people. Even with a good story, you've been off on your own too much for their liking, I'm sure. Try to buy back some trust."

Fidget nodded a bit, rubbing the morning chill from her arms, still a bit groggy around the eyes. "Finn?"

"Hm?"

"Thank you. For saving me last night. I know it was...I know it cost you something, so...just...thank you."

Finn shrugged one shoulder, turning back to the hearth, poking the cloth around to let the flames in the back get a taste. "Nothing to thank me for. Couldn't leave a friend behind, could I?"

A smile toyed with her mouth, and she tugged the too-long sleeves down to hide her knuckles, hugging her hands against her chest. "A friend?"

He groaned, waving her off. "Gods, don't make me regret it, will you? Take the win."

"Hmm." She came and sat at his feet, crossing her legs and staring into the fire, her toes wiggling as if basking in the heat. "Friends should probably know each other's names. Any guesses yet?"

"Hmm...Lorraine."

She rolled her eyes. "Be serious."

"Lorraine is a very serious name!"

"*Finn.*"

"Fine." He dipped a hand into his pocket before holding out a pair of shimmering crystal earrings—a very familiar pair she'd given up to save him last night. "Jade?"

A sparkle spun to life in her eyes. She didn't even ask when he'd managed to grab them back from Tomas—she simply hooked them back through her ears, rubbing them between her fingertips. "Mm...it was, once. But just for one night."

"Ah, a loaner. Okay, then. Let's think." He sat down beside her, mirroring her cross-legged pose, letting the arm wielding the fire poker dangle loosely over his knee. "Seraphina."

"Ooh, pretty. But no."

"Grace."

"Also pretty. Also no. One more try."

He considered for a long moment, though he had the answer ready. "Cistine?"

She laughed again, nudging her bare shoulder into him. "I've never even heard that name."

"It's from a book." His favorite book, in fact. He had so many bookshelves crammed into his room that he didn't even know what color his walls were painted, shelves packed with books on magic and warfare and politics and all the different recipes one could make with swordfish, but that one was one of the fantastical ones. A story about a gossipy princess who'd stormed an enemy kingdom and stolen the loyalty of their most renowned warriors for herself.

All right, so maybe that wasn't *exactly* how it had gone. He knew there'd been something romantic involved, something about stardust and blood oaths and the same heart beating in two chests, but he'd been more interested in the way the princess had fought her war. Not just with her weapons, but with her mind, with cleverness and well-wielded friendship.

He had to admire that idea, the other side to the coin of his treachery and tricks. But he wouldn't have been any good at it. All the loyalty he possessed was bought, either by coin or by fear.

Fidget's sigh distracted him from that spiral of thought, her shoulder pressing into his again, skin against skin, freckles to freckles. "Guess you'll have to try again tomorrow."

"A hint or two wouldn't hurt, you know." He bumped her a bit, chuckling as even that slight impact nearly sent her toppling.

"Nope! Not allowed," she giggled, pushing off the floor with one hand to give herself more momentum as she shoved Finn with the other. He mock-yelped, tumbling off to the side with a series of dramatic groans that melded with her bubbling laughter as she scrabbled over to him, leaning above his head with a grin that nearly touched both her ears. "I have faith in you."

He grinned back at her with ease that no longer startled him—and perhaps that should have worried him more than anything. He folded his arms beneath his head, gazing up at her with a raised brow and a cocky tilt to his head. "Well, I *was* told I'm the smartest of the Atlas family by this one girl…ah, damn, what was her name?…I think you might've been there. Do you remember?"

"Nice try." She flicked him between the eyebrows before pushing to her feet with a gusty sigh. "You think I'll be able to get back to my room without being seen at this hour?"

He shrugged. "I think you'll be fine."

"You already paid off the guards, didn't you?"

"Handful of gold apiece."

She sighed, her shoulders slumping. "I'll pay you back."

"You will not. I owe you for that dress, anyway." He jerked his thumb at the fire over his shoulder. "Just go quietly. I paid off the guards, but I didn't pay off my family…or your paranoid, noose-happy employer."

A light shudder traced a path up her body, and she hurried to the door, pausing with her hand wrapped around the knob. She looked back at him still lounging on the floor, a mischievous, more sincere smile spreading across her face as she offered the best semblance of a curtsy she could, pinching the hem of the pajama shirt between her fingers and spreading it a bit like a skirt. "Good day, Lord Lionett."

Something that was far, far too close to happiness fizzed in a forgotten corner of his chest, and he waved his hand in a dramatic flourish. "Lady Lionett. I'll see you later this evening."

"You'd better," she laughed. And even after the door shut, even after she was long gone, that foreign flutter of feeling in his belly didn't abate.

He cursed quietly under his breath, knocking his fist twice against his chest as if it could settle whatever had just woken up inside him. But whatever it was resisted soothing, a zipping sensation that soared through every vein, waking up parts of him he hadn't known existed. Like towing up a garden rock and discovering a host of living things beneath when he'd expected nothing but dead earth.

This was bad. This was very, very, very very very bad.

But worst of all…some defiant piece of him didn't really care.

Some defiant piece of him that was already counting down the hours till evening.

* * *

Vash was staying in the barracks like any other soldier, but thanks to his rank, he'd been granted the privilege of a private room rather than bunking with others. And thank whatever powers were worthy of gratitude for it, too, because Finn didn't want an audience for this: him and his Viper ally standing before a god-touched artifact, Finn's fingers pressed to his lips, Vash's folded in a position of prayer, both of them watching the quicksilver innards of the mirror undulate gently within the frame.

"What does it do?" Finn asked out of the corner of his mouth, almost afraid that speaking too loud would summon its power to the surface.

"No idea. I tried a few things, but nothing seemed to trigger it." Vash's eyes were flat and emotionless once more, their concern from the night before a distant memory—maybe even a hallucinated one. "None of my contacts had any clue, either."

"Nor mine." Finn scratched an itch behind his ear as he stared into the mirror's center, more perturbed than he should've been by its lack of reflection. After all, he'd been avoiding that very thing for weeks now. But it was just…*wrong*. It had all the qualities of a surface that should have captured his likeness in its panes, but there wasn't a trace of face or feature in it. Only endless, eternal silver. "Have you touched it?"

Vash shook his head. "Not bare-handed. It felt foolish."

"Hmm." Finn subtly pulled back the finger he'd started to extend toward the mirror. "Yes, agreed."

Vash gave him a look. "Prince."

Finn spread his arms defensively. "Well, do you have a better idea?"

"I don't have the utmost confidence in your judgement right now. Not after what I saw last night."

A chill stole all humor from Finn's tongue. "Bold words from a poisonmaster."

"Any blood I've shed has been in the name of Atlas. In the name of Soleil. What you did was…"

"I'm not going to talk about this with you. You're not paid to judge my morals, Maren."

Vash's jaw twitched, the only hint of emotion that bled through. "I would appreciate it if you proceeded with caution. That's all."

"You know, people keep saying that to me these days. I don't much care for it."

And with that, Finn reached out and touched the relic.

Instead of pressing flat to its surface, his hand plunged *into* the pool of silver, the utter cold within freezing his held breath in his lungs. He tried to pull away, tried to kick free, but that nothingness behind the silver façade held him fast.

Then came the pull.

Something tugged so sharply on his arm that he heard his shoulder pop, yanking him forward without warning, a stumble that drew a shout from Vash behind him—

And before he could shake his breath free to scream, he plunged face-first into the mirror.

CHAPTER 49

SOREN

"I understand your concerns, Josef, but we have to consider the ramifications of moving more troops to the border towns without direct threat..."

Normally, Soleil wasn't annoyed by the sound of her mother's voice. But just then, after hours of listening to it drone on about armies and soldiers and borders and Nyxians above the vibrations of feet and voices and skidding chair legs rumbling through the polished floor beneath her, she was getting sick of listening. What little she could see of the war room from behind this drapery in the corner didn't offer anything interesting, and she was about ten seconds away from sliding back through the hidden alcove in the back of her parents' closet and leaving this snooping mission behind.

But just as she turned to go, she found herself face-to-face with Finn, his glasses sliding down his nose, two goblets in his hand. "Did I miss anything good?" he asked breathlessly, using the back of his hand to shove his glasses back up the bridge of his nose, the liquid in the glass swishing dangerously.

"Just Josef Lionett being rude to Mama."

Finn scowled, ducking down in tandem with her, both of them peering out through the curtain around each other. "He likes to hear himself talk. Just like Jaskier."

Soleil mimed a gag. They'd been forced to entertain Jaskier Lionett, Lord Josef's son, on one too many occasions during formal dinners and meetings. He was spoiled and whiny and smelled like he bathed in his father's cologne. "At least Mama didn't make us play with him today."

"I don't think his papa brought him. None of the kids came."

"Wolf and Sage came with Aunt Genevieve and Uncle Cypress."

Finn frowned. "Where are they?"

"Sitting with Kal. Look." Soleil ducked down further so Finn could peer over her. Their two oldest cousins sat on either side of Kallias: Wolf watching Mama closely, dark-haired and solemn, while Sage took studious notes in his little book, his reddish-brown hair falling in his eyes. Or at least, he appeared to. Soleil knew that after the meeting her cousin would come and show off his ridiculous sketches if she asked, caricatures of all the stuffy lords and ladies who ruled over Atlas's major cities. She hoped he'd given Josef the ears of a donkey or something equally fabulous.

"This is beside the point," Aunt Genevieve finally interrupted. "Nyx has yet to actually commit an act of war. I say hold steady, Addie. Don't let him see you as easily provoked. Outright war with Atlas would be foolhardy…surely he knows that."

"In any case," Uncle Cypress stood, his long hair falling in thick braids down his back, his mahogany skin furrowed deeply between his brows, "Arborius must remain neutral. We can offer you medical supplies if it comes to that, as we would any kingdom in need, but we cannot offer military might. I'm sorry, Adriata, Ramses."

"Don't be," Papa assured him. "We don't expect you to break your oaths, Cy. We just wished to keep you informed."

That wasn't what Soleil had overheard Mama saying yesterday before everyone arrived. But Mama didn't argue with Papa; she just dipped her head to Uncle Cypress before moving on to other matters.

"Here." Finn drew her attention by sliding one of the long-handled glasses into her hand, and she frowned down at it.

"What is it?"

"Hot chocolate."

"In the fancy glasses?"

"It was all I could grab. Chef Abbi came back before I could find mugs."

Soleil sipped the warm cocoa, slurping up a couple marshmallows. Finn nudged her, hissing, "Quiet, kid!"

"I am being quiet, kid."

Every voice in the room beyond suddenly went quiet when Mama held up one hand. Her eyes roved over the table, across the room—

Right at the curtain they hid behind.

"Run," Soleil and Finn whispered at the same time, turning and bolting back out through the closet, Finn grabbing her wrist and dragging her faster as they plunged through their parents' room and barreled into the hallway, making a break for their rooms.

They reached Soleil's first; Finn flung the door open and shoved her in, but footsteps down the hall drove him inside as well. He twisted the knob and eased the door shut, slowly untwisting it so the latch wouldn't make a sound when it clicked back into place, then turned and hissed, "Act natural!"

When Papa opened the door, he found Soleil contorted in a hopeless position on the floor with a doll in one hand and a paintbrush in the other, looking like she'd attempted a handless somersault and failed badly. Finn was the picture of ease on the bed, holding a book open near the end, looking for all the world like he'd been sitting there for hours. The glasses of hot chocolate sat on the nightstand beside him.

"What's going on in here?"

"Nothing, Papa," Soleil said with an angelic smile.

"We're hiding from Jaskier," Finn said easily. "We heard Lord Josef was here."

"Well, lucky for you two, he left his boy at home. You've been here all day?"

"Not all day," Finn said before Soleil could even take in a breath. "Kal took us swimming earlier."

"Can that boy go a day without touching toe in the water?"

"Nope," Soleil and Finn chorused, and Papa sighed.

"Well, I'll leave you to it. Wolf and Sage are here, by the way. I'm sure you'll see them at breakfast tomorrow."

"Wolf doesn't even talk to us," Soleil complained. "We're too little for him now."

"Wolf doesn't really talk at all," Finn countered. "Did Sage bring his magic cards?"

"I have no idea. You'll have to ask them tomorrow." Papa came in and planted kisses on each of their brows before taking his leave, shutting the door behind him.

Finn and Soleil both exhaled in relief, Soleil dropping her doll and brush, Finn closing the book and sitting up. "That was close," he groaned. "That didn't look very natural, Soleil!"

"I panicked, okay?" She crawled up onto the bed beside him, grabbing one of her pillows and hugging it close to her chest. "What are we going to do if Nyx attacks us?"

Finn shrugged. "They'll probably start at the border, then work their way in. It'll take ages for them to get here, and we'll be long gone by then. Mama and Papa keep the country house secret for a reason."

Soleil blinked. "How do you know all that?"

Finn blushed. "I read. A lot."

"So you don't think they'll come here first?"

"Not if they're smart." Finn looked at her and frowned. "Hey…it'll be fine. Mama and Papa will fix it. And even if the Nyxians show up, we know all the best hiding places here. They'll never find us."

"I guess so." Warmth filled her chest, though she still worried. Pictures of faceless soldiers stomping into her room came unwanted to her mind, and she shivered, that warmth going cold.

"Besides…" Finn smirked. "They wouldn't bother with you, anyway. You're too shrimpy to worry about."

"Hey!" Soleil shoved him, the blankets bundling up as he caught onto them and held tight, laughing as he tried not to fall off. "I'm a whole inch taller than you!"

"You're going through a growth spurt, that's all. I'll catch up."

Lightning suddenly flashed across the windows, thunder crackling outside, freezing them both in their tracks.

"Maybe we should check on Kal," Finn said faintly, his eyes fixed on the window. "He's probably stressed after the meeting."

"Yeah," Soleil croaked. "Probably."

When the next stroke of lighting cracked open the sky, they both leapt from the

* * *

Soren

The flood of memories that came after Finn was not so jarring as Kallias; some part of her had always known Finn, a remembrance beyond memory, something in her heart that missed her almost-twin. But her chest still ached as she closed her eyes and let the memories crowd what used to be empty space— hot chocolate in wine glasses, games of tag that ended in several pieces of broken pottery, learning how to lie with a straight face because of his earnest coaching, escapades into the kitchen that left them with aching stomachs and lungs fit to burst from laughing through the slap-happiness of a sugar rush.

"Why are we doing this?" she whispered, knowing Jira was still beside her, both of them standing in the middle of an Atlas hallway while Soleil and Finn sprinted to Kallias's room, giggles edged with terror floating back to her as they ran.

Jira heaved a sigh that sent the curls around her face flying. "You never were the brightest star in the sky, were you?" At Soren's scowl, Jira quickly held up her hands. "But we all love you anyway!"

"Jira." She was tired of jokes. Tired of memories. Tired of this piercing, mind-numbing headache that only seemed to get worse with every trip backwards in time. "Please."

Jira's eyes softened, and she gestured to the floor, waiting until Soren sat before copying her, crossing her legs and slouching forward with her elbows braced against her thighs. "Do you know what's happening out there right now?"

"Elias went home." That, at least, was a relief. "Kallias fled with him. They're safe."

"Wrong." Jira scooted closer, the sword-shaped earrings dangling from her ears rattling with her movement. They were the one gift from her sister that she'd kept through every fight they'd ever had—so many other trinkets had made their way into the wastebasket after a famous Angelov sister spat, but never those earrings. "Elias is in Artem, fighting metal dragons and insulting his goddess and permanently denting his knuckles from punching walls. Kallias is with him, sleeping in the same room as my hag of a sister and picking fights with her—just another point in his favor, honestly—and Finn is dancing around a very dangerous queen and an even more dangerous goddess. They need help. They need you."

She blinked. Folded her hands and pressed them against her lips, watching Jira for any sign of her usual tells, waiting patiently for the lie to show through her sparkling eyes. When she merely stared back with bruise-black eyes, no light, no smile...

"Go to the pits, Jira." She crossed her arms tightly over her racing heart. "None of that is—"

"I'd know better than you, now wouldn't I? I'm not the one who retreated from a battle she was winning." The implication was so loud, so clear, Soren could hear it as voice and not silent intent: Unlike you, I'm not a coward.

"I wasn't winning." The words ached as they clawed out from between gritted teeth, her fingers curling into the thick carpet beneath her. The fibers rubbed uncomfortably between her fingers, her bones flinching inwardly at how real it was, and she flattened her palms instead. "I wasn't in control. Things were slipping—"

"So what? You think dying will keep them safer?"

"I don't gods-damned know, Jira!" She hadn't meant to shout, hadn't meant to stand, but she was—leaning over Jira and yelling, all the helplessness and rage and terror twisting her guts into knots until it hurt. "I don't know what in the pits I'm doing, and none of this is helping, all right? Even if I wanted to, even if I tried, I can't fight a goddess! I can't help them, and I won't watch her use my body to end them!"

Jira's hands gripped her shoulders and pulled her in until they were nose-to-nose—well, mostly. Jira had always been an inch or so shorter than her...and eternally disgruntled by it, too. "You're wrong about that," Jira said quietly. She twined her hand in Soren's hair and tugged, a gentle shake. "You haven't remembered everything yet. And I think once you have the whole picture, you're going to feel very differently about all this."

She highly doubted that. But Jira had never lied to her before...well. Not about important things. Not about family. Not about life and death.

She swallowed hard. Thought on everything Jira had said. "Elias and Kallias are in Artem? With Raquel?"

"Yes."

"And Finn is..."

"Unbearably attractive."

"Jira, I swear to whatever gods don't hate me—"

Jira held up her hands in surrender. "Fine, fine. Finn is losing a game he barely knows he's playing yet."

"Finn can handle a goddess." That much she knew. He was already playing Anima like a fiddle.

Jira's eyes flashed. "Not this one."

A quiet snort. "Anima is hardly—"

"Not Anima." For the first time, Jira's lip curled in disgust, and Soren's stomach dropped. "Someone worse. Someone you know better than you think you do."

"What does that mean?"

Jira pulled back, offering her hand. "Let me show you."

CHAPTER 50

FINN

A gasp punched into Finn's chest, and his eyes blew wide, blinking away silver to sun.

He was standing in a room filled with windows—sunlight poured in from everywhere, painting every surface in cheery shades of white-gold. The room lacked in décor—the scattered tables, the floor, even the walls were painted blank cream—but it was still lively with chatter and childish laughter.

Children. There were at least a dozen here—sprawled on the floor with toys in their hands, seated at the tables with paper and paints, running around and trying to tag each other while dodging the ones who played on the ground.

Where in the depths was he?

"Excuse me, sir," said a voice behind him, and he turned to see a stout woman watching him with a pleasant smile, her salt-and-pepper hair tugged back in a tight knot at the top of her head. "Are you here to volunteer for the day?"

Finn blinked. "Yes."

Questions may have been the better route to take—such as what is this place and how did I get here, exactly—but suspicion tended to follow questions. A quick lie might take him further.

The woman started rattling off instructions, and he listened with one ear while he took in the rest of the room, that horrendous itching behind his ears refusing to fade. The urge to scratch was almost unbearable, but he kept his hands at his sides, refusing to break the picture of composure and belonging.

But then his eyes found red hair, and his heart forgot how to beat.

A ghost sat at one of the tables. A little girl, no older than nine, golden-red hair tugged into pigtails that barely brushed her shoulders. Shorter than he remembered it. She wore a simple gray day dress, her mouth bent in a sullen frown, her eyes fixed on the paper in front of her. She clutched a paintbrush in her fist.

Finn didn't even manage to excuse himself from the woman's explanation. He drifted away as if caught in a dream, his eyes fixed on the impossibility sitting before him.

At Soleil, huddled at that table with her shoulders bent inward like she was trying to hide, her arms and legs and head patched with bandages and unhealed burns.

He was going to be sick.

Slowly, half-afraid to shatter this dream, he slid into the seat across from her at the table. "What are you drawing?"

His voice came out strangled, and he cleared his throat sharply, folding his hands on top of the table. She glanced up at him, and for some absurd reason, he held his breath. Waited for a flash of recognition, for his name to tumble from her lips.

None of it came. She simply looked away, mashing her paintbrush back to the paper. "I'm painting. Not drawing. It's different."

Oh, gods, her voice. He knew it as well as his own, remembered it as if he'd only heard it yesterday, had heard it screaming for him in so many nightmares. In it, he could hear the future to come—the sarcastic, abrasive timbre of Soren—but he could also hear the past long gone, the mischievous, sweet tone of Soleil.

"Right, of course," he rasped. "How silly of me. What are you painting?"

She kept her eyes glued to the paper. "My family."

Another kick to the gut. He swallowed down bile. "You remember them?"

She did look up then, giving him a look of caution that warned him he was seconds away from having an authority figure called over to get rid of him. "Right now I do. A little bit."

That was a very strange way to word it. "Can you tell me about them?"

Soleil hesitated, but he offered her a smile he rarely used, the silly grin that usually put children at ease; he didn't often come across children on his jobs, but when he did, he did his best to ensure they wouldn't be left shaken by the encounter. Children remembered monsters. He'd always preferred to be a forgettable friend.

Slowly, she eased herself out of her chair and came around to sit beside him, letting him see her paper. "That's Mama and Papa." Both taller than the rest, both with red hair. "That's my big sister and her best friend." She pointed to another red-haired stick figure and a dark-haired one beside it. "And these are my brothers."

Finn stared at the smallest of the redheaded figures for far too long, taking in the glasses, the exaggerated smile, the brown shirt that was drawn nearly to its feet. "Do you remember their names?"

"No." Soleil's voice pitched down with frustrated sadness. "But sometimes I don't even remember what they looked like, so…so I'm painting them. So she can't make me forget."

Cold flooded his veins. "What do you mean, she?"

"The mirror lady." Soleil didn't look up, too concentrated on the task before her. "I don't remember her all the time, either. But she can't make me forget them forever. I've gotta get home. I'm supposed to be…" Her voice trailed off into the curl of a question mark, frustration tightening her fist around her paintbrush. "Oh, I'm supposed to be something. I don't know. But I know it's important."

The mirror lady. "What does the mirror lady do to make you forget?"

"Magic." Her answer was simple, confident. "She comes in through the mirror and tells me it won't hurt, and then she makes me go to sleep. And when I wake up, I don't remember them again."

No. No, no, no. This couldn't be real. "Do you know the mirror lady's name?"

Soleil blinked, finally looking up at him, her gaze flooding with heartbreakingly earnest hope. "You believe me?"

"Don't the people here believe you?"

She shook her head hurriedly, scooting her chair closer to his, lowering her voice to a child's stage whisper. "No, nobody! They said I hit my head but I didn't, Mister. I didn't."

"Well, I believe you, all right?" Oh, gods, did he believe her. "Do you know her name?"

Soleil hesitated. "Well…no. But I know she's a goddess. She told me that, I think. Like Mortem, but she's not Mortem. Mrs. Angelov says Mortem can't make people forget things or walk through mirrors."

Every thought stilled, replaced by a hollow, furious hum, a hive of wasps knocked free in his head. But he forced another smile at her, because if she saw anger, he didn't think she'd keep talking. Soleil had always been timid in the face of aggression—a trait Soren had grown out of, clearly—but he wasn't entirely certain this was Soren in front of him. No, this was some between-girl, a child trapped between orphanhood and family, a child with one hand desperately clinging to a past that was trying to leave her.

That someone was trying to take from her.

And he thought he knew that someone's name. Because she was trying to take something away from him, too.

"That's awful," he croaked. He had to find something to say, had to find something to help her hold on. "Can I ask your name?"

"Why do you like names so much?" But she sighed, holding out one paint-spattered hand. "They call me Soren here, but that's not my real name."

So different from the woman she'd grow into. He took her hand, shaking it briskly. "Understood. What do you like to be called?"

She shrugged. "My sister calls me Soso."

His ribs caved in on his heart, but he nodded, letting her hand go. "Soso it is. So-so tell me, Soso—" He smirked while she giggled, hating how his soul ached at the sound. The little boy he used to be remembered missing that, so desperate to hear it again that he'd fallen to his knees in Life's temple and invited Death inside to bargain with him. "Are you happy here?"

Soleil frowned. "I mean…sorta. The people are nice. I like my friends. But it's not my home."

"You miss home? Even though you can't remember it?"

Soleil's eyes welled with tears, but her mouth twisted into a stubborn knot, her entire forehead creasing as she forced them back. She nodded once.

Whatever dream this was, whatever vision, it was utterly cruel. To have placed him within reach of something he'd wanted for so long…to give him the opportunity to see his sister again when he couldn't help her, couldn't save her…

Maybe that was the harsh power of the mirror relic. Maybe it gave you exactly what you wanted, but held it just out of reach, able to be seen but not possessed.

She was here. All along, for the entirety of those ten awful years, she was right here. Waiting for them. Missing them. Needing him.

"You'll make it back to them someday, kid," he croaked. "I know it."

Her eyes gleamed, shining with the relief of someone finally being heard. "You think so?"

"Finn," Soren—Soleil—said desperately, "what's going on? Why is everyone looking at me? Where were you?"

"You're okay," he'd said, forgetting all masks and tricks and chess pieces, throwing them aside to wrap his arms around her as she sobbed and leaned into him, and he thought he might never be able to make himself let go again. "Hey, listen to me. Everything's okay. I'm sorry I wasn't there, but I am now, okay? I'm here. And I'm not leaving."

"I promise you," he whispered. "You'll make it home someday, Soso. And your family will still be waiting when you do."

She laughed quietly, clinging tightly to her paintbrush with both hands. "What's your name, Mister?"

He debated for a moment, but what could it hurt? How likely was it that this was real, anyway? "Finn."

"Finn." This time, that smile was less sure of itself, tipping closer to sadness. "I like that name."

Damn all of this to the depths. He was here, and she needed him, and he could help.

"Soleil," he said, and her gaze snapped to his, widening in shock. "Your name is—"

Before he could finish, something tugged hard on his arm, jerking him straight out of that chair. Jerking him straight out of that time.

Carpet dragged across his cheek as he skidded against the floor, searing his skin with a friction burn, and he shouted in pain as he slammed at an awkward angle against the wall. He scrabbled up, one hand flying to his cheek, his breaths coming in uneven pulls.

Vash still stood by the mirror, but his arms were outstretched toward Finn, his eyes wide. "What happened? What did you see?"

Finn couldn't even begin finding the words to answer him. He stared at that mirror, at the quicksilver depths that had taken him somewhere else—sometime else—and the welling in his throat was the only warning he received before he bent in half and vomited all over Vash's carpet.

"Prince?" Vash knelt before him, but Finn threw one hand out.

"Wait," he said, the word rough from the acrid touch of bile.

So Vash did, lowering himself to his knees in front of Finn, ignoring the clump of vomit mere inches from his kneecaps. "What did you see?"

Finn might as well have swallowed kerosene for how his throat burned. "How do I talk to Occassio?"

"What?"

"How do I speak to your damned goddess, Vash?"

Vash blinked again at the venom in his voice, but his calm did not break. "You don't. You pray, I suppose. But with Occassio, it's mostly waiting for her to speak to you. Why?"

Finn swallowed the acid in his mouth. Relished the way it burned beside his fury, a match lighting an unquenchable fuse. "She's the one who really killed my sister."

CHAPTER 51

KALLIAS

R aquel Angelov had a lot of nerve telling him off for arguing with physicians.

"Angelov," he said tiredly, coming in just as another one went scurrying out with their tail between their legs, "they're trying to help you."

"They can help me by letting me do this myself," Raquel said through gritted teeth. She sat cross-legged on the physician's table, a soft-looking shirt cast across her lap, her brows furrowed in concentration and pain as she gingerly wrapped bandages around her upper torso.

He forced himself not to focus on the cotton undershirt rolled up just below her chest—or the well-muscled abdomen exposed beneath its hem. But that brought his gaze down to the shirt draped across her knees, and he paused. "That's my shirt."

"All of mine are too tight on my ribs. I asked Elias for a spare and he brought me this. Not my fault if he picked something of yours."

"But that's *my* shirt."

She glared at him from beneath black lashes. "Not anymore."

He let her keep the shirt.

When she tweaked her ribs, he saw it; she twisted just a bit wrong and stiffened, a harsh exhale escaping her lips, her movements slowing as she tried to adjust herself.

"Okay, enough." Kallias marched over and held out his hand. "Give it to me."

"I can do it, Atlas."

"I know you *can*. But you're *not*, because it's ridiculous. Give it here."

Her jaw flexed like she tasted something bitter and wanted to spit it out. But she slowly set the roll of bandages in his hand, her fingertips brushing his palm as she withdrew. The hair on his arm rose like he'd encountered static. "One wrong move, and—"

"And I'll be dead, I know, I know." Strange, how he wanted to smile at her threats. How they flooded him with relief now instead of anger. "Good to see that beam didn't knock the hostility out of you."

"Why in the pits are you *smiling* at me?" Raquel demanded, lifting her arms a bit so he could better reach around her, burying his fingers in her tangled hair while she watched him. She'd twisted it into a bun instead of a braid, loose strands trailing against her neck and shoulders, blue against brown, and he had to clench his fingers to stop them from brushing that hair aside.

Gods, he was such a complete disaster.

"If you're already feeling well enough to threaten me, then I think you're going to be just fine."

Raquel's tentative breathing paused, and he didn't think it was because of the pain this time. When he looked up from his task, she was already staring down at him, a new kind of crease carved into the space between her brows. Confusion instead of anger. "You don't make any sense to me, Atlas."

"I've heard that before."

"You came after me." There was a blankness to those words that suggested she didn't quite believe them. "You ran into *fire*. For *me*."

"I know."

"*Why?*"

Why, indeed. Why had he risked his own life for a woman who would have gladly left him to that same fate? Why had his fear of leaving her to the fire's mercy overcome his terror of the fire itself?"I don't know," he admitted, to her and to himself. "I guess I couldn't watch one more person burn."

He straightened up, eyes fixed on her ribs, both his hands braced on her back as he pinned the bandage in place. When his fingers brushed bare skin, he felt goosebumps rise beneath them, and his own breath stuttered in his chest; when he raised his head, he found her face only inches from his. Her dark eyes, for the first time he could remember, held no animosity. She only looked...frustrated. "You're nothing like you were supposed to be."

Kallias's heart winced, but he did his best to keep his voice light. "I've heard that before, too."

"No." Raquel shook her head, and his hands slid from her back to brace against the table instead. His thumbs brushed her hips, and an apology leapt to his lips, but she didn't move away or snarl at him; in fact, she leaned closer. Her breath smelled like the medicine they'd given her to fight off infection and pain, but her eyes were sharp as her blades.

He'd never longed to be impaled before, but for just this moment, he was perfectly willing to take her blows.

"You were supposed to be a monster," she whispered. "You were supposed to make this easy, and you're just...you're not. I *hate* it."

"What am I, then?"

Raquel's eyes wandered over his face—stopped on his lips just long enough for his heart to throw a punch at his ribs. By the time she raised them back up to meet his gaze, he was sweating. He flexed his damp palms on the table, praying to Tempest that he wouldn't accidentally freeze anything this time.

When she tipped her head to the side, he let himself lean into her space, following her guiding, his breath and hers coming together as a single gust of wind. "What am I, Raquel?"

Her lids fell to half-mast. Her mouth was so close he could practically taste the bite of the tonics she'd taken. His heart was going berserk; he was half-certain he was going to end up with a chest just as bruised and battered as hers.

Then the door opened, and the moment shattered.

They flung themselves away from each other in opposite directions—Kallias catching himself on another table, Raquel's back thudding against the wall behind her, both of them taking in quick breaths, Raquel's hitching painfully, his hitching in a different way.

"I come bearing gifts!" Safi's cheerful voice preceded her arrival, her grinning face morphing into a look of suspicion as she took them in: Kallias splayed against a table, eyes blown wide, excuses already poised to dive off his tongue; Raquel, huddled against the wall, one arm wrapped around her sore ribs while she breathed through the pain. "Um…am I interrupting something?"

"No," they chorused, but no matter how hard Kallias tried, he couldn't make eye contact—with her or with Safi.

"Right." Safi sounded entirely unconvinced, but she offered him the tray she'd brought in, a fine silver thing covered in even finer pastries. "Havi sent these. He feels bad that he didn't get there sooner."

"It's not his fault." Kallias slowly sank into a nearby chair, silently begging his body to relax, but a chill still leaked from his palms. He kept them folded in his lap; then, after further consideration, slid them a bit further down toward his knees. The last thing he needed was to freeze himself in a more *intimate* place.

Though at this point, a cold shower might just be in order.

"He couldn't have done anything," Raquel agreed as she tugged his shirt on, the excess cloth gathering in her lap. "It all happened so fast."

In spite of his protests, he had to admit…he liked the sight of her in that shirt. Liked it far more than he should.

"Have you talked to Elias yet?" Kallias asked Safi, forcing himself to focus elsewhere. He'd barely seen the man since their argument had nearly turned deadly; every time he tried, Elias ducked away with some mumbled excuse, refusing to look Kallias in the eye.

Safi's gaze gentled. "A little. He's been in the bakery a lot, talking to Havi. Pyromancy is…it's a difficult magic, especially as someone newly blessed. All magics respond to our emotions, but most of them aren't quite that…destructive."

"It wasn't his fault, either," Raquel said quietly, flexing her fist against her leg.

"We all know that. Artem is no stranger to outbursts like that one, believe me. But Elias being Mortem's cleric…his magic is different. His fire burns hotter, faster. It resists being extinguished by natural means. He has to learn to not let anger have its head."

"How can we help him?" Kallias croaked.

"Tell him you don't blame him, for starters. He's horrified about what he did—especially to you."

Kallias blinked. "Me?"

Safi smiled, but it didn't last nearly as long as it usually did. "He's fonder of you than you think, Prince. He keeps saying he almost killed his friend."

Friend.

Kallias stood, brushing his palms off, wincing at the gentle clicking of ice shards falling to the floor. "I should go find him."

"I'll come with you," Raquel announced, starting to slide off the table, but he crossed the room in two strides and stopped her with a firm hand on her shoulder.

"You're not going anywhere," he said. "You need to rest."

"I need you to get your *hand* off me."

He obeyed immediately, but didn't move away. "I mean it, Angelov. You'll be no good to anyone if you double over in the middle of the mountain."

"He's right, Raquel," Safi agreed. "Stay here. Eat. Enjoy my sparkling company. I'm sure Kallias will be back to check on you soon."

The meaningful look Safi shot him heated his ears with an embarrassed blush. He cleared his throat, gave an awkward wave, then ducked out, nearly hitting his head on the doorframe as he did. Before he closed the door, he heard Safi's cackle following him out—and Raquel's rare chuckle, too. Lower, raspier, but still a laugh.

His heart lurched in the wrong directions, and he rubbed his eyes with a quiet curse, the cold nestled in his palms soothing the irritation left over from the smoke.

This was bad. All of it bad, all of it well beyond him.

He went to find Elias. But even as he did, his ankles ached to turn around, his mind trailing behind, caught up in thoughts of a Nyxian soldier with beautiful eyes and a scowl that could stab through a heart.

CHAPTER 52

ELIAS

The nightmares had changed.

It wasn't just Soren anymore; it was Kallias and Raquel, all of them begging him not to burn them, all of them screaming as the pyre ate them alive. And no matter how hard he tried to stop, no matter how much he begged for help or forgiveness, his words poured out in molten gouts of flame, his very breath turned weapon, wreaking havoc he could not stop.

But not tonight.

Tonight, he dreamed about his father.

His mother always told him how he took after his father; until he'd reached his eighteenth year, he'd never seen it. He bore his mother's coloring, her broad nose, her well-built frame. But when he'd reached manhood, he began to see what his mother meant: he had his father's smile, his father's careful hands, his father's rumbling laugh that had startled him the first time he heard it from his own chest. Sometimes he caught his mother brushing a tear away when he laughed too loud or long at things. It had made him shy of enjoying a well-told joke.

When he opened his eyes to a river kissed with the light of dawn, his feet hanging in the icy water beside his father's, their shoes piled between them, he waited patiently for the ruin to begin. For the sunlight to catch flame. For the grassy bank to burn blue. For his father's easygoing smile to twist into a grimace of pain.

None of it came. It was only him, and his father, and the thin strip of the Vela River that ran through the plot of land behind their house.

"Do you know why I come out here every morning, Eli?" asked his father, one foot dangling in the water while the other rested on the muddy edge of the bank, the springtime sun gleaming off his olive skin. Though the winter snow had melted, its cold lingered in the numbing bite of the river, in the slap of the wind against Elias's bare arms.

Eli. Only his father ever called him that, something that eternally vexed his mother. "Elias is short enough as it is," Sera would scold. "I think you can expend the effort to make it all the way through." But Elias had secretly loved it, thought of it like a little joke between him and his father.

Why he'd used it in Atlas, he wasn't entirely sure. Why he continued to let Kallias use it was just as much a mystery. But there was something comforting about hearing that name again. Something that ached, but in a good way. A way that promised that wound, at least, had finally scarred over.

"Why, Papa?"

"To pray," said Evan. "To say good morning to Mortem, and thank her for bringing me through another night."

"You think she listens?"

"I know she does."

Elias rested his elbows on his knees, staring down into the river, watching tiny stones tumble past on their way to the much wider banks of the Vela further north. "I told her to leave me, Papa." He let the confession slip into the river like a skipping stone, its echo dancing across the water. "I...I gave up the faith you taught me."

He waited for the condemnation, the disapproving scowl.

"Do you feel free?" asked Evan instead, his head turning toward Elias, hazel eyes refusing to give up their true feelings.

Elias blinked.

He didn't know what he felt, but free wasn't it. He knew people who had long since given up their faith; knew they'd found peace in that, in the freedom it offered them to explore a new path. Many flourished in their faithlessness. But for him…the idea of stepping outside of his faith, of probing past it to see what lay beyond, only shoved a spear of terror deep into his belly. It offered him no semblance of rest. But neither did stepping back into the comfort of what it had been. He'd changed too much to believe the way he used to, but he hadn't changed so much that he could give it up.

He was angry with Mortem. He couldn't find it in him to trust her any longer. But that wasn't the same thing as casting aside his beliefs entirely. And he didn't know how to reconcile that, didn't know where exactly that left him.

"Nothing feels right anymore," he admitted. "I don't think I can follow her the way I did before. But I don't…I don't like the man I've become without her guidance, either."

"Hmm." Evan was quiet, birdsong and babbling water replacing their voices for a time. Then: "Are you angry with her?"

"Yes." The answer left him without hesitation; he'd never been able to lie to his father.

"Tell me why."

The story came so much easier when it was his father's ear listening. He told him of vows offered and promises broken; he told him of battlemates found and battlemates lost. He told him of temporary deathbeds and harrowing trials and the branding seared into his skin that had marked him as a man overstaying his welcome in mortality.

Before he could finish, his father's sturdy hand settled on his shoulder. "Eli. Look at me."

Even as a man, his father's stern tone made him flinch a bit inside. But he obeyed.

"You're fighting the wrong battle, son," Evan said, squeezing his shoulder in a bracing hold. "And until you figure out what the right one is, you'll never be able to claim your victory over this brokenness inside you."

"I'm fighting for my kingdom. How can that be—?"

"Not the trials, Elias. Not the war." His father's hand moved to settle over his chest. The beast within bridled at his touch, a painful swell of teeth and claw and spine. "You need to fight this."

"But Papa—" he started.

"Look at me, Eli."

He frowned. "I am looking."

"Eli."

"I'm—"

"Eli, wake up."

This time, Elias didn't wake to bile flooding his mouth or terror hurling him out of his makeshift bed. This time he woke to a cold touch on his back, opening his eyes to reddish hair and a green gaze filled with worry.

"Soren?" Groggy. Half-lost in dreams still. It wasn't until after he said her name that he realized those green eyes were tinted a bit blue. Wasn't until after that Kallias's face swam fully into focus, his brows bent, his mouth thin…and his heart thunked to the bottom of his chest. "Sorry. I was…I…"

"Don't worry about it." But for the first time, he heard the strain of grief in Kallias's voice—a strain that loosened quickly, replaced by gruff concern. "Havi said you weren't feeling well."

It hadn't been a lie, though it had been an excuse. After hours spent sitting with Havi, both talking through his actions the day before and learning the basics of controlling his…magic…he'd been so worn down that he'd had to find his way to their quarters with his hands out and his eyes closed, feeling his way down the corridor with the barest wisps of consciousness keeping him upright.

"Raquel's doing fine," said Kallias, though Elias hadn't asked. He was grateful for it, though—grateful Kallias hadn't made him muddle through layers of guilt and fear to ask the question. "Bruised up, and they think a couple ribs might've cracked, but nothing she won't recover from."

Elias's mouth twitched. "You sound relieved."

Kallias's cheeks pinked as he scowled, but even that bent toward a smile. "You sound like you need to mind your own business."

"And you?" The answer seemed to be standing before him, but it felt rude not to ask. "Are you all right?"

Kallias hesitated, holding up hands covered in leather gloves. At Elias's questioning look, he said, "Safi's suggestion. She says they might buy me a moment to stop myself if my magic gets out of control again. She sent a pair for you, too."

He didn't shape the words like an accusation, but they hit Elias in the chest all the same. "I'm sorry," he rasped, curling himself up against the wall. His body protested, sore from the tavern incident and from his insistence on sleeping on the rock floor. "I am…so, so sorry, Kal. I don't know what happened. I didn't mean to…"

Slowly, Kallias twisted and lowered himself from his knees to his haunches, sitting beside Elias and easing himself back against the wall. Elias wasn't sure if he imagined the way the stone chilled as Kallias leaned into it. "I am…intimately familiar with the hole you've dug for yourself. I've dug a few of my own. Most of them deeper than yours."

"This is a strange analogy."

"Yeah, well, it's been a strange few weeks. Bear with me, will you?"

That was truly the least Elias could do for him. He'd almost burned him alive.

Kallias's sleeved shoulder bumped against Elias's bare one, the prince letting out a gusty sigh. Even with that barrier between them, something had shifted. Elias could feel the cold pacing back and forth along Kallias's bones, his more feral magic brushing up against Elias's fire with a dangerous, tempting purr—a challenge that bloomed heat through Elias's skin like hovering a palm over a candle.

"I almost killed Finn," said Kallias suddenly.

Elias blinked. Had this just turned into a confessional? "What?"

Kallias shrugged the shoulder pressed to Elias's, raking a hand through his messy waves of hair. He hadn't braided it back or tied it up today. "It was a little over a year after Soleil died. He was…gods, he was only eleven. I snuck a bottle of wine into my room and drank the entire thing."

"How old were you?"

"Almost seventeen. A week shy of my birthday." Kallias breathed in shakily. "I barely remember it, but Mama made sure I knew. Gods, she made sure I knew exactly what I did."

Elias hated Adriata Atlas more and more every time Kallias spoke of her. He hadn't thought he had room for more loathing toward the woman who'd held his kingdom captive in a war they didn't want, but that look in Kallias's eye… "What happened?"

"He came to my room that night for some reason. I think he had a nightmare. But I was drunk, and I hadn't slept, and…I got angry. I threw the bottle at him. I didn't mean to, I wasn't looking and I didn't realize he'd moved, but…you try explaining that to an eleven-year-old with glass shards in his back." A laugh with no humor. "He didn't speak to me for months. Couldn't blame him, either."

Elias genuinely couldn't picture Finnick Atlas, mastermind and menace, as a frightened child seeking his brother's comfort. Couldn't picture him as anything but a smirking, dark-eyed terror who wore city shadows like a fine cape. But Kallias, he guessed, didn't know that side of his brother, and it didn't feel like the right time to enlighten him. "So what are you saying?"

"I'm saying a punch to the face is hardly the worst thing to come from a drunkard's grief."

"I don't know what got into me," Elias rasped. "I never...I never do that."

"Do what?"

"Throw the first punch." Only once, on a different terrible day, prodded into rage by a different redheaded royal.

Kallias snorted softly. "It's hardly the first punch I've taken."

Elias couldn't help scoffing. "Kallias Atlas, brawling? This I have to hear."

A laugh. "Not brawling, gods forbid. I was trained in grappling and hand-to-hand, the same as you. You thought sword-fighting was all I knew how to do?"

"Yes," Elias answered bluntly, and Kallias rolled his eyes.

Silence, for a beat. Then Kallias whispered, "I'm sorry, too. I know our beliefs differ when it comes to Soleil...to Soren. I shouldn't have said those things to you."

A lump formed in Elias's throat. "I would give anything—"

"I know." Gentle. So gentle it almost hurt. "And I know you believe she's gone. But can I tell you why I can't?"

It wasn't really a question, so Elias nodded, a silent gesture for him to go on.

Kallias's eyes found the ceiling, a bit of water gathering in the corners, threatening to take shape as tears. "I grieved her for ten years," he said softly. "Finding her on that battlefield...I thought I'd finally cracked. It should've been harder to recognize her—ten years older, Nyxian armor, that scowl on her face, but I just..." He shrugged lightly. "I would've known her anywhere. Anytime. One year later or fifty, I still would've known her."

Elias knew exactly how that felt. Had experienced it himself in an Atlas hallway, his knife an inch from cutting Finnick's throat, Soren's voice coming from a princess dressed in Atlas clothes, wearing an Atlas crown.

He knew the opposite side of it intimately, as well—the absolute certainty that had driven him to wrap his hands around Soren's throat, knowing full well that shy smile and timid laugh didn't belong to his battlemate.

"I didn't hurt her," Kallias added, glancing at Elias out of the corner of his eye. "I don't know if she told you that, but it wasn't me. She got my leg, and one of our soldiers came after her. They thought they were saving me."

"They were. She would've killed you."

Kallias only grunted, a sound Elias took to mean fair enough. "They dragged me off to get seen to by our medimancers, and by the time I fought my way back to her, she was…" A low, rattling breath this time, Kallias tightening his arms around his knees. "I thought she was dead all over again."

Green eyes with the light dying out of them. Bloodied lips moving with unbearable slowness: "Elias. Don't go."

Elias rubbed at his chest, wishing that pain would dull. He had enough fresh ones to carry without that one causing trouble. "I did, too. When I came back and she was gone."

Kallias turned his head to look at him this time, brows furrowed. "You were there?"

"I was her battlemate." Was. "Of course I was there."

Kallias nodded once, looking back to the ceiling. His fingers tapped lightly against his knee. "Twice I thought her dead, and twice she survived. I…I can't grieve her a third time. I lost faith in her before, and for ten years, she paid the price. I won't give up on her again. Not until I watch her body buried in dirt or burned on a pyre. I owe her that."

Faith. There it was again, that word.

"You were right," Elias whispered, avoiding Kallias's gaze when he glanced toward him again. "In the tavern, you were right. I don't want to believe she's alive."

"Why not?"

"Because if you're wrong, false hope will only make it worse. And even if you're right…to be trapped in your own body with no way out, that's…that's a suffering I cannot imagine. Something I wouldn't wish on anyone, least of all her. And it would be worse, because…" Elias swallowed thickly, bracing himself against a sickly shudder. "Because there still wouldn't be a way to free her besides killing her. There is no way to remove a goddess from her host without putting an end to her. And with Anima's magic settled by now…I don't think it's even possible."

And even if it was, how could he make that choice? Letting his battlemate live on in agony, or granting her mercy by ending her life with his own hands?

The first time had been instinct. Knowing she was already dead mixed with his need to give her soul peace. But this…this would not be instinct. This would be choice. And he didn't think there was any way that he could choose to harm her, mercy or not.

"I have to believe she's dead," he whispered, "Because if she's alive, I won't be able to let her go."

Kallias nodded, a slow bob that brought his chin nearly to his chest. When it came back up, his jaw was set in determination. "All right," he said softly. "I hear you."

"And I hear you."

Kallias offered his knuckles, and Elias couldn't help smiling as he bumped his against them, both of them wincing and cursing under their breath at the collision of already-bruised bone.

"Not the brightest thing we've ever done," Kallias moaned, shaking out his hand as a grimace cut across his face.

"I don't actually know if we've ever done anything bright."

"True enough."

A sharp knock on the door interrupted their laughter, sounding less like a request and more like an order.

Kallias frowned, but he hauled himself to his feet, brushing imaginary dust from his clothes before going to answer the knock. "Yes?"

"Prince Kallias," said Star, and Elias was on his feet in an instant, striding to Kallias's side. Star stood in the corridor with her hands folded, flanked by two more guards, her expression the kind of grim that normally preceded terrible news. "You two have been summoned."

"By the Priestess?"

Star's eyes flickered to him, and his heart dropped at the cold anger in her eyes. "By Empress Idris."

"But I haven't finished the trials," Elias started, but Star lifted a hand, her eyes trained on Kallias now.

"Our delegation has just arrived home from Atlas," she said, and the floor slid beneath Elias's feet. "And they brought some very interesting news with them."

Elias exchanged a look with Kallias, panic overcoming the prince's features in the span of a second. Elias's legs locked up with tension, ready to run the moment Kallias tried. But there was nowhere for them to go. They were cornered. They'd run out of time.

CHAPTER 53

ANIMA

B rae hadn't come to see her again since the mirror was taken, and Anima couldn't decide if she was relieved or frightened by that.

She took in a breath sweetened by one of the dozen chocolates she'd consumed in the past hour, the carnation-pink box nestled in her lap, the lid tossed askew against her pillows. She dug another truffle out of its slot, popping it into her mouth and chewing glumly. If not even chocolate could take the edge off of her worries, then she must truly be doomed.

She'd been hiding in her room for two days now, feigning a fever by leaning out the window and coaxing the sun to kiss her face until her cheeks and forehead glowed warm and pink. But she couldn't hide forever, and neither Jericho nor Brae would be fooled by a well-placed sunburn.

She might not have been the cleverest of her siblings, not by a long shot, but she was plenty smart enough to outthink a mortal or two. She could do this. She was a *goddess*, for crying out loud.

She sat up with a fierce nod to herself, but that movement knocked the chocolate at an odd angle, jamming into her windpipe. While she choked and punched uselessly at her own chest, the weakest laugh drifted from deep within her head.

"Of course you choose now to take a peek," Anima rasped to Soren past the burn of sugar in the sensitive parts of her throat, finally dislodging the chocolate and swallowing painfully, making a quiet *ack* sound as she cleared her throat.

No response, not verbally. But she felt Soren curl away from her, huddling as far from the wall between them as possible, like she was trying her best to go back to sleep.

It had been days since her cobweb had roused; she'd begun to worry—*wonder*—if she'd finally slipped away for good, finally crossing from Ani's realm to her sister's. Some part of her thought Soren might be wishing for that very thing herself.

She shook off those depressing thoughts with a huff. Day after day, she was beginning to feel worse about Soren's plight—worse because she understood the agony of being trapped somewhere you couldn't escape. She had to earn her way back out. And there was only one way to make progress there—she needed to talk to Jericho.

The hall to the First Princess's suite was ominously quiet; so much so that even Ani's silent footfalls seemed too loud.

That could only mean one thing.

Heart sinking gently to the floor of her chest, Ani pressed a palm and an ear to Jericho's door, surprised when it inched inward; unlatched, unlocked. The hinges were blessedly silent, and it was only for that reason that she felt bold enough to peek past the door, careful to angle as much of her body behind it as possible.

Just as she expected, Vaughn was propped up against the bed's headboard, the collar of his shirt soaked through with sweat, his damp curls lying limp against his forehead. His breaths rattled so loudly she could hear them from here, a horrific wheeze that made her own lungs wince. But he was awake, alert; his eyes were bright as they watched Jericho, curled up against her husband's side, her face tucked into his shoulder, her cheeks slick with silent tears to match his.

"You know we can't go back to the battlefields," Vaughn was saying, his voice ragged but patched up with a forced strength he only clung to for his wife's sake. She knew that much from his prayers. "It's too obvious. Someone will see. And it's too dangerous for you. You're nothing but a target out there."

"To the depths with me."

Vaughn closed his eyes. "Jericho—"

"Don't *Jericho* me. I'm not the one who's rotting from the inside out!" Jericho's anger slipped into sorrow by the time she reached the end of her protest, her voice quivering with tears yet unshed. She forced Vaughn to turn his head, to look at her, her hand fit perfectly to the curve of his hollow cheek. "There has to be a regiment that's lacking for healers. Any of them would be happy to have another medimancer, and a physician of your reputation—"

"I haven't practiced in years."

"But the knowledge is there." Desperation disguised as fervor struck a blow to Jericho's voice, forcing a wobble into it, but she kept going. "And they're hardly going to deny their Prince-Consort. I'm so close with Tenebrae, I'm almost there, but in the meantime—"

"Jericho." Softer this time. "If they were going to heal me, they would have done it by now."

"It's just this last thing, all right? This one last thing he wants, and then…then he'll—"

"He'll what? Love, this god has proven nothing but that there is no completion to his promises. He will only keep asking more of you. The only way this stops…the only way you're free is if—"

"I want no *freedom* from you," Jericho interrupted, a fresh wave of tears pushing dangerously toward spilling over. She held his face with both hands now, her brow bent to his, her lips pressed against a quiver. "There is no freedom to be bought. You are never a *burden* to me."

No bout of necromantic agony compared to the look on Vaughn's face now. This was a different kind of rotting away. This was a different kind of death.

"You knew from the start we were on borrowed time," he breathed, one hand rising to wipe away Jericho's tears, his thumb brushing gently against her glimmering lashes. "You always knew you would outlive me. So why won't you let me save you from this?"

Jericho shook her head against his hand, her lips near-white from her refusal to let them tremble. One last tear crept from her eye, tenderly kissing Vaughn's thumb, rolling down to his knuckle before dripping away from its chosen path.

"Why won't you let *me* save *you*? If we stop now, all of this—*all* of it, all the grief, all the pain—all of it was for *nothing*."

"It *has* all been for nothing! Jericho, it's time to cut our losses. This war has taken countless lives. Your bargain with Anima cost us Soleil a second time. Kallias, too, now that Eli told him the truth of my nature. Finn nearly died when I lost control at the festival, and the city…" A shudder tumbled from Vaughn's head to his toes, and he released Jericho to cup his hand over his mouth like he might vomit. "Gods know how many people have died or been hurt just to buy me another day. I'm sick of it—I'm sick of trading entire lives for one measly hour without pain. It's not worth it."

Jericho's hands dropped into her lap, fingers spread in silent plea. "Vaughn—"

"When he comes to you again, you will tell him your deal is *off*." A harsh breath—Anima didn't know if it was hers or Vaughn's. "And we will learn how to say goodbye to each other. Like we should have done ten years ago."

Jericho recoiled from him, and when he reached for her again, she put a hand up, her lace sleeve trailing on the sheets as she pushed herself away.

"Jericho." Vaughn's voice broke on his wife's name. "I love you so much, you know that? If love was enough—"

"I know." Jericho rose like a wraith drifting through the wind, like a woman trapped in a dream—a nightmare. She stood like that for several moments, her eyes on her feet, her fingers still splayed in silent reach for something that could never be caught.

"Jer." Vaughn pulled himself across the bed with no small effort, fresh sweat breaking out on his forehead as he dragged himself within reach of her, taking her hand in his. "Come on, love, look at me."

Jericho did not move.

"Look at me. Please?"

With unbearable slowness, Jericho obeyed, and Anima nearly flinched at the sheer agony wrenching her face from a vision of beauty to a picture of tragedy. An anguish that could not be replicated. Artists would go mad trying to capture such visceral suffering.

Vaughn's face crumpled in turn, and he held out his other arm. "Come here."

With an awful whimper that edged toward a sob, Jericho collapsed into his arms, curling up in his lap and burying her tearstained face against his neck, clinging to him so tightly Ani was half-sure Vaughn's frail bones would snap beneath the pressure. But he didn't wince; he only enveloped her in his arms, his face hidden in her hair, their shoulders lurching in sobs that might as well have wrenched free from the same chest; the same shared, shattered heart.

"All my best days belong to you," he whispered into her ear, and she bowed further into him, as if his words robbed the very strength from her limbs. "You have filled my life with beauty beyond measure, and you have done enough. Jericho, do you hear me? You have done *enough,* we have been given *enough.* Let it be enough."

Anima took one step back. Another.

What were they *doing*? What kind of person…what kind of *goddess* let her people suffer for her own gain?

Tenebrae needed a host; she knew that. But not like this. This was *wrong*.

She was forest-grower, wound-healer, life-giver. Not hope-killer and pain-maker. Her hands were meant to mend, not harm.

All their suffering was on her shoulders. And maybe she couldn't stop it, not without Tenebrae's permission, but she could at least do this: she could at least give Vaughn a day he did not have to purchase with someone else's blood.

She squeezed her eyes shut, reaching out in front of her, fingertips brushing against the air that carried bits of Vaughn and Jericho's breath within. She followed those piecemeal threads back to the royals themselves, feeling along the thin, fraying cord of Vaughn's life until her magic brushed against his body. She sensed him shiver a bit at her intangible caress, but he did not call out, so she kept going, easing that thread beneath his skin just as she had a few days ago. But this time, her magic had settled far deeper into this body's bloodpaths and bones. This time, it knew it belonged to her, and she would not settle for something as petty as alleviated discomfort.

It was the miasma of her magic wrapped around this world that had bound itself to this man, the one magic in the world that demanded to be fed, that craved life in such a similar way to its mistress; but where her need spurred her to dance in the ocean and bury her hands in rich garden soil and eat a boxful of chocolates just because she *could*, necromancy's need demanded satiation from darker, deadlier places. It hungered ceaselessly for the last desperate vestiges of life siphoned from the dying and dead, life at its most brilliant and bold; no one wanted to live so badly as when they no longer could.

She felt it: that constant pang of *need* tunneling through Vaughn's body, an appetite that was past pain, past suffering. How he could feel *anything* past it, let alone find the fortitude to beg his wife to stop trying to save him from it…

Her heart broke for him, this man who bore a curse sewn by her careless hands.

She could not lift it from him entirely, not yet. But she could feed it. She could buy him time.

The thread of her magic coiled around the gaping, shadowy maw in the center of Vaughn's being. She took the deepest breath she'd taken yet in this body, and when that breath touched the bottom of her lungs, she focused her entire will on that ravenous abyss. When it turned its attention on her, Life herself come to see it sated, she dug her magic in—

And she *lived*.

Chocolate and cinnamon and flaky fried fish. Flower crowns and embroidered dresses and sand burning the soles of her feet. Ramses kissing her head, Finn elbowing her in the ribs, Soren laughing as she fell into the ocean face-first. Silk sheets on smooth skin, her curls bouncing behind her in a high ponytail, the sun persuading her skin to pink beneath its invisible caress.

Elias's hands wrapped around her throat. Elias's hands wrapped around her waist. Elias's hands wrapped around the blood-soaked handle of a dagger, dying eyes fixed on hers, that beautiful smile threatening to stab her straight through.

I was going to ask you to marry me.

A gasp ripped out of her like a fisherman tearing a hook free from a worm, and she wobbled, her head suddenly weightless, spinning like a maple seed thrown to the mercy of a spring breeze. Her shoulders thudded into the wall, but she hardly felt it, her skin buzzy and numb, a wave of inexorable fatigue falling over her. It reminded her of some childhood memory, though she didn't know if it was her childhood or Soren's: a memory of plunging beneath the layers of blankets on her bed and tossing them upward just to watch them float back down and settle over her body oh-so-lightly. Yet another small, silly piece of magic hidden in simplicity.

But beyond the comfort of that memory, that exhaustion set off warning bells in her brain. This body remembered this feeling—fought against it with all it had, a silent roar of defiance blistering through that tender sleepiness—and even Soren stirred a bit in the back of her head, alarm raising her voice from the indifferent mumble it had faded to these past days. *What happened? What did you do?*

In the next room, she heard Vaughn catch his breath. Heard him inhale deeply, no wheeze, no rattle.

She thought she might have smiled, but her lips were too numb to be sure. "His magic was hungry. I gave it something to eat."

You what?

"Never mind." Rot and ruin take her, her whole body *ached*. "Was Elias really going to marry you?"

Now Soren was wide awake. *Excuse me?*

Anima didn't ask again. She simply closed her eyes, letting her mind drift away like one of those whirling maple seeds, seeking out a friendlier perch.

CHAPTER 54

FINN

There were one hundred and fifteen different places in the city where Finn was currently hiding stolen or secret goods.

An old sheet wrapped beneath his bed had just become number one hundred and sixteen.

Dust itched his nose as he shimmied back out from underneath his bedframe, and he scrunched his nose up against a sneeze; the force of it would no doubt fling his glasses from his face with the angle his head was bent at, and he really didn't want to tell his mother he was in need of yet another new pair. He was just about out of believable excuses; he was pretty sure he'd stretched her trust in him past its limit the last time, but to be fair, he'd been sleep deprived and a bit giddy from breathing in secondhand herb-smoke in the taverns all night.

Still, he probably could've done better than *a seagull ate them, Mama, glass and all!*

At any rate, the mirror was hidden. He hadn't told Fidget yet that he'd recovered it from Vash's possession, and he planned to keep it that way. If this was Esha's test, that was fine, but he'd pass it on his own time. Better to let her sweat a bit first. Nervous people were always more easily bent. Panic, when applied properly, made a fantastic interrogation tool; he'd get more from her if he dealt her an incomplete hand. Her itch to find that missing card would distract her from the fact that he'd already bluffed his way into a victory.

Besides, he already had plans tonight, and they involved the company of an entirely different Mirror.

He no longer fought the grin that came to play at the thought of her—gods, what was the point? He'd already shed blood for her, had already sullied his own hands to keep her safe. Compared to that damning fact, a smile was hardly something to worry over. And after spending so much time over the last day or so wrestling with the fact that Occassio was the one who'd stolen Soleil's memory...he needed a break from anger.

Besides, Fidget would be gone soon, spirited back to Lapis with her queen. There was only so much time left for him to indulge in thoughtless grins and thrilling hearts. Gods only knew if he'd ever feel it again.

One last night. Only one, and then he would finally put an end to this game. All the whispers planted and relics stolen, all the flirtatious looks and casual touches, all the laughter and jokes and borrowed names...all of that would end when he finally revealed his true hand. And afterward, she would hate him so thoroughly there would be no hope of salvaging what bits of this mask had actually started to meld into his true skin. The tricks he'd pulled off so well that he'd almost begun to believe them himself.

But that was all right. That was the nature of his work. She was never anything more than a pawn. And if it hurt when it was over...well, it was his own fault for letting her further across the board than she was ever meant to go. His own fault for promoting a pawn to a queen.

But that was for tomorrow. Tonight, he had one plan for her that didn't involve any bloodshed or thievery.

Well, maybe a little thievery. But all of it his own.

He checked one last time that the mirror was covered, tucking the sheet tight around its frame, careful not to accidentally press against that malleable center. He didn't need to take another trip into the unchangeable past.

Finally standing, he rubbed the itch at the tip of his nose while he went to his closet, rummaging past pomp and flash until he found the familiar purple yarn of his sweater. He changed into it quickly, stroking the static out of his hair as he reached back in for the scarf he'd stolen from Fidget...then paused.

He really should give it back. She'd earned the return of her collateral— more than earned it—but reluctance rusted the joints of his fingers before he could make himself grab it.

He closed the closet door, leaving the scarf inside. If she asked for it, she'd have it from him. For now, it stayed where it was, tucked into the hollow corner of a shelf near-bursting with other pieces from his years of costumes and disguises.

His entire closet smelled of lilac and crystal shoes and giggles that bubbled over like freshly popped champagne. He almost dreaded its inevitable fading away, the coming day when it would only smell of must and whatever tavern or shop or party he'd gone too last.

When he stepped into the hall and shut the door behind him, a voice made him pause, his fingertips lightly draped against the doorknob.

His father was talking to Vaughn.

Finn had been avoiding that man intentionally—him and Jericho. The potential arrangement with Esha had made it easy to form excuses, to allow him to dodge dinner invitations and beach trips and bedside visits on Vaughn's rough days with sheepish shrugs and reminders that he had a queen to court.

Not that he'd been doing absolutely any of that, but what they didn't know couldn't reveal him.

Thankful he'd forgone shoes for now, he silently stole down the hall toward the partially-ajar door to Jericho and Vaughn's chamber.

"Well, I'm grateful you're feeling more yourself," said Ramses, relief indeed flooding his father's voice, the clap of hand on shoulder freezing Finn in his tracks.

"As are we." But Vaughn didn't sound grateful, or even pleased, really. He sounded...dumbfounded. In shock. "I'm sorry to have caused—"

"Ah-ah! None of that. I told you before, you never need to apologize for things outside your control. We're thankful you're all right. That's all that matters."

Finn's stomach dipped low in warning, threatening to drop. If Vaughn was improving...had there been another necromancy attack in the night? Another grave robbery? He was supposed to be *watching* for that, gods damn him, had he missed it while dealing with the mirror? Surely Vash would have mentioned—

Maybe Vash had. Maybe *he'd* forgotten.

His hand gave a warning spasm. He clenched it shut before it could rebel in earnest.

"Finn!"

The sound of his name on his father's tongue melded with the sound of the door swinging open, and Finn dropped into a casual slouch against the wall, snatching his glasses off his face before the two of them crossed into the hallway proper, cleaning them on his shirt with an air of boredom, like he'd been at the task for ages. "Papa. Vaughn," he greeted without looking up. Concentrated on his task. Certainly not bothering to eavesdrop.

"Getting ready for your night with Esha?" Ramses's voice bent a bit oddly at the end, and Finn had a feeling the question he'd asked wasn't the one he really wanted an answer to.

"I'm not entirely certain I need to be present for that," Finn hedged. "For a woman pursuing a courtship, she's not too fond of…"

"Chatting?" Vaughn suggested.

A wave of anger flowed and ebbed in the span of one breath, inhale to exhale, rage to patience.

Whatever it took. He'd promised Soleil. And for now, it required him to shove down his pride where it could not challenge Vaughn's part in these lies, in this silent power struggle between Finnick Atlas and the divine.

"Speaking to me in general, really," he drawled, looking up with a self-deprecating smile, the most difficult of his many masks. Humility was simple, confidence easy, but putting himself down was harder.

Vaughn seemed to be struggling with his own imitations, as well…the smile he hung on his face was nowhere close to the real thing. But he did look better— better than Finn had ever seen him. His black curls were clean, swept up off his forehead, not a drop of fever-sweat to be seen. The muscle that had wasted from his body from weeks of bedrest was miraculously restored, hidden beneath folds of knit gray, and his eyes were gleaming with something other than pain for once. His cheeks had *color* in them, for gods' sakes.

A miracle, indeed. Finn knew only one goddess willing to hand out miracles lately, and from what he'd seen, they were only bought, never given.

He curled his tongue against the pungent tang of dread, holding his smile tightly in place. Vaughn would not be smiling if Jericho had given herself completely over to Tenebrae. Vaughn's adoration of his wife was the only thing Finn still trusted. So they must have paid another price to buy this moment of health.

Whatever it was, Finn hoped it was nothing that mattered to *him*.

"I'm sure she's just adjusting," said Vaughn. "Lapis has never been a forthcoming kingdom."

"Or," said Ramses, "she may have been thrown off by the rumors about you and one of her Mirrors."

Oh, depths. "You heard of that?"

Ramses raised one eyebrow—a warning flag he knew all too well. "Only from the mouths of every palace worker within the walls. You're lucky they don't whisper when your mother is near."

He should have expected that. Rumors could hardly be limited to the city; the palace was fortified against people, not whispers. "It's nothing, Papa. Just gossip. I've barely spoken to the Mirrors."

"That's not what I heard," Vaughn said.

"Come on, really? You think *I* of all people have been fraternizing with a stranger?"

"I know you haven't. But Finn, there's nothing wrong with—"

"Vaughn," Ramses interrupted, patting his son-in-law on the shoulder, his eyes locked on Finn, "would you give me a minute with my son, please?"

Depths.

Vaughn nodded, walking off with an energetic stride that curled Finn's toes inside the sheath of his socks. Darkness capped the light of his anger, a murderous instinct so similar to the one that had tugged his knife across Tomas's throat.

Tomas's lifeblood soaking into the creases of his palms. Fireworks of gore dashed across Fidget's dress. Her hollow, dazed eyes driving fear so deep into his chest he might as well have been stabbed himself.

"Finn?" His father's hand touched his cheek, fisherman's calluses rough against his freshly shaved skin. "Where'd you just go, boy?"

"Finn?" Her hands were touching him, one pressed to his chest, the other to his cheek, her eyes wide with worry.

He swallowed thickly. Did his best to speak without grinding the words against the rock in his chest. "Nowhere, Papa."

"Don't lie to me, Finn." That gentle warning added weight to the rock. "You've been different since Lapis arrived. And I don't think that's Esha's doing, is it?"

A delicate curtsy, a champagne giggle, a sparkling smile. Cunning eyes, fearless fingers redirecting a crossbow, cheap earrings she'd fashioned into treasure with only her words. "Good day, Lord Lionett."

"I don't know what you mean," he said. "Different how?"

"You're distracted. Distant. But you smile more." That very thing crept across Ramses's bearded face, nostalgia soaking his coffee-brown eyes in fond memories. "I know what it looks like when someone falls in love, you know."

That time, he outright laughed. "You're hilarious."

"It's not a joke."

"I think I'd know if I'd suffered such a terrible fall." Gods forbid. Even Astrid hadn't crept close enough to shove him off *that* ledge.

He could never let his guard down like that, not unless he trusted them implicitly. Not unless he could offer them every secret he had without fear. And that would never happen. Could never happen. His kingdom lived or died based on the secrets he held, and he had yet to meet someone he'd be willing to risk his kingdom for. If he put his trust in the wrong person, especially now…Atlas would be the one to fall.

He'd seen it happen to Soleil. To Jericho. To Vaughn. The madness love wrought had cost him half his family, and he could give it no quarter in his own heart. His own head.

Occassio's magic was driving him mad enough already.

Ramses shrugged one shoulder, pulling Finn to walk with him. "There's nothing wrong with having no desire for it. I've known plenty of people who took no pleasure from romance or intimacy; some who only desired the romance, others who only desired the intimacy. But I remember how you were when that Arborian girl was here; you remember her? The golden-haired one who was smarter than half your mother's council?"

"Papa, if you're trying to say something, will you please just say it?"

"We need this alliance with Lapis. But there are a hundred ways to buy allies, and I know better than anyone—as does your mother—that the heart does not always lead us down the most convenient path." Ramses chuckled, a smirk tilting his lips. "Imagine your grandmother's dismay when your mother had the pick of the kingdom, and she chose a fisherman in a moth-eaten, ill-fitting suit."

Finn snorted softly. "Amma adored you."

"She came to, in time. But she felt it would have been better for Atlas had your mother chosen a councilperson's heir, or another kingdom's dignitary. Someone familiar with the process of ruling a kingdom. But I brought something else that was more important to your mother: a perspective rarely heard by royal ears."

"She found this out before you called her ugly, I presume?"

Ramses pinked a bit, scratching the back of his neck. "I really shouldn't have told all of you that story."

Finn chuckled, but his chest tweaked a bit. His parents' love story was famous, the queen and the fisherman, the fire-haired Heir and her tenderhearted husband. As boys, he and Kallias had sometimes imagined out loud how their own arrangements would come about; Kallias had been endlessly excited, rambling about the honor of being chosen by someone as their partner in rule and in life, imagining grand weddings and passionate kisses and finally having a crown that truly belonged to him. Finn, more practical, had held different dreams cradled close to his chest: someone who saw all the crooked angles and dark hollows left behind by his life's great loss, someone who could peer beneath the layers of masks and never flinch at his true face. Someone who could love a man with no honor, no medals, no crowns but the ones he'd forged for himself. A villain wearing a prince's smiling face.

He wasn't sure even crafty, calculating Astrid would look at him with anything but fear or suspicion now, if she knew all the things he'd done to keep his kingdom aloft. But Fidget had watched him lie, and steal, and shed blood. She'd stood in the carnage left behind by his greatest sin, her gown greedily soaking up the stains, and her only concern had been to make sure his people didn't see him vulnerable, blood-bathed and rambling in senseless shock.

She'd protected him, laughed with him, put on every costume he offered her with a twirl and a giddy squeal. She was the face of a dream he'd never allowed himself to truly ponder having, and now that she was there, just within reach of grasping fingers...

But dreams were dreams for a reason. It was better that they didn't come true. If every one of his dreams came to fruition, he'd be a shopkeeper on the run from a Tallisian mountain cat intent on destroying his stock of papayas. And he'd have wings to boot.

"I made a friend within the Lapisian delegation," Finn allowed. His father needed at least a shard of the truth, or he'd keep pushing. "That's all. And it's...it's been better since Soleil came home, too."

Ramses's smile faded at that; not quite a frown, but enough of a dip that Finn's warning flag immediately flew back up its pole.

"What?" he asked.

"Has Soleil seemed strange to you lately?"

"She's always been strange," he hedged. Holy gods, how much had his father seen? "Why?"

"She's been...quiet."

"I'm sure she's just adjusting. The undead attack so soon after her memories started coming back, then her battlemate's betrayal, then Kallias leaving...she's probably just overwhelmed."

Ramses took his arm away from Finn and stood in front of him, halting them both in the middle of the empty hall. His eyes fixed hard on Finn's, the king's glasses reflecting Finn's own face back at him. "She's never been quiet," Ramses said, arms crossing over his middle. Suddenly Finn was a small boy again, caught performing some sort of mischief, about to be handed a punishment he wasn't ready for. "Even when she first arrived here, scared out of her wits and half-desperate to kill us all, she was never *quiet*."

Finn's throat closed up. "Grief is strange. She and Elias—"

"Finnick." His father never called him by his full name. Nor did he ever look at him *that* way, with a quiet dread that bordered on fear. "I know you keep things close to your chest. I know you keep secrets, and that's all right. Everyone does. But if something was wrong—I mean truly, deeply wrong—you would tell me, wouldn't you?"

That almost undid him. He was grown up now—grown up well before his time—but he wasn't sure a child ever outgrew that senseless confidence in their parents, that hint of surety that his father could lift any burden from his shoulders and make it better with a smile and a kiss to wherever the hurt was.

But what would his kindhearted fisherman father do against the combined might of two—if not more—gods?

"Of course I would, Papa," he croaked, and he hated this lie more than any he'd ever told. "I promise."

CHAPTER 55

ANIMA

"Help me understand."

Ani gritted her teeth, bracing her hands against the frame of her closet door, her eyes roaming over the various outfits available without really taking them in. Not that she was going anywhere—Brae hadn't let her past the walls since the mirror debacle. But even if he had, his tense, irritated tone would've put her on edge anyway. She'd known he would have some choice words when he found out she helped Vaughn, but he didn't have to be so *sharp*. "Do I need a reason to answer the prayers of my worshippers?"

"You do when it's *them*." Tenebrae shook his hands—Jericho's hands—in exasperation. He'd been stealing her body more and more often lately—he couldn't stay, not while she refused to give him permission, but he was still the most powerful god in their pantheon. He could still force his way in. "You do when it makes you lose consciousness in the middle of the hall. Your magic should have settled by now, it shouldn't have been hard—and *healing* him? Helping him when we were *so close*? You just set us back *weeks*. Who knows when Jericho will be that close to giving in again?"

"He was suffering, Brae! Because of my blessing!"

"Because of *his* magic—"

"Magic that belongs to *me*! Brae, what we're doing, it's not right. This bond isn't supposed to be forced, that's not how it's done! We don't blackmail people into letting us take their bodies. It's wrong!"

"We don't have a *choice*, Anima!" he snapped, grabbing her by the shoulder and forcing her to face him. "We are running out of time. We gave Jericho the chance to give herself willingly, and she's put it off every time. Rotting bones, the things I had to make her do just to get *you* a body—"

Anima blinked. "What?"

Brae paused. Cursed. Wiped a hand across his sweating forehead. "Nothing."

A hum thrummed to life in her head. She thought it might be anger. "You told me Soren gave herself up willingly."

"She did! Anima, she did. It just…it took some persuading, that's all."

Anima's hands fell from the wall. "What kind of persuading?"

Brae crossed his arms. "Nothing that wasn't undone quickly. We made it right."

"*Brae.*"

Brae sighed, shaking his head with a dismissive wave of his hand. "It was just that boy—the one Mortem is so fond of. He was dying anyway. She barely needed any pushing. All we did was promise her his life back. It was a *gift*, Ani— he was already dead, whether by our hand or not. She was rewarded as promised."

Horror arrested her breath in her lungs.

Her nightmares…those awful, twisted pictures of Elias Loch's broken neck, his bloody shirt, his lifeless eyes…

Not nightmares.

Soren's mind had been giving up some of her memories, after all.

"Brae." Anger built into fury, such an unfamiliar emotion for her that she almost thought Soren had woken back up. But no, those were *Ani's* words that spat from her tongue, Ani's hands wearing that fury between aching knuckles. "We can't fully settle without *willing* consent. Consent under coercion or threat isn't consent at all, you *know* that—"

"Those old rules?" Brae snorted, waving his hand dismissively. "Nothing but drivel fed to us by weaker gods. You're starting to sound like Mortem."

"It's not drivel! It's always been the rule, and if we don't follow it—"

Brae's intense gaze suddenly pinned her in place, silencing her. "Are you struggling to settle in your host body? Is there something you're not telling me?"

Ani's throat tightened in fear at the dark intent lurking behind his bright, borrowed eyes. "…No. No. It's just…it's not *right*."

Truth and lie in one. It wasn't right, wasn't fair—but it wasn't just that.

Now she knew why Soren hadn't faded away.

She didn't remember the moments before waking up in Soren's body. When it came to immortality, to switching bodies, she'd found memory to be patchwork at best—her clearest memories were still those from her first life, and the rest were just shadows. She left most memories behind with whatever host she made them in. She was fairly sure she could remember everything when she was without a body—when she existed somewhere *else*, in the place where she was more goddess than girl—but even that was fuzzy. Mortal minds were only capable of holding so much. They weren't built to contain centuries.

She'd had no idea. No idea that Soren had been threatened into this existence. No idea that her sacrifice had been forced.

When her silence stretched on too long after those words, Brae sighed, shaking his head. "I understand where you're coming from, Ani. I do. But things are different now. We have to adapt—we have to *change*. If we want to put our family back together, we have to cross some lines we don't want to cross. If you can't handle the guilt, then stay away from these two." He gestured at himself with a curl of his lip. "I'll handle them. Just focus on keeping the rest of this family fooled until we're ready to move on."

Anima looked down at her toes. "Fine."

Brae's hand slid under her chin, tipping it up until she was forced to meet his affectionate gaze. "Your heart does you credit, little sister. I know it's hard. But I'm proud of you, you know that? You've done so well. Don't lose your nerve now. We're almost there."

Anima swallowed down the guilt swirling in her stomach, squaring her shoulders. "I know."

"Good." He kissed her forehead, patting her cheek. "We're going to be a family again. And when we are, we can go back to being our better selves. I promise."

She wanted to believe him so badly. But he'd lied to her about how he'd gotten her this body—he could be lying about so many other things.

But she had no choice. He was all she had.

"All right," she whispered. The words tasted like dirt, like rotting bones, like blood spilled in her name. "I trust you."

CHAPTER 56

KALLIAS

"What did you do?"

If he wasn't so busy being petrified for his life, Kallias would have bristled at Raquel's accusatory hiss. She was already standing at the altar when he and Elias were herded in, flecks of light from the stained-glass lamps painting her in all kinds of colors, disguising the bruises and burns still healing on her arms. Still, that mottled light did nothing to muddle her scowl as Elias and Kallias came to stand in a line with her, Kallias to her right, Elias to his right.

"It seems the delegation that traveled to my kingdom arrived early," Kallias murmured, nodding in acknowledgment as her eyes widened. "I know."

"This is bad."

"I *know*."

"Maybe not," Elias croaked from his other side. Things must truly be dire if the only optimism was coming from that direction. "We asked for an audience. We're getting one. She'll understand once she hears what happened."

"Maybe," Kallias agreed halfheartedly.

"Unless your kingdom has labeled you a traitor and a necromantic sympathizer," Raquel mumbled out of the corner of her mouth. "If they've declared you an enemy—"

"They wouldn't." The answer came out too quickly, filled with a faith he didn't possess. "Finn wouldn't let that happen."

"Isn't your brother the lazy one? Would he really risk his own position by standing against your mother's word?"

"We should probably talk about that at some point," Elias said, rubbing his arm, wearing a scowl sewn shut with a grudge.

"Talk about what?" Kallias hissed, but before Elias could answer, the doors to the chapel opened behind them, the sound of clomping boots and clanking armor announcing the arrival of the Empress.

Chills broke out across Kallias's arms, and he folded his hands behind his back, pressing gooseflesh against his thin tunic. Leather creaked as he flexed his gloved hands, the wool lining turning crisp with frost while the footsteps drew nearer, and flame flickered in the corner of his eye—

Disbelief arrested his heart as the group rounded them, and he heard Raquel and Elias's matching intakes of breath as they took in Idris.

Armored dress. Diadem of flame. Eyes of coal.

"You?" Kallias rasped.

The High Priestess did not answer, or smile, or even nod. She came to stand before them at the foot of the altar, Star at her right hand, two guards behind her, two who stayed at the door.

"I would ask you to forgive the caution of dishonesty," said the Priestess— the *Empress*—"but it seems we have that in common, don't we, *Prince* Kallias?"

Steel bound his back, and he stood straight as he could, meeting her eyes without the flinch that tried to bend his head. "Caution is the word for it indeed, Your Majesty. I didn't believe you'd welcome me in if you were aware of—"

"And you were correct. General Aquila, escort them from the mountain. If they resist—"

"Wait!" Elias interrupted. Shock still glazed his eyes, but there was anger there, too. "You haven't heard us out."

"I have heard my ambassador, and the news he shared was most troubling." Idris leveled her glare at Kallias once more, and he felt Raquel and Elias shift on either side of him. "He claims you abandoned your kingdom in the wake of the necromancy attack, freeing an enemy spy and fleeing to Nyx to seek sanctuary under Queen Ravenna's banner. Do you deny this?"

His throat dried out. "Not the events, Your Majesty, only the implication of wrongdoing. You must listen. Your alliance is being sought under false pretenses."

"And what do you call this? Lying about your title, using an arrangement you never intended to see through in order to buy yourself access to my mountain?"

"Your Majesty, *please*," said Raquel—a word that sounded like a foreign language on her lips. "Hear us out. The fate of all our kingdoms rests on this news. At least let him speak."

Idris looked at Raquel for so long that Kallias itched to step between them, but Raquel wouldn't appreciate that, and he was sure Idris wouldn't either.

"Five minutes of your time," Raquel added firmly. "Five minutes may save your people and mine months or years of bloodshed. We will still be outnumbered in five minutes. If you wish to escort us out then, you may do so knowing you've heard all sides of this story."

Silence stretched on for at least two of the minutes Raquel had promised. Finally, the Empress climbed the altar and sat at the top step as if it was a throne, gesturing to Kallias in silent invitation. He looked to Elias, who gazed back with a firm nod, squeezing Kallias's arm before letting his hand drop back to his side.

This was what they had come for. This was how he saved his people.

So he told the Empress everything. And when he was finished weaving his tale, Elias breaking in to offer insight where needed, they fell silent, waiting with baited breath for the Empress to speak.

Idris was expressionless, but Star held her spear so tightly he thought it might snap, and even the guards were glancing at each other with nervous flickers of eyelids or twitching of fingers.

"Tenebrae," murmured Idris. "The Chaos God. You're certain of this?"

"We are." Elias fussed with his ring, but his eyes were locked on the Empress. "The threat is real, Your Majesty. Anima wears the body of my battlemate. I saw the gold in her eyes myself. I heard her voice come from my battlemate's mouth." A tremor ran through Elias's body, and it was Kallias's turn to reach out and brace him, pressing a palm to his arm. His friend's skin nearly burned with heat. "Princess Jericho has lied and killed and manipulated in order to feed her husband's magic. What Tenebrae's goals are in all this, I can't say, but I know we cannot let it come to pass. Something is happening with the gods, and whatever it is, they've infiltrated the throne room of a very powerful kingdom. And if they made their way that far, I imagine they may have infiltrated elsewhere…perhaps even here. I can't imagine the consequences will be limited to Atlas's borders."

"Mortem hasn't revealed more than this?"

Elias's mouth twitched downward. "Not as of yet."

The only sign Idris was troubled by this news was the slight wrinkle between her brows. She glanced to Star, who nodded slightly. "If this is true, we have many things to consider. However, it is your word against your queen's, Kallias. I would require more proof."

"What more proof can I offer?" Kallias demanded. "I have brought a witness to corroborate my story. I have given my word and staked my own honor. I have nothing else to give. If you doubt me still, summon one of your sanguimancers. They can tell the difference between truth and lies, can't they?"

He saw Elias and Raquel both turn toward him in his periphery, and a curse crept toward the tip of his tongue before he forced it back; he hadn't gotten the chance to tell them of his interaction with Zaccheus and Esmeralda yet.

Suspicion darkened Idris's eyes once more. "How do you know of the gifts sanguimancy grants?"

"I've told him much," Elias cut in. "He's a quick learner."

Elias Loch, lying on his behalf. Would wonders never cease.

Idris sighed. "Some sanguimancers have developed this ability, yes, but it isn't infallible. It's an informal skill that relies on them reading the reactions of someone's body accurately. I wouldn't trust it to inform my decision on this."

"Then what would you trust?"

Quiet fell for a minute that felt stretched into an hour, bloated with dread and dying hope.

"There is one way to test the truth of your heart," Idris finally said. "But it will require you to stand before a judge far less merciful than me."

Kallias's stomach twisted, his mother's eyes flashing through his mind.

Anyone with less mercy than this powerful Empress, with her fireproof hands and simmering glare…that idea cowed his determination a bit.

But if it was his heart they were to judge, they would not find it lacking. He had told no lies in this room, not today. He had nothing to fear.

"I'll stand before anyone you like," he said firmly. "My story holds."

Idris's eyes glimmered like the black diamond in Elias's ring. "So it shall be." She snapped her fingers, and the guards in the room converged on him and his allies, catching their wrists and pinning them firmly behind their backs.

"Take them to the arena," she said. "May Mortem smile favorably on them there."

CHAPTER 57

FINN

Fidget was early.

He'd told her to meet him at the kitchen exit after supper—an affair he'd spent with only Esha and her favored Dagger. After a discussion mostly between him and the Dagger, he'd almost allowed himself a single quip—*Perhaps you and I should get to courting, seeing as I've learned more about you in two minutes than I have about your esteemed queen in two weeks*—but it wouldn't do to offend Esha now. She might have refused to attend the event tonight and kept her Mirrors and Daggers shut in with her, and that would've ruined everything.

He'd expected Fidget to be late again. But this time, when he flung open the kitchen door, he found her already waiting, bouncing impatiently from one foot to the other.

"What took you so long?" she demanded, hands planting on her hips as he slowly eased the door shut, taking her in with one long look. "We finished eating *ages* ago, and I've just been sitting here like a—what are you staring at?"

There was that *smile* again, the rash one that refused to follow orders in her presence. He tugged a hand through his hair, silently cursing as he remembered the pomade he'd combed through it only a few minutes ago. "Nothing. You just look…very Atlas."

And she did: she'd donned black leggings and a knit tunic in the same shade of rich purple as the sweater he wore, her ringlets pinned behind her shoulders with a diamond hairpiece, kohl lining her eyes in sharp points. The sleeves themselves were loose, but the cuffs clung to her wrists; he was beginning to understand that she found that pressure comforting somehow. He hadn't yet seen her wear something so casual, though she'd still accessorized with finery; her usual sequins were all in place, and she wore the earrings he'd stolen back for her.

"Oh." Fidget cleared her throat, brushing imaginary dust from her outfit. "Thank you, I think. You fixed your hair?"

"You sound surprised."

"You washed the dye out, too."

"Don't need it." He offered her his elbow. "We're not scheming tonight."

Fidget's eyes widened a bit, and alarm pitched her voice higher. "Finn, I promised Esha back the mirror by morning, if she doesn't get it she's going to—"

"She'll have it, I promise." She wouldn't. But this was hardly the first lie he'd told Fidget; it was just the one that would hurt her most. "First, there's something you need to see."

"What is it?"

"A surprise."

She hesitated, but finally slid her arm through his. "Where are we going?"

"Do you understand the concept of a *surprise*?"

The golden sunlight didn't mesh well with her ensemble of purples and cool-toned colors—she was a painting best viewed in the moonlight. But the light did bring out the amber flecks in her brown eyes, and he was content to watch them while she chattered away, telling him all about her meal and her day and how her fellow Mirrors had accepted her excuses for her absence with only minimal questioning.

She seemed relieved by that. Him, less so—the lack of questions from a pack of wary seers was less likely to indicate trust and more likely to indicate patience. If he had to guess, they hadn't believed her story; they were simply waiting for the right time to reveal her lies to their queen.

But that wasn't a concern for now. All of it would be handled when he spoke to Esha in the morning.

"Here," he said, interrupting her just as she was giggling her way through a story about one of the Daggers choking on a fish bone. He tugged gently on her elbow to turn her in the direction of the beach; the evening wind had a bite of cold to it, but thanks to his sweater, it only managed to nip at his nose. With it came the familiar scent of salt and sand, the call of gulls, the roar of the water folding in constantly on itself—things he hadn't realized he missed until now.

He'd never loved the ocean the way the rest of his siblings did; but it was still the heart of his home, and the beat of its pulse—wave pounding steadily against shore—was still a comfort.

Fidget came to an abrupt halt, her feet arrested on the line of grass between city and beach. Her gaze fixed on the ocean beyond with a look he couldn't read; her dimple deepened, though not with a frown or smile, and she arranged her arms strangely over her middle, each of her hands clasped over the opposite wrist.

"What's wrong?" he asked.

"I…" She did not blink, barely breathed. "I've never seen it before."

Finn frowned. "Seen what?"

"The ocean." The words hardly made it off her tongue, snatched so quickly by the wind he barely had time to hear them. She inched one foot forward, toetip kissing the line between sand and grass. "They said it was huge, but I didn't…"

Finn moved to stand behind her, trying not to laugh at how far below his eyeline she was; she didn't hinder his view at all. He braced her shoulders, craning his neck a bit when her curls started to tickle beneath his chin. "You can't imagine it until you've seen it, can you?"

"No." Wonder steeped her voice, every word floating like dandelion fuzz on the breeze. "It's like a second sky."

And just now, it looked exactly that. Sunset bled over sky and sea until the entire world was bathed in gold and red and pink-tinted orange, like an artist had spilled a bucket of paint into a cyclone and turned it sideways.

"If you think that's good," Finn murmured, giving her shoulders a single squeeze, "wait until you see the real reason we're here."

"This isn't the surprise?"

"Not even close."

It took a bit of coaxing, but she finally removed her shoes and followed him onto the sand, her tentative steps quickly turning to giddy twirls and a full-on sprint down the beach that left him breathless, laughing as he tugged off his own shoes and ran after her, trying to shout directions over the roar of the wind. And just for now, just for tonight, he shrugged off the weight of the eyes that followed their reckless dash, shut out the whispers that trailed on their heels, ignored the seeds of rumor he was planting deep in fertile soil with every person he hurtled past.

Those were all problems for tomorrow.

Eventually, just as the sun sank beneath the horizon and the world faded from golds and reds to blues and purples, he brought her up a winding trail to the only place he knew they would be far from prying eyes: the abandoned lighthouse.

This one had been out of service since well before his mother's rule; a storm had rendered it inoperable, and a new one had been built not far down the cliffs. But Finn knew all its weaknesses and how to avoid them; he had climbed every groaning stair and rusted rail as a boy with his three siblings, Jericho leading the charge, Kallias taking up the rear to catch any of them that slipped, Soleil racing Finn up the stairs to the gallery. He could still remember his jaw dropping at the view that spread out before his eyes the first time he'd ever seen the entirety of Port Atlas in all its grandeur, an ivory-scaled beast slumbering alongside the unending shore.

That view was exactly what he needed tonight.

When they reached the top of the lighthouse, he slung the pack off of his shoulder and set it on the gallery floor, a soft cloud of dust poofing up from the impact. Fidget's eyes hung on his every movement as he opened it, taking his time arranging the picnic blanket, weighing it down with rocks he'd plucked from the shoreline to combat the sea winds trying to buffet them from the edge of the gallery.

"Finn, we already ate," she laughed as he started pulling out the food he'd packed, followed shortly by a bottle of fine champagne that would definitely be missed from the palace cellar.

"If I recall," he said, opening one of the tins to reveal a pile of glistening chocolate-covered strawberries, "when we first came into the city together, you mentioned something about an extra dessert stomach."

Her delighted squeal had him checking over his shoulder to ensure what glass remained in the windowpanes hadn't shattered. She sprawled onto the blanket before he could finish arranging everything, feet kicked up in the air, greedy fingers exploring what treasures he'd brought: the strawberries, caramels coated in sea salt, taffies in all colors, cookies of all kinds.

All kinds but simple sugar cookies, anyhow. Finn never bothered with things quite that plain.

"It's an apology," he said as she rummaged through the treats, two taffies already stuffed in her mouth before he could warn her that she'd chosen to mix banana and black licorice. Her expression morphed from euphoria to disgust in an instant, and he held out a napkin for her to spit the taffies into, chuckling at the disappointment on her face. "And a thank-you."

She frowned, propping herself up higher on her elbows, craning her neck to look at him. She really did wear dusk well; the blueish light settled over her eyes until they nearly gleamed violet. "What am I being thanked for?"

"For your quick thinking the other night with…with Tomas." *Blood, hatred, blackness.* "And for getting me inside before anyone could see me."

"You don't have to keep thanking me for that. I'm the one who almost ruined the whole mission. You saved *me*, remember?" Fidget offered him a smile that revealed her dark-stained tongue; that black licorice taffy at work. "We can call it even, I think."

He reached out and hooked one finger around the bowl of candy, tugging it out of her reach with a raised brow. "Well, if this is you refusing my gift…"

"No!" she squeaked, hurriedly snatching the bowl back, swiveling herself into a sitting position and setting the bowl in her lap. "What I meant to say was *yes, well, you certainly do owe me a great debt, and I think this lovely picnic will do quite nicely.*"

He chuckled. "That's what I thought." Ravenous little creature. "Try the strawberries, will you? They're the pride of our pastry chef."

She obeyed, the resulting moan of ecstasy drawing another laugh from him as he snagged the champagne bottle and uncorked it with a smooth flick of his wrist, letting the foam spew off the edge of the lighthouse to pool somewhere on the cliffside below. He poured and passed her a glass. "Try not to get it on my pants this time, will you?"

"No promises," she laughed, putting the glass to her lips and sipping, eyes closing in quiet pleasure, and he forced himself to keep breathing. To resist the urge to pluck that loose strand of hair from where it stuck to the corner of her mouth. To ignore the sudden, insatiable curiosity rising within him, the notion of what that champagne might taste like on her tongue…a question he refused to even consider asking.

They lounged on the floor of the lighthouse gallery for gods-knew how many minutes, Fidget sampling every dessert he'd brought with equal praise, though she kept going back to the strawberries, just as he'd thought she would. She even convinced him to sip from a glass of champagne himself, though he still wasn't so much a fool as to let himself drink to any point of intoxication. He might be mad now, but never *that* mad. A drunken Finnick Atlas was as good as an army bent against his kingdom. Secrets slipped far too easily between drink-slick lips.

Still, it was good champagne, though its bubbling bite hardly answered his forbidden question.

It was only when starlight fully drowned out the sun that he finally stood, offering his hand to her. "Come on. You're going to want to see this."

"See what?" But she took his hand anyway, and he led her to the railing, draping her fingers over it with gentleness he rarely wielded. Something strange was nibbling at his stomach, and he didn't think it was the champagne, though the bubbles certainly weren't helping. It wasn't entirely unpleasant—it didn't *hurt*—but it wasn't something he'd felt in a long time, and it wasn't until she smiled over her shoulder at him that he found its name:

He was nervous.

"Do you remember," he asked, quickly dodging her gaze to look up at the sky, coming to lean against the railing beside her, "the story you told me before?"

"Which one?"

"The one about your brothers and sisters. The city. The fireworks."

"Oh." Sadness painted her voice in shades of gray, but he held steady. If all went according to plan, that color would change soon enough. "I…yes. Of course I do. Why?"

He took her chin between his thumb and forefinger, his lips twitching as her eyes widened a bit, a thousand thoughts teeming in her eyes like the silver fish that swam beneath the dock. He carefully turned her head toward the city, directing her gaze to what he hoped was the right place. "I can't fix that memory for you. I can't bring them back. But…I figured I could at least offer you that view you were looking for."

And as the first fleck of blue light ignited from some far-off launching point in the city…as the first firework screamed triumphantly into the sky, its cobalt starburst reflected in the pupils of Fidget's wide eyes…he decided this was one memory he was happy to keep forever.

The sky ruptured into dizzying color, supernovas of scarlet and emerald and amethyst and sapphire exploding between the stars. The sparks danced in the shadows of their own smoke, and he could hear the distant cheers as the spectators on the beach took in the splendor.

But when he looked to Fidget again, his stomach dropped at the sight of tears freckling her cheeks, her jaw steeled against a barely-controlled quiver, her hands gripping the railing so tightly he feared she'd break straight through the rusted metal.

"I thought…" Her voice was so faint he couldn't hear the rest past the pop and shriek of the fireworks.

"What?"

"I thought they were cancelled," she said again, and the blankness in her voice took him back to another night they'd stood together underneath the moon—a night filled with rage and blood and terror that Tomas had somehow broken her.

"They were. I…I arranged for them to be rescheduled. I thought that…Fidget. Fidg, hey…was this a mistake? We can go. We'll go right now."

But as he started to duck away, to pack their things and get her away from whatever terrible memory he'd unintentionally brought her back to, she snatched his hand in a grip that could've shattered steel, a demanding hold that stopped him in his tracks. "You did this?" she asked, her eyes still fixed on the sky, tears streaming freely down a face that was utterly devoid of feeling.

"I did," he croaked. "Clearly that was—"

"Shut up."

"All right."

Fidget took in a sharp, unsteady breath, lacing her fingers through his and squeezing. "You did this for me? All because I told you some silly story?"

Finn hesitated only a moment before following what little leading his instincts gave him; he put his other hand over hers, bracing her in place. "Nothing's silly if it matters that much to you."

"But how did you…you couldn't have…" She finally turned to look at him, brows knit together, some puzzled anguish in her eyes that he didn't understand. "How did you *know*?"

Equally confused, Finn met her gaze, silently trying to prod his way through that look. Trying to find his way to the answers hidden behind it. "I…I know what it's like to lose a sibling. And I know what it sounds like when you're so desperate to have them back that you'll look anywhere just to get a glimpse of them. I just thought I could make that search a bit easier for you."

Fidget laughed, but it didn't sound anything like the giggles he was used to; it was a sound of disbelief, of thunderstruck wonder. "Finnick Atlas," she whispered, "you…you are more brilliant than you know."

He cracked a grin even as his heart raced, still half-sure he'd taken some terrible misstep. "I hear that a lot."

"No, I mean it. This is…this is…it's the best gift I've ever been given." She pulled her hand away only to gather both of his in her grip, braiding their fingers together, meeting his eyes with a broad grin that reached straight into his heart and pulled a hidden thread, threatening to unravel him. "Thank you."

He swallowed hard, that smile turning him stupid. "Did you know you have double dimples?"

A startled laugh. She blinked so hard, two more tears leapt from her lashes. "What?"

"When you smile. There's one here…" he touched one fingertip to the further dimple, "and one here."

As he traced his finger down the dimple closest to her mouth—just shy of the strand of hair caught at the corner of her lips—she caught his hand again. Held it right there, pressed against her cheek, as her other hand reached up to caress his chin, her smooth thumb settling in a dimple of his own.

"Finn," she whispered, "I would like it very much if I could kiss you."

The world stopped spinning.

She might as well have stolen his heart from his chest and thrown it off the ledge of the gallery for how far it fell—no, not fell, this wasn't falling, he *would not* call it falling. This was plunging, jumping, a reckless hurtle toward an inevitable shattering on the rocks so far below.

And it was then that he knew he'd truly gone mad. Irredeemably, dangerously mad.

Because he nodded.

And when she stretched up on her tiptoes to catch his mouth with hers, he was already leaning down to meet her, his hands cupping her face as hers cradled the back of his neck.

He got his answer.

That champagne tasted damned near perfect on her lips.

He pulled her away from the gallery railing, not trusting it to hold both their bodies, heady thrill pouring through him as his mouth became a different kind of lockpick, seeking out the combination required to coax one of those exultant gasps from her throat. He wasn't half as sweet as any dessert, but as her teeth found their way into his bottom lip, he had the wild thought that she might be hiding a craving for bitterness somewhere beneath her taste for sugar.

They kissed until one of them had to come up for air—he wasn't entirely sure which of them pulled away first—and they dragged in a harmonized inhale, both of them exhaling in a breathless laugh. Finn's forehead fell against hers, their noses brushing, her sweet breath mingling on his champagne-sour tongue.

"Beautiful," she whispered.

"Me or the fireworks?"

Her only answer was a wicked chuckle pitched so low that it hit him right in the gut. "Do it again."

"I don't take orders from Mirrors," he rasped, grinning at her frustrated groan as she gripped his sweater in her fists.

"Do it again, *please*."

He didn't take orders, but he could appreciate a well-placed *please*. He lifted her against the wall, bringing her mouth up to his, delighted satisfaction curling in his chest as she sighed into the kiss, bending her body to better fit against his.
If this was foolishness, fine. It was hardly the first time he'd played the fool for her. And he hoped—gods, he hoped—it wouldn't be the last.

CHAPTER 58

ELIAS

The arena looked much different from the stands.

He and Raquel were seated on the ground floor, where they'd held Raquel and Kallias back from running to him during his second trial. They were flanked on either side by guards—and by Idris, who was playing the part of High Priestess once more, stoic as ever as she watched a handful of soldiers clearing the arena and raking the dirt until it was smooth. The jagged teeth of stone were already gone; Elias couldn't imagine how anyone had managed to move them, but that curiosity was at the bottom of a very long list.

The setting sun outside cast reddish-gold light through the hole in the cavern's ceiling, dappling Idris's simple black ensemble; armored chiffon still, but lacking the extravagant embroidery of her other gowns. Her hair was bound in a cascade of locks down her back, and she wore no crown or circlet of fire around her head today.

"Why the guise of the Priestess?" he asked, keeping his eyes on the arena as the soldiers worked. He couldn't see Kallias yet, and she'd refused to tell him where his friend had been taken. If she wouldn't answer his other questions, she might at least answer this. "Why lie?"

"My father," said Idris; surprise sparked at her quick, frank answer. "He died paranoid and terrified, convinced he was poisoned, not simply ill. I was away for some years before he died...I left as a girl to study my magic in a city far from here, rumored to be the birthplace of Mortem's magic."

"Sanctaviv," Elias said softly. He was familiar with the lore.

Idris dipped her head. "When I arrived home after receiving word of his illness, he hardly recognized me after so much time apart, and neither did many others. He implored me to shield my identity, convinced someone had it out for the crown. He begged me to keep to myself, to rule from the shadows, but after coming home to find such deep wounds still struck into my people from the war...how could I serve their needs as Empress without walking among them?" She shrugged. "We compromised and came up with a story together—I was a priestess who arrived with the princess to continue her training when the crown passed to her, and the princess herself was buried so deeply in grief that she refused to take audiences after her father died. She passed that duty on to her priestess, and I carried out her will as needed."

"So not even your people know the truth?"

"Not many."

Elias nodded. "May I ask another question?"

"You may."

"My father." He met her gaze. "You said he was Mortem's last cleric?"

Idris smiled then. "Evan Loch. He took the trials when I was small."

"I...I was never told..." The ache in his chest built until he could hardly speak. "I never knew that side of him. I didn't even know he had magic."

"He was a young man when he came here—close to your age." She studied him, locks swaying as she leaned forward, clasping her hands in her lap. "He was the opposite of you; he passed the Trial of Fire, but failed the Trial of Blood. It was combat against a champion back then...less easy to trick."

What he'd done in the arena hardly counted as *easy* in his book. "So he didn't earn...this?" He waved his hand, wincing as a flame sputtered to life in his palm before dying just as fast. He hadn't quite mastered calling it at will. He'd barely started to believe that he was capable of it at all.

"Not until the third Trial. But he passed in the end. He met your mother while he was here; it's rare that one of our own chooses to leave Artem, you know. She must have loved him dearly."

Dearly didn't cover it. "He was her world. And she his."

It was a love they'd demonstrated every day, even the bad ones—fights never escalated past sharp tones and quiet frustration, and they never lasted past sunset. He'd seen it in the way they made gifts for each other, in the way his father reminded his mother to eat when she lost herself in the forge, in the way his mother let his father hog all the blankets in their bed. It was a love they'd built, a love they'd taught, a love he'd learned.

A love he'd done his best to show Soren, whether she'd recognized it as such or not.

"Elias." He raised his eyes to find Idris gazing at him with strange, nearly familiar softness. "No matter what happens here, you were chosen by Mortem. You will be allowed to attempt the third Trial. But whatever is gnawing at you, whatever has its claws in your peace…find a way to kill it. The third trial is the hardest of all. You cannot go into it alone."

The words escaped before he could swallow them. "I have no one to bring with me."

Raquel wouldn't escape unscathed if Kallias was judged harshly. And without them, Elias would truly be alone again.

Idris's eyes fell to his sternum, and he instinctively reached to hold his ring, flanked on either side by what remained of his mourning braids.

"The people we love are not so easily shaken from us," she said. "You carry them with you as surely as you carry Mortem's fire. They're closer than you know."

The sound of a bell pealing through the cavern kept him from answering. He turned just in time to see Kallias escorted out by six guards—a ridiculous number for one man. Had he fought them? It didn't seem like Kallias, but maybe panic had taken over.

Raquel tensed beside him, and the hairs on his arm that touched hers suddenly stood on end. He glanced over to find her eyeing Kallias—and the manacles of fire around his wrists—while her jaw twitched, her gaze lit with fury.

"He's terrified of fire," she said through gritted teeth.

Not fury toward Kallias. Fury *for* Kallias.

Idris glanced at her as well, and after a heartbeat, she reached out one hand and clenched it closed. As she formed a fist, the manacles around Kallias's wrists vanished, and he visibly relaxed, his broad shoulders slumping forward.

"Thank you," Elias said. Raquel merely grunted, eyes never leaving Kallias, every muscle in her body stiff as stone.

"Raquel," he said. She didn't look at him. "He's going to be fine."

"He'd *better* be." He blinked at the ferocity in her tone, and she cleared her throat, loosening her grip on the railing in front of her. "His death still belongs to me."

Probably best that he left that alone.

Idris made her way to the outcropping she'd stood on during the Trial of Fire, the crowd in the stands settling with a hush that sent a bolt of adrenaline down to his toes. He'd lived this once; though the crowd was smaller this time, the sudden silence still felt like a drop from a precipice with no rope.

While she explained the judgment that was about to take place, Elias shifted closer to Raquel. "I need to apologize to you. For the tavern."

She shook her head. "You don't."

"I do. You were hurt because I couldn't keep my anger in check. And you went in to get me out. I'm sorry. It won't happen again."

Raquel snorted softly. "I know a thing or two about anger, Elias. If I was a pyromancer…the day Lily died would have seen a city burn. You shoulder no blame from me."

Before he could speak again, a shadow passed over the hole in the mountain's cap, interrupting the golden rays of sunset for a moment.

A blazing tendril of adrenaline started to tunnel through Elias's limbs, and he stood, tightening his hold on the railing.

The shadow passed again. And again.

The fourth time, the shadow dove.

A torrent of hot, smoke-scented wind buffeted the arena, sweeping dust from the floors and nearly bowling Elias to his knees. The shadow crashed downward, landing with a *boom* that vibrated through the floor, climbing up Elias's bones to shake his very spine. His legs went numb, his heart stopping clean in his chest as his eyes tried to make sense of what he was looking at.

Ebony talons curled into the ground, bracing a mass of bristling black feathers that towered over Kallias at the height of a two-story house. It paced forward, the firelight catching on glistening reds and golds and oranges buried among the black, its four legs almost wildcat-like in their musculature despite their feathered visage.

Wings that fanned out from its back, spreading a shadow over the arena like a shroud. A beak that came to a razor point. Golden eyes that glowed in the light of sunset, staring at Kallias with unnerving intelligence as it lowered its head to look him dead in the eyes.

"Phoenix," Raquel breathed, echoing the stunned realization in Elias's head.

A phoenix. One of the mythical mounts of Mortem herself.

Deathless.

That Kallias didn't run was the truest testament to his courage Elias had seen yet; there wouldn't be any more jabs of *prissy* thrown his way. Though he shook so badly Elias could see it from here, he stood straight and tall, shoulders back, chin up. He met the phoenix's eyes as an equal.

"Are you to be my judge?" Kallias's soft words traveled easily across the arena, as if the wind itself was tasked with carrying them to every listening ear.

The phoenix blinked slowly. A dip of its head seemed confirmation enough.

"Go on, then." Kallias raised his chin another inch, and Elias's stomach caught somewhere between terror and pride. "I have nothing to hide."

The moment seemed to last forever, clinging by its fingernails to the edge of the present, refusing to move on and become the past. The phoenix paced a slow circle around Kallias, every footfall sending new tremors through the floor, every ruffle of its feathers or snap of its beak nearly yanking Elias's heart straight out of his ribcage. The beast living in his chest mimicked the creature's movement, circling the opposite way, claws scraping Elias's ribs as they waited with held breath and coiled muscles to see what judgment was passed—and what the consequences would be.

Kallias would be fine. They'd told the truth.

He *would* be fine.

Elias would accept nothing less.

The phoenix circled once, twice, three times before coming to face Kallias again, but something had changed. Its eyes no longer blazed gold; instead, a bloody scarlet glow cut through the twilight now falling over the peak of the mountain. Rows of feathers slowly started lighting up, fire outlining them with deadly light, catching and spreading upward toward its head.

No.

Elias was moving before he thought about it; moving before Raquel could shout, moving before the guards could catch him. Moving before he really understood what he was choosing to do.

As he vaulted the railing and lunged into the arena, tearing toward Kallias at a dead sprint, he watched the prince's eyes close. Watched him shudder with fear—then control it. Watched as Kallias Atlas accepted that his fate would mirror his younger sister's; that not only would he die a traitor to his kingdom, so far from the ocean he loved like nothing else, but he would die in flames.

As the phoenix reared onto its hind legs, opening its beak and releasing a scream that broke open the world, the Nyxian spy threw himself in front of the Atlas prince, hands empty, weapons still sheathed.

And when a torrent of fire flooded after that horrible scream, Elias embraced it with open arms, throwing his magic outward to meet it.

Fire met fire, and everything blazed goddess-eye-gold.

CHAPTER 59

ELIAS

The unmaking began at his fingertips.

Flame gnawed his nails down to the quick, tearing past his knuckles to his wrists, devouring bone and flesh and scar like they were nothing but chaff long-dried.

As Elias Loch burned, he dreamed.

He dreamed of stepping into Mortem's temple for the first time as a boy, escorted by both his parents. He remembered clutching his little holy book and the prayer beads his father had hand-carved for him, stomach filled with excitement and nerves in equal measure, churning like his mother's stew while she stirred it.

"Papa," he said, "what if Mortem doesn't like me?"

His father knelt before him, offering that smile his mother said Elias had inherited so flawlessly. "Elias," he said, "Can you be faithful?"

He didn't quite understand the meaning of that word yet, but something flared in the core of him at the question, even that young. He gripped his beads tighter. "Yes, Papa."

"Can you be strong?"

He helped his mother in the forge all the time; she was constantly impressed by how much he could carry at once. He puffed out his chest. "Yes, Papa."

His father tapped his chest with a chuckle. "I don't need to ask about your heart. You have a good one. Mortem values three things most, Eli—faith, strength, and love. Do you know what love is?"

Elias hesitated, clutching his things close, glancing up at his mother for a hint. She gave him a warm smile, but no help.

"It's when you like someone a lot?" Elias guessed meekly.

His father laughed out loud that time, and Elias blushed, embarrassed. He'd thought it was a good answer.

His mother flicked his father on the back of the head. "Evan. Don't laugh at him."

"Sorry. I'm sorry, Eli. That's not a bad answer, but it's not quite right. Do you have another guess?"

Eyes still smarting, Elias shook his head. His father smiled again, much softer that time, framing Elias's face with his hands. His father's hands were always warm, no matter the weather or season.

"Love," his father told him, "is sacrifice. Love is being willing to give up anything for what matters to you."

* * *

As Elias Loch burned, he dreamed.

He dreamed of Life's temple filled to the brim with death. He dreamed of a dagger buried deep in his belly, of desperately dragging in the breath he needed to tell Soren the last secret he owed her, of hearing her sobbing out her anger as she tried to hold in his lifeblood.

"I was going to ask you to marry me."

"I would have said yes."

He dreamed of closing his eyes and tiptoeing into Mortem's realm. And worst of all, he dreamed of being forced out; forced back into a world without his battlemate, a world without stolen socks and cookie dough and *smartass* and *jackass*. A world filled with empty beds and twisted nightmares and punching walls to make *something* pay for her being gone. A world of one-sided prayers and pretending he could hear her whispering to him when he knew there would never be anything but silence again.

The flames crept up to his elbows, his shoulders, his venom scar, consuming the proof of Soren's own sacrificial love.

If he let the fire burn, he would see her again.

He could leave grief and war and pain behind him. He could lay down the responsibility that had been shoved onto his shoulders, tasked to help save the world by a goddess he no longer prayed to.

You're not done, jackass, Soren had told him the last time he'd been ready to give up. But he didn't hear her now.

New flames caught at his feet, melting his boots, sinking their teeth into his feet. They clawed up his legs while the old ones spread up his shoulders, jumping to his hair, each spark hunting as a pack until nearly all of him was consumed.

But there was one part of him that had not yet burned away.

His heart.

* * *

As Elias Loch burned, he dreamed.

He dreamed of a different fire, a different night, cross-legged on a rug in an Atlas sitting room. He was surrounded by snores and mumbles slurred by sleep; Jericho and Vaughn were curled up together on one couch while Soren and Finn were stretched out on the other, her feet resting by his head and vice versa, each of them sporting crumbs and flecks of powdered sugar on their faces and shirts from trying to out-eat each other. But he couldn't sleep; the heaviness of the tale he'd told them that night still haunted him, every creak of a couch cushion or a too-sharp exhale from one of the sleepers making him start.

"Still up?"

Elias glanced over his shoulder, grimacing at his stiff neck as Kallias came back into the room, rubbing his ear with a towel, his wet hair soaking into his fresh sleepshirt. He'd been the first to fall asleep after Vaughn, which had marked him as the one to be thrown into the palace's pool. The prince still looked a bit put out, but the smile he offered Elias was kind, if edged with tiredness. He held two glasses of wine in his hand.

"Don't you think you've had enough?" Elias asked diplomatically. He'd already had half a bottle before his dip in the pool.

"Cold water has a way of sobering you up. Besides, this one's for you." He handed Elias one of the glasses before sitting down beside him, staring into the fireplace with furrowed brows. "I wish there was another way to heat this place in the winter."

Elias grunted, sipping politely at the wine, his nose wrinkling at its sour bite. "It's too bad you can't harvest all the hot air Seamus seems so full of."

To his surprise, Kallias laughed so hard that he spat out a bit of wine. The prince quickly mopped his face, his embarrassed blush overtaken by his cocked grin. "Eli, did you just make a joke?"

Elias couldn't help it; he smirked back. "I do that from time to time. Seriously, though, maybe slow down. I don't want to be responsible for dragging you all to your rooms tonight. Feels like a lot of responsibility for a lowly guard."

"Mm." Kallias was quiet for a moment. "You're not lowly."

Elias shrugged one shoulder, gazing down into his wine, admiring the way the flames played with the red liquid in the glass. It was far nicer to look at than to taste. "That's kind of you to say."

"It's not kindness. I mean it. I appreciate everything you've done to help me with this…necromancy." The prince shuddered lightly, but he did set aside his glass, wrapping his arms around his knees instead. He gazed into the fire. "I'll sit with you for a bit, if you like. I know how it is to have sleep escape you. Insomnia is better with company."

"I didn't think you were allowed to flirt with guards," Elias deadpanned.

Kallias started, then threw his head back and *cackled*—a laugh so close to Soren's that Elias almost looked over his shoulder to make sure his battlemate was still asleep. "Another joke! I think maybe we're growing on you."

A slight smile tugged at his unwilling mouth. "Maybe a little."

Kallias clapped his shoulder, shaking him a bit. "I think we may just end up being friends, Eli."

Elias couldn't say anything in protest; couldn't explain just how much of an impossibility that was. So he clapped Kallias's shoulder in return. "We may just, Your Highness."

"Please, call me Kal. Everybody else does."

It was worth keeping in mind that the prince had drunk quite a bit of wine. "Maybe we can compromise with Kallias?"

Kallias chuckled. "If you insist...sure."

* * *

Love is sacrifice.

He'd always thought of sacrifice in terms of death; had always thought of it as laying down his life for his fellow soldiers and friends. Or his father dying protecting innocents from an Atlas invasion. Or Soren offering her body to a goddess in exchange for his life.

But as the flames burned closer and closer to his core, he thought of something else.

His mother releasing him into the temple, her mouth smiling while her eyes wept. Kaia letting him borrow her schoolbooks over and over, even though he often absentmindedly dogeared the pages. Soren letting him burn his incense in her room even though it made her head hurt, running her fingers through his hair until he found dreamless sleep in her arms.

And what of you, Elias Loch? A voice he hadn't heard since he'd ordered her away from his side. *What are you willing to sacrifice?*

If he gave in here, now, he would find Soren again. He knew it in his bones. The ache in his chest, the guilt, the beast that had tortured him for all these weeks...he could put an end to it all right now.

No more suffering.

But if he let this fire consume him, it would hunt Kallias down next.

Kallias, who had sacrificed his time to keep Elias company on a warm winter night in Atlas; Kallias, who had sacrificed sleep to see him through his first trial; Kallias, who had sacrificed his title to protect Elias's people.

Kallias. His friend.

He could practically feel Soren's arms around him. Could practically hear her voice, see her smile.

Together or not at all, jackass?

A tear escaped his eye, sizzling to steam before it could find a path down his cheek.

I'm sorry, smartass.

He opened his eyes to fire, just as he had in the Trial of Blood. But this time there was no automaton, no ruby eyes or metal teeth—there was only the phoenix, watching him through the flames with eyes gold as Mortem's, looking for all the world like it was waiting for something.

"Faith," he rasped. "Strength. And sacrifice."

He could have sworn the phoenix's eyes gleamed with approval.

So Elias Loch did not burn. Instead, he cast his arms out to either side, commanding with all his strength, all his will: *Be gone.*

And in a blink, the fire obeyed. But it didn't rush away from him—it rushed *into* him, punch after punch of fire driven into his chest until he'd absorbed every spark, his heart taking on that blaze as its own, pumping its heat through every vein.

The roar of the flames was replaced by the roar of the crowd as the world crashed back in all at once. Elias looked down to find his clothes untouched, his skin unmarred; no evidence of what he had endured in that inferno.

Nothing but the pain that continued to burn in his chest, on and on and on, no longer protected by numbness.

As he caught his breath against that agony, the world still dull and ringing and a bit distant, the phoenix lowered its head once more, the edge of its beak brushing against Elias's forehead—deathless to deathless.

Then, with one powerful swoop of its wings, it was gone.

Kallias's arms crushing him from behind shook his mind out of its daze, the prince's startled laughter too loud in his ear. "That...that was...I don't know what that was. You're a fool. A mad fool. Did we...I mean, was that acceptance? Did we pass the test?"

"Indeed." And there was Idris. She crossed the arena with a broad smile, a twinkle of something tricky in her gaze.

"That was the third trial," Elias croaked.

"The Trial of Fire tested your faith. The Trial of Blood tested your strength. The Trial of Death tested your heart—your willingness to sacrifice for what matters." Idris folded her hands behind her back. "Mortem would never grant her final blessing to a man loyal to a kingdom of necromancy. I decided it would be the best way to test your truth."

His breaths were coming fast, too fast; his lungs hurt. Everything hurt. "I need—I need a moment, please."

Idris's smile faded to a cautious frown. "Of course. Kallias, escort your friend out the door you came through. It should be empty. I'll send Officer Angelov to join you in a moment."

No weeping. No weakness.

He'd finally been given the chance to have her back. He'd given it up.

No weakness.

His breathing came faster and faster, and his feet followed suit, carrying him past Kallias toward the familiar door he'd come through his first time in the arena.

Kallias was still babbling on excitedly about what he'd seen out there; how Elias had shielded him from the fire and how the inferno had wrapped around Elias without burning him, just like Havi could do, and *holy gods, Elias, a phoenix! No one's ever going to believe us!*

Elias barely heard any of it. His pulse was pounding in his head, the beast in his chest suddenly *rabid*, beating at the walls of his ribs with howling, horrible cries he felt in every bone as it burned to death.

"Elias?" Kallias's voice dropped from excited to worried, and it was only then that Elias realized he was muttering out loud, a chant that grew more and more frantic with every step he took.

"No weeping. No weeping. No weeping, no weeping, no—no…no weeping…don't. Don't, Kallias, don't…don't…"

But it was too late. Kallias turned him around, forcing him to look his friend in the face. Forcing him to reveal his quivering chin, his tear-filled eyes, his hands clasped around the ring that would never find its way to Soren's finger.

"Eli," Kallias said, so pained, so gentle.

"She *left me*," Elias sobbed.

And when he collapsed into Kallias's arms, a broken cry wrenching out of the beast's melted cage, Kallias caught him without question, holding him close. Holding him up.

And Elias wept.

CHAPTER 60

FINN

Finn woke up the morning after the fireworks with a pillow shoved over his head and a rock of dread settled over his heart.

What in the depths had he done?

He forced himself to sit up, rubbing the sleep from his eyes, blinking blearily around his sun-coated room. Empty, thank all the gods—he hadn't been that rash, he'd escorted Fidget back to her own quarters like a perfect gentleman—but that didn't change the mistake he'd made last night.

Sleeplessness and distractions and gods-damned magic. That was what had brought him here. That was what had tossed him so far off the deep end he'd allowed a mark to…he'd let Fidget actually get him to…

No. He could still save this. It was all a natural part of the plan, that was all. He'd always intended on seducing her somehow—that was the entire damned con. She fell for him, he plied her queen's secrets from her with sweet smiles and flirtatious winks, and he used those secrets to turn her queen's head toward other prices for her alliance. Prices that would allow him, the only Atlas royal left capable of stopping these godly advances on his kingdom, to stay right where he was. That was always the plan.

But he'd never planned on growing fond of her.

He'd never planned on kissing her, depths take him.

He needed to talk to her. Today. Now. She had to understand that could never happen again. Had to understand that he was…that he could never…

He shook his head with a groan, throwing back his covers and sliding out of bed, his aching soles wincing at the brush of wood. The climb to the lighthouse hadn't been kind on his feet.

He dressed in a hurry, silently building the final stage of this plan back up in his head, forcing the slip-up last night to become part of the tapestry he was weaving…letting it become the nail holding up the scaffolding, the roots feeding the tree. He could salvage this—he would.

And when she spat in his face for it, he would not flinch.

He was Finnick Atlas, Trickster Prince, builder of his own throne, forger of his own crown. He would not lay his kingdom down for the sake of some girl who wouldn't even tell him her name.

He burst into the hall with renewed purpose flooding his limbs, stalking down the hall, determined to track Fidget down before his private breakfast with Esha. But before he could even make it three paces, he heard the soft slither of a snake quick on his heels.

He sighed. "Morning, Vash."

"Vidia is home."

Finn's heart jerked, and he whipped around to face Vash. The Viper wore an actual smile for once—only the barest hint of one, but enough that Finn could tell he spoke the truth. Vidia was only ten minutes younger, but Vash felt every second of those ten minutes, and he took the responsibility of them seriously; it was the one weakness Finn had managed to extricate from Vash's web of secrets. Vidia was the same; the Maren twins' only true weakness was each other. It made them formidable when they were together, vulnerable when they were apart. "Is Kallias—?"

"He isn't with her."

Finn's anger flared even faster than his hope. Had she even listened to his instructions before he sent her off? "That was her entire mission. That was the whole point of sending her to Nyx, why didn't she—?"

"I don't know. She says she has to tell you herself."

Typical. "Fine. Broken Conch, after breakfast. I have to find Fidget first."

Vash blinked. "Who?"

Right. He hadn't told the Viper her nickname. "Fidget. The Mirror who was with me at the auction the other day."

Vash continued to blink at him as if he hadn't spoken.

Finn sighed, irritation clawing at his already-raw temper. He didn't have time for this. "Maren, did you not get your coffee this morning? The Mirror you helped drag me back in here after you got the relic. The little one in purple."

Vash stopped blinking now. Stared instead, something dark welling behind his eyes.

That didn't bode well. Then again, nothing did these days.

"Prince," Vash said slowly, "none of the Mirrors wear purple."

"What?" A laugh barked out of his chest, hitting every wrong angle on the way out, sounding nothing like him by the time it hit the air. "I thought I was the one with a spotty memory here. The one in the alley, Vash, the one we had to—"

"Finn," Vash said urgently, stopping him with a hand on his shoulder; Vash never touched him unless it was life or death, unless he absolutely had to. "None of the Mirrors wear purple. They're not allowed to. It's Occassio's color. And there was no one in the alley with you that night—no one but the man you killed."

Everything became so, so, so quiet.

Not allowed.

Occassio's color.

No. No, no, no no no no.

He couldn't have…he couldn't possibly…

"Vash," he rasped, "I swear to every single god dead and alive, if you are lying to me—"

"Prince, I swear it on my life, on my sister's life, on everything that is and has ever been precious to me. No one was with you in that alley."

His pulse beat in his head like a war drum. His skin felt transparent, ethereal, like his soul was slipping free from the fetters of his bones.

A dream. A nightmare. This had to be…

He was Finnick Atlas, Trickster Prince. He was better than this. He had to be better than this.

Vash was wrong. Vash had to be wrong.

He pushed past Vash, shock crystallizing into something colder, sharper, a boy turned blade, danger turned dagger.

"Where are you going?" Vash hissed after him.

Finn did not look back. Could not look back. Did not trust his eyes to give him the proper picture.

"To find a Mirror."

* * *

He found her trying to pick a lock.

At first, he just stood and watched, letting himself breathe in the sight of her. Letting himself come to understand exactly what was happening here; exactly what had been happening to him for weeks now.

The Trickster Prince, tricked. No longer a fool in play; a fool in truth.

A fool in so many ways, because he knew this Mirror's name. Had always known her name. Had cursed it, mocked it, paid good coin to have it whispered over crystal balls and tarot cards.

Fury, hotter and fiercer than the fire that had scorched his life to cinders, sharpened his voice to an arrowpoint, roughened it to a rasp, barely able to make the journey from his mouth to her ears: "Occassio."

Her ever-fidgeting fingers stilled on the door.

Her shoulders loosened. Her head tilted. And before she'd even turned around, before a single word left her lips, he saw her shed the skin he'd come to search for in the halls: the girl who had surprised him with her quick hands and quicker mind, the girl he'd stolen and lied and murdered for, the girl who'd held his face and called him brilliant, called him beautiful.

By the time she turned around, nothing remained of that girl but the freckles on her face and the keen, wicked gleam in her eyes.

And Finn hated her. Gods, he hated her.

"Clever boy," said Occassio, goddess of time and trickery and making jesters out of men who thought themselves kings. "I'll be honest—I thought you'd catch me faster."

He should have. He should have. All the signs were there, all the little tells, but he'd named them all wrong. Like trying to read a book held upside down, he'd followed all the clues to the wrong conclusion, the story he'd been reading entirely different from the story that was truly there.

A familiar quaking seized Finn's hands in a vicious hold, forcing his fingers to splay apart. He started to slip his hands into his pockets, but Occassio put one finger out, wagging it in a playful tick-tock motion. "Ah-ah," she tsked. "Come on, Finn. After all we've been through, you think you can still hide behind your pockets? The shaking's unfortunate, I know. But it would go away if you'd just stop fighting me."

As she stepped forward, a glimmer started at the crown of her head and fizzled downward like a bandage unwrapped from a wound. Beneath it, she was still the same girl Finn had come to know, but the slight changes were just enough to shift the entire picture: longer ringlets that sparkled in the light, sharper cheekbones and narrower eyes, knives of kohl drawn on her eyelids. Her simple lavender top and dark leggings vanished to reveal a gown that looked like she'd fashioned it from shattered panels of opaque stained glass. Triangular slits were cut at the waist and beneath the knees, revealing smooth brown skin that shimmered like she'd coated herself in some kind of cosmetic oil. She wore no crown. She didn't need one.

"Esha doesn't know I've been looking for her mirror, does she." Flat. Without feeling. "She doesn't know anything."

Occassio gave him a viper's smile, that traitorous tongue poking through the gap in her teeth. "If we're being technical, love, it's my mirror. And I am oh-so-grateful for you putting it back in my hands. I like to have a little leverage when dealing with my big brother these days."

All at once, the entirety of these last weeks rolled out before him, the fabric of reality laid out like a rug over the false images he'd been fed:

The night of the welcome ball, he hadn't drifted after a shy, sad Mirror with hands full of cookies. He'd abandoned his family and his duties to sit on a balcony alone, had spilled champagne on himself, had bowed to thin air while his mother dragged him back inside. He hadn't accompanied Fidget to a tavern and studied himself in her mirror pendant to mimic base admiration; he'd sprawled at an empty table and talked to himself and stared at the chair across from him while the barkeeps cautiously slid him the water he ordered and wondered out loud to each other how many other taverns he'd already visited.

He hadn't found Tomas leaning over a terrified girl in a rat-infested, shadow-thick alley…hadn't been confronted by Tomas at all. She'd taken his hand on the tavern stairs and flooded his vision with her magic, knitting together the illusion of an enemy, testing how deeply she had him under her spell—testing whether he'd choose her safety over his. The people at the auction had stared at him because he was laughing to himself, rambling to himself before finding his seat.

And Fidget's scream…he hadn't come upon Tomas threatening her. He'd sprinted away from Vash to stalk a stranger through the streets, a man Occassio had cloaked in the veneer of Tomas, and when that man stepped into an alley to take a shortcut home, Finn had plunged his knife through the man's windpipe, silencing him for no greater crime than being the unfortunate object of Occassio's illusions. And that was the sight Vash had come upon that night, the reason he'd treated him with such reproach afterward: Finn, wearing blood and shock like silken gloves, his hands cradling invisible elbows and his lips muttering nonsense about fireworks, asking the alley shadows if they'd been hurt by the innocent man who'd bled out so quickly his body didn't even have time to twitch.

All this time, he hadn't been losing his mind at all.

No. It was already long gone, and he had no idea when or where he'd let it slip through his fingers. No idea how long he'd been trying to run a game he kept forgetting the rules to.

"But Luisa," he croaked. "She spoke to you. She…"

"Luisa is an extremely talented former Mirror who knows how to keep her mouth shut. You really think she'd go up against her precious goddess? For you?" Occassio snorted. "All the gold in the world couldn't buy you loyalty like that."

Fury and betrayal tied twin nooses around his throat, but he refused to let them tighten. Not yet. He needed answers as long as she was giving them, and there was only one question left that mattered.

"Why."

He did not have to elaborate.

"Because it turns out that you were telling the truth." Her voice dropped into an imitation of his, so close it was startling, so real his hand flew to his throat to make sure it wasn't actually his mouth speaking her words: "Anything that could have broken me is already gone. At first I thought, well, that's bullshit, of course, but it's true, isn't it? You made sure of it. You either drove them away or let them die out, one by one by one." A sanctimonious smirk took a nauseating curl across her face. "So. How else to break a man with no weaknesses but to become his weakness?"

He didn't decide to draw the dagger from the hidden sheath beneath his shirt. There was no plan, no scheme, no careful steps plotted out in the map of his mind. There was no ace up his sleeve, no path to checkmate, no mask he possessed that would be good enough to trick the Trickster Goddess.

This was foolishness, pure and simple. But seeing as he was done playing the fool—had worn the mask so long he'd somehow become him—he didn't care to shove it down.

He lunged with a speed that would have left most people pinned to the wall, his dagger sunk to the hilt in their chest. But not Fidget—not Occassio.

She waved a hand in the air, a lazy drift that should have done nothing to block his blow. But just as her fingers stopped their arc, the air congealed around him; less like air, more like water. More like tar.

He ground his teeth against the weight, straining with every muscle to force himself forward, but the movements were sluggish, heavy. Even blinking took longer, his eyelids struggling to meet, only a sliver of the world disappearing with every handful of seconds.

Occassio chuckled, a resonant, preening thing that itched the back of his ears with the unbearable urge to scratch, to claw, to block out her maddening voice. She prowled up to him with alarming speed, coming right up to his face as if she couldn't feel the resistance holding his body down. "Time magic really is my favorite. Nearly impossible to use as a mortal, but so gratifying to wield as a goddess."

He could feel it; not just the thickening air around him, but the magic that stretched across it like well-tuned strings, her fingers plucking idly at whichever cord happened to be tied to the limb he was trying to move. It reminded him of the sensation he'd felt while passing through the relic—the mirror with no reflection, his body plunging through quicksilver into an impossible past.

A mirror he'd managed to traverse once already.

If this was a matter of strings, he played a damned decent fiddle.

With unbearable slowness, he reached for one of those threads, keeping his eyes fixed on her while she chattered on about this magic, her eager tone digging sharp nails into his stupid, useless heart, a grief for something that never even existed. And the moment he hooked his finger around one of the strings, he tugged with all his might.

Snap.

The sound of the cord breaking tore through his skull, a wordless cry, a suffering without pain. Every muscle locked up, throwing him to one knee, and it wasn't just his hands that shook now; no, his entire body went rigid, quivering, his breaths coming in frenzied gasps he couldn't control. Something warm gushed from his ears and nose, copper and salt creeping across his tongue.

"Oh." The disgust in Occassio's voice brought his chin up, blood dripping from it like rain. She regarded him with a displeased scowl, those pert eyebrows drawn together in annoyance. "You already used the mirror. Ugh, you wily bastard. I hate how lucky you are. Then again, I guess that's my fault, isn't it?"

He didn't wait for her to reach into her bag of tricks again. He drove himself up from the ground, bleeding and breathless, dagger extended—

His body passed straight through hers, colliding with the wall so sharply that pain sang through his teeth at the impact, the breath driven from him with a harsh oof. Not a moment passed before manacles clamped down on his wrists, pink light pinning him to the wall, and a pair of shrewd, thieving hands soon followed. She leaned up to whisper in his ear, her curls tickling his cheek, the scent of champagne on her breath a temptation that had lost all power over him in the span of a moment: "This isn't over yet, Trickster Prince. Be grateful—you still have a little time left to say goodbye. But I already know how this game of ours ends, and trust me…there's not enough aces in the world for you to cheat your way around me."

Dizziness twirled his mind in ballroom circles, and when he parted his lips to answer, he spat out the words soaked in blood: "You will not have me."

Her giggle was a dagger straight through the center of his back. "Oh, Trickster," she purred, pressing a tender kiss to the back of his neck. "I already do."

He blinked, and everything changed, the scene before him rearranging like an artfully shuffled deck.

He was no longer pinned against the wall. Instead, he sat on the floor of his room, cross-legged before the footboard of his bedframe. Propped up against it was the mirror relic, its covering removed, and in the center of that quicksilver pool…

He saw his reflection staring back at him, a grin that didn't belong to him hung crookedly on its face, its eyes glowing with golden divinity.

The cry that burst from his lips was not a decision, not a scheme, not a plan. It was desperation, a hopeless grasping into the dark, what little remained of his boyhood reaching out with all its might:

"Kallias!"

CHAPTER 61

FINN

Everything hurt.

Every drag of his feet across the cobbled street sent new pains clattering down every fiber of sinew and bone. Every note of a fiddle or pound of a drum strengthened the headache trying to thrust an axe through his skull. Every laugh that wandered too close to a cackle brought his hands to his ears with a jolt of dread, his stinging eyes searching the streets for a flicker of lavender or a gleam of too-white teeth.

He had yet to stop shaking. It had been three hours.

People stopped to stare, taking in the limping man with blood crusted in his nostrils and across his lips, his cloak barely fastened, flinching away from laughing children and people dressed in purple. But he couldn't stop. Couldn't blink. If he blinked, this could all disappear, and he'd find himself back in his room, staring down a reflection that didn't match reality.

His grasp on his mind was tenuous at best. If he closed his eyes now, it might take that chance to slip away once more.

He stumbled into the Broken Conch like a man already several cups deep, and he didn't have to look up to know every eye had fallen on him, the horrified judgement of upper city folk settling heavy on his shoulders.

So many eyes. Too many eyes. All of them looking at him, taking note of him, seeing him—

Two pairs of hands found his shoulders, and he couldn't even find the strength to fight them as they guided him down into a chair, one pair lingering while the other pulled away, footsteps clapping against the floor as the figure circled the table.

A beat of silence, then: "Everyone out."

Vash.

His command must have been accompanied by a flash of steel; the tavern emptied in a stampede of steps that felt like they pounded over the bruised flesh of Finn's abused mind, ache after ache grinding deeper through his skull.

Pestle against mortar. Hammer against stone.

You will not have me.

Oh, Trickster…I already do.

"Finn."

He raised his eyes to meet Vidia's fearful gaze, strands of her satin-smooth hair falling across her face as she slid into the seat beside him, her hand never leaving his back. She wore a thin cotton top the color of mirror frames and false tears, an armored leather vest strapped over the top of it, a new piercing in her left ear and a yellowish, healing bruise mottling her jaw.

"Where is he." He couldn't bend the words into a proper question.

"We can talk about that after you tell me what happened here."

"We'll talk about it now, Captain Maren."

Vidia scowled at his use of her formal title. "If you think playing princely is going to intimidate me—"

"I don't have time for your gods-damned jokes, Vidia!" He hated the break in his voice, the terror that flooded out from it, a fear he'd tried to leave behind in his boyhood. "Tell me where my brother is!"

Vidia blinked. And blinked again. And just before he could erupt, she let her hand slip off of his shoulder, leaving his back exposed. "Artem."

Shock cleaved his stomach into two parts as he pressed his back against the chair, shielding himself from any teasing fingers that might try to spider up his spine. "*What?*"

That was the last thing he'd expected to hear. *Imprisoned in Nyx's dungeons* had been at the top. *Killed by Elias for saying something stupid* had settled somewhere in the middle, a compromise between Kallias's prowess with a sword and Elias's senseless grief. *Married some Nyxian peasant and settled into a cozy life as a sheep farmer* had even landed higher on the list.

But *Artem?* The home of Kallias's betrothed? The place he'd given up his crown to avoid?

"Seems he and the Nyxian spy were only in Nyx a couple days before they were sent off on a new mission. The royals sent them, I think—though some say it was Mortem herself."

Mortem. Tempest's mildewed sandals, there were *four* of them now?

Bad idea to invoke that fifth god's name at this point, probably. Who knew what could summon Tempest into this mess? For all Finn knew, that night he'd bowed to the moon and called Occassio a name, she'd decided it was as good as an invitation to ruin his heretical life.

He swallowed. Shook himself. Wished he *hadn't* shaken himself the second his head protested. "Artem," he said again. "He's not coming home."

Vidia exchanged a look with her brother. Finn *hated* that—their silent communication that was either a result of sharing a command or sharing a womb. He couldn't pick apart the motivations and honesty of words left unspoken.

"Not yet, anyway," Vidia finally agreed. She said it like she was trying to turn it into good news. Like she was afraid anything less than optimism might shatter him.

But it was too late for that. The shattering was over; the pieces of his mind were scattered across Atlas by now, and without his brother there to fill in the cracks…

He swallowed hard, dry throat finding no relief. "He's not coming home."

Quiet, this time. So quiet he could hear their breathing—even that they did in tandem.

I can't save you! No one can save you!

But some childlike, damaged part of him had hoped for it anyway. The part that still had a shard of wine-soaked glass burrowed inside it. The part that still wanted his older brother every time he dragged himself out of a nightmare by the tips of his nails.

"Prince Finnick," said Vash, in the gentle way people spoke to the sick, "you're not well."

Laugh. Make a joke. Threaten him. Do something—anything.

"Did you know?" Not what he meant to say.

Vash did not blink. "I don't know what you mean."

"Occassio." Even saying her name sent a shiver through his bones, his eyes twitching with the need to look over his shoulder. "Did you know I've been…seeing her?"

"Oh," Vidia said knowingly, relief flooding her features as she settled back in her chair, propping her leather boots up on the table. The soles were crusted with dirt and greenish needle-like objects. Some kind of plant matter, maybe. Likely left over from tromping through Nyx's winter woods. "You've just gone mad, that's all. For a moment I thought you were poisoned, you're looking so pale and strange—"

"Vidia," he said calmly. Too calmly. The kind of calm he'd felt just before his knife tickled the inside of an innocent man's throat. "This is not funny."

"No one is laughing," Vash interrupted before his sister could shove her muddy boot even further into her mouth. "No, Prince. I didn't know anything about it until you mentioned the Mirror this morning."

Vash made his trade in deceit and masks, just like Finn. But liars knew how to read other liars, and Finn knew all Vash's tells. Not one of them showed on his face now.

One small relief. Not all of his allies had betrayed him.

"You remember what I said about Anima taking my sister," he rasped, and the Maren twins bobbed their heads in affirmation, all amusement leaking from Vidia's face. "I don't believe she's the only one. Occassio has made no secret of what she wants from me."

No secret, not anymore, but that truth had come too late. She'd told him a hundred lies before it, and he'd fallen for each and every one of them.

Finn, I would like it very much if I could kiss you.

He'd never touch a drop of champagne again. Even the memory of its taste soured his stomach.

"The gods walk among us again," Vash croaked, awe and fear wrestling each other in his eyes. "All of them?"

"Tenebrae, Anima, Occassio…now Mortem." Finn gestured to Vidia, who looked ready to run all the way back to Nyx, mirroring her brother's fear now. If she did, Finn honestly thought he might just join her. "I doubt Tempest will be content to keep to himself."

Silence took the crown from Finn's head and made itself king of this tavern, fashioning a throne from barstools and sticky table legs. Its reign lasted until Vash shook himself from his stupor, folding his hands in a praying pose, something bleak draining the awe from his gaze. "Why now? Why like this? The gods have never been violent about taking hosts before, not in any legends I've ever heard. What's changed?"

What, indeed.

"I don't know." Three words he hated most in the entire world. "But there's someone who might, and he's currently inside a mountain with our favorite deserter."

Vidia raised one eyebrow. "You think Elias would know?"

Finn blinked at her. "You're on a first name basis with him now?"

"You told me to make friends. I made friends. One by the name of Evanna Loch." Vidia smirked faintly. "Lovely woman. Very proud of her little brother. Has a tendency to worry out loud if you slip a little something into her drink."

"You *poisoned* her?"

Vidia shrugged one shoulder, clearly wearing a bit of pride where she shouldn't. "Only a little. Just a pinch of something to loosen her tongue."

For the first time since the night before, Finn actually thought he could manage a smile. "Yet again earning your reputation, Fang."

Vidia bared her teeth in a grin of her own, flashing her canines. "What can I say? I'm a biter."

Vash wrinkled his nose. Finn would have chuckled if he had any laughter left. "How much longer can I keep you two here?"

"We're owed a leave for a couple more weeks," Vash said. "But even if we weren't, this…this is bigger than the war."

"Good answer." He gathered up the fallen strings of his self-control and tugged them taut once more. There was still a game to play. Still a victory to claim. "Go to my room and stay there. Guard that relic with your life."

Vash nodded once. "Understood."

"Vash," said Finn, and the man paused as he was standing. "I know you worship her. If you are going to bow to her if she walks in that room, I would just as soon send you back to the army."

Vash's expression didn't change. "I bow to no one who harms my friends."

Finn's throat tightened. He cleared it with a dismissive nod. "Vidia?"

"I'm not the religious type," said Vidia, a gleam in her eyes as she cracked her knuckles. Almost like she'd been waiting for a reason to fight a goddess. He didn't know whether to curse or thank the gods for her and Soleil never being in the same room. "But what are you going to do?"

Finn forced his hands into fists, his gaze falling to his empty ring finger.

One game he hadn't yet lost. And his plan to win it remained the same.

"I need to have a chat with my future wife."

CHAPTER 62

FINN

F or someone so distrustful, Esha Levine didn't see through shadows very well.

It was no difficult feat to lurk deep in the silhouette of her armoire, watching as her favored Dagger and Mirror did a quick sweep of the chamber, the Dagger's hands probing in every nook and cranny of the furniture, the ruby girl's eyes gleaming pink as she searched over the rest. Esha's chamber was grand for a guest room—the walls were painted maroon, every piece of furniture crafted from Arborian darkwood and furnished with gilded detailing. It was the perfect room to find a shadow to slip into.

Finn didn't think he was imagining the way the darkness clung tighter to him when he wished it to; didn't think it was luck that the Mirror's piercing eyes slid right past him without so much as a blink.

I've already seen you do it. So do it.

A silent breath slid through his gritted teeth, and it took work not to try and bat her voice out of his head. *I don't want your damned magic.* Though it was proving itself to be useful at the moment.

There was no answer—there hadn't been since he'd woken up in his room after he'd called her by her true name, her fingers teasing memory free from his iron-clad mind the same way his liked to flirt with the inner mechanisms of a lock.

Gods knew how many hours he'd lost over these past couple weeks. Gods knew what all he'd done under her influence.

Well. One *goddess* in particular knew.

He tucked that away for later. He only trusted his failing mind to handle one thing at a time right now.

Once the Dagger and Mirror seemed to be satisfied with the safety of the room, the Mirror lit the kerosene lamps on the desk and nightstand, bade her queen goodnight, and left. The lamplight caught the edge of the ruby Mirror's dress, casting chips of scarlet light across the wall, and Finn's heart stumbled at the memory of sanguine streaks cast across a kaleidoscopic dress.

Curse Occassio straight to her older sister's smoky pits.

The Dagger lingered, just long enough for Finn to catch the stiffness to his shoulders, his dark eyes scanning the room as if he was dissatisfied with it somehow. Finn held his breath until Esha finally touched the Dagger's shoulder— the only time he'd ever seen her touch one of her attendants—and guided him toward the door. The Dagger still looked reluctant, but he finally bowed to his queen before leaving, shutting the door behind him.

Esha herself only relaxed once she thought she was alone. He watched in silence as she eased herself onto the gold silk bedspread and reached up to unbind her hair from its coil at the top of her head, letting it unfurl down her back, the onyx strands brushing the duvet. With small, nimble fingers, she started to untangle bits of hair from the silver curls of her decorative tiara, cursing softly at the tug against her scalp.

"Pesky things, crowns."

Before the first word had fully left his mouth, a hot streak of pain cut across his ear, warmth oozing down the side of his neck a moment later. He raised a hand to his ringing ear to find a knife buried to the hilt in the inch of wall between his head and the armoire. Esha stood in a defensive stance, her hand still outstretched from the throw, her skirt still settling from the retrieval of the blade from some hidden sheath.

"Good aim," he offered as he stepped out of the shadows, unruffled. He had two goddesses as his enemies now. A quick end by mortal steel would be a mercy at this point.

"Prince Finnick." At her slightly frantic tone, at the panicky glance she shot back and forth between him and the door, it suddenly struck him how young Esha was. Younger even than him, only just eighteen. "I-I did not invite you here."

"And yet, here I am." He shoved his hands into his pockets and tipped his head to one side, letting the wolf's grin he'd learned from his Nyx-raised sister curl across his face. "Funny how that works."

Esha tried and failed to claim that same cold look that she'd worn every day before this, betraying a hint of the paranoia Fidget—*Occassio*, damn him to the depths—had mentioned to him. So there'd been a pinch of truth sprinkled over her lies, then.

"What do you want, Prince?" Her pealing-bell voice lowered along with her hand, her fingers dipping into another fold in her skirt. He wondered just how many blades she was hiding within its layers of jewel and gossamer and silk. Wondered how many warning throws she would make before her weapon landed true.

Enough scaring her. He'd made his point, and mercy or not, he'd do Atlas no good if he was dead.

He raised his hands in surrender, walking with careful steps until he stood directly across from Esha, between her and the door. "No screaming," he warned just as her lips began to part. "I'm not here to hurt you."

"And yet you skulk in the shadows like some kind of—"

"Thief?" He raised one eyebrow suggestively. "Had a bit of trouble with that sort, have you?"

Fury swept away all fear from the young queen. "*You*—"

"Did not take your mirror," he interrupted. "But I know who did. And if you want it back, Your Majesty, you'll sit and listen to what I have to say."

Esha's eyes were wide, her sharp jaw twitching, her black eyes shuttering with their usual layer of ice. "I don't care to be blackmailed."

"I like to think of it as *negotiation under duress*."

"The words of a cad, not a prince."

This time, his grin wasn't fake. "I wear many hats, Your Majesty, and my crown is the one I use least. Will you hear a prince's offer, or must the cad continue to lay threats at your feet?"

Oh, that irked her. He could see it in the grind of her jaw, the narrowing of her eyes, the curling in of her shoulders. But she was young and alone and terribly, horrifically vulnerable. She had nowhere to go. And he could see something else behind her anger: desperation. He'd dangled the idea of having her most prized possession back just out of her reach, and he knew from experience how that kind of temptation could tunnel one's focus to a pinpoint.

She nodded. Sat. Gestured for him to do the same. "You have three minutes to explain yourself, Prince Finnick. If I am not satisfied with your explanation for threatening a queen, you can consider this alliance lost."

Exactly what he was about to request, but it was too early to flip that card over. "I only need thirty seconds."

Her silken hair and gossamer-coated skirts rustled against the duvet as she shifted to face him more fully, her mouth pinching like she'd bitten into something sour. "Is *braggart* one of your many hats?"

"My favorite, in fact."

"Hmm. Go on."

"Tell me what the mirror does."

Now both her eyebrows reached for her hairline. "That is not an explanation."

"You said I have thirty seconds." Mentally, he tossed up a middle finger to the memory of the moon. "You didn't say I had to use them now."

"The mirror is a precious relic of my family," Esha said, ignoring his words with a dismissive blink. "I will not reveal its secrets to—"

He held up a hand. "Perhaps I did not make myself clear: I currently have my two best guarding this precious relic of yours. And if you do not tell me what it does, I'll be forced to assume it's worthless to me, and I'll return it to those who saw fit to steal it from your chamber in the first place."

Esha's fist clenched against the duvet. "You'll never make it out of this room to give that order."

"The order has already been given. If I do not safely return to them to tell them otherwise, the relic will be returned to the thieves at midnight."

A lie, all of it. But he knew that look in her eye. When what was most precious to someone was taken away, they lost all faith in their ability to read a bluff. She would not risk it.

He was relying on that.

Esha was quiet for a heartbeat too long, enough that his own threatened to stop. But finally she said, "The mirror is…many things. But it is guarded so fiercely for what it can give, not for what it can do."

"And what can it give?"

"Have you touched it?"

A lie would do him no good here. He nodded.

Esha leaned back an inch, new wariness rattling her a bit as she breathed in. "Where did it take you?"

"I don't know." Not a lie, not really. "I…I saw my little sister."

"The Heir?" At his nod, she added, "Before the fire, or…?"

"After. Just after. When…when we already thought her dead."

Esha nodded as if she understood precisely. "I saw my parents, the evening before they were killed. I think it shows you the moment you most wish you could change."

Gods.

"The mirror is a vessel, of sorts," she added. "As are all the godly relics. They each contain a magic or ability borne only by the gods."

"And the mirror contains…?"

"Chronomancy. The ability to manipulate time." Esha raked her eyes over him once. "Wave to me."

Finn did as she asked, not seeing the harm in it. Esha raised her hand and closed her eyes, moving her hand in a slow arc, just the way he'd seen Occassio do in the hall.

His hand grew heavy, as if his bones had been transformed to iron. He strained to continue the waving motion, but he could not force his way through. Remembering the threads of magic he'd seen Occassio manipulate—watching Esha's fingertips twitch in nearly the same way—he tried to probe outward with his mind, a clumsy attempt at using this godsforsaken magic he'd been forced into carrying. But he hadn't yet recovered from his encounter that morning, it seemed; the moment he tried to wield that power again, a shattering pain cracked through his skull, nearly drawing a cry of pain from his lips.

Esha gasped out a breath, her hand dropping into her lap at the same time a trickle of blood slid from her nose, painting her pale lips in crimson. Finn's hand jerked too far to the side, suddenly free from that unbearable weight, and it nearly threw him to the floor. He only just caught himself with his other hand.

"It does mortals precious little good," panted Esha, dashing her hand across her nose, frowning down at her bloodied fingers as if they were a mere inconvenience. "I can only use a bit before it drains me. We're not built for magic of that sort, it's meant for the gods alone. It's how they fully settle themselves into their bodies when they take hosts."

"What do you mean?"

"My mother used to tell me stories…tales of Occassio taking her first host. Human bodies can't bear the weight of godhood all at once; it takes time to adjust to carry it, even for those born strong enough. If all their magic flooded the body at once, it would give out beneath the weight. So each of the gods stored their most powerful abilities within objects and entrusted them to their most devoted followers to protect. And every time they took a host, they would journey to obtain the last of their magics from their relics. Until then, their magic was limited to what their body could bear."

Finn's throat dried out. "What if the host had already used the relic?"

Esha's eyes flicked to him. Narrowed. "I assume it would save her time," she said slowly. "If the host was prepared that way beforehand."

Damn it. Damn it, damn it, damn it.

Every step a misstep. He couldn't get ahead.

"I'd like to use my thirty seconds," he croaked.

"Go on."

"I want you to leave. Find any excuse you must, any reason you can give my mother for your hasty departure and delayed negotiations. But you will not ally with Atlas against Nyx."

Now Esha looked truly taken aback. "You wish to cripple your own kingdom's war effort?"

"It's a long story." A long, long, *long* story. Not one he planned to offer to this cold-hearted, time-bending queen. "But yes. I want you to abandon this alliance."

Esha stood in a sweep of skirts, wiping her blood off on the golden duvet. She crossed her arms, ducking her chin to look at him from beneath long lashes. "I came here for a consort."

"So I was told. But you and I both know you don't want a consort; you want another target between you and a vial of poison. Maybe a well-timed blade in the dark or a noose looped around your neck." Finn stood as well, shuddering as he placed his hands on his hips. "And while I wanted to be many strange things when I grew up, *dead* was never one of them."

Esha's lips pursed. "I don't suppose telling you that you are uniquely suited to the role would convince you otherwise?"

"Alas, I'm newly immune to flattery."

"It's not flattery. Prince Finnick, I did not make this offer without intention. I have heard many things of you…things your own kingdom will never appreciate. Word of your exploits were murmured between my Mirrors for weeks before we made this offer. I chose you because I felt you, of all royals, might actually manage to survive a reign at my side." Esha stepped around the bed to approach him. They were the same height—her dark eyes bore into his without looking up or down. "The Trickster Prince who wears a thousand faces. The liar who can reel the truth out of anyone's mouth. The charmer who can bring anyone around to his side of things. Lapis needs a king to put their faith in. I need a partner my kingdom will love to stabilize my rule. And I chose *you*—out of dozens of others, I chose you to share space in my throne room. I fear I cannot leave here without accomplishing that goal. All the power you hold here, with nothing to show for it—surely by now you must be craving a true crown."

He'd been afraid of that. This was about to get much messier. "Of course I am," he said softly. "But my ambition has been carefully leashed for some time now. If you set it free, I fear it will not be content with second-best."

Her brows bent inward. "I'm afraid I don't follow."

"Neither do I. So consider this carefully, because I promise you, Queen Esha: if you force me into this marriage, I *will* go through with it. I will go back to your kingdom with you. And you will be nothing more than a figurehead within a week of my setting foot in that throne room. You want a partner? You'll get a tyrant. I suggest you take my counteroffer."

It was the most carefully crafted threat he'd ever made—one perfectly done up for a paranoid queen on the brink of civil war, tied with a dagger-sharp smile and a promise he could most definitely fulfill. If she was unwilling to bend, he would become the thing she feared most: usurper. Betrayer. The unrightful king of her crystalline queendom.

He'd pulled off more taxing schemes on any given day of the week. He almost hoped she'd let him try.

Esha's smile had frozen in place, the sheen of rage in her eyes nearly blinding. But she only said, cold and clipped, "And what is your counteroffer, exactly?"

"I will return your mirror to you, under the condition that you take it far, *far* away from here." Best to get it far from Tenebrae's clutches—and his own. He had no intention of allowing Occassio to snatch up his body as hers, but he was in his right mind less and less these days. He couldn't even trust *himself* anymore. "Take it, take your Mirrors and Daggers, and return to your own kingdom. If word from Atlas comes again under *any* name but Kallias Atlas, for the sake of yourself and your people, you ignore it."

Her ire gave way to unease the longer she stared at him, and again he saw the orphan beneath the sovereign. A kingdom of masks and illusions, Lapis; he really might make the best king for it, if he only had the time to waste on such an endeavor. "Something is very wrong here."

"Yes." He held her diamond-hard gaze. "And I'm giving you one chance to escape it. Only one, Your Majesty. I cannot guarantee you will have an ally in me by morning."

A beat. "You'll return my mirror?"

"Yes."

"And your only price is my absence shortly thereafter."

"Yes."

Esha stared at him so long that his ears and neck began to itch, the blood on his left side starting to dry.

"You really would make a brilliant king," she said, almost wistfully.

"As you make a brilliant queen. You need no consort to make your kingdom love you, Majesty. What you need is to let down a wall or two. Get to know your people. I've learned more sitting with my subjects in taverns and bakeries than I ever have sitting on a lumpy throne behind the palace walls."

Esha's mouth twitched, just a bit. "My throne is quite comfortable, actually."

"Diamond?"

"Velvet."

Finn hesitated. "Is it too late to reconsider your offer?"

Esha laughed, looking as though she was just as surprised by it as him, and the sound was twice as terrifying as any look she'd ever thrown him across the breakfast table. "My escort and I will be gone before breakfast. But my mirror..."

"I'll see it returned once I know you've spoken to my mother."

"Fair enough."

It wasn't. None of this was even slightly fair. But it was necessary, and that was all he needed to know.

"And Finnick," she added as he turned to leave, "just so you know . . . you do not have an ally in me now, let alone by morning."

He rested one hand on the doorframe. The other on his hip, where he still wore his dagger. "Do I have an enemy?"

Esha only smiled, a demure thing he didn't trust for a moment. "We'll see how this game of yours plays out, won't we?"

Indeed they would. Yet another problem for yet another day.

But he had one problem left, at least, that could not be shoved aside or told to wait its turn:

Kallias was in gods-damned *Artem*.

CHAPTER 63

FINN

"What do you mean, Kallias is in *Artem*?"

Seamus's incredulous voice was doing Finn's exhaustion-fueled headache no favors. He slumped back against his seat in the private dining room, watching Seamus pace by the curtain-covered window, his blond hair gleaming in the light of the chandelier above, and even that much of a reflection stirred nausea in Finn's stomach.

He hadn't slept in two days. Hardly the first time he'd gone so long without shutting his eyes, but it was still beginning to take a toll.

Esha was gone, her excuses made and her people gathered. His mother was livid, his father baffled, and Finn had only managed to play clueless for a full ten minutes before claiming he needed some time to think and practically fleeing the throne room.

Esha had taken the mirror with her. Good riddance, too. But there were still four more relics out there, and gods knew—literally, only the gods knew—where they could even start looking for them.

"Captain Maren was on her own mission for me these past couple weeks," Finn explained, wrapping a loose thread in his sweater around his forefinger, watching as the tip went pale from lack of bloodflow before he loosened the string and let it pink up again. "I sent her to Nyx to assist Kallias in case his welcome was…less than warm."

Seamus stopped halfway through his next pace, utter disbelief in his eyes. "You sent *Vidia* over me? She couldn't act her way out of a—"

"Seamus, you and I both know that if I send you over the border to Nyx, you're not coming back," Finn snapped with a roll of his eyes; he was truly tired of Seamus acting like he was dense. "Besides, they know your face there. After all these years, there'd be questions, most of which I certainly don't want you to answer."

Seamus's scowl deepened, but he wouldn't meet Finn's eyes. "I'd come back for Alia."

"Alia would go there to get you," Finn corrected, watching her wince a bit out of the corner of his eye, "and then you'd both be lost to me. Vidia was a fresh face. Stop playing like I hurt your precious feelings and listen, will you?"

Seamus stewed for a moment longer before kicking a chair away from the table and dropping into it, scooting over until it was pressed against Alia's. He rested his head against her shoulder, and Alia reached up to stroke his hair without breaking Finn's gaze. "So what now?"

His chin tingled with the memory of fingers cradling it with that same tenderness, and he ground his teeth until the sensation faded. "Artem's delegation will return to their kingdom with the news of Kallias's abdication any day now, if they haven't already. Gods know what Kallias is thinking, but my guess is that he hasn't been forthcoming about that, if they let him over the border even with two Nyxian escorts. I might be able to—"

Seamus suddenly bolted up in his seat, hand resting on Alia's thigh, his eyes trained on the door. "Did you hear that?"

"Hear what? Seamus, I swear, if you're being petty about—"

Seamus was up before Finn could finish, and he watched in disbelief as the captain of the palace guard bolted from the room, not even bothering to catch and close the door on his way out. He exchanged a look with Alia, who looked just as confused and far more worried, lifting one shoulder before getting to her feet. Her wiry form slipped out without a sound, and Finn cursed quietly, shoving his sleeves up above his elbows and adjusting his glasses before hurrying after her, doing his best to look purposeful but not harried.

He heard it once he crossed the room's threshold—shouts, scuffles, sounds of a struggle coming from the direction of the palace's entrance. Seamus had already vanished from the hall, the door ahead swinging on its hinges; Alia wasn't far behind.

Gods, what now?

When he strode into the foyer, he found Seamus standing frozen in the middle of the room, Alia's fingers clasping the back of his uniform and *pulling*, on her tiptoes and whispering urgently in his ear. But even as Finn came up behind them, he couldn't hear what Alia was saying over the commotion at the door.

"What in the depths is happening?" he snapped, pushing Seamus and Alia apart to look between them. Alia twisted out of his way, moving behind him to set herself behind Seamus, but Seamus's bulk barely swayed, his eyes fixed on the palace doors, his face entirely drained of color.

Finn followed his gaze to where a knot of guards was struggling to make their way through the foyer—three, four, maybe five of them surrounding one man. A man with the faintest hint of gold hair shaved close to his head, his clothes stained with blood and dust, a tattoo climbing from his exposed collarbone up his neck and around his ear, the guards restraining him so desperately that his shirt had torn at the collar. He had a deep gash across his forehead and a dazed look in his eyes, but he was *fighting*, fighting harder than any injured man had a right to.

And his face…Finn had to do a double take to ensure Seamus was still standing beside him.

Shit.

He'd no sooner had the thought than the shouting, writhing man in the guards' clutches caught sight of Seamus. His body went suddenly limp, and the guards surged forward to get better grips on his limbs as he sagged, his eyes widening in a desperation familiar to Finn as he shouted: "Jax?"

Seamus jerked forward as if by instinct, and only Finn's iron grip on his sleeve kept him in place.

Shit. *Shit.* Anyone who looked twice was going to see the resemblance between the two in an instant.

"Seamus," he said into his informant's ear, but Seamus didn't blink. His breathing was heavy, labored, wild eyes fixed on the man who was back to struggling against his captors, tearless sobs robbing the strength from his blows now. "*Seamus*. Do not even think about it. Walk away."

"Jax!" roared the captured man again, but one of the guards finally got a proper grip and wrestled him down to his knees, shouting for someone to bring something to bind him with.

He could *hear* Seamus's pounding pulse, the rage and terror radiating from his skin in waves of heat. The captain's arm rose, reaching out, but Finn struck it down, twisting it subtly behind his back and turning so no one could see him hiss: "*Jaxon*. I will handle it, do you hear me? I will *handle it*. Walk away, now."

Seamus swallowed visibly, his hands curling into fists at his sides. But he turned slowly, calling over his shoulder, "Who've you got, Harlen?"

"Looks like a spy, sir," said one of the guards. "Caught him trying to enter the city with Nyxian propaganda on his person."

Seamus kept walking—Finn sent vague thanks to some higher power that at least *one* person was still following his orders—but he could see the tension in the captain's shoulders. He was an inch from snapping entirely. "Dungeons, then. I'll handle his interrogation personally."

"Not without me," Finn muttered to him. Seamus barely acknowledged him, but his chin did dip, and that was good enough for now. "Smart, Seamus. Play this smart. We'll get it sorted." Whatever *it* was.

"Jaxon!" The man wouldn't stop *shouting*, damn him. "Please, it's me, it's Jakob—"

"What's that he keeps calling you?" Finn asked—loudly. Casually.

"No clue." Seamus kept his eyes fixed forward. "Probably delirious from that head wound. Looks nasty."

The man—Jakob—finally fell silent then, and Finn finally breathed easy, keeping himself between Jakob and Seamus as they made their way down to the dungeon. If anyone cared to ask why he was following, he simply told them he was curious to speak to a Nyxian, and that seemed to satisfy their curiosity well enough.

This was going to be another long night.

* * *

"Seamus."

After an hour spent watching a tearful reunion between brothers—angry accusations and questions on Jakob's part quickly giving way to sobs—he was feeling twice as murderous, some strange jealousy spurring him to bury his hands in the yarn of his sweater.

This was what their reunion with Soleil should have been. Joy and sorrow and tearful laughter mixed with demands to know why they hadn't come for her sooner. Instead, because of Occassio, they'd really only gotten the anger.

Seamus—Jaxon; it seemed everyone was wearing more than one name, lately—was sitting in Finn's room, eyes fixed on his boots, a look in his eyes that promised a foolhardy plan was forming. Alia sat cross-legged behind him, rubbing his back; Vidia and Vash were propped on either side of his windowseat, each one leaning against a different bookshelf, their eyes tracking him simultaneously as he paced.

All his remaining allies in one room. It made his army suddenly feel pitifully small.

"Seamus," he said again, finally drawing the captain's eyes. "We will get him out, all right? I'll figure it out. But it's going to take a couple days to do it properly."

"That's too long," Seamus said. "His wound is already infected, and gods know what they'll do to him down there—"

"You heard me, Seamus. If you want him to get home safely, we do this my way, am I clear?"

Seamus's jaw flexed. Finn didn't like the look in his eye.

It was Alia who said, softly, "You're clear, Prince. We do it your way." Seamus shot her a look of betrayal, but Alia met it with a look of her own and a press of her lips to his hand, and whatever protest he'd been about to voice died on his lips.

"Who is this boy to you?" Vidia asked with a frown. She and Vash had been privy to Seamus's Nyxian background already, but the brother was new—to them and to Finn.

"My younger brother." Seamus ran a hand over his face. "My only brother. He was barely in training when I got sent here, when I got...caught."

Another glare at Finn. He simply stared back, unmoved.

The nature of war. He wasn't sorry for what he'd done.

"But what is he doing *here*?"

"You think I know?"

"Enough," Finn muttered into his palm. "We have bigger problems than your brother right now, Seamus."

Seamus scowled at him. "Like *your* brother?"

"Chiefly, yes!"

"Someone has to go to Artem," Vidia said.

"We'll never make it before the delegation arrives," Vash pointed out, running his thumb over the jeweled hilt of his sword. Finn was too tired to flinch at the way it sparkled. "They're likely already there. This would be a rescue mission."

"You two aren't going," Finn croaked. "I need you here, defending Atlas from the inside. Seamus and Alia too."

Vidia blinked at him. "Are you saying—?"

"One person will move faster than a group." Finn shrugged. "And I...I have ways of moving without being seen. I can get in."

"Atlas cannot afford to lose both its princes," Vash muttered. "Especially when both its princesses are under hostile influences."

Finn met Vash's gaze. "As of two days ago, at least one of its princes is falling prey to one too. You were right—I'm not well. I...I trust Atlas more in your hands than I do in mine."

Something he never thought he'd say. Something he never thought he'd *believe.*

"If you have that little confidence in your state of mind," Seamus said, "that's all the more reason for you not to go alone."

"And who would I take with me? Are you volunteering?"

Seamus's mouth shut. He hadn't thought so.

"Vash and Vidia are needed here. Alia goes where you go, she's made that clear. And I have no one else I trust here," he said, aware even as he infused confidence into his words just how bleak this situation was. This felt like a surrender, a retreat. "I believe I can get there. Atlas...Atlas does need its prince. Someone has to get Kallias home, and he'll come if I ask him to. I know he will." *I hope he will.*

Seamus sighed. "Lead on, then," he said. But there was no confidence in his words, and the worst part...

Finn wasn't sure yet if he'd told them the truth or not.

CHAPTER 64

SOREN

S he was nine years old with no name when she first met the mirror girl.

Or at least, she was nameless when the girl left…but had she started out that way?

There was no way to know. All she knew was there had been a flash of purple, a girl with a soothing voice that lulled her toward sleep, promising an end to the agony and fear. Promising to keep her protected until she was big enough to protect herself.

Then nothing. Nothing before and nothing after, a girl who only existed a day at a time, a girl with no name or past or family to speak of.

They said her family died in a fire.

She believed them. She forgot.

* * *

She was twelve when the mirror girl came to visit again.

She'd been drawing more pictures—pictures of dreams she had, dreams she couldn't shake, dreams of redheaded mothers and fathers and brothers and sisters. Dreams of a river with no bank, a river full of waves that could hold up ships and floating boards.

The mirror girl told her that dreaming was dangerous. It wasn't time for dreaming yet.

The mirror girl put her to sleep again. She stopped dreaming.

* * *

She was fifteen when she first realized the mirror girl was an enemy.

It was deep in winter, and she was ill, sick with a fever she couldn't seem to shake. It had been a week of sour tonics swallowed and hazy dreams muddling her waking thoughts and her mother and sisters coming to dote on her, assuring her constantly that this wouldn't put her too far behind in her training.

At the end of that week, when the fever broke, so did something else.

She woke from her slumber already sobbing, coated in sweat, a fog she hadn't known was present clearing with a flash of light, memories flooding her mind until it hurt, hurt, *hurt*—hurt so badly she thought she would die. And even when they settled, finding their way back to their proper places in her mind, still she thought the pain might tear her heart to shards.

Finn. Papa. Mama. Kallias. Jericho. Vaughn.

She'd forgotten them. She'd *forgotten them*.

She raked a hand through her hair, clinging on tightly and tugging at the roots, panic tingling through her scalp as she leapt from her bed, pacing as she did the math.

Six years. She'd been gone *six years*.

Six years Jericho had to be Heir, something she'd promised Soleil she never wanted to be. Six years…Kallias was twenty-one now. Had they already married him off to some other kingdom? After she'd *promised* him he'd never have to go. And Finn…he'd been alone. All this time, he'd been alone, no notes to read, no games to play.

Six years her parents, her *people*, had fought a war. Because of her.

Her fingers were flying before she fully decided on her path, tugging her pack out of her closet and shoving in what belongings she would need, a plan already forming brick by brick in her mind. She would find Jira in the barracks tonight—*now*. She would tell her everything, the entire truth of who she was, and she would help because she was Jira, because they'd already promised their battlemate vows to each other when they completed training, because they were family too. She would go home, and once they saw she was alive—

"Oh, Soleil," sighed a voice, and she twisted to see another face she'd forgotten—a girl donned in purple who stepped *through* the mirror on her vanity, dancing lightly from the table to the seat in front of it, hopping down with the crystalline grace of a music box ballerina. "Aren't you tired of fighting yet?"

A shard of pain stabbed into her mind, and her hand flew up to cradle her forehead.

"I know it hurts." A hint of sympathy, of apology. "I can make it stop, darling. Come here."

Soren—Soleil—oh gods, her name, she remembered her *name*—took a step back as the girl stepped forward. "I know you." Anger replaced fear, and she took a step toward the sword propped at her bedside, rage bristling down her back. "You...*you* did this. You made me forget them!"

The mirror girl's smile curled from sympathy to condescension. "It's not time for you to remember yet."

"Go to the pits," she choked. Her hands shook as she raised her sword, and she nearly cursed again at her own fear. "Don't come any closer."

The mirror girl ignored her. Kept walking as if Soleil held a toothpick and not a blade. "I'm sorry," she said, and for just a moment, it sounded true—there was a remorseful twist to the girl's mouth, but it didn't quite reach her eyes. "I really am. But for the sake of the future, you can't go home just yet, Princess."

"I won't let you take them again." A harsh sob. She coughed past it, shaking her head as that feverish haze tried to creep back in. "You can't have them."

The mirror girl stopped an inch away from Soleil's blade. Her pitying look reflected in the polished steel, but the reflection didn't quite match the face—the girl's eyes were brown, but in the reflection, they glimmered hundreds of colors, her pupils haloed in gold.

As the girl stepped forward—stepped into the blade, *through* the blade—sob after sob punched out of Soleil's chest, and she kept backing up until she collided with the wall, helpless fury banding her chest as the mirror girl came closer.

"Please." From furious denial to desperate pleas. From Nyxian warrior to lost princess. "Please don't take them."

The mirror girl slid her fingers into Soleil's hair, and no matter how she fought, she couldn't break free from her grip. Her eyes captured Soleil's attention against her will, arresting her gaze, and she couldn't look away…didn't want to anymore.

"Please." A faint whisper.

The mirror girl hesitated. Sighed. "One memory," she said. "You keep fighting off my magic…that's no easy feat. I'll reward it. Pick one thing for me to leave."

"My papa," she blurted, terrified that if she took too long, the girl would change her mind. "L-let me remember my papa."

"As you wish."

When she woke up the next morning, the fever had broken. And while she couldn't remember most of the dreams she'd had the night before, she recalled one…her sitting in her father's lap at his desk, helping him write letters, ink soaking into her braids.

She clung to it with all her might.

* * *

From then on, once a year—on her birthday, she came to realize, her real birthday—Soleil earned a memory back.

At sixteen, she chose to keep her brothers playing hide-and-seek with her at the Saltwater Festival. At seventeen, she chose the ocean. At eighteen, she tried to choose her sister, but the mirror girl refused her—said it was too close now, that one more memory might tip the scale too far. To appease her, the mirror girl offered her something else: not a memory, but a promise.

"One year more," she told her. "Just one, and then you'll go home."

* * *

She spent the night before her nineteenth birthday in a war camp near Ursa, taking her turn at watch in the forest, and only one thought weighed heavy on her mind that night:

She *hated* numb toes.

No amount of hitting her boots together or stamping her feet helped. For all she knew, her useless stubs had completely fallen off, leaving her with two toeless feet.

She said as much to Elias, who sighed so hard his breath puffed white even through the thick scarf covering the lower half of his face. "You'd know if they'd fallen off. Toes are necessary for balance."

"Do I want to know how you know that?"

"My sister lost two of hers in a forge incident. She had to relearn how to walk."

Soren snorted, tugging her own scarf up higher, resisting the urge to yank it down to wipe the stream from her nose. They'd been on the treeline at the edge of their camp for hours, taking their shift for watch while everyone else slept or sparred or ate. It was nearly dusk—Jakob and Varran should've come to relieve them by now.

But here they were, sitting with their backs against one of the rustusk trees, its broad trunk big enough for both of them to huddle there together. These particular trees were sights to behold under most conditions, some with trunks spanning wider than the average house. But tonight, Soren didn't want to see the moon-pale trees or their strange, fur-like leaves that made the forest look like the pelt of a great beast from above. With homesickness sitting at an uncomfortable angle in her stomach and her mother's farewell tears still traced through her hair, she ached for the stars.

Elias nudged her, his thick coat shedding snow with the movement. "What's bothering you?"

She narrowed her eyes at him, wishing that the bone-dry, frigid wind hadn't stung them to the point of tears. "Nothing."

His eyes crinkled at the corners. "Yeah, right. The day you can't find something to complain about is the day they bury you in a box." A pause. "Actually, no, then you'd come back to life to complain about the stuffiness of the box."

"It's my gods-damned *toes*." She stamped both feet against the snow for emphasis. "What if they're frostbitten?"

"Oh, sure, now you worry about frostbite, Miss I-Can't-Sleep-With-My-Feet-Covered."

Soren pouted. "They get sweaty."

"Under one blanket? In a tent? In the dead of winter?"

"Yes, jackass." She elbowed him hard enough that he had to wave his arms to catch his balance back, the ridiculously-puffy layers nearly tipping him over. "As if you ever sleep with less than four blankets in the tent."

"I only sleep with *three*, smartass." He stomped his foot on top of hers, which seemed pointless considering what they were arguing about. She barely felt the pressure at all. "The quilt my mother made, the quilt my *grand*mother made, and—"

"And the one I knit you for your birthday, I know." Her best work, really. The ugliest thing she'd ever seen. Elias hadn't even flinched when he opened it, the useless bastard. She'd have to work harder next year. Maybe she could knit expletives into the pattern.

Silence settled between them, the popping of firewood and the hum of hushed chatter barely reaching past the blanket of quiet at the edge of the clearing. Elias's eyes were fixed on the forest ahead; Soren's eyes were fixed on him, on his arm, still too weak to hold a sword. He could wield almost as well with his left hand as his right, but not just as well.

The cold stirrings of dread began to prick at her insides.

"Maybe you shouldn't go out tomorrow," she tried, but he shook his head.

"Where you go, I go," he said. "Wounded or not."

Damn him and his stubborn loyalty. "I'm just saying, there's commitment and then there's stupidity. Going out with a bad sword arm is asking for trouble."

"So is letting you go out alone."

She closed her eyes, then wished she hadn't. Images of Elias cut down, relieved of his guts or his head, flickered in the darkness behind her eyelids. "Elias—"

"Don't." The rawness of his voice tugged her insistence to a halt. He turned his eyes to her, midnight-dark gaze burning hotter than the fires warming their fellow soldiers. "Don't ask me to sit back while you fight. You know I can't, and you know damn well why."

The crunch of snow heralded Jakob's arrival before she could argue more, and she turned to see him swaggering over, his arm looped around Varran's shoulders, his stupid grin and Varran's flushed, flustered face telling her exactly what had kept them so long. She scowled at them, tossing snow at Jakob's leg. "You're a pain, you know."

Jakob winked at her, ruffling Varran's hair, ignoring his battlemate's affectionate protests. "We do our best. Go get some sleep, all right? I'll see you two tomorrow."

Tomorrow.

Pre-battle jitters weren't common for her, but tonight, it felt like grasshoppers had taken up residence in her throat. It didn't bode well.

Elias offered his hand, and she took it, letting him tug her to her feet. "I don't suppose you brought an extra pair of socks with you?" she asked meekly, her thoughts turning back to her frozen toes.

He put his hands on his hips and arched to crack his back, groaning. "You do this on purpose, don't you? You forget an extra pair every time."

She gritted her teeth against a guilty grin, pushing her lip out in a pout instead. "You have better socks."

"You're unbelievable."

"And you love me anyway."

His only answer was a longsuffering sigh.

That was how Soren entered her nineteenth birthday: fast asleep beside her battlemate, bundled up in his arms, his socks covering her still-functional toes and his heart thumping against her cheek.

And when she bolted awake in the middle of the night with a gasp that bordered on a cry, it was his arms that caught her, his hand that forced her to meet his gaze even as she scrambled to try and free herself from her bedroll.

"Soren?" His eyes and voice sharp with concern, he caught her again when she tried to push away, her breath coming in hysterical gasps. "*Soren*. Look at me, smartass, it's me, you're all right—"

"They're not dead," she choked, squirming free of his arms and staggering upward, cursing wildly when the bedroll caught around her ankles. She kicked free and stumbled to her pack, adrenaline striking her core over and over and over again, a flurry of blows she couldn't dodge. "They're not dead, they're not dead, I—I have to go. Elias, I have to go."

"Who's not dead? Go where? Soren, hey—*stop*." His arms caught her around her waist, pinning her arms to her sides, holding her firmly as she tried to escape. "Soren. Listen to me, smartass, *listen*. It's just a night terror. Look at me— it wasn't real. Do you hear me? Whatever you saw—"

"No, no, you're not hearing me!" Soren's throat constricted, thinning her voice to something weak and embarrassing, but she couldn't help it—couldn't think past the utter *certainty* pounding in her head, not memory but something close, a knowledge that seeped all the way to her bones. "Elias, it's my family. My family. They're not dead."

"I know." His brow furrowed over his worried eyes. "They're back home. They're safe."

"Not Enna. Not my sisters, I—my *first* family. My birth family. They're not dead." A sob escaped, cloaked in the shoddy costume of a broken laugh. "I have to go, I have to get back—"

"Elias?" Jakob's groggy voice came from outside the tent. "Soren? Everything okay?"

"Everything's fine, Jakob," Elias called, still holding her down, still keeping her from *finding them.* "She's just..."

Sympathy softened the grumpy edge to Jakob's voice. "Another night terror?"

"I think so." Elias's hand soothed over her hair, and another sob tore out of her, this time wearing a growl of frustration. "I've got her."

"All right. Call if she gets violent."

"She's always violent."

"True. Call if you can't handle her."

"I will." He wouldn't. She could hear it in his voice. A sliver of sense cut through the fog of desperation, memories of this happening before, nightmares that presented themselves to her as reality until Elias calmed her down. It was a routine he'd mastered by now, a side of her she only trusted to his hands.

But this wasn't like that. This was *real,* gods damn it, this was *true.*

"Elias," she sobbed through gritted teeth, bucking against his iron hold, "you're not *listening.*"

"I am. I am, but you're not making sense, smartass."

Vaguely, she realized she hadn't responded the right way yet—hadn't returned his insult with *jackass,* their code to signal that she was clear-headed again—and that was probably why he wouldn't let her go. But she couldn't get any word to tumble off her tongue past *"They're not dead."*

"Soren." No, no—she knew that sweet sadness borne on his breath, and she couldn't hear it. Wouldn't hear it.

"No, they're—they're looking for me. I have to go home, I have to go home and find them—"

"I hear you! I hear you, Soren. Now you need to hear me. All right?"

Relief flooded her, and she stopped fighting, easing into his embrace. He would help her. Of course he would. It was Elias. "All right."

"It's too late to go anywhere tonight."

"But—"

"If you still want to go in the morning, we will go. Do you hear me? We can go in the morning."

"You'll go with me?"

"Of course. I'll go anywhere with you. But we can't go tonight." Now that she was calm, he turned her around, brushing her hair out of her eyes and pressing a kiss to her forehead. "If you wake up in the morning and you want to go—and you can tell me *where* you need to go—we'll leave. We'll tell Jakob whatever he needs to hear, and we'll go."

She took in a deep, shuddering breath that rattled her ribs as she leaned against him, pressing her forehead against his good shoulder. "You promise?"

"I promise." His hands guided her back to their bedrolls, and the moment her feet brushed against her blankets, fatigue crashed back over her with a power that dragged her eyelids shut long before she even knelt. Elias pulled her close again, tucking the blankets around her and rubbing her back to warm her, his lips pressing against her hair again. "Get some more sleep. We'll talk in the morning."

They didn't talk in the morning. By the time she opened her eyes to dawn, whatever certainty she'd possessed the night before had fled, and all she remembered of her episode was Elias gently talking her back to sleep. And when he mentioned it to her—asking her if she could remember where she'd wanted to go so badly—she'd simply shrugged, laughed, and said, "Only the gods know."

Or at least, one did. One who'd plucked it from her head before she could follow it back to the memories she'd fought for years to regain.

* * *

She'd fought her. All these years, all this time…she'd been fighting to get back to them.

Soren crumbled to her knees in the snow, staring after herself and Elias as they packed up to move on to Ursa. Emotion tore through her body with such ferocity she couldn't name it, couldn't understand what it *was*. Rage? Grief? Elation?

Love?

Memory.

Realization struck like a sword through the gut, like a confession in a bloodsoaked temple, like coming back to life.

The two halves of her…they were no longer halves. Soleil and Soren knit together, memory and memory colliding, melding until her life stretched out before her as one unbroken thread. One she could follow from beginning to end.

"Welcome back, Soleil Marina Atlas." Jira's voice was so soft, so warm. She settled her hands on Soren's shoulders, her gaze also fixed on the parting company she was once part of. "And Soren Andromeda Nyx."

Soren had to brace herself against her knees, shivers wracking her body, shock keeping her on the ground. "Which one am I?" she rasped. "Which one do I pick?"

Jira snorted softly. "You don't have to pick. You can be both. You *are* both." She knelt before Soren, resting her hand over Soren's heart. "This is the gift Mortem gave you: wholeness. Now, when you make your choice, you *both* get to make it."

A choice. Her choice.

Between living or dying. Between fighting or losing.

But she *had* made that choice. Had made it several times, over and over again—every time Soren and Soleil came together, memory twining them into a whole, she made the same choice: she chose to fight for her family.

Even when it hurt. Even when it seemed impossible.

Even against a goddess.

They needed her. They still needed her.

All these years she'd fought to come home. To get back to them. And she hadn't yet, not really…that fight wasn't over.

She owed it to herself to finish it.

"I can't have two names forever." The only choice left to make.

Jira smirked. "True." She sat back, crossing her arms patiently. "So what will it be, Soren-Soleil-whoever-you-are?"

It should have been easy to think of herself as Soleil. That was the first name spoken over her when she was born, joyfully sobbed from her mother's mouth as she pressed her lips to her new daughter's head. It was the first name she'd learned as a toddling child, cheered by her parents and gaggle of siblings as she took her first steps into Jericho's arms. It was the one she'd worn for the first nine years of her sunkissed life, this princess of light, this Heir of saltwater. It should have slipped back on easily, like a favorite shirt, like a well-worn quilt.

But Soren was the name she'd chosen, the name Enna had offered her when she'd woken without one, the one she'd grown into rather than out of. It was the name Jira had found more nicknames for than she should have been capable of. It was the name that the crowd at her official coronation as a princess of Nyx had roared, thousands of boots stomping a rhythmic beat on the ground as they welcomed her into their hearts with open arms. It was the name her barracks leader had called when accepting her into training. It was the name Jakob shouted when he picked her to be part of his company.

It was the name Elias had muttered into her mouth while pinning her against the wall of a supply closet, the name he'd used when he swore to fight at her side the rest of her life and his, the name he'd screamed on a battlefield outside Ursa, the name he'd coughed out through blood as he asked her to marry him with his final breath.

Soren was the name that bound her to him. That bound her to Jira. That bound her to the family she'd built, the family that had raised her from lost girl to soldier and princess.

She remembered Soleil. But she *was* Soren. That name fit her better than any other, and she didn't think she could ever get used to something else.

"Both," she whispered. "Soren Marina Atlas."

"That's more Atlas than Nyx."

In spite of everything, she had to restrain herself from whacking Jira upside the head. "So am I, you hag."

Jira threw her head back and laughed, one of the full-body laughs Soren missed so desperately. She flung her arms around Jira, pulling her close, hugging her so tightly it would've stopped her breathing—if she wasn't, well, dead.

Jira hugged her back just as fiercely, burying her face against her hair. "Soren Marina Atlas," she whispered. "Good to make your acquaintance. Andromeda's an ugly name anyway."

"I hate you."

"And I you." Jira pulled back to frame her face with her hands, pressing a kiss between her brows. "You know what this means, don't you?"

Tears pricked her eyes. A knot tied in her throat. "I have to go back."

"Yes."

"You can't come with me."

"No."

A fragment of her chest caved in, and she caught her breath against it. This wasn't fair. She'd said enough goodbyes—she was *so sick* of goodbyes. "How long can I stay?"

Jira—in spite of her tough, unflinching grin—had tears welling in her eyes too. She wiped away one of Soren's with her thumb. "Not long enough."

"I'm scared." An admission she could only give to Jira. It broke into shards on her tongue.

"I know." Jira laughed shakily. "But what good is life if you're not doing things that scare you?"

"It's going to be hard, isn't it?" She didn't have to ask; she already knew. But she'd never been good with subtleties or silences. She needed to hear it.

"The hardest thing you've ever done." Jira took her hands, leaning forward, her thick brows furrowing as she gave her a fierce shake. "And you're going to survive it. Because that's what you do, Princess—no matter what, no matter when, you *survive*."

Soren flipped her hands so she was holding Jira's, bringing them close, squeezing her eyes shut as she memorized the way they felt. The way Jira's laughter always stirred hers. The way she'd never coddled Soren, had never treated her as breakable, had always believed with her entire heart that they would conquer every mountain set before them.

Knowing that faith had carried on into death—knowing that no matter what, no matter who she lost or gained, no matter how she changed, Jira *believed* in her— that meant everything.

"I don't want to say goodbye to you," she murmured, and Jira shook her head, those tears finally welling over, sparkling on her cheeks like droplets of starshine.

"Then don't. I'm not going anywhere. Together or not at all, you remember that?" Soren nodded, trying to steel her quivering chin, but another harsh sob escaped. "I've never left your side." Jira reached up to her own hair, gripping a strand Soren hadn't seen before—a braid wound with cloth. A mourning braid that matched her own. "And I never will."

"You do realize you're going to have to fight Elias for custody once we're all dead?"

Jira snorted. "Please. That boy never had a shot at beating me a day in his life."

She wasn't wrong. Elias's ass, while not half-bad to look at, was one easily kicked.

"I love you," Soren choked.

"And I love you." Jira's smile was full of pride. "Now go. I think I hear your pretty brother calling."

Soren groaned. "Gods, you're really the *worst*. Why am I crying over you?"

"Because I'm the light of your life. Now *go*." Jira's amusement tensed into something darker, and she pushed to her feet, taking several steps away—steps that built the ache in Soren's chest with every inch between her and her first battlemate. "He needs you. Can't you hear him?"

She could. Faint as birdsong on a winter wind, but she could: *Soleil. Soleil, I'm sorry.*

"One more thing," said Jira as everything began to grow dark at the edges, dimmer and dimmer, until Soren found herself squeezed in a box of blackness. "Tell my sister to cut poor Kallias some slack, will you? I've forgiven him. It's all right if she does, too."

She didn't answer—couldn't. Because the second Jira's voice faded, Finn's came back, louder but...agonized. Desperate.

Dying.

"I tried. I tried, Soleil. I'm sorry."

He needed her.

They all did.

Finn. Mama. Papa. Kallias. Jericho. Vaughn.

Enna. Yvonne. Ember. Auralee. Jakob. Varran. Raquel.

Elias.

So Soren Marina Atlas shored up her courage. Her strength. Her ferocity and her love.

And she shattered the cage of blackness with a single blow.

CHAPTER 65

FINN

S eamus, Alia, and Jakob were gone by morning.

If Finn ever saw Seamus again, he was going to kill him on sight.

He'd been woken with the news from Vash: sometime in the dead of the night, Seamus and Alia had broken Jakob out and escaped into the dark. Guards were combing the city now, but Vash's grim expression told Finn there was nothing to find.

Two more allies, gone in one fell swoop.

It was in that state that Jericho had the misfortune of finding him: sitting at the head of the siblings' dining table, sipping a mug of black coffee with a plate of untouched breakfast in front of him, scoring tally marks of every game he'd lost in the past few weeks into the table with a butterknife.

Soren finding out he'd lied about the antidote. *Scratch*. Vidia failing to catch Kallias in time. *Scratch*. Keeping Seamus under his thumb. *Scratch*. Gods knew how many of Occassio's schemes he'd fallen for while she was under the guise of Fidget. *Scratch, scratch, scratch.*

He jammed the tip of the knife into the wood, staring at it while he contemplated the one game he had left.

Revenge for Soleil's second death.

"Gods, Finn, what did the table do to you?"

The hairs on the back of his neck bristled, but he held his voice steady, eyes fixed on the wood shavings scattered across the table. "He insulted my mother and suggested some things about my heritage. I had to teach him a lesson."

"Ah." Jericho lowered herself into the chair to the left of him, leaning forward until she entered the edge of his eyeline, offering a smile he couldn't return. "Is this about Esha or Seamus?"

"Guess."

"Seamus, then."

Finn shrugged one shoulder. Part of him was perfectly content to keep his eyes glued to the table, but she'd only keep pushing, and he was still playing the role of clueless boy. He looked up at her . . .

And almost forgot to be angry.

She looked...awful.

Cheeks sunken, eyes stamped with dark moons, bottom lip chewed to the point of chapping. Her hair was stringy, braided but unwashed, strands sticking out in every direction. Even the smile she put on was wan and sickly. "He played his part well. We never would've known."

"Never," he mumbled absently, eyes roving over her in disbelief. Gods, what had happened to her? Was this guilt? Or something more godly? Was she the one who'd paid the price for Vaughn's handful of good days? "I thought Vaughn was the sick one, not you."

Jericho's brow furrowed, and she tensed, her shoulders curling inward. Defensive. Anxious. Her fists gathered handfuls of her skirt, fussing at the creases. "I'm fine. I don't know what you mean."

"You look like you used a jellyfish as a powder puff."

Jericho's lips pursed. "That's not very kind."

Finn raised one eyebrow, gesturing to himself in silent demonstration.

She smiled for real then, if ruefully, knocking her elbow into his. "Right, right. Forgot who I was talking to."

He shouldn't have been worried. He had no time to waste worrying over a sister who'd thrust a knife through the rest of their backs. But… "Jer, really," he said quietly. "Are you okay?"

One chance. If she came to him now, he'd give her one chance to repent. One chance to earn his help.

Jericho met his gaze, her lips parting, and for just a moment, he could see her deciding whether to tell him the truth. He could *see* the confession forming on the tip of her tongue, could sense the tearing apart happening inside her, the war between her vows and her desperation.

And he sensed her making the wrong decision before it had even left her lips.

"Yes," she said firmly. "I will be. Once Vaughn is well again."

Pain nibbled at his ribs, the beginnings of hurt feelings, of betrayal…of anger.

And it was anger that made the mistake for him. The anger that was sick of playing dumb, sick of acting like he'd fallen for her tricks, sick of repeating unfulfilled promises to a dead girl's journal in his room.

He was Finnick *gods-damned* Atlas. And he was sick to death of being lied to.

"Tenebrae's not too keen on keeping promises, is he?"

All the air whooshed out of the room, leaving behind a ringing silence broken only by Jericho's choked, half-formed gasp.

He raised his eyes without lifting his head. She stared at him in mute horror, and behind her eyes, he could see her scrambling. Trying first to find a proper lie, then realizing it was pointless, then changing tack to try and find the right questions to ask instead.

And there it was: that expression of dawning fear he ordinarily enjoyed so much. But on his sister, someone who should have known him well enough to learn her way around his masks anyhow, the shock in her eyes felt like an insult.

"Jericho," he said before she could find her voice again, "tell me everything right now, and maybe, *maybe* I will consider helping you get out of this mess."

She blinked at him.

Blinked again. Cocked her head at just enough of an angle that it felt wrong.

On the third blink, her eyes opened up to reveal gold irises, someone else—some*thing* else—looking out through his older sister's eyes.

"Occassio was right," said a voice like the buzzing of wasps and the crumbling of cliffs, a deep rumble that made up the bedrock beneath his sister's gentler tones. "You really are too smart for your own good, Prince Finnick."

For the very first time in Finn's life, true mortal terror thrust itself deep into his gut.

This god wasn't like Anima. Anima was a girl wearing godhood like a fancy costume, a girl easily manipulated, easily won with a false smile and a bad joke. When Tenebrae stood up from the table with Jericho's body, moving between Finn and the door with a languid sigh and a roll of his head, the very room shook.

The windows rattled in their frames. The walls groaned. Two of the table's legs splintered at their centers, putting the table on its knees with a deafening crash as Finn flung himself away, tumbling to the shaking ground while Tenebrae casually stalked toward him. Finn drew his knife as he rolled to his feet, pain barking through his still-sore chest, that visceral terror battling with his refusal to bow to this creature who'd toyed with both his sisters' hearts, who'd torn his family apart stitch by fragile stitch.

Tenebrae laughed, a mocking, vile thing that sounded nothing like Jericho at all. "A knife against the god of chaos. That's cute."

"Not the first time I've been complimented by a god." He twirled the knife, palming it carefully. "But your sister's much better at it."

"Well, it's her job."

A flutter of movement near Tenebrae's feet caught Finn's attention, and his heart dropped. A dark vine slithered across the floor like a viper on the hunt—not the usual vibrant green of Jericho's biomantic plants. It twitched and shuddered as if in the midst of death throes as it crept after Tenebrae's coaxing hand, unnaturally long thorns emerging while it grew, a sickening hook curling at the end of each.

"You should have kept your mouth shut, Prince," Tenebrae sighed.

"Or what?" At least his brazen tone hadn't died with his courage. "Your sister won't be pleased if you kill her precious host. She went through a lot of trouble to get me this far. And from what I've seen of her, she's not someone you want to cross." Complimenting Occassio nearly heaved his stomach up to his throat, but he managed it anyway.

"Hm. That first murder does do a number on you, doesn't it? Makes killing seem like the easy solution to everything." Tenebrae came closer, the grin that crept across his face twitching in time with the creeping vine, Jericho's mouth trying desperately to twist into something other than a smile. "I don't have to kill you, Prince. I just have to make sure you can't tell anyone what you know."

The vine rubbed against the toes of Finn's shoes, and he recoiled, pressing himself to the wall. Tenebrae still blocked the door—there was nowhere to go. Shouting for help was pointless; no one was going to save him from a god.

The vine curled around Finn's leg and climbed upward, thorns scratching lightly through his clothes, snagging on loose threads and drawing blood as they hooked themselves in. It took everything in him not to start hacking at it—he'd only succeed in stabbing himself.

He had to think. Had to think. *Come on, Finn, something. Anything.*

"Hard to write without your hands," Tenebrae murmured as the vine split into three, two stretching from Finn's legs to tease his wrists, one continuing to climb. "Hard to speak without your tongue."

Finn's chest tightened, his breathing coming faster and faster as that third vine caressed his chin with a lover's softness, the claw-like thorn at its tip tracing upward toward his lower lip.

Then he remembered the fiddle. The mirror.

It was his only chance. Either it worked or it didn't.

Squeezing his eyes shut, he forced himself to ignore the prodding of the thorns against his skin.

If you don't want a host who can't lie, you'll make this work, Cassi.

When he opened his eyes, he was surrounded by strings.

Shimmering threads stretched in a dazzling loom from floor to ceiling, from wall to wall, a dense weave he could barely see through.

He'd already endured this magic twice in these past couple days; had broken it once, at a cost. He had no idea if this would work. No idea what it would do to him if it did.

But when the tip of that thorn pierced his lip, he raised his hand. Flexed his fingers, strumming those spider-silk thin threads, pushing his entire will into the action: *Faster.*

And without looking to see if it had worked, he swiped his dagger, hoping with all his might that the thorns were slower than his hand.

In a blink, he severed through all three vines.

In a second blink, he was bolting for the door, unable to tell if his feet were even touching the ground.

After the third, Tenebrae *roared* in realization, in fury, a feral scream that only spurred Finn's feet faster.

He made it all the way to the ground floor of the palace before the same sensation of a thread snapping jolted him, a wave of limb-deadening fatigue flooding him with an intensity that was almost painful. He tumbled to the ground with a wheezing cough, a globule of blood plopping onto the carpet as he gasped and choked and drooled red, his lungs and throat and heart *burning*.

Like he'd run a hundred miles without stopping. Like he'd fought a week-long battle and taken more than one blade to the chest.

A red haze fell over his vision, pulsing in time with his frenzied heartbeat, that organ working desperately to keep his body from giving up beneath the weight of the magic he'd just torn from the world to wield as his own.

Through that red haze, he saw pale toes enter his vision, stopping just short of his spat-up blood. "Finn?"

Anima.

Shit.

He coughed harder, spitting more blood on the carpet before raising his head, letting a baleful glare go free. What use was there in hiding it anymore? "Goddess," he rasped, rising to his knees only to dip in the mocking semblance of a bow, complete with a flourish of his hand. "How's my little sister's corpse treating you?"

Anima's face dropped at the same time Tenebrae's voice roared from behind the closed door at the end of the hall, still a ways off but getting closer, closer— "*Ani, stop him!* He has the relic!"

He didn't. But better that they thought he did, if it bought Esha time to get it back to Lapis.

He tried to bolt past Anima, but his legs didn't have anything left to give. He barely staggered two steps before a vine—healthy and verdant this time—wrapped around his calves, pulling him back to his knees and wrenching a groan out of him as pain hurtled through his entire body.

This was it. There were no guards around, no siblings, no parents. Just him and a goddess in an empty hallway.

Kallias will fix it. It's all right. Kallias will fix it without me.

That ridiculous belief turned circles in his head as Anima dragged him around to face her, a look of utter concentration and uncertainty nearly foreign on Soleil's irreverent features, her hands shaking as she mimed pulling him back toward her, the vine following her silent command without question. His knees burned against the carpet until he knelt before her once again, staring up into his favorite sister's face.

"I tried," he told her. "I tried, Soleil. I'm sorry."

Fear flashed in Anima's eyes, and the vine tightened around him. It had wrapped itself around his entire torso by now, creeping toward his neck. "Stop talking."

He looked her directly in the eye, searching for any fleck of green, any hint of memory. "I'm sorry, Soleil." His voice quivered. There was no one left to hide it from. No one left to trick. "I broke my promise."

"I said *stop!*" Fear climbed the ranks to panic. The smell of grass and bark and the subtle rot of autumn foliage forced itself up Finn's nose.

He could only offer her one more thing. The goodbye he'd always wished he could have given her, the farewell he was never allowed to have.

He smiled at her. Not a mask. Not a trick. The smile that only belonged to them, to Finnick and Soleil Atlas, twins born a year apart, deceit and honesty, villain and hero, brother and sister. "You are my best friend." A single tear escaped, the final mark of his failure, the period at the end of his confession. "I love you."

The next cry that escaped Anima was wordless, guttural, less a shout and more a scream. Finn held his head high. Refused to bow or break. He closed his eyes, waiting patiently for the darkness behind his eyelids to deepen to something more permanent, waiting for the pain to stop…

Nothing happened.

For what felt like an eternity, Finn sat there on his knees, Tenebrae's furious shouts rattling the hall he'd abandoned, the echo of Anima's scream ringing through this corridor that would serve as his coffin.

But that vine did not tighten. Did not crush his windpipe in a godly grip. Did not grow thorns and rip out his tongue.

When he opened his eyes, he found Anima's hand hovering before his face, her hand glowing with spore-like bits of greenish energy.

Her opposite hand was wrapped around her wrist, white-knuckled, *shaking.*
Holding herself back.

When he raised his eyes to hers, everything inside him hollowed out.

One eye was still brilliant, sickening gold.

But the other…the other was green.

Familiar, sharp, sea-tinted *green.*

"Finn," gasped Soleil, her entire body trembling with the effort of holding the goddess back, her expression twisted in agony and determination, *"run."*

"Soleil," he choked, reaching for her as she forced herself back a step. The vine retracted from around his body, whipping across the floor to snap taut across the door instead, holding it shut just as someone—presumably Tenebrae—attempted to shove it open. The vine held fast, and Tenebrae's scream of rage made Finn want to crawl out of his skin. "Soleil, you—"

"*Run!*" she snarled again, tears streaming freely from her one green eye, her teeth gritted so hard he could see the muscle twitching in her jaw. And when she looked at him…

He knew.

This wasn't the sister Kallias had dragged kicking and screaming from a Nyxian battlefield. This wasn't the sister who'd only cautiously allowed them in, who'd only recovered one memory or two, who'd barely begun to settle here before she was so cruelly snatched away from them again.

He knew the girl behind that green eye. And she knew *him*.

And that made this *so much worse*.

He couldn't leave her. He had to leave her.

He was going to kill everyone who'd dared betray him in this city. Everyone who'd helped twist this moment from a choice to a necessity.

He stood on shaking feet. Took a step in the opposite direction he wanted to. "I'm coming back for you." Another promise—one he would not break. "Do you hear me? I'm coming back."

Soleil laughed. A shattered sound that made him remember what it was to be murderous. "Don't," she whispered, so softly. "Don't ever come back here."

Her body spasmed, dropping her to one knee. That green eye glinted gold, and Finn staggered backward, one hand still outstretched, tears of his own tracing hot trails down his face. "Soleil—"

"*Go!*" she roared.

And even though he hated himself for it, even though it killed him…Finn obeyed.

He fled. Ignored guard and palacefolk alike as he barreled into the foyer, pushing his trembling legs nearly to their breaking point, diving into the city like he'd seen Kallias plunge himself from the end of the pier.

But even as he ran, even as his body threatened to break beneath him, elation rose up in him; useless, but entirely, beautifully welcome.

Soleil was alive.

Soleil was *alive*.

CHAPTER 66

ANIMA

She wasn't grateful for pain anymore.

That thought pounded like a hammer across the surface of her skull, a wake-up call not half as pleasant as the birdsong she was used to. Ani groaned as the world spun back into existence, waking new pains, little agonies that burst to life in every limb. Bruises all over. Little stings that suggested cuts. An ache that patted her head apologetically to inform her she'd hit it on something.

She opened her eyes to the infirmary walls and four pairs of worried eyes: two green, one brown, one gray.

"She's awake!" called Ramses over his shoulder, relief cracking through his words so sharply that her chest twinged. It was his hand that rested on her head—his fingers were coasting gently across her hair, a tenderness that nearly brought tears to her burning eyes.

It took an alarmingly long time to find her voice. "What happened?"

"We aren't sure." Jericho. The princess was hovering over her, hands splayed horizontally above her body, green magic dancing around her fingers— Anima's magic. Jericho was healing her wounds, slowly but surely. "You had some kind of fit."

Jericho shouldn't have needed to do that. Ani's body should have healed itself already.

Welcome back, Goddess Great.

Every inch of her stiffened at the sound of Soren's voice—no longer distant and weak, no longer hidden, no longer dying. Determined. Arrogant.

Strong.

What did you do? Ani didn't voice the thought out loud.

I decided I'm not quite through with my body yet. Soren's voice dropped from smug to snarling. *And nobody hurts my family while I'm still breathing.*

All at once, the memory of what happened crashed over her: the hall. Tenebrae shouting. Finnick bent on his knees, coughing up blood, glaring up at her with eyes that weren't fooled by her familiar face. His tears, his words—*I'm sorry, Soleil, I love you*—stirring a presence within her that shook her to her bones. Reaching out to silence him, her magic following her guiding—

A hand catching her wrist.

Her own hand stopping her blow.

Ani's hand rose to her mouth now, nausea flooding her as she realized—

Soren had spoken with *her* mouth. Had used *her* magic to trap Tenebrae the next hall over.

I'm not done fighting, Soren hissed. *This is my body. My life. My family. And you will not have them.*

Perhaps seeing Ani's building panic, Jericho quickly said, "She needs rest. Let's come back later. Someone should find Finn and let him know, too."

Finn. What had happened after she blacked out? What had Brae done with him?

Reluctantly, everyone obeyed: Vaughn leaving first, casting a suspicious look over his shoulder—Ramses next, after planting a kiss on her forehead and promising to come back later with food—and Adriata last, settling her hand on Ani's shoulder in an awkward pat before going after her husband. But Jericho stayed, closing the door behind them, her shoulders rising and falling in a long breath.

When she turned around, it was Tenebrae who looked back at Ani, his golden eyes unreadable.

"What happened," he asked flatly.

Ani eased herself up, relieved to find her body was beginning to heal itself again, the pains winking out one by one. She gathered the blankets up over her chest, hugging them close, avoiding his gaze. "I don't know."

"Don't lie to me, Ani. I can't help you if you lie to me."

A shiver played with the hair at the nape of her neck, but she couldn't make herself meet his gaze. She was half-sure he'd be able to see Soren hiding behind them. "I'm not lying. I don't remember what happened."

"I broke through that door to find you convulsing on the floor and that little *bastard* already well past the palace gates."

Soren's relief came out in a rush of Ani's breath. *He made it out.*

"Ani." Tenebrae's voice, much gentler now, finally brought her eyes to his. He sat down at the edge of her bed, running a hand over her cheek, frowning as his thumb caressed a bruise that had yet to heal. "Talk to me. Is this guilt? I told you already, if you don't want to deal with the messier side of this, that's fine. I'll take care of everything."

One shoulder relaxed, Ani's fear soothed by her brother's touch. The other stayed stiff. "You mean it?"

"Of course." He kissed her forehead before standing, frowning at the door. "With both princes gone, they're going to start realizing something is off here. I wouldn't put it past Finnick to have left some kind of failsafe in place. I didn't want to do it so soon, I wanted to wait for Cassi, but it might be time to rid ourselves of the rest of these royals. We don't need the queen or king for this."

Soren caught on before Anima did.

No words this time—only stunned, deafening silence.

Then...fire.

Every vein, every organ, every facet of her caught *fire* with a ferocity that Anima had never felt before. Her jaw went stiff. Her spine snapped straight. Her entire body shifted, her entire bearing changed, her hands curled into claws and reached out, lunging—

Lunging to claw at Brae.

"Try it, you pits-damned bastard!" The voice that roared from her was *not* hers. "Try it and see what I—"

A heartbeat before her nails could rip into Brae's face, Anima gasped in a breath, snatching her control back, leashing Soren with a hard, vicious tug. Her nails stopped an inch from Brae.

Chest heaving, horror trembling through every limb, Anima pressed back against the cot's frame, clutching her hand to her chest. "I am...I don't...Brae, it's not—"

His eyes were wide. "Your host is still alive."

Ani caught her breath against a whimper. "She's—"

"Anima. Do not *lie to me*."

She lowered her head. "Yes."

"This whole time?"

"Yes."

"*Ani.*" Frustrated affection drifted through Brae's voice as he sat down again, framing her face in both hands. "Why didn't you tell me?"

Ani swallowed, trepidation tightening her throat almost beyond speech. "I don't know." She did. "I thought she would fade on her own." She hadn't.

Brae's brow furrowed. "Well, the solution is simple. Just burn her out."

Now the fear that locked their limbs belonged to both Ani and Soren. "I...I don't want to."

Brae sighed, closing his eyes and pinching the bridge of his nose, rubbing it like he had a migraine. "Anima."

"You saw what it did to Mora!"

"Mortem."

"Whatever!" She'd never understood Brae's insistence on leaving behind their old names. "You saw how broken she was. She didn't speak for *weeks*. I don't want that to happen to me!"

"What are weeks compared to eternity?"

"They're *weeks*. Weeks of suffering I don't want to go through. I can control her, all right? I can. She's barely even here."

"I want her gone, Ani."

A pause followed, a torturous silence longer than any eternity she'd lived through.

Yes. She tried to bend her tongue to the mold of that word, the thing that would buy her a pleased smile and a comforting hug from the brother who'd bothered to stay. *Yes, Brae.*

"No." The refusal was not soft as down feathers—no, it was padded in iron. Strong as a stubborn cobweb. "I won't."

For once, Soren didn't offer a smartass remark. She just lurked behind the wall between them, her tension leaking into Ani's muscles, her fingers twitching habitually toward the place she used to wear a sword.

Brae studied her for a long moment, expressionless, eyes narrowed. Finally, he stood. "Do you feel well enough to walk? You'll likely recover better in your own bed."

Relief loosened the knots in Anima's shoulders, and she nodded, carefully sliding off the cot. "I think so."

They took the walk to her room in silence, but that was fine with Anima. Silence meant no more talk of burning or hosts that wouldn't die.

Thank you.

Anima blinked, shock slowing the blood in her veins. *What?*

Thank you. Soren sounded just as surprised. *For not agreeing to do…whatever it is he wanted you to do.*

I didn't say no for your sake.

Rot take her, she wished that was true. This wasn't the first time Brae had pushed her past the limits of her comfort for the sake of their cause. But it *was* the first time she'd told him no.

Sure, Goddess Great. If she didn't know any better, she almost would've called that note in Soren's voice *affection. Either way, I'm…grateful. Ish.*

Well, you're welcome…ish.

Soren's quiet laugh had just finished echoing inside her mind when they came to a halt outside her room. Anima slipped inside with a deep breath, both of them relishing the familiar smells of sea wind and fragrant candles scattered around, a welcome reprieve from the unpleasant, sanitary smells of the infirmary.

The door clicked shut behind them, and Anima turned, another question for Brae poised on her tongue—

But he wasn't there.

"Brae?" She frowned, going to the door, turning the knob—

It jammed against her hand.

"Brae?" She rattled the knob, frustrated, but it wouldn't give. "Brae, the door locked."

"I'm sorry, Anima." But he didn't sound sorry, and the cold dismissal in his voice twisted her stomach. Soren surged to the front of the wall with such force that it sent a pulse of pain through her head. "But as long as you have her in your head, I can't trust you out here. When you're ready to get rid of her, then we'll talk."

510

Anima blinked. Tried the knob again. Began to breathe faster when it refused to give. "Brae, let me out."

No answer.

"Brae, let me *out*!"

Nothing.

She pounded on the door for what must have been hours, shouting herself hoarse, begging for someone—*anyone*—to get her out. But Brae must have done something—either something magical, or by using Jericho to give strict orders that she not be disturbed, because no one came.

No one came.

She was trapped.

That bastard, snarled Soren.

Anima couldn't even find it in her to protest. Panic was clenching down on her chest, forcing her to struggle for every breath. Her hands folded over her heart as she turned, her eyes landing on the open window.

Fresh air. She needed fresh air.

She took one step toward the window and crumbled, her knee buckling beneath her as her body fully gave in to terror, nausea rumbling deep in her stomach while she dragged herself to the window seat, forcing it open and leaning out, taking in the smell of the sea in great, gasping breaths.

She wasn't trapped. She was trapped. Brae was protecting her. Brae had trapped her.

Breathe. Soren. *Breathe, Ani. Listen to me. In, out. Control what you can.*

"What can I control?" The words barely made it out past a hysterical sob.

Breathe in for ten seconds. Hold it for ten seconds. Breathe out for ten seconds. Do that until you're calm again, and then we'll figure out the rest.

She didn't want to listen to her, this cobweb that had ruined everything. But she didn't have much of a choice. She was new to this body, and if Soren said this would work...

In for ten, hold for ten, out for ten.

She could do that.

She could do that.

And afterward, she would figure out what else she could do to fix this.

* * *

We need to get out of here.

It wasn't the first time Soren had insisted on that, and Ani guessed it wouldn't be the last.

"How?" she said, pacing the same path she'd been walking for nearly a full day.

I would like to once again suggest—

"No."

Coward.

"It is not *cowardly* to refuse to jump out a window."

You have all this magic and absolutely no *creativity. It's such a waste. If you have some planty things climb up the wall—*

"Planty things?"

Shush. I've only got half my mind to work with here.

"You only had half a mind to start with."

Soren paused, a surge of delight telling Ani she'd made a misstep. *You just said something mean!*

"It wasn't that mean."

I'm so proud.

Ani blushed, crossing her arms over her chest, wishing Soren couldn't feel the heat in her face. "Just keep going."

If you have some vines crawl up the wall, we can use them like a rope and climb down.

"And it's a fifty-foot drop if you're wrong."

Sixty-five, actually. At Ani's whimper, Soren quickly added, *But like you said, you can't die, right? Your magic won't let it happen.*

"I can still feel horrible pain! And thanks to you trying to steal your body back, my magic isn't fully settled. It might take a while to heal, and someone will probably catch us if our legs are crushed from the fall!"

I have a solution, if Her Greatness cares to hear it?

"Her Greatness will allow it."

Don't fall.

"Ugh!" Maybe burning her out *would* be worth it.

I heard that.

"You were supposed to."

But after several more moments of deliberation between them, Ani's fear finally caved into admittance: Soren's idea was the best they had. Short of breaking down the door, which would likely result in a damaged limb or two anyway, they didn't have another way out of this room; and if anyone was going to find them, to free them, they would have by now.

Brae would be furious at her for disobeying his orders, for risking her safety. But if she got that mirror back, he would forgive her. He would see she could handle this—even if she had to deal with an unwanted passenger.

"Okay," Ani relented. "But you can't fight me like you did before. If we have another fit like that, we'll never catch up to your brother."

I'm not letting you drag him back here—

"No. Not him. Just the mirror."

Soren's hesitation slipped beneath the wall between them, weakening Ani's resolve. But after a moment, the answer came: *Let's climb.*

CHAPTER 67

ELIAS

He didn't know how long he cried in Kallias's arms, how long he bled grief before the wound stanched. All he knew was that at some point he fell into a fitful sleep that lasted days, only waking in blurred spates of time before exhaustion shoved him back into darkness.

And after gods-knew how long, he finally woke in truth, finding himself tangled in his nest of blankets on the floor. His eyes were puffy but dry, stinging a bit, but still he woke feeling oddly...calm.

He'd slept dreamlessly. No nightmares.

He walked around their chamber on silent feet, half afraid any sudden movement would crack his chest open again, like he might startle his anguish awake. But nothing happened; he bathed and dressed in the company of silence, both in the room and in his mind.

By the time he'd finished the breakfast Kallias had left for him—a sandwich with bacon and egg accompanied by a note that said he and Raquel had gone to speak with Idris while he rested—he knew what he had to do next.

He went to his pack and dug around inside it, brushing past maps and supplies and scraps of aged food left over from travel rations until his fingers brushed smooth, rounded wood.

He slid his prayer beads over his head, and when the skull charm settled beside the ring and the braided cloths, his chest lifted and fell in his first sober deep breath since Soren's death.

He could never give it away or deny it—faith was more than a word to him, more than a ritual or a prayer. It was the thing that made up the core of his being, the spine that supported his soul, the ribs that guarded his heart. Faith was as inseparable from him as his blood and bone. It was the essence of all he'd ever hoped for, ever loved, ever needed.

Mortem had been right. Faith had not failed him. He had been blaming the wrong weapon.

So after making sure the door was locked, he knelt before the fireplace carved into the far wall. Only embers remained from the blaze that had warmed them the night before, but there was a pile of fresh wood in the basket nearby.

Another deep breath.

He reached out and picked up a piece of firewood, closing his eyes, calling to the fire he knew lived inside him. Something had shifted after his encounter with the phoenix; the magic didn't feel foreign anymore, something to fear or push away. It was just another part of him—another muscle to be trained, if a less familiar one.

When he opened his eyes again, flame leapt between his fingers, just the way he'd seen Havi do the first time he visited the Sugar Spinner.

A smile stretched across his face, and it didn't even hurt.

He set the log inside the fireplace, plucking up embers and arranging them to his liking, his smile spreading into a grin as giddy wonder claimed him for the first time in gods-knew how long. He pulled back his fingers, marveling as he took in the lack of pain or injury.

"Welcome back, Elias Loch." He heard the smile in Mortem's voice even before he swiveled to see it. "May I?"

He swallowed hard, turning away from the fire, never leaving his knees. He clasped his hand over his prayer beads and bowed low, his forehead nearly touching the floor. "Forgive me. The things I said to you were—"

"Perfectly natural," Mortem interrupted him. "Grief brings out the worst in us, Elias. I don't judge the whole of people by what they became at their lowest."

He didn't—couldn't—look up. "You were right about me."

"I know." No boasting; only truth. Her thumb pressed into the divot in his chin, gently tipping his face up. Her eyes, for the first time since he'd met her in that run-down tavern with whiskey on his breath and fire in her hair, were gentle. Kind. "You're not angry with me, Elias. You were never angry with *me*."

His chest shuddered, catching painfully on a sob. "It's not fair. How…how can I…?"

"Who are you angry at, Elias?"

Shame bent him before her once more, his head curling towards his knees, his entire body slowly beginning to quake. "I don't…I don't know how to say it."

"Tell me the truth," Mortem prompted. "Tell yourself."

His next words cut his mouth like broken glass. "I am so angry at her for leaving me."

And there it was. The truth of the ragged, burning hole inside his chest; the thing that had withered him into this wretched creature of guilt and rage.

He wasn't just angry at Soren; he was furious with her. Such terrible, all-consuming fury that he could hardly grieve for anger. And that made him the most ungrateful, horrid person to walk this world, because how could he deserve the life she'd given back to him when he hated her so much for trading hers in exchange?

He didn't deserve to wear her braid in his hair or her ring on his chain. He didn't deserve to have loved or been loved by her. She'd given every inch of herself for him, for *him*, and he felt nothing but *this*: a simmering in his stomach, a ravaging in his chest, a pounding fury in his head.

Slowly, two black-clad knees hit the dirt before him. A delicate hand slid over his chest.

Mortem was kneeling in front of him.

"Anger is a natural part of grief," she said quietly. "Her choices caused the pain you're suffering. When the living hurt us, we get angry. When the dead hurt us, we feel we've lost the right to that anger. But that's not true."

"She saved me. How can I—?"

"If Soren was alive, what would she say to you? If she knew you were angry, would she be hurt?"

He swallowed. "No."

"What would she say?"

A dry laugh rasped from his throat. "She loved making me angry. She'd probably laugh."

Mortem smiled, ever so faintly. "Honesty, Elias."

Again, his breath snagged painfully in his chest. "She'd make me fight it out with her, even if I didn't want to. We'd fight until we were too tired to do anything but talk. And then we would find a way to solve the problem."

"So because she's not here to defend herself..."

"There's nowhere for it to go." But it had, hadn't it? He'd spent it everywhere else: to Kallias, to Mortem, to himself when all else failed. Yet it kept coming, a fount without end.

"Have you tried talking to her?"

He blinked. "She's dead."

"So? You've been praying to her for weeks. What makes you think you can't fight with her the same way?" Mortem's eyes flickered with warmth. "You've done it with me."

He hadn't considered it that way. "You said yourself that she can't hear me."

"Maybe not. But I think you'll find the exercise helpful."

He doubted that. But he'd done enough doubting her these past weeks; he didn't think it would do to say so to her face.

Mortem sighed, resting her hand on his cheek. It was warm, calloused, comforting. It reminded him of his mother's hand, or his older sister's. "Forgive her, Elias. Forgive her for loving you too much. Forgive her for choosing you over herself."

Elias closed his eyes, dipping his head to her. And when he lifted it again, she was gone, leaving behind only the faint smell of roses and a lingering sense of comfort.

After a long, long moment, he found that feeling's name.

Peace.

CHAPTER 68

KALLIAS

I dris agreed to halt negotiations with Atlas.

They'd spent days talking in circles around each other while Elias slept off the strain of the trial and his subsequent breakdown, Star and Raquel flanking them on either side of the negotiating table while they bartered over the finer points. Raquel had proven herself surprisingly adept at formulating convincing arguments, weaving her opinions into Kallias's in a way that complemented rather than contradicted for once. Afterward, Idris had dismissed them so she could speak with her trusted few on next steps, and he and Raquel had come back to the chamber to find Elias absent. But the food they'd left this morning had been eaten, which was a relief, and nothing looked out of place in a way that made him worry.

So they'd collapsed on their respective beds, and Kallias had promptly slipped into a deeper sleep than he'd managed in some time; even nightmares of the phoenix's fire coming at him couldn't rouse him. His body had given in fully to exhaustion, and fear was going to have to wait its depths-damned turn.

Unfortunately, that message didn't manage to reach his other commitments.

"Atlas." Something hard nudged his ribs.

"Umph," was his incredibly eloquent reply, and he heard a sigh that practically had *Raquel* written on it in fine calligraphy.

"Zaccheus is at the door for you."

"Mmm."

"Are you even awake?"

He considered for a moment. "No."

She nudged him again, harder this time—was she using the pommel of her *sword?* "He says it's important."

"*Sleep* is important," he mumbled, but raised a hand before she could jab him a third time, catching what did indeed feel like a pommel. "I'm *up*, woman, gods."

Since he was holding her sword with one hand—and his eyes were still closed—he wasn't able to stop the pillow she brought down on his head. Above his cry of protest, she said, "Be up faster, then. I can't sleep with all the knocking."

"All right, all right," he relented, finally prying his heavy eyelids open through sheer force of will. He released her sword and swung himself up to a sitting position, rubbing his eyes and tossing her pillow back to her. She caught it, still scowling, but it almost seemed...softer than before. Less a weapon and more a smile. She was wearing something different than she'd gone to sleep in—maybe she'd left the room while he slept?

"Your hair looks lovely this morning," he said. He'd never seen a more impressive case of bedhead.

"Shut your mouth." But her lips twitched too as she turned away, stalking back to her bed—was he imagining the extra sway to her hips? Gods, why was he looking in the first place?

He cleared his throat and got up, snatching up a change of clothes and ducking into the bathing chamber. By the time he came back out, Raquel was asleep again, still wearing her day clothes, stretched out on her stomach with her face half-buried in her pillow. Her lips were parted slightly, so he knew she wasn't faking to get out of talking to him—she'd never let him see her so unguarded if she had the choice.

So he was comforted with the knowledge that when he saw the plate and steaming mug sitting on the end table beside his bed—a blueberry muffin and coffee heavy with cream—she wouldn't see the grin that stretched his lips nearly to the point of pain.

* * *

"We have a problem."

When do we not? Kallias thought, frowning as Zaccheus paced the floor in his living room. Ignis trotted alongside him, glued to his heels, watching him with those bright eyes that still slightly unnerved Kallias. The sound of Esmeralda's humming came from the kitchen, where she was fixing tea for all of them. "What problem? Idris agreed to halt negotiations."

"With *Atlas*, yes." Zaccheus dragged a hand through his hair and looked to Kallias, eyes stoked with fury. "I just spoke with Safi. She says her mother came home talking about an alliance being offered to *Nyx* instead."

Kallias blinked. His breakfast did a nauseating flip in his stomach, and he braced himself against the arms of his chair. "What?"

"She hasn't let go of war. She merely shifted her intentions—to the *losing* side." Zaccheus shook his head, a wild edge to his eyes, but his voice was calm as he stalked to his fireplace, leaning one elbow against the mantle and staring into the flames. He ran a hand over his bearded chin. "We made it worse, Kallias."

"I…I could talk to her again." Thoughts whirled through his mind in a waterspout, and he rubbed a hand down his own beard. "Maybe we weren't clear enough. I can—"

"No." Zaccheus shook his head, the fire expanding and contracting with his inhale and exhale. "If she's this set on war, nothing will sway her. It's the emperor all over again. This only stops if someone else sits on her throne."

The frantic thoughts stilled in Kallias's mind.

"Zaccheus," he said slowly, "that's treason."

Zaccheus glanced at him out of the corner of his eye. "Is it treason to protect one's kingdom at all cost?"

Soft. Desperate. A hint of the ruthlessness he'd seen before in Zaccheus, but never truly considered something to worry about.

Kallias swallowed. "I cannot be party to…if this is where your thoughts lead, I can't…I should go."

Zaccheus blinked, and his face shifted in an instant to apology. "Oh, gods, no, I—I'm sorry. I'm not serious, Kallias, gods—I would never—I'm just thinking out loud. I hear how it sounded, but…I'm sorry. Don't go. Mal's been asking when

I was going to bring you back to visit. I didn't mean to imply such sinister things, I'm just..." He raised a hand, then dropped it in a helpless shrug. "I don't know what to do."

There wasn't much to be done, really. Zaccheus was right; he'd seen the difficulty of changing Idris's mind. "We'll think of something. My companions and I can discuss this as well—they've lived through what you're trying to avoid." He tried not to wince at the memory of Elias bound in chains in their flooding dungeon. "They'll help. We all will."

"Thank you." Zaccheus nodded, finally straightening. "I'll call a meeting tonight or tomorrow, I think. See if anyone else has ideas short of outright protests. Though, if the soldiers refused to fight—"

"Zac!" Esmeralda called from the kitchen, cutting him off. "Come here and help me carry these! I only have two hands, you know."

"You could always have Safi build you a third," Kallias called as Zaccheus left the room. He had no doubt that woman could do it.

"That's not an awful idea," Esmeralda mused as she came into the room, carrying two cups. Zaccheus followed with a third, handing it to Kallias before taking one from his wife, planting a kiss on her cheek and nuzzling his nose against her temple affectionately. Esmeralda grinned as she sat down on the couch opposite Kallias's chair, Ignis curling up at her feet. "I'm going to need it once this one comes along."

Kallias frowned, sipping his tea as he tried to puzzle out that remark—he took in Esmeralda's now-empty hand, which had fallen to rest on her stomach, and Zaccheus's softened smile. He smacked his forehead. "Oh, gods, I'm so dense. Congratulations! That's wonderful news."

"It would be, if not for all...this." Zaccheus swallowed and pulled Esmeralda closer. Suddenly Kallias understood the dark shadows under the man's eyes, the pallor to his skin, the flayed skin around his nails that looked like he'd been picking at it.

The sight tickled at his memory, pulling at loose threads, trying to tug a conclusion free. But no matter how he pulled, he couldn't seem to follow it to its end.

"We'll figure it out," Kallias promised, purpose seizing his heart in a clenched fist. "I promise you that."

They talked for an hour or so after, every worried look from Zaccheus and flash of fear in Esmeralda's eyes tightening that fist around his heart, squeezing until he could barely breathe for fervor. By the time he bade them goodbye and walked out, heading back toward their chamber, every thought felt muddled with heat, emotion crashing through him in vivid colors, clearer and better understood than any he'd ever felt.

So he was no longer a prince. That was fine. He could still help—he could still do good for people who could not do it themselves.

He could have a new life; a different one he'd never even allowed himself to imagine, one where he could have anything he wanted. Everything he wanted.

And there were so, so many things left to want.

CHAPTER 69

ELIAS

The bell on Havi's door rang out cheerfully as Elias pushed his way inside, a disjointed addition to the melody Havi himself was singing, and for the first time, he didn't flinch at the lyrics. There were a couple scattered customers, but most had taken up the outdoor seating today—likely to watch the preparation being done in the center of the common area. People were milling about everywhere, preparing for the feast to be held that night.

The feast. His feast. They'd waited to celebrate his success in the trials until he was awake. He was grateful for all this kingdom had done for him, but *gods* was he tired of being the center of attention.

"There you are, cousin!" Havi's grin, as always, was brighter than the white-gold flames that lit his shop. But there was a bend to his brow that spelled worry. "You slept a long time."

"I think I needed it."

"You're feeling better now?"

Elias nodded, glad for the ability to offer him a true answer for once. "Much."

"I'm glad. No nightmares?"

"None."

Havi nodded, still smiling, but his eyes took on the thoughtful look Elias knew preceded an invitation to the kitchen to talk. But before his cousin could say it, he interrupted: "I was hoping I could visit for a minute?"

"You can visit for even longer than that, if you like." Havi's eyes lit up as he stood, gesturing toward the kitchen. "Come on. I've got some bread baking."

As he slipped behind the counter after Havi, Cherry unwound from her bed and padded after them, her scarlet scales glimmering as she coiled herself around Elias's legs, purring and chirruping her hellos. Elias bent to scratch her behind her ear as he carefully stepped around her, his legs used to making room for pets; the Loch family cat, Scythe, was just as clingy to him when he was home. Evanna claimed the cat really loved her best, but Elias knew better. Scythe was *his*.

"So, what do you need?" Havi asked as he wandered to the oven and pulled out the pan, setting it on the counter in front of him. Cherry flapped her wings and propelled herself straight into the oven, curling up with her tail tucked over her nose, beating her wings once more to flare the embers before falling back to sleep.

Cautiously, Elias reached out and grabbed the bread pan bare-handed. He could feel the immense heat of it, could tell it should be blistering his skin, but no pain came.

He wasn't sure he'd ever get used to that.

"A couple things," he admitted, watching Havi slice up the loaf of molasses bread, taking the offered slice. "I'm nervous about the events of today. I was hoping you'd have some insight."

"I'm afraid I don't know many details. I do know that part of it is forging your own Artemisian weapon—with help, this time, if you want it," Havi added with a chuckle at Elias's groan of dread. "Safi's already offered up her forge and her assistance. And I believe you'll be sent to complete your tattoos—with your input on design, of course. Beyond that...I don't know."

Those two things, at least, sounded like blessedly private events. "One more question?"

"No need to limit yourself. I'll answer anything I can."

"How much longer until you'll be able to afford the ring you want for Ember?"

Havi's rapid blinking was the only sign of his surprise. "Well...hang on." He went to his desk in the corner of the kitchen, moving the portrait of Ember hanging on the wall to reveal a small alcove behind it. He dug inside for a moment before pulling out a jar full of coin, frowning at it like it was speaking to him before he finally said: "A few more months, I think. Custom pieces are more expensive, so I—"

By the time Havi turned around, Elias was already standing behind him, holding out his open palm. In the very center sat the ring—Soren's ring—free of its chain now, polished and carefully cleaned of the grime and blood that had built up on it over these past few weeks.

It was like holding his still-beating heart in his hand, and it hurt just as desperately as he'd guessed it would. But it was still the right thing, the best choice he could make for himself and for her—to honor what she was to him while also thanking Havi for all he'd done. "I've carried this ring with me for months now. Longer, honestly. It...it's the first thing that bound my battlemate and I together."

He told Havi the story of the first time he met Soren; of falling in love with her smile and falling in hate with her attitude, of how he'd kept that ring as his own for years; never wearing it, only holding it. How shortly before he'd been injured by an Atlas Viper, he'd turned it over to Ember for resizing and restoring, entertaining exhilarating and terrifying notions of getting down on one knee and laying his last bit of pride at Soren's feet. Of asking her to spend the rest of her life driving him absolutely mad—though she would have done that anyway. Of asking her to drive him mad as his wife, not just his battlemate, not just his best friend.

And he told Havi how those dreams were stolen with the swipe of a Viper's blade. How by the time Ember gave the ring back, he couldn't bring himself to ask Soren to give a dying man a set of vows that belonged to the living. How he couldn't take anything more from her than what he would already take with him when he died. And by the time he finished the story, forcing the ending out in whispers, tears were carving new paths down his cheeks.

I was going to ask you to marry me.

I would have said yes.

"I know who Soren was," he rasped, "and I think if she couldn't wear this, she would want me to make sure it went to someone deserving. She loved her sisters with her whole heart, and I know...I know it would make her happy to see Ember happy. And I know she would have loved you. I want you to have it. Take it, do what you have to with it, and marry Ember. Don't wait."

I was going to...

"Really," Elias whispered, his throat tightening, regret closing its grip around his throat. "Don't wait. If you truly want to prove your love for her, then sacrifice your pride. Sacrifice your idea of what love should look like. Mortem may be merciful, but death is not. It won't wait for you to be ready. You have to beat it to the punch."

For a long moment, Havi only stared at him, his eyes flickering through a hundred emotions. His eyes lowered to the ring, and Elias's stomach punched up into his throat.

Could he really let it go?

Havi reached out, and Elias's fingers ached to close, but he held firm. Soren would want this—and in truth, he did too. He owed Havi a debt he wasn't sure he could pay back any other way; and Ember too, for telling him to go see the baker in the first place. Havi was in large part responsible for him making it through these past few weeks.

Havi reached out, opened his hand...

And closed Elias's fingers over the ring.

"I hear you," Havi said softly, shaking his fist a bit, "and I agree. But that ring...that belongs to you and yours. I wouldn't feel right taking it."

Elias swallowed. "I have no use for it."

"Maybe not." Havi met his gaze with that same knowing look that always preceded some piece of wisdom that would sock Elias in the gut. "But something tells me...call it an instinct...that Mortem's not quite through with her ten thousand tasks on your behalf. Hold on to it. I don't think you'll regret it."

Elias hesitated, looking down at his hand, now covered with Havi's.

"Besides," Havi added, "if Ember worked on this piece, she'll know where it came from, and I don't know if she'd ever feel it was truly hers. And, honestly— don't tell her I told you this—but she's pickier than you think. She wouldn't like it." He cracked a smile. "I'm leaning towards a design with rubies. She likes red."

The laugh that came out of Elias was small, but it was real, and it surprised him so much he almost forgot to answer. He swallowed again, nodding, and tucked the ring back in his pocket. "If you're sure."

"I'm rarely not."

Elias looked up at Havi again, studying his face carefully. "What did that letter from Ember really say?"

Havi smiled knowingly. He shrugged, crossing his arms over his broad chest, baring those rose tattoos that climbed from his wrists upward. "Now, that belongs to me and mine."

Elias sighed, shaking his head. "Fine. Keep your secrets."

"I will, thank you." Chuckling, Havi offered his hand again, and Elias clasped it. Havi pulled him in for a hug, clapping him on the back, and he returned it, surprised by how easy it felt. How comforting. "You're going to be all right, cousin," Havi said into his ear. "I promise."

And for the first time since he'd seen the gold in Soren's eyes…Elias thought he just might believe that.

* * *

His second attempt at forging with Artemisian steel went much better than the first.

When he told Safi what he wanted, her eyes lit with the fire of accepted challenge, the crack of her knuckles making him wince a bit. He wasn't sure he'd ever shake the memory of his neck breaking, or the *sound* of it, but…the burden of that memory was a bit lighter now than it used to be.

Handing over his daggers—his last gift from Soren—was almost harder than trying to give the ring to Havi. But Safi took them with such gentleness and respect that the ache in his heart eased enough to let them go. She studied them carefully, worrying her lip with her teeth. Then: "Yep, these will work fine. Get your stuff on. We've got work to do."

And work they did. Safi's guidance showed him what was missing from his first trial—he'd handled the steel with such hesitation that he'd overthought every stage of its forging, ignoring instinct in favor of caution. Safi forged with utter confidence, not a chip of uncertainty to be found, making decisions in the snap of a finger where Elias would have agonized for a few seconds too long. But after hours of working alongside his cousin, melting down his old blades and reworking them, he found himself catching on to that boldness…and before long, he was leading the charge, Safi shifting back to give him room to work, easily changing from leader to assistant without a single hiccup in their rhythm.

And at the end of it all, he lifted the finished products, turning to find Safi grinning from ear to ear, pride threatening to stretch her face beyond its limits.

"They're perfect," she declared.

And they were. Elias held his new weapons up, admiring the way the forge-fire lit up their contours: twin obsidian scythe-like blades, scaled down to be handheld weapons rather than perched on the end of a staff, the curve of the blades deeper than traditional scythes. The handles were what Safi claimed to be carved dragon bone, supposedly fireproof, which she assured him was going to be necessary.

"Try it," she urged when he gave her a doubtful look. "It's what Artemisian steel is built for. Why do you think it's so hard to melt down?"

Elias hesitated a moment longer—if this ruined the steel, he wasn't sure he had it in him to forge yet again—but he finally called to the heat that lived in his chest now, the ever-burning flame that had scorched away the beast when he faced down the phoenix.

That heat flared, tunneling through his veins until fire burst to life in his palms, and he sent it up the blades, grinning as the fire coated them without biting down, the metal glowing without softening.

Safi looked utterly giddy. "My best work, easily." Elias raised one eyebrow, and she hastily amended, "*Our* best work. But mostly mine. Like, eighty-five percent mine, and then you—"

Elias banished the fire with a quick thrust of his arms, sheathing the scythes across his back before bending and hugging Safi with all his might.

She froze beneath his touch for a moment before relaxing, throwing her arms around him and hugging back, so tightly he thought a rib might crack. But he didn't care.

"Thank you," he croaked. "For everything. For making me laugh when I didn't think I could do that anymore. For taking care of Kallias and Raquel. Just...thank you for everything."

"Well, someone had to make sure Kallias's sword stayed in its sheath." Elias wrinkled his nose, and Safi smirked before adding, "But seriously, Elias, they're either going to kill each other or kiss each other, and I honestly don't know which."

"Both, maybe," Elias muttered.

"Probably both."

He pulled back, keeping one hand on her shoulder. "Is there anything I can do to repay my favorite cousin?"

Safi laughed, shoving his palm off and untying her knot of braids, letting them fall across her shoulders. "You can tell everyone you come across about the lady who helped forge your blades and how she's talented beyond measure, and which crest they should look for when purchasing Artem-forged weapons. I make royalties on every piece sold, you know."

"I'll spread the word far and wide."

"You'd better. Now get going. You're going to be late for your tattoo appointment." Safi shoved him toward the door. "Also, you're sitting with us at dinner tonight. You and your friends."

He cocked one eyebrow. "Don't you mean, *Elias, would you and your friends care to join us at dinner tonight?*"

Safi snorted. "Have you met me?"

He smiled. "We'll be there."

* * *

The tattoos took longer than his scythes.

Raquel came and sat with him—when he asked where Kallias was, she shrugged and simply said he'd gone to talk to one of Artem's captains he'd apparently befriended.

He should have sent her to find Kallias and make sure he wasn't getting into any trouble. But she'd brought food and water with her, and her steady presence was comforting, and Kallias could handle himself.

He didn't want to be alone for this, at least not to start. If there was one thing he'd learned over this ordeal, he didn't do well with *alone*.

He positioned himself as comfortably as he could in the chair, slinging off his shirt to reveal his back and shoulders to the tattooist, shivering lightly as cool air coasted over his bare skin; the tattooist worked in one of the cave-shops further from the heart of the mountain, so the ever-present heat didn't quite find its way this deep. But that was all right. Cold was familiar; cold was home.

The tattooist herself, a woman by the name of Kodi, looked around Evanna's age; her dark scarlet hair was tinted blue at the roots, and her skin the same cool-brown color as the mountain stone outside this city. Her right arm ended with a ring-decorated hand, each of her fingers sporting glimmering gold and silver jewelry; the left arm ended in a shining steel prosthetic limb, a piece that seemed to be a meld of magic and metal like Safi's automaton. While he watched, she took off its current attachment—a simple hook—and replaced it with what he recognized as a tattooing needle. It even had a vial of ink attached to the underside.

"That," he said, "is the most badass thing I've ever seen."

Kodi smirked. "Isn't it, though? Hold still."

The pain of the needle was, oddly, another comfort—this too was a reminder of home, of his first session beneath a tattooist's hands, receiving marks that were remnants of an ancient magic older than the gods known to so very few—magic that lay in the power of certain words inked in an old language, runes that allowed him to resist the effects of more sinister magics. With them, he could see through illusions and resist magic that affected memory, mind-magics that very few Occassio followers were blessed with.

He could have chosen different runes. Could have chosen to be given symbols that would prevent his body being puppeted by necromancers. But he'd thought them extinct, or at least near it; he'd been far more afraid of Occassio and the things the Trickster Goddess could do, knowing her followers were scattered through all kingdoms.

He'd given a similar rune to Kallias, cutting it carefully into his skin for lack of better tools and time so he could see through at least minor illusions—just enough that he could see the truth of Anima in Soren. It wouldn't work against anything more powerful, but he'd been rushed, and the most important thing was that Kallias believed him.

Finn had refused the same symbol. He'd claimed he'd seen the eyes just fine without it, and arguing with Finnick Atlas was a task well beyond him. What the tricky Second Prince risked was entirely on his own shoulders.

Hours trickled by, Raquel leaving after she was sure he was well-situated, and the pain of the needle faded to the back of his mind as he lost himself to memory…and to wondering what came next.

They'd done what they came for. They'd stopped Artem from joining hands with Atlas, an alliance that might have obliterated Nyx in a few quick blows. He'd made it through the trials. But they hadn't thought much out past that; stopping this alliance had been a finger pressed to a stab wound, only adequate enough to slow the bleeding, not stop it.

They weren't done yet. But he had no idea what the next step was.

Kodi finished his back and shoulders before tapping him to turn over, allowing her to reach his arms. While she busied herself with that, his mind turned to something else—something that had been formulating in his mind for a while.

And as she finished his arms and moved aside to let him out of the chair, he croaked, "May I request one last thing?"

Her eyes softened as he explained his hope; the eyes of someone who understood the intent behind it. She gave a firm nod before turning to refill her ink, and Elias leaned back, closing his eyes once more as her needle found its way above his heart.

When it was done, Kodi guided him to the mirrors in the corner of the room, three of them arranged at different angles so he could see every side of himself.

And what he saw...

Across his back and shoulders, flaming feathers extended in the shape of wings, the dark ink blending flawlessly with the runes and geometric shapes already inked into his skin. Down his arms were more flames, layers of fire that climbed from wrists to shoulders and across his chest and collarbones, lapping at the hollow of his throat. His venom scar was entirely hidden, the thorny knots of tissue devoured by fire. And over his heart...

A simple braided circle stamped over his heart like a shield, like an oath branded in blood.

He rested his palm over his heart, closing his eyes, the heat swimming in them threatening to become new tears.

"Thank you," he rasped.

Kodi shook her head. "It's my pleasure."

Elias turned to look at himself once more, gazing at that braided circle. The burning pain ingrained in his skin melded with the heat of his magic beneath, pulsing steadily with every beat of his heart—a heart that wasn't quite whole, and might never be, but...this marking was a patch to a hole he hadn't known how to close before. A mourning braid no one could cut from him.

He may have been the fire, but Soren was the flint and steel, the thing that brought him to life. This was for her as much as himself.

He had no idea what came next. But wherever he went, he carried her with him, and that was enough.

CHAPTER 70

KALLIAS

Raquel was awake when he shoved open the door, but she still jumped as he lurched inside, hurriedly shutting the door behind him. Giddy, near-feverish energy pulsed through every limb, and he could have run a hundred miles. Could have danced at a hundred balls.

"Atlas? What's wrong?" She stood with slow, careful movements, and her caution irritated him. Who had the time to be cautious, to be careful? He was through being careful. Through being *afraid*.

He was sick to death of terror. He wanted to make fearless mistakes.

"I like you," he declared, and the change in her was immediate; the tension in her body loosened as her scowl deepened, her arms crossing over her chest, which was honestly terrible for the sake of his focus, drawing his eyes where they didn't need to be.

"You're drunk," she accused.

"I haven't touched a drink since I left home." And every torturous day might have been worth it to make this declaration cleanly. "I mean it. I like you. Even though you yell at me—gods, even *when* you yell at me. Maybe *because* you do, I don't know…there's something about you when you're angry. I never understood that, people telling other people that they look good angry. Nobody looks good angry, but you do. It's like watching a lightning storm tear through a town." A laugh spun wildly from his loose tongue; there was no biting it back. He didn't want to. He was tired of tasting his own blood every time he had a truth to tell. "You drive me absolutely *mad*, Angelov, do you know that? You make me so angry I could scream, and you want me dead, and that's ridiculous, isn't it? To like someone who wants me dead?"

She stepped toward him with her arms out, and Kallias took it as a good sign. His hand hooked around her waist and pulled her close, his grin an inch from her scowl, and her breath hitched at the same time his body did, a jerk toward falling that he quickly righted. "Care for a dance?"

"Atlas, stop." She pushed his hand off with uncharacteristic gentleness—a gesture he didn't fight, though he did frown in disappointment. He took a step back to give her space, all that heat in his chest rushing up to his head, dizzying him. Robbing him of that reckless abandon that had dulled his senses with warmth. "You're drunk. Shut up and go lie down. Sleep it off."

His frown deepened. "Raquel, I told you, I haven't had a drop."

She snorted. "I'm not a fool, Atlas. You can't…" She broke off, frowning, and he tried to make sense of the look she was giving him. Everything was starting to blur unpleasantly around the edges, a familiar sensation without the familiar cause.

He hadn't lied. He wasn't drunk. But his body sank into it with the same ease, embraced it like a man dying of thirst wandering into a rainstorm by chance.

Raquel's hand suddenly flew to his face, and he flinched a bit, expecting a slap; but instead she pressed her fingers into the crook of his jaw, raking her eyes down his form, taking in the state of him: the smile he could feel starting to contort into a grimace. The unsteadiness of his limbs. The ruddy, feverish tint to his cheeks.

She swore so loudly he jumped. "Your pulse is weak. Where did you just come from? Who were you with?"

Kallias blinked hard, heat flooding everywhere now—that fist around his heart had yet to release him. Its grip had only tightened since he'd left Zaccheus's house, and it was starting to pinch. He reached up to rub at the knot. "My chest...hurts," he muttered, distracted.

"Kallias!" Her hand moved from his forehead to his cheek, the other coming up to join it, shaking him until his eyes found hers. In the torchlight, he could see every fleck of brown buried in the darkness of her gaze. "This is important. You need to tell me where you were. Was this Zaccheus? Were you with anyone else?"

His lips were sluggish, heavy. "You're beautiful."

"*Kallias*," she said again, sharper—not angry. He thought it might be fear.

But he didn't have the chance to find out before the blackness in her eyes flooded outward, claiming every sense until he was consumed by it.

CHAPTER 71

ELIAS

He only made it halfway back to their chamber when Idris summoned him to the chapel.

She didn't stand at the altar today; instead, she sat in one of the pews at the front, eyes on the eternal flame burning in the brazier, twiddling something between her tattooed hands. Without turning to look at him, she gestured with her head for him to join her. "Safi says your forging went well."

"Better than the first time, certainly." He sat beside the Empress, following the direction of her gaze. The flames in the brazier were lower today, colder, burning more red than gold. "You look troubled."

"A ruler is always troubled." Idris turned to look at him, smiling as her eyes fell on the feather tattoos peeking out from beneath his shirt. "I see your encounter with Sempir was impactful."

"Sempir?"

"Our best-kept secret. My phoenix." The fondness in Idris's voice—and the ease of her smile—caught him off guard. "He's bonded with every ruler who's ever sat on Artem's throne."

"Your people know this?"

"My people believe he lives somewhere on the mountain, the last of his kind left behind by Mortem to protect us. And when Mortem must test the hearts of those who serve her, she sends him where he's needed. They don't know of his bond with me." Idris looked at him. "But you didn't come here to ask about me."

Elias shrugged. "I came because you summoned me."

"Hmm." Idris looked down at her clasped hands, and Elias followed her gaze once more. Cradled in her hands was a black feather—but when she held it up to the firelight, that color seemed to shiver, undulating into waves of scarlet and gold and cerulean. "Have you ever been told of the Divine Relics, Priest Loch?"

"I have." A mirror with no reflection that once belonged to Occassio; an ice shard that wouldn't melt even beneath the harshest sun, belonging to Tempest; a bloom that had been crafted from a mystical tree deep in the heart of Arborius, belonging to Anima; a music box that contained a song of chaos, belonging to Tenebrae. And...

"My family has protected Mortem's relic for centuries...since it was gifted to my ancestor, the first to sit on Artem's throne after Mortem ascended to goddesshood." Idris held the feather out to him. "A feather plucked from Sempir's first form."

Awe dried his throat to dust, and he moved from the pew to drop to one knee, gazing at it in wonder. This was more than powerful, more than magic. What Idris held in front of him was holy, and his hands shook at its nearness.

"You know of Mortem's magics, I presume?"

He swallowed past the lump in his throat. "Pyromancy. Sanguimancy. And..."

"Mortemancy," Idris finished for him, as if sensing that he'd run out of voice. "Power over death itself."

Elias looked up at her, caution dulling the yearning ache in his chest, curling his fingers back from their longing reach. "Why are you sharing this with me?"

"Mortem has chosen you as her cleric, years after her last, just as you bring news of her siblings snaring hosts for the first time in decades, if not centuries. They will be after their own relics, of that I'm certain. You will need this as you move forward in your task."

"And what task is that?"

"To stop them," Idris said, as if he was testing her patience. "Why else would Mortem have brought you here? Why push you down a path you were so unwilling to follow? You have a purpose, Elias Loch—she does not choose her champions idly. And I fully believe you have more yet to do."

"You would trust me with a precious, ancient relic...based on what? A hunch?"

Idris's smile cooled, but her eyes gleamed. "Call it a leap of faith."

A leap...more like a plunge. This feather was imbued with Mortem's goddesshood. Whomever carried it would have to be trusted beyond measure.

"Tales of Tenebrae are told more freely in the Sanctaviv temple," Idris added, a frown carving notches of unease into her imposing features. "Tales of selfishness and foolhardy bargains and recklessness beyond measure. You must see his plans foiled at any cost. He cares not for the fate of those he deems lesser; only for his siblings, and them only barely. Chaos serves no master."

"And how am I expected to stand against a god?"

"This will be a start." Idris held the feather out once more, the bristles tickling against his knuckles, slashes of heat branding wherever they touched. "This feather grants its bearer the three magics of Mortem. If you wear this, you will be known to all as one who carries the full power of Mortem's blessing...her chosen cleric. The Phoenix Priest."

Another breath of hesitation; one last heartbeat tainted by fear.

There would be a cost to wield such magic. He knew that without being told. But to be entrusted with this...it was a privilege as much as a burden. One he would not refuse to carry.

Elias bowed his head and took the feather.

The moment his hand closed around it, his heart surged with a blazing gasp of power, heat flooding from his fingertips to his chest to his gut, spreading until his entire body sang with holy flame; magic that danced in the gaps between bone and vein, muscle and flesh, spirit and soul. The heady thrill that brought him to both knees was like nothing he'd ever known, and when he looked down, he found the lines of his tattoos flooding with molten light, a glow of gold and crimson that tiptoed up every inch of ink until his very skin shone with rivers of pyromantic power.

He raised his eyes to find Idris already watching him, the oddest mix of pride and sorrow in her eyes, like a woman watching an innocent man walking to the gallows with his head held high.

"Elias Loch," she said softly, "the Phoenix Priest. You have accepted the blessing of Death herself. Mortem keep you…Mortem save you."

* * *

As he walked back to their chamber, his tattoos faded, the feather now attached to the chain he wore…Elias prayed.

"Hey, smartass."

One last heretical prayer. One more, and then he would lay her to rest.

Rest—he almost laughed at that thought. Soren had never been the sort of person who worried about *rest,* unless he tried to rouse her anytime before dawn. She'd never lacked for energy; it had always been her running ahead and him following behind. The idea of laying her to rest was nearly as foreign as the idea of walking through a future without her leading him by the hand.

Since the day he and Kallias had left Atlas, he had often been accosted by the same thought, over and over and over—*I cannot live without her. I cannot live in a world where Soren does not.*

That had not changed. The man he was could not breathe past her absence; the man he was could not take a step without her leading him through it, without her dimpled smile and freckled crooked nose and her ugly cackling laughter goading him on.

But then his mother's words floated back to him on the winds of memory— what she'd told him after Kaia's death, when he'd sobbed through gut-wrenching tears that he could not go on without his battlemate.

We live and die a hundred times in our lives, she'd said. *If there was a part of you that couldn't live without Kaia, that's fine. Let him die. Rise again as someone new.*

The man he was could not live on past Soren, because she had formed him, was such a crucial part of him that his lungs collapsed without her horrid jokes making him laugh. His fingers broke without her grip twining between them. His sleep was plagued with nightmares fueled by the absence of her warmth wrapped around him, the cinnamon-and-peach smell of her faded from all but one of his remaining shirts, one he had yet to wear again for fear of erasing the last trace of her from his life.

But that man had been consumed in phoenix fire. The man who'd risen from the ashes was different; he still longed for her, still grieved her, still refused to wear the shirt that bore her smell. But he also chose his own place. He walked his own path. And wherever it led, he would carry her with him; her laughter, her love. The memory of her would become a fuel rather than a weapon held against him.

She was the strength in his bones and the fire in his heart. She was the flint and steel to his flame. She was the smartass to his jackass. And he would not rest until he ensured her sacrifice had not been wasted on him.

So he gripped her ring in his hand. Pressed his lips to it and closed his eyes, letting his mind roam back over all that had happened between their first meeting and now; letting himself feel the love that had built and built with every laugh and joke, with every bowl of cookie dough consumed and every sparring session lost, with every pair of socks stolen and every shirt borrowed.

"There's this little cottage just outside Andromeda," he whispered. "It's got this gorgeous stone on the outside, and the door is orange—can you believe it? I've never seen anyone paint their door orange before, but they did…that burnt sort of orange you like to wear. It's got a lake outside that freezes in the winter, the kind you can skate on, and there's a barn in the back I could easily build into a forge…before the Viper bite, I was talking to the owner about buying it. I know I should've asked you first, I should've waited on the ring, but…it was perfect, Soren. It was perfect for us. I wanted…I wanted it to be ours."

He barely managed to get those words out before grief wrapped its hand around his throat and tried to choke his breath, to stop him from getting out his final confessions. But he pulled himself free from its iron grip, breathing in and out until he could speak again, until his voice found its strength past the pain.

"You are my life's only love," he whispered into the ring. "I miss you every second. And I meant the vows I swore to you…together or not at all. But the people who took you from me are still out there, and I can't…I can't stop until they're gone. I *will not stop* until they pay for it. You have my new oath, and any oath I swear after: together when the fight is won. Until then…wait for me, smartass, all right? Wait for me. I'm coming. Just…wait for me."

There was no response. There never was. But Mortem was right—he felt a bit better talking to her anyway.

So he gave that ring one last kiss. Brushed his fingers against the feather, reminding himself of the path he had yet to walk.

Elias Loch, the Phoenix Priest.

He walked into their borrowed chamber, smile ready, finally prepared to ask after their next mission—

And what he saw stopped his heart dead in his chest.

Raquel was on her knees beside Kallias's limp body, her hair tied in a messy bundle of curls behind her as if she'd hastily bound it to get it out of her eyes. Her navy sleeves were rolled up past her elbows, her eyes harsh with the focus of a woman fighting a battle, shoving the heels of her palms into Kallias's chest over and over again, a rhythmic series of blows meant to save rather than kill. Kallias himself was flushed, bursts of feverish red blotching his bearded cheeks, and his chest...

Whenever Raquel took a pause between thrusts to shove her own mouth against Kallias's, her chest heaving as she forced air into his lungs, Kallias's chest did not rise.

He wasn't breathing.

No.

It was not a word, not a feeling. It was a demand. It was an *order*, and it came again as he rushed to Kallias's side, falling to his knees and fumbling against his neck, searching for his pulse.

No. No. No.

There. There was a pulse, but it was so weak, fading fast, fleeing from Elias's fingers like it was afraid to be caught.

"I don't know what happened," Raquel snarled as she pulled back once more, her hands forcing Kallias's heart to beat. "He showed up rambling, delirious, and seconds later he collapsed. I think someone poisoned him."

No.

"Kallias," he said, his voice less plea and more growl. "Open your eyes."

Nothing. Not even a flutter.

"Open your eyes, Kal."

Nothing.

"Move." Elias tried to push Raquel, but she pushed back, eyes fixed on Kallias's face, a wet sheen to them that belied her composed features.

"I can't," she said.

"Raquel—"

"I *can't.*"

Fine. He would work around her, then.

This feather grants its bearer the three magics of Mortem.

Three magics. That included sanguimancy—a magic that could filter toxins from the blood.

Elias clasped his hands around Kallias's wrists, seeking out the places where his pulse pressed against the thin sheath of his skin, squeezing his eyes shut with a harsh prayer expelled between trembling lips. "Mortem, guide me."

Warm, now-familiar hands slid over his, invisible but tangible. And as Mortem closed her fingers around his, a sound built in Elias's head with slow, deliberate precision—a *thud, thud, thud* that mirrored Kallias's pulse. And the tighter Elias held on, the more he could see in his mind's eye: every vein in Kallias's body mapped out in lurid red, and the clouded blackness that began in his stomach and pumped throughout his limbs, his lungs, his heart.

The poison had already consumed so much of him.

Elias's gut tightened in terror, but he pushed through it, forcing himself to focus on the path of the poison.

"Kal," he croaked, "fight it."

And then he lit Kallias's blood with cleansing fire.

Kallias's body arched beneath their hands, a ragged moan ripping free of his chest, his hands contorting into claws that scraped against the floor as if he was trying to tear himself away from their grasp. But both of them held on, Elias forcing his magic through Kallias's corrupted bloodpaths, Raquel forcing his heart to beat against the smothering hold of the poison. Ice crackled across the stone Kallias dug his fingernails into, chilling Elias's knees like he'd taken cover in a snowdrift, but he ignored it.

He'd already lost Soren. He would not lose anyone else.

Least of all Kallias.

They fought the battle for gods-knew how long, Elias wielding his newfound fire, Raquel wielding what knowledge she had received from her battlefield physician father, both of them refusing to surrender to the poison trying to force Kallias into an unearned grave. But eventually—just as Elias was starting to feel the beginnings of magic-induced exhaustion crawling under his skin— Kallias's chest heaved under his own power, a gasping breath that set Raquel back on her heels with a choked curse, her hand coming up to her mouth as if it burned from touching Kallias's.

Elias fell back as a wave of fatigue crashed over his body, softening his limbs until they bent easily beneath its blows. But he still managed to feel the crook of

Kallias's neck, seeking that elusive pulse with a desperation that surprised even him.

Kallias's pulse answered him with fervor that time, an even beat that threw itself against Elias's fingers without pause, and Elias nearly crumbled beneath the weight of his relief.

"I think it worked," he choked. "Thank Mortem it worked."

"What now?"

He didn't get the chance to answer Raquel, because right at that moment, the door flung open without so much as a knock. Star stood there in her full uniform, her expression stoic even as she took in Kallias's unconscious form. "What happened?"

Elias opened his mouth, but Raquel beat him to the punch, her voice casual as anything. "A bit too much to drink, is all. What do you need?"

Star's eyes drifted between Elias, who couldn't stop shaking no matter how hard he tried, and Kallias, who still looked dreadfully unwell. But she simply said, "Someone just arrived at the entrance to Mount Igniquit. He claims he must meet with Prince Kallias immediately."

Elias's brow furrowed, and he rubbed his eyes, trying to clear away the fatigue. "Did they give a name?"

"Yes. Prince Finnick of Atlas." Star folded her arms. "And he's brought a prisoner with him."

CHAPTER 72

FINN

All right, so…the arrival in Artem hadn't gone quite as planned.

The first part was flawless. He'd found the entrance to the tunnel the Artemisians used to get up and down the mountain fairly easily, then hiked up to the entrance to the actual capital city and presented himself to the guards with his usual flourish, putting on his best haughty tone and demanding to be taken to his brother immediately.

The part where they pointed spears at him and relieved him of the prisoner he'd picked up along the way had gone considerably less in his favor, but at least he was inside the mountain now.

He leaned against a stone wall with his arms crossed, raising his eyebrows as he looked down at the spear tips positioned an inch from his chest on all sides. "One man against seven spears. Did Prince Kallias put you up to this? I'm flattered by the implication, truly, but this seems a bit extreme."

"Empress Idris no longer looks favorably upon Atlas," said one of the guards coolly.

Gods help him, had Kallias really managed to mess up *that* badly already? It had only been a handful of weeks. "Well, that was not my understanding when I departed to serve as witness to their marriage."

"Clearly." Finn didn't care one bit for the condescending amusement in the guard's tone.

"Excuse me," spoke Finn's prisoner meekly, looking up with golden eyes they likely saw as green, "but I was brought here against my will, and I—I didn't intend to trespass. So if you could let me go—"

"No one is leaving until I am given permission from my general to release you."

Slumping, shooting him a scowl that reflected the body she was holding captive, Anima crossed her arms on her knees and rested her chin on them. "This is ridiculous."

"Well, you should have done a better job following me," said Finn. "I tried to let you do your thing, but come on, Your Godliness—you snapped a twig. If I'd let you get away with that, you'd never learn your lesson."

"And what lesson is that?"

"Don't step on noisy twigs."

Anima's scowl deepened, ever-petulant. "I *know* that."

"Well, you should see about your memory, then. You certainly didn't know it yesterday."

"I'm not exactly the pinnacle of grace here." Anima gestured at Soren's long-legged body, frustration drowning out her fear.

"And yet Soleil's always managed."

"Soren," Anima corrected.

Finn blinked, his smirk threatening to fall from his face like a withered leaf. "Excuse me?"

"Her name is Soren." Anima avoided his gaze, cinching her arms tighter around her knees. Her hair was coming free from its braid, and he would have laughed at all the branches and leaves stuck in it from when he'd pinned her to the ground if not for the look on her face. "That's the one she chose."

"Forgive me if I wait for her to confirm that rather than believe it from you."

"Prince Finnick?"

He looked away from Anima, barely managing to drag a penitent smile over his lips in time for the general to return—but the person trailing behind her told him he needn't have bothered.

All urge to joke vanished as Elias Loch pushed through the gathered guards—not the same man who had left Atlas with deadened eyes and merciless, murderous hands. This man stood straight-backed and solemn-faced, a chain around his neck that sported four strange tokens: a ring, two strips of braided cloth, and a black feather. Just above that collection sat the skull pendant on his prayer beads, and as he held out one arm to warn the guards back, Finn's eyes caught on his tattoos—fresh, by the look of them. There were new scars, a new beard, a new haircut…a new way he carried himself. He could have sworn fresh heat throbbed through the already-warm air as Elias's eyes found Anima, and the Nyxian man halted with a jerk like he'd been shoved, a flicker of desperate agony crumpling his features before he wrenched them back into stoicism. But his eyes…his eyes stayed haunted, the look of a man seeing someone he'd thought long-buried.

Finn's mouth dried out as he took in another change—another piece of Elias he didn't recognize.

A ring of light blazed in a molten halo around his right pupil, a rim of gold separating black from black.

"Elias," said Finn. The Nyxian didn't look at him; his hand merely crept toward his back, where Finn could see twin pommels sticking out over his shoulders, and Finn raised his voice to match the building emotion in Elias's eyes. "*Elias*. Whatever you're thinking of doing, you'll have to get past me first."

Anima swallowed thickly. Her expression was taut with fear, but her eyes…now that Finn knew what to look for, he saw the pinch to her brow, the twitch of her eyelashes. Soren had to be making a racket.

Good. He hoped she screamed until Anima fled to whatever ether realm she'd crawled out of.

Elias swallowed thickly. "Why did you bring her here?"

"That's not the first question you should be asking."

Elias's eyes snapped to him, and Finn actually found himself blinking against the muted fury burning low in his gaze. "I am not in the mood for your gods-damned games."

"Neither am I." Not in the mood for any games at all. "If you'll let me speak to my brother…"

That fury banked, cooling into something that had him holding his breath. "I tell our story first. And *she* doesn't leave my sight."

Finn glanced at Anima, who shrank even further beneath their combined glares. "Done. Take me to Kallias."

* * *

Poison.

He was going to murder Kallias for being foolish enough to accept food or drink from strangers. After he was done murdering whoever had thought they could poison a member of the Atlas family and get away with it.

No longer empty threats, those. The color of blood flattered him. He was willing to wear it again.

Finn sat at Kallias's bedside, watching him breathe, timing them carefully to make sure they weren't slowing or speeding in a way that would suggest oncoming death. Kallias's pallor was alarming, and the rapid movement of his eyelids suggested his sleep wasn't easy, but he was breathing; and according to Elias, that was a great improvement.

And while he watched, he listened to Elias tell the story of his trials while avoiding looking at Anima; she sat with her wrists tied, guarded with a blade held to her neck by another Nyxian—Raquel, Elias had introduced her as—who, based on the way she was watching him, had no fondness for Atlas. Though her glances toward Kallias—out of the corner of her eye, clearly unwilling to stare outright—suggested those feelings were newly complicated.

It was hard to hate a noble man, even one who had wronged you. He knew that struggle intimately.

Just as Elias was finishing his tale with a story involving a phoenix that Finn wouldn't have believed if he didn't know Elias's tells so well after months spent watching him lie, Kallias's eyelids fluttered.

Everyone in the room froze as Kallias pried his eyelids open, blinking dazedly, his gaze wandering about the room before settling on Finn, staring without any real recognition. The look was too similar to the way Soleil had first looked at him when she'd been brought home. Like he thought he might know him, but couldn't place how.

Cold speared into Finn's stomach, and his fist curled against the edge of the bed.

Don't panic. Don't panic.

"Kal?" he croaked.

Kallias frowned, and Finn's stomach dropped another notch lower. Then:

"I think I'm still feverish," Kallias announced in a voice that scratched horribly against his throat. "It looks like Finn is sitting next to me."

Relief swooped through him so violently he nearly vomited, but he forced a haughty expression instead, leaning back and putting his hand over his pounding heart. "Aw, you dream of me? That's so sweet."

That hazy look cleared in an instant, replaced with utter shock—and a hint of alarm. "Finn?"

Finn glanced downward, patting himself as if checking to make sure he was real. "Last I checked, yep."

"What in the *depths* are you doing here?" Kallias surged up halfway before freezing with a pained grunt, his hand wrapping around his middle as his face went a shade paler. "What happened? You look awful."

That much was probably true. He'd gone back to avoiding mirrors after escaping the palace, and he'd been on the run for days since, staying in barely-passable inns and failing miserably at his attempts to sleep. "No worse than you, you utter *moron*. I let you go off alone for a few weeks and you managed to get yourself *poisoned*?"

"Finn," Kallias said through gritted teeth, "why are you *here*? You're supposed to be at home with—"

"With Anima?" Finn pointed to their prisoner, who was watching with a distinctly put-out look. "Things went a bit awry on that front."

"I can see that." Kallias blinked again, looking to Elias first, then Raquel, and—oh, gods help him. The way he looked at her...

A few weeks, and his brother had managed to get himself poisoned, had managed to piss the Empress off against Atlas...and he was giving a Nyxian *that* look?

Disaster. He never should've let him go off alone.

"We were just about to hear that story ourselves." Raquel looked back at Kallias with considerably colder eyes, but there was a bend to her mouth and a hitch to her breath that didn't match her glare. Then she looked to Finn and waited, a patient silence that suggested he continue before patience turned to something more demanding.

He would deal with that mess later.

There was too much to tell them—too much he didn't want to tell them. So he kept it short and simple: the arrangement with Esha, how one of her Mirrors had *befriended* him, how he'd found out later that she was in fact the Goddess of Time in disguise. He told them about the relics and the mirror and his confrontation with Esha…then his confrontation with Jericho. With Tenebrae. With Soleil.

"I already told you, I don't—" Elias began, his teeth gritting his words into gravel, but Finn interrupted him with a hand held up.

"I heard you," he said coolly. "This isn't a game. Soleil's alive. I spoke to her—to *her*, Elias, not Anima."

Elias was quiet for a long time—too long. "That's not possible."

"I'm struggling to remember when Soleil ever cared about sticking to what's possible."

Elias stared at him for several moments, his jaw working like he was holding back some choice words. Then his gaze shifted to Anima. "Well?" His voice was still low, hardly more than a growl. "Is that true?"

Anima avoided his gaze. Didn't speak.

Elias walked to her with slow steps, his feet going through each motion like they were weighed down with lodestones. He sank into a crouch in front of her, taking her chin with a firm grip, forcing her gaze up. He stared at her without flinching.

"Is it true?" A raw, broken demand. "Is my battlemate still alive?"

Anima tried to recoil from his touch, but he held her fast, his fingers tightening around her chin until her skin paled beneath the pressure.

"Yes." Hushed, terrified. "She is."

Kallias's breath burst forth in a rejoicing laugh. Elias, however, didn't flinch. Didn't so much as blink. He dropped Anima's chin and stood. "It could be a trick. A lie to save her own life."

Finn groaned. "Elias, no offense, but I think we both know I'm a bit sharper than you when it comes to reading people. If it was a lie, I'd know."

Elias glanced at him briefly before looking away, a cold dismissal. "You've been fooled by a goddess once already. *No offense.*"

Finn hated, hated, *hated* that there was no good comeback to that. No argument he could offer or insult he could trade.

"Fine," he said. "You don't have to believe me. But I know you, Elias; better than you know yourself. And I know your faith in her is only second to your goddess. If you can't believe in me, fine. Believe in *her*. And believe that I'm not going to let you harm a hair on her head until we've found a way to remove that goddess from inside it."

Elias watched him carefully. "You really believe she's in there."

Elias could posture and play suspicious all he liked; Finn could see straight to the desperation hidden underneath. Whatever he said, whatever he thought was the truth, he *wanted* Finn to be right. Whether he knew it or not, he wanted that more than anything.

He wouldn't try to kill Anima. Not now that Finn had planted this doubt in his head.

So Finn eased back, propping one leg over his opposite knee, crossing his arms and shrugging. "I do. She saved me from Anima and Tenebrae; she fought them off long enough for me to run."

His voice caught a bit at the end, but he swallowed hard to loosen the snag. He'd already admitted enough weakness in front of these Nyxians.

While he and Elias were having their standoff, Raquel had moved to Kallias's bedside, checking his pulse and temperature while speaking to him in quiet, stiff tones. Kallias's still-groggy gaze locked on her, his attention entirely captured as she leaned in closer, strands of her hair brushing his face as she pressed a hand to his chest to check his breathing. With slow, timid movements, Kallias reached up to move those strands aside, tucking them behind her ear. As his fingers brushed her temple, Raquel's throat bobbed, and she cleared her throat hard before pulling away, muttering some excuse and walking—fleeing—back across the room.

Finn shot a look at Elias, finding his own exasperation mirrored in the Nyxian man's face—a shared opinion between them, for once. Finn jerked a thumb over his shoulder with a raised eyebrow. *What's going on there?*

Elias raised both hands in a sign of surrender, a silent *Don't look at me* written all over his face.

So this was beyond his understanding, too. That was something of a comfort.

"Kallias," Elias said, bringing Kallias's confused attention back to him, "I need you to try and remember what happened. We need to know who did this to you."

"And why," Raquel added while she briskly folded a discarded shirt on her bed—then unfolded it, then refolded it. Despite her unruffled expression, her movements screamed *flustered*.

Kallias rubbed his temples with a grimace. "I'm trying. It's all…fuzzy. I remember leaving with Zaccheus…"

"Who?" Elias and Finn asked together, at the same time Raquel said, "You were gone a couple hours with him."

"Captain Zaccheus Janus," Kallias croaked. "We've been…we were working together to try and get an audience with Idris faster. He's desperate to keep Artem out of another war, and when he realized I wasn't keen on the alliance, we struck a deal."

"But if you were helping him, what reason would he have to poison you?" Elias sat at the foot of Kallias's bed, frowning, one eye still on Anima.

"I don't know. I don't remember…I think we went to his house…" Kallias huffed out a frustrated groan, rubbing his eyes with the heels of his hands, strands of sweat-matted hair falling to frame his face. "It's all a blur."

"Excuse me," said Anima meekly, and they all turned to look at her. She shrank beneath their gazes, but cleared her throat, forcing herself to sit up straight. "I could try to heal him. It might help."

"No," all three of them chorused in unison, and Anima's face twisted into an expression much closer to Soleil's familiar glower.

"Fine." She tried to cross her arms, but blushed when she seemed to remember the ropes making that impossible. She let them fall into her lap instead with an awkward throat-clearing. "Good luck figuring all this out, then."

Silence held the room captive for long enough that Finn's head started to spin into a dangerous space, a space where daydreams and half-formed prophecies could tangle him up in visions before he had the chance to resist them. So he broke it with a sigh. "I mean…it might not be the worst idea."

"We are not letting her magic into anyone else's head," Elias snapped, but Kallias shot him a look.

"Eli, we might not have a choice. We need to know what happened."

"And what if she harms instead of helps, hm? Do you know what she can do? I'm certainly not confident enough in my education anymore to trust—"

"Minds are not her realm of expertise," Finn interrupted. He knew full well who governed over *that* sort of magic. "You know that. And she already has her host. What more harm can she do?"

"I'm not willing to risk it," Elias insisted.

"It's not your risk to take," Kallias reminded him, a stern edge pushing through the lingering grogginess. He looked to Finn. "You've been around her the most. What do you think?"

Finn made sure to meet Anima's gaze slowly, intentionally, letting her feel the full force of having Finnick Atlas's attention solely on her. "I think she knows any one of us will cause great pain to her if she does anything other than help you."

Anima's face paled, but her eyes flickered green for a moment; he could have sworn he saw approval there.

"I trust you." Kallias held his gaze for a moment too long—long enough for the guilt to creep in, for him to think of all the reasons his brother should never trust him again. Then he leaned toward Anima. "Let her try."

Raquel went to Anima and tugged her up by her shoulders, guiding her firmly over to Kallias. She leaned in and whispered something in the goddess's ear before pulling back, keeping one hand clamped on her shoulder.

Still pale, a bit shaky, Anima reached out and touched a timid hand to Kallias's temple. Beads of green light formed between her fingers and trickled upward like raindrops falling in reverse, rolling up to Kallias's head and soaking into his skin.

The entire room held its breath while Kallias closed his eyes.

When he opened them again, his gasp tore the held breath from all their lungs.

"We have to go." He lunged to his feet, nearly toppling over before Elias and Finn caught him, each of them grabbing a shoulder. "We have to find Idris, we have to warn her—"

"Warn her of what?" Elias demanded.

Kallias met his gaze, dread shining in his now-clear eyes. "I think Zaccheus is going to try and take the throne. And I think he tested his method on me first."

Elias blinked. "She said her father thought he was poisoned, not ill. He begged her to stay hidden, he thought..."

Kallias shook his head. "We need to find her," he said. "*Now.*"

CHAPTER 73

ELIAS

He couldn't gods-damned focus.

They sprinted through the stone tunnels of Mount Igniquit as a unit, he and Finn and Raquel arranged in a triangle around Anima while Kallias took the lead, rushing to stop what could be an impending assassination...and all he could think about was Soren's body running beside him. Soren's eyes sneaking looks his way as they ran. Soren's hands that were close, *so close*, hands he'd desperately wished to have within reach these past few weeks...

And he could take comfort in none of it. Because her eyes were still gold. Because she spoke like she was afraid that the air would shove her words back down her throat. Because she looked at him with terror in those gilded eyes he hated so hard it hurt.

Soren had *never* been afraid of him. Infuriated, irritated, worried…but never *afraid*.

He'd earned that fear the day he'd wrapped his hands around her throat. He knew that.

It shouldn't have mattered. It shouldn't have bothered him.

It mattered. It bothered him.

Just as the noise bothered him; the common area was packed full, tables scattered throughout, laden with food and drink and people. Laughter and chatter and calls of greeting crowded him as he skidded to a halt, the rest of the group following suit as he searched the flood of people for Idris.

There—at the head table, wearing her armored dress and diadem of flame, the guise of the Priestess once again set in place. She was smiling, laughing, chatting with Star while pulling apart a roll with her fingers.

Relief nearly choked him. They weren't too late after all.

He'd barely taken a step toward Idris when he saw Star suddenly frown, her hand fumbling up to cradle her throat. Her mouth opened, but it looked to him like no sound emerged; her eyes widened in panic as she clawed at her throat, her hand shooting out to knock Idris's cup over before she tumbled backward, her chair crashing to the floor while she choked and scrabbled at her neck.

A scream broke through the surge of voices, and even as Elias picked up his pace, he saw Havi wheeling Safi toward their mother, their faces contorted in terror. And then a shadow rose to his left, something dark and angled in their hands—

He recognized the shape as a handheld crossbow just before pain exploded in the center of his chest, a familiar kind of agony searing a path from his sternum to his back.

He looked down to find an arrow sticking out of his heart.

Anima screamed as he collapsed to one knee. A raw, unbridled roar of rage that he'd only heard once before, the last time steel had found its way beneath his skin: *"Elias?"*

In the daze of shock, of pain, he almost thought he heard two voices chorusing as one in that cry.

Before he could think better of it, he'd jerked the arrow from his chest, his vision blurring in patches as he cradled the arrow in his palm, blinking at the droplets of blood plopping from the arrowhead to his oddly steady hand. As he stared at it, his brow furrowing while he tried to comprehend the fact that he'd been dealt a mortal blow…the pain in his chest changed.

No longer a deadly numbness, but a scalding heat.

He looked down to see smoke drifting from the hole in his armor, in his chest. He caught his breath against a surge of pain as the wound flooded with fire, an agony that exceeded the death blow before slowly leeching away…

Leaving a cauterized hole in its wake.

Deathless.

Mortemancy—power over death itself.

"Gods," he whispered in awe.

Then everything went to the pits.

Screams broke out all around as more people in the crowd turned on their peers—some with bows and spears and blades drawn, others wielding fire in their hands. Shouts of "Keep the hearth burning!" rang out on all sides, but louder than all of them was the horrible wail from Safi, a howl that slowly built from devastation to rage—a rising that told him it was already too late for his aunt.

Before he could even take a step in that direction, a familiar body crashed into him, red-gold curls shivering as Soren—*Anima*—shoved the heels of her hands against his chest, lighting them up with healing magic before he could protest. He watched her expression shift from wild-eyed frenzy to befuddlement, her fingers seeking out a wound and finding nothing.

Then her eyes settled on the feather. Widened. Sharpened.

"You're her cleric?" So soft, those words. So quiet he only understood them because he'd learned long ago to read Soren's lips, something they'd practiced to keep themselves entertained during important meetings.

He shoved her hand away. "Do not touch me."

Her face twisted with hurt, but it didn't matter. It *couldn't.*

"Elias!" Kallias's shout drew his attention toward the table. Idris was standing, thankfully, but one hand was pressed to her chest, the other wrapped tightly around the top of the chair to steady herself. Kallias was bracing her by the elbow to keep her standing. "I need you!"

Elias pushed past Anima, drawing his scythes and looking over his shoulder at her. "Do you know how to fight?"

Clipped. Cold. He couldn't let her into his head.

Anima nodded, a jerky bob that was far from convincing. After a heartbeat, her brow wrinkled, her lip protruding in a slight pout before she finally shook her head.

He cursed under his breath. "Great. Stick close to me. Keep your head down. Don't lose it."

"Lose what?"

"Your *head*."

Then he was running, and he refused to look behind him to make sure Anima kept up. He had living friends and allies he needed to protect; people he could still save.

He jumped over wounded and dying and dead, another arrow finding purchase in his shoulder while his feet found gaps between legs and arms in an artful battle waltz. He ducked under a swung blade and kicked a fallen chair back onto its legs, launching himself up and over it, drawing his scythes as he flipped and landed atop the table in front of Idris and Kallias, dispatching two attackers coming at them in as many blows.

As he heaved in a breath and straightened his back, Kallias's eyebrows rose in fear, and he reached for another arrow in Elias's shoulder. "You need—"

Elias yanked it out with a quick jerk, grimacing as fire flared and fizzled, leaving only a cauterized scab behind. He tossed the bolt to Kallias, who caught it with a blink and a comically dropped jaw. Elias merely shrugged his reply, hopping down from the table and bracing Idris's other shoulder; it jerked in jagged breaths beneath his hand, her eyes ferocious but glassy, one arm wrapped tightly around her middle.

"Star," she gasped out, a wheezing whistle accompanying her next breath out. "See to—see to Star first—"

"It's too late." Tact was for later. Grief was for later. "Let me help you."

Kallias reached out and touched his shoulder; a shudder went up the prince's arm as he brushed his thumb over the burned-over wound. "Elias…"

"I have her," he said. "Find that Zaccheus person."

Kallias swallowed, squeezing his arm below the wound. "Be safe."

Elias's throat tightened. He took Kallias's hand and pulled him closer, bumping his forehead against his. "And you."

Kallias's gaze softened, and he clapped Elias on the shoulder once before tearing away. He was gone by the time Elias turned his full attention to Idris, the cacophony of the rebellion rising above the Empress's pained gasps. And it wasn't until he was already extending his new magic into her body that another pair of hands joined his—freckled, scarred, calloused. More familiar to him than even his own.

He raised his eyes to meet a golden gaze buried in a beloved face.

"Let me help," Anima whispered.

"I don't need your help."

"No, but she does."

Gods, he hated her voice—Soren's still, but pitched high in all the places it should have been low, timid where it should have been brazen, apologetic where it should have been annoyed. But worse than all that was the fact that he couldn't come up with a good enough reason to refuse her.

"Fine," he muttered. "But keep your hands to yourself. You touch me, you lose them."

Anima's mouth bent downward. And when she said, "Fine," she mimicked his Soren so perfectly that his fingers curled sharply into Idris's armored sleeve.

Later. Later.

For now, he had an Empress to save.

CHAPTER 74

KALLIAS

*I*s it treason to protect one's kingdom at all costs?

This was Atlas all over again. A more classic coup, but a coup all the same. What he'd witnessed in Zaccheus's house had only been a sliver of the true picture—there were more Hearth-Keepers than he'd been allowed to see, each of them skilled in either weapon or magic, each bearing old scars dealt by Tallisian hands. His one consolation was that many were not dealing mortal blows—they struck to incapacitate, not to kill—but he could not find Zaccheus or Esmeralda.

He'd been played.

Again.

Kallias Atlas. Always the fool. Always handed the jester's hat, never the crown.

Fury chilled his gloved fingers until he had to peel the leather off, ice coating the insides to the point that they held their shape even after he removed them. He tossed them aside with half a thought, but his stride stumbled a bit as he looked down.

His fingertips were bluer than an Atlas summer sky, his nails lacquered in ice, hoarfrost coating his hands like fur.

Breathe, thunder murmured into his ear. *It cannot harm you. Only our enemies.*

"*Our* enemies?" He could not obey that command. His lungs crackled with cold.

You and I stand on the same side, Prince. We merely have different priorities. The thunder rose from a growl to a boom: *To your left!*

Kallias whirled in time to see Finn thrown to the ground, his body rolling until he collided with the stone wall with a bark of pain. He struggled to stand, but his attacker kicked him back down with a foot to his chest, pinning him to the floor with his boot. Finn's shirt twisted as the boot did, his face contorting in pain as he swung one of his two daggers up—a move so quick and vicious that Kallias had to blink, unsure suddenly if that was really his brother. Finn had always been clumsy with blades, his fingers better suited to pen and paper.

But whether he was sure about Finn or not, he knew exactly who was attacking him. And when Zaccheus kicked his other foot around, trapping Finn's arm against the stone floor and bearing down with a merciless twist of his foot, Finn's shout of pain drowned Kallias in such frostbitten fury he could barely see for blue.

"Zaccheus!" he roared.

Zaccheus's head jerked around, eyes widening in telltale shock at seeing Kallias alive—then narrowing, returning to the younger Atlas prince. He rotated his wrist as he raised his arm, and the flame that sputtered to life...Kallias had never seen fire like it. Not clean orange, but oily black, a sooty blaze that writhed in agony, struggling in protest against its very existence.

Corrupted. Wrong. The way it moved made him nauseous.

Finn's eyes widened, and for the first time since a wine-muddled night nine years ago, true fear lit his little brother's gaze as Zaccheus thrust that fire down toward his chest.

In the moment that fire touched Finn's tunic, in the moment Kallias's cry of terror drew ripped through the world, Finn's gaze found his.

Desperate. Pleading.

Time slowed.

We can stop this, murmured the thunder. *If you let me, I can stop it.*

How? The word didn't make it to his tongue, but the thunder replied all the same.

You know how.

He did. Gods, he did.

I can't save you! His own voice, ragged with rage and grief. *Stop looking at me!*

That much was still true. That much had always been true. Kallias could not save him—not then, not now, not from that fire or this one.

But a god could.

Tempest could.

"Save him," he rasped. "Save him, and that's *all.*"

There was no warning. No pain. Only a gentle push, a guiding that led Kallias's consciousness away from his eyes, his vision tunneling until it vanished entirely.

Save him, he begged Tempest, clinging on long enough to force his body toward Finn, one hand stretched out toward the corrupted fire that burst to life over his brother's chest.

You have my vow, said Tempest in return.

And as the god cracked open his skull and climbed inside it, making himself a home in every hollow place, Kallias suddenly remembered what it felt like to be cold.

CHAPTER 75

RAQUEL

When her god tore his way into the world, Raquel Angelov felt it in her bones.

The dry heat of the mountain dropped away, cold sapping the sweat from her skin and lifting a hint of the homesickness that had dogged her since she stepped over Nyx's border with Artem. An old aching began in her stomach and rippled outward like a stone thrown into water, a yearning that reminded her how long it had been since she'd tasted magic.

Long, and longer still to go.

She struck down one of the defectors before whirling, probing the crowd with her good eye, her grip on her sword tightening the longer she went without finding her quarry.

What in the pits did you do, Atlas?

There was no flash of golden-red hair to be found amongst the feast-turned-battlefield, but he was here somewhere. Ever since she'd met him, she'd always known when he was close; she could taste an oncoming blizzard in the air wherever he was, a shiver coaxing goosebumps to her skin whenever she met his earnest, solemn eyes. Worse when he was angry. Worse still when he was inches away, his breath cold as winter wind against her mouth, his hands braced beside her hips—

She discarded those thoughts with a sharp shake of her head, cursing quietly under her breath. Damned Atlas bastard. If he'd done what she feared he had, she was going to *kill* him.

Her feet jerked, missing a step, and she nearly stumbled before recovering herself, cursing again as she picked up her pace, scanning the cavern with building anger…building fear.

When had killing him, the only thing that had kept her walking forward since her sister's death, become an *if*?

There. A flash of red.

A flash of gold.

Raquel's stomach punched up into her throat as she met Kallias's gaze across the cavern…

Not Kallias.

Eyes of gold held hers just long enough for feral terror to spear from head to stomach, and suddenly she was a girl again, stone digging into her back as she screamed and screamed and screamed, writhing against the white-hot agony in the pit where her eye once was. The noise of battle faded, replaced by dozens of voices chanting, a sick kind of rejoicing as the thing she loved more than life, the thing she cherished beyond friends and family and self, was unspooled from her like hundreds of hands tugging her guts out inch by torturous inch.

Her knee buckled, but she caught herself, eyes still locked on Tempest's.

She would not kneel before the god that had abandoned her in the darkest pits of her life. And she certainly wasn't going to do it while he wore Kallias Atlas's face.

Tempest raised his hand as if in greeting, and the expression on his face was one she'd never seen Kallias wear. It was calm, confident, the look of one entirely assured in their purpose. He didn't flinch beneath her glare—didn't match it, either.

That look made her small.

His hand surged forward, and her breath cut off in preparation as lightning arced toward her like a thrown javelin, crackling blue heat that seared her cheek—

And speared straight past her, punching into an Artemisian defector who had crept up on her blind side. She spun just in time to see him fall, mouth gaping, smoking pits where his eyes and heart once were.

By the time she spun back, the path before her was clear, revealing a sight that spread an oily sickness through her stomach: Tempest and Zaccheus circling each other, Tempest's hands coated in ice, Zaccheus's in blackened fire.

"You claim that you wish to avoid war at all costs." Kallias's voice boomed across the cavern like thunder, echoing with deeper bass tones that didn't belong to him. "Yet you've thrown your lot in with my brother. You think the God of Chaos is fond of peace, Captain Janus?"

Zaccheus's hands trembled a bit—he was facing a god, after all, and had hardly struck her as foolish enough to do that without fear—but his voice was strong when he replied, "I have my orders...and my promises. If I ensure my people don't offer aid against him, he will spare us from his designs for the rest of the kingdoms. My people will be safe."

"Chaos is a liar," said Tempest. "Promising freedom and only offering turmoil. You're being lied to. My brother's war will find you yet, and it will be the end of you."

"I thought Occassio was the one with all the prophecies," Zaccheus said, his lip curling, doubt flickering in his gaze before solidifying to steel.

"It's not a prophecy." Tempest bent Kallias's mouth into a vicious, primal grin, and not for the first time, she wondered if Kallias could be dangerous if the notion struck him. "It's a promise."

Zaccheus paled, and in that moment of pause, Raquel caught sight of the younger Atlas prince sprawled on the ground beyond them. He was sitting up, braced with one arm against the ground and one over his chest; his shirt appeared to have been partially eaten away by flame, the cloth blackened and curled in on itself. The flesh beneath was angry and red—definitely burned, but hardly as bad as it should have been. When he shifted, she caught the glimmer of water droplets sliding down his torso.

Oh.

She looked back to Tempest, understanding and anger cracking her heart open.

Of course he had. The way Kallias talked about his family...of course he'd given in to save one of them.

"You're wrong," said Zaccheus. "We made a deal."

"He makes many deals with many desperate people."

"He told me about you…about all of you." Zaccheus took a step back, and Raquel's fingers dipped into the pouch at her belt, ready to throw one of her knives…or rather, Jira's knives. "How you refused to help him. How your family nearly perished for it. You don't understand what it is to be willing to do anything for your family."

Tempest's confidence bent a bit, revealing a hint of pain before snapping back into place. "More would have perished if we had. More will perish if I do now."

"Let them," Zaccheus rasped. "This world isn't black and white, God of Nature. I won't sacrifice me and mine for the sake of strangers. Tenebrae can do what he likes with the rest of this gods-damned world. As long as my people are safe. *I* will keep them safe. And you're not welcome in *my* mountain."

Tempest pulled his hands back, blue sparks of energy leaping from his fingers. But before he could release the bolts, Zaccheus shoved his hands toward the ground, and black flame roared up into an impassable wall. Tempest cursed, letting the lightning fizzle out and calling to water instead, dragging it from the puddle left by a discarded water jug nearby and flinging it at the fire.

The flames sputtered…then roared up again, unhindered.

Flames that couldn't be smothered by water.

Raquel got closer in time to hear Tempest mutter, "Rot take it—" before he clasped his hands together, squeezing them shut, his brow furrowing in concentration. He pulled his hands apart after a moment, revealing a spinning orb of sourceless water, liquid that nearly glowed against the backdrop of the dark flame. He cast it out once more, and this time the flames died without protest, revealing an empty space where Zaccheus once stood.

Fire that could only be put out with divinely created elements. Pits.

Blood leaked from Tempest's nose. He wiped it off without looking away from where Zaccheus's fire had been, a cold look in his eyes she hated, *hated*—and hated even more because she couldn't explain why she did.

He started to step away, and her voice leapt from her throat before she could stop it, because she was a fool and a blood-traitor and a hundred other distasteful titles she'd earned by letting Kallias live this long: "Stop!"

He did, but the halting didn't have an air of obedience—instead, when he looked over his shoulder, his incredulous look suggested he'd only listened out of shock.

Raquel swallowed, forcing her chin to rise a notch, meeting his gaze head-on. "Did he give you permission?"

"Yes."

Her heart stumbled. "What were his exact words?"

"*Save him*," said Finnick, who'd clambered to his feet, his own glare settled on Tempest. The cold in his eyes put Tempest's to *shame*. "*Save him and that's all.* That's what my brother told you."

A knowing look came over Tempest's eyes. But he didn't speak; didn't give in.

She shifted to stand beside Finnick, crossing her arms over her chest; hopefully it would hide her shaking. "That doesn't sound like consent to me. Not for you to stay."

"He allowed me in. Those are the rules. He gave his permission."

"Well, *I* don't!" Wherever this fury was coming from, the anger that kept rising up on Kallias's behalf, she didn't know. All she could think of was the smile he'd given her when he'd found her alive in that burning tavern; the fever-emboldened declaration he'd thrown out when he was poisoned, the words *You drive me absolutely* mad, *Angelov, do you know that?* almost making her forget to breathe; the tenderness with which he'd brushed her hair aside in the aftermath and whispered *Are you all right*, those unbearably bright eyes watching her with worry— worry for *her*, when he was the one bedridden.

"His death belongs to me," she hissed. "I claimed it long ago. And I do not relinquish it to you. He is *mine*."

Tempest met her gaze head-on. Stared for what felt like minutes…hours.

All the while, her own girlish screams echoed in the back of her head.

"Raquel Angelov," he mused softly. "I remember you."

Her fists clenched, her back twinging with spectral pain. "Then you remember what I endured for you. And you remember that I do not give up what is mine without a fight."

Tempest smiled—not menacing this time. No, she could have almost sworn it was pride.

There was no warmth in it. But then, there wouldn't be; Nature was not kind.

That was all right. Neither was she.

"I'll offer you this." He crossed his arms, his head held at an angle she remembered from hunting trips; it was the way a predator studied their prey. "A boon for your boldness…and a repayment for what you have lost. I will honor your claim, Raquel Angelov…this time. But the next time he offers himself to me—and he will—I'll ensure the wording is definite. And if you do not claim your life debt before he can, I will consider it void. Do we have an understanding?"

Still her knee tried to bend. Still she held herself up. "We do."

Tempest nodded, sighing as he bent his neck back and forth, the cracking noise startling both her and Finn. "This prince carries so much weight," he said with a wink. "Might as well give him a bit of relief, hm?"

Before either of them could speak, Kallias's eyes closed, and his body shuddered sharply before slumping forward, dropping toward the floor without any attempt to catch himself.

"Kal!" Finnick swore, diving forward, and Raquel followed a half-second later, both of them seizing Kallias beneath his shoulders, Finnick catching his head before it could snap forward. They moved in tandem, ducking into an empty shop to hide from the rebels, and Finnick glanced out the door while she held Kallias up. His skin was *freezing*, ice-cold and clammy, and adrenaline shot through her as she fumbled for the crook of his neck, not relaxing until she found his pulse—thready, lurching, but there.

He should have been dead. Every legend she knew stated that a god taking a host forced the mortal soul out of the body. But here he was, breathing...and according to Finnick, Soren had survived her own possession, too.

So many things they'd gotten wrong. Gods only knew what else they could be wrong about.

"We need to get him out of here," said Finnick, who didn't look entirely well himself. His eyes were distracted, his teeth chewing absently at his abused bottom lip, and his hands trembled against Kallias's chest when he came back to help her support him. "We need to get him out *now*."

He'd barely gotten the words out when Elias lurched through the door, supporting a hooded figure with Soren—no, Anima—shadowing right behind him. It wasn't an unfamiliar sight; Soren and Elias had been attached at the hip for years, and Raquel wasn't able to see through the green-eyed illusion like Elias could, but the timid look on Soren's face still made it difficult to reconcile memory with reality. Her almost-sister had never been *timid*, not since her first year in the orphanage.

"What happened?" Elias's eyes widened as he took in Kallias, stark panic striking through his eyes like lightning. "Is he hurt?"

"Later," Raquel said through gritted teeth. "What's the plan?"

"The tide is turning, and not in our favor," croaked the hooded figure—she recognized Idris's voice, weak as it was. "Those who remain loyal have been ordered to regroup outside the mountain. Zaccheus had over half of *my* gods-damned army on his side, and many of the common folk…while quite a few are skilled enough to fight back, it's not enough. We're outnumbered here. The mountain is lost."

Raquel's stomach dropped. "Already?"

Idris's eyes shone with pain as she raised her head. Raquel didn't think it was because of the poison. "It seems my removal from my people made it very easy to turn their opinion against me. And Zaccheus…it seems he's been planning this for some time."

"So we run?" Finnick rasped.

"I don't think we have a choice." Elias's gaze was still raking over Kallias's limp form, but her and Finnick's lack of outright urgency seemed to calm him. He stood straighter. "Havi and Safi are already out, and Star…Star is gone."

"Damn," Raquel said softly.

"Yes, we're all devastated," Finnick said curtly, grunting as he shifted to better hold his brother's weight. Kallias's physical prowess clearly didn't extend to this other Atlas prince. "If we're going to go, can we go?"

She'd expected Kallias's younger counterpart to be more like him—straight-backed, serious-eyed, angry and empathetic in equal measure, bashful when he was allowed to be. This boy was different. He stood with an air of laziness, yes, but not the slothful sort; he held an air of impatience that suggested he'd already solved a problem and grew tired of them struggling through all the steps to catch up to him. His mind was already out of this mountain while his body remained trapped with them.

Dangerous. Finnick Atlas, somehow, was the more dangerous prince.

Jira had been like that, too—cleverer than most, her mind faster than her hands, a girl bound for the war room if she'd ever seen one. Jira would've made general in a couple short years. Jira would have turned the tides of the world.

Gods, she was starting to sound like her mother after a drink too many.

"Let's go," she agreed, and quiet as it was, it seemed her vote tipped the scale—everyone finally started moving, Idris muttering directions in Elias's ear, leading them out of the mountain through passageways known only to its Empress.

And all the while, Raquel clung to Kallias, knowing she could claim what belonged to her any moment. A dagger into his heart. A slit cut into his throat. A sudden jerk of her arm to twist his neck.

Instead, she pulled him through threshold after threshold, careful to keep his feet away from burning patches of ground. And as they fled from the captured

Igniquit, she wondered to herself what in the pits had rotted her mind—and her bloodlust—in just a few short weeks.

CHAPTER 76

KALLIAS

W hen consciousness came back to him, he knew immediately that they were no longer in the mountain.

Fresh air played hopscotch over his face, caressing him with playful fingers and tender kisses, promising him he would never be so far from its touch ever again. And with it came pain—an aching that tugged ceaselessly against his bones, against his lungs. A hunger that demanded to be satisfied.

With the aching came a memory: *Save him.*

But when he opened his eyes, he only saw rock above.

"Water." The request burst from him as if his throat had a mind of its own. "Water."

Moments later, liquid seeped between his lips, guided by the metal rim of a flask. He drank greedily, desperately, consuming until the flask would give no more. And even then, he still thirsted. He still needed *more*.

"Kallias?" Finn's voice cut through the buzzing need in his head. "Are you awake?"

He blinked, that thirst abating a bit as his senses trickled back to him. Uncertainty phrased his answer as a question. "I think so?"

"He's all right," Finn called over his shoulder before muttering, "and dull as ever."

"I heard that," Kallias said.

"You were supposed to, dumbass." He hadn't heard that raging edge to Finn's voice since the day he'd brought Soleil home, when Finn thought he was pulling some sick prank on them all. "What in the *depths* were you thinking back there?"

He was about to ask what exactly Finn was talking about before the memory crashed over him like a breaking wave: Zaccheus shoving dark fire into Finn's chest. Finn's terrified eyes. His own pleas of *save him* answered by a god who hadn't needed to be invited twice before snuffing him out, quick as a candle flame robbed of its air.

Nausea clamped down on his stomach, effectively putting an end to hunger or thirst of any kind. "What happened?"

Bandages peeked out from beneath Finn's half-unbuttoned shirt as he leaned forward, and alarm shot through Kallias, his fingers moving up to pull the shirt aside. Finn batted him away. "I'm fine. You're the one who had to get his ass saved from a god by a *Nyxian*, of all people."

"I heard that!" called Raquel's voice from somewhere nearby, but her annoyance toward Finn was far duller than what she tended to throw Kallias's way.

"You were *supposed* to, that's how insults work!" Finn called back, muttering something rude under his breath before returning his scowl to Kallias. "I'm gonna need you to stop making friends with violent Nyxian soldiers."

"Unfortunately, those seem to be our only options for allies at the moment."

"Damn." Finn rubbed his eyes. "How far the mighty have fallen."

"We're a damn sight better than your former options, and you know it, bastard." Was it his imagination, or did Raquel almost sound...amused?

Finn snorted, his scowl tipping toward a smirk. "I hate to admit it, but she's actually sort of cool."

"She wants to kill me," Kallias said.

"So, definitely cool, then."

If not for his lingering fear over those burns on Finn's chest, he would've hit him. "Where are we?"

"Depths if I know. A cave somewhere." Finn looked over his shoulder again. "Elias! Where are we?"

"Just left of *stop asking me questions when I'm trying to sleep*," came Elias's muffled growl.

Finn pouted. "It's Kallias asking."

"He's awake?" Elias's voice came much clearer then, and a few moments later his head joined Finn's, both of them hovering over Kallias at an angle that made him a bit dizzy. "What in the pits were you *thinking* back there, you—?"

"Save it," said Finn. "I already asked."

"Did he answer?"

"No."

Elias punched him in the shoulder, drawing a pained grunt from him. "What in the *pits* were—?"

"What else was I supposed to do?" Kallias demanded, pushing Elias away and drawing himself up into a sitting position, noting the bedroll he was currently wrapped in—and the startling number of people scattered around them. He cleared his throat, lowering his voice. "I don't know if you noticed, but that wasn't natural fire. And I'm hardly in control of this magic, I…I didn't think I could…I couldn't save you, Finn. Not on my own."

The light in Finn's shadow-circled eyes dimmed. He sat back a bit, one shoulder coming up in a strange almost-flinch. "I'll get you more water," he muttered, standing up with an unsteady lurch, hitting Kallias's hand aside again when he tried to offer it. The Second Prince walked off without a backward glance, passing Raquel, who was huddled close to a small fire beside Idris, the two of them deep in conversation. Her eyes wandered past Idris and locked on his, and he found he couldn't look away. There was something different in the way she looked at him now—he would've called it worry if he didn't know any better.

Elias's heavy sigh finally drew his gaze back to him. The Nyxian sat back against the cave wall, cocking one knee up, staring at the fire—at Havi and Safi, who were huddled close together, both of them hollow-eyed. Havi's face was heavy with grief; Safi's was contorted with silent rage.

"It's not your fault," Kallias muttered, following the thread of guilt in Elias's eyes to its source. "Star was gone by the time you reached her, wasn't she?"

"I should have moved faster."

"Even if you'd made it, gods know if it would have helped. You're still new to this. We're lucky you were able to help Idris."

"I didn't even do that well enough. She's still fighting off what's left of that poison."

"You did enough," Kallias argued. "She's alive."

Elias shrugged one shoulder, but didn't argue.

It was then that he realized there was a face missing from those huddled around the fire. "Where's Anima?"

Elias jerked his head in the direction he'd come from, and Kallias had to squint to make out the fire-limned form of a cloak-wrapped girl with her back tucked against the stone wall. She was curled up like a cocoon, everything but half her face covered in the cloak, her eyes shut tightly. "Asleep. Finn wanted to tie her back up, but she doesn't seem inclined to run."

"What are we going to do with her?"

"I don't know."

"Finn said—"

"I know what Finn said." Sharp. Quick. "But your brother's a more talented liar than you think."

Whatever the depths that meant, Kallias didn't know. But that question would have to wait its turn. "So where does that leave us?"

Elias gazed into the distance, his jaw working; after a minute, Kallias realized he was staring at Anima's sleeping face. At *Soleil's* face. "I don't know," he repeated, a soft whisper that barely rose above the quiet chatter around the fire. "I really don't know anymore, Kal."

Silence took over for a time, the two of them sitting in companionable quiet—so different from the way they'd spent their first journey together, tension keeping them glancing at each other from the corners of their eyes all the way from Nyx to Atlas, blades always within reach in case of a betrayal.

Neither of them were the same men who'd made that journey. And Kallias found he was glad for it.

"Do you know why Nyx started the battlemate custom?" Elias asked suddenly.

Kallias shook his head, his eyes wandering to the braids of cloth hanging from Elias's chain.

"It's based on an old story...older even than the gods. It speaks of the idea of soulmates...how some people believe you're born with a soul that matches someone else's. That there's someone out there who...not completes you, exactly, but who...complements you. Fills in the gaps. Someone who gives what you lack yourself." Elias shrugged, his thumb wandering over the ring he still wore, his eyes never leaving Soleil's face. "But the story challenges that belief a bit. It suggests that you're not born with a soulmate, but that you can choose them. That if you choose to commit yourself to someone else with your whole heart, you *become* what the other needs. You choose each other every day. You choose to grow together, to walk together, to protect each other's backs as you would your own."

Kallias nodded once, thinking back on the times he'd seen Soleil and Elias together. Even before he knew who they truly were to each other, their connection had been clear as day—they moved as two halves to one form, a call and echo, a question and answer. "That's beautiful."

Elias quieted again for a moment. Then, without looking away from Soleil: "I'm not ready to take another battlemate. I don't know if I ever will be. But...if I did..." He took a deep breath, clenching his fist against his cocked knee. "If I asked..."

Kallias's heart warmed, and he squeezed Elias's shoulder. "I would be honored if you ever asked that of me."

Elias smiled faintly, and he lifted his hand to cover Kallias's. "Thank you."

"Elias, Kallias," called Raquel, and they both looked up as she stood, crossing over to crouch in front of them. Her hair was tugged up into a knot, revealing a barely-scabbed-over slice across her cheek, and Kallias had to catch his breath against a surge of anger.

At who, only the gods knew.

Idris followed Raquel, helping Havi maneuver Safi's chair across the cave floor, and Finn returned soon after. They all circled Kallias and Elias, each of them wearing different degrees of pain on their faces.

He hated it. He hated that he could not help...and that he hadn't seen what Zaccheus truly was until it was too late.

"We will not let this lie," Idris said after a long pause. "My people are scattered along these caves for the night…before dawn, we plan to flee toward Sanctaviv. Igniquit is our crown city, but Sanctaviv is Artem's heart. There are people there who will rally to me if I ask."

"Havi and I plan to go to Nyx after seeing Empress Idris safely to Sanctaviv," Safi said, her voice uncharacteristically dull. But her eyes gleamed, and she kept fondling the knives belted at her waist. "If this *Tenebrae* bastard is the reason my mother is dead, then I plan to do whatever I must to join that fight."

"I want to bring the news of my mother's death to Aunt Sera myself," Havi added softly. "And…and I need to see Ember. I need…"

He trailed off, but they each nodded their understanding—except Finn, who seemed distracted, his eyes fixed on something far away.

"Tenebrae's gaining ground," Finn said to no one in particular.

A shudder from Idris pulled Kallias's eyes to her—and Elias's, who asked, "What do you know of him?"

Idris, for the first time, wore a hint of fear in the crease of her brow. It sent a pang of dread straight to Kallias's toes.

"The priests and priestesses in Sanctaviv are…less superstitious than those in Nyx," said Idris. "I was taught much about Tenebrae and his history. The origin of the gods lies in Sanctaviv, you know—it's where they were born."

Finn leaned in, attention suddenly rapt. "The gods were once human?"

"I told you that," Elias muttered. "Back in Atlas."

"Bold of you to assume I've ever once listened to you."

"Let her finish," Kallias scolded, and Finn rolled his eyes before obeying, crossing his arms gingerly over his chest and leaning back once more.

Idris ran one hand rhythmically down one of her locks, her onyx gaze locked on the fire. Then, in a rasping whisper that scraped a sharp nail down Kallias's bones: "Centuries ago, before the six kingdoms came to be, there was only the Empire. A collection of nation-cities under the rule of a single man, Emperor Solomon. And Sanctaviv was their holy city, built to honor their only god: Sancta. It was there that our gods were born—but only one born with magic.

"Emperor Solomon was a hateful and bigoted man; he believed only those trained in priesthood held the divine right to magic, and if anyone outside the clergy was caught practicing it, they were punished swiftly and cruelly—often by a torturous death. This is the fate that befell the gods' mother, in fact. So when the youngest of them began to show signs of being blessed with magic of her own, the four older siblings banded together to hide her from the Emperor's soldiers."

Kallias glanced to where Anima slept, and a shiver ran down his back that had nothing to do with the mountain air.

"The five of them—Braeden, Peter, Mora, Cassandra, and Annelisa—scraped by for many years, hiding in abandoned hovels and taking odd jobs. Mora herself was a woman of faith, and she took a job cleaning the church in Sanctaviv, spending most of her nights dusting an empty altar and whispering prayers where no one could hear. Only those educated as priests and priestesses were allowed to worship in the church in Sanctaviv, but Mora's mother had taught her faith, and she'd declared that it belonged to all in equal measure. This was the one rebellion that Mora allowed herself: she worshipped against the decree of the Emperor.

"But one night, she was caught by a priest—a young man named Arthur who'd only recently been sent to serve in Sanctaviv. She begged him not to turn her in, and he agreed to keep her secret. In exchange, he only asked that she keep him company during his own prayers." Idris's mouth quirked. "He claimed he was afraid of the dark."

Kallias glanced out of the corner of his eye to see Elias's gaze drift to where Anima slept on, blissfully unaware of her life's tale being spun only a few feet away.

"They fell in love," Idris said, "as most stories go. But priests and priestesses back then were not allowed to marry, and beyond anything else, Mora dreamed of being a priestess. They were forced to keep their liaisons secret. And it worked—until the day a plague came to visit Sanctaviv.

"Arthur fell terribly ill. And the nearer he crept to death, the more desperate Mora became, until finally she took him to her home. There, Annelisa healed him, bringing him back from the brink. But when he asked how it was possible, Mora claimed it was her who had the magic to protect her sister, believing he wouldn't betray her to the crown. This was her fatal mistake.

"The next day, Arthur returned to the hovel with soldiers, and they dragged Mora out onto the street, accusing her of wielding heathen magic and attempting to corrupt one of Sancta's holy priests. She pleaded with Arthur to stop them, for him to tell them the truth, but he clung to his story, claiming she'd bewitched him with her unholy powers. They dragged her to the middle of the city and tied her to a stake. Her siblings heard her screams across the city and came running—all of them tried to fight their way through to crowd to reach her, but none made it through before they set the fire beneath her feet."

Horror curled Kallias inward, his stomach churning. Such punishment was…worse than savage. He'd never heard of a practice like that. Elias, too, looked sickened, his hand pressed over his mouth and nose like he could smell the burning flesh even now.

"Mora stared out at the crowd, seeing the faces of each of her siblings twisted in horror—and Arthur, watching her burn without shame. And in that moment, her grief turned to rage. As she burned, she threw her head back and screamed out to Sancta, reminding him of her faithfulness and demanding that he reward it. That he prove to her that he was indeed what her mother had told her he was. And Sancta did.

"The flames of the pyre bellowed out with her prayer." Idris reached out one hand, and a piece of the campfire reached back, curling against her palm. "And in one fell blow, Sanctaviv was scorched to cinders—the city and all its people. All but Mora's four siblings, who stood unharmed amidst miles of ash, their own magics surging to life within them as their sister stood over the carnage she'd wrought. What happened after is of some debate, but all accounts claim Tenebrae was corrupted by the touch of his own magic. His ambitions for himself and his family grew until they could not be sated within the confines of mortality, and they've continued to grow ever since. Even now. I dread to dwell on the possibilities of what hungers may have woken in him after this long."

Silence wrapped the cave in a stranglehold, seeming to snuff out even the sound of their breaths in the stale air.

"So, where do we go next?" Kallias asked, desperate to shove off the weight of that dreadful quiet, looking to Elias. "Has Mortem given you any direction?"

To his relief, Elias engaged immediately, shaking off his own shroud of thought. "No. Tempest?"

Kallias's muscles tightened. "No." He looked to Finn next. "Has Occassio…?"

"I will throw myself off this mountain before I even *think* of going anywhere she tries to send us," Finn said, with such venom that Kallias blinked.

"I have a suggestion," Raquel said, "but you may not care for it."

"We haven't cared for any of our options in some time," Elias said tiredly. "By all means."

"Tempest spoke to us while he was in possession of Kallias's body." Gods, it never failed to punch him in the gut when she said his name. "He promised us that he would have Kallias permanently, one day…that he would give in to him eventually." Raquel looked at him, her brows furrowed over a serious gaze. "And I think he's right."

Kallias gritted his teeth. "I would never—"

"You already did," Finn interrupted. "Raquel's right. I've seen firsthand the way these gods break you down...how easily they can dig into the heart of you. He'll find a way to make you feel robbed of all other choices, Kal—and I know you. You'll give yourself up in a heartbeat for us, for Atlas. You've done it before. You just *did*."

He had no argument for that.

"I think I have a way to stop it," Raquel continued, "but it would mean traveling to Nyx, northeast of Ursa. And...it's not an easy thing. It will be like nothing you've ever endured. But it might be enough to force Tempest to seek out a new host."

"Did Tempest seem like he was on Tenebrae's side?" Elias asked.

"No," Finn answered this time. "But he's an enemy to me as long as he's trying to take Kal's body."

"And Occassio?" Kallias pressed again. "Where does she stand?"

Finn's mouth curled in anger...in *hate*. "As far as I can tell, she stands on whatever side serves her best. But I'd rather burn to bones than take her as an ally."

"I agree," Elias said—perhaps the first time he and Finn had ever agreed on anything. "And really, I wouldn't trust Tempest, either. He's known to be brutal, to justify any means by the ends he'll achieve. He's not one to rely on. He's not on our side, he's just not on Tenebrae's, either. And even if he was, Finn's right. We're not giving up one more person to them. I'm done losing friends."

Fair enough. "I'm willing to try it, if you think we should," Kallias said to Raquel. "I...trust you."

Finn muttered a vague plea to some higher power, pinching the bridge of his nose in exasperation. Kallias ignored him.

"If I may," Idris interjected, "if we're entering into a war waged by a deity...you'll need more than swords to bring him down. Even if you kill the host body, it won't kill the god; it will only force him to seek out a new one."

The image of a blade plunging through Jericho's chest flashed through his mind. His stomach twisted back into a tangle, and he wrapped his arms around his middle, willing himself not to throw up.

"And what do you suggest we do about that?" Finn asked, his tone far too scathing to be addressing an Empress. Kallias shot him a warning look, but Finn took his turn to ignore Kallias.

Idris raised her chin, looking down her nose at Finn. "Do not condescend to me, boy."

Finn's jaw worked, and the strangeness of his expression—a darkness Kallias didn't recognize—worried him deeply. But Finn looked away first, and a quiet breath of relief escaped Kallias.

"There have been rumors for years that Tallis is in possession of an unnatural weapon...something that can reach through all layers of the world," Idris continued. "A weapon that can kill a god."

Elias's eyes shot to Idris, and his hands slackened in shock. "That isn't possible."

"None of this is possible, Elias," Finn muttered. "We passed *possible* about three atrocities ago. Try to keep up."

"I don't know if it's true," Idris reminded them, shooting a look of distaste Finn's way. "But my father believed it, and many rumors are at least partially rooted in fact. Tallis has *something*, I'd stake my life on it—something you'll need if we're to have any hope of defeating Tenebrae."

"So where first?" Raquel demanded. "Tallis or Nyx?"

"We haven't even discussed the relics yet," Finn added. "The mirror is handled, and Elias has the feather...that puts us ahead by two. I don't know what he needs them for, but he was *pissed* when he realized the mirror was gone. There's still three left—one in Arborius, two in Nyx."

Raquel ran a hand over her ruined ear. "I think we can kill two birds with one stone in Nyx."

"How?" Kallias prodded.

"Because I know where Tempest's relic is." She met Finn's gaze. "And it's the same place we need to go for Kallias."

"Then let's do that," Elias cut in. "We go to Nyx first. Get Kallias out from under Tempest's thumb and find that relic. Then we can double back to Tallis. I doubt Tenebrae will be eager to reveal a weapon that could be his end. The relics should take priority."

"I agree," Raquel said quietly.

"Me too," Kallias said. He looked to his brother next. "Finn?"

"I'm in," he said. "As long as we return to Atlas fast as we can. I left defenses in place, but they're paltry at best. We need to get back...*you* need to get back, as soon as Tempest is out of your head. But on top of that...I want to add an item to our list."

"I don't know that we have room for more," Raquel sighed.

Finn looked to Elias, crossing his arms in a stance Kallias knew well from both him and Soleil—a sign that there would be no budging him. "We find a way to get Soleil free from Anima."

Elias held his gaze steadily. "If we come across something, I will be the first to make sure we try it. You have my word on that."

Finn blinked, then slowly nodded. "Then we have a plan."

"Before dawn, then." Kallias looked around his gathered allies, wondering how exactly his life had come to this. But somehow...grateful for it, too. These weren't the people he would have chosen to have his back, but now that they did, he found he wouldn't wish for anyone else. "If Tenebrae's smart, he'll be having nightmares about *us* tonight."

CHAPTER 77

FINN

K allias's prediction was wrong. Over the next few days traveling toward Nyx—traveling adjacent to the Tallisian border by Kallias's advisement, since Zaccheus was less likely to chase them in that direction—the only nightmares involving Tenebrae were Finn's.

When he finally dragged his eyes closed on the fifth day of foot travel, a task made difficult by the lingering discomfort from his burns and the constant adrenaline pulsing through him, he did not find rest. Instead, he found himself back in the palace, back in the private dining room he and his siblings had claimed as their own. The table had been fixed, and Jericho was perched in one of the chairs—but not Jericho, not really. Her eyes were solid gold, indicating Tenebrae was in control; and standing before him, her dainty body bedecked in purple velvet, every muscle belying the coiled grace of a snake…

His heart curled in on itself, withering at the sight of Occassio.

"He doesn't have the mirror," he heard her say, so much different than the way she spoke as Fidget—still with that Lapisian accent, but every word was a knife thrown, efficient and primed to kill. "But it doesn't matter. He's already used it."

"It matters," Tenebrae snapped. "If you aren't able to take him as your host, you'll need to hunt down another, and without the mirror—"

"Relax." Now her voice held emotion; still cold, but bored now, annoyed. "I have this under control, brother. I'm not Ani."

"Not anymore, anyway." Tenebrae shook his head with a sigh. "The way you change yourself is truly frightening, you know. You almost had me convinced you cared about that fool prince."

Was it his imagination, or did her eyes narrow in a glare? "He's not a fool."

"What would you call it?"

"You think I'd take a fool as my host? It takes a rare mind to match mine, Brae. It took work to win him. Don't downplay my accomplishments."

Tenebrae's smirk only grew. "I wouldn't dare, sister. So tell me, then—why does he still walk under his own power?"

"Like I said, it's a rarity to find a true adversary." Occassio's lying mouth curled into a pretty pout. "Don't rush me, will you? I haven't had this much fun in *centuries*. Give me a bit longer to play my game."

"So long as you don't draw it out too long." The amusement dropped from Tenebrae's voice in an instant, a cold front crashing over what he guessed was false affection. "You know what to do. Toy with him for a while, if it makes you happy. But when the time comes…"

"Break him," she agreed, so casually confident that Finn's chest spasmed with dread. Her head turned, and he found himself captured in her gaze—multicolored facets of light buried in the brown.

He didn't blink.

She was not better than him. She could not *break* him.

He wouldn't let her.

She smiled then—the same wicked grin that had first stirred him to an attraction that had resulted in his ruin. She gave him a slow, taunting wink. "Believe me, brother…it will be my absolute *pleasure*."

He started awake, a scream already building in his throat, but his body had learned this pattern—before the scream could escape, he'd already clamped a hand over his mouth, muffling the sound to nearly nothing. That hand caught the blood trickling from his nose, flowing hot and coppery, warming his frigid fingers. The closer they got to Tallis's evergreen mountains, the colder it became; even the tents they'd procured from a merchant caravan they'd passed along the way did little to keep out the cold, though the reprieve from the merciless wind was nice.

He'd hated calling in quite so many favors before fleeing the city, but necessity couldn't be bargained with; he'd needed coin, and he'd needed it fast. And thank the gods he'd gotten it, because since his own escape, Kallias had reportedly spent a good chunk of what he'd taken from the palace treasury on marked-up inn prices and Artemisian baked goods.

A muffled snore reminded him that he wasn't alone in the tent. Speak of the spender.

He glanced over to see Kallias still asleep, sprawled on top of his bedroll rather than inside it, his thick blanket tossed aside. He seemed perfectly comfortable without it, only his sleepclothes left to shield him from the cold…well, not perfectly comfortable. Sweat had gathered on his forehead and soaked through the armpits and back of his shirt, and his brow was furrowed even as he snored on.

Sweating. *Sweating*, while Finn continued to shiver even while bundled in his bedroll and a knit blanket that reminded him a bit too much of the one he'd left behind in his room.

Whatever Raquel had in mind, they needed to accomplish it—*quickly*. Atlas couldn't lose all of its heirs to fickle, feral gods.

And after Kallias was saved, Soleil was next on the list.

He curled back up into his bedroll, wiping his blood on his sleeve, snatching up Kallias's discarded blanket. If Tempest insisted on making Kallias immune to cold, there was no reason it couldn't benefit him.

He'd only just started to drift back into sleep—dark, blessedly dreamless, marginally warmer sleep—when a familiar scream split the air.

He and Kallias bolted up in one movement, meeting each other's gazes with equal horror.

"Soleil," they said together, before snatching up their weapons and racing out the tent door.

CHAPTER 78

ELIAS

"I still think we should elope."

Elias snorted, burying his smirk in Soren's hair and wrapping his arms around her waist. "And break both of our mothers' hearts?"

She leaned her whole weight against his chest, sitting in his lap with her legs crossed over his, her left hand raised while she admired the ring sparkling on her fourth finger. "I mean, I'd love it. A whole day for me to be the center of attention—"

"You know this involves me too, right?"

She ignored him as she nestled closer, soft and warm in her fleece pajamas. "All those people bringing me gifts, telling me how beautiful I am…it'd be great. It's just that the planning takes so *long*."

"We could do it secretly." He freed one hand to steal hers, thumbing her ring while pressing absent kisses to the crown of her head. "Get married on our own, then let them throw the big ceremony anyway. You get your party, and I get to call you my wife."

The small, delighted noise she made deep in her throat nearly undid him. "Say that again."

Elias chuckled, dipping his head to the side, leaving a trail of kisses down her collarbone. Her jaw. Lower.

"My wife," he murmured into the crook of her neck, and the goosebumps that rose beneath his lips stirred a molten heat that churned deep in his core. "Mrs. Soren Loch."

He barely finished saying that name before she twisted around, catching his lips with hers, grinning into the kiss. "I think technically you'd take *my* name. Prince Elias Nyx."

Elias pulled back to catch his breath, the flush climbing up his face starting to make him dizzy with heat. "The name, I'll take. I'm not so sure about the title."

Soren laughed, shoving off of his chest and sitting back in his lap, hooking her hands around his neck and playing with the ends of his hair. She wrapped her legs around his middle, crossing them behind him and using her grip around his neck to keep herself from falling backward. "I think you'd make a fabulous prince. The sight of you in a crown alone would be worth it."

"You're making fun of me."

"I'm not! You'd look so handsome."

"I'd look a fool, and you know it full well."

She snorted, sidling closer until her lips were right beside his ear. He closed his eyes, waiting for the next joke, the next kiss, contentment radiating through him in waves of warmth.

All of it broken as her ear-piercing scream jerked him straight out of sleep and onto his feet, darkness meeting him as he fought his way out of his bedroll, his head spinning with lingering dream-fog.

Another scream.

"*Soren!*" The roar burst from him at the same time he tore out of the tent, only to be met with chaos—shadows moving in blurred relief against deeper darkness, the only indication of danger the occasional glint of moonlight on drawn blades.

They'd been surrounded.

Still delirious from sleep, still half-sure he was trapped in a nightmare, he couldn't form a clear thought before that scream broke through the freezing night air again, a desperate shout that honed his fear into fury: "*Elias!*"

And suddenly, it didn't matter where he was. Didn't matter if he was dreaming or awake. Didn't matter if he was still in Artem's mountain halls or bunking down in the Nyxian barracks or staggering half-conscious through a makeshift camp beside the Tallisian mountains. Didn't matter if her cries were stolen or sincere.

That was Soren screaming for him. His Soren.

Elias Loch, the Phoenix Priest, unleashed himself on his enemies with a roar that shook the mountains.

There was no thought. No plan. Only blade and blaze and bloodlust, a triumvirate of death that cast judgement over these intruders and named them men already dead.

His scythes bit through skin and bone and blood. He palmed one man's face and shot fire straight into his snarling mouth and widened eyes, burning until there was nothing left but a smoking crater of melted flesh. He cut and burned and cut and burned and cut and burned—

And still, *still* he could not see her. Still he could not find her.

He cut and burned and cut and burned.

"Elias!"

He whirled, his hand already lit with a brand of white-hot fire. But when he threw the punch, another hand caught it—a shaking hand coated in ice, an explosion of steam hissing into the air as they collided, the flickering fire revealing Kallias's pale face.

"You can stop," he said, and it sounded like he'd said it more than once. "It's over. You can stop."

He blinked, the haze of sleep finally clearing away as he took in the clearing they'd chosen as their camp—a clearing now filled with smoking, bloody, or frozen dead. Some more than one. Some all three.

Ears ringing, chest heaving, Elias clung on to Kallias's hand, half-afraid he'd collapse without the support. "Soren?" He cleared his throat with a curse. "I mean—I—where's Anima?"

"Gone," came Raquel's grim, furious voice. She marched across the frost-crusted grass, every movement stiff with anger, kicking one of the corpses' arms and breaking it at the elbow. "Tallisian mercenaries. They snatched her out of our tent and ran."

"What would they want with her?" Finn demanded, rubbing his eyes as he stumbled up to join them. He looked as disheveled as the rest of them, hair rumpled and clothes askew, but his eyes were clearer—like he'd already been awake.

"It doesn't matter why," Raquel hissed. "The Tallisians despise the gods. If they find out what she is—"

"They might already know." Dread overcame him until his legs finally gave out, and he sank into a crouch, rubbing his hand over his jaw. "Tallisians have dozens of ways to ward off god-magic, including illusions. Gods, one of those merchants…if they saw her golden eyes, they would have spread that rumor to any ear that would listen."

"Damn it," said Kallias. Then again: "*Damn* it."

They all stood in silence for a moment, only the buzzing of their own thoughts to keep them company.

Soren's screams—Anima's screams—echoed between his ears, a dirge that twined with Idris's whispers of a weapon made to kill gods.

He rocked to his feet. Ducked into his tent.

Kallias followed him, watching as he started throwing things into his pack. "You're going after her."

"Yes." He didn't need to explain why. Kallias knew. The nosy bastard always knew.

"We're coming too. We'll be packed in five minutes."

"No."

Kallias stopped; Elias couldn't see it, not focused as he was on his own packing, but he heard the halt in his breath. "Don't be stupid."

"I mean it. Look at you, Kal." He turned enough to gesture to Kallias's ice-coated hand, the patches of sweat on his clothes. "This isn't something that can wait. You need to go."

Kallias's head shook, even as his eyes darkened with defeat. "She's my sister. I'm coming."

"And what happens when Tempest takes you and wants her for his own purposes? You think we can fight off two gods? We're lucky Anima hasn't used her magic against us thus far." And now that he thought about it, that was strange.

He'd seen her use her healing, but nothing offensive—at least, not toward them. He had no idea what she'd done during the Artem battle…or this one. He tossed on his coat and hefted his pack over his shoulder; he'd slept in his clothes, anyway. "You need to go to Nyx. I'll meet you there when I have her."

"And what if we've left Nyx by the time you find her?" Kallias demanded. "Or what if they take you too? You're one man, Elias. *One.*"

"One man with a goddess's blessing." He patted his chest above his prayer beads.

Kallias stayed in the tent's entrance, arms spread, blocking his way. "Eli…"

"Kal. You know I have to go. And you know you can't come with me."

Kallias looked at his feet—as much of an admission as he was going to get. "We need…we need a better plan. We need to think about this."

"Where's the other relic?" Elias pushed past Kallias, raising his voice to call to Finn: "Finn! Where's the third relic?"

"Arborius," Finn said, eyeing Elias's pack. His face was calm, but his eyes were frantic.

"We're going after her?" Raquel asked.

"*He's* going after her," Finn and Kallias corrected at the same time. Finn raked a hand through his hair, agonized eyes darting between Kallias and the direction of the Tallisian border.

"Find her," Finn said, suddenly spearing Elias with such a severe look that he had to step back. "Promise me you'll find her and bring her back to us, Elias Loch, or I swear to whatever god or goddess you worship that it will be the last time you fail."

Elias, for once, believed him wholeheartedly.

"I will," he said. "Raquel, get Kallias well and meet me in Ursa. If I don't meet you there in time, make for…Kallias, is there a city where we can charter a ship to Arborius without passing through Port Atlas?"

"One," Kallias croaked, rubbing his neck, still looking stunned. Their plans had all fallen apart and come back together so quickly, Elias could hardly keep up himself. "Sirena. It's much smaller than Port Atlas, but there's an academy for physicians and healers there that rely on imports from Arborius, so they have a small harbor…if we had the coin, it wouldn't be too hard to charter a private ship."

"Good. If I don't get to Ursa by the time you finish up there, head to Sirena. I'll meet you there instead."

"And if you don't?" Of course it was Finn who had to ask.

Elias looked at each of them for several seconds, lingering on Kallias the longest. The Atlas prince looked ready to either rage or weep, and suddenly the thought of leaving him and Raquel…unbearable.

But…

"I will," he said. "And if I don't…"

He locked eyes with Kallias. Smiled. Put a fist over his heart—Atlas's salute.

"Save our kingdoms," he rasped. "Save all of us."

Kallias's eyes welled with tears barely visible in the moonlight, but he matched Elias's gesture. "I will see you again…Nyxian peasant."

Elias barked out a tearful laugh. "Atlas bastard."

When Kallias enveloped him in a hug, Elias embraced him back, a bone-crushing thing that somehow felt like all of his broken pieces were being shoved back into place. And when he let go, even though a part of his heart was ripping away, he felt more whole than he had in some time.

"Mortem keep you," Raquel called after him as he started off into the night.

The prayer beads seemed to warm against his chest, a gentle flame nestled against his heart. A constant companion. An unfailing promise. "She will," he said.

He believed it.

He had faith.

EPILOGUE

ANIMA

S he didn't know where she was.

She'd hardly had the time to scream—her and Soren of one mind for a brief moment, Anima's breath and Soren's words melding to form a shout for *Elias*—before the gloved, grasping hands snuffed out her air, choking her until something sharp pierced her neck, sending her into a restless darkness that held her prisoner for gods-knew how long.

When she woke up, her head pounding and her thoughts sluggish, her tongue heavy and parched, Soren's thoughts were somehow clearer than hers: a furious hiss that slid past the wall into Anima's groggy mind: *They* drugged *us*.

Anima only realized she'd echoed the thought out loud when a face entered her blurry span of vision: a leering man's face, young-ish, golden hair and stubble distracting her with its shine in the lantern light. He would have been handsome if he wasn't making that awful face.

Not even then, Soren disagreed.

"Wakey wakey, Goddess Great," he laughed—gods, his breath stank of something sharp.

Ale, Soren supplied. Anima's teeth gritted of their own accord, an old instinct bracing her for what might come next.

Goddess Great. She preferred that taunt coming from within her own head.

"What a pretty body you stole," he purred, tugging on one of her curls. Soren's instincts guided her again; her teeth snapped at his finger, barely missing, a jolt of aching pain shooting through her temples when they cracked together. "And feisty, too? You'll fetch a good price in Craghaven, that's a sure bet. A goddess with bite worse than her bark."

You haven't heard my bark yet, Soren hissed. Then, after a moment of thought: *Well, actually, you're in charge of the bark. So he's probably right.*

"Please stop talking," Anima mumbled to Soren, her tongue thick with exhaustion. "It hurts."

"Oh, you think that hurts?" The man's voice darkened suddenly, and Anima's breath seized up, fear cutting through the haze in her mind. "I can make it hurt, pretty girl. I'd love to test how far that healing shit of yours can go."

Anima, Soren whispered, all amusement gone, *you need to let me take over.*

I can't, Anima reminded her, finally remembering to answer in her head. *Last time we almost* died, *remember?*

I think that's a bit dramatic. We passed out.

We were bleeding.

Not the first time. Not the last, either.

Anima was saved from having to argue further by a light creaking outside the door. Now that her vision was clearing, she could see where they were: a tiny room, barely large enough for both her and this stranger and the chair she was tied to, made of log walls and a cold stone floor that chilled the tips of her bare toes.

The man cursed quietly, shoving up to his feet, wobbling the chair and nearly knocking her over. "You stay put and stay quiet," he ordered, listing to the side before straightening back up, making his way out the door and shutting it behind him.

Anima tried to lift her head, to hold it steady, but her neck felt weak. Everything was dizzy and slow, like she'd danced around a maypole one too many times before being tossed in a vat of syrup.

She didn't remember closing her eyes; she only realized she had when raised voices and a crash outside the door dragged them open again.

"What was that?" she mumbled, her voice sounding slurred even to her own ears.

Maybe he passed out, Soren guessed, but she didn't sound convinced—she was pressed up against the wall again, her presence pushing at the ache in Ani's part of their head. *Listen hard. If he did, we have to take our chances and try to get out of here.*

"They'll come for us," Ani whispered. "Any minute now. I know it."

Soren was silent for a long moment. *No one's coming, Anima. Not for either of us.*

Before Ani could argue, the door swung open again, and every muscle tensed like well-tuned fiddle strings, taut beneath the shield of her skin. She forced her limp, boneless fingers to twitch, trying to call her magic, but only the barest green sparks spat from her fingertips—nothing usable.

Fresh panic bloomed in the hollow of her throat, cutting off her air. A drug that kept her from using her magic? *Her,* a goddess?

"I'm sorry about my brother," said a new voice, and Ani dragged her gaze upward to see another man duck into the room. He was tall and lithe, the dark cap his hair a startling contrast to the vivid blue of his eyes, the youthful cast to his complexion not matching the grimness of his face or the frown lines dug into his mouth. "He's a mean drunk—and a foolish one. He knows better than to lay hands on you."

Ani swallowed, wincing at the dryness of her throat. The man frowned, deepening those lines, and he dropped to one knee in front of her while untying something from his belt—a canteen. He raised it to her lips, and she made a tiny noise of relief, stretching for it—

No! Soren's bark preceded a sharp jerk on the muscles of her neck, tugging her head back against the back of the chair. *Did you miss the part where they're drugging us?*

The man's eyes sharpened, and he pulled his canteen back. "I am so sorry for this," he said, an apology twice as earnest as the first. "I know it isn't fair."

Anima swallowed thickly. "Thank you."

The man's lip curled, and he shook his head, leaning in closer. "Not you, Goddess. I'm speaking to *her.*" He reached out for her face, and she was too tired to pull away again—could do nothing but stare dully as he ran his thumb down the center of her forehead. "The poor girl you have trapped in there with you."

Shock thumped through her chest, twice as strong with her and Soren sharing it. *How does he know about me?* Soren hissed. The suspicion in her voice, rather than relief or excitement, almost warmed Ani's heart.

"It's rare for someone to survive a deity taking their body. Most don't believe it's even possible...you must be so lonely in there. Frightened." The man sighed, and she almost thought the grief in his eyes was...genuine.

Soren scoffed. *Oh, please. Get a load of this guy.*

I think he's actually trying to be kind, Ani argued.

I think he's being condescending. Frightened, my ass.

"I am sorry," the man repeated—again. "Sorry that you'll be forced to share her fate. But we can't allow the divine to walk the world again. My king gave us a mission, and we have to carry it out. But I'll make sure your body finds its way back to your loved ones, wherever they may be."

I'm sorry too. Sorry you're still wasting our damned time, Soren muttered. *Anima, let me punch him.*

No.

Just one little broken tooth.

We're tied up, remember?

"Colin!" barked the other man from outside the door. "Stop wagging your tongue at the goddess and come help me skin this."

The image of *skinning* turned Anima's stomach, and she fought a retch.

Colin offered his canteen once more, and drugged or not, Soren's snarling or not, Anima's parched throat won out above all sense. She guzzled it, her tongue only barely registering the sickly sweet taint to the water, and she only stopped drinking when her head grew too heavy to hold up. She let it drop, her damp chin touching her clavicles, darkness muffling all sight and sound until it was just her trapped in a haze of cottonmouth and smothering night.

"They'll come for us," she whispered again.

This time, Soren and Colin spoke together, grim tones melding into a promise that coaxed twin tears from beneath her closed eyes:

"No one is coming, Goddess."

They were right. No one did.

THE END

ACKNOWLEDGMENTS

To God:

To my siblings:

To my parents:

To Miranda:

To Kristin:

To Renee:

To Marcia and Mike:

To Aunt Shawna:

To my beta team :

To my ARC readers:

To Katie Marie and Sapphire Ink Press:

To Fran (@coverdungeonrabbit):

ABOUT THE AUTHOR

Cassidy Clarke is a proud Michigander, freelance editor, and NA author who subsists on chicken tenders, ketchup, and fantasy books. She recently graduated with her BA in Creative Writing, which has allowed her to pursue her passion for storytelling and helping others make their books the absolute best they can be. *THE SALTWATER HEIR* is her debut novel, a high fantasy love letter to the lost princess daydreams of her childhood and an attempt to put her experience growing up with three younger siblings to good use. She spends her days writing like she's running out of time, binging Critical Role on Youtube and GBBO on Netflix, and baking the world's best chocolate chip cookies.